Two Lifetimes as One

ADST MEMOIRS AND OCCASIONAL PAPERS SERIES
SERIES EDITOR: LISA M. TERRY

In 2003, the Association for Diplomatic Studies and Training (ADST), a nonprofit organization founded in 1986, created the Memoirs and Occasional Papers Series to preserve firsthand accounts and other informed observations on foreign affairs for scholars, journalists, and the general public. Through its book series, its Foreign Affairs Oral History program, and its support for the training of foreign affairs personnel at the State Department's Foreign Service Institute, ADST seeks to promote understanding of American diplomacy and those who conduct it. Irving Tragen, author of the 35th volume in the series, spent most of his 55-year Foreign Service career specializing in inter-American relations, culminating his career as Executive Secretary of the Inter-American Drug Control Commission (CICAD).

RELATED TITLES FROM ADST SERIES

DIEGO & NANCY ASENCIO, *Joys and Perils of Living Abroad: Memoirs of a Foreign Service Family*

JANET C. BALLANTYNE, ed., *Fifty Years in USAID: Stories from the Front Lines*

GORDON S. BROWN, *Toussaint's Clause: The Founding Fathers and the Haitian Revolution*

JOHN GUNTHER DEAN, *Danger Zones: A Diplomat's Fight for America's Interests*

HARRIET ELAM-THOMAS, *Diversifying Diplomacy: My Journey from Roxbury to Dakar*

BRANDON GROVE, *Behind Embassy Walls: The Life and Times of an American Diplomat*

JUDITH HEIMANN, *Paying Calls in Shangri-La: Scenes from a Woman's Life in American Diplomacy*

ROGER KIRK, ed., *Distinguished Service: Lydia Chapin Kirk, Partner in Diplomacy 1896–1984*

JOHN G. KORMANN, *Echoes of a Distant Clarion: Recollections of a Diplomat and Soldier*

NICOLE PRÉVOST LOGAN, *Forever on the Road: A Franco-American Family's Thirty Years in the Foreign Service*

For a complete list of series titles, visit adst.org/publications

Two Lifetimes as One
Ele and Me
and the Foreign Service

Irving G. Tragen

ASSOCIATION FOR DIPLOMATIC STUDIES AND TRAINING
MEMOIRS AND OCCASIONAL PAPERS SERIES

SCARITH

NEW ACADEMIA PUBLISHING

Washington, DC

Library of Congress Control Number: 2019920718
ISBN 978-1-7333980-6-0 paperback (alk. paper)

 An imprint of New Academia Publishing

 New Academia Publishing, 4401-A Connecticut Ave. NW, #236,
Washington, DC 20008
info@newacademia.com - www.newacademia.com

Two Lifetimes as One is an autobiography of Irving Tragen and his late wife, Eleanor "Ele" Dodson. Irving, who suffered a severe hearing loss from the aftereffects of scarlet fever, relives their odyssey from their first meeting at International House at the University of California, Berkeley, through a dozen appointments in the United States Foreign Service and the Organization of American States. Ele and Irving lived in seven Latin American countries. Irving worked in all thirty-three Latin American and Caribbean countries on diplomatic, development, and drug trafficking-control assignments over nearly sixty years. He details each of those assignments and the lessons he learned and makes it very clear that he could not have carried out those assignments without Ele's support.

To Ele (1922–2005)
to Whom This Remembrance Is Dedicated

My love, my dearest one
What emptiness as you leave my side
The rock on which our lives are built,
The conscience of our deeds and thoughts.

Dearest Ele, you shaped our union
Your mind willed us to strive and endure
Your strength drove our every day
Your star piloted us through good and ill.

You inspired me from boy to man
Challenging me to cope with handicap and mood
Gently replacing bitterness with vision and humor
Overcoming gloom with understanding and peace.

Dearest Ele, my light in darkness,
Your heart and soul abide with mine
To love you is my gift through eternity
Bountiful and divine.

From Ele
A Fragment Found Among Her Papers

KNOWLEDGE

If each generation had to learn alone, little progress would
be made. Writing, art, and math allow us to accumulate
knowledge as we do property and money.
Knowledge is our greatest wealth.
Knowledge is learning how others have solved problems and
how to solve those of our day.
Knowledge includes simple faith in God and respect for all his
creatures.
Knowledge tells all that government is a contract among
people acting in good faith. People need ready exchange of
knowledge as information, with clear how-to books graced by
simple illustrations and giving pleasure.
Knowledge should be valued more than commodities.
Knowledge should be our sixth sense. The 3 Rs form the basis
for all learning and the search for truth. Prize and teach the 3
Rs to continue the search for truth.
Knowledge teaches us the acceptance of life's gifts.
With charity, enjoyment, and proper use, the cycle of
Knowledge ever renews itself.

Contents

Preface

Welcome to our lives. This is a simple love story of two people who helped implement U.S. foreign policy—how we worked and lived to advance the interests of our country and to better relations with our neighbors in the Western Hemisphere. This does not cover policy making at the White House or on the Seventh Floor of the State Department. There are no revelations of great foreign policy secrets. It is the story of two human beings and their twentieth-century relationship, set against the backdrop of careers, aspirations, and other forces. This is my remembrance of what happened to Ele and me, from our first encounter to our current temporary separation.

This relates the coming together of two opposites, two very different personalities and spirits, who for some unknown reason found themselves drawn to each other and who shared their lives. It is not a superficial sexual drama in the style that preoccupies our contemporary world, but something far more profound: the gradual melding of two human beings who found, in their official and personal lives, that they shared common interests, common values, and mutual respect.

She is Eleanor May Dodson Tragen and I am Irving Glenne Tragen. She was the Sparkle. I was the Nerd. Our life together started in the fall of 1944 and lasted over sixty years, including fifty-seven years of marriage in which we shared the joys and sorrows of everyday living. Fate took Ele on April 15, 2005, at 10:30 a.m. I am now in my mid-nineties and still feel a terrible emptiness without her, even though her spirit and loving memories have become part and parcel of my everyday life.

This memoir started as an effort to relive our wonderful, if not always happy, years together. I have tried to imbue each page with the values and objectivity that Ele made the central force of our relationship. I hope my prose is adequate to tell our story. She was the true writer in our family and I wish that we could have written this chronicle together. Unfortunately she is not here to edit it and give it the style and verve that were her trademark.

Almost all of this autobiography has been drawn from memory. Once in a while, I reviewed files and the internet to check names and dates. Occasionally I called on friends like my editor, Anna Chisman, to help me refresh my recollection, clarify confusions, and place a name on a face branded into my brain. My objective is to tell the story of the life Ele and I lived together, not to give a scholarly commentary on U.S. relations with Latin America, although I do not hide my perceptions and disappointments.

Most of Ele's and my life was lived in or revolved around the U.S. Foreign Service and relations with Latin America. We lived through the Cold War, the Alliance for Progress, and the onset of the war on drug trafficking. My forte was not the traditional Foreign Service functions of reporting and analysis, but rather development efforts to support governments and people in building institutions and programs to enhance economic, social, and political development—especially in enhancing popular participation in the processes of development. Ele and I worked to build bridges to the countries in which we lived and worked, and to help our Latin American and Caribbean counterparts build their own bridges to and with their countrymen.

In our overseas assignments, our lives were enriched by being part of the official U.S. family. This was before the computer, cell phones, and instant communication with family and friends at home. It was the official U.S. family that had to be there to fill many immediate needs that beset each and every member of our community. The quality of life at an overseas post depended in great measure on the support and kindnesses of one's colleagues. Oh, yes, there were good friendships built with wonderful people from the host country, but our family at post was our coworkers in the U.S. establishment. Throughout these remembrances, I have tried to spell out the importance and depth of those relationships.

There have been five eras to our lives. Each era is covered separately in the following parts of my memoir:

Part I simply tells who we are, how we met, and how miraculously Ele fell in love with and married me.

Part II is about our adventures as a newly married couple who left the security of our homes and routines in California to build a new pattern of life for ourselves and acquire the knowledge and experience that permeated our fifty-seven years of married life. Chapters 7 through 15 cover the years in Mexico, our first experience in Washington, D.C., and assignments in El Salvador, Chile, and Venezuela, and, almost, in Peru.

Part III summarizes the excitement and challenges of the years of the Alliance for Progress, President's Kennedy initiative for inter-American cooperation for development. Chapters 16 to 26 spell out our tours with Institutional Development in Washington, D.C., as USAID Mission director in Bolivia, in the State Department Senior Seminar on Foreign Policy, as director of the State Department Office of Argentine, Paraguayan, and Uruguayan Affairs, as the first vice president of the Inter-American Foundation, as director of the Regional Office for Central American Programs (ROCAP), and finally as economic counselor and USAID director to Panama.

Part IV covers nearly two decades of association with the Organization of American States (OAS). Chapters 27 to 32 deal with the years when I served as deputy U.S. representative, then as executive officer of the OAS Secretariat for Economic and Social Affairs, and finally as the first executive secretary of the Inter-American Drug Abuse Control Commission (CICAD).

Part V deals with the last years of our life together. Chapters 33 to 35 relate our return to California in 1995 with Ele's health in decline, our move to San Diego in search of better health care, and my persistence without her.

The five phases of our lifetime were a learning process for both of us, as individuals and professionals. *Two Lifetimes* tells how we came to know, love, and respect each other through the fifty-seven years of marriage, and relives the joys, sorrows, and misunderstandings that cemented our relationship.

Ele and I welcomed each new assignment as an opportunity to enrich our lives by learning about the people and institutions of the country in which we were posted. We learned that each was unique, requiring us to adapt and reshape our thinking and actions in light of its values and realities if we were to help better relations with our country and to promote U.S. principles of respect for human dignity and rising living standards. We are creatures of our democratic roots in California.

The assignments we most cherished were those related to development. Ele and I had a constant dialogue about development. From our first assignment in Mexico, experience showed us how complex and long-term the process is, especially for countries transitioning from feudalism and mercantilism to a new political, economic, and social order. We were witnesses to the impact of modern telecommunications, transportation, and technology on traditional communities and the upheavals they spawned. We learned that helping those countries deal with this change is much more comprehensive than providing funds, sharing technology, and training people.

In this recounting of our experiences, I show what led Ele and me to see development as a political process in which economic, social, psychological, and human resources needed to be blended together to build a solid base for development. As a political process, it is essentially a national dynamic—the interaction of government and people. Foreign assistance can help accelerate or broaden the process, but the leadership cannot be imported.

I recount the difficulties we faced in helping governments move the development process forward, break down the resistance to changing traditional practices, and overcome the obstacles caused by inexperience as well as entrenched interests and corruption. I detail the importance of knowing the terrain before testing out a development project, and why a project on sheep shearing using manual implements succeeded while another applying power tools failed. There are also examples that demonstrate why access to the marketplace is critical in designing projects.

A central lesson our experience in country after country illustrates is that development requires time—often generations—as shown by the centuries it has taken Europe to progress from the Age of Reason to build functioning capital-formation democratic societies. Decades, not years, are needed to mobilize the financial base for self-sustaining growth, build institutions and infrastructure, set up education systems, and train and season managers and technicians. To buy that time and minimize the threat of derailings, the middle class and grassroots have to feel part of the process and need concrete evidence that giving up their traditional way of life is worth the pain. That is why Ele and I became convinced that governments needed more than top-down policies and actions. They needed to design and support systematic programs that enable the grassroots to participate through better access to education and upward mobility, improvements they themselves instituted at the community level, and rising family income. The essential counterpart to macro-financial solvency and self-sustaining national growth is enabling the people to raise their horizons and quality of life.

Welcome to *Two Lifetimes as One: Ele and Me and the Foreign Service*.

A Word of Appreciation

Since I began drafting *Two Lifetimes as One* several years ago, I have been blessed with the support of many people. My thanks to my neighbors at my senior residence, the Pacific Regent La Jolla; to my nephews Gary and Ray, and to the many friends who encouraged me to draw from my memory this recounting of my life with Ele, much of it in the U.S. Foreign Service. My thanks also to the late Dr. Ben Holmes and the late Herb Klein, director of communications at the Nixon White House and publisher of the *San Diego Union Tribune,* for helping me to shape and organize my writing. To Stella Villagrán and René Gutiérrez, Librarians at the Columbus Memorial Library of the Organization of American States, for checking elusive names and dates. To Judy Rubenstein, wife of playwright Howard Rubenstein, for guiding me through filing the application for a copyright, my very first. To each and every one, my special thanks for their interest and helping hands.

Writing on the computer has been a constant challenge, and many a time I had to call for help to reclaim a chapter from its voracious maw. At those terrifying times when I pressed the wrong key, I called for help from my good Samaritan Tracy Atherton, and sometimes from Pacific Regent staffers Cindy Russell, Amy Grant, Holly Travis, and Josue Salgado. They showed the computer that it could not take advantage of an old man like me. Without their help, I would still be writing new versions of texts drifting somewhere in the never-never land of my nemesis.

Getting my initial version ready for prime time reading has required the assistance of my editors, Anna Chisman and Lisa Terry. As you will find out in my account of the creation and building of

CICAD in Chapter 30, Anna was one of those with whom I worked most closely. She has lent me that same dedication and good judgment in her critique of my writing as she did in the CICAD years. To Anna and Lisa, your skill and patience have earned my heartfelt admiration.

Finally, special thanks are extended to Susan Johnson and Margery Thompson of the Association for Diplomatic Studies and Training (ADST) for their support and decision to include this book in ADST's Memoirs series.

Without the generous support and kind deeds of so many, this story of our Foreign Service adventure would never have been completed.

PART I

SPARKLE AND THE NERD, 1922–1947

1

As First We Met

This is the chronicle of the quiet, unsure boy from the Big City, San Francisco, and a special auburn-haired gal from a small California Central Valley town, Tulare, whose paths crossed by some divine ordinance at I House on the campus of the University of California in Berkeley.

I House is what Cal students called International House, the seven-story cream-colored stucco tower on Piedmont Avenue at the edge of the campus. Without its presence, the Nerd would probably never have met Sparkle.

I House was founded by the Rockefellers in the 1920s to contribute to international understanding and world peace by providing a residence in which students of all nationalities, races, and cultures could share their ambitions and experiences, their values and life styles, and their visions for the future. Essentially, the Rockefellers believed that building personal friendships through shared university experience could lead to lifetime cooperation of not only individuals but also of peoples around the world. The Rockefellers financed the creation of three such centers: the one at Berkeley, the original at Columbia University in New York, and the third at the University of Chicago.

I House was always coed, with an about equal group of male and female students, about half of whom came from the United States and the rest from foreign countries. Prior to World War II, the majority were graduate students. I House traditionally had a population more mature than the general university community and had become a special meeting place on the south side of campus. Some called it the "zoo" because of its unique blend of residents and its richly diversified cultural activities, including dance and art, reflecting life styles from the far corners of the world.

In World War II, the physical structure of I House was taken over by the U.S. Navy for a special training program for officers. I House stayed alive by renting four fraternity houses that had been vacated as their members joined the Armed Forces and waged the war against the Axis. During the war, the student body at Berkeley changed. There was a shortage of U.S. graduate students and very few available men. There were specialized foreign students, mainly from Latin America. These changes created a very different mix of residents, but the principles and vision were unchanged.

The Nerd was one of only a handful of U.S. male students at I House when it made the transition into the fraternity houses. He was classified 4F (not acceptable for service in the Armed Forces) and was essentially deaf. He had lived at the original I House during his senior year as a cum laude Phi Beta Kappa Political Science and Economics student where his room overlooking the Golden Gate had become his refuge from his despair at not being with his confreres fighting the Axis. He lived at one of the fraternity houses while he studied at the University's prestigious Boalt Law School.

Sparkle was admitted to I House in 1944. She moved to Berkeley in 1943 for her last two years of university after earning her AA degree from the College of Sequoias in Visalia, California, a few miles from her home in Tulare, a farming center in the San Joaquin Valley. When she first came to Berkeley, she lived for a year in a boarding house with an old friend. They were traditional WASPs and were rushed by several sororities, but found the sorority lifestyle not to be their cup of tea. They wanted to savor new experiences and meet people of different backgrounds and lifestyles. When Sparkle and her friend discovered I House in the fall of 1943, they were intrigued with the program and environment. They became non-resident members and in the spring of 1944, were accepted as residents for the fall semester that year.

The Nerd faced a terrible challenge at law school which, because of the demands of World War II, set up an accelerated study plan: three semesters a year instead of the traditional two. Having lip-read through most of his undergraduate years, he coped by burying himself in books and lecture notes to make sure that he had the subject matter of each course well under control. He studied nights and weekends, even when he went across the Bay to spend time with his family. The library and his I House room were the centers of his universe. Law school meant more of the same routine for twenty-four consecutive months without a break between semesters.

The I House director appointed the Nerd to be graduate counselor at one of the two fraternity houses designated for male residents. The house, set high on the Berkeley hills and surrounded by extensive gardens, was designated I House #4. He moved into a suite of bedroom and bath, just inside the front door, with ample space for his desk, books, and other personal effects. The new law student also became advisor and overseer for forty Latin American, Icelandic, Chinese, and other students, many of whom were double his tender age of twenty-two.

Life at I House during World War II was very informal. The facilities of the four fraternity houses brought all of I Housers together in a true adventure of international living. In the big I House, each person had had his or her own room and could revel in his or her privacy. In the new set-up, there were really no private rooms, with each dorm room shared by two men. Many slept not in their rooms, but on large sleeping porches. Residents of different races, creeds, and nationalities truly came to know each other much more intimately than in the original building. This sharing crafted many lifelong friendships. Unfortunately, as in any setting where humans live so closely together, it also spawned a few unfortunate confrontations and animosities. The Nerd never knew what new adventure each day would bring.

Even during World War II, I House brought together a wonderful combination of personalities and talents. I Housers included physicists working on the cyclotron, sons and daughters of international diplomats, and veterans who had been wounded and discharged by the U.S. military. There were doctors and engineers from countries around the world on post-graduate fellowships as well as undergrads from the Middle East, Europe, Southeast Asia, China, Africa, and Latin America. There were luncheon discussion groups, dinner language tables and guest speakers from the university and the world community. Imagine the exciting opportunity that I House offered in the depths of World War II! A special dividend came in 1945 during the San Francisco Conference that created the United Nations, when diplomats from various countries took time to visit their countrymen at I House and share with us the latest news. I House was a center of ideas and those living there loved it.

It was in this environment in the fall of 1944 that the Nerd first saw Sparkle. Sparkle had just moved into I House #3, and he saw her one day in the dining room. The I Housers in all four fraternity houses convened daily for breakfast, lunch, and dinner at I House #3. He was impressed but too shy to say hello.

Meeting her was almost an accident. With the University operating twelve months a year to speed up the preparation of specialties needed for the war effort, the dining room was a diversion from the pressure of studying. I House scheduled special activities at lunch and dinner hours and on weekends to enrich this special time. One of the weekend activities was the bi-weekly dance at House #2, usually on a Friday night. A number of gifted Latino musicians provided live music to supplement our collection of records. One Friday evening, a farm dance was scheduled. Let's not confuse an I House farm dance with an Iowa hoedown. A farm dance meant blue jeans and everyday dresses. The music ran the gamut from foxtrot and rumbas to waltzes and sambas. There was a simple buffet and soft drinks, but there was usually someone who spiked the punch just a little.

For this particular barn dance, the Nerd had no plans for attending. He was burdened with law school midterms. He was anxious to keep up his good grades; oh, yes, he had excellent grades and was on a fellowship. His progressive loss of hearing, the aftermath of scarlet fever from when he was four, required him to complement his lip reading with reading and re-reading the cases covered by his professors to make sure that he had not missed critical issues in each of his five courses.

The Nerd had no particular girlfriend at the time. He had never really met Sparkle. Yes, he saw her almost every night in the dining room. She waited table several nights a week and, on the other evenings, was deeply involved in discussions with friends. He had often lip-read conversations, and admired the positions that Sparkle had taken. The truth was that he had wanted to meet her ever since his eyes lit on her beautiful auburn hair and baby blue eyes; and on her smile that twinkled like sunshine.

They had spoken, but only casually. At each of the meetings, she seemed so sure of herself that the Nerd was inevitably drawn to her, as opposites inexorably attract. He was struck by the ease with which she seemed to relate to people.

The first date

One evening in the crowded dining room, one of the doctoral candidates in House 4, Bill West, sat down to dinner with him and asked for a favor. While they talked, he watched Sparkle clearing a table. The Nerd was willing to oblige but begged off because of his need to study for the upcoming exams. Bill persisted, so the Nerd said, "I have to run to the law library now and I'll stop by your room when I get back." As he walked to the law library, her smile lingered with him.

On his return, his friend explained that he had made two dates for the Friday night barn dance and needed someone to take one. The date was Sparkle. The Nerd was overwhelmed and filled with doubt. Would she accept? Would she like being with him? What would they talk about? The Nerd accepted in principle if Sparkle was agreeable.

So, the next day, he sat at the table where Sparkle was seated with a Latin American medical grad student who was anything but pleased by the intrusion. The conversation started awkwardly, but she said smilingly, "Don't go, there's plenty of room." The Nerd sat nervously through lunch not jumping much into a conversation. Reading their lips was difficult, but he perceived that Sparkle was giving the doctor, several years her senior and already married, serious advice about the need to be faithful to his wife!

After lunch, the Nerd trudged back down to law school, chiding himself for not telling her that he was interested in being her surrogate date. He had been truly impressed by the intelligent and warm person she was. He promised himself to talk to her again that night at dinner.

And he did! He walked into the dining room late. Sparkle was seated with a group of friends, still lighting up the whole room. Her companions were men from Europe, Latin America, the Middle East, and the United States. The Nerd convinced himself that he could never compete with them. When dinner ended, he asked Sparkle if he could talk to her and got up the nerve to ask her if she would allow him to take her to the dance in place of Bill. He was prepared for a turn down. He was nonplussed when she said yes. A bolt of lightning had just struck!

For the next several days, before the dance, they talked casually in the hall, in the dining room, and on the way down to campus whenever their paths occasionally crossed.

How Sparkle spent her day getting ready for the big dance will always be her secret, but the Nerd spent his waking hours trying to think of excuses for not going. He tried to draw out law school assignments so that he would have a pretext not to go. He even asked friends for excuses not to show up. No one came up with an appropriate ploy.

Even on the Friday night of the dance, the Nerd was still waffling, telling himself that he had assignments to be ready for Monday morning, and that he was too tired after his three classes that day, and so on. But somehow he jumped into the shower and put on a pair of old pants and shirt, bandana, and straw hat to fit the mood of the Fall Barn Dance. He even combed his already thinning hair. Then, still protesting to himself, he made his way down to dinner at I House #3 to gulp down some sustenance before facing the witching hour of 8:00 p.m. when he had arranged to pick Sparkle up. Oh, how he would have loved to scamper back to the sanctuary of the law library or the obscurity of his own residence quarters!

But he did go. And that night began sixty-one extraordinary years in which Sparkle let the Nerd share her life.

At 8:00 p.m., he was waiting on the terrace at the entrance of I House #3. Lo and behold, right on time appeared Sparkle. She smiled and said how much she had looked forward to going with him to the dance. The Nerd read her lips with great surprise. She said that she had seen him at other dances that spring and thought that he had a great sense of rhythm and that she had wanted to dance with him. His mood was transformed, and he wondered why he had not approached her before. Joy spread through his no longer anguished soul.

They walked over to I House #2, the other I House hall for ladies. It had an imposing entrance, with an outer staircase and terrace. It was blessed with a large living room that lent itself to large social events like dances. Its inside staircase wound down to the living room and gave the room an aura of elegance.

They danced every dance that evening, from foxtrot to samba, from waltz to merengue. His loss of hearing had not impaired his ability to feel the beat. Sparkle and the Nerd fought off those who wanted to cut in as they warmed to being with each other. She followed him with an ease and grace that made him feel like he had never felt before. They just seemed to enjoy being together.

They sat out only two or three dances, and had only one drink all evening. The usually innocuous I House punch had been liberally laced with some God-awful firewater to give it a heroic character that neither felt necessary to make them happy. Somehow, they never tired of dancing and both seemed equally frustrated when the phonograph played "Goodnight Sweetheart" at midnight to announce the dance was over. The dance was a wow, if memory serves reasonably well!

In the cool night air, Sparkle and the Nerd walked the two blocks back to I House #3. It was an exercise in lighter-than-air movement. They chatted arm in arm up to the front terrace and then sat on the wall at the entrance of I House #3 for a few minutes. What they chatted about the Nerd really didn't know, because it was almost too dark to read her lips. All he knew was that she was more fun to be with than anyone he had ever dated before and that she seemed to like being with him. The Nerd even got to kiss her goodnight. The Nerd didn't feel like a Nerd anymore.

2

Getting to Know You

The dance was only the first step in a long process of coming together. The Nerd was so absorbed in getting through his second year of law school that he really didn't give much attention to non-academic ventures such as dates and girlfriends. He kept convincing himself that nothing mattered much besides having each assignment ready for the next class. Nonetheless, in the middle of a lecture on property law or civil procedure, he found himself thinking about auburn hair. While searching precedents for a class on constitutional law, he began wondering about when he could make time to talk with Sparkle, if only at dinner or walking to campus. Could it be that there was something more important to his life than getting through law school?

Well, he tried resisting the temptation and buried himself for the week after the dance as fully in the routine of law classes as he could. Boy, did he study each night for the next day's assignment! Nonetheless, he found himself asking Sparkle's friends about her schedule of classes. By the next weekend, he began replacing case reading with scheming about how he could rearrange his day to accompany her as many times a week as possible from the dining room in House #3 to her classes. He was astounded to find that she was becoming more important to his wellbeing than an "A" in corporation law.

Ten days after the dance, the Nerd found himself in the dining room delaying his sprint to law school, hoping that Sparkle would come down early for breakfast. He had been informed that Sparkle had arranged her schedule so that all of her classes and seminars were on Tuesdays, Wednesdays, and Thursdays. This gave her time to go home by train to Tulare occasionally over weekends and take jobs on her free days to cover her expenses.

That morning, Sparkle came to breakfast at the last minute, gulped down some juice and toast, and headed for the door. The Nerd was waiting. He asked if she wanted company going down the hill to campus. She said that she was in a rush to get to her 9:00 o'clock psych class, but she welcomed the company. That began a routine that repeated itself several times a week, off and on, for several weeks.

Walking together allowed them to get to know each other. They talked about everything under the sun. Sparkle was up front in letting him know that she was not interested in romance. She had two boyfriends. Sparkle had a long time boyfriend from her hometown high school, Tulare Union. He was a navigator flying the dangerous "Hump" route of Burma to China. She also had a second beau who was a real estate developer and stockbroker in San Francisco, a Stanford graduate who had recently proposed marriage.

The Nerd felt a real outsider. He was at least number three in line for her attention and affection. He really thought that he could not aspire to much more. After all, he was not a dashing Romeo. He was a 4F who was full of guilt about not being with his buddies in the fight against the Nazis and the Japanese. He had to walk sideways in order to read her lips and try not to appear awkward as they trudged down to campus. In fact, all too many times, Sparkle had to grab his arm to warn him not to run into someone or jump into trouble as they crossed the streets. He accompanied her, but often she was actually looking after him!

The first few days, the conversation was uneven, almost artificial and stilted. He asked about her classes and her interests. She regaled him with details about journalism, business law, and child psychology. She flowed on about her life in her hometown and her work at the Tulare Advance Register as society editor during her senior year at Tulare Union High. How she enjoyed getting around the town of 40,000 to find out who was entertaining whom and what civic events were being held. She talked about her favorite teacher, Miss Thompson, who awakened her interest in English and writing. We chuckled over her favorite scoop in the Advance Register about a cow munching calmly in the town park in the wee hours one night as she returned home on a date. She painted a vivid picture of those special social events of the summer season.

By the third week of walking together after breakfast, the Nerd felt less and less uptight as they came to know each other better. Sparkle filled the pauses with warm comments about her interest in law and queries about his plans and classes. He spilled out his uncertainties about his own future and his ability to meet the demands of being a deaf lawyer in the courtroom. His insecurity seemed to be a challenge for a woman who appeared ready to face anything that life might offer. She reminded him that the courtroom is not the alpha and omega of the legal profession. She made him feel that she was genuinely interested in him, as a good friend.

By their fourth week walking down the hill, the Nerd felt that he had made a new special friend and looked forward on the weekends to seeing her the following Tuesday. Sparkle was busy most of the weekends on dates with her friend in San Francisco. On weekends, the Nerd spent most of the time with classmates at the Boalt Law Library. His wartime Class of 1945 had only thirteen members, twelve of whom were 4F men and one woman. The distinguished faculty in 1944 outnumbered the students. Students had to be prepared for every class because the odds were that you would be called on at least once in every session, and the professors read every test and made no secret in class of their opinions of the responses by the would-be lawyers.

As the second month of the walking relationship took shape, the Nerd found that his thinking about Sparkle was crowding out his study time. Sparkle was everywhere in his little world, taking part in dinners at I House surrounded by friends, sitting in on discussions about world affairs, and participating in the Spanish or French language tables. Rushing back from the library in late mornings and afternoons, he watched her light up the living room or the dining room with her smile and animated conversation. He felt very lonesome even as he poured over his studies. Sometimes, even a citation or a paragraph in the case under study brought her back into his consciousness.

It was in the second month that the scholastic pace slowed a bit. They both had taken most of their midterms. They both had time for more leisurely breakfasts and, to his delight, Sparkle came to the dining room about the same time he did and joined him without his having to ask her. It was on one of those mornings when one of the kitchen staff came over to the table to tell him that he had a phone call. Since he was unable to take the call, he asked Sparkle if she would talk for him and serve as intermediary. She smiled as they walked to the phone. It was his mother calling from San Francisco.

After Sparkle introduced herself, his mother Hazel replied that she wanted him to come home to San Francisco for the weekend. She had invited guests to dinner and thought that they would like to see him. There was still one midterm pending for the following Monday, and the Nerd felt that he needed the time to study. He also wanted to stay on campus because there was a dance that Friday night and he wanted Sparkle to be his date. Despite his excuse, his mother persisted, and Sparkle served as an ideal foil between the reluctant Nerd and his persistent parent. Sparkle was inventive and a warm flow of conversation convinced Mother of the need to respect the Nerd's concerns. In fact, his mother liked her so much that she invited Sparkle to Sunday dinner. Sparkle declined because she already had a commitment.

When the call ended about twenty minutes later, both of them had to gulp down their toast and coffee and almost run down the hill to avoid Sparkle's being late for her class. They spoke little as they sped across streets and past Faculty Glade, but Sparkle asked about Hazel and life in San Francisco. That began a much more personal series of discussions about their families and their lives before Berkeley and I House.

They said little that day. All the Nerd could muster up was that Hazel was a superb cook who loved having company. She worked with his father in their deli business and loved interacting with the customers. That was all they could cover by the time that they reached Wheeler Hall where Sparkle's class was scheduled. Just as she was turning into the building, he blurted out a request that she go to the Friday dance with him. She smiled and said that she had a date in San Francisco that night and doubted she would be able to join him. She smiled and said she was sorry. Well, the Nerd apparently put on a long face and waved goodbye, hurrying on to get ready for his 10:00 a.m. class.

That evening he got back late for dinner. Quite tired and a little depressed from the long day at law school, the Nerd sauntered into the dining room and immediately saw Sparkle waiting table. She waved at him and signaled for him to come to the table she was serving. As soon as he got seated, she came over and told him that her date in San Francisco had been moved to Saturday night. As he read her lips, his cares seemed to melt away. She confided that she asked her boyfriend to move the date since she was going to start a new job at a nursery school the following Monday and needed to see the director of the school Friday afternoon. The Nerd never found out whether his invitation or the new job was the real reason for the shifting of the date. But, by God, she did it!

That Friday night was a special treat. It was great fun. They danced almost every dance and just enjoyed each other. Most of the talk was trivial and touched on little more than experiencing the moment and enjoying each other's little jokes. The three hours rushed by and the feeling of her beauty in his arms made the Nerd happier than he remembered from other dates. When "Goodnight Sweetheart" closed the dance, a group of I Housers decided to go down to a late night spot in Emeryville that served beer to Cal students, and Sparkle and the Nerd went along. The car in which they went was Gwendolyn, a late 1930's black sedan with thousands of miles of use. The car belonged to Carlos Bee, a medically discharged veteran and a recent addition to I House. Eight people crowded into Gwendolyn and off they all went. They drank beer and laughed at all the antics that went on around them. When the 2:00 a.m. closing hour arrived, the Nerd felt closer to Sparkle than ever before. And when they got home, they snuggled a while and then agreed to have lunch together the next day.

The Nerd got to bed after 3:00 a.m. Saturday and was up at 7:00 a.m. to get to the law library as soon as it opened. When he got back for lunch, he found a message from Sparkle that she had to leave early for her date in San Francisco and wished him luck on his Monday midterm. He was disappointed as he ate a light lunch and at the last minute went with I House friends to a football game at Cal Memorial Stadium.

For the next several weeks, they had only glimpses of each other in the dining room. At that time, the Nerd was not only feeling the overload of three years of law school being compressed into two but also doing research on a law school article; he had been selected by the eminent Professor of Constitutional Law D.O. McGovney to do research for his precedent-setting article on the unenforceability of racial exclusion clauses in real estate contracts. He ate and ran for almost the rest of 1944. He spent most of his nights at the law library and fell into bed exhausted.

So tired was he that he had messed up on his responsibilities as the graduate counselor at I House #4. As graduate counselor for four semesters, the Nerd had tried to become friends with each and every I House #4 resident and used reason and persuasion to try to keep their activities more or less in line with the rules and regulations. He kept the I House director informed but, whenever possible, tried to insulate him from some of the day-to-day antics that would upset a man who was an ordained Presbyterian Minister. There were unscheduled parties that he had to break up many a night when he got back from the law library. There were nights when he was locked in his room by certain partying residents so that he could honestly say that he had heard nothing. There were confrontations between two of the Icelanders and the Latinos when the Icelanders, under the influence of too much firewater, asserted that they were part of the Nazi Super Race and Latins were not. There were complaints by the Chinese that the noise caused by informal Latin parties stymied their studying efforts. He tried to work out such incidents without involving the director, only generally telling him that there had been problems that he had had to deal with.

In the fall of 1944, as study demands multiplied, he occasionally lost track of what was going on. He was caught by surprise when, coming back at 11:00 p.m., he found that someone had organized a big, noisy party and coeds in various states of undress were running all over the dorm. He cleared out the house before neighbors were disturbed. He reported the incident to the director the next morning and asked him to consider warnings to the two principal perpetrators.

Several evenings later, when he trudged up the hill from the campus, he found another party underway with loud Latin music and lots of bottles stashed in various corners of the library. He barely got the ladies out of the building before the Berkeley police arrived to investigate a complaint about the noise. This time the director issued warnings to all the residents.

Enough kooky, but innocent, things happened regularly around the house so that it was not unknown to the Berkeley police. A couple of Latin American men, whenever it rained at night, took showers running around the block in their birthday suits. A group of fellows after a long night of studying climbed the trees in the backyard and played Tarzan. Sometimes a few of the men sneaked their girlfriends into the house in the wee hours of the morning. On several occasions, the Nerd had been summoned to cool down a sizzling lovers' quarrel. Eating into study time for his second-year law exams made being graduate counselor an ever-greater trial. Receiving his room and board was increasingly less tempting. He was afraid that he couldn't pass his law courses with the pressure and distractions at the House.

Then, one day, on returning from the law library, the director of I House left a message for him to come urgently to his office. What a shock it was to learn that one of the Latin American doctors on a post-graduate fellowship had performed an abortion in his dorm room in House #4 and that the tragic young lady was the daughter of a minister in a neighboring Northern California city. This event happened without even an inkling from the other housemates that the apparently mild-mannered doctor, with a family of three children at home, had gotten himself into such a terrible mess

That was the final straw! The Nerd felt that he couldn't stay on as graduate counselor and had to make an imminent decision about continuing for another semester. What to do? He needed the room and board; or else he had to find other sources of income for the remaining half-year that he planned to be in Berkeley and at I House. But, he felt that he could no longer balance his study time and his duties overseeing House #4.

Well, that night as he was groping for a solution, he quite by accident ran into Sparkle as he was leaving dinner. She took one look at him and asked why he was so worried. She took him by the hand, sat him down in the living room, and quietly asked him if there was a problem at law school. He said no, rather that it was connected to something unspeakable that had occurred at House 4. She urged him to tell her what happened and promised not to tell anyone. She let him talk it out. She assured him that the problem was not of the Nerd's making and that he had nothing to be ashamed of.

Her advice was simple and direct: tell the I House director the next morning that the law school workload made it impossible to continue as graduate counselor the next semester. She said, "Do it now so that the director can line up a replacement in time. He will understand. Don't get him down on you for not giving adequate time to line up a replacement. Maybe this is the right time to get yourself ready for the world beyond law school and I House."

The next morning he had the talk with the director. It was agreed that a new graduate counselor would be named for the next semester and that the Nerd would stay on as a House #4 resident for his remaining time at law school.

That night Sparkle and the Nerd talked for hours. They began sharing life experiences on a totally new level, discussing the future. Somehow it was no longer a casual campus relationship, but something much deeper.

Sparkle had been very busy during the last weeks of 1944 before the conversation. She was one popular coed. The Nerd would see her at I House dinners, dances, and bridge games as he left nightly on his way to or from the law library. She had one date after another. Her involvement in I House affairs went far beyond social life. She participated in many of the serious discussion groups that dealt with the range of issues that permeated our concerns as we approached the end of World War II, from the Four Freedoms to the Breton Woods accords. She was active in organizing discussion groups about the direction of the post-War world community. She had that special knack of getting people who didn't like or trust each other to talk with her and then be drawn into spirited dialogues.

At one lunch session, she tried to get two Palestinians, one Jewish and one Arab, to talk about what was needed for coexistence in the Holy Land. In spite of her sincerity, earnestness and smile, she could get them to do little more than acknowledge each other when she first invited them. But she persisted and gradually helped them to open a limited conversation that seemed to break the ice. When they left I House at the end of the fall 1944 semester, they were able to talk to each other. And both of them went out of their way to thank Sparkle for being a friend.

It was during the fall of 1944 that her long time Tulare boy-friend, the navigator on the Hump flight from Burma to South China, came home on leave. The Nerd observed their comings and goings for several days. But Sparkle never mentioned the visit until after that special conversation. Most weekends, Sparkle also went on dates with her San Francisco boyfriend. The Nerd noticed that she was away and heard the gossip that she was almost engaged. Since there had been no commitment between them and their relationship was so casual, he had remained quite detached as he was drudging away on the seven-day-a-week law school routine.

Sparkle also had two jobs of her own. She began working as a nursery school teacher at a federally run facility in South Berkeley. She worked three afternoons a week and really enjoyed the children. She applied her course work in child psychology to the task at hand. She regaled us fellow I Housers with her adventures with the children, many of whom were African-Americans, and how adorable she thought they were. She loved to tell us of the games she played with her young charges to get them to behave without the threat of force.

She was especially amused by their efforts to manipulate her and the other nursery school teachers so that they could get out of something they had been told to do. The game was precisely "who could outsmart the other!"

One evening, Sparkle arrived at the dinner table with a glint in her eye. She was chuckling over her trip home that evening. She had been waiting for a late parent to arrive and she was afraid that she would miss her bus home to I House. So, she picked up Alvin, a handsome young black boy, and carried him a couple of blocks to his grandmother's house. She was very amused when a white man did a double take as he drove by, then went around the block to see if his eyes had deceived him and then looked with dismay at the sight of Sparkle with the black boy in her arms. Sparkle just smiled and went on her way. Many years later, when we remembered the incident, she would wonder what had happened to Alvin and whether his world had become a better place for interracial coexistence.

She also had a second job a couple of days a week to do clerical and typing work for one of the original world renowned environment giants, Dr. Jepson, who with John Muir had saved the Sequoias and started the Sierra Club. She talked little about the substance of her work with the famous botanist, who was at the time a Professor Emeritus, but she told us of her admiration for his contribution to California and the recognition of his scientific eminence. She told us of the large number of incoming phone calls he received almost every day from distinguished academics and government officials from all over the country. She reported that she seldom saw the reclusive scientist, but she made no secret of her problems in deciphering and transcribing the almost unreadable scribbles she found awaiting her.

After that fateful night when her advice had guided him to give up his job as graduate counselor at House #4, they made more time to spend together. Gradually they began sharing other confidences, much more personal. One evening as they walked home from the library, she began to tell him about her parents and her concerns about her life before coming to Berkeley. She confided that her father Haskell had been killed in a work accident when she was nine years old and that, after his death, her mother Mabel and grandmother Addie had reared her. In turn, he told her about his family: his mother, a third generation San Franciscan and his father, a newcomer from England. They talked about their schooling. Both were products of public schools. He had gone to only three schools, from kindergarten through high school. She had attended only two schools in Tulare, from the first grade through high school, except for a year in Long Beach, the year after her father's death.

The Nerd and Sparkle began having dinner often together at I House. In addition, she was becoming a frequent guest for Sunday dinner at his home in the city. His mother Hazel embraced Sparkle. From their first telephone conversation, Hazel had become an ardent admirer of Sparkle and did everything possible to draw the two together. If she got wind of a dance to which Sparkle had agreed to go with the Nerd, a corsage—often a butterfly orchid—would be awaiting Sparkle on the afternoon of the dance. The Nerd, bless his naiveté, never thought of such niceties.

From that first phone call with Sparkle in the fall of 1944 through the first half of 1945, the Nerd's mother Hazel periodically invited a gang of I Housers, always including Sparkle, to Sunday night dinner. The invitees made their way—frequently in Carlos Bee's Gwendolyn—over the Bay Bridge to the Nerd's dinner table on 29th Avenue in the Richmond District of San Francisco. Hazel, a great cook, prepared gourmet treats of baked hams, roasts, crab, and shrimp dishes. Hazel came from a large family, and she always enjoyed having a large number of people at the dinner table. The dinner table was always full of good conversation and great food. For Sparkle, the dinners were extra-special.

3

Sparkle's Family

Sparkle introduced him to her close-knit family in a way that made the Nerd feel that he knew them, even though he had never seen or talked with anyone in Tulare.

Sparkle was born on April 1, 1922, Easter Sunday. When her father first laid eyes on her, he called her his Easter Bunny. And, Bunny was the nickname her family and friends always called her. It was the name that everyone at Berkeley and I House called her. She was Sparkle to me, but she was Bunny to the world.

Her father Haskell had been born into a large family of Welsh-English origin with roots in the Blue Hills of North East Tennessee that went back generations. He was the youngest in a family of thirteen siblings, his mother being the second wife. After World War I, he, like many of his brothers and sisters, moved westward and settled in Tulare.

Haskell had been in the signal corps in France during World War I and was a mechanical whiz who loved to tinker with motorcycles, cars, and anything electrical. Above all, he was a personality kid and made friends easily. He was a joiner and belonged to just about every veteran, service, and fraternal organization in the Tulare area, and everywhere she went with her father, people would greet them with a smile and friendly talk. He was active in the Methodist Church where his wife, although a Presbyterian, taught Sunday school. Sparkle recalled how her father loved to go to revival meetings, especially at the nearby predominately black community, and sing at the top of his lungs. She speculated that he would have gone into politics if he had lived.

Sparkle recalled trips in the family Hupmobile, highlighting those on which the family went overnight to conventions and meetings of the various organizations of which her father was a member. On travel days, it was her mother who did the packing, constantly calling to Haskell to make sure that she was including everything he needed. Her mother would then get the family up and pack snacks for the trip. Sparkle would just smile as she described trips in which she felt like a queen. She was never car sick, and loved the changing panorama as her father told her about what was growing in the cultivated fields they passed or what the principal activity was in the small towns they passed through. She developed a real love for travel.

Her remembrances of her father also included his temper: how mad he got one night during Prohibition when some bathtub beer he and some friends were brewing in the family bathtub blew up after one of his co-conspirators added the wrong ingredient. His flow of invectives ranged from the unholy to mean. On another occasion, Sparkle told a story about her father being arrested for punching a businessman who tried to cheat him. She also recalled how irate he became when he heard of someone being evicted from his home for missing a mortgage payment in the early years of the Depression and his efforts to raise the money to help his friend out. She was especially proud of her father's sense of justice and his willingness to help those in need.

She also described daylong trips to the country with her father when he took her hunting or fishing. She never developed a taste for either. To her dying day, Sparkle truly disliked the gutting of the fish or stalking a deer or a rabbit. One night while Father was taking her home, a rabbit crossed in front of the truck. Father turned on his searchlight and reached for his rifle; Sparkle screamed that he should not hurt the bunny rabbit; her father stopped to console his daughter and the bunny escaped. After that, her father became reconciled to her not following in his footsteps. With her father's urging, she tried baseball and other sports, but she was readily bored. In fact, Sparkle was not an outdoors or sports type. She preferred to read, play with her dolls, and be with Mother and Grandmother.

Her father Haskell had become district service manager for the Southern California Edison Company before he was killed in a work accident when Sparkle was only nine. As part of his job with the utility company, he went out to fix milking machines and other equipment on the dairy farms in the area. There he met the owners, many of them recent immigrants from the Azores and many of whom spoke only limited English. He admired them for their initiative and often talked of their backbreaking work and frugal living conditions as they built up their own dairies. He saw them as his friends.

Sparkle reminisced about her parents being awakened at 3:00 a.m. by a dairyman barely able to speak English. The voice would say, "Please Mrs., I need him urgent!" Mother would hand the phone to dad, who would say, "Morning, what's the matter? ... Uh, uh, uh… Yes, Tony, I understand. I'll be there as soon as I get dressed." Then mother would ask, "Are you sure that was Tony?" "Of course I'm sure that was his voice." He would dress, crank up the car, and be on his way. He always had breakfast with the dairymen and their families and would only get home after his normal workday.

Sparkle vividly remembered his funeral. So many wanted to pay their respects that the Methodist Church was filled to overflowing. She recalled the large numbers of Catholic Portuguese standing in the street outside the Church when her father's casket was carried down the steps. In those days, Catholics couldn't enter Protestant churches, even for funerals. Those sidewalk mourners were the immigrant dairymen who paid their respects to the man who went out at 3:00 a.m. to fix their milking machines.

For years after Haskell died, her mother Mabel would find hams, pork chops, and fruit on her back porch. No one ever left a note. It was just the way the dairymen remembered their friend and saw to it that his family was never short of food. Years later, when Sparkle would run into a dairyman who was helped by her father in the 1920s and early 1930s, she would always be greeted as good Haskell's daughter.

After her father's death, Sparkle was reared by two ladies: her mother Mabel and her grandmother Addie. Her mother's family, the Luneys, was Scottish-Irish who had emigrated from Belfast in Northern Ireland, and settled in Denison, Iowa before the Civil War. They had sold their cooperage business, carried the cash proceeds in a paper bag across the Atlantic and out to Iowa where they invested it in farmland and a grain mill. Her grandmother came from English-Welsh stock who had pioneered in Kentucky and then Western Iowa. Both of her grandparents had been Presbyterians with a strong sense of individual responsibility and morality.

Her grandparents had lived on the family farm in Denison until the patriarch of the family passed on. Her grandmother, Addie Jones, had been reared on a neighboring farm and remembered riding as a little girl with her parents in a wagon across Iowa to see the Lincoln funeral train. Addie's mother passed away when she was quite young, and when her father remarried, she and her stepmother didn't get along. So, Grandmother packed her satchel and headed to town to find a job. Walking along the road, she was passed by a wagon and offered a ride. The wagon driver, James Luney, asked what she was planning to do and then told her that his family needed a hired girl. She accepted and not too many years later, the wagon driver proposed and she accepted.

At the wedding of her grandparents in 1883, the patriarch sat with his back to the Presbyterian ceremony in the family parlor because he felt that Addie was not well born enough for his eldest son. In spite of this initial disdain, Grandmother soon became the family favorite—not only of her father-in-law, whom she nursed during his final illness, but also of all the brothers and sisters and their spouses. By the time the patriarch died, Grandmother had become the apple of his eye.

The family farmed and operated mills in Iowa and the Dakotas as a de facto family corporation. Her grandfather had been the family treasurer and went regularly to Chicago to sell the crops. As the family grew older and the offspring increased, he believed that the family operation was getting too complicated and divided up the land equally among his brothers and sisters. Her grandparents, with their two surviving children, left Iowa for the state of Washington. After exploring business opportunities, Grandfather bought an island in Puget Sound and built a sawmill. Unfortunately, as sometimes happens in the waters there, the tides shifted and the island became submerged.

So, about 1900, he picked up his family again and migrated to Los Angeles where others of his siblings had already moved. Long Beach became their new home, and he went into the real estate business on Central Avenue in then downtown Los Angeles. Grandmother loved Long Beach. She had found the ideal place to live. She no longer was bound to the rigid routine of farm life. She had left the old days behind her and she set out to rear her two surviving offspring as urbanites. Her son Tom was to be a lawyer and her daughter a bookkeeper. She urged her husband to buy a home near the beach.

That was the family situation for several years until Grandfather went on a real estate trip to the lower San Joaquin River Valley of California and found a ranch with artesian wells outside a small rural community called Pixley. Without even consulting Grandmother, he purchased the land with the money that Grandmother expected would be used for buying her home in Long Beach. And, as Grandmother repeated many years later, "I spent all my life trying to get off the farm. But after I found the good life in Long Beach, there I was back on a dairy farm in the Central Valley!"

The children got their education and their careers off the farm. When Grandfather died in the late 1910s, Grandmother returned to Long Beach with her bachelor son and resolved never to leave the seashore again. Sparkle's mother Mabel met and fell in love with Haskell, the handsome Tennessean. They married after World War I and settled in Tulare not far from the Pixley dairy ranch where he and Mabel had met. The family kept the Pixley ranch and the farmland in South Dakota that Grandfather had allocated to himself on liquidating the family corporation. Her mother and Grandmother sharecropped that land after Grandfather's death and those returns were a significant portion of the family's income for the next thirty years.

Sparkle grew up an only child and an only grandchild. The death of her father and her bachelor uncle left her as a teenager entirely in the care of her mother and grandmother. She was the apple of both their eyes—truly the center of their lives. Even so, as she told the Nerd, she often felt very much alone.

After her father's death, she spent several long spells in Long Beach with her grandmother and uncle. Her mother wanted to move the family to Long Beach but fate conspired to keep them in the Valley. Sparkle's parents had purchased a home financed by the California State veterans program. Under the rules at that time, a veteran or his widow was entitled to one subsidized mortgage for only one home—and that mortgage could not transferred to another property. So, her mother's plan of selling the Tulare house and transferring the mortgage to another house in Long Beach was denied by California authorities and she had to remain in Tulare.

Sparkle loved the company of her grandmother. She told me, "Grandmother had a quick wit and an adventurous spirit." Sparkle loved the hours they spent on the beach together talking of life and observing the people. The hours just seemed to roll by—and Sparkle never tired of her grandmother's stories of the family in Denison and the trek to the West Coast. Sparkle's eyes shone as she remembered those experiences and how each day on the beach Grandmother and she waited each afternoon for a frisky but friendly Scottie that, once set loose by its master on the hill, would run across the beach to greet the sunbathers. He always came over to the two ladies for a caress and a frolic.

Sparkle and her family had a weekly ritual in Long Beach, which was to go on the red interurban train to Los Angeles or Hollywood to see the latest movies. Even more special were those Saturdays when her uncle took her all dressed up to Grauman's Chinese Theater and she could feel a real part of the fervor sweeping across the world from the make-believe factories of Hollywood. She had her autograph book with her just in case she might see one of the glittering stars on those Saturday treks to Tinseltown.

It was during this interlude that Sparkle experienced the terrible fury of the 1933 Long Beach earthquake. She recalled the shocks that rumbled through the family home and the panic she felt as she was awakened by the jolt. Leaving her bedroom, she heard Grandmother urging everyone to be calm and stand under the doorways. From the corner of her eye she could see into the living room where the family baby grand was sliding from one end of the room to the other, blocking escape through the front door. When the shaking ceased, the family had to live in the car for several days until it was safe to return to the house. She would describe the damage to the houses in the neighborhood and the cave-in of the roof of her elementary school. The quake colored her sense of security for the rest of her life, and every time she moved to a new house, her instinct was to identify her possible escape routes in the event of an emergency.

The earthquake closed the schools in Long Beach so her mother had to take her back to Tulare. That is where she was born and it was destined to be her home.

Then, her uncle Thomas had an accident and was disabled. Grandmother took care of him until his death. In her 70s, she decided to come up to Tulare to be with her daughter and granddaughter. She built a house next door and settled in. But she, like Sparkle, never forgot Long Beach and the life that they had so lovingly lived together there.

In Tulare, Grandmother became the center of the family. Ele told me that it was Grandmother who made the family decisions and frequently maneuvered her mother into doing something mother was not inclined to do. Sparkle told the Nerd that Grandmother was always willing to try something new while her mother would try to pour cold water on anything that went beyond her normal routine.

One evening walking back from the law library to I House for a soda, Sparkle told the Nerd the story of her spectacular trip to the two World's Fairs of 1939. She said that one afternoon in the spring of 1939, as she was coming home from high school she passed by the Greyhound Bus Depot. She saw an announcement of a special rate of $69.95 per person for a round-trip from Tulare to San Francisco for one fair and then to New York for the other. A trip around the U.S. and a visit to both fairs! She talked to the depot master and found out that, as long as a passenger was headed east, he or she could go north or south when headed to New York. Coming home from New York, the route could include any locale that was of interest in the westward direction. Well, Sparkle raced home to sell the trip to Mother and Grandmother. Grandmother captured the same enthusiasm as Sparkle while Mother hemmed and hawed about the expense and the time she would lose from her duties with the garden club and Job's Daughters. The debate went on all through dinner until Grandmother said that she couldn't take her money with her and that she would help pay Mother's expenses if that would resolve the impasse. Grandmother smiled at Sparkle as mother reluctantly agreed.

Over sodas with the Nerd, Sparkle described the six-week trip around the country, from San Francisco to Seattle and Vancouver, eastward through Montana, the Dakotas to Chicago, Detroit and Niagara Falls to New York City. A week in New York City before heading to Washington, D.C., Richmond, Miami, New Orleans, and Denison, Iowa, for a family wedding, before travelling to Denver, Salt Lake City, and home.

Sparkle then smiled broadly as she exclaimed, "Can you imagine that we made the trip for under $150 per person? Well, we did! We each took $150 from our respective bank accounts and covered our own expenses. You know that mine is a Scottish family and we watch our pennies very closely. Why, we even bought a wedding present for the Denison wedding at Marshall Fields in Chicago, and we went shopping in Macys in New York. We never missed window-shopping or taking advantage of a bargain. We economized whenever we could, but we really skimped on nothing."

For almost an hour, she told the Nerd some of the highlights of her trip. Her eyes aglow with enthusiasm, she spilled out her thrill with seeing so many wonders of the U.S. and Canada. The bus went through national parks from Yellowstone to the Smokies. She loved Marshall Fields in Chicago for its elegance and the style of its clothes. The New York Fair impressed her much more than San Francisco's.

And the adventures in New York! When they arrived at the New York Port Authority Terminal, her mother walked over to the Astor Hotel to see if they could get reservations. The clerk said that the best rate he could offer them was $6 per day for the three of them. Well, said mother, that rate would break their budget. The clerk replied that the Astor managed a residential hotel, the Flanders, on 50th Street that had weekly rates, and he called to see if any rooms were available. Yes, he reported, there was a three-room suite of two bedrooms and a bath at $27 per week for the three people. Mother agreed to the offer and returned on foot to the Terminal. They splurged and took a cab to the Flanders—Grandmother paid for the taxi.

Sparkle took real pleasure in having taken the coast-to-coast trip during the Great Depression when meals at Horn & Hardart Automat could be purchased for less than fifty cents per person. The subway cost a nickel and buses a dime. The first day in New York, the three ladies decided to go to the Fair by subway. Grandmother and Sparkle got on the train before the doors closed, leaving mother on the platform. Mother started to scream and was terrified at being lost. Sparkle called out to her to take the next train and that Grandmother and she would be waiting on the platform. Mother ran toward the front of the train crying and pleading to be let on. The motorman just drove off. When the next train arrived, the three ladies were reunited. But they never rode the subway again. Mother agreed to pay the extra nickel each day for them to go around New York by bus, no more subways!

The ladies spent a week in New York. They went down to Wall Street and up to the Cloisters. They enjoyed Sunday services at St. John the Divine Cathedral. They shopped at Macys and Gimbels, and spent three days visiting almost every exhibit at the Fair. Sparkle loved the displays from countries around the world. She waxed eloquent about those from Europe and Latin America. Wanderlust had been awakened and Tulare would never be enough to satisfy her vision of her life. She said that, as a little girl, she had a dream of going to China as a missionary. The two Fairs had revived her taste for seeing the world.

The Nerd was captivated by the story of the trip to the World's Fairs. He tried to find examples that paralleled her adventures. But he usually ended up talking of unrealized dreams, like the one he had as a little boy growing up on the edge of the Golden Gate and wanting to get on one of the ships heading for the Orient. He confessed that, while he loved San Francisco and his family, he wanted a taste of much more of the world. A new horizon had been opened in their ever-closer friendship.

Each conversation seemed to touch a new element of their lives. Sparkle introduced him to her interest in music and the theater. She told him of her experiences at Tulare Union High School and how much she enjoyed writing and acting. Sparkle had been in the band but her real love was taking part in school plays. She especially remembered her role in Thornton Wilder's *The Happy Journey to Trenton and Camden*. She favored playing character roles that added light touches to the entertainment.

Sparkle had taken piano lessons since she was a little girl. When she entered high school, she found that the piano was not part of the school band. But the band was where all her friends participated. So she took up the flute. Always practical, why take up a new instrument that weighed a lot? Mother bought her a classical German flute, and Sparkle became one of the flutists. The band at high school was fine, but the marching got boring and once she graduated, the flute got put away. At Berkeley, when she needed money to cover expenses, she sold it to the second flutist in the San Francisco Symphony. Grandmother understood right away why the instrument was sold, but mother was heartsick that Sparkle would not be able to play her flute at future Tulare events.

Sparkle had been active in the social life of her town. Her family seemed to know all the right people and she had a lot of friends, both boys and girls. She had served as the Honored Queen of Job's Daughters. She was involved in most high school and church dances. She regaled the Nerd with details about decorating for dances and the many girl and boyfriends who populated her life.

With all the social life, the family lived on a tight budget. Expenses in the Depression in Tulare were quite low, but the income from the farms and savings was equally low. Sparkle said that the family lived well but watched the pennies. She never wanted for anything since her mother was an excellent seamstress and made most of her clothes. Sparkle said that she wanted to add to the family income and found jobs in her senior year in high school and during her two years at the College of the Sequoias as a window dresser at the Tulare Penney's store and at the local newspaper, the Tulare Advance Register.

As they began to trust each other, Sparkle confided that she did not make close friends easily. She had lots of acquaintances, but only a few real friends. She said that she had a close circle of girl friends at high school, but only in one did she have a real sense of kinship. That friend she had known since early grade school, the daughter of Danish-Americans, Marion "Mimi" Nielsen, with whom she felt a special bond. Indeed, Mimi was her only attendant at our wedding. She confided that people often found her easy to meet and talk to and that she enjoyed meeting them. However, meeting them and sharing her feelings with them were two different levels of relationship. Trust, she said, was something that had to be earned with her and that only those few people she truly trusted would she share her real inner thoughts and feelings.

Sparkle said that she had always enjoyed being with older people. She told me of adults she felt especially comfortable with. She especially enjoyed the company of the Librarian at the Tulare Public Library, Elizabeth LaCell, and Elizabeth took extra efforts to help Sparkle prepare papers and enjoy great literature. She also enjoyed the company of a distant cousin, Jim Leonard, a few years her elder, whom she admired for his intelligence and resourcefulness. She also talked about the Campbells, whose son Charles had often been her date. Charles's parents treated her like the daughter they didn't have, and Sparkle said that she always considered Charlie more as a brother than a boyfriend. The Campbells often took her on family excursions, including her first trip to San Francisco.

Sparkle developed a great interest in travel. She was interested in different cultures and understanding what made people tick. When the Nerd asked her what she wanted to do in life, she didn't hesitate one minute. She said, "I want to write. I want to be a journalist. I want to see the world and tell people about what is happening out there." She volunteered that her choice of courses had focused on subjects that helped her better understand people and social conditions that she deemed critical to being a good writer.

Then she shared some of her writings—some personal and others related to her classwork. She had a wonderfully easy style of writing—quite simple and easy to read and understand. She had none of the Nerd's stilted language and complex sentences. Hers were to the point and down to earth. She was always writing short notes and stashing them in her binder—a practice she continued through her lifetime. Unfortunately she never got around to expanding those notes into the books and articles she had hoped to write.

4

The Nerd's Family

Sharing his thoughts and fears, even with his parents and aunts, was something the Nerd did not do easily. As a young teenager he had found it impossible to talk about the terrible inadequacy and emptiness he felt after learning that he was losing his hearing. He felt that he was somehow to blame for the scourge. Coupled with his physical awkwardness and lack of coordination that had kept him off sports teams, he really believed that he was incapable of doing anything significant in life. The opportunity Sparkle gave him to share feelings awakened a level of confidence that he hadn't experienced before.

The Nerd was a city boy—born and reared in San Francisco. His only real experience until he went to Berkeley had been in the city. The family traveled a bit, but neither his mother nor father drove a car, so that leaving the city meant a ride with friends or going on a train. He lived in the Richmond District, having been born at St. Mary's Hospital just a few blocks outside of the District. He knew all the streetcar routes and was a devotee of everything San Franciscan. He even fought with other young friends who said that there was some place better than his city in which to live.

His early life revolved around his mother Hazel, who was the strong person in his family. She was from an old San Francisco family that dated from the Gold Rush days. Her grandfather had migrated from Rotterdam and settled in the 1850s in the Mission District. Her grandmother and mother, Jenny, he had been told, had been born in the city. Jenny had married twice, having been widowed when she was in her early 20s. Still in her 20s, she remarried an elegant German, Isadore Asch, whom his mother considered the epitome of a dashing gentleman. Isadore had emigrated from Germany and had become one of the premier cigar merchants in the Bay Area. After the Earthquake and Fire of 1906, he became the proprietor of the cigar shop in the Palace Hotel and later owned a prestigious store on Market Street near the corner of Sansome. His grandmother Jenny passed away when he was a year old.

The Nerd remembered his grandfather as an elegantly dressed gentleman, almost Prussian in his bearing, carrying a cane and with a baby rose in his lapel and a pocket full of silver dollars. He also recalls the day when, as very little boy holding his grandfather's hand, they walked along Montgomery Street when a chauffeur-driven car parked next to where they were walking and a distinguished man got out of the car. Grandfather said, "Good morning, Mr. Gianinni." And, Mr. Gianinni, founder of the Bank of America, replied, "Good morning, Mr. Asch. This must be your grandson." His grandfather died of pneumonia when the Nerd was about seven.

The Nerd's mother was one of seven siblings, four girls and three boys. She and one brother were only ones who married. Two of the brothers, who were twins, his aunts told him, had died within weeks of each other in their early 20s. One of the sisters had died young. His Uncle Melvin had fathered one son, his cousin Robert, who was fifteen years older than the Nerd; they lived across Golden Gate Park in the Sunset District.

The Nerd was very fond of the maiden aunts whom he had known. The oldest, Aunty Paula, was crippled by a disease in her hipbone. She had stayed home for years, taking care of her mother and father and younger siblings. She was gentle and loving and a wonderful cake baker. Oh, how the Nerd loved to lick her cake batters and savored every bite of her chocolate Viennese Tortes! His younger aunt, Net, worked as a secretary-administrative aide in an insurance company until she was carried away by kidney disease in late 1930s. When the younger sister died, Aunty Paula, having cared for her parents and siblings, became a companion to older women who needed someone to take care of them. He admired her courage and indomitable spirit.

The Nerd's father, Hyman (Hymie), had immigrated to San Francisco from England in the early 1900s with his older brother Morris. They were invited by their uncle and his family, the Harrises, who had immigrated in the 1880s. The Tragens and Harrises had come from Eastern Europe. Relations between the brothers were not close, Morris returned to England in the early 1930s after a divorce to rejoin the family textile and apparel manufacturing business in Manchester.

The Nerd never met his father's parents or siblings. His father spoke warmly of his mother but never of his relationship with his father. After his mother died and his father remarried, Hymie never contacted his father again. Occasionally one of his sisters would write from England, but the information was never shared with the Nerd. Occasionally an old-fashioned English-style raincoat or other apparel would arrive from England, that the Nerd was told came from the family's factory in Manchester.

Hymie's family did not approve of his marriage to Mother, because, as Orthodox Jews, they did not believe that my mother and her family "were Jewish." You see, my mother's aunt had married a Mormon; her uncle, a Swedish Lutheran; and her brother Melvin, a Lutheran. An English cousin told me a few years ago that my mother's family was too "unique" to be accepted.

Hymie was a workaholic: he left early every morning to open his food market and the deli department he personally ran. He was ambitious, but never seemed to achieve what he had hoped for when he emigrated from England. His Harris cousins were quite well-to-do and had offered different investment possibilities to him, but he never seemed to take their advice or offers of business deals. One of his cousins involved in San Francisco real estate wanted him to join as a partner in developing what is now the western end of the Sunset District. His mother once told the Nerd that his father had rejected her urging to accept the offer with the comment, "Who would want to live on those sand dunes!" The Nerd seemed to follow in his father's footsteps when in the early 1950s, on being offered the opportunity to buy a two-level house above the Sausalito ferry slit for less than $10,000, queried, "Who would want to live there?"

The Nerd's mother, Hazel, had been reared in a very open and cosmopolitan household. Her parents with their large brood usually had lots of guests at their dinner table, from all the various nationalities and religions that populated the seaport city. Her family was nominally Jewish, but they celebrated Santa Claus and Christmas trees, never a menorah. They had Easter hams and hunted for Easter eggs, never a Seder.

The Nerd's father came from an orthodox Jewish family, but his mother knew so little about Jewish customs that she served her husband ham and eggs for their first breakfast after they returned from their honeymoon. None of his father's traditions seemed to rub off on the couple. As long as the Nerd could remember, even his father participated in the Christmas festivities. Christmas Eve was a family celebration with his aunts who spent weeks preparing homemade cakes and candies for their friends as Christmas presents. Mother's family was truly ecumenical and many of their closest family friends were Irish-Catholics. Hazel's first great love had not been Jewish and she commented one day to the Nerd when he was a teenager that she still remembered that man and still regretted their breaking up.

The Nerd really knew very little about his mother's family other than his aunts. Neither Mother nor aunts ever spoke of family relationships. Outside of his mother's aunt by marriage, no one was contacted or discussed. No one ever mentioned what happened to that aunt's husband or why he left his wife and child. One day when he and his mother were on Grant Avenue in downtown San Francisco, a lady said hello to his mother and, after a short exchange, walked on. When asked who the lady was, Mother replied: "Just one of my cousins. Don't worry about her." She would often say: "You can choose your friends, but you are stuck with your relatives."

His nuclear family consisted of his mother, father, and one sister, Jacqueline or Jackie. An older brother, Gordon, had died of a glandular disease before the Nerd was born. His mother had suffered miscarriages between his birth and that of his sister. Jackie had been born four and half years after him in late 1926. His mother lavished attention on him and was very protective. In her rocking chair, she would croon over and over again that nothing would harm this little man. She did not want to lose the Nerd as she had lost Gordon.

Whenever he was sick, Mother took him right to St. Mary's Hospital where he had been born. He still recalls the attention of the nuns and the sense of protection he felt in their care. One of his trips to St. Mary's was to have his tonsils removed. He still recalled the incredible sensation of orange water ice on his throat after his tonsils were taken out. He recalls the Sister coming to his bed and asking if his throat hurt. When he nodded "Yes," Sister said, "Don't tell Mother" while feeding him orange water ice. And, then a few minutes later, Mother Superior asking how he felt and then saying, "Don't tell Sister" while feeding him more orange water ice. Orange water ice is still his comfort food.

When he was four and a half, just before his sister was born, he fell ill with scarlet fever and was returned to the hospital. In the back of his mind, there is an etched memory of the love and attention by his mother and the nuns. He will always remember the warm embrace of his mother as the doctor told him that the fever had damaged the optic and hearing nerves and that, when he was better, he would have to spend some time having a lot of tests. Those tests lasted for many years until he was told at the age of thirteen that he had irreparable damage to his hearing and that he should learn lip reading.

As he recovered from scarlet fever, his baby sister was born. He quickly got used to Mother spending more and more of her time with the blonde-haired, blue-eyed baby. Mother got a live-in girl to take care of the two youngsters while she went back to work as the Great Depression clutched the family in its grip. They moved from their spacious flat to a small apartment.

As family finances further declined, the girl had to be let go and the Nerd became a baby-sitter for several years. He had the chore of house cleaning on Saturdays and had to forego the playground or movies to look after the little one. And they had tiffs. Jackie had learned early on how to get her brother's goat. For years, phone calls to the parents were a constant feature of Saturday mornings whenever brother tried to get sister to do something that she didn't want to do. Sister loved to play with her dolls and saw no reason to clean up her room or help with dusting. How often he was told that he was the big brother and had to be responsible for taking care of his sister. And, when he asked for daddy's help, dad would just say, "Talk to your mother!" Those Saturday skirmishes ended in the mid-1930s when Mother met a wonderful lady, Frances, whose family was down on its luck, and she moved in and took care of both of us for the next several years until she married a Navy man and started her own family.

Brother and sister were fond of each other and never deliberately hurt one another. But their interests were very different from the beginning. He loved books, especially biographies and history. While Jackie was smart and learned very quickly, she was never a bookworm, but was interested in playing and shopping. He was a straight A student in the only three schools he attended from kindergarten through high school—Alamo, Presidio Junior High, and George Washington High School—all within walking distance of the family flat. He loved to study. She thought it a bore. Little sister always felt that she had to live up to the reputation of her egghead older brother. Jackie had a special relationship to her daddy and knew that she was the apple of his eye.

Neither of his parents had been to university. Mother had been to business college and cherished her ten-year career as a buyer for the Women's Department at the venerable White House department store on Grant Avenue. The Nerd never knew how far Father had gone through the British school system. Both parents encouraged his career aspirations and interests in reading and academics. The Nerd always received encouraging gifts when he brought home report cards with all "A's," and his parents listened lovingly to the reports and debate arguments he prepared in Junior and Senior High School. No parents could have been more supportive.

Early in his life, Mother made certain that the Nerd came to know a lady, Alicia Woods, with the education and intellectual experience that Mother had not received. That lady became the grandparent he did not have and one of the most important influences in his young life. She asked him to call her Grandma Woods.

She was an elegant former schoolteacher from one of San Francisco's elite families. Her own daughters and grandchildren lived in the Midwest and East and the Nerd got most of her grandmotherly wisdom and direction. She arranged for him to be invited to programs at the de Young Museum and other San Francisco institutions that held special events for young people. She told him to "Keep your mind open and make your own judgments." And she was a disciplinarian. The Nerd remembered throughout his life the day when Grandma, Mother, and he were walking on Grant

Avenue, and like many a tot, he lingered and was lagging behind. Grandma said only once, "Young man, you do not loiter. Come here and take my hand." He continued to tarry. So, Grandma reached out for him and pulled him to her, took down his pants and gave him a couple of firm slaps. He never lagged behind again and never needed to be spanked again.

It was Grandma who truly nurtured his interest in the world of books and the annals of human history. She challenged him to think about the world around him and the social drama inflicted on the people by the Great Depression. She would talk to him about political and economic issues, including the drama unfolding in Germany in the early 1930s. She was a lifelong Republican, as the Nerd's Mother had been, and she worried about the role of government in the lives of people. She believed strongly in individual responsibility, but recognized that the Great Depression required government to help people unable to take care of themselves. She also would occasionally take him with her to a service at Grace Cathedral so that he would be exposed to different religious creeds and rites. "Never be afraid to try new experiences, but also be sure of what you believe in your heart," she once told him.

When the Nerd was a young teenager and before he had truly confronted his hearing loss, Grandma passed on and left a terrible void. When he tried to discuss such thoughts with his parents or aunts, they listened and tried to respond, but somehow they lacked the insights that came from his sessions with Grandma. It was a strange sensation that, when the Nerd talked to Sparkle, for the first time since Grandma's death, he found someone whom almost immediately related to what concerned him and could help him find peace and guidance that he felt essential for dealing with this needs.

The Nerd had always loved sports, especially baseball, swimming, and tennis. He admired the good players on the playground. He wanted to be part of their teams, but he always ended up being the last one chosen because he was not well coordinated and wore glasses from a very early age. Probably contributing to his physical distress were the effects of his scarlet fever. These were concerns that he talked about with Grandma, never his mother or aunts. Mother would get panicky about her little boy and go talk with the athletes about letting her boy play. The Aunts would tell him not to worry, and that time would take care of the problem. Grandma would talk sympathetically and try to explain that he needed to find the strength within himself to overcome his limitations and to concentrate on things that were attuned to his own abilities.

The Great Depression impacted the Nerd's growing up. He never forgot the long bread lines on Market Street and all the talk among his parents' friends about their problems. More immediately, his father lost a great deal of money and was unable to develop his plans for a chain of specialty delis. Father had also invested on margin and the family savings were wiped out. The family had lived in a spacious, elegant flat, but had to move to a much smaller nearby one-bedroom apartment.

The Nerd had been very happy in the spacious flat. He had made good friends and enjoyed the nearby playground. He loved the upstairs neighbor, Mrs. DeNegri, who was always making pastas whose aromas lured him up the backstairs to sample what is still his favorite food. His parents were always having dinners and parties: mah jongg and bridge parties in the afternoon for Mother and her friends and poker nights for Father. The Nerd helped to set the table and enjoyed the excitement until sent out to play or go to bed. All of that ended when they moved.

During the Depression years the Nerd tried to find jobs to earn money as well as do the household chores that Mother or the maid had done before. For several years, the Nerd sold the Pictorial Review magazine. He would walk around the neighborhood asking everyone to buy a copy at 25 cents each. He made a few bucks a month. One day walking on California Street near 23rd Avenue, he asked a man if he would buy a magazine. He smiled and said, "I'll buy them all." Then he gave him a $5 bill. "I have no change," answered the Nerd. "Keep it," said the man. "Say hello to your parents. I'm your uncle Mo Harris." He was my father's first cousin and became my best customer until I gave up my magazine career. He and his family became lifelong friends and loved Sparkle from the first day they met.

The second job that the Nerd got was delivering telegrams for Western Union in San Francisco, at 36 cents an hour, when he was just sixteen during the summer of 1938. The job was arranged through family friends of his mother and he delivered messages on skates in downtown San Francisco. The Nerd recalled taking a message from the office on Geary Street near Mason up the hill to the Mark Hopkins. Going up was a strain, coming down on skates was the killer.

Then he got a 50 cent an hour job as an usher at the Grand Theater on Mission Street that carried over until he graduated from high school in 1939. A friend of his father owned the movie house that showed re-runs. It opened at 11:00 a.m. and ran until midnight. The job five days a week included opening up the theater in the morning, cleaning the foyer, checking the restrooms, taking the tickets, and calling the police if there was an obstreperous patron. If the Nerd was asked to do other tasks normally assigned to the Head Usher, he made 75 cents an hour. Each shift lasted seven to eight hours. The clientele often included ladies who smuggled wine into the theater and often passed out during the movie—and the Nerd became quite adept at getting them to leave without calling the cops. Clients also used the fire exit doors to sneak in friends during the movie—and the Nerd never quite figured out how to thwart that scam. The big attraction was a sixteen-week run of King Kong in the summer of 1939 that kept the movie house full—and lots of ladies came every day to toast the King with cheap wine.

By 1935, the economy improved enough for the family to move to a lovely large flat just down the street from Presidio Junior High School. There were two bedrooms and a sunroom. The sunroom was the Nerd's sanctuary with all his books and other treasures. His parents began to entertain again, but it was very different from the old days. No mah jongg or poker, only dinner, talk and drinks, usually on Sunday evenings. Mother would cook a roast, bake a ham, or serve cracked crab—her spectacular main courses. She didn't serve the deviled crab, crepes, soufflés, or other specialty dishes than he remembered from pre-Depression years, but the dinners were still great.

The Nerd's senior year in high school coincided with the opening of the Golden Gate Bridge and the 1939 World's Fair. He had watched the bridge being built as he walked to school every day through 1937 and 1938, and marveled at the progress in putting down the foundations and finally the span itself. As he climbed the bluff on which George Washington High School was built, he saw the miracle crossing to Marin County and wondered how it would change the flow of life in his city.

During the high school years, he often dated. He loved to dance and seemed to feel the music that sometimes he could hardly hear. He had a couple of short-lived romances and a small circle of friends, but he often felt like an outsider. Because of his hearing loss, he was unable to take drivers' education. His family did not own a car and his father had been a poor driver. He never became a respectable driver.

He got through high school in two and a half years and finished at the academic head of the class. He was selected to be valedictorian of the Pioneer Class of George Washington High School, then the newest secondary school in the city. He knew he wanted to go to college, the first in his family. He was earning money as an usher in order to pay his university expenses. He was offered scholarships to several universities, but financial reality made the University of California Berkeley the only feasible, affordable choice—just across the Bay Bridge from home and the lip reading courses that had become a staple in his life.

He was accepted at Berkeley in the spring of 1939, just as the World's Fair was opening. The Nerd was almost as excited about it as he was about his selection to deliver the valedictory address at the elegant Opera House—you see, the new high school had no auditorium. His parents thought his address was smashing. He was overawed by the occasion.

On the night the World's Fair opened, there was a great parade headed by Mayor Rossi. His parents' store on Market Street had a big picture window that was made available for people to watch the parade as it moved from the Ferry Building to City Hall. His parents made room for Jackie and the Nerd to enjoy the parade. The Nerd remembers seeing the first float arriving when a pair of hands reached over and covered his glasses. It was his mother's hands—and they were there to protect her sixteen-year old son from seeing the Sally Rand Nude Ranch Float with its bare-breasted beauties riding by. Mothers can be mothers!

The Nerd enjoyed the Fair on the days he didn't work and although underage, he did get to see Sally Rand and the Feathers, as well as the inhabitants of the Nude Ranch. But much more exciting for him were the exhibits of the foreign countries and the scores of restaurants serving exotic foods. He spent time observing the latest industrial advances and the display of the new inventions, like television. The Fair only exacerbated his itch to travel and see the world beyond San Francisco Bay.

When UC Berkeley offered the Nerd a scholarship, the die was cast. The Nerd decided to live away from home and get the full college experience. UC Berkeley had only one men's dormitory at that time and its cost was beyond his budget—and the people living there were among the elite of campus life. Late that summer, he and Mother looked for housing in Berkeley. After visiting several boarding houses, they found a cooperative dormitory that cost $4 a week coupled with four hours of chores. He was in.

By the second semester, through friends, he found a boarding house on College Avenue that cost $30 a month, with three meals a day. The cost was within his budget. UC Berkeley cost him $27.50 a semester for incidental fees and free medical care at Cowell Hospital, and his scholarship paid him $20 a month. He could swing the remaining costs with his savings and a few bucks from home. And, he usually went home for the weekends and had his Mother's cooking.

World War II broke out as he began his freshman year. He applied for ROTC, which he had taken in high school, but was turned down because of his hearing problem. He was eager to be part of the war effort, but found his options limited. He studied hard. He got all "A"s except for a "C" in Philosophy—a subject he didn't understand until just before the final when it finally dawned on him what the subject was all about. The second semester was almost identical, except that he got a "B" in Social Philosophy. He joined the Forensic Society and made the Freshman Debating Team—and usually sat in the front row to read lips.

When Pearl Harbor occurred, the Nerd sought to leave Berkeley and join the military, but he was not accepted. So, when the semester ended, he applied for a job with the U.S. Army at Fort Mason, San Francisco. He was hired as a GS-2, for $1,220 per annum to check on the checkers who checked on the checkers for Army shipments to the Pacific Theater of Operations. He worked for several months until one night he was locked into the icehouse overnight after checking a shipment of beef. When he was found the following morning, he was almost frozen and had a bad case of pneumonia. Six weeks later when he reported back to work, his boss—and his Draft Board—told him that his best contribution to the war effort was to get his degree at UC Berkeley.

The Nerd had spent 1942 and 1943 getting his AB in political science, economics, and history. He was accepted at the UC Berkeley Boalt School of Law in 1943. In 1942, he had applied to and was accepted by I House as a resident. Law school had become the center of his life when he met Sparkle.

During his adolescent and university years, one of the most complex problems that the Nerd grappled with was his moral and religious conviction. As a little boy he had been taken to Christian Science Sunday school with an old friend of his family. Grandma took him once in a while to Grace Cathedral. He had a classmate whose father was a Presbyterian Minister, and his mother allowed him to go to church with him several times. With his family observances and his experiences, he was drawn to Christianity and the message of Christ. He was proud of the Jewish traditions that flowed in his blood and mindful of the role that Judaism had played in the evolution of modern ethical and religious thought. But he did not know where he belonged.

Then, when he was about eleven, his mother and father spoke to him about his being Jewish and the tradition of bar mitzvah. He then went to Temple Beth Israel, a reform synagogue, for religious education and instruction. When qualified by the rabbi, he was honored with the bar mitzvah. However, he sensed an uneasiness as the impact of his deafness became more pronounced. And he found solace not in the Jewish tradition, but in the Sermon on the Mount and the words of Jesus.

When he went to Berkeley, he spent many hours visiting various religious centers—Newman Hall, Hillel House, and a number of churches. In 1941, he found a church and a Minister who spoke to him as no one else had. It was Reverend Loper at the Berkeley Congregational Church. For nearly two years, he went to the church and even had private chats with Dr. Loper. Then as he passed his twenty-first birthday, he advised his parents that he had made a personal decision to join Dr. Loper's congregation. In early 1944, he made a public affirmation of his commitment and joined the Congregational Church.

It was later that year that he met Sparkle. And, he found a kindred soul who understood the problems that plagued him and began to help him relate to the world that engulfed him.

5

A Budding Romance?

One evening as they walked back from the university in the fall of 1944, Sparkle and the Nerd got to talking about religion. Sparkle talked of her family commitment to Presbyterianism and individual responsibility, and the Nerd told her about his dilemma and his respect for Dr. Loper. Sparkle said that she had many friends in Tulare who were Congregationalists and that she was comfortable with that church's doctrine and practices. They agreed to go to hear Dr. Loper the next Sunday and then go to lunch and a movie. Her only admonition was that a preacher does not a church make. She told of her own experience with the Tulare Methodist Church where she had respected a minister for his courage and his message. However, when he was transferred to another church, his successor was a pastor that her mother, her grandmother, and she could hardly tolerate. She said that she followed the teachings of Jesus, but was not sure that she ever wanted to belong to a specific church again.

Even as their friendship blossomed, there was still no real romance. Sparkle was still weighing two marriage proposals: one from her San Francisco banker, the other from her long-time boyfriend flying the Hump from Burma to China. She told him little of her feelings for either of those men and never talked of a relationship with each other.

Sparkle also had her share of other problems. She had been diagnosed at Cowell Hospital, the University medical center, with a thyroid problem that left her constantly tired. Her mother wanted her to go home to Tulare where she could be properly cared for. Her mother, Sparkle confessed, had ulterior motives because she was worried about the influences of Cal, I House, and foreigners on her little girl. Mother wanted Sparkle to come back to Tulare and take her place in the town's society. But Sparkle's horizons had been so expanded by her I House experience that she was not eager to go home. She would occasionally sob when she talked of her mother's scolding, but was reassured by her grandmother who advised her to make her own decision. Sparkle had already earned her AB degree and wanted an MA in child psychology. Above all, she wanted time to make up her own mind about what she wanted to do with her life. The Nerd agreed with Grandmother and urged her to take the time she felt that she needed. Can you imagine, the Nerd and Grandmother were giving the same advice!

As Christmas approached in late 1944, Sparkle decided to go home to Tulare for Christmas, but come back for New Year's Eve. The Nerd invited her to be his date at the I House New Year's Eve Party. When she accepted, for the first time, the Nerd felt that Sparkle and he were an item.

Classes at law school were over several days before the holidays. Sparkle had her last afternoon at the nursery school on December 22 and the Nerd went down to South Berkeley to accompany her home. They had dinner with a group of friends and then piled into Carlos Bee's sedan Gwendolyn for a drink at their favorite tavern in Emeryville.

The next morning, the Nerd accompanied her to the Southern Pacific Valley train and well remembers carrying her little black suitcase. In those days people dressed up for a train ride, and Sparkle wore her new black fur jacket and a beautiful black dress. She was a vision of light and beauty, with her auburn hair and blue eyes sparkling. That was the image that he took with him as the train departed the Berkeley station and he wended his way home across the bridge to San Francisco on the Key Route F Train.

Christmas was a blur as the Nerd awaited Sparkle's return. The Nerd spent three days at home and then buried himself in the law library to get ready for the finals of his first semester of his senior year in law school. The grind was wearing the Nerd out and his thoughts of Sparkle easily distracted his concentration.

Sparkle returned unannounced on December 30, and he met her unexpectedly as they arrived at the I House dining room almost at the same time. They dined together and made arrangements for the New Year's Eve party. One of their I House mates offered to drive them to the dance in his 30's touring car with a rumble seat. The I House Party was not formal, but college elegant. The Nerd's mother sent Sparkle a beautiful orchid for the dance. Knowing the Nerd's lack of social graces, his mother didn't want him to blow his chances. Sparkle was amused by his mother's gesture, and never mentioned it to the Nerd until after they were married several years later.

The Nerd picked up Sparkle about 6:30 p.m. and they climbed into the rumble seat. It was a cool December evening, thankfully without rain. She gave the Nerd a peck on the check and said that she loved rumble seats. They reminded her of her family's old Hupmobile and the many happy days she spent riding around as a young girl with her mother in the rumble seat. He put his arm around her to help keep her warm and they just laughed as they rode to the restaurant. Dinner glided by with good conversation and then off to the dance at House 4.

And, what a dance it was! Almost everyone who lived in the four I Houses was there. There was not only the music from the hi fi, but several of the Latin Americans had brought their guitars, maracas, and drums so that there was a constant stream of boleros, sambas, rumbas, merengues, and congas. Sparkle and the Nerd danced every dance with each other and shared snide comments about some of the other dancers.

The weather dropped sharply about midnight and Sparkle was driven home inside the touring car. The Nerd walked the two blocks from the dance at House 4 to House 3 to say goodnight one more time. Too cold to stay outside, they nuzzled for a while in the living room until the room filled up with so many other couples that there was no privacy and they had to say goodnight.

On New Year's Day 1945, they walked down to the Congregational Church to hear Dr. Loper's words for 1945 and his vision for the New Year. World War II was on everyone's mind and the Battle of Bastogne had raised serious doubts about ultimate victory. Sparkle was very concerned about her long-time beau and his safety in the Burma-China theater of operations, but said that she was not sure how she would react when he came home. From church, they went to the Black Sheep Restaurant for brunch and a leisurely walk home in the cool Berkeley afternoon. They kissed and went back to the routine that would govern their lives through the winter and spring at the University. The interlude was over and the question still remained unanswered. Were Sparkle and the Nerd friends or a couple?

As January went on, Sparkle and the Nerd fell into the routine of class work. Sparkle had graduated in October 1944 and planned to get an MA in Child Psychology by 1946. Her mother continued to pressure her to return to Tulare. Her grandmother was in her mid-80s and almost blind and was no longer able to support Sparkle's decision as she had done only a couple of months earlier. Sparkle told the Nerd that she had to prove to her mother that her decision to get an MA was right for her life and that she planned to study very hard for the next two semesters to prove it. To underline her determination, she refused further financial help from home and planned to pay all her university expenses from money she earned. So, she increased the hours she worked each week in both the I House dining room and at the nursery school.

The Nerd was fully absorbed in the last semester of law school and exhausted by the strain of eighteen consecutive months of law studies without a break. To cover his living expenses at I House, he picked up a teaching assistant job in Money and Banking. Several hours a week at the Economics Department were added to the workload of three classes almost every weekday. He also was deeply concerned about where he would fit in the profession. As experienced lawyers repeatedly advised him, his prospects as a lip reader were not good, at best a job in the back room of a large law firm writing briefs. Jobs in the public sector were limited in those days, and for handicapped persons even more bleak. So, he began doing research work for various professors in addition to his regular classes in order to gain more experience that might interest or influence a potential employer. The grind and stress were getting to him.

By mid-March, the strain was starting to affect both of them. Sparkle's thyroid problem was slowing her down and even required a short stay at Cowell Hospital. The doctor said that she had to lighten her schedule and rest a good deal more. She didn't share this warning with anyone, not even her family. She continued to run on all burners, except that she decided to cut down on dances and dinners out.

About the same time, the dean of the law school, Edwin Dickinson, called the Nerd in for a long talk about his future. The dean advised him that his options for jobs were not good because of his hearing loss and urged him to stake out a specialty that would make him a specialist needed by major law firms. The Nerd confessed that his association with I House for nearly four years had made him especially interested in international law and comparative legal systems. The dean then proposed that he apply for a Travelling Fellowship in Comparative Law that the law school offered for graduate law students.

That night the Nerd asked Sparkle to have coffee with him, and asked her what she thought of the proposal. She asked him what he wanted to do and how he looked at the future. Neither mentioned their personal relationship. She told him about her thyroid concerns and the possibility that she would have to take some time off from school and return to Tulare in order to recoup her health. Finally she urged him to apply. She simply said, "If you don't, you'll spend the rest of your life wondering what would have happened if you had." The Nerd did apply and was awarded the Fellowship.

That spring was very hard on all students. The death of Franklin Delano Roosevelt in April shocked all of us. The growing sense of Allied victory was tempered by our deep concern about the loss of the leader. University classes were suspended for the three-day mourning period and Sparkle and the Nerd joined in many I House group sessions of students from many countries around the world, who poured out their concerns for our still unsettled world without FDR. They felt that an era had ended, but they had no time to mourn since final exams demanded their urgent attention.

Then in early May, VE Day occurred on the eve of finals. That was a joyous occasion, but still overshadowed by concerns about the continuing conflict with Japan. Both had friends fighting in the Pacific and periodic notices of deaths kept the mood very somber. Nonetheless, they joined in the celebration that swept the campus community. They went to an impromptu dance at I House 4 for a while and then joined in an alcoholic toast for peace in the nominally dry environs. The defeat of Hitler truncated studies for several days until it dawned on all that finals had not been postponed.

Cramming for those finals was a real chore. Studying for three years without a break left the Nerd nearly exhausted; and working twenty hours a week to cover her expenses while weakened by thyroid issues undermined Sparkle's stamina. Neither did as well as they had hoped. But they passed with respectable grades.

Sparkle's mother learned of the thyroid problem and pressed her to go home to Tulare for the summer. But Sparkle decided to stay in Berkeley to support the Nerd while he studied full-time for the State Bar Exam. She remained involved in the social life at I House, which was especially intense in May and June as delegates from countries around the world drafted the Charter of the United Nations. Delegates from European, Middle Eastern, and Latin American countries came over regularly to I House and joined us for dinners and discussed the great issues being weighed in the deliberations across the Bay. Sparkle was at all the dinners and lunches, and the Nerd often had to rely on her for reports on the briefings that his Bar Exam seminars prevented him from attending. It was a heady time for all of us.

Among Sparkle's friends at I House was Ali Samy, a distinguished Egyptian, cousin of King Farouk and Egyptian Consul in San Francisco. They played bridge together whenever their schedules permitted. Their foursome usually included a South African and an Indian who remained friends of both Sparkle and the Nerd throughout their lives. At one of their bridge games, in early June, during the UN conference, Ali proposed that the foursome get dressed up as if they were delegates to the Conference and go to San Francisco. The foursome laughingly agreed to tempt fate.

The following Saturday night, the four left I House at 7:30 p.m. in Ali's official Cadillac for the adventure of a lifetime. Ali as Egyptian Consul had a generous gasoline ration. The three men were in white tie and tails, and the distinguished Egyptian wore his bright red sash of princely office. Sparkle wore her best evening gown of soft green tulle that glamorized her auburn hair and blue eyes.

They drove over the Bay Bridge and up to the circular driveway of the Mark Hopkins Hotel. Ali got out of the car and advised the doorman that they had arrived for dinner at the Ballroom and handed him the keys to the Cadillac. Then Sparkle, on Ali's arm, swept into the foyer of the hotel and asked for directions to the Ballroom. The assistant manager left his post and led the foursome into the Ballroom where they were given a floor-side table. Ali ordered champagne for his guests and a soft drink for himself. Society photographers from the major San Francisco newspapers rushed in to take pictures and the orchestra played a special medley for their international visitors. Sparkle danced with each of her companions to the applause from the patrons. At 11:00 p.m., Ali announced that it was time to depart, and they swept out of the Ballroom to return to the routine of college life. On Sunday morning, both the San Francisco Examiner and the San Francisco Chronicle published pictures and articles of the pseudo-UN delegates at the Mark Ballroom. The I Housers had conquered the social life of San Francisco!

In late June 1945, the Nerd graduated from law school. The ceremony was very simple, with only fourteen in his graduating class: thirteen 4F men and one lone lady. At graduation, the Nerd was awarded the Boalt Law School Travelling Fellowship to study comparative corporation law at the University of Chile. The Nerd's family came over the Bay Bridge for the ceremony, and Sparkle went back with them for a family celebration. A happy day that ended a cycle of life!

How fast the summer of 1945 passed into history! The Nerd was not only preparing for the California Bar Exam but also his forthcoming trip to Chile. He had to leave in late September to spend several months learning lip-reading in Spanish, improving his limited Spanish, and orienting himself to the Chilean way of life before the University of Chile Law School academic year began in March 1946.

Then on the eve of the Bar Exam came V-J Day and the end of World War II. Sparkle and the Nerd celebrated with a group of I House companions the end of the terrible conflict that had disrupted so many lives. The incredible relief gave way to joy as they joined tens of thousands of swirling people on Telegraph Avenue in Berkeley and Market Street in San Francisco. They cheered and mingled with other celebrants, reassembling periodically to make sure that all the I Housers were accounted for. What a joyful night!

When they got to Berkeley in the wee hours of the morning,

Sparkle and the Nerd cuddled together for the rest of the night. For the first time, they truly felt that they were in love. Sparkle said for the first time that she had deep feelings for the Nerd and that she felt a real bond between them. They went to breakfast together and the Nerd didn't want the heart-to-heart connection ever to end. They stayed together talking of the new world about to unfold until neither could keep their eyes open. As Sparkle and the Nerd kissed good night, they talked for the first time seriously about a life together after university.

In August the Nerd took the Bar Exam in San Francisco. It lasted three days, with a three-hour morning and a three-hour afternoon of answering questions about every aspect of his law school course work. Each night he went to his parents' home and his mother gave nightly bulletins to Sparkle, who sent her encouragement. After the last question was answered, he went back to I House and celebrated with Sparkle and a handful of close friends. He was so exhausted that he fell asleep at the table in the Emeryville bar to which they migrated after dinner.

After the Bar Exam, the Nerd stayed in San Francisco but took the F Train to Berkeley almost every day to spend time with Sparkle. He was unwinding from the grind of law school, but had not begun the mental transition from student to lawyer. I House was receiving a new crop of residents, many of whom were returning veterans, and one or two men were already inviting her out. The Nerd saw a new generation of competition!

Excited as he was for the trip to Chile, he was almost more concerned about leaving Sparkle. They went to a few parties, but mainly they just talked. They made no commitments. They just agreed that, when the Nerd returned from Chile, they would see how they felt about each other. Her beau was returning from Burma and she was honest in saying that she just didn't know how they would react to each other after so many years of absence.

In mid-September, they said their goodbyes at I House after a bon voyage dinner with his family. The next day the Nerd flew off to Los Angeles as the first stop on his way south. Sparkle left the next day for a visit with her mother and grandmother in Tulare— and a reunion with her beau on his return from Burma.

Chapter 6

Love and Marriage

From September 1945 to December 1946, weekly letters were the bond that linked Sparkle and the Nerd. He was absorbed with a world very different from the one he had known. Sparkle stayed in Tulare until the summer of 1946 when she returned to big I House for the fall 1946. She had a new ardent suitor, and the Nerd was meeting and dating some very elegant Chilean ladies. Neither was sure of what would happen when they would meet again.

On her visit to Tulare in September 1945, her mother and grandmother helped her control her thyroid problems, relieving her of all household chores. Her aviator returned and they found that the old spark had died. They went out together on several dates and agreed that they had separate lives to lead, and different visions and expectations from life. He wanted to make the Air Force his life, and Sparkle was drawn to other interests. As Sparkle described it some years later, "We agreed to disagree." They parted as friends. He moved to Florida and had a successful military career and a happy marriage.

Sparkle remained in Tulare until her health improved. In June 1946, she wrote the I House director that she was ready to return and asked if there was a room available for her. He told her that not only was a room was waiting for her, but he also invited her to join his staff as a weekend receptionist, with free room and board. It was a Godsend! Room and board meant that she didn't have to work two jobs at the same time she took classes. She could plan her schedule of graduate seminars and find part-time employment that would allow her to keep her thyroid under control.

Sparkle was back in her room at I House 3 in mid-July and she wrote the Nerd that she loved her job and her life. Meeting people had always been one of her special talents and the opportunity to greet and help students made her especially pleased. A friend later told the Nerd, "Her smile permeated the House."

As soon as she settled back in her routine, one of the returning veterans became an ardent suitor. A geology student, he had taken her out many a night over the summer of 1945 when the Nerd had been tied up studying for the Bar exam. When Sparkle returned that July, he told her that he was determined to marry her. He took Sparkle to meet his family and his mother was as captivated with her as the Nerd's mother had been. The Nerd in Chile heard only bits and snatches about developments in letters from Sparkle, I House friends, or his own mother.

Sparkle was clearly once again trying to make up her mind. Sparkle later told the Nerd that she was very fond of the geologist, but had misgivings about life as the wife of a geologist in petroleum camps or small towns near petroleum operations. She confessed that she was very attracted to him, but something induced her to wait until the Nerd got back. She decided not to accept the geologist's marriage proposal.

In the first three months in Berkeley she helped make the move back into the big I House. Then, working as the weekend receptionist in the Great Hall, with its array of windows and sunlight, gave her joy and satisfaction. She had found a part-time job doing clerical work, nothing too demanding, so she concentrated on studies in Child Psychology. Her letters were upbeat and exciting, full of descriptions of the new generation of I Housers, mainly veterans, men and women whom she came to know and whose experiences fascinated her. She became convinced that academic life would not satisfy her any more than being an Air Force officer's or geologist's wife. She wrote of her desire to get a much broader taste of the world.

The nerd was also getting a taste of a new world. It had started in late September 1945 with his flight to Chile. Traveling by DC 3 to South America at the end of World War II was an adventure. The airports did not have night lighting, so one flew from sun-up to sundown. The plane ended the day whenever the pilot decided that there was not enough light to move on.

The trip to Santiago took seven days. After Los Angeles, there was an overnighter in Mexico City with customs stops in Calexico, California, and Aguascalinetes, Mexico. Arrival at the Aztec capital at noon allowed for an afternoon of exploring the center of the city before bed and a 4:00 a.m. Pan Am wake-up call for the dawn take-off to Central America. After six fueling stops in Tapachula (Mexico), Guatemala City, Tegucigalpa, San Salvador, Managua, and San José, he arrived at dusk in Panama. All of the U.S. passengers were put up at the Tivoli Guest House in the Canal Zone and all of us were in bed by 9:00 p.m.

Panagra, an airline owned by Pan Am and the Grace Line, awakened him at 4:00 a.m. and before dawn he was loaded onto the plane for a 6:00 a.m. departure with the cabin windows covered as a security measure as he flew out over the Canal. That day the goal was Lima, Peru. After stops in Cali, Colombia and Quito, Ecuador, bad weather forced an early end of the flight day in Guayaquil, Ecuador. All of the passengers were put up at the Panagra Guest House. Hot and humid, with lots of bugs and lizards, is the Nerd's only remembrance of that night. At dawn, the flight resumed to Lima, with stopovers in Piura and Trujillo. That night, the Nerd stayed at the Hotel Bolivar with its bar called the "snake-pit," famous for its Pisco Sour cocktails—and how he enjoyed them and a good night's sleep! Up at dawn again, the plane flew on to Santiago with stops in Tacna, Peru, and Arica and Antofagasta, Chile. Seven days after leaving the Golden Gate, he had arrived in Chile. And, as the mother of Fernando Walker, his close friend at I House, who met him at the plane, reported "he was pale green and a day late."

The next sixteen months were a wondrous time for the Nerd. The middle class kid was thrust into elite circles of Chilean society. He met many entrancing people not only from Chile but from all over Latin America, Europe, and the United States. He spent months deepening his knowledge of Spanish and learning to lip-read that language. By the way, Spanish is much easier than English because of the regularity of pronunciation and only five vowel sounds. He spent days wandering around the various neighborhoods of Santiago and learning the bus and tram routes. He began his study of Chilean corporation law, with its roots in learned treatises on Civil Law, often written by French and German scholars.

He met University of Chile officials to understand the structure and dimensions of Chilean university life, all very different from the experience he had had at Berkeley.

When he arrived, Fernando's mother, Josefina "Chepa" Walker, settled him in her home for over a month until Fernando's sister, Blanca, became engaged to the grandson of Chile's greatest naval hero. He then was invited to live for several months in the home of Agustín Edwards, owner and publisher of Chile's renowned newspaper *El Mercurio,* and a member of one of Chile's most famous and wealthy families. There, he met statesmen, poets, artists, and businessmen. He had a chance to meet some elegant ladies and was exposed to a social life quite different from his upbringings. Central to this experience was a close, lifelong friendship with the Walker and Edwards families.

Early in 1946, he met a young U.S. Embassy officer who invited him to share an apartment in the center of the city and that apartment became his home for the rest of his stay in Santiago. By the opening of the academic year he was settled into a routine of studying Chilean corporation law and the preparation of a thesis comparing U.S. and Chilean law. In the process, he heard from U.S. corporate executives in Chile that they could access all the expertise they needed on corporation law from established Chilean firms, but they needed someone who understood the labor code and labor-management relations. So, he added that dimension to his study program.

Through it all, the Nerd never stopped thinking of Sparkle. He missed their time together. He missed sharing the Chilean experience with her. He became certain that he wanted to build his life with her. So, on Valentine's Day in 1946, he sent her a proposal of marriage. A simple letter! She didn't answer! As she said later, "Couldn't you have done something more romantic?"

The experience in Chile ended in late 1946 when the Nerd flew to New York to look for a job before he returned to California. Almost all of the legal firms active in Latin America were based in New York and he had met representatives of several while in Santiago. He spent two weeks in New York and received a couple of offers, but returned to California after a senior partner in a prestigious firm took him to lunch to explain what would be expected of him as a junior member of the firm. Without roots in New York, the Nerd felt that he would be unable to make a go of it. Besides Sparkle was in California and, with her help, he hoped to build a different sort of career.

Before Christmas 1946, the Nerd and Sparkle were reunited at the San Francisco Airport. She had an I House male friend accompany her in the Cadillac of her Egyptian buddy. The Nerd was immediately jealous, but Sparkle gave him a warm embrace and a kiss. There was only a happy scene. Sparkle, her friend, and the Nerd went to his parent's flat in San Francisco for a welcome home drink and dinner. Sparkle and the Nerd spent the next two to three weeks talking about themselves and the future.

The Nerd delivered the thesis he prepared on comparative U.S. and Chilean corporation law to the dean of the law school and consulted him on the next steps in his career. He told the dean of the advice given him by corporate executives about their need for legal experts in labor law. The dean volunteered to contact an associate in the U.S. State Department about that Department's interest in the Nerd's plans. He suggested that the Nerd return to Berkeley for the next few months to take a couple of courses on labor law and international law while awaiting a reply from the State Department. To cover immediate expenses, the Nerd proposed to open his own law practice in Berkeley. He shared the plan with Sparkle and she was supportive.

The State Department contact advised the dean that the subject matter was of interest and suggested that the Nerd apply for a State Department grant to round out his studies. After reviewing the situation in Latin America and U.S. investment patterns, Mexico was selected as the appropriate site for a comparative study, in view of the Mexican Labor Code and the high volume of U.S. business in investing across the border. The grant proposal on comparing U.S. and Mexican labor law and labor-management relations in that country was submitted to the State Department, and acceptance came in a matter of weeks. The grant was for a year or two, beginning on September 1, 1947.

When he told Sparkle of the acceptance, he proposed marriage again and this time she accepted. They began making plans for a wedding in Berkeley in August. Sparkle chose the date of

August 7, 1947, one day after her grandmother's birthday. After the honeymoon, they planned to visit her mother and grandmother in Tulare before going on to Mexico. They also planned a work and study schedule together to prepare for Mexico.

To build cash reserves, the Nerd got three teaching assistant jobs at the university, including one on labor economics. His law practice netted all of $200 from three divorces, a couple of wills, and drafting an inter-vivos trust. While the law practice covered most of his expenses, he was quite discomforted handling divorces and learning the intimate details of the proximate cause. He told Sparkle that opening his own law practice was not his cup of tea. She just laughed and said categorically that as far as she was concerned, the Nerd was a lawyer and that law practice as an option should never be off the table. She had taken two commercial law courses at Berkeley and was extremely interested in all aspects of the law. Then, she made it very clear that one of the elements in her decision to marry the Nerd was because he was a lawyer.

The months leading up to the wedding were very busy. The Nerd didn't drive and had never owned a car. His parents gave the about-to-be-weds a 1936 reconditioned Dodge as their wedding present. The Nerd took driving lessons and almost always froze when he took the wheel.

Sparkle continued to work as the weekend hostess at I House, and the Nerd moved back in when the I House director asked him to room with a graduate engineer from Peru on a fellowship who needed help in learning English and adapting to university life.

They spent most of those months together, often having serious and sometimes explosive discussions about the future. The Nerd was not sensitive to the concerns that Sparkle felt about wedding plans and beginning life in a foreign country. They had many a fight, usually provoked by the Nerd's lack of understanding. Sparkle wanted a formal wedding and an exchange of rings. The Nerd demurred. Sparkle agreed to an informal wedding with a single ring placed on her finger. All sorts of little issues arose, and the Nerd seemed to find reasons for not agreeing. Despite all the tensions, Sparkle seemed to find the way to bring them back together.

Sparkle and the Nerd were wed at St. Clement's Episcopal Church at 4:30 p.m. on August 7, 1947. Sparkle was a luminous and radiant bride. Her auburn hair and blue eyes shone as she walked down the aisle. The congregation was made up primarily of friends from the Berkeley campus and I House. Estelle Carlson, a dear friend of Sparkle's and a senior staff member at I House, offered her home in the Berkeley Hills above I House for the wedding reception. The Nerd and his family met the new in-laws at the reception held in the open air on a sweeping lawn overlooking the Golden Gate.

It was a truly lovely party, with tables laden with special treats and the wedding cake from a San Francisco pastry shop. The fruit punch prepared by Sparkle's mother was soon spiked by a culprit never identified, but presumed to be from I House. The flavor was sufficiently identifiable that Sparkle's grandmother told the groom that it was the best punch she had tasted since her husband died. Sparkle's mother and the Nerd's mother were upset that the punch had been doctored, but they seemed to enjoy the toasts.

The couple departed in the early evening. Thus began a life and partnership that lasted fifty-seven years.

PART II

THE YOUNG MARRIEDS, 1947–1962

7

Mexico

The newlyweds left the reception about 6:30 p.m. for the two-and-a-half-hour drive to the Ben Lomond Resort in the Santa Cruz Mountains for a brief honeymoon. I started the drive while my bride cringed on the other side of the front seat. So I pulled over and let her drive the rest of the way. My choice of honeymoon resort was lovely, but not what Ele would have picked, as I learned not too many days later. She would have preferred the first night at the Claremont Hotel in Berkeley and a couple of nights in the city. This was my first lesson: happy married life is what we both decide, not I alone.

During those four special days in the mountains, we rested and enjoyed the resort. We spent most of the time with each other, making plans for our trip to Mexico in the 1936 Dodge. We took some drives as Ele tried to sharpen my driving skills for the long drive ahead of us. I didn't improve much.

Then we (mostly Ele) drove back to the city for a farewell three nights with my parents. My mother had special dinners each night for close family friends who had not been able to attend the wedding. Then, we were off to Tulare for five days with Ele's grandmother and mother. Ele never let me touch the wheel on Highway 99.

It was over 100 degrees when we reached Tulare. Her mother's and grandmother's houses had desert coolers, not air conditioning, and the heat hit me very hard. Ele's mother put out all our wedding presents in grandmother's living room and organized a reception for family friends. I remember that very hot evening with more than a hundred people coming and going. Most had known Ele all her life as the Sparkle I had come to love.

The few days in Tulare were spent firming up our travel plans. Ele knew the head of the local auto club and he gave us a trip plan and indications of where to stay on the drive to Mexico City. In 1946, the highway system was not well developed; most of the route was on two-lane roads and overnight facilities were few and far between. The auto club gave us a plan for stopovers at approved motels and reliable service stations all the way to Mexico City.

Our other immediate chore was to set up bank accounts in Tulare so that Ele's mother could keep an eye on our finances while we were away. Inter-country banking arrangements were not highly developed, and we found that in Tulare, the only bank that could help us in Mexico was the Bank of America. This bothered my mother-in-law because she did her banking across the street at Security Pacific Bank. After some hemming and hawing, we opened our account and received letters of introduction to its corresponding bank in Mexico City.

After a tearful farewell, we started out for a couple of days with Ele's Aunt Leora and Uncle Julius Lehmann in Whittier, part of the Luney clan who had migrated from Iowa and settled on a Whittier avocado grove. Uncle Julius had taught her to play golf and gave her first clubs. Golf was the only sport Ele really enjoyed. All of the Luneys in the Los Angeles area dropped by to wish us well at Aunt Leora's open house.

All too soon we were on Routes 90 and 83 to Phoenix, El Paso and Laredo before crossing onto the Pan American Highway. Ele did almost all of the driving; she would tolerate my driving an hour or so over the desert or on stretches with little traffic. We stopped at motels recommended by the auto association—some were little more than rustic cabins with clean beds and showers. The stretch of washboard roads in New Mexico threw our wheels out of alignment and in El Paso we had to pay $20 to realign them.

On September 1, a day behind schedule, we crossed into Nuevo Laredo and onto the Pan American Highway, which to our consternation consisted of two lanes—not much different from the roads of the past several days.

We overnighted at a recommended hotel outside Nuevo Laredo and had a long night's sleep before setting off the next morning for the two-day drive to Mexico City. My mother had told us that friends who had recently made the same trip recommended that we spend the first night at "Tom and Charlie's" motor court. So, before we left our hotel we asked about it at the front desk. We got a sly smile from the clerk who volunteered the correct name, "Tamazunchale," and phoned ahead to make a reservation.

Ele drove all that day through hilly terrain until we entered the mountains. It was a hard eight-hour drive, and we arrived after dark. Fortunately, our room was waiting for us. In talking with other travelers, we learned that much of tomorrow's driving would be tough, as it would be raining as we drove up the mountains to get to the Valley of Mexico at 8,000 feet. They urged us to get to Mexico City by 3:30 p.m. before the rush hour. The clerk also gave us directions for reaching the *pension* where we had made reservations for our first couple of weeks in the Mexican capital.

Getting Settled

In spite of our best efforts, the weather conspired to delay our arrival in the Aztec Capital. It rained all day and the curvy roads made for slow driving. We reached the entrance to the city at about 5:00 p.m. and hit Reforma about an hour later. Our windshield wipers chose to go on strike amid a terrible downpour just as Ele turned onto Reforma into three lanes of bumper-to-bumper traffic. For the next half hour, I gave her directions from the information given us at Tamazunchale the night before. We reached the Diana Glorieta about 6:30 p.m. and found the *pension* around the corner.

When Ele got to the front door of the *pension*, I jumped out to summon help. The lady answering the door said, "We have been concerned, but welcome." Her assistant helped us unpack the car and then parked it in the *pension's* parking lot. The *señora* showed us to a lovely Spanish colonial style room, elegantly decorated and with large comfortable beds. She invited us to come down to dinner as soon as possible. We washed up and went to the dining room, where several other American couples were sipping on cocktails before dinner at 8:00 p.m. Ele and I joined them, enjoying our first drink since leaving San Francisco. The margaritas were wonderful. Dinner was excellent. Baths were divine. We slept like good little kids. We had arrived a day late but all in one piece!

The next morning, I went to the embassy to report in. Ele stayed in bed and told me not to disturb her until dinner. The *señora* sent her some breakfast and said that she would look in during the day to make sure Ele received anything she needed.

The embassy was in the Zona Rosa, just off Insurgentes. I walked in the front door and introduced myself to the lady who operated the switchboard. There were no Marine Guards or other controls in those days. She directed me to the Cultural Section where a young officer, Bill Calderhead, met me (Bill is now in his late 90s and is still a friend). He gave me an orientation package and some general instructions about filing my per diem claim and arranging to pick up my monthly stipend of $150 for the next twenty-four months. I filled out the papers and was introduced to the embassy payroll officer who was to give me my monthly check. He then took me to the security office where I was given instructions about applying for a *carnet* for Ele and me (the *carnet* was our official identity card from the Mexican government and verified our legal status in Mexico). I needed to bring Ele to the embassy, and we needed to bring photos and sign the documents in the presence of the security officer.

With all the administrative procedures complied with, Bill took me to meet Cultural Attaché Cody. We talked for about an hour about my proposed research plan. Mr. Cody said that several officers in the embassy were interested in my work and suggested that Bill arrange appointments with the labor attaché, Dwight Dickenson, and the Economic Counselor, Mervin Bowen. Before I left Bill's office, I had the appointments as well as an invitation from Mr. Cody to a reception that Friday night at the embassy.

When I returned to our lodgings, I told Ele about my day, the need for her to go with me to the embassy the following day and the invitation from Mr. Cody. Then she suggested that we take a walk and, following the directions given us at the *pension*, we made our first excursion into Chapultepec Park. Walking at that altitude could be tiring, but Ele with her thyroid problem found it exhilarating. Her concern was finances: I was making $150 a month and the *pension* cost $7 a day. We would soon blow our nest egg!

At the embassy, after we completed the paperwork for our *carnets*, Ele asked Bill if he knew of any accommodations we might find that would fit our pocketbook. He suggested we call the Gurza family. In prior years, other grantees had been pleased staying there. He had his secretary call the Gurzas and found that a room and bath were available. We made an appointment to visit them the following afternoon.

I then had my first meeting with the labor attaché, with whom I talked for over an hour about the Mexican labor political scene. Dwight was a political officer closely following the critical developments in the labor movement. The one-time secretary general of the *Confederación de Trabajadores de México* (CTM), Vicente Lombardo Toledano, had broken with the governing political party, *Partido Revolucionario Institucional* (PRI), and formed a new Stalinist political party, the *Partido Popular* (the People's Party) and was challenging the PRI for political power and control of the CTM.

Preparing for my project, I read a great deal about the organization of rural and urban unions since the end of the 1910–1920 Revolution, including Mexico's first significant union movement, the Regional Confederation of Mexican Workers (CROM), led by Luis Morones, Mexico's first national labor leader, and its links with the political movement that ultimately emerged as the PRI. The PRI deemed labor one of its three bases of power—together with farmers and the army. I also studied reports of the power struggle within the PRI over Lombardo Toledano. During the tempestuous 1930s when President Cárdenas and the PRI expropriated the foreign oil companies, Lombardo Toledano enjoyed a close relationship with President Cárdenas and masterminded the strategy to unify the labor movement under the umbrella of the CTM. In the 1940s, the PRI leadership moved toward a more pragmatic and market-oriented economic system while Lombardo Toledano pressed for an alliance with the USSR and adoption of the Soviet economic model. Lombardo Toledano had been the secretary general of the CTM until the early 1940s when he named a handpicked successor, Fidel Velázquez. Even in 1947, some PRI insiders had serious doubts about the loyalties and orientation of Fidel Velázquez: would he stay with the PRI or would he follow his mentor into the new *Partido Popular*?

I assured Dwight that the focus of my study was technical and legal, but my analytical work required my understanding the political reality of the Mexican labor movement as well as the direction in which the PRI was taking the economy. He reiterated that my project was of special interest to him since it would help him better understand the Mexican Labor Code, the government's enforcement processes, and the framework for labor-management relations in Mexico. He said that he had recently discussed these issues with the economic counselor, Mervin Bowen, at which point he picked up the phone and suggested that Mr. Bowen talk with me. Mr. Bowen invited me to come right over.

I ran out of the embassy to find Ele who was window shopping in the adjoining tourist area around the Hotel Geneva so that she could accompany me to my meeting with Mr. Bowen. We hurried back to the embassy to take the next embassy shuttle to the Economic Unit, then located on Reforma near the monument to Christopher Columbus.

Mr. Bowen welcomed us and suggested that Ele acquaint herself with the Mexico-U.S. Cultural Center, just a block away. His secretary called the director, Andy Wilkison, and Ele went to see him while I laid out my work plan. Mr. Bowen and his chief deputy, Harry Turkel, then questioned me for some time. When they finished, Harry Turkel said that my study would be of great interest to the Economic Unit and asked me to meet periodically with him. Mr. Bowen then asked how I would feel about working out of the Economic Unit building. He had an empty office on the third floor if I wanted to use it. He could supply typewriter and office supplies but no secretarial services. I was delighted. He then had me escorted to a third floor office overlooking Reforma and I was given a key to the office I used for the next nine months.

Then I walked down to the Cultural Center and found Ele in deep conversation with Andy Wilkison. Andy was also a University of California Berkeley graduate as was his wife Dorothy. They had three children and their youngest, Jeanne, had hearing problems. Ele had volunteered my help for Jeanne. Andy arranged for Ele to begin in-depth Spanish lessons. Two very happy people returned to the *pension* that night.

The following day, Ele and I visited the home of don Jaime Gurza. It was located on Hamburgo, across Reforma from the embassy—a great location for us. Don Jaime and his family had come to Mexico City from Coahuila with President Francisco Madero in

1911 when the Porfirio Díaz dictatorship was overthrown. He had been minister of Economy in the Maderos government and was a respected public figure, known for his competence and integrity, someone who had not personally profited from public service.

It was a two-story, solidly built house, comfortably appointed but not elegant. We were shown a large airy room at the back of the house with a huge double bed, an armoire, dressing table, chest of drawers and several comfortable chairs. The bathroom adjoined with tub/shower. The Gurzas asked $90 a month for the two of us, including three meals a day. Don Jaime also offered to arrange parking for our car in a nearby lot for $10 a month. We arranged to move in on the following Monday.

I then arranged for an appointment to meet the master specialist of Labor Law of Mexico, Dr. Mario de la Cueva. It was he who wrote the labor provisions of the Mexican Constitution, Article 123, and oversaw the drafting the Mexican Labor Code. He was currently the chief Judge of the Mexican Labor Court. I had written him from Berkeley and asked to study under his direction. In his response, he merely agreed to see me.

That first meeting was quite stiff and formal. I sensed an initial reluctance, if not resistance to my studying under him. However, he finally agreed to allow me to join a group of senior year UNAM (Autonomous University of Mexico) law students who were interning at the courts. He said that he would try to meet with me whenever I had specific questions to ask him. However, I only saw him once or twice during the next nine months.

We had been in Mexico City only one week and we were settling into a new life.

Adjusting

September 10 we made our move to the Gurzas. We got settled easily and had dinner with the family. The daughter was an elegant lady who was the manager of the clothing department at Sanborns, the prestigious shop on Juárez at the entrance to the Zócalo. Hernán, the son, was a fifth-year student of medicine. *Señora* Gurza was a plain but gracious lady. The discussions at the table were all in English. Mrs. Gurza was dressed in black—indeed, I never recall her not being dressed in black. The family was a traditional Catholic family that mourned their family dead for a year, and Mrs. Gurza wore black because death seemed to be an ever-recurring happening in the extended family group.

Conversation covered world events and developments in Mexico, as well as family news. The daughter invited Ele to come to Sanborns after her Spanish class. Hernán invited us to join him on September 15 for the *Grito* in the Zócalo. The *Grito* is the annual repetition from the presidential palace of Father Miguel Hidalgo's proclamation of Mexico's independence from Spain in 1815. The talk was pleasant, but there was no levity. They were serious people engaged in the serious business of living. At the Gurza table, we never left hungry. We never wanted for conversation or compassion. We learned to love tortillas for breakfast, lunch, and dinner as well as chilies and rice as part of our everyday diets. Those fine people went out of their way to make us feel at home.

Hamburgo Street was only two blocks from Reforma and we learned the second week in Mexico City how to ride the buses up and down Reforma. Getting on and off was often a challenge, but we took the more expensive ones at a peso a ride. By the way, we received 4.85 pesos for a dollar. We kept the car in the parking lot most of the time because traffic was so heavy and parking in the center of the city was difficult. Three days a week, Ele went to the Cultural Center with me after rush hour, about 9:30 a.m., and we came back to the Gurzas for lunch at noon. The days Ele did not go downtown, I left about 8:30 a.m. Each afternoon I either went to the Labor Courts on Arcos de Belén or to other offices to do research.

The first week that we lived at the Gurzas, all official business was suspended for the Mexican Independence celebration. The streets were festooned with red, green, and white banners and stalls selling patriotic wares covered the sidewalks throughout the center of the city. There were people everywhere and wending one's way took time and energy. Ele and I had never experienced anything quite like the exuberance and excitement of this September celebration, and we looked forward to our adventure with Hernán at the *Grito* ceremony.

That evening, after a wonderful Mexican dinner, Hernán drove to a garage owned by one of his friends and then we set off on foot for the Zócalo. What Ele and I had not anticipated was that the people throw lighted firecrackers at ladies' legs—and Ele had on her nylons and was terrified that they might catch on fire. As we moved further down Juárez toward the Zócalo, the crowd grew to monstrous proportions with ever more firecrackers and larger fireworks. Ele just couldn't go any further. We never got to the Zócalo that night and never tried again to witness the ceremony in person. Hernán took us back home and we listened to the ceremony on the family radio, drinking hot chocolate.

Once the Independence Day celebrations were over, I settled into my third floor office. I had a monthly progress report to write, organize my research, keep notes on my studies at the Labor Courts, and set up other records for the study that I planned to use in drafting the Comparative Labor Law study for the State Department and the law school. This was my first really professional office.

I have never been a good typist, and early on I needed technical advice on how to adjust something on the typewriter. So I went across the stairwell looking for help. I found it at the Department of Commerce, Weather Bureau, Mexico City Office, in the person of Helene Phipps, the secretary to its local chief. I popped my head in and asked for a favor. She gave a warm hello, asked who I was and how long I had been in Mexico.

Then the phone rang. Helene answered: "Department of Commerce, weather." The caller posed a question about the weather. Helene went to the window and looked out before replying, "Slightly overcast about 65 degrees and small chance of rain." After a brief pause, she said, "You're welcome. Any time." I looked surprised at her response. She just smiled and said, "We're only starting to set up scientific facilities here, and my guess is as good as theirs." I started to laugh.

Helene said, "So what is your problem?" She fixed it right away, and then asked whether I needed any more help. I told her that I could not use the telephone. She just smiled and volunteered to take my calls. Then she called the secretaries of the Cultural Office, the labor attaché, and the economic counselor to advise them that if they wanted to see me, they should call her extension and she would convey the message.

That started one of the great friendships of Ele's and my life.

Helene wanted to know all about Ele and me. Then, she said, "Bring Ele to dinner Saturday night. I live nearby, and Sally, my daughter, will love to meet you." That Saturday night we drove the few blocks to Helene's. We drank tequila cocktails and ate one of her casserole dishes. We exchanged stories and laughed all evening. That was the first of many evenings we spent together. Helene and Sally became parts of our lives for decades.

What was so intriguing about Helene was how she never let adversity get her down. She was from Grosse Point, Michigan, had married a much older man against her family's wishes, and had joined him in Mexico when he bought a cattle ranch in San Luis Potosí. She walked out when she found out he had a mistress, came to Mexico City with Sally without working papers, but finagled a local hire job at the embassy anyway. She joked about always having a Mexican immigration agent on her tail and told us how she kept him out of reach, in spite of his knowing where she lived and worked. When she got the job at the embassy, she was not put on the diplomatic list, so the immigration agent persisted in pursuing her. She said, "We reached a truce. He comes around every so often for a drink and a try. He gets his drink but no try." And we roared with laughter.

Her one recurring headache was a drive to the border every six months because of her car. It had Michigan plates and was a "tourist" whose papers had to be renewed every six months at the border. She asked about our car, also a tourist with California plates. However, since we were in Mexico on a State Department grant, the car did not have to return to the border until the grant ran out—and the embassy would renew it every six months for us. Unfortunately, the Department of Commerce did not yet have a similar relationship with the government of Mexico for local hire U.S. citizens like Helene. So Helene just smiled and said, *"Méjico, mi Méjico. Así es la vida."* (Mexico, my Mexico. That's the way things are.)

Getting settled in Mexico meant opening a bank account. That was an involved procedure in which Ele and I went to the bank, presented the manager the letter from the Bank of America, and identified ourselves with passports, *carnets,* and other IDs. The bank then called the embassy to verify our identities and told us the rules and regulations. Each check required the approval of a supervisor before it could be cashed and that could take some time, often half an hour if the bank officer was otherwise engaged. This was definitely not contemporary U.S. banking procedure. It took us over an hour before we received a checkbook and a passbook in which to record each deposit.

Banking became a regular two-week procedure. I would receive my check from the embassy and deposit it. I think it was the third time that I went to the bank that fate dealt me a surprise. I had endorsed the check in front of the teller and handed him my *carnet* when an arm reached over my shoulder and picked up the *carnet*. The arm was covered by a gray uniform—and when I turned around, I faced a colonel in the Mexico City Police and Traffic Department. He looked at my picture and at me. Then he looked at the license number of my car. There was an awkward silence until he said in Spanish, "*Señor* Tragen, I see that you are losing your hair." I replied, "Yes." He also noted that the car had special status for the length of my grant. He said something about the strange arrangement and noted the license plate number. Then he said, "In addition to my work at the Police Department, I manufacture the best hair tonic in Mexico and you need to buy it." I stammered as he continued, "I will be coming to your office once a month with a bottle for you. It is very inexpensive for the service I will provide you—only 25 pesos a bottle (a little over US$5). I will be by tomorrow in the morning." I was had! When I got back to the office, I told Helene about it. She said, "Pay him and your car will be protected—and besides, it's not a very expensive *mordida* (bribe)."

The *mordida*, as Ele and I quickly learned, was a fact of daily life in Mexico. You paid on the side for just about everything. The very low wages, especially for those in public service like policemen, made the *mordida* an essential component of their family subsistence income. If you had a traffic violation, a couple of pesos solved your problem because if you went to the station you would probably be expected to make "accommodations" there to get your problem solved. When you had a traffic violation or parked in a prohibited area, the policeman took your license plates and you had to go to the station to pick them up. We heard of so many cases of licensed plates "being lost" until the *mordidas* were paid. Mexican friends told us they often did not have to pay fines once the arrangements were made to "find" their lost license plates.

So, I paid our protection for almost eight months and we never had a problem. As Helene would say, *"Méjico, mi Méjico. Así es la vida!"*

Another extraordinary family came to play an equally important part in our life: Andy and Dorothy Wilkison. Ele's visit to the Mexico-U.S. Cultural Center paid us incredible dividends. The Wilkisons invited us to dinner and we just clicked. I offered help to Dorothy in her care of Jeannie, whose hearing had been impaired from birth. I helped Jeannie read my lips and she responded warmly. Moreover, all of us had the Berkeley experience and enjoyed similar things. We played bridge together and discussed books and the adventure of living abroad.

Andy observed Ele's progress in the Spanish classes and her interaction with both his Mexican and American staff. One day, he called her into his office and advised her that one of the Americans on his staff was returning to the States and asked if she would be interested in the job. "It only pays about $100 a month in Mexican pesos, but it is yours if you want it." Ele was delighted. What those extra pesos did for our budget! So, we started 1948 with an income of almost $250 a month—enough for us to splurge.

Over the Christmas holidays, Dorothy invited us to dinner and bridge at their home in Colonia del Valle out beyond the bullring. Theirs was the only completed house on a block with new two-story houses under construction. After a wonderful dinner, the Wilkisons put their three youngsters to bed and opened a window to air out their bedroom. We played bridge for a couple of hours before leaving at about 11:00 p.m. While we were playing bridge downstairs, someone broke into the upper story through the open window and stole every piece of clothing that the Wilkisons owned, without disturbing us. The next morning, as I deposited Ele at the Center, Andy and the embassy security officer took us to the police station to make statements. It seemed to us that the police blamed Andy and Dorothy for the robbery for not having bars on their windows!

Petty theft was a constant problem. Ele and I were always on the alert for pickpockets and learned not to leave windows open that might invite adventurers. The car was a major concern. We never left it parked on the street unless we hired a watchman or *sireno* to protect it while we went on an errand or saw a movie. We were told that the *sireno* split his income with the policeman on the beat. We were also told that, if we failed to pay, offended the *sireno*, or offered too little money, the license plates would be removed and taken to the police station where the cost of recovery was many times higher than the "tip" to the *sireno*. In our two and half years living in Mexico, our license plates only once ended up in the police station. The reason, we learned from the embassy security officer, was a dispute between the *sireno* and the cop on the beat over the cop's share. The cop took all the license plates on the street to embarrass the *sireno*. It seemed that the dispute was resolved and the two were back working together.

Each day our life in Mexico added new experiences. It was not easy for Ele because she was just learning the language and the customs of a culture very different from Tulare, Long Beach, or Berkeley. There were real tensions during those early days and the tightness of our budget did not give us much chance to relax. We had a few invitations from embassy officers for cocktail and dinner parties, and most embassy people reassured her that things would work themselves out. We also met a number of Mexican and U.S. businessmen, political leaders, and Mexican government officials who usually tried to put us at ease. During those first three months in Mexico, Ele had her routine of studying Spanish and window-shopping. She began to explore the handicraft centers and silver shops, always on guard from pickpockets.

Living in someone else's home also had its challenges. While the Gurzas did everything possible to accommodate us, Ele and I were unaccustomed to an environment always in mourning. We found it difficult to converse at the dinner table when the recurring topic was the life and death of a family member. We were often the only people at the table with don Jaime and *señora* Gurza. Hernán was at medical school and the daughter often worked late at Sanborns and ate downtown. We were told of the illness and passing of family members from Coahuila, up to and including third and fourth cousins. When I tried to ask don Jaime about Maderos and the Mexican Revolution, his wife would frequently seem uncomfortable. As a result, we learned little about his experiences or why the family never returned to Coahuila after the Revolution.

The Gurzas always lit votary candles during their mourning pe-

riod. They had eighteenth and nineteenth century religious paintings on the walls outside our bedroom and lit votary candles under
each of them. Ele had never been exposed to votary candles before.
So, our the first night when we returning from dinner with friends
in the late evening the Gurzas had turned in, Ele saw the candle
and said to me, "How thoughtful to help us see our way upstairs."
Then, she blew out the candle. I gasped and relit the candle as fast
as I could, explaining scoldingly what the votary candles were. After we got into our room, Ele said, "Never talk to me like that again.
I'm learning as fast as I can to understand how to live in another
person's house—and this new culture."

Ele asked me if we could look for a place of our own. We made
inquiries about a small flat that we might rent. No luck on our budget! Ele got cold as winter approached. The house was not heated, and November, December, and January in Mexico City can be
cold. The Gurzas solved the problem by sitting outside in their car
with the heater on, pretending that they were in Cuernavaca, the
semi-tropical city across the mountains. We just cuddled in bed and
assembled all the covers we could find in the armoire.

When Ele was hired at the Cultural Center, we began to look in
earnest for an apartment. We asked at the embassy if they knew of
any listings in our price range. An embassy officer left a message
for me with Helene Phipps about a small one bedroom furnished
flat on the ground floor of his apartment house on Lerma Street. Ele
and I arranged to see it that very evening. It was tiny, with a small
living room, dinette, bedroom, full bathroom, closet-sized kitchen
and maid's room with shower and toilet. The furniture was simple
but adequate. The landlady, distinguished looking and bilingual,
lived on the third floor, asked Ele what we could afford. Ele said,
"$100." She said that would be fine. Ele asked about the car and
was advised that there was a parking lot around the corner and
assured her that there was a parking space available. We agreed on
the lease, starting the following week.

Then we went around the corner to the parking lot and met
Eduardo, who lived there with his family and took care of the cars.
He was bilingual, seemed smart and very accommodating. We
rented a space for $10 a month.

When we told the Gurzas about our plans, they were extremely gracious. Señora Gurza said that she had expected us to "want a place of our own when we could afford it." They wished us well, and we moved the following Monday.

The apartment building at Lerma 247 became our home for the next two years. When the embassy officer who lived on the second floor was transferred that June, and Ele had a new job, we were able to move from our small unit to the second floor. Now, we had two comfortable bedrooms and baths. Our apartment house had large water storage tanks on the roof, so we were never without water, whereas more modern and elegant buildings ran dry during the almost perennial water shortage those days in Mexico City.

When we got our small apartment, I thought we needed a maid. Through the Mangolds, we hired a cousin of their own maid, Altagracia, a young country girl with a small baby. *Altagracia* means "high grace." She was roly-poly, less than five feet tall, with a lovely face. We found that she really knew little about keeping even our small apartment. She could cook a little, especially rice and beans. Ele always confused her name and called her *Altagrasa* ("lots of fat"). She lasted only about a month, and we then enjoyed being alone for the first time in our married life.

I also thought we needed a dog for protection. We bought a puppy that whined and cried all night. He lasted two days.

Ele talked to our landlady who said, "I'm here all day. I will look after your apartment for you." We never had another maid or dog during our remaining tenure in Mexico City.

Getting to Know the Labor Law

Two to three times a week I gave up my reading of documents and textbooks on Mexican Labor Law to witness its application. Those were visits to the Law Courts and my interaction with my fellow interns and the staff of the courts.

The experience at the Labor Courts in some ways paralleled my introduction at the University of Chile Law School. Most of my colleagues sounded Marxist and pro-Soviet. At first, they made a point of their anti-U.S. sentiments, but as we worked together, they seemed to become more tolerant of the gringo in their midst. Some even confessed that they admired the progress and political stability of the Colossus of the North and had a few kind words for the late President Franklin Delano Roosevelt, the New Deal, and his support "for the Soviet victory in World War II." But, even as we seemed to develop personal friendships, most of them often found opportunities to remind me of U.S. aggression in the Mexican War of 1846–48; the "theft" of California, Texas, and the Southwest; and U.S. "capitalist" support of the Porfirio Díaz dictatorship. So, many of our afternoon discussions went far beyond the subject of labor law and the labor courts. I don't remember the number of times I was told the old Mexican lament, "So far from God, so close to the United States."

I tried to listen without becoming provocative and often found that once my colleagues had made their points, we could settle down to the process of learning together. The environment, which had been quite formal if not hostile at the beginning, thawed enough for me to have long discussions with my fellow interns, labor judges, and administrative personnel about the workings of the court and the problems they faced. I rapidly absorbed the written materials, especially the judgments that settled individual cases. There was no *stare decisis*, and each case was settled on its "merits." I was allowed to sit in on some cases and observe the proceedings in which the judge usually doubled as the prosecutor and relied much more on the evidence presented by his administrative staff than on the statements by the parties.

I reread Article 123 of the Constitution and the law. There are no legal frameworks more favorable or beneficial to the rights of workers. I saw provisions drawn from the Australian, Swedish, and German legislation that clearly apply to the most developed economies on the planet. However, Mexico was a developing country, with a relatively small urban labor force and empirical signs of substantial under- and unemployment. I began to ask myself questions about the relevance of this body of laws and procedures to the current stage of Mexican development and whether there were not higher priorities for government attention such as job creation and training workers for mid-twentieth century jobs.

Those concerns led me to the Banco de México, the country's Central Bank. In the late 1930s, it had set up an economic think tank that had become one of the most prestigious in Latin America. Harry Turkel introduced me to one of its top specialists. When I arrived at his office, I ran into two old friends from I House Berkeley: Gustavo Polit and Carlos Quintana. They were working together on research projects at the Bank. How fortuitous! We spent the morning talking about my concerns. They gave me some reports and the names of several studies that they felt relevant.

It turned out that Gustavo, his wife, a UC Cal grad, and two small sons were returning to Ecuador by ship when it burned up in Veracruz harbor and the family escaped with only the clothes on their backs. Carlos had completed his doctorate at Columbia University, married Lulu, a Hawaiian-born student at Columbia, and returned to Mexico shortly before Gustavo's disaster. Carlos helped Gustavo get a contract at the Banco de México until he could raise enough money to continue on to Ecuador.

Over the next few weeks, I read countless economic studies by the Banco de México and unclassified embassy reports that Harry provided me. The data showed an essentially agricultural country, with perhaps 15 million of its 23–24 million people engaged in agriculture and living in rural areas and small towns. In the rural sector, most of the large land holdings had been expropriated during the revolution of 1910–1920 and converted into *ejidos*, a form of collective farm that was supposedly based on pre-colonial farm practices—collective not individual land ownership. The data on agricultural production were dismal, with Mexico importing crucial food supplies, including corn, its basic staple.

The capital market structure was incipient, with only a limited number of industries and manufacturing facilities, many of which were owned or managed by foreign corporations. The principal source of government revenues and foreign exchange earnings were from extractive industries, petroleum, and mining. The larger companies appeared to be well-equipped and competitive; one gap was the lack of information from the state petroleum company, PEMEX, about capital expenditures to modernize equipment after the industry was nationalized in the 1930s.

I tried to relate this economic reality to the dispositions of the Mexican Labor Law. I understood the motivation and thrust of the 1910–1920 Revolution that ousted the thirty-year dictatorship of President Porfirio Díaz, and ended the feudal structure of rural Mexico and the mercantile model of the Mexican economy, but why did the revolutionary Mexican leadership place such great emphasis on an advanced labor regime in such an underdeveloped country? I could see its relevance to the extractive sector, but not to the rest of economy.

In the United States and Western Europe, labor legislation had emerged to correct excesses and abuses by management. Bread and butter unionism, championed by Samuel Gompers and the U.S. labor movement, was an effort by workers themselves to raise their standard of living and improve the futures of their families. European unions, while more ideologically influenced, emerged as the worker response to working conditions and remuneration. The Mexican experience was totally different, and the rationale for the labor code was obviously political, not economic.

The Mexican Revolution had been heavily influenced by the socialist and communist internationals. Its leadership enunciated goals such as a new Mexican society with the rights for rural and urban workers enshrined in Article 123 of the Mexican Constitution. The Labor Code that followed spelled out the application of the legal framework. But, that framework was not attuned to the development needs of the 1920s, 1930s, and 1940s. That led me to conclude that Article 123 and the Labor Code were essentially declarations of political principles rather than norms and procedures for resolving immediate labor or labor-management issues.

Hence, I reshaped my study to reflect both the political setting and a comparison of provisions in Mexican and U.S. legislation. This required me to make a balanced analysis of the intent, coupled with an objective look at the applicability of key provisions to socio-economic reality of the country. A simple study of the comparison between the provisions of Mexican and U.S. laws would be relatively easy to do, but of little practical value as it would not focus on the fundamental differences between the two economies. I had to go beyond a simple formulation that Mexican law served ideological objectives and that U.S. law intended to resolve immediate problems in the work place.

Oversimplification can be deceptive, if not dangerous. So, I amplified my study to: (1) compare the actual provisions of the labor laws in both countries, then (2) examine the Mexican urban and rural workplace, the adequacy and appropriateness of the provisions to the reality of Mexico, and the manner in which the Labor Code was applied.

The only person with whom I regularly discussed my concerns was Ele. She was always pragmatic and practical. She understood the situation and warned me that I needed to avoid being seen as an ideologue or anti-Mexican. She kept me focused on an objective, constructive comparison of legal provisions, and the regime for enforcing them.

During the two-to-three-hour sessions at the Labor Courts, Mario de la Cueva was frequently out of the office. So, in our discussion groups, different judges and administrative officials substituted for him. The most notable for me was a judge whose name I remember as Lorenzo Maya. Unfortunately, in the many moves that Ele and I made during our years of Foreign Service, many of my notes disappeared, so I must rely on my memory of a thoughtful man who took so much of his time to help me understand Mexican labor law and labor court system.

I am not sure how the dialogue began between us. It may have been a question I asked in reaction to one of his presentations after which he invited me to his office. We had several lunches together during the fall of 1947 and he began to give me insights into the political direction of the government of Miguel Alemán. He acknowledged that the Labor Code was more a political declaration than a pragmatic response to labor needs in the current state of the developing Mexican economy.

Judge Maya seem to know the origin and purpose of almost every word in Article 123 and the Labor Code, as if he partnered with Dr. de la Cueva in its drafting. From our discussions I learned that he seemed to know all the key leaders of the PRI and he arranged for me to meet several high government officials, including ex-President Lázaro Cárdenas. He arranged for me to meet the minister of Labor and observe various ministry functions, especially the labor inspection service. He allowed me to sit in on Labor Court hearings he conducted. When I mentioned his name to embassy officers, they all seemed to know of him and told me that he was one of the PRI inner circle.

In our private discussions, we talked a great deal about the issues facing the Labor Courts. I told him of stories I heard about the undue influence and bribes in individual case decisions. He reminded me that under Civil Law, the accused is not presumed innocent and the burden of proof is on the accused to prove his innocence. Under the principles of Article 123, the Courts usually presumed the defendant guilty, especially when the claimant was a poor worker. But he finessed my questions on the power of money and the influence of CTM affiliated unions in adjudicating cases. I learned not to press or cast judgment, but accept as much information as he was willing to share.

I complemented those discussions with Judge Maya with periodic conversations with my I House colleagues, Gustavo and Carlos, about the state of the Mexican economy and plans for development. In December 1946, the administration of Miguel Alemán announced a major program to develop Mexico's infrastructure—especially roads and power facilities—to overcome the shortages that a decade of the Revolution and two decades of political transformation had sown. It also called for greater private and public investment in industrial enterprises. Plans were being advanced to overcome the shortage of trained personnel that had resulted from the migration of large numbers of professionals, technicians and middle class families out of Mexico during the Revolution. Many of the plans of the Alemán administration had been drawn from the reports and proposals of the *Banco de México*. From Gustavo and Carlos, I was able to get first-hand analyses of those reports and proposals.

Making Friends

Having the Polits and the Quintanas enter our Mexican experience was very enriching. Ele had not known them at I House since they had already left by the time she moved in. But Lulu, Lesley, and Ele enjoyed each other's company from day one. Being with them gave us insights into the lives of young professionals like ourselves. Both couples were busy tending to babies and making do outside of the diplomatic arena. Visiting their homes and discussing their problems helped us understand the challenges that middle income Mexicans were facing. They were very generous to spend a part of their busy lives with us. The Polits even came to trust us enough to allow us to babysit their young sons when they had official functions to attend.

Every day we seemed to meet some new people. Ele found some interesting Mexican ladies at the Cultural Center with whom she enjoyed talking about Mexico and their lives. Occasionally I would walk down from my office to have a sandwich or taco with Ele and get a chance to meet them.

We also received a surprisingly large number of invitations from embassy officers to dinners and receptions. One young officer, Toby Belcher, had two sons with hearing problems and we spent some time with them discussing their education. At an embassy reception, we met the Mangolds who not only found our apartment for us but also had us to dinner with the landlady to facilitate our obtaining it. The Bowens invited us to their home where we were truly dazzled by the elegant colonial furniture from Peru, with ceiling to floor mirrors that seemed to encompass the whole room. Bowen's sister told us that their family's long association with Peru accounted for their acquisition of fabulous colonial era pieces. The Turkels also had us to a family dinner during which Harry's wife, Margaret, and Ele talked about their own career interests outside of the Foreign Service.

One memorable evening, the Dickensons invited us to a reception for Mexican business and labor leaders. When we arrived, Ele led me around the room introducing ourselves to all the other guests. We chatted with everyone in the room before the reception ended. That made an impression on Dwight and he invited us later to help him when he was assigned as the control officer for a visiting dignitary. The control officer in the embassy is assigned to meet VIPs at the airport, accompany them on appointments, and see to it that their visit is as comfortable and productive as possible. Ele and I helped out on visits by two U.S. senators and one U.S. Labor Department official.

At another reception hosted by the Dickensons, we met one of the most fascinating ladies imaginable, Josephine Littlejohn. Josephine looked the epitome of a *grande dame* and was a leader of the expatriate U.S. community in Mexico City. Her uncle, John Hudson, from a Topeka, Kansas abolitionist newspaper family, had come to

Mexico in the 1890s and founded the first English language paper in the Mexican capital. As a young girl, Josephine had spent her summers with Uncle John at his home in San Ángel, then a suburb outside the city. On one visit in the 1900s, she met and fell in love with Ken Littlejohn, an engineer hired by the Porfirio Díaz government to chart the route for a railway from Mexico City to Acapulco. They got married. Porfirio Díaz was overthrown. The railway never was built. The Littlejohns left Mexico for Arizona where Josephine became the Republican National Committeewoman. In the late 1920s, the Littlejohns rejoined Uncle John in San Ángel, and had lived there ever since.

That evening Josephine never left our side. People would come to greet her and she would say, "Have you met my friends Ele and Irving?" She regaled us with stories about life and experiences in Mexico and told of her great love of the country and its people. Before we left, she invited us to her home in San Ángel on the following Sunday. We had no idea where San Ángel was, so she drew us a map on a cocktail napkin. She said, "Come about 1:00 p.m. We shall have a great time and I have some people I want you to meet." Her introduction usually led to friendships that lasted decades.

That Sunday, we found the sprawling residence that Uncle John, Ken, and Josephine called home. It was Spanish colonial with gracious rooms, furnished mainly with old comfortable furniture and Mexican handicrafts. She told us that the silver has been stolen so many times they didn't bother to replace it! As she led us into the living room, we were met by Uncle John, Ken, and the couple she wanted us to meet, Ruth and Henry "Kiki" Wright. Kiki was the son and grandson of one of the first U.S. industrialists to settle in Mexico. His grandfather created La Consolidada, the first steel mill in the country. Kiki had studied at the Colorado School of Mines and Columbia University, and had met Ruth at the International House in New York. Josephine was right: we liked each other from the start and remained friends throughout our lives.

When we went into lunch, we had Mexican staples served on Mexican plates. Josephine said: "All the good china has been stolen." We just laughed. Uncle John told of life in Mexico City before the Revolution. He recalled auto races on dirt streets from San Ángel to Reforma whenever a prominent Mexican personality purchased a new car. In response to questions from Ele, he told us of the challenges and hazards he faced running an English language paper during the Revolution. Ele's love of journalism just seemed to whet Uncle John's memory. As we left, Josephine said, "You will have Christmas dinner with us. It is black tie." When we headed back to the Gurzas, we were all smiles.

The Wrights had small children and were very busy. Ruth worked at the American School. Kiki was an executive at Sears preparing for the grand opening of its first store in Mexico. But they still invited us to drop by the following Saturday for potluck at their home. We saw the Wrights frequently over the next two years.

One evening before Christmas, Ruth and Kiki invited us to dinner at the Wright family mansion in Colonia del Valle. It was truly elegant, a multi-story building occupying a full city block. Conservatively furnished, it reminded me of a stately English men's club that I had seen in a movie. It had an impressive collection of antique Mexican silver and Spanish colonial paintings. I suspect the mahogany dining room table could comfortably have seated 16 to 20 people. And it had a full movie theater where we saw home movies taken by Kiki's uncle of the birth of the Volcano Parícutin as it emerged out of a cornfield near Uruapan not two years previous.

December in Mexico was a delight. It was cold and crisp. The spirit of the season permeated the life of the city. Decorations with the unique flavor of Mexican handicrafts festooned the streets and shops. The season truly begins on December 12, the feast day of the Patron Saint of Mexico, the Virgin of Guadeloupe—the day on which in the sixteenth century, the image of the Virgin Mary was said to have appeared in the Grotto of Guadeloupe. Andy and Dorothy Wilkison took us with them to the Grotto on the outskirts of Mexico City where we observed the zeal of tens of thousands of pilgrims and worshipers. The fervor of their devotion belied the schism that had existed between Church and State since the Revolution.

On Christmas Eve, we celebrated with Helene and Sally, with the traditional hot chocolate and sweet tamales.

On Christmas day we drove out to San Ángel all dressed up. Ele had on a floor length dinner dress that Lesley Polit had lent her: it was a forest green velvet that showed off her auburn beauty, and she was radiant. I wore my best blue suit; I didn't own a tux then. The Hudson-Littlejohn home was adorned with traditional Mexican decorations and had a great fir tree in the far corner of the living room. We were two of more than ninety guests, including the ambassadors of Canada and Australia, American business leaders, some U.S. Embassy officers, and the Littlejohns' daughter, Cricket. We were astounded that we had been invited.

The large, impromptu dining room consisted of three long saw-horses covered by boards and adorned with typical Mexican ta-blecloths, Mexican glassware and dishes, and alpaca cutlery. There were fifteen chairs of assorted sizes and varieties on each side of the three sawhorse tables, with a place card at each chair. Amid great fanfare, Josephine invited us to sit down—and we were served a feast. We had different wines with each course. After the main course was served, Josephine got up and told us how pleased she was that we were sharing Christmas with her and her family. Then she announced in a loud voice, "Shift! It is time to eat dessert with new friends." And everyone scurried around to find a new chair before dessert was served. Ele and I never had another more joyous Christmas dinner!

A Year of Surprises

We were truly beginning 1948 on a high note. Ele was to take up her job at the Institute in January. Our family finances were about to improve. Christmas with Josephine so overwhelmed our own New Year's celebration that I don't remember what we did to ring in 1948. Living in our own little apartment on our own schedule was a joy. Our newfound income let us begin to do things that we only had hoped for during the first six months of our married life.

When Ele started her job, Andy Wilkison arranged for us to have a parking space in the lot in which the Institute parked its ve-hicles. So now we would drive down Reforma every morning, turn into the parking lot and walk to our respective offices.

Ele became Andy's administrative aide. She did everything from keeping the books to filling in as an English teacher when someone was ill. She typed Andy's letters and prepared stencils for the mimeograph machine. She took classes in Spanish and met with

U.S. and Mexican students at the Institute to get their assessment of the programs and classes. She loved every minute of it. When I picked her up every afternoon before we drove home or occasionally went out to dinner, she was invariably smiling.

One particular job, helping to keep the accounts, brought her into regular contact with the embassy financial officer, Billie (whose last name escapes me). Billie and Ele became good friends and occasionally lunched together. One day in April, Billie called Ele and said that the newly established Mexico-U.S. Commission to Eradicate Foot-and-Mouth Disease in Mexico (the "Aftosa Commission") was looking for a payroll clerk—a job that paid $2,500 a year plus a housing allowance. Billie had recommended Ele to the Commission's financial officer, Dorothy (last name also escapes my recollection). Ele asked Andy and he said, "Go for it!" Ele arranged to meet Dorothy at the Commission's offices near the Zócalo, on 20 de noviembre Street. I accompanied Ele to the interview and saw immediately that Dorothy and Ele hit it off. Ele was hired then and there to begin work the following Monday. She was now earning twice as much as I.

During the early months of 1948, Ele and I worked about the same hours. While she was at the Institute, I worked out of the Economic Unit and made my daily rounds. My usual weekly routine included two afternoons a week at the Labor Courts, three days working on the framework and contents for a comparative study of U.S. and Mexican labor laws, and a few hours each week with Gustavo and Carlos absorbing all I could about the Mexican economy and development plans.

At the Labor Court, I often was getting an insider's in-depth view of the functioning of the Court and the application of the provisions of the Labor Code. With my fellow interns and occasionally Judge Maya, we discussed the whys and wherefores of various decisions by the Court and the positions of some judges that had attracted my attention. It was evident that PRI policy favored labor and the Court adhered to that policy. After reviewing a significant number of cases, I asked Judge Maya why they almost all involved individual complaints. He wryly responded that politically sensitive disputes were usually settled at a "political" level, not in a hearing before a Labor Judge.

I also asked Judge Maya why in the cases I observed there had been so few instances in which labor inspectors had been invited to provide expert evidence. I understood their absence in cases brought by servants against families, but not in factory or commercial situations, especially those involving work accidents.

So, he arranged for me to meet the minister of Labor and ask him about the inspection service since enforcement was a responsibility of the Ministry of Labor, not the Labor Courts. After a brief conversation with the minister, he called in the chief of the Inspection Service and asked him to show me his operations. What I found was a loose organization of a few semi-trained inspectors. I found no systematic plan of plant inspections, and got the impression that many inspections were made on instruction from the minister. I was not shown manuals or inspection forms to guide inspectors in identifying possible violations. When the chief of the Inspection Service called me back to discuss my observations, he seemed interested but not surprised. I think that he saw me as a gringo who did not understand the true political nature of his operation.

Let me add that one day, I arrived ten minutes before the hour the chief had scheduled our appointment. I reported to his secretary and took a seat. An hour later, one of the attendants in the office noted my concern about waiting and suggested that I make a slight offering to the secretary to facilitate her announcing my presence to her boss. I slipped her a five-peso note and was immediately received by the chief, who chided me for being late.

I reported most of my experiences in the monthly report required by my grant. Many of them were shared with Economic Counselor Bowen, Harry Turkel, and Labor Attaché Dwight Dickinson. My observations apparently coincided with their experience and reports by U.S. businessmen operating plants in Mexico.

I also tried to talk periodically with the labor attaché about developments in the labor movement. 1947 and 1948 was still a time of considerably uncertainty about the political direction and control of the CTM. Fidel Velázquez had been elected secretary general, taking over from his mentor, Vicente Lombardo Toledano. At the Labor Court, I heard many rumors about Fidel's political loyalties. As the Cold War was getting underway, his decision was not merely a domestic Mexican concern but could have repercussions throughout the Americas. In the Western Hemisphere, Secretary of State General George Marshall was organizing a hemisphere-wide alliance against Soviet penetration. The support of Mexico mattered. CTM support weighed heavily on the political climate within Mexico.

I seldom raised trade union political issues with Judge Maya, but as our relationship matured, he would comment on national labor policies and the role of the CTM. When I asked about CTM President Fidel Velázquez, he merely said that Fidel was committed to the PRI and commented that he had participated in the PRI's decision to expel and isolate Lombardo Toledano. In one of my discussions with the labor attaché, I told him what the Judge had told me—and although Dwight said nothing, I got the impression that the Judge's comments coincided with other embassy intelligence.

When I met with Harry Turkel or other officers in the economic unit, our discussions usually ran in the direction of the economy and the implications of Labor Court decisions on private investment. Harry joined me once or twice in meetings with Gustavo and Carlos and asked penetrating questions about the direction of economic policy. Successive administrations since the Revolution had not been friendly to the private sector or private investment. Government planning of economic development was the cornerstone of its philosophy and strategy. Both Gustavo and Carlos were U.S.-trained economists who favored private sector investment, but supported a central role for government in economic planning and import substitution. Harry would challenge them to consider a more open market system.

Harry also occasionally invited me to sit in on a meeting with an American investor or businessman to understand his attitude toward the Mexican Labor Law and the Labor Courts. One morning, he called me down to meet an American entrepreneur who was having productivity problems at his plant outside Mexico City. He had purchased the plant during World War II and wanted not only to make money, but also to raise the standards of living of his workers. He decided to pay more than the minimum wage and raised his workers' income substantially to $1 an hour, which he believed to be a reasonable base wage. Once established, he could not lower it without facing a labor dispute.

The result was that, with their newfound income, many of his workers didn't show up for work on Fridays and/or Saturdays, because they had made enough money working four days to cover their normal expenses. The decline in production was affecting his bottom line. The few that did show up did not take the additional money home to their families, but spent it on the traditional Mexican *casa* system: when income increased, many men added a new love to their lives and added a new household, or *casa*. The most successful men had *la casa grande*, the large house for the family; *la casa media*, the medium-sized house for his second love and her family if it came along; and *la casa chica*, the small house for a third younger love as soon as his income permitted, his wife and family notwithstanding. Harry slyly asked me if I could offer any suggestions to the entrepreneur. I took up the challenge. I said that I would try.

Drawing on insights I had gleaned from reviewing labor court cases, I suggested trying an incentive system. For example, when a worker completed the full week, he would earn points toward bonuses for each full week of work. After six months or a year, the bonuses would enable a worker to receive a refrigerator or washing machine or tuition for his children's education in a private school. I also suggested that the company should make sure that the *casa grande* learned of the incentives. The employer thought it worth a try after he calculated the potential costs and benefits.

He kept in touch with me and was quite pleased with the results. After three months, he had almost 90 percent of his employees earning bonuses and that meant 90 percent was working the full week. His production was rising and his profit margin had improved. When we left Mexico, he invited us to dinner and told us that my proposal had improved labor-management relations and, even with the additional costs, improvements to his bottom line.

This incident apparently impressed Harry sufficiently enough to earn me an occasional invitation to sit in on an unclassified discussion at the Economics Unit. It also resulted in a recommendation from Mr. Bowen in June 1948 for a job at the Aftosa Commission. The U.S. co-director asked the embassy to recommend someone whom it could hire to help it deal with the Mexican government on labor problems. He proposed that the co-director talk to me. Well, the U.S. Department of Agriculture had no such post authorized, but it had a vacant post for a job classification and wage administration assistant. Mr. Bowen set up an appointment with the personnel officer, Jim Anderson, who offered me the job as a trainee level at $3,737 per year. Counselor Bowen, Labor Attaché Dickenson, Cultural Attaché Cody, Harry Turkel, and Ele urged me to take it even though I had not fulfilled the objectives of my grant. So, the Tragens were about to have another substantial injection of income into their monthly budget.

Harry Turkel also suggested that I take the Foreign Service Examination. He talked to Florence Finney, the embassy personnel officer, who queried Washington and found that my hearing disability would probably prevent an appointment even if I passed the examination. Harry minced no words about his disapproval of the policy. He understood the need for healthy foreign service officers, having spent three years as U.S. liaison with French General LeClerc in his campaign from Dakar to Paris. He told me that he had no doubts about my ability to serve in the U.S. Foreign Service.

Another morning that spring, Dwight and Harry asked Ele and me to help out with a VIP coming to Mexico City from the U.S. Department of Labor—the director of Labor Standards, Ms. Gertrude Schermerhorn. They knew that I had already met the Mexican Ministry of Labor officials, and they thought Ele might be able to help Gertrude get around. Andy Wilkison said that he would give Ele time off (with pay) for the few days that Ms. Schermerhorn was in town. Gertrude turned out to be one of the special people in our lives, especially after we left Mexico for our next assignment in Washington, D.C.

Gertrude spent three or four days in Mexico City. I accompanied her on some of her visits to the Labor Ministry during which she negotiated the first technical cooperation labor arrangement between the two governments: cooperation in labor statistics; work safety and industrial health; administration of labor standards; and labor inspection services. Ele and I had dinner with her almost every evening, and Ele took her shopping. She told us stories about the "old days" when she was engaged in lobbying to improve child labor and minimum hours of work for women during the first three decades of the twentieth century.

Meeting interesting people like Gertrude were high points. Most of the time focused on adapting to life in Mexico, taking care of ourselves, and keeping house. Our weekly routine included a Saturday visit to the sprawling Merced market to buy fruit, vegetables and tortillas. We had visited the Merced when we lived at the Gurzas; then it had been a lark, now it was our sustenance. What arrays in stall after stall of tropical, semi-tropical, and temperate zone food to choose from! Ele always wore her pedal pushers, which was a bit radical for the era, and the market ladies called her the "*gringa* who wore pants." We soon settled on a few market ladies who greeted us warmly and offered "*gangas*" or bargains. Sprinkled among the food stalls were artisans who sold their handmade ceramic wares — and they enchanted us. There were days when we decided to buy an *olla* (bowl) or *jara* (pitcher) we couldn't resist, instead of a food item on our marketing list.

When we went to the Merced, we never took wallets or purses, only the cash we needed. One Saturday, the transit police had put up a No Left Turn sign at a corner where we had always been allowed to turn left before. Ele made the left turn when she heard a police whistle. She stopped, and two policemen came over to the car. They had been standing in front of the no-turn sign, shielding it from the view of drivers. They had apparently selected our car with its tourist California plates as their pigeon for making a deal.

One of the policemen told us that we had just made an illegal left hand turn. Ele said the sign had not been there last week. The policeman said that the change had been made that morning. He asked for our IDs. Ele said that they were at home since we were going to the Merced. He said that we then had to go to the police station and got into the back seat. Ele took over: she drove straight for our apartment while the policemen objected. When we got to the apartment house, she sent me upstairs to get our official *carnets*. The policemen panicked and wanted out. Their ploy to get a bribe had gone awry. I gave them a couple of pesos for bus fare back to their "tactical stand" at the No Left Turn sign. We left them at the curb while we proceeded to the Merced.

Sunday mornings we sometimes went to a nearby Anglican church, but more often to Plaza de las Madres where most of the artists of Mexico City set up displays of their works. Everything was on sale for half of what the painting had been priced at during the week in one of the many galleries in the Zona Rosa or San Án- gel. With our new opulence, we began purchasing paintings, many of which lovingly adorn my walls today.

The first painting we bought at a prestigious gallery not far from the Cultural Institute in early 1946 was a green acrylic group- ing of pheasants. Ele fell in love with it and we truly splurged. We spent about 500 pesos (US$100) for it, one month of her salary then and there. Many Sundays we were invited to Josephine Littlejohns' for dinner. She told us that Bill Buckley and his brother had lived nearby in San Ángel when they were writing *God and Man at Yale* and she expected my study to be no less compelling than that great book! So, she set me up in her library to work on my *magnum opus*. I would work for a couple of hours at her old Underwood Upright typewriter and then she would say, "Time for tea!" Often at teatime she invited other friends and introduced us almost as part of her family.

On Sunday evenings, she often invited newcomers to Mexico City. One of those evenings, she introduced us to Perrie and Ed Beyer. Ed was the manager of a W.R. Grace chemical plant near Mexico City. Perrie was the daughter of one of Josephine's old friends. The Beyers lived a couple of blocks from us in a beautiful modern apartment house across from Chapultepec Park off the Di- ana Circle. They loved their apartment, but often it ran out of water by midday and Perrie mentioned that many an evening, they had to go out without a shower. Ele responded that our building never ran out of water because of tanks on the roof and invited them to come over to use our guest bathroom in an emergency. That invi- tation began a friendship that lasted for decades. The Beyers did come over several times to take showers. We kept in touch for many years.

Other frequent visitors on Sundays were Ruth and Kiki Wright, sometimes with their small children. Kiki, as chief of personnel for Sears in Mexico, was hiring staff for its first store in the country. He invited the Littlejohns, Ele, and me to the ribbon-cutting ceremony for that store on Insurgentes. It was a significant event, attended by Mexican ministers and city officials. The store had the first escalator in the country. When the doors opened, the people poured in and I will never forget the awe on the faces of the many indigenous people as they stared transfixed by the movement of the escalator—too afraid to try to get on and too much in awe to move away.

When Ele got her job at the Aftosa Commission, we had money to enjoy the wonderful restaurants in the city: Sanborns, Tacuba, La Cazuela, and La Fonda for typical Mexican fare—and how I loved the *enchiladas suizas* and *chilis rellenos*! We found Yucatán, Oaxacan, and Veracruzana restaurants to enliven our taste buds. And we never tired of Mario's and Chalet Suiza for more European dishes.

Ele took me to the Teatro Lírico so that she could hear Pedro Vargas and Agustín Lara. I couldn't hear them, but I enjoyed the spectacle as much as Ele relished listening. We went to performances at the *Bellas Artes*, the cultural center of Mexican life. We bought tickets for five pesos (about US$1.00) in the upper gallery, and thoroughly delighted in the new folklore musical performances even though the world-famed *Ballet Folklórico* had not yet been created. Our most entrancing evening at *Bellas Artes* was to experience the great Cuban ballerina, Alicia Alonso, dance with the newly formed ballet of Mexico. Alonso was superb in spite of the corps de ballet's inexperience.

We also took some weekend trips. Before each trip, our trusted mechanic Eduardo checked the car and filled the tank with gas. Our first overnight outing was to Puebla, the lovely colonial city. We stayed at an elegant old hotel near the center of the city, walked cobblestone streets, and visited the ceramic factory that made Mexico's version of the famous Spanish Talavera pottery. The second trip was a three-day excursion to San Miguel de Allende, Guanajuato, and Querétaro. We stayed in old hotels with great charm and walked our feet off, seeing the Gothic cathedral and art center in San Miguel and climbing through the unique colonial city of Guanajuato built over centuries-old silver mines. In Querétaro, we visited the historic area where Emperor Maximilian was captured and shot, and visited an opal dealer whom Helene had recommended. Ele bought five opals and designed a gold ring studded with opals; she had a jeweler convert the design into a ring that she never tired of wearing throughout her lifetime.

Before I went to work for the Aftosa Commission in early July 1948, I was allowed to take a vacation. Helene and Ele planned a trip to Acapulco in the off-season, with stops in Cuernavaca and Taxco—the silver jewelry center that William Spratling had made famous. So, in late June we made reservations for six days at Las Gaviotas, a *pension* in the hills behind Los Hornos Beach. Helene volunteered to do the driving in her faithful convertible. It was just Ele, Sally, Helene, and I.

The first day, we lunched in Cuernavaca and made it to Taxco for dinner before the silver shops closed. Ele bought herself a silver necklace, earrings, and a pin at Spratlings. We left a deposit and they agreed to have everything ready when we came back on the return trip in six days. From Taxco, we dropped to the semi-desert en route to the Pacific. It was hot and the two-lane highway was no pleasure trip. There were reports of bandits along the route so we went as fast as possible to get through to the coast. The *pension* was not elegant, but it was comfortable. Our rooms overlooked the Pacific and the breeze kept them reasonably cool in spite of the bright sunlight that poured in.

The next morning, after a good Mexican breakfast of papaya, *huevos rancheros,* and *bizcocho*s (Mexican sweet breakfast rolls), we saw the sights of Acapulco and its central market. After lunch we went to the *Los Hornos* Beach. *Los hornos* means "the ovens," and it was so hot that we gave up after only 30–35 minutes, but that was enough to inflict the worst imaginable sunburn on both my auburn-haired Ele and brunette Sally. Helene and I escaped the torture somehow. When we got back to the *pension,* we tried all the recommended cures on our lobster-red charges. The owner of the *pension* lent us his support. We tried cooling them with wet sheets and all kinds of salves, but to no avail. Ele and Sally spent the next few days bemoaning their fate in their respective bedrooms—they wanted nothing to eat and survived on bottled water.

Not Helene and me. We went out to dinner each night, danced at one of the hotels, and played *caucho* (a Mexican dice game) at the *pension* each night with our nightcaps before turning in. We noticed three university students who were staying at the *pension,* and we said hello to each other each night when they came back from dinner. They would politely ask how Ele and Sally were.

By the third day, both were recovering enough to be interested in getting out of their respective rooms and getting a bite to eat.

After dinner, when we got back to Las Gaviotas, Ele and Sally said goodnight while Helene and I had a nightcap and played *caucho*. When the three young men arrived, they greeted us and said that they had seen Ele and Sally go to dinner with us. "How are they feeling?" one of the young men asked me. I replied, "Much better." Then he asked me if I would mind if he asked one of my daughters to go dancing with him, the redheaded one. Helene and I smiled while I explained that the redheaded one was my wife and Sally was Helene's daughter. The young man was embarrassed, but we put him at ease by suggesting that the following evening all seven of us go out to dinner together, and, if Ele felt well enough, I was sure that she would have a dance with him. When I told Ele the story, she just smiled. We all had dinner together at a lovely hotel on the beach the following night, and Ele danced with the young man. We had a *copita* together back at Las Gaviotas before turning in. Alas, we never saw the young men again.

The following day, when we returned to Taxco, Ele's beautiful silver necklace, earrings, and pin were ready. We also spent the final day of our trip touring around Cuernavaca, the lovely city of eternal spring, before climbing up to Mexico City.

I started my new job the following Monday.

The Aftosa Commission

Ele and I were now working in the same building down near the Zócalo on 20 de noviembre Boulevard. Most of the block around the building was restricted parking limited to use by Aftosa employees, with a specially picked *sireno* to watch over our cars. Ele, the payroll clerk, worked on the fourth floor in the Accounts Office and I—the trainee in Job Classification, Wage Administration, and Employee Relations—was assigned an office on the third floor in the Personnel Office.

Ele had grasped the job quickly. She joked that the preparation of a Master's thesis in Child Psychology had qualified her to tabulate wages and hours for hundreds of American cowhands engaged in eradicating foot-and-mouth disease in Mexico. She learned her job so well that her boss delegated to her most of the responsibility for putting together the bi-weekly payroll, orienting new employees on the payroll system, and answering employee questions about calculations, deductions, and special charges. By the time I was hired, every U.S. national at the Aftosa Commission knew Ele. Up to that job, her nickname had been Bunny, but Bunny prompted sly comments by those cowhands—and her nickname transitioned to Ele.

Almost the same day that I received the offer to work at Aftosa, our friends and neighbors the Mangolds were advised by the State Department that they were being transferred to a new post. They called us to ask if we would like to move into their apartment two floors above our small nest. The rent was within the housing allowance that Ele and I would be receiving, and the landlady told the Mangolds that she would welcome our renting it. It took us about five seconds to say yes. The Mangolds invited us for dinner the following night to show us their furnished two-bedroom, two-bath apartment that occupied a full floor—a veritable mansion for us. We moved up a few days after I reported to duty at Aftosa.

My immediate boss in the new job was the assistant chief of personnel, Leonard Greene. He was a South Carolinian who was an experienced federal personnel officer and a specialist in job classification and wage administration. He and the chief personnel officer, Jim Anderson, introduced me to what they expected me to do.

They briefed me on Aftosa's mission to eradicate foot-and-mouth disease in Mexico and to prevent the disease reaching the U.S. border. North America had been clean of the disease since a devastating outbreak in the 1920s. After that event, the governments of Central and North America had agreed to prohibit the importation of beef from countries like Argentina where the disease was endemic and virulent. Unfortunately in the mid-1940s, a brother of then Mexican President Ávila Camacho used his influence to get a permit to import a herd from Argentina. Shortly thereafter, his herds and those of his neighbors were infected and the disease spread like wildfire across central Mexico. The outbreak posed an imminent threat to the cattle industry in Texas and the southwest United States. The two governments agreed to work together to eradicate it.

The Aftosa Commission was truly a bi-national undertaking. Two governments joined together to deal with a critical problem in Mexico that directly threatened the economic wellbeing of the southwestern United States. Policy and administrative decisions were made jointly. The U.S. financial contribution was much greater than Mexico's, but Mexico provided most of the personnel and field facilities.

The U.S. Department of Agriculture (USDA) was to provide technical and financial support for a national campaign in Mexico to quarantine the infected areas, kill the diseased and exposed cattle, and develop vaccine(s) to protect animals from its recurrence. The USDA appointed a co-director to share with his Mexican counterpart responsibility for directing the effort. It was now at the critical stage of building an administrative and technical staff to help plan and implement the eradication program, and U.S. livestock and quarantine specialists were to reinforce Mexican personnel in getting the job done. At the same time, the two governments were to build and operate research laboratories and vaccine production centers capable of analyzing the field problems across Mexico and producing the vaccine(s) capable of dealing with a recurrence. Since there was no known vaccine for attacking the strain of disease virulent in Mexico, the laboratory was to develop an appropriate new vaccine.

My immediate job was to draft job descriptions for each category of work to be carried out by a U.S. employee and propose appropriate grade levels in accordance with the job specification standards of the U.S. Department of Agriculture. Len instructed me on the USDA classification standards for setting grade levels and gave me copies of existing job descriptions already approved by the USDA for jobs similar to those being set up by the Commission. I had six weeks to have drafts ready.

I was assigned a small interior office and a young bilingual secretary, Ana María. She was as new to the job as I. She was one of those gifted people fluent in both languages and able to write them correctly and grammatically. She took dictation in both languages and adroitly corrected my Spanish, making sure that the English and Spanish said exactly the same thing. And she took the time to help improve my Spanish, especially before a meeting with officials of the Mexican government. Ana María made my job much easier.

Len next set up appointments for me with key U.S. and Mexican officials so that I could hear firsthand about the various categories of personnel to be hired, the work to be performed, and the technical and administrative requirements.

Before I left that day, semi-shell shocked by the assignment, he introduced me to the other two U.S. citizens working in the Personnel Office: Alan Parkinson, a former FBI agent in charge of security, and Max Winkler, the employment officer. Both spoke Spanish. Alan married the daughter of a long-time U.S. businessman in Mexico City. Max was from South Texas and had grown up speaking Tex-Mex.

I had a lot of learning to do in a few weeks. I just applied the discipline I learned in law school to get the facts and apply the law to the facts. Although I was apprehensive, I delivered the package of work a week ahead of schedule. Len and Jim completed their review with only minimal changes. Then U.S. Co-Director Dr. Noyes, and USDA Washington approved them as submitted. I was commended for their clarity, scope, and comprehension. I was promoted from trainee on my 120th day on the job. My income swelled!

The second component of my job was to accompany Jim Anderson to his meetings with his Mexican counterpart and advise him on the impact of Mexican labor law on U.S. rules and regulations, especially in dealing with the Mexican national personnel hired by the Mexican government to work with U.S. field and research personnel. This was a very delicate area because many U.S. staff members had limited understanding of Spanish and little prior experience with Mexican labor law or with their Mexican counterparts. Problems were arising every day, and the USDA wanted to minimize on-the-job friction that might lead to political tensions.

The third component was to help draft rules and regulations for conduct by U.S. personnel with their Mexican counterparts in the field and to help design training programs for existing and new employees, both U.S. and Mexican. Field operations were carried out jointly, with Mexican and U.S. counterparts. Such cooperation was a new experience for many and there were frequent cases of misunderstandings and occasional conflicts. Many were cultural, involving different work habits or different perceptions about how to do the work. Neither government was sensitive to such issues, and the Aftosa Commission had no orientation program for the U.S. personnel assigned to field operations.

As part of the third component, I visited field offices and operations in fifteen states of Central Mexico. I made farm visits to observe the interaction of Mexican and U.S. personnel with each other and with Mexican farmers. The disease was so virulent that tens of thousands of cattle had to be killed and their carcasses burned. It affected not only large herds, but also small farmers who lived outside the cash economy. The big and medium-sized cattle raisers could reinvest the money they received for the slain animals, but subsistence farmers barely participated in the cash economy and saw little value in the money given them for the slaughter of their milk cows or other animals.

In some of the *ejidos*, there were instances of strong resistance, sometimes with armed force and more often by using political influence. To deal with this problem, I was asked to participate in a small bi-national task force. One of those consulted was a PRI expert on working with rural communities, Enelda Fox. After our official discussions, she invited me to lunch; I took Ele with me. We had a far-reaching conversation about changing rural life in Mexico and the beginning of the rural-to-urban migration. She said that, in spite of the macho image of Mexican life, the key to introducing change in rural communities, including *ejidos,* was to convince the most influential senior woman. This became one of the recommendations of the task force. I never knew if anything was done since the task force was dissolved shortly thereafter.

When I was assigned to investigate a reported flare up between a Mexican livestock inspector and the U.S. counterpart in Oaxaca, I asked Ele if she would accompany me. We had discussed going to Monte Alban and the Oaxacan craft center with Perrie and Ed Beyer. When I told them of the assignment, Ed said that he had some free time and offered to drive us down. We spent four days in Oaxaca. After my Mexican counterpart and I found the problem was primarily poor communication between the two inspectors, we jerry-rigged a solution by adding a third Mexican technician to the team whose English bridged the gap. We also had time to climb Monte Alban as well as see Mitla, explore craft shops, and talk with master craftsmen.

On another trip, I was sent to Michoacán, Guadalajara, and Nayarit to look at some local problems. My counterpart and I spent a week on the road resolving issues that had more to do with personalities than policies and practices. We also found resistance among some key local *caudillos* (political bosses) to killing cattle and once were offered a sizable amount of money to go away. In Nayarit, we were detained by the local police for being members of the Aftosa Commission until the honorary British Consul came to our rescue—my father had been a British subject and the consul came to his son's rescue.

On all my field visits, the U.S. inspectors invariably asked me if I knew Ele, the lady who ran the payroll office. Their respect for her made my job easier.

Then, in late October I was given a different kind of assignment that was not in my job description. I was sent to recruit livestock inspectors and quarantine control officers in the Southwest of the United States. The city boy who knew little or nothing about cattle was to hire hundreds of personnel to staff the program throughout Mexico. Aftosa was offering $3,737 per annum plus a housing allowance and other benefits in a U.S. Southwest that was in the grip of the post-World War II recession. The money looked attractive to cattlemen, who were barely scraping by on low cattle prices and rising costs.

USDA County Agents identified areas where the Commission might find qualified recruits and made the arrangements for my visit. I read USDA background information about the cattle business and developed a set of questions to ask each applicant. Then, I flew to Tucson, Arizona, and on by bus to Deming, Albuquerque, and Las Cruces, New Mexico. The County Agents alerted local cattlemen and put up announcements of my visit in their offices. There were plenty of applicants. Quite a few were just unemployed and had little experience with cattle. Many were experienced cowboys or ranch owners. Only a few had a working knowledge of Spanish. I recommended over seventy for hire.

One of high points of the trip was my three-day stay at the Amador Hotel in Las Cruces, one of the most unique establishments I ever had the opportunity to enjoy. The lobby was home to the owner's collection of animals he had bagged, from bears to antelopes. The rooms did not have numbers, just the names of the great Mexican female movie stars. He assigned me his finest room, the

Dolores del Rio, one of my all-time favorite film stars, and I spent three nights in Dolores' bed!

I did such a good job on that first recruiting mission that I was sent back a second time—this time over the 1948–49 Christmas-New Year holidays.

This trip was to New Mexico and West Texas: Albuquerque, Marfa, and Uvalde. I had been to Albuquerque on my first recruiting trip two months before and the pickings this time were quite slim. I had to rely on Texas for most of the recruit's this time. I was in Marfa, Texas, between Christmas and New Year. The recruiting office in the County Court House was next to that of the county sheriff, Everett Copeland. On my first morning, Everett came to see me with a cup of coffee and offered his help if I needed him. He helped interest ranch owners in the Aftosa program, took me to lunch my first day in town, and invited me to dinner at his home on New Year's Day. What a treat! I had spent Christmas alone at a hotel in Albuquerque. That New Year's Day, my alma mater UC Berkeley, was going to play in the Rose Bowl and Everett promised to give me a running commentary since I couldn't hear the radio transmission myself.

New Year's Day at the Copelands was festive, fun, and joyous. No alcohol because Marfa was a dry county. My alma mater lost the Rose Bowl while I feasted on turkey and the fixings. As we ended dinner, Everett asked me about the job in Mexico. It paid more than his sheriff's salary and he needed capital to buy "some more cows." His Spanish was good enough, as was his son's. The two signed up and helped reduce the number of recruits needed.

Uvalde was notable for the large number of qualified candidates who showed up from various parts of West and South Texas. I saw the former vice president of the United States, John Nance Garner, in his lavender Cadillac going into his bank near the Court House. There were enough qualified candidates for me to reach the number needed so I was able to return to Mexico City on January 5.

Mexico City College

Shortly after I was hired by Aftosa, I was approached by the president of Mexico City College, an English language institution, to teach a course on comparative labor law. He said that the Cultural Office at the embassy and Judge Maya had recommended me. He asked if I would teach a seminar two nights a week. After consulting the USDA, Jim Anderson authorized me to accept the offer—provided that I did not receive any cash remuneration. If the College chose to give an equivalent recognition, there was no rule prohibiting me from accepting it.

So, between field trips and recruiting adventures, I taught the course and was "recognized" each semester with a silver tea set, silver service plates, a silver punch bowl and water pitcher, and other silver pieces that became lifelong treasures and are now gifted to the Museo de las Américas in Denver, Colorado

Car Problems

In late 1948, Aftosa moved its headquarters office from the Zocalo to a spanking new building off Reforma and across from the Monument to the Revolution. Ele and I had more commodious working spaces and windows with panoramic views of the great city. The new offices were very convenient and reduced our commuting time by half.

More important, we had a government-controlled parking lot with our own *sireno*. We had learned from sad experience that, even when we parked in a designated parking area with a *sireno*, we were sitting ducks for shrewd con men. They would watch the gringos park their vehicles each morning and then follow them home at night. Once they had established the route, they struck. When the *sireno* was otherwise occupied, they opened the hood of the car and punctured the membrane of the oil pump, so that the car would run only a few blocks before petering out. Once the car sputtered and died, the con men would miraculously appear, identify the problem and replace the oil pump with a "new" one (actually an old one barely able to get one home). Well. They had got us!

One night, we barely made it home to our parking garage. We told Eduardo what happened. He took one look under the hood and told us, "You have been conned!" He explained the ruse and told us never to park regularly on the street and/or take the same route home every night. "You vary your routine and they will leave you alone," he said.

Ele had come to rely on Eduardo for everything related to the car. He knew cars inside out and could fix any problem that arose. His English was as good as ours, and he was as smart as he was dependable. He had demonstrated that from day one of our relationship. Ele and I had taken several trips outside Mexico City and often found the car sputtering and sometimes stopping for no good reason. It was exasperating. We would pull into gas stations and for a few pesos get the car rolling again. It happened when we went to Puebla. It happened when we visited the Pyramid to the Sun. It happened the first Sunday we went to the Plaza de las Mujeres. It happened when we drove to Cholula to see the city of 365 churches built on the ruins of 365 pre-colonial temples.

On our return from Cholula, Eduardo met us at the gate and asked why the *señora* was so upset. After Ele explained what had happened, Eduardo said: "*Señora*, it is your gas line. The PEMEX gas you buy is watered and full of junk. Let me clean it for you and let me show you how to fill your tank." Then he emptied the gas line and a parade of nails, metal parts, water, and gunk appeared. He advised us to buy a five-gallon gas can and a piece of chamois leather. He showed us how to filter the gas from the can through the chamois into the tank to remove the impurities. Then he added, "When you are in town, just bring me the can and I will fill up your tank." Thereafter, we paid Eduardo one U.S. dollar each time we had to fill the tank. On the road, we followed his instructions and we never had another problem with PEMEX gas in the city or on the road.

Enjoying Mexico

Ele and I worked very hard in 1949. We also had a substantial increase in our take home pay when the Mexican peso was devaluated to 8.65 for US$1. We were also earning three weeks' vacation time that the Commission doctor urged us to use "to get out of the altitude every few months."

So, for Ele's birthday on April 1, we took a long weekend at the thermal baths at San José Purua: pure luxury at prices we could afford! We spent long days soaking in the baths and being pampered. One Sunday we drove over to Patzcuaro to admire the lake and its fishermen, rummage through the weekly market and marvel at the enameled, colorfully painted trays. The tray we purchased still greets me every morning when I walk into the living room.

Then in May, in connection with a field trip I had to make to Veracruz, we made plans to drive down to the port city, stopping off one night in the famous resort Fortín de las Flores. Ele would take three days' leave while I made the assigned inspection. Ele enjoyed the drive, even the incredible hairpin turns as we descended from the highlands to sea level. The night at Fortín de las Flores was a delight, with margaritas, superb food, soft breezes, and bright moonlight. When we arrived at our hotel in Veracruz, we entered an elegant older building near the harbor with Talavera-like tiles in the lobby, lush foliage, and cane furniture that seemed to be out of a 1930's film shot in the tropics. Our room was spacious and airy, with high-ceilings and broad windows in front of which hung two hammocks. We enjoyed that room and we enjoyed Veracruz. The seafood was fabulous. Seeing the historic city and its colorful Caribbean setting was a delight.

The Mexican official with whom I made my inspection was a pleasant, urbane man who served as our city guide as well as my colleague. We worked out the problem in one short session and Ele and I took him to dinner on the waterfront for red snapper (*huachinango*) and giant prawn cocktails. We drove contently back to Mexico City on the highway that does not involve the horrendous hairpin turns.

Our third excursion out of the altitude was a return to Acapulco in the rainy season. Ele saw an advertisement for a long weekend at the Hotel de las Américas, then queen of the resort city. Friday night through Monday evening was $150 per person, including room, meals, airfare and airport-to-hotel transport. The offseason, yes—but the price, incredible! So, in spite of the memories of the sunburn of the preceding year, we made reservations for a weekend close to our third wedding anniversary on August 7.

Our room had a glorious view of the Pacific. The hotel was not full and the service was impeccable. The weather during the day was just right, and we had the pool with the bar in the middle almost to ourselves. The hotel organized an excursion to the arts and craft market. We danced in the open air during dinner—between rainsqualls.

Ele and I worked hard that year, never missing a day at the office, even when our tummies were uneasy. We suffered occasional attacks of what we gringos called "Montezuma's revenge." Ele's worst bout gripped her when were still living at the Gurzas, and Mrs. Gurza's cure was a heavy dose of green chilies. The Aftosa doctor gave us more traditional medications.

My worst attack occurred one Sunday in 1948 during a visit from my Uncle Mo and Aunt Tillie Harris from San Francisco. Uncle Mo was that generous man who had purchased all my *Pictorial Reviews* when I was a wee lad entrepreneur. Since then, he and Aunt Tillie had kept in close touch with me and had welcomed Ele into their lives. They made the visit especially to see us. Ele and I took them sightseeing in and around Mexico City. That Sunday, we took them to Xochimilco and hired one of the colorful riverboats to wend our way through the canals. We had lunch at a restaurant famous for its *mole poblano.* I got a terrible case of Montezuma's revenge. On the way back to the city, I thought that I would explode. Fortunately we were close to the Wilkisons' house. They took pity on us. Dorothy gave me Pepto Bismol to settle my stomach. We spent a couple of hours there before I felt able to face the trip back to the center of city. I shall never forget that day!

The Tour Ends

Ele's and my workload at the Aftosa Commission seemed to get heavier as 1949 wore on. Ele was the junior on the payroll when she was hired. Her immediate supervisor was a grade or two higher than she, but Ele got things done and solved problems. Her supervisor was getting on in years and seemed more interested in her retirement plans than in tackling problems. And she had no interest in learning Spanish or becoming really acquainted with the work going in the field. Ele talked with the technicians when they came in to pick up their checks; she listened to their concerns and problems and made suggestions for helping them over difficult times — including a plan to facilitate sending their checks directly to their banks at home. Ele recognized the special conditions under which they worked and tried to find ways to adapt traditional USDA procedures to accommodate those special circumstances.

My big job for 1949 was to design and propose a wage scale for Mexican nationals or U.S. local hires that was compatible with U.S. statutory requirements and current Mexican salary levels. That involved extensive research of U.S. laws and regulations as well as compiling information about wage levels not only in Mexico City but also in the other geographic areas in which Aftosa operated.

Len Greene was once again my mentor in the process, and he kept a careful eye on each phase of my work. The wage proposal was submitted to the co-directors in April or May and then to the governments for their consideration, amendment, and approval.

Jim Anderson and Len then decided that I needed a deputy to help me do job audits in the field as well as Mexico City, oversee the application of the new local wage/salary plan, and deal with employee grievances. I got promoted and Len Pouliot was hired as my assistant.

All through 1949, I kept in touch with Judge Maya. We would get together every couple of months. He was interested in my work at the Commission and Mexico City College, and our conversation usually extended to the political scene in Mexico and labor developments. Our friendship had reached a point where I felt comfortable spelling out my reactions to government policies and disgust with the ever-present *mordida*. When I asked at a lunch one day if the PRI leadership was aware of the need to reform and eliminate the *mordida*, he offered me this perspective, "The reforms you want will take time. We are the first generation of the Revolution. Our goal is to consolidate power. The second generation will concentrate on getting rich and adopting policies to make that possible. The third generation will enjoy power and money, and our grandchildren will have the luxury of being born powerful and begin to think of reforms to make the system work better. The fifth generation will be the true reformers who attack the structures and systems that inhibit progress and broad-based popular participation in the fruits of the Revolution. Real change comes slowly."

We returned to that theme the last time I saw the judge in 1963. He urged me to be patient and try to understand what was going on in Mexico.

What a rich experience our life in Mexico was! Our jobs were satisfying, our income was good, and we met so many interesting people. Our new apartment was quite comfortable and we could invite six to eight people for informal dinners and evenings of bridge. As we were both working, we never tried to have fancy dinner parties or large receptions.

We were specially privileged by the friendship of my colleague, Allan Parkinson and his wife Peggy. Peggy's father had established the Packard agency in Mexico and she had been reared in Mexico City. She knew all the special places to visit: the out-of-the way museums, the mariachi haunts, the jai alai courts, and the hole-in-the-wall cafes that had extra special *tacos* or *enchiladas*. Her parents had purchased a historic town house in Cuernavaca and restored it to its colonial glory. Every corner had a special gem, whether it was a ceramic or a painting. The Parkinsons invited us down for a couple of weekends, which were just wonderful relaxing interludes. One Saturday night we went to the fights at the downtown arena. Another Sunday lunch, Peggy took us to the restaurant where the deposed King Carol of Rumania and his mistress, Madame Lupescu, dined regularly—and we saw them that day as they royally lunched.

Our ties to Helene Phipps, the Wilkisons, and Josephine Littlejohn never wavered. We often joined Helene and Sally for dinner. Sally was a beautiful girl who was just beginning to date, and one of her early suitors was the son of President Miguel Alemán, whom Ele and I met one Saturday night when he picked Sally up for a dance. Helene had met a businessman from Los Angeles, Bob Tubbs, and she was clearly falling in love. She shared her feelings with us, and we found that she was never available when Bob was in town. In the fall of 1949, Helene began considering marrying Bob and moving to Los Angeles—which she did shortly thereafter. We visited them each time we visited Los Angeles, and our friendship lasted our lifetimes.

The Wilkisons remained our refuge. Hardly a week passed by without our getting together. We shared with them most of our personal joys and sorrows. The Wilkisons were our favorite bridge companions. We occasionally spent an evening with the children when Dorothy and Andy had to be at diplomatic or official appointments. Our established routine included periodic checks of the house to make sure that the Wilkisons never had another break-in while we played bridge or socialized downstairs.

Sunday afternoons at the Littlejohns were less frequent. We celebrated Christmas 1948 at their home as we had in 1947. I purchased a tux for the evening and Ele had a dressmaker make a dinner dress for the occasion. Josephine regularly called to check on our wellbeing and remind us that she wanted to see us. We never turned down a call from Josephine. She always intrigued us with some new project that caught her fancy.

One Sunday afternoon Josephine asked us if we had met Diego Rivera. When we said "No," she said, "He lives around the corner. Let's see if he's home." So, off we went to the master's house. She rang the bell. The servant who answered the door apparently knew Josephine and told her that he was in his studio. Josephine said, "Good. We'll go see him." She smiled at the servant and we burst into the studio where the great artist was resting. And that is how Ele and I met Diego Rivera.

Ele and I never had a dull moment during our tour in Mexico. A thoroughly fascinating and varied country! Its artisan handicrafts captivated us. We never tired of visiting craft centers in every community we visited. The differences in concept and form whetted our interest no matter where we visited. We often ignored other attractions to visit workshops and markets. We collected every piece of artisan handicraft we could afford. We became convinced that plastic would drive out many traditional ceramics, and feared that future generations would not have a chance to experience these everyday art objects. Those purchases became the core of the handicraft collection that Ele accumulated and savored in her lifetime.

Ele and I never talked about leaving Mexico. We liked our jobs. We had great friends and an exciting routine. I had the teaching post at Mexico City College, and, in preparing my lectures, the opportunity to complete my study of comparative labor law.

Then, one morning in November, Jim Anderson called me to his office. He told me that the World Health Organization (WHO) had appointed him personnel director for its Western Hemisphere Office about to open in Washington, D.C. He invited me to be his deputy. He would be leaving in two weeks and needed to know my response as soon as possible. I told him that I would need to consult Ele. He invited us to dinner the following night so that we could discuss the new job. Following that evening, we agreed to make the move.

The timing was tight. We had to be in Washington by Christmas. We had a lot of arrangements to make. Ele decided to buy furniture for our living room, dining room, study and bedroom at the Domus furniture store, in blonde mahogany *primavera* wood with striking Mexican fabric upholstery. WHO would ship our household furnishings and clothes to Washington, but not our Dodge. Selling a car with foreign license plates, like ours, was prohibited. So we had no alternative but to drive it back to the States. Friends helped plan our route to Brownsville, Houston, across Louisiana, Mississippi, Tennessee, and Virginia to Washington, D.C.

In a month of farewells, it was hard to leave so many good friends. Closing the first chapter of our married life was bittersweet. We arrived with uncertainty and were leaving with the basis for careers that would not involve the back room of a law firm.

Mexico has continued to intrigue us since our tour ended. Ele and I never missed an opportunity over the next fifty years to return, and we visited all the States of Mexico except Chiapas. We watched the succession of administrations introduce economic and social changes and then consolidate them. We tried to keep up with the urbanization of the country, the massive increase in population, the development of the middle class, the emergence of a multi-party political system, and the deadly violence of the drug wars.

As I have observed those changes, the words of Judge Florencio Maya have echoed through my mind and I wonder if the fourth and fifth generations of post-Revolution leaders will undertake the changes needed to open up the political and economic systems and to convert the Mexican government into the "enabler" of equitable political, economic, and social development.

8

Washington, D.C.— Our First Experience

The drive from the Aztec Capital to the Yankee Capital was grueling. Ele didn't let me into the driver's seat once during the trip. She valued our lives too much. After a five-day drive, we arrived at the Nation's Capital on a cold and rainy Sunday afternoon. Sylvia Anderson had found a room and bath in a small rooming house in an older Foggy Bottom building that was replaced some years later by the headquarters of the International Monetary Fund. She also rented a parking space in nearby garage for our faithful old Dodge and left some snacks in our rooms, making our arrival as pleasant as possible.

We called the Andersons and Jim drove down to pick us up for dinner. We had a comfortable family evening as they intrigued us with details about the new life we were beginning. He told me how to get to the office, but said that he didn't expect me to appear until Tuesday, "Just rest and get acclimated to the city." After all, this was our first experience of living in the United States outside of California. Ele had visited Washington in 1939 after enjoying the New York World's Fair, but I had never been anywhere near the Potomac.

My Job

That Monday was a dismal, grey day. We planned to walk over to the White House only a couple of blocks away and take a streetcar ride to the Smithsonian. But after a brisk walk in the cold air before breakfast, Ele decided that she needed the day to rest. So, I decided to see my new office. I took the Connecticut Avenue streetcar up to

Columbia Road, where the Pan American Sanitary Bureau (PASB), the regional office of WHO, was located in an old mansion on the hill where Columbia Road merges into Connecticut Avenue. Next door on Connecticut were two three-story town houses that had been rented to handle the growing staff of the merged international organization. I found the Personnel Office on the second floor of the first building adjoining the mansion and said hello to Jim. The Personnel Office was brand new. Before the merger with WHO, PASB had no Personnel Office, relying on the Pan American Union, the predecessor to the Organization of American States (OAS), for its administrative services.

After showing me our three-room office, he took me to meet Chet Guthrie, the newly named director of administration, who had served as deputy archivist of the United States. Chet told me that we had a ton of work to get done in the next few weeks to meet the UN and OAS budget cycles . Then, he warned me that the marriage of WHO and PASB was a bumpy one since WHO was turning PASB working habits upside down and the PASB leadership didn't like it one bit.

When I checked into work the following morning, it was clear how challenging the immediate job would be. In accordance with United Nations rules and regulations, all of the specialized agencies like WHO were required to have compatible administrative and personnel systems. The UN's structure and regimen were much more formal than those of the OAS, and its wage scale was substantially higher.

My immediate assignment in less than two months was to prepare new job classification standards for professional, administrative, and clerical staff that met both the worldwide UN standards and those set by the OAS for such positions in the format required for submission to WHO headquarters in Geneva and the OAS in Washington, D.C. for approval. In addition, I had to prepare a wage scale for clerical personnel who, under UN rules, were to be paid in accordance with the wage scales prevailing in each locality. Both were preconditions for triggering WHO funding for personnel and programs of PASB/WHO; and, under the merger agreement, a substantial portion of the budget was to be paid for with WHO funds. In the weeks leading up March 1, I had to learn UN and OAS standards, rules, and regulations while I surveyed the jobs to be set up, their duties and responsibilities, and minimum qualifications. I also had to understand the pertinent U.S. federal standards and job descriptions for public health workers. Only then could I draft job descriptions to cover every anticipated post. Then, I had to collect data on pay scales in federal and local governments as well as data on private sector wages.

In late February, I presented the drafts for Jim and Chet's review. With their additions and corrections, the drafts were presented before the deadline to the PASB director, Dr. Fred Soper, a renowned leader of the inter-American efforts to control yellow fever, and his deputy, Mr. Murdock, equally well-known for his work in designing and building the Pan American Highway. Their professional and operational skills made the PASB a respected inter-American technical institution for improving environmental health conditions throughout the hemisphere.

Dr. Soper and Mr. Murdock, both PASB veterans, were suspicious of the bureaucratic requirements of the UN and WHO. They headed a group of dedicated doctors, engineers, and health technicians who had been used to working in a loose, low-cost operation, and were uncomfortable with the new rules and with those who owed their loyalty to Geneva. As Dr. Soper told me, you are loyal to the one who pays you. I was on the PASB payroll while Jim Anderson was paid by WHO.

Since PASB had always operated with great flexibility, Dr. Soper had pretty well made his own administrative decisions and operating rules. He was used to hiring personnel in the field when an outbreak occurred that needed immediate action, expecting that his administrative staff would come up with the funds to pay the people even though no *a priori* appointment papers had been cut. It may have taken months to get technicians paid, but the OAS had always managed to accommodate such commitments. Dr. Soper was scrupulously honest —he just did what he thought was needed to get an outbreak under control. This style of personnel administration was contrary to UN and WHO regulations that prohibited salary payments for any work prior to the appointment date on a personnel action and *ex post facto* appointment papers. Personnel management of two organizations of such different operational cultures posed major challenges.

I recall my trepidation when Chet and Jim took my drafts over to the director, whom I had only met once when I came on duty. He had seemed cold and formidable. When Chet and Jim returned to the office, they had very little to report—only that Dr. Soper took the drafts under advisement and said that he and Mr. Murdock would study them and call back when they completed their review. They were also instructed us not to contact Geneva until they had made known their reactions.

Two days later, Dr. Soper called me to his office, without Chet or Jim. He looked at me very sternly and asked me to go over the drafts with him. He and I spent the next hour reviewing every item line by line, especially the grade levels for each professional job. He asked me the source of my recommendations and about the relationship of the proposed local wage scale to the UN's in New York and to prevailing wages paid in Washington by the U.S. government for commensurate jobs. When he finished his questioning, he relaxed and said to me, "Thank you for patience and your honesty. You know that you work for me and that PASB pays your salary." After leaving Dr. Soper's office, I reported to Chet and Jim what had transpired—they seemed quite surprised.

From that meeting on, my relationship with Dr. Soper was cordial but also quite formal, never really relaxed. He seemed to trust me and I respected his role as the decision-maker. What we discussed in his office remained between us.

About a week later, with a series of minor adjustments by Dr. Soper and Dr. Murdock, they authorized us to submit formal proposals to WHO and OAS for review and clearance. There were several weeks of transatlantic consultations and clarifications. In early June, my proposals, with some minor adjustments and editing, were approved by both WHO and OAS.

Over the next three years, I had a unique apprenticeship in public health. I worked with some of the most distinguished inter-American specialists in public health and learned a great deal about programming technical assistance projects. Dr. Soper had no ego problem in surrounding himself with the best minds available to assist him in charting the transition of the Pan American Sanitary Bureau from a body primarily dedicated to combating yellow fever into the regional center for raising health standards and supporting the public health agenda of Latin American and the Caribbean governments. WHO/PASB is now called the Pan American Health Organization (PAHO).

In Latin America and the Caribbean of the early 1950s, the primary economic activity was agrarian and extractive, with 75 percent of its 150,000,000 people living in rural areas. In little more sixty years, the area has grown to over 600,000,000 people with diversified economies and over three-quarters of its population living in urban areas. Public health problems are dynamic and new ones are constantly arising. Dr. Soper helped shape the institutional framework capable of responding to those ever changing public health needs.

Getting Settled

While I was being baptized into my new job, Ele was finding us a place to live. Sylvia Anderson introduced Ele to a real estate agent who agreed to show her housing possibilities in and around the city. Sylvia and Jim had returned to their home in Silver Spring and suggested that we look first in the area near them. I told Ele that I wanted to live in a red brick two-story Cape Cod house, with three bedrooms and two baths. Ele said that she would try.

On the first day out in mid-January, the real estate agent took Ele to see several houses. The first four or five were the typical Cape Cod two-story brick houses that I believed we should "like to live in." Ele found them cut up, too dark, and not to her liking. When we got together that night in our temporary room, Ele was pretty discouraged.

The next day, when the agent picked her up, he said, "Mrs. Tragen, I have a listing that you might like. It is not a red brick Cape Cod, but a new California ranch style house on three-quarters of an acre of land in a rural setting. I know your husband wants a Cape Cod with two bathrooms, but this one may be better suited to you, your furniture, and your lifestyle."

The agent took Ele to Scully Lane, to a one-story beige brick house with floor-to-ceiling picture windows, an attached garage right next to the kitchen, set back twenty-five feet from the street, and surrounded by trees. There was a small farmhouse on the lot next door and a 180-acre farm across the street. There were woods to the rear and on the other side. Ele walked into the house and fell in love with it. The walls were painted in soft pastels, in harmony with the upholstery of our furniture that was en route from Mexico. She could arrange the furniture in her mind's eye exactly as she had hoped. The house had a large living room-dining room, two large bedrooms, a state-of-the-art electric kitchen and one bath. It had been built by a plumber who had installed radiant heat, air vents under the windows, and efficient, state-of-the art plumbing. She found the bedroom a delight with floor-to-ceiling windows over-looking the woods. Its price was $16,500, with a $3,000 down pay-ment and a 3 percent mortgage for the balance—a price we could afford.

She called Sylvia whose home was about twenty minutes away, and Sylvia sped over. She also loved the house. Ele said that Irving had his heart set on a Cape Cod with two bathrooms. Sylvia said that Ele should make a bid on the house then and there, "Don't let it get away! We'll deal with Irving later." The agent said that he would tie up the house for twenty-four hours and that he would pick Ele up the following morning.

About 4:00 p.m., Jim told me that Ele and I were having dinner with them that night at his home and that Ele had a house to show me that was not far from where he lived. He drove me to Scully Lane. In my inimitable style, I exploded, "Ele, how could you bring me here? It is not a Cape Cod. It has only one bathroom and no third bedroom if we were to have company or an addition to our family." Ele just looked at me with her best nursery school look— and said that I was wrong. I played stubborn for a while

She identified all the salient features of the house, and pointed out that, if we needed to, we could build an addition on the left side of the house to accommodate future little Tragens. She pointed to the quality of the workmanship, the light and openness given by its floor-to-ceiling windows, the appropriateness of the house for our Domus furniture, the lovely brick fireplace in the living room, and the uniqueness of the design in a world of two-story cracker box Cape Cods. And, then she turned to the *pièce de résistance:* we could afford the house! A few tears at strategic points, and I was vanquished.

When we got back to our room that night, we made an agreement that lasted throughout our married life: Ele would keep her property separate from the community and she would manage the community property. She had a fine business mind and recognized good investments better than I.

The next day, she called her grandmother and mother to tell them that we had found our first home. Grandma was so happy for Ele that she gave her $3,000 for the down payment, advising us to save our money for our next problem. How do you ever truly express your appreciation to anyone so selfless!

That afternoon, Ele and I signed the agreement to purchase the house and the thirty-year, 3 percent mortgage.

When I told Chet about the purchase, he said that he would like to take a look. So, Chet invited Ele and me to a Saturday lunch to meet his wife Dorothy and daughter Gayle and then examine our purchase. That day, we learned that Chet was adept at all the construction trades and that Dorothy was a gifted artist. They, like we, were native Californians. Dorothy was from Lake County in Northern California and schooled at the Art Institute in San Francisco. Chet had grown up in Fresno, not far from Ele's hometown of Tulare. They approved of the design and construction of the house, and enthusiastically supported Ele's choice.

The day in February when we moved into the house, Washington had one of its typical ice and sleet storms. Ele knew where each and every piece of furniture was to be placed. Jim allowed me to stay home with Ele on that miserable day. The moving van sat outside the garage and the pieces came into the house through the garage. The radiant heat in the floors kept us comfortable and the arrangement of the house on one floor sped up the process.

Ele did a spectacular job arranging the furniture and hanging the pictures. She had already decided where each piece was to go. All we had to buy were a couple of mattresses, the drapes for the picture windows, area rugs, and some kitchenware. The weather didn't bother her as she oversaw the unwrapping and installation. She put me to work on moving out boxes and packing materials. Even that first night, the house looked special.

Sylvia helped us that night by bringing dinner and some food supplies that we had not had time to buy. Then our neighbor down the road, Mr. Robb (he never used his first name) also brought us a casserole that his Belgian-born wife had baked. They became good friends.

We spent the next several weeks unpacking and decorating. Ele was the planner and supervisor and I was the peon. The peon seldom behaved as selflessly and obediently as he should—and Ele had to put her foot down quite often. And, being contrite usually set the stage for my apologizing. We worked very hard through March and April, buying the odds and ends that we needed to complete furnishing our castle. Ele's taste was very special, with the soft pastels in the living room walls to set off the paintings and furniture that we had brought from Mexico.

Unfortunately not everything we had packed in Mexico City ended up in our new home. Some boxes just disappeared en route. In this case, missing were a couple of special Tree of Life ceramics that had captured Ele's eye in an art shop near the Hotel Genève, two woolen blankets, and a box of my notes on Mexican Law and the operations of the Labor Courts. It was all probably worth no more than a few hundred dollars but was quite dear to us! We fretted and fumed, but no trace of them was found. Over the next half century as we made other inter-country moves and some inside the United States, we had many other "disappearing items." I was told in one country that movers always like a small remembrance from each job.

For Ele's birthday on April 1, we had a house warming party for old and new friends. They included colleagues from WHO/PASB, I House friends living in D.C., the Andersons, the Guthries, Gertrude Schermerhorn, and new neighbors who had been so gracious. Ele converted the garage into a barn and we had an old-fashioned barn dance, with our record player supplying the music. The bar was limited but the food was plentiful. We had a fun time and none of the neighbors complained to the police. We had settled in.

PASB's Fiftieth Anniversary

One morning in April 1950, Dr. Soper informed me that he was planning a reception for the staff at the Sulgrave Club to celebrate PASB's 50th Anniversary and that I was to stand to his right and introduce each staff member on his or her arrival. I scurried around to make sure that I knew each of my fellow staff members and would not disgrace myself by not recognizing them as they passed through the receiving line. On that momentous night, decked out in my best dark suit, Ele and I arrived early. We had a pleasant chat with Dr. Soper, and then my colleagues began arriving. I did well on the first five or six—and then Jorge Vivas arrived, whom I introduced in the English translation of his name, "George Life." From that point on, my foot was in my mouth. By the fifteenth or sixteenth arrival, Dr. Soper put his hand on my shoulder and advised me to join Ele, saying that he could do better on his own. I was never again invited to perform such a lofty task while I was with WHO/PASB.

The fiftieth Anniversary coincided with the date for the Inter-American Conference called for every four years under the Agreement that created PASB. The site was Ciudad Trujillo in the Dominican Republic (its name was Santo Domingo before and after the dictatorial era of Trujillo). Dr. Soper chose me to be the headquarters advance man to go down six weeks before the opening of the Conference to negotiate with Dominican officials the arrangements and local personnel needed for the meeting.

When I told Ele that I would be away for six weeks, she invited her grandmother and mother to come east and stay with her during my absence.

The flight to the Dominican Republic was routine. I had some trepidation about going to the Dominican Republic since I was well aware of Rafael Leónidas Trujillo's reputation as a bloody dictator. I had read of his flirting with Hitler for a spell and how he was kept in camp by Sumner Welles and some U.S. largesse. On my arrival, I did not hear the call for diplomatic passports and just waited in line. I saw how those not on the Dictator's A List were subjected to body searches and other indignities in the plain view of the remaining passengers waiting to be cleared. When I finally reached the control window and handed over my OAS diplomatic passport, the official left his post and escorted me to the diplomatic waiting room into the care of a representative of the Ministry of Health, who then rushed me to an official car before I could catch my breath. The representative found my bags in Customs and we were off to my hotel. We never alluded to my arrival experience once the Dominicans became aware that I was essentially a lip reader.

My hotel was the Jaragua, where my counterpart was waiting for me. He explained that, pending the return of the minister from Paris, I was to provide him with the list of personnel, equipment, vehicles, and other resources needed for the Conference. When I proposed that we have our first working session later that day, he merely commented that I must be quite tired after my trip. After I checked in, he rather pointedly asked if I needed anything for the night. I smiled and said no. He left a phone number to reach him in the morning and had me escorted to my room. I had dinner and went to bed.

The Jaragua was the top hotel in the country at the time, comparable to the Nacional in Havana for food, accommodations, and nightlife. The facilities were luxurious and, as I later learned, equipped with bugs to allow my counterpart, as part of his regular assignment, to listen to goings-on in each room.

That I discovered when I thought that I had lost a cuff link and told my counterpart. He immediately decided that one of maids had taken it. He took me to his inner sanctum where he read the riot act to the maids and staff. I asked a simple question about some equipment on a desk and he matter-of-factly told me how he used it to listen in on guest rooms—a technique he had learned in Germany when he trained with the Gestapo during an interlude in which Trujillo flirted with Hitler. When I returned to my room, I found the lost object on the dresser—I've never been sure whether I had misplaced it or whether it had been returned. Anyway, I realized that all of us would be under surveillance and must behave.

The second morning, I asked my counterpart to set up a meeting with the officials at the Ministry of Health who were supposed to be in charge of arrangements for the Dominican government. He convened a session with the acting minister and his advisers. I provided them with the extensive list of requirements for the Conference that the conference staff had prepared. The list placed top priority on the number of Dominican multilingual personnel that were needed to supplement the conference officers coming from Washington. It also listed the number of vehicles required for operations, the number of meeting rooms, the size and configuration of the rooms for plenaries and committee meetings, the required sound equipment, the amount of paper needed for meetings, and so forth. Dr. Soper had also asked me to arrange for all delegations and staff to be housed in the same hotel and that the Dominican government negotiate with the hotel a special rate. Dr. Soper had specifically instructed me to call him directly if the Dominican government was unresponsive.

The acting minister had expected PASB to pick up all the costs and do all the work. I then produced the note of the Dominican government through its ambassador in Washington in which the government had agreed to assume all of the costs, with only certain designated expenses to be borne by PASB. I also pointed out that this was to be the first major inter-American meeting to be held in Ciudad Trujillo since the president had come to power. A representative of the Foreign Ministry was then summoned—and he confirmed that the ambassador had been instructed by Trujillo himself to present the offer. The meeting was adjourned while the Dominicans consulted among themselves.

That afternoon, I reported the gist of our initial discussions to Dr. Soper. And then I waited and waited in my Jaragua Hotel room! What were we waiting for? The return from Paris of the minister of Health! No one dared take any action until the minister returned. The minister was the president's brother-in-law, and I was confidentially told that he had taken one of the president's sons to Paris to be initiated into the arts of love.

It was about the fourth day that I heard from my counterpart, who said that we would have daily meetings starting the following morning. I asked about the actions being taken to fulfill the government's commitments, but got nowhere. At the beginning of the following week, the minister took personal charge and the logjam began to break.

He took me to a meeting with the president's right hand man. We went over the lists. Aides were ordered to line up vehicles, space, and personnel. The minister arranged for me to talk to businessmen, university professors, bankers, and government officials in order to identify qualified multilingual people to work in the Conference. I was consulted about equipment and vehicles, chairs, and tables and all the other items on the list. I was overwhelmed and asked Dr. Soper to send down a conference specialist to help me.

Ten days before the Conference was to begin, the first senior public health officer from WHO/PASB headquarters joined me, as did the senior conference officers from PASB's parent, the Organization of American States. Then the Dominican government moved. Friends in the Dominican diplomatic service told me that the word had come down from on high. All the personnel we needed were ordered to close their businesses, release their multilingual secretaries and even bank managers. I was told that some businesses were ordered to volunteer at no cost the vehicles and drivers needed for the Conference, as gestures of support for President Trujillo.

The Conference opened on time, operated like clockwork and set the tone that Dr. Soper had wanted. I can claim little credit in retrospect, but I learned how a dictatorship works and how things happen when the dictator wants them to happen. I remember little about the proceedings except that all of the initiatives proposed by the WHO/PASB were adopted without much dissent. I also remember being invited to lavish social events, including the inauguration at the National Palace, presided over by Trujillo himself. I vividly remember a reception hosted by Trujillo at one of his residences outside the city where for the only time in my life, I saw a bathroom in exquisite sea foam tile with fourteen-carat gold faucets. It was a far contrast from the evident poverty in the poorer sections of the city and the farm labor conditions on the sugar plantations.

Ele's Career

Once settled in Washington, Ele told me that she wanted her own career, building on her university training in journalism and psychology. She prepared her resume while I was in the Dominican Republic. She delayed her job search while I was away and her mother and grandmother were with her. They arrived the morning after I left for Ciudad Trujillo. Ele became a tour guide, showing them the sites in and around the city and explaining their historical importance. She became an encyclopedia of the most convenient routes, the good inexpensive restaurants, and places to park. When I returned, we spent a week together before they returned to Tulare. All four of us came to know each other better, and bonding was very easy.

The Monday following their return to California, with resume in hand, Ele went to an employment agency, with great trepidation. After she presented her university training and experience, the agency sent her on a job interview. She got the address wrong and found herself in the business office of Allied Youth and was hired on the spot for $175 a month.

When she told me the name of her new employer, I was quite uneasy: Allied Youth! Well, this was the McCarthy era, and yours truly was concerned that it might have been a "pinko" front group on McCarthy's infamous list of subversive organizations. Far from it! Allied Youth was the last vestige of the Carrie Nation Methodist Church campaign to turn America into a non-alcoholic bastion. It was dedicated to convincing teenagers that they could have a good time without drinking. She was no stranger to the environment since her father had been a Methodist and she had gone to Wesleyan Sunday school and church most of her life.

That afternoon, Ele met Ken Weaver, the man who was to become her boss. She told him what her interests and experience were. He laid out what he expected of his editorial assistant—to help him plan the layout of publications, crop photos, draft captions for photos, and occasionally prepare texts for feature articles. This was exactly her cup of tea and she liked Ken. When she advised the employment agency of her mistake she agreed to pay its fee even though she had gone to the wrong potential employer. The agency told her that she signed on for a job that paid $25 a month less than the one to which she had been referred. Ele wasn't upset because she discovered the other employer really wanted a secretary, not an editorial assistant.

Ele considered this a learning experience. Ken took the time to train her in the editorial technicalities and techniques that many would have kept to themselves. She found herself helping athletes, including famous football players from Texas universities, draft testimonials about the evils of drink.

Her office was not far from mine and we drove to and from work every day. We would brief each other about our adventures on the drive home. Some days when we reached Scully Lane, she would mutter a bit before announcing that she wanted a dry martini.

Another feature of Allied Youth was its annual convention for high school students at Buck Hills Falls, Pennsylvania. High school students from across the east and south came for a weekend dedicated to programs on how to better enjoy their lives without drinking. In July, Ele and her companions at the Washington headquarters served as discussion leaders and chaperones. Ele worked with Ken in preparing the report on the proceedings.

Many of the delegates were from wealthy Florida communities and from families whose parents were near-alcoholics. They had witnessed the scenes their parents caused and knew precisely why they preferred not to drink. Moreover, as wealthy teenagers, they had learned other ways to enjoy themselves. When Ele returned the following Monday night, she was exhausted. She reported that neither she and nor any of her office colleagues had had much sleep for three days as they chased boys and girls out of each other's rooms. She succinctly said, "No need for the conference or a convention. They already know how to have a good time without drinking!"

Ele worked with Ken for well over a year before he took a job at National Geographic. She was offered Ken's job, but without his remuneration. Revenues were drying up and the future of Allied Youth was uncertain. So, she decided that it was time for a new challenge.

In May 1951, Gertrude Schermerhorn invited us to dinner at her apartment on Connecticut Avenue. She asked Ele if she were interested in working for the Bureau of Labor Standards in its publications division. Ele said yes, and Gertrude arranged for her to be interviewed by the chief of the Bureau's Publications Division. It was another love at first sight. The interview included the Division's principal writer, Olive Clapper, the widow of World War II journalist Raymond Clapper, and a well-known author in her own right. Before they could invite Ele to join the staff, she had to earn the approval of the associate director of Labor Standards: Mrs. Clara Beyer. Mrs. Beyer—Ele and I always called her Mrs. Beyer—was the first woman graduate of the University of California Engineering School. No one was hired in that Bureau without Mrs. Beyer's authorization, even an entry-level editorial clerk. After a twenty-minute interview, Mrs. Beyer was satisfied and had Ele escorted down to the Personnel Office. She was offered a Civil Service entrance level job, CAF 3.

Some weeks later, Ele was formally installed in a job she loved. She respected and enjoyed the people with whom she shared the working day. She used all the skills and techniques that she had learned at Allied Youth. She also learned many more about editing technical papers and articles prepared by subject matter experts of the Department of Labor. The job lasted almost two years until we left Washington for my next assignment in El Salvador.

Ele's job was to review papers or articles as drafted, and identify lacunae and unclear passages. She would then show them to her boss, who would review the passages with the authors. In only a few months, her boss discovered that Ele was as good as she in dealing with the authors, and by early 1952, Ele had become the real Tragen diplomat who could tame many an unreconstructed tiger!

WHO/PASB

As Ele developed her editorial career, mine at the PASB grew. Much of the day-to-day personnel management work was delegated to me. I was placed in charge of recruitment, job classification, and personnel grievances. My bosses, Chet Guthrie and Jim Anderson, handled the relations with the senior public health staff and advised them on the body of rules and regulations that the UN system was introducing to replace the more informal procedures and practices of the Pan American Union.

Chet Guthrie was a highly regarded specialist on the design and implementation of governmental systems and procedures. Chet had rewritten the classic textbook about the separation of powers, pointing out the reality of Federal government operations. As he pointed out, the Presidency devotes most of its time to drafting and shepherding legislation through the Congress, while the Congress spends most of its energies on trying to run the Executive Branch through its appropriations and oversight powers. Chet described how Congress used the power of the purse to influence and define the operations of Bureaus throughout the government and how Bureau Chiefs made alliances with key congressmen to protect their turf. He also introduced this naïve neophyte to the power of lobbyists and moneyed interests on the Executive Branch and Congress to make sure their sacred cows were not gored.

Chet and I had long conversations about the complex relationship between the U.S. government and the emerging international organizations. In 1950, the UN was in its infancy, and was one of the first world organizations that the U.S. had joined. Congress had never authorized membership in the League of Nations. The first inter-American organization was the Pan American Union, and the U.S. looked at it as a means of pushing U.S. trade interests. The United States was a nation state that resisted initiatives of international organizations to set standards or regulations that would be binding on it, even in public health. We discussed the threatening Cold War and the requirement for new international alliances to protect vital U.S. national interests, including the transformation of the Pan American Union into the Organization of American States (OAS), with the collective security and military commitments to build a western hemisphere alliance against communism. How far and how fast the U.S. would accept the UN, the OAS, and WHO/ PASB was not clear.

My relationship with Jim Anderson centered on personnel administration. His interests were on his job, and he was a first-rate specialist. He had been schooled in the U.S. Department of Agriculture with its old-line career civil service in which change was resisted and promotion came slowly. He taught me how the Civil Service Commission and the U.S. Department of Agriculture did it—and that was how WHO/PASB should do it!

Both men made my learning process much easier that I had expected. However, neither one lasted long at the PASB. Chet tried to lead Dr. Soper from his traditional one-man leadership role to that of a regional leader in a worldwide body. Chet was used to the culture of the U.S. government, not that of the Pan American Union. Chet became frustrated and in late 1950, returned to the U.S. government. He was replaced by a competent long-time civil servant who knew his role was to support, not to lead. His name was Harry Hinderer.

Jim Anderson was selected for his job by the WHO director of Personnel, a long-time colleague at the Department of Agriculture. While Dr. Soper consented, he was never sure whether Jim worked for him or for WHO/Geneva. Jim tried every way possible to reassure him, but the relationship had never been easy.

In mid-1951, Harry Hinderer called me to his office and advised me that Jim had been relieved of his responsibilities and that Dr. Soper was naming me as the new personnel officer. He asked me to move into Jim's office. By the way, I was to remain on the PASB payroll and would communicate with WHO only through him. This was one of the worst days of my life. I felt that, in loyalty to Jim, my mentor and friend, I should also resign. That night Ele on the way home urged me not to take abrupt action. Instead, she took me out to dinner and we saw a fine movie, *The Quiet American*. As we left the theater, she suggested that we talk to Jim. So, we drove by his house. The lights were still on, so we rang the bell and had a drink together. Jim was very philosophical. He had seen the dismissal coming and urged me to stay on. He had trained me and thought that I could do a good professional job. Above all, he said that I had the confidence of Dr. Soper and the Latin American public health specialists. The Andersons and the Tragens remained friends for many years.

WHO/PASB continued to grow exponentially. WHO money was financing new activities and a new cadre of professional and administrative staff. Dr. Soper moved the headquarters down Connecticut Avenue to Dupont Circle, to a mansion and an adjacent residence on New Hampshire Avenue. The adjacent residence was converted into office space for technical and administrative staff. On its second floor the Personnel Office was installed, and my private domain was a converted walk-in closet.

Neither the mansion nor the adjacent buildings had air conditioning. As Washington's summer engulfed us, Assistant Director Murdock, established a rule that we would close our offices when the first lady employee fainted from the heat and humidity. Many a day during the summers of 1951 and 1952, I was alone at work until Ele picked me up. On the hottest, most humid days, I worked in my skivvies behind a locked door with the blinds drawn! Her offices at the Department of Labor were air-conditioned.

As we built up the Personnel Office, we were fortunate to find an extremely competent Mexican national, fluent in French and English as well as Spanish, to head our employment unit. He was so competent that I never had to discuss a procedure or rule twice. He did his job superbly and allowed me to concentrate on training the less competent staff that we frequently had to replace. In 1952, when I was the personnel officer, he resigned. I urged him not to. He replied that I had taken him for granted and had not adequately made known to him how much I appreciated his efforts. That taught me a lesson that I remember to this day: never take anyone for granted and never forget that each of us needs friendship and encouragement when we are doing a good job.

Most of the work of a personnel officer was routine. Job classification, wage administration, and employment were carried out in accordance with the standards and procedures set by the UN, as the OAS basically withdrew from the administrative area. There was very little room for innovation or variation by a regional office. Under Mr. Hinderer, we operated by the book. Occasionally, Dr. Soper would hire a yellow fever specialist in the field without advising us and we would have to improvise a way to cover his back wages. However, everything settled into a routine.

Only when there was an employee grievance did we deviate from the routine. I was called once to the director's office because of a grievance by a clerical employee against a professional staff member. The UN had established an intricate grievance procedure that the Personnel Office administered. The most common case was an allegation by a secretary that her boss (usually a public health officer) had mistreated her on the job. The Personnel Office investigated the complaint, tried to mediate between the parties and, if mediation failed, convened a grievance panel to hear the complaint and propose a solution.

Dr. Soper and almost all the other public health officers (Latin American and U.S.) had never worked in an organization with such a grievance procedure, and invoking the procedure usually resulted in their objecting to the questioning of their professional judgment. This made my job very uncomfortable whenever a grievance arose. Usually, I was able to find a solution. Once, the aggrieved employee was transferred to the Personnel Office. Another time, I had to shade the truth in order to protect the process and the employee. Ele usually had to suffer my black moods while I tried to reconcile the parties or work out compatible solutions.

Life in Washington

Living in Washington was a brand new experience for two Californians. It wasn't only the four seasons, but we arrived knowing only three people—all through work contacts. It wasn't like Mexico with the embassy contacts that helped us find our way through the assimilation process. In Washington, in spite of the great support from Sylvia and Jim Anderson, we were on our own. We were two young marrieds on our own in the process of building our fortune.

Yes, we made friends at the office and in the neighborhood who were helpful, but they had families and lives of their own. Most of them did not appreciate the problems of a young couple far from home in meeting the challenges that life in Washington posed. We found that understanding from my colleague Chet Guthrie and his wife. We could talk out our challenges with them since they had already faced similar ones when they migrated east from Berkeley. They allowed us to become part of their extended family and guided us through the adjustment process. We were invited to share family events at Thanksgiving and Christmas and trips to the Eastern Shore to delight in Captain John's oysters and soft-shell crabs and visits to Williamsburg—a relationship that lasted over forty years.

And then there were the old friends from I House Berkeley. Shortly after we arrived in the nation's capital we got a call from an I House friend saying, "Welcome to Washington!" and invited us to an I House reunion at which over a dozen people came to greet us. Most of those who came to meet us were in government jobs and they were living the same experience as we. They were the catalysts that helped us adjust to and understand the Washington scene and gave us a sense of continuity in that new life.

One of those who joined us that evening was a special favorite of Ele's, Rollo Rush, who was working in personnel administration for the U.S. government. We not only maintained a professional relationship, but I was his best man when he married another friend from I House, Joan Obidine. They had their wedding reception in our house.

Shortly after Joan and Rollo married, Ele and I received a surprise phone call from another I Houser, our best man, Fernando Walker. He was about to be married at the Naval Chapel to Barbara

Rhea, whose stepfather was Vice Admiral Woods, and asked me to be his best man.

The I House ties permeated much of our life during our first tour in Washington. We had periodic visitors who overnighted with us. People who helped us understand the world beyond Washington and the changes emerging in our economy and society. Bill Escherrich and Hal Kerber working in the private sector and Carlos Bee entering the political arena kept us in touch with developments in California. We in turn took them to visit the highlights of the nation's capital, especially the Smithsonian.

Friendship also paid a major role in improving my ability to hear. I depended on lip reading and my secretary or Ele handled all my phone conversations. My job required extensive use of the telephone and I searched for a way to use it personally. I shared that concern with Gertrude Schermerhorn, whose family had hearing disabilities, and she introduced me to the editor of the national magazine of the American Hearing Society who arranged for me to test the post-World War II generation of hearing aids. In early 1952, I found a Teledyne model that worked for me. It was a compact instrument with a small microphone for my shirt pocket and a cord to the earpiece that fit inside my ear—so unlike the bulky five piece apparatus that I wore in the 1930s and 40s, with a microphone hanging around my neck with a cord to headphones and another cord to two large batteries in my pants pockets. It was expensive, but we bought it. Then, Ele became my teacher in learning to identify sounds and then words in both English and Spanish—a tedious process that lasted several years. The editor followed my progress closely and decided to make my story the lead article in a 1952 edition of the magazine and Ele co-authored the piece with him.

Our life during the first couple of years concentrated around the house and our offices, and we sought more time to enjoy the cultural and historical sites in the area. Ele pointed out that we spent most of our free time working in the yard or cleaning the house. She bemoaned that we had very little time for vacations; indeed, in two years, we had made one two-week trip to California to visit our parents, a weekend with friends in Philadelphia, and an overnight excursion to see the Army-Navy game. Ele proposed that we consider how we wanted to live before we started our family. We were debating what we wanted to do when an offer for an overseas assignment came from the U.S. Department of Labor.

Our interest in enjoying the unique resources that abound in and around Washington was one of the reasons that we decided to sell our house in 1952. The house required constant attention when we would have preferred to see an exhibit at the National Gallery or a play at the Folger Library. In addition, our experience in Mexico had whetted our taste for foreign service.

Changes Are Coming

I assumed the duties of personnel officer in 1951. I began dealing on a daily basis with some of the most eminent public health doctors, engineers, veterinarians, hospital administrators, and nurses in the hemisphere. I was their agent to solve their personnel needs, not a colleague with whom to discuss public health problems or help program multidisciplinary approaches to solving the underlying social and economic issues. Being their administrative agent was not my career choice. I was a lawyer who was smitten by substantive development issues and the impact of change on the lives of people. I shall always be grateful for this chapter in our life, but it was time for the next phase to begin.

The change began one day in the spring of 1952 at the Department of Labor when Mrs. Beyer called Ele into her office to inquire whether she thought I would be interested in becoming a technical adviser for the Department of Labor in Latin America. Gertrude Schermerhorn had given Mrs. Beyer some papers I had written on labor law in Mexico. Ele asked me, and I was excited.

So, I took a few days leave when I was invited to meet the senior staff at the Bureau of Labor Standards. I was questioned and then briefed by line supervisors and technicians from not only Labor Standards but also the Bureau of Labor Statistics and the Employment Service. A lengthy session with the Safety and Occupational Health specialists was my final interview. A week later, Ele was advised that Mrs. Beyer wanted to talk with me and asked that I make an appointment, and that Ele was to join us. Mrs. Beyer began by telling me that her colleagues were impressed with me and my work to date. She laid out her vision of the role the Department of

Labor should play in implementing President Truman's Point Four Program through technical support for creating jobs and improving labor standards to promote safe, healthful working conditions. She saw the U.S. Department of Labor leading a worldwide effort to help less-developed countries evolve as democratic, economically strong societies that respected the rights of all people. Her formula simply was that jobs gave people the means to support themselves and their families, and good labor standards served to improve working conditions.

We talked for nearly an hour before she said to Ele and me, "The Bureau wants to send you to Bolivia as an advisor to the government on labor standards in the mining industry." I was flabbergasted. I knew little about mining and mine safety standards. She assured me that the Bureau believed that I was capable of doing the job needed. She called in the chief Safety Engineer who said that he agreed with Mrs. Beyer that I could do the job and that he could backstop me with mine safety specialists as needed. He stressed that they needed someone who could gain the confidence of the Trotskyite union leaders and convince them, as well as the management of the principal tin mining companies, that working conditions and mine safety standards needed to be improved. Mrs. Beyer added that sending safety engineers to Bolivia before the preparatory work had been done with the union and the mining companies was premature. They thought that I could do the preparatory work. I asked for some time for Ele and me to talk over the offer. Ele just nodded and urged me to accept. So, I did.

Mrs. Beyer then called the director of the Institute of Inter-American Affairs (the IIAA), the organization that administered the U.S. technical assistance program for Latin America. It had been created during World War II to support the war effort and consolidate support of our Latin American allies for the Allied cause. Its director had been Nelson Rockefeller.

An interview was set up for the following week. I ran a gauntlet of questions about my age and experience. The IIAA activities were concentrated in agriculture, health, and education. I was to be its first labor specialist, and there was little enthusiasm for expanding beyond its three central specialties. And, since I read lips, there was skepticism that I could do a field job. But, IIAA had no health requirement like the Foreign Service that had thwarted my taking the entrance examination in 1948. I was advised the following week that the IIAA acceded to the request of the Department of Labor.

I was later told by one of the top IIAA officials that the article published about me and my qualifications in the American Hearing Society's publication had influenced their decision. I suspect Gertrude Schermerhorn sent them a copy.

I was called back to the IIAA Personnel Office to fill out the employment forms and detailed security background information on both Ele and me. This was the era of McCarthyism, and anyone with links to Labor was especially suspect and subject to special investigation. The IIAA personnel officer advised me not to say anything to WHO/PASB for the time being, because it was taking IIAA up to two years to complete the security clearances, especially for anyone who had lived or worked abroad. I went back to my job with high hopes that in the not too distant future, I would be starting next chapter of my life.

Ele suggested that this was the time to sell the house and make a visit New England and Quebec where some of our I House colleagues had settled. The house sold quickly at the price Ele set. We rented a two-bedroom apartment in a complex conveniently located for access to our offices and laid plans for our vacation during the summer of 1952. The trip as a wonderful interlude during which Ele fell in love with New England covered bridges and red barns and I devoured the treats of Quebec and Montreal.

I remained at WHO/PASB during the clearance process. Changes at the top were coming there. The assistant PASB director, Dr. Murdock, retired and was replaced by Dr. Helio Candau of Brazil, whose vision of health and integrated development captured my imagination. Unlike many of his public health colleagues, Dr. Candau saw development as a multidisciplinary process in which he attributed to public health a pivotal but not always central role. He talked with me on several occasions about his interest in building teams of public health, agricultural, education, public administration, and other specialists to work in designated pilot areas to provide the people with all of the technical tools they need to raise their wellbeing and their standard of living. In addition, he was an excellent administrator who had the knack for getting bureaucracies to accept challenges and experiment with new ideas and approaches. I was not surprised when in 1953 he was elected director general of WHO and moved to Geneva.

I remained with WHO/PASB until the spring of 1953. My security clearance had been delayed because of no response from the U.S. Embassy in Mexico City. Someone made a call to the embassy and got action on my papers. In the meantime, the Bolivian Revolution of 1952 occurred: the political system was in upheaval and the tin mines were nationalized. My Bolivian opportunity vanished.

When informed that my security clearance was in hand, Mrs. Beyer made a decision to send me to El Salvador as the Advisor to the minister of Labor. Mrs. Beyer through Ele asked if I would accept. Ele and Gertrude told me to accept—no ifs, ands, or buts. In March 1953, I was offered a contract by IIAA, one of the first cleared by the Eisenhower administration. I gave a month's notice at WHO/PAHO. Ele gave similar notice on her job. We were scheduled to depart for Central America in mid-April. We were bound for El Salvador.

We enjoyed several farewell parties. I was honored at a reception and given a gold Longines wristwatch. Dr. Soper and the public health staff held a luncheon in our honor during which he told me that, had I not accepted the El Salvador assignment, WHO planned to transfer Ele and me to one of its regional offices outside of the Americas. The big send-off was from the U.S. Department of Labor at a dinner at Olive Clapper's home. Olive had just successfully published her delightful inside look at Washington political and social life, *Washington Tapestry*. She not only hosted the farewell but helped write the high point of the evening: *This Is Your Life, Ele Tragen, and Where Is El Salvador?* What more could anyone ask!

9

El Salvador

Ele and I were never more excited about any assignment than that to El Salvador. We both played roles in my being selected for the appointment, and we looked at it as the beginning of a career in the U.S. Foreign Service. We both strongly supported President Truman's Point Four Program, and optimistically believed that we could contribute not only to raising standards of living and democratic development but also to strengthening U.S. interests throughout the developing world.

El Salvador turned out to be the pivotal period of our life. It was in El Salvador that I became a competent technical adviser and learned the ropes of foreign relations. It gave me the confidence to accept whatever opportunities might come for us. I learned that my disability was not an insurmountable impediment to doing a complex professional job when the minister of Labor, Mario Héctor Salazar, overlooked my disability and provided me with the support I needed to advise him.

This was also the period in which I began to hear reasonably well with the new hearing aid. It was Ele who spent much of her time helping me to relearn the meaning of sounds and hear words once again in English and Spanish.

It was in El Salvador that Ele and I realized that our life would probably not involve children. We made several attempts to start a family but were unsuccessful. I suspect that the problem was mine. Ele merely said to me that she and I are our family. We drew closer together and I can vouch that my love and respect for Ele grew over the years—she was my best friend and the priority of my life.

Washington Orientation

We were allowed two weeks in Washington for orientation. We were to be in El Salvador by April 15. The briefings on El Salvador were handled by the Institute of Inter-American Affairs (IIAA) and the U.S. Department of Labor (USDL). In those days, there was no provision for orienting spouses and families, so it was up to me each night to brief Ele on what I had been told. It was almost twenty years later that wives and families were included in Foreign Service briefings—and then only after years of lobbying by the American Association of Foreign Services Wives (AAFSW), in which Ele was actively involved.

The first week of orientation was at the Department of Labor. Ele was allowed to join me for most briefings about the activities, resources, and training programs by key technical personnel of each of the major Bureaus. Each explained its policies and procedures, as well as the possibility of lending support to El Salvador. A couple of Bureaus had been actively engaged in training programs in Europe under the Marshall Plan. The Office of Foreign Labor Affairs had developed a specialized research staff on trade union developments worldwide and was interested in information about the labor movement in El Salvador.

The second week was spent at the IIAA, where I was given detailed briefings on its policies, procedures, and budgetary processes. A special lecture covered its creation in World War II and its mission to support U.S. military forces stationed in various Latin American countries. Those troops needed healthy living and working conditions, an adequate local food supply, and trained local personnel to provide services at the military installations. That led the U.S. to negotiate agreements with the host countries to help them improve health conditions in and around the installations, increase production of food crops, and train personnel in the skills needed for base operations.

The mechanism created for assisting governments in meeting those objectives was the *servicio*. It was a unique inter-governmental body made up of administrators and technicians of the two governments. The *servicio* management made up of U.S. and host government officials planned and implemented projects in country. The U.S. essentially financed operations.

The success of the *servicios* in World War II led the governments of almost all the Latin American countries to call on the U.S. to continue the program after the end of the war. By 1949, as part of the Point Four Program, and as a measure to win Latin American support in the Cold War, the United States acceded to Latin American governments' requests to revive the *servicios*. The IIAA was designated to administer the program. Agreements were signed with almost all of the independent countries of the hemisphere, including some that had not been allies in World War II. The program remained focused on public health, agriculture, and education. At first, the U.S. agreed to pick up almost all of the costs and then developed a long-term plan to increase host government financing of *servicio* operations and to transfer completed projects to host country ministries. The IIAA program provided only technical assistance, with no capital or financial aid.

The *servicio* planned, designed, organized, and implemented multiyear programs made up of specially designed projects that provided essential public sector services. I was briefed on projects in all of the countries, and pointedly reminded that I was the first labor technician ever hired by IIAA and that there was no specific project experience to be shared with me about the impact and results of similar projects in other Latin American countries.

My briefings covered mainly agriculture, public health, and education field projects. In agriculture, activities were concentrated on research stations and extension services. In public health, maternal and childcare and rural health programs were priorities. In education, the World War II emphasis on vocational education shifted to teacher training and elementary and secondary curriculum development. The objective was to build public sector agencies that would be transferred to the respective national ministry and then be financed by the host government within its national budget. Over time, the U.S. directors and technical personnel were to be replaced by host country nationals. The *servicios* were to be phased out as the national ministries became more technically and financially capable of implementing the various projects.

These *servicios* produced effective transfers of technical expertise, but national budgets had not been able to absorb the more sophisticated programs and trained technicians. In addition, almost none of the countries had civil service laws to ensure job security for the trained national technicians. Public sector wage scales in each country were substantially less than those paid in the *servicios*. The trained nationals resisted the transfer of their programs to their own governments, and governments increasingly pressured the U.S. to fund the *servicios* indefinitely or to make block transfers of funds to finance their ministerial programs.

In my briefings, I asked about IIAA access to the overseas lending programs of the U.S. government, like the Marshall Plan. I was concerned that the absence of a loan component prevented financing of critical dimensions of government services, such as schools, health centers, research stations, and farm-to-market roads. As programs began to deal with more complex development issues, such as farm credit and the construction of dams and infrastructure, what would be required were loans, not grants.

In my briefing on the U.S. Operations Mission in El Salvador (USOM), I was advised that its budget was about $1 million a year. It had a technical staff of about thirty, mainly in education, public health, and agriculture. It had a mission director, a program officer, and an economic adviser. All of its activities had been in place for many years. Most of its funds went to pay the salaries of U.S. technical personnel. A small percentage was earmarked for supplies and equipment for technical projects, such as agricultural research experiments, supplies for experimental health programs, equipment for model schools, and scholarships.

My last briefing was at the State Department. I arrived early on my next to last day in Washington. The specialist who met me asked what I was going to do in San Salvador. I replied, "Adviser to the minister of Labor." He countered after reviewing his notes with, "I didn't know San Salvador had a labor ministry. After all, it is just a small colonial island." Then it dawned on him that I was going to El Salvador, whose capital is San Salvador, a Central American Republic, and not to the Caribbean island! He excused himself and I waited an hour until a young foreign service officer came to apologize for the mistake. He told me not much more than I already knew about El Salvador: the smallest country in Central America in land area, but its most densely populated. The country had had a bloody uprising in 1931–32 in which most of its indigenous population had been wiped out, and had lived under the repressive dictatorship of General Maximiliano Hernández Martínez until 1946. A military coup took place in 1948, with progressive military officers allied with young "liberal" civilians taking the reins of government. Then he reminded me that the "suspect" Arbenz regime in Guatemala was next door, and there was concern about the possible spread of Arbenz's influence since his wife was the daughter of a Salvador-an coffee planter. His carefully worded briefing avoided telling me much about the current political situation.

Ele also did a good deal of research on her own at the Library of Congress to get a picture of the country and its history. No larger in square miles than the state of Maryland, it was second only to Haiti in population density per square mile. It had many mountains and small valleys in the interior, and its coastal plain was largely unde-veloped because of yellow fever and malaria. What most impressed her was the concentration of productive farmland in the hands of a few powerful landowners, known as the Fourteen Families (even though there were probably three score listed in the various books and monographs we read). Coffee was the lifeblood of the econo-my, providing up to 95 percent of foreign exchange earnings and most of the revenue for public sector and development programs. She found little information about the urban economy or agricul-tural crops other than coffee and only footnotes about the former importance of indigo whose industrial uses were aborted after Ger-many during World War I developed a chemical substitute that was cheaper and more uniform.

The history of the country showed little democratic develop-ment. Its indigenous populations, the Pipiles, were related to the fierce Aztecs of Mexico and were noted warriors in pre-colonial times. The Spaniards imposed the *encomienda* (feudal plantation) system and divided up the land among a handful of families. They became the powerful oligarchs who ruled the Republic from its independence from Spain in 1821 and Mexico in 1825. In the nineteenth century, these landowning families rotated in political power, under constitutions that assured them supermajorities in the legislature and allowed them to consolidate their landholdings by divesting small landowners of their land, which created a large landless population. She found a report of a petition to the U.S.

Congress by El Salvador in the late 1840s, for admission to the United States as a slave-holding state, even though slavery had been abolished in its initial Constitution after independence!

She found an analysis of the power of the Fourteen Families and their influence with the Army and the Church. It described how they led the suppression of two indigenous uprisings, one in the 1830s and another a century later. Both resulted in major losses among the indigenous population. In 1931, when a liberal reform government was elected—the first and only in El Salvador's history, the Fourteen Families were reported to have induced General Maximiliano Hernández Martínez to stage a coup and take power, killing an estimated forty thousand indigenous people in its wake. He then became dictator and governed ruthlessly for the next decade.

By the late 1940s, a group of young military officers, influenced by the Mexican Revolution, led a reform movement to modernize the country and open up the political system. They were supported by university students who called for democracy and economic development—some were Christian Democrats, some were socialists, some were influenced by Franklin Delano Roosevelt and the New Deal. A reform government under Colonel Oscar Osorio was elected in 1950, and one of his key civilian supporters was Mario Héctor Salazar, the minister of Labor, with whom I was to work.

Each evening, after Ele briefed me on her research for the day, we did some packing. Ele organized and supervised the packing of all our worldly goods. They were to be shipped by air to El Salvador and scheduled to arrive by late April. The rainy season was to begin in mid-May. We were told that the customs warehouse at the airport had been destroyed by fire a few weeks earlier and that the new one would not be built until the following year. When we boarded our plane south, we were both conscious of the need to find a house in less than a month to avoid damage to precious household effects by being left in the open air at the airport, especially after the rainy season begins.

Getting Settled

Pan American Airways delivered us that evening in mid-April at the San Salvador Airport. Ele had celebrated her thirty-first birthday on April 1, and I was to be thirty-one on May 18. We had no idea what to expect as we disembarked at San Salvador, a city located at 2,400 feet above sea level and noted for a pleasant climate for most of the year.

We were met at the plane by the USOM administrative officer and hustled out of customs to the Nuevo Mundo Hotel. As we looked out the windows of our hotel, we saw a Third World capital. There were few buildings higher than two or three stories, almost all of which were in the Spanish rural colonial style, and built of adobe and wood. The walls of the houses lined the sidewalks, any gardens or patios behind those walls. There were few gaps between buildings downtown. Many residences had been converted to businesses. There were only a few multistory cement buildings like the Salvadoran Club, the Association of Coffee Growers, the National Bank of El Salvador, the National Theater, and the Ministry of Labor.

It was very warm night, with not much of a breeze. So we took our first walk around town. Most of the stores looked more like Arab bazaars than modern businesses. The streets were full of people. Everyone was doing some kind of street business, but not much of the begging we had seen in Mexico.

When we returned to our rooms, we had a power blackout. My briefing had warned me that power failures were not uncommon and that there might be water shortages in the mornings: the infrastructure was not in good shape. We soon learned that the city offered few diversions, with only three movie theaters, another acceptable hotel, the Astoria, and a couple of sports clubs.

The next morning, Ele and I were picked up and taken up to the Operations Office (USOM). We were introduced to the director, Mr. Green, and then taken over by Dr. William E. Schenk, the Economic Adviser. Bill had been a Professor of Economy at the University of Illinois and his Ph.D. was in development economics. His job was Adviser to Enrique Sol Castellanos, the minister of the Economy, who later became a senior economist at the Inter-American Development Bank and the World Bank.

Bill briefed us on the Salvadoran economy and said that El Salvador was working on its first development plan. He pointed out the significance of the labor component to the development plan and questioned me about my development philosophy and economic interests. Ele and I liked Bill from the beginning. He invited us to dinner, and we bonded with his wife Hildreth just as quickly when we met her.

Bill told us that he and I were unique members of the USOM. We were not members of *servicios* and our role in the Mission was suspect. He told us that the *servicios* were in trouble. To meet their objectives, they needed to refocus their activities. In addition, key Salvadoran politicians were envious of the progress made by the *servicios* and complained that their technicians were earning more than they. Bill added that the popularity of the *servicio* personnel in the countryside made them potential political threats. Bill then alerted us to the opposition of the coffee owners to the current government and its efforts to raise government revenues to finance development projects. He also warned us that many politicians would raise arguments like, "Why do we need the *servicios?* Just give us the money to fund development in accordance with our own political and development priorities."

Ele then asked for help in finding a house. Bill told us that the USOM and embassy did not have a listing of available houses or apartments and that there was a shortage of available housing. We would need to find a residence on our own, as USOM had no cars available for us to use. We would have to wait until ours was flown in as soon as a freight plane became available. We were alarmed.

The Hotel Nuevo Mundo was not our cup of tea. It was hot in the rooms, with no cross breezes and no air-conditioning, and the meals were not that appealing. So, the next day, we asked about a possible *pension* at which we could stay until we found a house. The USOM director's secretary told us about a family residence in which she had stayed.

We went there after work and were told that no rooms were available. As we were leaving, almost providentially we ran into Jorge Molina, a friend of Ele's from I House. Jorge had studied architecture at UC Berkeley and lived at I House while I was in Chile. Because of the Arbenz regime in Guatemala, he was living in exile. He was delighted to see us and said that he was living at the *pension* for the time being. Ele invited him to join us for dinner. Hearing our plight, Jorge offered to help us find a house starting the following evening. He had his Beetle with him, and the three of us could squeeze in. He proved to be our savior.

For nearly two weeks, we drove up and down every residential street. His strategy very simply was to ring the bell at any house that had the lights off. We went through the elegant Los Pinos, the emerging upper class residential Escalón district, Flor Blanca, and even Los Andes, perched another 500 or so feet above the city. In Escalón, we saw several quite comfortable new houses. Some of them were too large for us; many asked for rentals beyond the allowance provided by the U.S. government. Several sat alone on a block, and Jorge warned us, "Too exposed. You'll be robbed within the first week after you move in." Jorge's excellent training in architecture served us in good stead.

By the end of the second week, we were beginning to despair when Jorge stopped at a house in Flor Blanca, about a block from the National Stadium. It was a solid, two-story concrete structure in the middle of the block and backed up on a house facing onto the next street. Jorge said that this looked like a good possibility since there was no light shining in the front window. We could see a flickering of candlelight faintly weaving in the background. He walked up the steep driveway and the front steps. He rang the bell and, after a few minutes, a man opened the front door. He was the owner of the property, and he advised Jorge that his mother had died several hours earlier and was lying in her bedroom awaiting burial the next day. Jorge expressed regrets and asked if the house was for rent. The owner said that he had not given any thought to what he would do with the house, but invited us to return the following evening to meet with him and his wife at his house situated across the street.

The following evening at the appointed hour, we appeared. He and his wife were gracious and told us that they would show us the house in a day or two, but were not sure that they wanted to rent it. We paid our respects and agreed to return two days later.

In the meantime, Jorge discovered that the landlord had been educated through high school in Brooklyn and ran a dry cleaning establishment, one of the best in the country. His mother had made the family fortune as the premier Madame of El Salvador. On her retirement, she set up her son in business and lived a quiet, respectable life amid the families of her many former clients.

On our return two days later, the owner and his wife had decided to lease the house to us, with rent payable in dollars, not in Salvadoran *colones* (the local currency). He then showed us the house. It was quite large and built with solid cement walls. It had a large interior patio right opposite the living room and his late mother's bedroom. A large, winding staircase went to a second floor with two bedrooms and a bath. There was a dining room and pantry, with room for a refrigerator. At the end of the front hall was a locked gate beyond which was a smaller patio flanked by the maid's room and shower on the left side and the kitchen on the right. At the rear, off the red-tiled patio, was a three-story high back wall to discourage potential intruders. The floor in the main part of the house was made up of mottled pink ceramic tiles and the walls were an off-white color. There was no hot water and the upstairs bathroom toilet was broken. It was not exactly our cup of tea, but it was certainly the best possibility that we had seen.

Ele and Jorge talked with the owner and they agreed on a rent within our allowance. He also agreed to install a hot water tank on the main floor and repair the upstairs toilet, providing we shared part of the installation expense. Agreed! He mumbled that he saw no reason for the hot water tank, since his mother had lived there without it. Ele was superb in dealing with him, and he ended up making just about all the changes she requested, at his expense, except for installing the water heater. He thus became our landlord.

Our furniture was then called forward from Tampa. It arrived in late April and was moved from the airport directly to the house the same day. The rain started two days later! Without Jorge's help we would have lost the Domus delights we had bought in Mexico, and I would not be able to say that the furniture is still gracing my current home.

When we settled into our new home, we invited Jorge to use the second bedroom until he found a place of his own. When I informed the USOM that we permitted an I House friend exiled from Guatemala by the Arbenz regime to live temporarily in our home, I was excoriated by the administrative officer and told that, since we were receiving a U.S. government housing allowance, no one not of our family could live there. This was the McCarthy era in U.S. politics and, when I sought an appeal from the mission director, he declined to intervene. So, with a heavy heart, I had to tell the person who helped us find our home that we could not help him until he found a place of his own.

The Ministry of Labor

On the third day after our arrival in San Salvador, Bill arranged for me to be presented to the minister of Labor, Dr. Mario Héctor Salazar, and his chief advisors. The introduction was cool at best. The minister made it quite evident that he was not enthralled by having me assigned to advise him. The vice minister, Dr. Fernando Castellanos, was even less cordial. The minister's two aides, Dr. Ramón Ávila Ajacio and Dr. Rogelio Chávez nodded casually to me when I was presented to them.

The minister raised questions about my age and experience (though he was thirty-six and the vice minister was under forty). He then asked me to take a careful look at the Inspection Service and to report back to him in thirty days, and asked his Administrative Assistant, Dr. Chávez, to show me my office.

With formality and little cordiality, I was taken to a large office on the main floor. I was introduced to Dr. Augusto Ramírez and Alberto Monti who were to be my liaisons with the minister. I shared my office not only with them, but also with the ILO (International Labor Office) expert who had been brought to El Salvador to write a Labor Code based on ILO policy recommendations. Bill Schenk and I thanked the ministry officials for their cooperation, and I said that I would be back to work the following morning.

In my first month at the ministry, I arranged private appointments with the minister's immediate staff and his advisers. The ministry was made up of dedicated young professionals. I found out the vice minister was also the secretary general of the then governing political party, PRUD; that Moncho Avila was very bright and had the full confidence of the minister; and that Rogelio Chávez was the minister's brother-in-law. The inner circle also included Dr. Napoleón Albéñiz, legal adviser to the minister, and his assistant, lawyer-to-be Luis Olmedo; Dr. Miguel Angel Molina, chief of the Inspection Service; Dr. Funes, chief of Worker Health Services; Dr. Hugo Navarette, chief of Labor Statistics; and chief of the newly formed Women's Program, Doris Campbell. I also dropped in on several of the young technicians who were designing new services for workers and their families, as well as the Argentine who created the Workers' Theater and was training young workers to act in live performances on social subjects.

I spent hours reviewing the activities of each of the ministry's units and took a series of trips with labor inspectors and technicians to get a hands-on feel for the ministry's work, the labor market, and labor-management relations. I made no effort at that time to get to know the labor leaders or the union movement.

I met once a week with Bill Schenk, attended periodic USOM staff meetings, and prepared a monthly report for USOM/IIAA and the Department of Labor. Bill Schenk provided logistical and sec-retarial support to meet USOM/IIAA requirements, while don Augusto provided secretarial and other administrative support for my work at the ministry.

By mid-May, after consultation with Bill Schenk, I requested an interview with the minister to bring him up to date with my inves-tigations and to share with him my initial reactions. I was very ap-prehensive because I was still being treated almost as an intruder.

The afternoon that the minister granted me an interview, my apprehension had turned to almost panic. As I entered his office, he sat at his desk with a very stern look on his face. He was flanked by Rogelio Chávez and Ramon Ávila. There was a definite chill in the air! After thanking the minister for the chance to present my views, I said, in essence:

El Salvador does not need more labor laws at this time. The economic effects of the two laws recently enacted have produced results that benefit the few at the expense of the many. The wages and hours legislation was certainly desirable for those few workers that benefited from its provisions. However, there are only ten to twenty non-agricultural establishments in your country with more than one hundred employees that were impacted by the law. All agricultural enterprises (coffee, cotton, and sugar) were exempted. Of the ten to twenty, two were railroads: IRCA (the International Railways of Central America, owned by United Fruit Company) that runs from Puerto Barrios in Guatemala to La Unión (the Salva-doran port the Gulf of Fonseca), and the Salvadoran Railways Company, which hauls coffee and other products from the interior of the country to the port of Acajutla. Before the new laws, the time for a rail trip from Guatemala to San Salvador was under eight hours; now, with the overtime provisions, the trip takes fifteen hours and fifty-nine minutes. The brewery and one or two other companies are the only ones with a sophisticated enough management to set up records that the new laws require, while the other affected businesses are almost too small to absorb the additional costs involved. Even before the law, most of the enterprises affected already operated on forty to forty-eight hours normal workweek.

I then pointed out that most Salvadoran wage earners were seasonal farm workers who followed the crops from Guatemala to Nicaragua, and received cash income for fifteen to twenty weeks per year. That's your real labor force today and that is the group you have to convert into year round workers. They have to be reoriented and trained to provide the manpower required to make your development plans work. The proposed new agricultural labor law proposals do not deal with them. What the proposal would cover is only the small year-round core of workers living on the coffee and cotton plantations, who receive a house, a plot of land for their own crops, and a small cash wage, supplemented by a daily ration of corn and beans. They need assistance, but does a new labor law provide what they need? I fear that a new agricultural wages and hours law could be counterproductive and create an incentive for landowners to reduce their core labor force and create a new body of unemployed that the urban sector is incapable of absorbing.

Then, I suggested that the ministry should consider shifting its priorities and work to create the services that workers need in a country in process of development, including statistics to understand the labor market, manpower planning, employment services, and skill training that would facilitate worker participation in the emerging economy and help them raise their income and living standards.

I agreed on the need for an efficient, objective inspection corps that knows the working conditions in the few existing urban industrial and mining enterprises and urged him to professionalize the staff and build its reputation for honesty, openness, and objectivity. The inspectors should be your eyes and ears, but your long-term core program should be manpower development.

When I finished, there was no immediate response. Moncho began questioning me in detail about my core ideas and strategy. He was very precise, almost surgical, in his probing. I thought, "Ele, we will be packing up very soon!" Rogelio followed with a series of other less technical, but relevant legal and practical queries. I remember saying in response to one of Rogelio's last comments, "A law is only effective when it is enforceable."

The minister then offered me a demitasse of strong Salvadoran coffee and said, "Thank you for your frankness. We will consider what you have proposed. One of us will call you back in a few days." The meeting ended somewhat abruptly on that note.

When I went home later that afternoon, I was ambivalent about what to tell Ele. I didn't want her to be unduly worried but felt that maybe I had struck out. She took one look at me and said, "Relax. You did what you had to do." We had dinner with the USOM director and Mrs. Green that night. I was not in the mood for a festive evening, but Ele kept us focused. Bill and Hildreth Schenk took us home after dinner and told me to relax. The next few days, I went to the ministry every morning not sure what to expect.

I think that it was four or five days later that the minister himself called me up to his office. He was alone and he invited me very formally to sit down. Then he said that he had a great responsibility to help create conditions that would ensure that there would never again be the bloody dictatorship that had ruled his homeland for so long. He said that his country needed a body of laws to ensure protection for all of the people, especially labor laws that give workers respect and rights. I replied that I agreed but that the law needed to be relevant to workers' needs. I repeated that the inspection staff was not yet trained to enforce effectively the current labor laws, much less try to oversee new, more complex or comprehensive ones. I also reiterated what I thought the role of a labor ministry should be in the development process.

He said that he agreed that his country had to build a technically competent labor force that was capable of earning good wages and providing their families with the basis for higher living standards. We talked for several minutes about the problems of rural workers, and I remember asking where and how rural laborers would find urban employment at that time in El Salvador if the new rural labor laws under consideration were viewed by the landowners as the pretext for reducing their work force. As the conversation evolved, his tone changed and he began to call me Irving.

He then called Moncho and Rogelio in to talk about my proposal. The four of us talked for well over an hour about the policies and programs the Labor Ministry should undertake to become a meaningful participant in the development of the country.

This happened over sixty years ago, and the precise words are not important. But that morning we formed a willing partnership to design a new strategic role for a ministry of labor. They seemed to like what I had said and the ice was broken. Oh, we had sharp discussions and disagreements over the next four and a half years, but always at a level of civility and friendliness that made reaching an accommodation possible.

A few days later, the vice minister invited me to his home for a drink and an afternoon of "let's get to know one other." A few days later, Rogelio and Moncho invited me for a drink after work to talk about my role in the ministry. Rogelio said that the senior officials had made a bet before I arrived over how long I would stay. Rogelio picked four months—the longest of any of them. He said that the minister and the rest had concluded that Rogelio was the winner since they unanimously agreed that I could stay as long as they ran the ministry. And from that day forward, I was never excluded from important policy discussions about the direction and programs of the Ministry of Labor—through three ministers: Mario Héctor Salazar, Fernando Basilio Castellanos, and Ramón Ávila Agacio.

I prepared the first draft of the strategic plan for the ministry over the next month. I discussed it with Bill Schenk and sent a copy to Gertrude Schermerhorn for Mrs. Beyer, for it involved both extensive training for ministry personnel and additional U.S. advisers to work with me. When I got clearance from my bosses to proceed, I reviewed it with Rogelio and Moncho step by step. It called for immediate action to (1) train the Labor Inspection Service to ensure more effective enforcement of existing labor laws and (2) develop a Salvadoran labor statistics and research unit to identify trends and problems in the work force and identify problem areas that needed attention. It proposed that we spend 1953 preparing a detailed plan for ministry action on manpower development.

The U.S. Department of Labor sent one of its senior labor standards officers to help me put the package together. We worked with Rogelio and Moncho and prepared an outline for the minister's consideration. In return for the minister's agreement to provide the necessary personnel and support services, the Department of Labor offered to provide technical services and training for key technicians. The ministry adopted it as its plan of action. In the work plan, my immediate job would be to advise on improving the technical competence of the Labor Inspection Service. I was also tasked with preparing an operations manual for the inspection service. Since *de facto* it was the only ministry activity that touched every potential and actual employer and worker in the country, the behavior of its personnel significantly influenced how businessmen and workers would react to the ministry and its other programs. I had already heard allegations that certain inspectors had received bribes to look the other way or even invent a problem to get paid off. Moncho and Rogelio agreed that the ministry had to train and carefully oversee personnel and minimize the chance of corruption.

The second component of the plan was to upgrade the quality and scope of labor statistics. The ministry published series on wages and hours, work accidents, and labor-management relations that had technical flaws and were incomplete. A priority would be to train the staff and advise on and develop a comprehensive database. The third component of the plan was to build the ministry's capability over the next three to four years to create and operate an employment service to match employment prospects to workers seeking jobs, and to organize a workers' job training program that would equip workers with minimum skills needed for available and planned jobs under national the development plan.

Moncho Ávila and I prepared a four-to-five-year plan of action on manpower. Moncho obtained clearance within the Salvadoran government while I worked with Bill Schenk in obtaining clearance at the USOM, the U.S. Embassy, and IIAA Washington. Bill in turn worked with the minister of the Economy to incorporate the manpower component into the emerging five-year national development plan, the first such blueprint in the history of El Salvador. Moncho and Rogelio refined the work plan to conform to their country's political and budgetary realities. When we had all our ducks in order, the USOM director and the minister met. They agreed that we had a full-scale proposal for both governments to consider.

The response from the U.S. Department of Labor was positive, and it agreed to a multiyear commitment to provide technical support, training facilities, and in-country advisors. The IIAA was supportive even though we were not proposing a *servicio* as the mechanism for implementation. As we were receiving the green light from Washington, Mario Héctor was obtaining political and budgetary clearance within his government.

I can't remember exactly all of those painstaking negotiations and how many times I felt that we had hit a brick wall. I do remember the heady experience of accompanying the U.S. ambassador, the USOM director, and the minister of Labor and the minister of Foreign Affairs to the office of the president of El Salvador at the *Casa Presidencial* for a signing ceremony.

Now the real work was beginning. I was working directly with the Inspection Service to understand its structure and operations, the format for plant inspections, and the background and training of each of the inspectors. With the director the Service, we developed a plan for plant visits to the principal industrial, mining, and commercial enterprises in the country that employed over fifty workers. Both ministry and USOM colleagues helped me select the sites to visit. In geographic terms, El Salvador is about the same area as the State of Maryland; most establishments reachable within a day or two.

With the head of the Inspection Service, Miguel Ángel Molina, we made inspections in just about every business in every corner of the country on my list, including two railways, the brewery, the cement and other construction material plants, the few oil storage facilities, and small factories. Most of the banking and service industries were centered in the capital. We looked at plant layout and potential risks to workers. Most of the businesses were hand-to-mouth entrepreneurs. We examined their work requirements and practices. We met with workers, and found that very few were unionized. We discussed labor-management relationships, and developed a framework for adapting inspection systems and practices to the reality of an unsophisticated industrial and business environment.

Whenever our schedules permitted, we visited coffee mills (*beneficios*), sugar mills (*ingenios*), and cotton mills. Coffee remained the backbone of the economy, providing 95 percent of foreign exchange earnings. The only other large-scale agricultural crops were cotton and sugar cane. Bananas had never become a large commercial crop. Some owners of coffee *fincas* diversified into other activities, but most of the new plants were owned and operated by a new generation of entrepreneurs, not by the Fourteen Families. In fact, many of the traditional families had lost their landholdings to moneylenders in the Great Depression—the concentration of power merely moved to new names and faces.

After observing the plant visits and seeing the inspectors at work, I then began drafting the inspection manual with Ele's help. Fortunately, in one of her assignments at the Department of Labor, she edited the upgraded manual for inspection services by the various state governments throughout the U.S. and arranged to have a copy in Spanish sent to me. Ele gave me a good deal of technical assistance as we extracted and cut out sections of the U.S. manual. We studied the Puerto Rican guidelines. I drafted new sections and reshaped others to meet Salvadoran reality and needs based on my experience with the inspectors.

Then, with the help of Miguel Ángel Molina at the ministry and Bill Schenk at USOM, my oversights were identified and my Spanish corrected. Once the chief of the Inspection Service, Miguel Ángel Molina and I were satisfied with the text, we took the proposed manual to the minister for his approval.

The minister and his aides took a week to analyze the proposal before giving their approval. Miguel Ángel and I then reorganized the Inspection Service, creating a small supervisory staff to oversee field operations and set minimum qualifications for appointment. A training program was also initiated.

The second activity in which action began in that first year was on labor statistics. To evaluate the limited statistical program, the Bureau of Labor Statistics agreed to send down one of its experts, Lloyd Procknow. The USOM director, Bill Schenk, and the ambassador were so pleased with the proposal that they dug up money for Lloyd to come down.

Lloyd was an imaginative and understanding technician. He

surveyed all the statistical series published by the ministry, carefully examined the state of development in the country, and presented a plan for building a labor statistical database for the labor and manpower component of the Salvadoran economy over the next three to four years. In his plan, Lloyd proposed that a statistical specialist come down from Washington for three months a year over the next three years to work with the chief of the Unit to organize and develop the data base. He further proposed that the ministry and he identify Salvadoran statisticians who needed specialized training in Washington, D.C. or Puerto Rico. Since few of the Salvadoran statisticians were proficient in English, Lloyd decided to work with counterparts in Puerto Rico to design the proposed training exercises.

If the plan was approved, Lloyd committed himself to return for the next two years to appraise the progress made, identify problem areas that needed to be addressed, adapt the training plan to cover problem areas, and recommend the development of additional statistical series, primarily related to manpower.

Lloyd's proposal was enthusiastically supported by the ministry, USOM, and the Bureau of Labor Statistics. The ministry included personnel and funds in its budget, USOM agreed to include it in its submission to IIAA.

The Labor Program was underway.

My Real Assignment?

As I became more involved in my assignment, I began to wonder why I had been selected for it. Yes, I knew the labor law. Yes, I knew Spanish and had some experience in Latin America. But no, I was not a crackerjack Labor Department technician. No, I was not a veteran labor inspector and had little field experience in enforcement. I came to suspect that I was chosen because I had demonstrated an ability to work with Latin Americans and had the right mix of age and experience for the job that the U.S. government wanted done. And I further thought that the job had more to do with getting to know the minister of Labor and any possible ties he might have with the regime in neighboring Guatemala.

Guatemala was seen as potential ally of the USSR in the Cold

War. President Jacobo Arbenz led a regime in which several cabinet positions were occupied by communist party members or fellow travelers. He was pursuing anti-U.S. policies at home and abroad. In regular contact with key members of the Guatemalan government was Vicente Lombardo Toledano, the Mexican labor leader who had founded the Mexican Communist political party, *el Partido Popular*. There were reports that, with Soviet financial support, Lombardo Toledano was training cadres of Guatemalan labor and agrarian leaders to spearhead the next phase of installing a Soviet-style political and economic system in that country. Arbenz and his Salvadoran wife frequently appeared in pro-Soviet settings. A major program of the Arbenz government was land reform, expropriating large properties, including those of the United Fruit Company. The new secretary of state, John Foster Dulles, had been a long-term corporate lawyer for United Fruit and his brother, Allan, was head of the CIA.

Guatemala was a major concern of the U.S. government. In the McCarthy era, no one wanted to be charged with "losing" Guatemala—losing China was terrible enough. When we arrived in El Salvador, in our initial contacts at the U.S. Embassy and the USOM, the Guatemala question was on everyone's agenda, and there was concern about any of Arbenz's allies in El Salvador.

As I became acquainted with my colleagues in the U.S. Embassy and USOM, I found that many had doubts about the minister of Labor, his political inclinations, and his possible Guatemalan connections. They warned me about the difficult man with whom I had to work. In my only meeting with then U.S. Ambassador Angier Biddle Duke, he confided that mine was not an easy assignment; he wished me luck.

I also learned that, prior to my arrival, no one had been able to establish a relationship with the minister of Labor—not the ambassador, the embassy political section, the USOM director or Bill Schenk. The most they could tell me was that he was young, in his thirties. His father had been a powerful general in the Hernández Martínez dictatorship. He had been a "radical" student leader at the University and played a major role in building civilian support for the Young Turk Colonels who assumed power in the late 1940s. It was he, with his vice minister, Fernando Basilio Castellanos, who had organized the PRUD party and rallied students and workers to its support. In fact, the PRUD was run out of the Ministry of Labor.

The U.S. Embassy with its military missions and training programs had close ties to the people around President Osorio and his military cohorts, but no one really knew the key civilians who provided him political support. Everyone knew the minister of the Economy, Dr. Jorge Sol Castellanos, a U.S.-trained development economist, but they also knew that he was not close to the leadership of the PRUD party or the minister of Labor. They knew that Reynaldo Galindo Pohl, the minister of Education, was a leftist but not a political activist like the minister of Labor. No one was sure about the powerful minister of Labor.

So, I speculated whether my real mission in El Salvador was to get to know Mario Héctor Salazar and the cadre of young professionals, like Moncho Ávila and Rogelio Chávez, whom he had molded into his ministerial team. That might explain why my appointment in the early days of the Eisenhower Administration had been expedited while my USOM colleagues bemoaned the delay in getting replacements cleared for other assignments.

I recognized my technical limitations early on, and I felt that my value to both governments lay in understanding the Salvadoran reality and using that knowledge to help the minister design and implement a program that he would support. I never anticipated being more than adviser to the minister and opening a dialogue with him. I tried to be honest and upfront about what I thought. I never tried to play games with him. My decision to lay out what I felt the ministry ought to do was the turning point not only in my relationship with the minister but in his perception of the government I represented.

From that day forward, the minister and I had many long conversations, not only about political matters but many personal situations. He became my valued friend. I was pleased to have opened the way for many other U.S. officials to come to know him and appreciate his intellectual depth and dedication to democratic principles. To this day, I believe that opening this dialogue was one of the most important achievements of my assignment to El Salvador.

An Additional Assignment

The third U.S. ambassador under whom I served in my first year in El Salvador was Robert C. Hill, a businessman turned diplomat. He was a Republican Party stalwart married to the daughter of Peter Grace, the CEO of W.R. Grace.

Shortly after Ambassador Hill's arrival at post, he called me to his office. At the meeting were the new USOM director, Edgar Hackney (a former stockbroker and treasurer of the Eisenhower election campaign), and Bill Schenk. The ambassador commended me on the job I was doing and asked me to set up an appointment for him with the minister of Labor. He also instructed me to keep him and the State Department informed of labor developments in El Salvador. He said that he had assigned me a desk in the embassy that I could use whenever I needed to prepare a report. So, now I had an office at the ministry, a desk at the USOM, and a desk as needed in the embassy.

I arranged the appointment and accompanied the ambassador to the meeting with the minister, serving as interpreter. It went beyond formalities. The ambassador expressed the support of the U.S. government for the minister's initiatives and asked for the minister's views on recent labor developments in Honduras and Guatemala. He inquired what the minister thought of having a representative of the U.S. labor movement assigned to support democratic unions in Central America, and mentioned that Andrew McClellan of the AFL-CIO was under consideration. As the meeting closed, the ambassador confided to the minister that he planned to have me serve as liaison between them and would be using me to keep up on labor developments in El Salvador. The minister nodded. As he was leaving, the ambassador invited the minister and his wife to dinner at the embassy.

The minister later told me that he had received a private letter from Serafino Romualdi, the AFL-CIO director of Inter-American Affairs, about possibly assigning one of his close colleagues to work in Central America, and had sent him the bio-data on Andrew McClellan, a leader of the food and beverage workers in Southern Nevada (Las Vegas), a Scotsman by birth, and fluent in Spanish. Andy later told Ele and me that my reports on cooperation by the minister in the development of the technical labor program had encouraged Romualdi to write directly to the minister.

Up until the arrival of Ambassador Hill, I had scrupulously avoided any involvement with the union movement. I was concerned about the impact that this additional reporting function would have on my principal job. I also consulted USOM Director Hackney and Bill Schenk, whom Hackney had promoted to deputy mission director, about their reaction to my taking on the embassy reporting assignment; they told me that they had already agreed to the ambassador's proposal. When I asked the minister if he was comfortable with my new dual duties, he smiled and said he saw no conflict, implying that he suspected that I had been doing it all along. Then, he offered to arrange for me to meet the two men the PRUD was grooming to head the Salvadoran labor movement: Sarabia of the Teamsters and El Negro Cordero of the Meat Cutters.

From my office near the front door of the Labor Ministry, I had seen Sarabia and Cordero many times as they climbed the stairs to the minister's offices on the second floor. I learned that they were union leaders who were active in the PRUD. I had also observed going up and down those same stairs several young lawyers whose faces appeared in the local press quite often as "leftist" opponents of the Labor minister and the PRUD. Just being in the ministry on a full-time basis had given me a passing look at some of the principal actors in the labor movement. Now, I had to get know who they were and what their interests were.

In addition, I needed background on the labor movement in El Salvador. I talked to several of the ministry officials who told me more about ministry relationships with individual union leaders, but very little about the history of the labor movement itself. So I consulted the anti-PRUD Professor of Labor Law at the University of El Salvador, Francisco "Chico" de Lima. Fortunately, Ele had met his wife and invited them to our house for cocktails. Chico suggested that I read a couple of recent histories on the country that touched on the limited development of unions in El Salvador.

I followed his suggestion and read that unions had never played an important role in the country. Given its agricultural economy and limited industrial and commercial activity, there was not a large enough concentration of workers to build a base of potential members. Agriculture had been dominated by small independent indigo producers and family-managed coffee plantations, which had small "in-house" work forces and large numbers of seasonal workers. Before World War II, El Salvador had no large banana, sugar, or cotton plantations or mining operations that had sparked the union movements in other Latin American countries.

The first unions had appeared in the early twentieth century among teachers, printers, and railway workers. They did not fight for bread-and-butter issues but for political and ideological objectives, based on anarcho-syndicalist, socialist, or communist manifestos. Unions had not been legally recognized except for a brief period in the early 1930s, and then they were crushed by the Hernández Martínez dictatorship in 1931–2. Those leaders who were not killed fled the country. Most went to Mexico where Vicente Lombardo Toledano and his CTM sustained them. They followed him into the communist orbit.

With the overthrow of the dictatorship and the installation of the Osorio administration, the surviving exiles, now well into middle age, returned home and set up a center of operations for building a trade union base independent of the PRUD and the government. During their years in exile, the CTM had trained them in organizing and running unions, and they were probably the only experienced union leaders in the country. Rumor had it that the Soviet Embassy in Mexico City was the primary source of their funding since unions in El Salvador had no structure for the payment of dues.

Nando, the vice minister, told me that the PRUD planned to build a new union movement based on the PRI model in Mexico. He wanted the unions to be one of the legs of the PRUD political power. He was identifying potential labor leaders and using PRUD funds to form a new generation of union leaders. He and the minister were supporting those new leaders to counter the exiles and their "illegitimate" association. Nando talked little about his tactics, but I heard stories of how PRUD money was used to keep union leaders in line, play one off against another, and even lure some of the returned exiles to support the PRUD. He planned to create a new pro-PRUD confederation of labor led by Sarabia and Cordero.

While my primary activity was implementing the technical

labor program, I now kept an eye on trade union developments. Whenever Andy McClellan came to town, we spent time together. Ele and I always had him to dinner, usually alone, or occasionally with another embassy or USOM couple. Andy wanted to be seen by local labor leaders as a representative of the AFL-CIO, independent of the U.S. government. His message was that unions should focus on bread-and-butter issues and labor-management relations, and be independent of political parties. I respected his wishes and maintained a low profile in dealing with union leaders.

One event that did project me into the union scene was in the summer of 1954 when Vice President Richard Nixon made his official visit to El Salvador. Ambassador Hill called on me to prepare a meeting of labor leaders with the vice president. When I advised the minister and Nando of the assignment; the minister told me that he had already talked with the ambassador and saw no problem. I met with Sarabia and Cordero, who helped me select about a dozen of their colleagues to participate in the meeting. I also talked with Chico Lima and added a few whom he recommended. None of the former exiles were invited.

The meeting was held at the EL Salvador-U.S. Cultural Center across the street from the U.S. Chancery. The meeting turned out to be a large assemblage of various civic groups, not a private meeting with union leaders. The vice president opened his presentation by expressing U.S. interest in and support for democracy in Central America. He praised the Salvadoran government for its efforts and thanked it for its support in the overthrow of the "Arbenz Communist Dictatorship" in Guatemala. His main theme was U.S. determination to combat communism anywhere in the world. When he finished, he asked whether there were any questions or comments and no one asked a question. There was no shaking of hands at the end of the meeting. I ushered the union leaders out of the room and asked for their observations. There were none, either positive or negative.

After the Nixon visit, for the next several months, Andy McClellan was a regular visitor. He was headquartered in San Pedro Sula, Honduras, close to the banana plantations on the north coast. The United Fruit Company also had its principal offices there. Honduras was the epitome of a Banana Republic and the north coast of

Honduras was its most important production center. Union activity had been ruthlessly suppressed for decades. Then, the succession of events in Guatemala to the democratic opening in Costa Rica brought winds of change that had shaken the status quo throughout the region. Arbenz's moves to expropriate United Fruit lands were widely watched in the other Central American countries. Political activists, including well-financed Soviet-backed groups, championed the expropriation of United Fruit company holdings throughout Latin America.

Those events apparently led United Fruit to consider changes in its paternalistic, anti-union policies. I learned from Andy that United Fruit consulted the AFL-CIO and was advised to let their workers build their own union, one that could operate independently of both the Company and local governments. The AFL-CIO offered to help form and nurture such a union. Andy also told me that United Fruit and Serafino Romualdi had encouraged him to leave his post with the hotel and beverage workers union in Las Vegas for this assignment.

In November 1954, I learned that Nando had authorized and approved the financing of the first national convention of Salvadoran labor unions since 1931. Nando was intent on making sure that his handpicked duo would control the meeting and set up a pro-PRUD body that would exclude the exiles returned from Mexico, and Andy was assisting in the process. I was not involved in planning or staging the event.

The convention started auspiciously. I was asked not to make an appearance since I was so identified with the minister. Sarabia and Cordero seemed to be in control. Andy was working behind the scenes, and everything seemed to be going well when Andy took a break just before midnight. Then all hell broke loose. The former exiles produced pictures showing the same femme fatale seducing both Sarabia and Cordero when each had believed that she was his exclusive mistress. The PRUD majority split. The exiles called for a vote after Sarabia attacked Cordero, who then walked out. The seasoned former exiles took charge and elected a slate of anti-PRUD, pro-Communist leaders for the Confederation of Labor of El Salvador (CTS). When Andy got back from his break, the new leadership had adjourned the convention. As Andy said later, "Never leave too soon and never take anything for granted."

From that morning forward, the labor movement went into recess. Sarabia and his family moved to Costa Rica. El Negro Cordero
stopped appearing at the ministry. The PRUD abandoned its efforts to create a labor confederation. Andy McClellan dropped over
occasionally from San Pedro Sula, but with little to do. In my new
assignment, there was very little to report on trade union activities.
No meetings! No strikes! Only an occasional political announcement from the otherwise moribund CTS!

Shortly thereafter, Ambassador Hill asked me to prepare a paper for him about farm labor conditions in El Salvador. I prepared
a short description of conditions on coffee *fincas*, about the tenant
families who lived permanently on the property, living essentially
as serfs, and the facilities and remuneration provided to seasonal
laborers who picked the coffee crop each year. Our best data indicated that the daily wage for the permanent families was about 75
cents in cash, two fistfuls of beans for each meal for each member of
the family, a few tortillas, rice and other food allotments. I provided him with a WHO report that called for milk to be provided for
babies and that with milk selling at 75 cents a liter, no farm family
could afford it.

The ministry had very limited data at that time about the new
cotton plantations or the small sugar industry. The only information I could provide was that the workers were essentially day laborers, were paid about a dollar a day, and lived in communities
near the farm operations.

He asked me if there were any farm unions. I replied that there
was no evidence that the landowners or the army would tolerate
them.

Then Ambassador Hill arranged for Ele and me to accompany him and his wife to the Vides *finca* for Christmas 1954. Jorge
Vides was from one of the original Fourteen Families. The family
estate was in the Department of Santa Ana, a three-hour drive from
San Salvador. Ele and I rode with Ambassador and Mrs. Hill to
the estate where we overnighted and participated in the landlord's
Christmas Day greeting to his tenants. Ele and I were seated to one
side of a large room, with the Vides and the Hills seated on a dais.
Don Jorge Vides greeted the families and wished them a Merry
Christmas, and then each family came up to the dais and was given

a present by the landlord: each girl received a doll and each boy received a ball. Each family thanked the Vides, curtsied and left. On the way home, the ambassador said that my report really told it as it was.

Renewed for a Second Tour

The progress that we were making in the labor ministry project received strong commendation in both San Salvador and Washington. I was instructed to prepare a plan of work and budget for two additional years of operations. It was approved with little or no modification. It included my continued assignment, a three-month in-country consultancy each year by Lloyd, and the assignment of two more full-time technical advisers: one in job skills training and the other on creating a national employment service.

The Department of Labor could not identify specialists on its staff who were fluent in Spanish or even had a working knowledge of the language. Because of the importance the minister attributed to implementing the program, he agreed to the assignment of two senior officials of the Department of Labor. The first was Al Burt, a specialist in worker skills training; the second was Josh Levine, a senior official of the U.S. Employment Service. Al and Josh joined me in 1954.

Their assignments were unique. There was no other similar project activity in Latin America. And the challenges facing us were monumental.

The skills training activity was intended to introduce new accelerated training to meet immediate manpower needs in the public and private sectors. We had to identify available training facilities functioning in country and the willingness of those facilities to cooperate. We consulted the chief of the education *servicio*, Peter Allemano, who identified the few training facilities in operation, namely, the vocational high school system that the U.S. government had helped create, and Catholic schools devoted to vocational training programs in the capital city and one or two other communities.

Next, we arranged a meeting of the minister of Labor with the minister of Education to discuss the new initiative and see if and how the two ministries might work together. The ministers found common ground and a common interest, but the Ministry of Education professionals were not enthusiastic. They raised objections to not using the established curriculum and argued that adult training was less likely to succeed than placing more money in vocational education for youngsters. They rejected allowing their facilities to be used for skills training outside the traditional school curriculum and raised objections to setting up night school courses for accelerated training on their premises, even if funded separately.

A further challenge came from the lack of reliable statistical labor force and manpower data. Lloyd was only beginning to set up the statistical series and there was no trained staff yet in place. Given the lack of data, Lloyd experimented with drawing together whatever information might be available. We asked the Ministry of Education to show us the data they used to select their vocational courses, but found that they had made no recent surveys. They had maintained the same curriculum of auto mechanics, building trades, and tailoring for over a decade.

Additional discussions with the Ministry of Education proved fruitless. Training the work force was not their priority—educating the children was. The budgetary resources for educating the children were hardly sufficient, and the Ministry of Labor could not mobilize the additional funds to overcome the teachers' reluctance.

Although Al was a product of the U.S. apprenticeship program, he had a broad knowledge of training systems for various vocations in different sections of the United States. He saw possibilities of breaking down skills components to make short-term, cumulative courses for unskilled and semi-skilled workers. He was willing to train vocational teachers and technicians at the Ministry of Labor and the Ministry of Education to test out a new approach. Al pointed out that such an endeavor required a multi-year commitment.

Unfortunately, Al became frustrated and asked that his assignment be terminated. His concerns were compounded by the problems his family experienced in adjusting to life and school in El Salvador. Without the language and no experience in living abroad, life had become too difficult for them on all fronts. Unfortunately for all of us, Ele had family problems that required her to return to California for several weeks as the Burt family problems mounted, and I was not as sensitive to them as I probably should have been.

The Burts' departure put a hiatus on developing a long-term plan for skills training. Al's replacement came in 1955—Tom Walsh, a veteran of the U.S. labor movement who had strong experience in worker education programs. And we started at step one all over again.

Josh Levine's assignment was to create from scratch a national employment service. El Salvador had neither public nor private employment agencies in 1954. There was no basis for matching those seeking employment with those needing employees. The absence of such a mechanism and the scarcity of data in the labor statistical series had been also serious obstacles for Al Burt.

Josh had to design an employment service in a developing country preparing its first development plan and beginning the process of promoting new urban factory and commercial activities. He could do the manpower aspects of the job after he trained a staff, prepared operations manuals, selected sites for offices, and developed a financial framework for making the service self-sustaining. Josh laid out all the challenges he faced to the minister, who gave him the green light to try.

To provide the Salvadoran staff for these new activities, we sent a steady stream of ministry technicians to Washington and Puerto Rico for training. Our plan was to train the staff at the same time as we did the preparatory work in country. Step by step, the new activities would get under way and the U.S. advisers would groom the Salvadorans to take charge.

Just as Josh was getting started, our first two-year tour in El Salvador was to end. The ministry and the USOM asked for me to return for a second two-year tour. Ele and I agreed. In April 1955, we were awarded our first home leave.

Home Leave

U.S. legislation governing service abroad requires each foreign service officer and his or her family to take one month's leave at home in the United States every two years. This is aimed at keeping U.S. officials attuned to and aware of what is happening at home. Our home leave in April 1955 consisted of one week of consultations in Washington, D.C. and four weeks in California.

On arriving in Washington, my first priority was to obtain medical clearance for my return to El Salvador for the second tour. I had received a medical waiver for the first tour, and was to undergo a careful review of my hearing capability before a second waiver would be considered. Ele's and my physical examinations were scheduled on our first day in Washington. My hearing test was slightly better than the one that I had taken two years earlier, and no other problems arose for either of us. The director of Medical Services advised my supervising office that same day he saw no reason to revoke the waiver. So, my week of consultations began.

Our home leave coincided with a major reorganization of the U.S. international aid programs. In 1954, President Eisenhower consolidated the worldwide economic and technical assistance programs into one agency—the Foreign Operations Administration (FOA). His strong support of foreign assistance grew out of the success of the Marshall Plan in reviving post-war Western Europe and Japan. He had seen first-hand its effectiveness in reviving public and private institutions and economies that had been devastated by the Nazis, and was committed to using them to support anti-communist governments and private institutions around the world.

In this reorganization, FOA was being replaced by a new organization—the International Cooperation Administration (ICA) that merged FOA with the Marshall Plan Mutual Security Administration (MSA). Its role was to apply and adapt the expertise and experience gained under the Marshall Plan to the underdeveloped world of Latin America, the Middle East, Africa, and Asia.

My old base of support in the IIAA had been dispersed to new technical and geographic bureaus within ICA. The Office of Labor Affairs, headed by a veteran U.S. labor leader who had successfully helped European democratic union leaders fight off communist inroads, now oversaw my project. Most of its the staff came out of the U.S. labor movement and were veterans of the MSA. I was quite unsure how these new support officers would react to the program taking shape in El Salvador.

Tuesday morning I reported to the office and was met by Harold Walker, responsible for overseeing Latin American programs. Harold was a railway brotherhood union official from Arkansas. After World War II, he worked on trade union programs in both

Japan and Iran. When I described the challenges facing us in El Salvador, indeed almost all of Latin America, Harold understood their similarity to the problems he had faced in Iran. Harold was savvy and knew who to call and how to approach them when one needed help.

Harold made appointments with key officers at the Department of Labor. At each appointment, he assured my counterparts of support for the Salvador program, and we worked on plans for the next two years. At ICA, Harold made sure that I met all the decision-makers who had a voice in analyzing and funding Latin American country projects. The final day included a meeting with the State Department Latin American regional labor officer, John Fishburne, whom I previously met and who provided me guidance for my reports on the Salvadoran labor movement.

Harold Walker made one other appointment during that week. It was my first meeting with Serafino Romualdi, the AFL-CIO director of Inter-American Relations. Andy McClellan had already briefed him on my work in El Salvador, and he greeted me like an old friend. We talked about AFL-CIO plans for supporting democratic unions in the hemisphere and for opening a training center for Latin American democratic labor leaders. He was an encyclopedia of trade union developments throughout the Western hemisphere, with decades of experience beginning with his emigration from Italy to Uruguay. He gave me an overview of the labor scene in Latin America including his own evolution from an Italian anarcho-syndicalist to a Gompers-style unionist. He was anti-socialist and anti-communist, with lots of friends and plenty of enemies throughout the region. Serafino promised to visit me the next time he came to Central America.

After getting her medical clearance, Ele spent her days seeing old friends at the Department of Labor and visiting the Smithsonian. Every night, good friends invited us for dinner. Ele also spent time at the U.S. Department of Agriculture investigating farm prices and farming conditions and getting information about services offered by county agents. She was gathering information needed to manage her family farms in Claremont, South Dakota and Pixley, California.

Before we left San Salvador, we had ordered a new Plymouth

under the Chrysler Diplomatic Overseas Purchase Plan. Ele settled on a sleek white Plymouth with minimal "upgrades" such as heating or air conditioning, which we would not need in semi-tropical San Salvador with its comfortable June-like temperature most of the year. We arranged to pick up the car in early May.

Our plan was to spend ten days driving across the country, stopping in South Dakota for a couple of days so that Ele could inspect her family's farm there, spend five days with my family in San Francisco, five days with Ele's family in Tulare, and three days in Los Angeles with our dear friend from Mexico City, Helene Phipps and her new husband, Bob Tubbs. In Los Angeles, we would turn the car over to the state department agent for shipment by boat to El Salvador.

On completing my Washington orientation, we took the train to New Jersey where we picked up our new car and started west to Aberdeen, South Dakota. Ele was the first member of her family to meet with the long-time farm agents since the 1930s. Before meeting with him, she got briefings on farm conditions and crop forecasts from the county agent and the farm management specialist at the Aberdeen Bank. Thoroughly armed with information, she and I kept the appointment with the family agent. She questioned him in detail about the low income her mother and grandmother had been receiving and asked why his accounts over the last decade listed prices well below the averages given her by the county agent. His answers were evasive. Then Ele said, "I shall consult my mother and grandmother as soon as I reach California and we as a family will advise you whether your services will be needed in the future." She then went back to the bank and talked at length with its farm management specialist about terms and conditions for its managing the farm and the prospects for finding a new tenant for the next farming season. Within two days of our reaching Tulare two weeks later, the old agent was fired and the bank took over the management of the farm.

The drive west took longer than expected, which meant that we had to reduce our visits in San Francisco, Tulare, and Los Angeles by one day apiece. When we arrived in San Francisco, we found that my parents had moved to a larger flat, around the corner from my sister and her family. We made no plans other than to spend time with the family to see the sights of the City by the Bay and enjoy family dinners. The only business we did was to open our first stock brokerage account with Merrill Lynch and bought our first share of stock. Every night we sat up with Mother to watch Jack Paar. She snoozed while Ele and I smiled at each other: Mother could never go to bed until Jack Paar signed off!

Little did we realize when we left that it would be the last time all of us would be together. My sister died two years later. My father's grief devastated him and led, I believe, to his affliction with Parkinson's disease that ravaged his nervous system until his death in 1962.

The drive to Tulare took just five hours down Highway 99. Ele had a full schedule of activities for our days, mainly connected with the business related to the nearby Pixley ranch. We made a couple of trips to the Pixley ranch with USDA and irrigation specialists. She checked out local farm conditions with close friends before selecting a new tenant on terms she set. Every evening we were feted with fried chicken, Swiss steaks, tossed salads, and apple pie à la mode. By the time we left for Los Angeles four days later, everyone knew that she was now the decision-maker on her family's farm business.

10

Living in San Salvador

Now that I have recalled how we found our first house in San Salvador and how the labor program took shape, let me reflect on why we always remembered that first tour as one of the most enjoyable periods of our life. It was enriched by the many Salvadoran, American, and European friends who became important parts of our lives. Those friends came from the Ministry of Labor, the U.S. official family, and the business community.

Ele and I found San Salvador in the mid-1950s to be a comfortable but sometimes challenging experience. We had expected to live in a tropical setting with heat and humidity. We were certainly unsure what our reception would be or how we would make out. Well, we did just fine. We found a city set on a livable plateau 2,400 feet above sea level, with a climate of almost eternal spring. We found people with whom we could interact easily. Salvadorans told us what they thought and expected up front. They were prepared to extend their friendship when you made the effort to offer yours. We could live comfortably most of year without air-conditioning or heating our house. There were a few hot nights each year, but usually it cooled off by evening with soft breezes. The humidity was usually bearable. We had occasionally heavy storms, called *"nortes"* during which it poured for days, but usually daily afternoon showers cooled us down and led to pleasant evenings. The environment suited us very nicely.

When we arrived, the city had few accommodations or restaurants, and there were only two hotels that were of acceptable quality. There were few places for an evening on the town, and the few nightclubs were places to which a man brought his lady friend of the evening, not his wife or mother. San Salvador had three movie houses, one of which was the National Theater, which doubled as the only legitimate theater in town when needed. There were a couple of golf clubs, with restricted memberships and an *ancien régime* atmosphere. The Club Deportivo was the tennis club for internationally minded Salvadorans and the foreign community. The Club Salvadoreño was the meeting place downtown and the site of many large social events. Many of stores and markets were like bazaars, where you could find cheap shoes and Rosenthal Porcelain sitting side by side. In short, one created his/her own life style and entertainment.

Running Our Household

Setting up a household meant finding a live-in maid. A maid was not a convenience, but rather, an essential defensive measure. The embassy warned us that any empty house invited burglars. Break-ins were every day occurrences, especially if there was no one home. So, having a maid was the alternative to Ele and me having to stay home all the time .So, we asked for help from the Schencks and two of their friends, Ellen Dutriz and Carlene Williams. Ellen was married to Bob Dutriz, one of the four brothers who ran the leading Salvadoran newspaper, *La Prensa Gráfica*. When the family was exiled during the Hernández Martínez dictatorship, the brothers lived in San Francisco where Bob and Ellen met and kept an apartment. Carlene was married to the coffee buyer for Folgers. The Schenks, Dutrizes, and Williamses were people we came to depend on. They suggested that we talk to Ellen's maid Hortensia because she had a niece, María, who was looking for work. Hortensia had worked for the Dutrizes for years, and Ellen found her to be honest and dependable. Ellen arranged a time for us to discuss our situation with Hortensia. When we arrived at Ellen's house, we found Hortensia cutting grass in the front yard. She was middle-aged, tall, gaunt, with a tangle of long black hair, barefoot and with a machete in her right hand. She smiled and her one front tooth stared at us as Ele asked her about her niece María. She replied that she would send word to her village that we were looking for a live-in maid. She opined that María would serve us well since she had been housekeeping for the nuns since she was five years old. Maria, we were told, would need little or no training!

A few days later, Ellen called to say that María had arrived and was ready for work. Ele interviewed the roly-poly smiling María, and they agreed on salary and living conditions. Ellen and Ele went to town to purchase a cot and other furniture for the maid's room. María was delighted to get her own room and furniture. She oohed and aahed at the cot, commenting that with the nuns, she had slept on a straw mat on the ground and didn't have an inside bathroom. Ele then took María to buy some all-white uniforms and shoes. More aahs and oohs as she said that this was the first time she had ever been provided "job" clothes. When I got home, Ellen and Ele were sipping a drink and discussing the young woman Ele had just hired.

With María, we learned not to take anything for granted. In spite of having been raised by the nuns, she was totally unprepared for our household. On her first morning with us, when Ele went down to check on breakfast, María was cutting up the fruit and throwing the peels out of the window. "Oh," María explained, "the nuns felt that the vultures on the roof would eat them and help keep the house free of garbage." When Ele came back up to the bedroom, her eyes were glazed over. She knew that she had to start from square one. Weeks rolled into months as Ele tried to teach María how to keep house, and how to clean a bathtub, toilet, stove, and refrigerator. She introduced her to a modern broom, vacuum cleaner, and dust cloth. She taught her about washing dishes in hot water, and showed her how to scrub a pot and clean the sink. She taught her how to write her name and the basics of reading when she found that Maria could not sign an employment agreement required by the embassy. "You see, *señora*, no one taught me that—reading and writing was for the nuns and their paying students."

Ele decided to find out if María could tell the time. One morning, when Ele was making lunch in the pantry and María was cleaning the study, Ele asked María, "*Qué hora es?*" (What time is it?), knowing that there was a large electric clock in the room. Ele said that there was a pregnant pause while María apparently looked at the clock and then scurried into the adjacent open patio, before calling back, "*Señora, son las 10:30.*" (It's 10:30 a.m., madam.)

Ele waited a prudent ten minutes before going into the study to check the time for herself. It was then only 10:05 a.m. María crept into the room and asked, "*Señora,* was that the right time?" Ele responded, "No, María, it is now only 10:05." Maria responded, "Ay, *señora,* I have such difficulties with those English-speaking clocks."

Ele and I believed in paying a decent wage and treating a servant with firmness but dignity. Ele always provided the shoes. Servants tried to get by on basic sandals that cost very little. Ele had edited the U.S. Department of Labor manual that spelled out the importance of appropriate shoes for each job. She took María to a shoe store where she was fitted for her first pair of good quality shoes, and María was delighted. When Ele caught her doing the housework in her old sandals, Ele scolded María, who responded apologetically, "But, *señora,* they are too nice to work in."

We also believed that a servant deserved a day off each week. This was not the custom in El Salvador: normally a maid got one afternoon a week to take care of personal matters and see the family, but was always back to serve dinner that evening. In our case, we not only respected the maid's right to her Sabbath but also gave ourselves a day each week without the wear-and-tear on our privacy that having the maid around generated. So, María had a day off every week.

María was sad one day, and Ele asked why. María said that she had not been to her village for some time and wanted to see her people. When I got home, Ele asked me which weekend suited us best to allow María to visit her family. I checked my schedule and we blocked off a three-day "stay-at-home" weekend. Ele told María, who was beside herself with happiness, bustling around like we had never seen her before. She said that she would be taking presents to her family, so Ele advanced her the wages for the month. Hortensia and María went shopping.

After her weekend at home, María returned right on time Monday morning, bringing a twelve-year old boy with her. Ele was perplexed, and called me at the ministry. Don Augusto advised Ele not to take any action until I got home at lunchtime. When I came in, I found María in a quandary and my wife quite upset.

I asked María who the young man was. She replied that he was her brother, Juan José. I said, "What do you expect Juan José to do here?" Oh, she replied, "I intend to send him to school." I asked, "Where do you expect him to stay?" María simply looked at me as if astounded by the question, "In my room with me." Where did she expect him to sleep? Very matter-of-factly, she replied, "In bed with me." She must have seen the surprise in my eyes and added, "Tell the *señora* not to worry. He will wear his swimming trunks to bed." The bed was a cot, barely wide enough for María, much less a bed for two innocents. Hardly able to contain my laughter, I said that Juan José could not stay and would have to return to her family in the village. She was heartbroken for a day or two. We never heard of Juan José again.

Hortensia later told us that María had been a "naughty" girl when she was twelve or thirteen years old and that Juan José was her son. She wanted him near her so that she could educate him, "Just as the *señora* had helped Maria to learn how to read and write." Cast bread upon the water and you never know what you will get back! When I was preparing a working paper for Bill Schenk for the manpower component of the Salvadoran five-year development plan, I found a population study that indicated the average age of first pregnancy for a country girl was twelve or thirteen.

On one of María's subsequent overnight visits to her village, we had a burglary. Someone came over the back wall and stole several sheets and other linens that were drying on the line in the back patio. Because there was a locked gate between the patio and the main section of the house, that was all that the enterprising intruders could steal.

As soon as we discovered the loss, I advised both the embassy and the Ministry of Labor, as per our instructions. The embassy asked me to file a written report so that it could contact the police and request an on-site investigation. Within twenty minutes of my call to the ministry, the minister himself and the head of the National Police Force, Colonel Tenorio, were in our living room, making sure that Ele and I were fine.

Colonel Tenorio and a couple of his aides surveyed the damage, and the Colonel asked us whether we had a firearm in the house. When we replied no, he offered me his sidearm and his personal card. He then advised me, "If you have another break-in, shoot the intruders and call me. I will arrange to pick up the bodies and deliver them to the morgue as unidentified vagrants."

I thanked him for his advice and generosity, but declined his offer of the sidearm. We never had another attempted burglary. After the break-in, police cars checked our house regularly. The word got around that we had influence in high places, so don't mess with the Tragen house!

María's tenure ended after another visit to her village. It was Easter and she wanted to spend it with her family. So, we gave her extra money to buy gifts and saw her off on a Saturday morning with bags of goodies. She was due back Monday morning, but didn't appear. Tuesday and Wednesday passed. Mid-morning Thursday she appeared smelling of *aguardiente*, the local sugar-based alcoholic drink. Ele took one look at her and recalled her time at Allied Youth. She put her to work and made her sweat out the results of her lost weekend. María said that the *señora* was very mean; she had been delayed by the high waters of the river, and she shouldn't be treated so harshly when the delay wasn't her fault. By the way, the headline in *La Prensa Gráfica* that day read, "Threat of drought. Rivers at record low."

Ele told me that night that she had lost confidence in María. She also told me that in recent weeks, María had slipped out of the house several times without telling her, and that she once found the house unattended when she returned early from a shopping trip. The next day, María was given a month's pay and told to leave the following morning with all her possessions, including the shoes and uniforms Ele had provided. Lots of tears, but no reprieve!

A few weeks later, Aunt Hortensia came over to tell us that María had been a naughty girl again, was pregnant, and would have to live in her village until she learned her lesson. Then she said to Ele, "*María perdió un bueno empleo por causa propia. Vd. la trató muy bien.*" (María cost herself a good job. You treated her very well.) To close María's story, if she had not been discharged that day and she had learned that she was pregnant while still employed by us, by Salvadoran custom we would have had to keep her employed and cover the expenses of the delivery.

We now needed a new maid. Our good USOM friends, E.W. and Gladys Ranck, had a fine cook, Josefina, who couldn't get along with other servants. Gladys had told Ele of the problems in her household. So, Ele called Gladys while María was packing up.

Gladys suggested that Ele come over to talk with Josefina, and she did.

Ele told Josefina that she would be the only servant in the house and that she would have her own room, eat the same food that we did, receive a wage higher than she was earning at the Rancks, and be provided with uniforms and shoes that the two of them would pick out together. Ele emphasized that she expected absolute honesty and diligence. If a problem were to arise, Josefina was told to advise us immediately. Ele emphasized that anyone can make a mistake, but to hide that mistake would not be tolerated. Those were the ground rules and for the last half of our assignment in San Salvador, we had a well-run, happy household!

Josefina was the antithesis of María. Josefina could not only read and write but also could keep accounts and do marketing. She knew how to organize her day and quickly learned how to relate to Ele. She had a temper and did not take criticism easily, but she accepted Ele's suggestions without argument. Ele had never considered allowing María to plan a meal, especially when we had guests for dinner. Now, Ele could tell Josefina who was coming over and Josefina would suggest what the meal should be. Ele had never considered sending María to the market; now, she never thought twice about asking Josefina to go to the market downtown or the grocery nearby called Hamers.

Josefina also taught us a great deal about the social security system in the country, one that has seldom been described in scholarly dissertations or state department briefings. Josefina had already told us that in El Salvador the men enjoyed themselves while the women earned much of the family income and reared the children. She said that a woman could never depend on a man staying around once she got pregnant—a comment in line with a report from the public health *servicio* that projected, from its sample, that over 80 percent of children were born out of wedlock, in part because of the large migratory population that followed the crops and in part because, under Salvadoran law, once married, a woman lost control of her money and children to her husband.

Our confidence in Josefina grew to the point where Ele would give her money to buy something that Ele had forgotten to get at the market. One Friday morning we ran out of eggs, and Ele sent

Josefina to the market to buy a dozen. Josefina preferred getting on the bus and going to the downtown market where she had old friends and where she could bargain. Josefina always accounted for every purchase, down to the last penny. So, instead of going around the corner to Hamers, she took the bus downtown to the public market where she got the eggs for half the price Hamers was charging. She gave the change to Ele when she got home.

The following Saturday morning at breakfast, Ele was seated across the table from me with her back to the kitchen door. Josefina came in with breakfast. I had soft-boiled eggs with my fruit and toast. While Josefina asked Ele about our plans for the day, I cracked open an egg—and it was fertilized. I interrupted Ele and Josefina by complaining about the fertilized egg. I reminded Josefina that Hamers' eggs from the new poultry farm weren't fertilized.

Josefina looked at me very intently and questioned, "If chickens are now laying eggs without a rooster, why can't I have a baby without a man?"

Ele smiled at me and said on her lips without making a sound, "You got yourself into it. Now you get yourself out." With that, Ele took her cup of coffee and went upstairs.

Josefina responded to the confusion on my face by telling me that she had a son, now twelve years old. When she got pregnant with her son, her mother resigned her job as a live-in servant to take charge of rearing him and she gave up her studies to earn the money to keep the family together. Now, she continued, "I have my son enrolled in the vocational high school so he can earn a good living and soon he will find a woman of his own and leave my mother and me. You can never depend on a son to take care of you in your old age. I need a daughter now while I can still work so that she can take of my mother and me when the time comes."

I innocently asked Josefina why she didn't want to get married. She looked almost astounded by my question. Her reply was matter-of-fact, "Get married and lose my independence? A husband would control the baby and me. That's no assurance of help for my old age. He would take my wages and spend them on drink and other women. No, I need a baby girl, with no strings to the father. She will be mine and she will be raised by my mother to look out for us both when I have to retire."

I told her that I doubted that science had yet developed a system for her to have a baby without a man. Then her next question was, "Do you know any American man who would like to father my child? An American is far more desirable because he probably has a family of his own in America and would not want to bother me about my little girl." I demurred and said that I didn't know of anyone. But she asked me to let her know if I had any ideas.

Josefina had touched on the hard reality of the social system not only in El Salvador but also for lower-income men and women in urban areas in much of Latin America. Whatever the traditional peasant family structure had been in rural areas, it had not persisted in the cities.

Let me add that Josefina got pregnant after we left the country. She had another son. After his birth, she went to work in the home of a member of the U.S. military mission. Then she had a little girl, reportedly after an affair with a U.S. sergeant. After that birth, she worked for a group of secretaries at the U.S. Embassy where I last saw her. Her little girl was five years old. Her employers told me that she never went out except for half a day a week to see her family. All she talked about was her daughter. The secretaries said that she showed absolutely no interest in men. When we last met, after a hug and some reminiscing, I asked her about her mother and her children. She extolled her little daughter, whom she planned to educate as a bilingual secretary. Her older son had a job; she saw him once in a while and he was a good boy: he was still living with the mother of his children!

A New House

We had lived almost two years in the house in Flor Blanca. While it was built to withstand earthquakes, it was open to the elements and the animal life that surrounded us. The big patio off the living room could not be closed off and one never knew what we might find walking around the patio. Our large bedroom windows let in cool breezes, but none of the windows had screens and we often had uninvited guests from bats to flies and mosquitoes. The patio roof sometimes hosted *sopelotes* (big black vultures), who would occasionally investigate some movement on the ground. Even so, we had been quite happy in our house, and the landlord and his wife had become friends.

We had learned to endure heavy rainstorms during which the main floor flooded. Protecting our carpets and furniture was a dreary, time-consuming ordeal. Finally after a particularly bad storm, Ele called the landlord over to inspect the damage. As he looked over the carnage, he mused that his mother never had such problems, but agreed to try to find a solution.

The following day he brought over a workman and instructed him to put up a structure over the patio. The man worked for days to put up a slanted steel frame and large steel screens on top of the frame. The landlord announced that the problem was solved; the frame and screening would keep the rain out of the main floor. Just as he declared the problem solved, a storm blew in, a torrent of rain came down, and the water rushed into the patio. Ele explained that screens keep out flies and mosquitoes, but not water. She simply said that a solid structure was needed on top of the frame to redirect the rain. After a lengthy discussion, the landlord agreed to put corrugated tin roofing on top of the frame instead of the screens. Well, that worked most of the time; but when we had heavy rains for several days, the cleanup brigade had to be mobilized to sweep out the rising waters.

Then, in 1955, for Ele's birthday on April 1, we decided to celebrate with the Schencks, the Dutrizes, the Williams, and the Salazars. After dinner at the Club Deportivo, we invited our guests home for coffee and brandy. As I opened the front door and turned on the light, we saw a field mouse scamper across the floor away from a vulture calmly eating his dinner on the patio. Entering the living room, we found a new decoration on our coffee table—a bat feeding on a cockroach. We all laughed at the unexpected floorshow. But when we went upstairs, Ele said that she thought it was time to move.

The following Tuesday night, we learned from friends that their neighbor, a German-born coffee planter, had built a house for his daughter but the daughter had decided to live in Europe. The house was not on the market, and the father had not decided whether he would rent it. Our friend Jackie took Ele to see the owner, and it was love at first sight! After he and his wife showed Ele the house, they said that they would welcome our renting it, with the understanding that our tenancy would terminate if the daughter decided that she wanted to come home.

The new house fronted on an unpaved street and was two and half stories, with a small front yard and a large enclosed back yard. On the first floor were a large living room, a dining room, a study-bedroom with full bathroom, large kitchen, two maids' rooms with bath, and a covered patio opening to the garden. On the first landing of the staircase going to the second floor was the guest room and bath, overlooking the garden. The second floor had two large bedrooms and baths. All of the kitchen and bathroom equipment was brand new, and there was hot water.

The amount of the rent, he said, was not important; he and his wife wanted someone compatible living there until the daughter came home. Ele and he reached agreement on an amount that we could afford and much less than he could have received if he put the house on the market. So, for our final two years in San Salvador, we had a fine house and a good neighbor.

When we gave thirty days' notice to our landlord, we had a very uncomfortable confrontation. The less said, the better. We were grateful to him and his wife, but we couldn't get him to understand that our moving was not a personal rebuke to them or lack of appreciation for their kindness. Ele and I regretted that our association ended on such a sour note. It demonstrated how personal a relationship can become in Latin America, even one related to renting a house.

The Market

Ele did almost all of the shopping while we lived in San Salvador. She loved the market experience, especially the bargaining over the cost of each papaya, carrot, potato, or orange. She enjoyed getting to know the market women and earning their confidence. She was *la rubia* (the redhead) to the market ladies, and they generally expected her on a Friday morning. Bargaining was a very formal process, part of the market experience. The market ladies expected Ele to bargain: no item had a fixed price, and I think that the women admired buyers who brought them down to the "right price." The conversation was essential to finding the "right price." The market was as much a social experience as a commercial transaction.

Most of the women confided to Ele that they were not married and had children in Catholic boarding schools in the States. When she asked questions about how they were doing, she always got detailed, substantive responses. They would share stories and show pictures of their children at school in the U.S. as well as the latest gossip. They knew what was going on in the country and had strong opinions about them. Sometimes she saw political personalities we met at social events in conversation with the ladies, and the market women who had befriended her would whisper that the politician needed another loan or some other favor. Ele frequently brought home information extremely useful for me in doing my job, information such as who was in favor one week, and out of the favor the next. It was usually more reliable than the U.S. embassy intelligence reports!

At first, Ele went to the central market in downtown San Salvador until she was introduced by a friend to the market in the neighboring town of Santa Tecla. She soon found that it was more convenient to make the ten-mile drive from our house to Santa Tecla. Parking was easier and the market was more orderly, cleaner, and less crowded.

Whenever I went with *la rubia* to Santa Tecla, I was greeted warmly. I was amused when the market women referred to Ele fondly as *Mamacita*.

The Tragens Go Social

As I reflected earlier, in 1953 San Salvador, there was no television, few movie houses, no symphony or ballet, few restaurants, and not too tempting black volcanic beaches down the twisting highway to the coast at La Libertad. There were the two golf clubs and the tennis club (El Deportivo) for some relaxation. The football (soccer) teams drew often-unruly crowds to the National Stadium, down the street from the house in Flor Blanca, and gringos joining in could bring unforeseen consequences. So, we made our own entertainment.

At one of the dinners to which we were invited shortly after our arrival, our hostess asked us whether we were interested in joining a little theater group. Ele said rather hesitantly that she had been in several high school plays and that we both liked the theater. The hostess said that it was great fun, with nineteen different nationalities participating. She offered to take us to the next presentation the following week—and we were hooked.

The group put on about eight plays a year. The actors read their parts in all but the one big production per year. The plays were performed in the main auditorium of the American School on a very adequate stage. For the seven performances in which parts were read, there were usually two or three rehearsals under the direction of the member who had proposed the particular play. Each actor was expected to perform, not just read. Under the discerning eye of the director, stage sets were designed for each new play and adjusted as needed after each rehearsal to help create the mood and support the action of the play. Performances were always sold out and the audience included all the different English-speakers living in the country, including many Salvadorans who had been schooled in the U.S. or Europe.

It was joyful to interact with people of such different nationalities and backgrounds. Finding a common interpretation for a play and its characters made every rehearsal and performance something to look forward to. Visualize *The Tea House of the August Moon* with Italian, English, Rumanian, German, Salvadoran, and U.S. cast members! Picture a set designed by a Belgian importer who used the straw wrappings from his Chianti bottles shipped from Italy to make the coolie hats, and wrappings and crates to create the Tea House. It was sheer delight!

For almost four years, we had our monthly commitment to work on or off stage in the production being presented. Ele played the Marilyn Monroe role in the *Seven Year Itch*. I read Androcles in *Androcles and the Lion*. Ele often played the ingénue lead: she had a photographic memory and could get into character at once. I was not so fortunate, and could be used only to collect tickets when a role had to be memorized. Over those four years, the theater group put on many sterling performances from Shaw's *St. Joan* to Agatha Christie's *Ten Little Indians*. All of us enjoyed sharing the experience together, even when things went wrong. We turned *Ten Little*

Indians into the comedy hit of the year as every snafu imaginable occurred, but the appreciative audience roared its enjoyment as the exasperated director stormed out of the theater.

Ele and I were usually actors, except for one gala that Ele directed: *East Lynne*, complete with villain and hero. With the help of our military attaché's wife, who had been a Rockette, a bevy of beauties formed a chorus line and did the Can Can. Ambassador Hill played the villain.

The theater group raised enough money to buy a curtain, lights, and sound system for the school auditorium.

Another stimulating monthly endeavor was the reading group. Peter Allemano, the head of the education *servicio* organized the group, which met once a month to discuss interesting books or articles that had intrigued or stimulated us during the preceding month. It included a Salvadoran who had lived in the U.S. and Europe, a specialist from the UN Food and Agriculture Organization and his wife, a British diplomat and his wife, the Allemanos, and the Tragens. We had potluck dinners one Saturday night per month at each other's homes. Such a variety of interests and opinions!

Thanks to the British couple, we got on the British Embassy's invitation list. Right after the first reading group in May 1953, we received an engraved invitation from the British ambassador for the lunch at the Club Salvadoreño to celebrate the queen's coronation. It was our first diplomatic invitation. It was an elegant sit-down luncheon at which we were shown pictures of the event that had just taken place only hours before in London; we were astounded at how quickly the ambassador had received them. Thereafter, we were always invited to the queen's official birthday celebration so long as we were in El Salvador.

The reading group lasted almost four years until the Allemanos and the British couple were transferred. Over those four years, we came to know each other very well. We looked forward to the opportunity to be together and share not only a reading but also a piece of our lives. Then suddenly we were dispersed. Christmas cards were our annual greeting for a few years. Such is a pattern of life in the Foreign Service.

Another important dimension of our social life was with my ministry colleagues. From the initial aloofness, we came to know each other well and many of our social activities involved them. Shortly after we got settled in Flor Blanca, we invited the minister and his key advisors to a small cocktail party to break the ice. Then the minister's wife, Yolanda, invited us to a small dinner where we met the wives of his inner circle. Although they were busy raising children and had their extended family relationships, we got together often enough to feel that they had accepted us as friends. We went to weddings and christenings and waited in hospital waiting rooms with the father-to-be for the birth of a baby. We reached a level of friendship that ministry officers told their spouses that they had been at our house when they in fact had a rendezvous with another lady. I recall an evening at the U.S. Embassy when a wife came over to Ele and thanked her for having had her husband to dinner the week before when she, the wife, had been indisposed. Without skipping a beat, Ele responded that her husband was always welcome at our home. We exchanged Christmas notes until they passed away in the 1980s.

Ele and I preferred small dinner parties where we could get to know people and learn about their lives, interests, and aspirations. We never really like cocktail parties. Even so, we threw occasional cocktail parties when we felt it would cement ties between our ministry colleagues and the USOM and the U.S. Embassy. The minister even asked us to have cocktails with other ministers with whom he needed to work out arrangements to move a project forward. For those cocktail parties in our house, I always had eighteen bottles of scotch for every ten Salvadoran invitees. Ever prudent, Ele attempted to discourage too much drinking by serving food savored by Salvadorans, like *pupusas* (tortillas stuffed with ground meat) and hot dogs. Ele and I learned to nurse a Scotch for the evening, and how to graciously turn down refills or new drinks.

Besides our ministry colleagues, we were fortunate to develop a number of Salvadoran friends. We often met Salvadoran couples about our age who had lived or studied in the United States. Ele and I wanted everyone to feel that they were guests and friends, not business acquaintances or protocol invitees—and she urged me to limit business to office hours.

Ele made a rule that anyone entering our house, whatever their nationality, had to divest themselves of their guns or other weapons at the front door. El Salvador was afloat with guns and machetes. Violence was common, and Ele wanted everyone to know that in our home there was zero tolerance for violence. She did not intend to have lights shot out by some guest who in his "enlightened" state might do something he would regret the next day. Every guest, including bodyguards, respected our rule. One evening when we invited a Salvadoran couple from a coffee plantation and other business friends, we had a machine gun, several carbines, and two hand guns stashed away in our locked library. We never had an incident in our home.

Being part of the official U.S. community also enriched our lives. We made three life-long USOM friendships: Hildreth and Bill Scheck; Gladys and C.W. Ranck, the market and credit specialist of the agricultural *servicio;* and Irene and Peter Allemano, the chief of the education *servicio.* We thoroughly enjoyed small dinner parties where we could dance after dinner or play bridge. Someone had a dance party every so often and records were the primary source of music. Both the Schenks and the Rancks liked playing bridge and we had many evenings at their houses. Every time we saw each other after El Salvador, we quickly picked up from wherever our last meeting had been.

Ele and I were rarely called on to squire visitors from Washington, especially congressmen. Occasionally a congressman from the home district of one of my USOM colleagues would inspect our activities and we would be included in entertaining him. One such visitor was an Indiana republican congressman, an old friend of Gladys and E.W. Ranck. He had a political agenda primarily related to issues that the embassy covered, but also wanted to spend time with the Rancks. So, Gladys organized a Sunday dinner for him, with Ele and me among the invitees. In his briefings before coming to San Salvador, he had been advised that there were rumors of possible coups. We had the usual late afternoon storm, followed by the usual interruption of electric service. A normal day for all of us, but a real jolt to the congressman who thought that a coup was underway! We quieted him down while Gladys induced him to enjoy some of the wonderful Indiana dinner she had prepared. On his return to Washington, he made special note in his report about the perilous conditions under which his fellow Indianans had to live and work.

We also had a few I House friends at post, like Guillermo "*Cuate*" Galván and his wife Dolores Molina. *Cuate*, which means "friend" in Mexican Spanish, had been my roommate for one semester while I was studying for the State Bar Examination. He was a civil engineering student, specializing in irrigation and water management. After graduation, they decided to build their life in El Salvador since there was a shortage of hydraulic engineers. Cuate and Dolores were raising a rapidly growing family, and those demands gave us limited opportunities for getting together.

When the U.S. Embassy Commissary was reorganized, its board asked the Commissary members (that is, all those official U.S. personnel assigned to El Salvador) if we could recommend a Salvadoran for the job of manager. Ele immediately proposed Dolores. Ele arranged for an interview, and she was hired. She became not only an effective and dependable manager, but also the friend of almost all the commissary members.

We included weekend trips to just about every corner of the country. We saw the landmarks from Mayan and Pipil relics to Lake Coatepeque and Lake Ilopango. One weekend we would go to markets in neighboring towns and villages just to get a feel for the variety of foods available and the prices. We went to local fairs and often ate in local markets. We learned that the lady potter who had won the grand prize for artisan handicraft at the 1939 San Francisco World's Fair lived in the small town of Ilobasco, so we drove out there to meet her. She lived in a straw hut with a dirt floor, no running water or plumbing, and there she sat molding the most delicate ceramic pieces imaginable, called *sorpresas* (surprises). A *sorpresa* is a miniature sculpted pottery that depicts a country or religious scene. She allowed us to buy only two of the pieces she had that day. They are now at the Museo de las Américas in Denver.

One weekend trip took us to Sitio del Niño, a small rural village an hour or so northeast of San Salvador where we met a group of young professionals from Europe and the United States working under the auspices of the American Friends Committee, to help the community raise family incomes and improve living standards. Their team included John Planck, later a noted professor at the University of Connecticut; Helen Sanford, sister of a future governor and senator from North Carolina; and Rolf Wilhelm, later director of the Swiss International Technical Cooperation Program.

Their big project was to develop a poultry production center, with an incubator for hatching the chicks, which would provide steady income to help finance improved living conditions in the village. The week before the inauguration, Ele and I spent our Saturday working on the chores required for the official inauguration. Everything looked just great when we left late that Saturday afternoon. The incubator had arrived, a new power line had been attached to the incubator, and the new chicks were arriving from the U.S. the following Friday. President Osorio had agreed to come out on Saturday to formally inaugurate the project. The chicks arrived on time in fine condition and were placed in the incubator. The European and U.S. advisers went to bed exhilarated. The next morning all the chicks had died: no one had shown the community how to turn on the switch for the electric power!

When we arrived at about ten o'clock that morning, everyone was in tears. But we all learned a very important lesson—in a development project, never take anything for granted.

The Trip to El Tenorio

Ele and I made two trips as tourists to Costa Rica and Guatemala during this assignment. Our first trip was to Costa Rica in 1954. We visited our old friends, Mary and John Stelzer, who after leaving the Aftosa Commission in Mexico, joined United Fruit Company to manage its large cattle ranch in Guanacaste, Costa Rica, known as *El Tenorio*. When they heard of our assignment to El Salvador, they invited us to come down to Costa Rica.

On the way to Costa Rica, we spent a couple of days in Managua, Nicaragua, to visit with our close I House friends, the brothers Luis and Humberto Carrión. The Carrións met us at the airport and took us to the Grand Hotel. We had dinner at Luis's home where we met both of their wives. They invited us to a picnic the following day on the banks of the Tipitapa River that runs between Lake Managua and Lake Nicaragua. Our conversation at the airport, in the car to the hotel, and at dinner was very circumspect and non-political. The Carrións focused on our adventures, and parried any question that Ele and I asked about life in Managua.

Only when the picnic was unpacked and we were set up several yards from the highway, did the conversation become more than polite generalities. As we watched the fins of fresh water sharks swim past us in the river and Luis kept an eagle eye out for any inquisitive caimans, they told us about life in Somoza-run Nicaragua, including his tyranny and graft. They advised us to be very careful what we said in the hotel and reminded us that in the Grand Hotel, none of the walls reached the ceiling. That was not merely to improve air circulation but also to facilitate eavesdropping. They and their parents were not Liberal Party members, and Somoza never trusted anyone who was not a dues-paying member of his party. The following morning Ele and I were relieved to board Pan Am for San José, Costa Rica.

Arriving in San José was like landing on a different planet. The police presence had been ever-present in Managua and there was always tension in San Salvador. In San José, from the moment we entered the lovely old airport just on the edge of town, the environment was different. The warmth of the greeting in immigration and customs contrasted sharply with the military brusqueness in Managua. San José felt like being in the U.S., except that everyone spoke Spanish. We grabbed a cab to the *pension* in the center of San José that the USOM in Costa Rica had recommended. The owner then suggested a restaurant not too far away for dinner and we walked over. Just walking the streets indicated how different San José was from the other neighboring capitals. The people on the streets were comfortably dressed, and we didn't see the extreme poverty that lined the streets in Managua, San Salvador, and Mexico City. The stores were well stocked but not opulent. We walked past street cafes in which people were speaking openly about politics.

While our primary purpose was to spend a week with the Stelzers, we set aside two days to see San José and its environs. We checked into the embassy, since registering there was required of all U.S. government officials on leave in the country. We met with USOM officials who asked about my work in San Salvador. We then took in the sights from the Opera House to the central market, from the Hotel Colón to the steaming Irazú volcano. The time went by quickly as we enjoyed the sense of freedom in San José.

Mary Stelzer drove us to El Tenorio, about two or three hours away, down to the Pacific port of Punta Arenas and then up the

Pan American Highway in Guanacaste surrounded by scrubland that runs all the way to the Nicaraguan border. About an hour up the highway, Mary turned into the large cattle operation run by the United Fruit Company, through a complex of houses on stilts, the traditional housing provided by the United Fruit Company on all of its estates, to a brand new California style ranch house.

Mary beamed as she showed us her new home. We were her first personal guests. She related how she had convinced the company to allow her to build a non-stilt house after an initial effort ended in failure. The District Manager turned her down since the standard company housing for field managers was wooden and built on stilts. Petition denied; case closed.

Then, the board of directors held a meeting at El Tenorio. Two of them were put up in the Stelzer house on stilts and others in adjoining stilted structures. During the night, bats and owls foraged around the rafters of the buildings, disturbing the directors' sleep. The next morning, several directors asked Mary how she was able to cope with the nocturnal problems. She explained that they were one of the principal reasons for her request to build a new manager's home in the California ranch style. She said that she could build a house, using materials available in El Tenorio, for no more than $10,000. The directors agreed to consider her request at the next board meeting in Boston. The board authorized the construction, provided that the Stelzers absorb personally any costs above $10,000. Mary supervised the construction and it came in under $10,000.

A footnote to the house construction was that Mary was able to put in a porcelain bathtub, not one made of floor tiles as in the stilted residence. When the district manager who had turned down Mary's original request, came on an inspection visit, Mary showed him the new bathtub. He was aghast and advised Mary, "One has to be with the company ten years before authorization is given for a porcelain bathtub in one's residence."

Ele and I spent a wonderful week with the Stelzers and their growing brood. We did some horseback riding, but mainly we rested. During the day, shortwave radio messages arrived from San José and Boston. Guanacaste was experiencing a terrible drought, and the government of Costa Rica banned any burning of pastures even though they were infested with insects and pests. I recall frantic calls from San José asking John if he had burned yet. John said no, because of the government ban. The voice on the shortwave warned, "When Boston says to burn, you burn!"

That incident remained with me all my life. It illustrated the terrible hiatus between the interests of headquarters and the reality on the ground. On so many occasions, I found myself in similar situations, especially when special interests for their own purposes pressured the powers-that-be in Washington to "get something done." Instructions would come down to take action that would save face in Washington but would make it more difficult to solve the problem on the ground.

Our return trip to San Salvador took us back through Managua. The weather was bad between San José and Managua. Most passengers had upset stomachs and had been forced to remain seated. Everyone had urgent need to use the bathroom. When the plane landed, we were rounded up by the Nicaraguan *Guardia Nacional*, herded into an open area of the airport where we were forced to stand in the heat and humidity and refused access to the bathrooms. Then we learned that someone had tried to assassinate President-Dictator Somoza and a state of siege had been declared. Everyone was suspect. Finally, after an hour, a Pan Am representative arrived with a senior Nicaraguan official, who apologized for the inconvenience and allowed us to use the facilities. Then, all the passengers were forced aboard the plane to San Salvador, no matter what their destination may have been.

Family Business in California

Ele made a trip to California later in 1954. Her mother sent her a letter announcing that she no longer wanted the responsibility of overseeing the two farms and that she planned to sell them. Her mother reported that she had been offered a deal for the California ranch, and the price was clearly inadequate. Ele was furious—in fact, I had never seen her so upset.

The letter arrived in one of the three weeks per year in which El Salvador shut down—and I mean totally shut down. For Holy Week, the Festival of Salvador del Mundo in early August and

Christmas-New Years, the government closed its offices. Doctors left the country on vacation. Home telephone service was cut off. Newspapers ceased publishing, and restaurants closed. People who got sick headed for the airport and took the next plane to the Ochsner Clinic in New Orleans.

After receiving the letter, Ele decide that she had to act to protect the primary source of her mother and grandmother's income. So we drove down to the main telephone office where one overseas operator was on duty. We were given a number and had to wait our turn. When Ele finally got on the phone, she read her mother the riot act and announced that she was catching the next plane to California. She ordered her mother not to discuss the sale of the ranch until she arrived.

When Ele reached Tulare, she found that her mother had signed an agreement with a real estate agent to place the ranch on the market for $10,000. Ele checked with farm realtors who said that the ranch would be a giveaway at $50,000. She called in the real estate agent, paid him his commission, and signed him to an agency agreement to look after the property for the following year. She kept the property off the market.

Then Ele went to work. She took over selling the 1954 cotton crop. To sell the cotton crop, the seller had to have a USDA marketing card, and Ele's mother had not given the card to the tenant. So, Ele talked turkey to the manager of the cotton gin, with whom the tenant had done business for the past decade. The gin manager told her that he had already purchased the crop from the tenant and that there was nothing she could do. Ele said, "Oh, yes I can. I have the marketing card and any transaction you carried out with the tenant is illegal without the marketing card." The manager balked. As Ele walked out she heard him muttering about doing business with old ladies.

She returned the following day with the USDA marketing supervisor and told the manager that she wanted all the weight reports for the 1954 crop and raised questions about the price per bale paid, which she pointed out was below what the manager paid other farmers for cotton of the same quality. Ele forced the manager to recalculate the payment and make out new purchase statements in the presence of the USDA agent before allowing him access to the marketing card. The amount was significantly higher than the previous arrangement with the tenant. As she walked out, she said in a very loud voice that the gin manager could hear, "This is the last time that gin manager will have to deal with this old lady!"

Ele then found a new tenant and another gin with which she could do business in future years. She also persuaded her mother to agree that she, Ele, would run the farms from that point forward. She would negotiate the farm contracts, agree on the crops to be planted, market the crops, and deposit the proceeds into her mother's and grandmother's accounts. Ele's grandmother was so pleased that she gave Ele her share of the California ranch. She spent the next six weeks reviewing her mother's and grandmother's finances, checked their wills, and made sure that they had a current list of their assets and liabilities. When she left them in October, she had her family's affairs in first-rate order.

On the night before she left Tulare, she had dinner with her closest friend Mimi Hoffman and her husband to tell them what she had done. They gave her three pats on the back and several gallons of extra creamy ice cream from their dairy to bring back to San Salvador. What a treat for us because a modern ice cream dairy had not yet opened there!

Getting the ice cream back to El Salvador was a logistic nightmare. When Ele arrived at the Visalia Airport, United Airlines agreed to put the precious cargo in its refrigerator. Helene and Bob Tubbs met her at the airport and took her out to dinner at Chasin's; Bob arranged to have the ice cream stowed in the restaurant's freezer and it was returned wrapped in dry ice. At the airport, Bob also arranged for Pan Am to take the package at check-in and put it in the freezer on board the plane. Ele had alerted me that she was bringing the cargo and the embassy helped me to get the authorization of Salvadoran Customs to move the ice cream directly into an official USOM car. We were able to get it home to Flor Blanca without losing a drop. In return, we held an ice cream social that Salvadorans and Americans alike thought was the big social event of the year! I doubt that, under today's security regulations, such a delivery could have been made.

The Guatemalan Highlands

Our second trip outside of El Salvador was to see the lakes and highlands of Guatemala. With the fall of the Arbenz regime, we were told that U.S. personnel were once again welcome; so we decided to go during Holy Week in 1955 to Antigua, Lake Atitlán, and Chichicastenango.

When I consulted the USOM administrative officer about our making the trip, he contacted his counterpart in Guatemala, who saw no reason why we should not go but warned of bandits in the rural areas. He suggested that he book us a five-day tour with a well-known local agency, starting the Wednesday of Holy Week.

The representative of Clark Tours met us at Guatemala City's Aurora airport and, with our official U.S. passports, whisked us through Immigration and Customs. As we drove to town, we noticed the streets deserted and heavy police and military presence on almost every street corner even though it was Holy Week. We were taken to the Pan American Hotel, then the prime tourist hotel in the city, just a block from the Zócalo where the presidential palace is located. We were just about the only guests in the hotel and were treated royally, including a special luncheon show of marimbas and folk dancers.

The Clark representative advised us that one other couple from the U.S. would join us and that couple was due at the airport shortly. He asked us not to leave the hotel until he returned with the other couple and would then go over our itinerary. Ele and I looked at each other and realized that the situation in Guatemala was far from normal. Ele put her finger to her mouth and smiled. We took a siesta.

About seven o'clock, the Clark representative called to invite us to join him and the other couple for cocktails and dinner. The dining room was almost empty. Over dinner, the representative told us of the plans for a city tour and drive to Lake Amatitlán on Thursday, then on to Antigua, Atitlán, and Chichicastenango (known as "Chichi") for the rest of the week.

Thursday morning we left fairly early, toured the high points in the city and visited the Central Market. Ceramics and textiles were everywhere and were so attractive. When Ele tried to discuss the wares and the prices, the market ladies didn't respond as she had expected, but instead said, "All prices are fixed." No interest in bargaining! Ele suspected that this was standard treatment for gringos on that tour.

That night, we stayed at the Hotel Antigua, a lovely oasis with only a handful of other guests. The low-rise hotel was among the ruins of the eighteenth century *Capitanía General* (the seat of government) of Central America, which had been devastated by volcanic eruptions and earthquakes. Its plain outer walls disguised the garden beauty of its interior. We had a bungalow in the center of the garden. With its typical Guatemalan menu and reputation for care in food preparation, it had long been a favorite of foreigners visiting Guatemala.

We walked the streets of Antigua as they were decorated with carpets of flowers over which the processions on Good Friday would walk. We wandered through the market, with its unique ceramics and traditional *huipiles* (ladies blouses) and other textiles. Then we went to the Crocker studio, where we marveled at his stylized portraits of indigenous people in their native dress and bought a collection of his prints. Ele later framed them in black lacquered window box frames, and they adorned our homes for over fifty years. They are now in the collection of Latin American handicrafts at the Museo de las Américas in Denver.

Even in Holy Week in Antigua, we sensed tension. The Hotel Antigua was only half-filled and management told us to be careful when we left the front door. The ever-present soldiers reminded us that the military had taken absolute control following the overthrow of the Arbenz regime. No one mentioned anything on the street, but the tone in the market was restrained. As we watched the initial processions on Friday morning, people were pious but wary.

We motored up to Lake Atitlán in the afternoon, arriving before dark. We were housed at the Hotel Panajachel, which projected out over the lake. Our elegant room overlooked the lake, allowing us to absorb one of the most dramatic vistas in the world: the great volcano rising out of the deep blue waters. The sunset was spectacular. When we went down to dinner, we found that we were almost the only guests in the hotel. During dinner, a series of shots rang out in the bar adjoining the dining room. The hotel manager rushed in to reassure us that there was nothing to be concerned about. Then, the electric power went off. Hotel employees led us to our rooms by candlelight and asked us to remain there for the night. We were not very sure of what was happening and who was doing what to whom. At breakfast the next morning, our guide told us that a minister, drunk at the bar, shot his companion because "he offended him." The incident was not reported in the press, apparently because of the people involved.

After a visit to two of the twelve indigenous villages around the lake, we took off for Chichicastenango, climbing up to the highlands through Sololá. How handsome were the black jackets embroidered in white that the men of Sololá wore! Many years later I bought one for myself, and was very unhappy when it was stolen from our shipment when we were transferred to Panama from Guatemala.

We arrived Saturday afternoon in Chichi and were installed in one of the most charming hotels in the world, the Mayan Inn. Our room with its corner fireplace enchanted us. Chichi, in the highlands, gets cold by early evening so the room attendant lit the corner fireplace early in the evening. When we went down to dinner, we were surprised to see only a handful of guests because to stay at the Mayan Inn even in the 1950s one usually had to make reservations months in advance.

Sunday was a magical day at the indigenous market. Ele and I went to the market early, surveying the booths and admiring the hand-woven *huipiles* and jackets from all over the highlands. Almost everything on sale that morning appeared to have been woven on hand looms. The ceramics were mostly utilitarian, but brightly glazed with intricate designs. The silver and gold ornamental jewelry in the booths were native design and uniquely Kaqchikel. We were restrained from buying because not only of the weight limitation on flying home but also we had already blown our not so extensive finances on the Crocker prints. We oohed and aahed to each other until it was time to join our fellow tourists for a visit to the Church.

And what a scene as we entered from the infirmary side of building! It was like no other Catholic church we had ever been in. There were no pews, no altar, and no priests at the altar. The kneeling Indian parishioners were facing each other in a line from the front door of the church to the base of the altar. They were making their own individual altars out of flowers and flower petals, lighting their candles and spreading incense, in an almost supernatural aura as they talked directly to God about their problems. Some were pious and others were shaking their fists at the heavens.

We were told that the *shamans*, native spiritual leaders, controlled admission to the church and placed supplicants according to the seriousness of their problems: those with life and death issues given places closest to the altar, while those with economic concerns were usually half way between the altar and the front door, and those with lesser personal concerns closer to the entrance. The *shamans* shuffled in and out of the church, giving comfort to some and advising others that their time of intercession was over. Ele and I were entranced by the sincerity, directness, and piety of each of the supplicants.

Later, with our guide, we went up into the hills above Chichi to watch many of the same *shamans* and supplicants repeat their prayers and requests to the animist gods of their Mayan and Kaqchikel ancestors. The aroma of incense and smoke exceeded that in the Church. No harm in trying both routes to receive the grace of God!

That afternoon, we walked back into the center of town and watched as the unsold wares were carefully folded and loaded on to backs and straps around the heads of the bearers in preparation for the hours-long treks up the mountains to their homes. The poverty and the humility of the people left their mark on us.

By chance, we crossed paths with a Canadian priest who oversaw the work of the Chichi Church. Ele told him how deeply the ceremony that morning had touched us. He told us that in the early 1900s, before his order had taken over the church, it had been operated traditionally, and few indigenous people ever entered it. When his order took over, the priest in charge consulted the *shamans* on how to attract his people to the Church. So, the people's church was conceived as a way to reach the animists and introduce Christ into their lives, without the symbolism of the establishment. Over time, health and other services had been added for the indigenous people. Early the next day, we left Chichi for the airport and the flight back to San Salvador.

For years thereafter, this visit stuck in our minds. No matter how justified the case may have been to help remove the Arbenz regime and its pro-Soviet baggage, the U.S. had allowed Guatemala to become a police state. We sat by as the military erased the democratic reforms introduced in the mid-1940s by the popularly-elected government of Juan José Arévalo aimed at enabling the indigenous Indian peoples to participate more equitably in the economy and society. U.S. support for the police state in Guatemala was every bit as disturbing as my experience in the Dominican Republic of Trujillo and our visit to Somoza-led Nicaragua. Ele and I resolved that in our work, our goals would be to contribute positively to the rights and dignity of people.

11

The Second Tour
in El Salvador

Our second tour began with word of change at the embassy and in the government of El Salvador. Director Hackney and Bill Schenk informed me that several important developments occurred in our absence. First, U.S. Ambassador Hill would be leaving short-ly for the embassy in Mexico and that my labor reporting might be affected. Second, minister of the Economy, Jorge Sol Castellanos, had been offered a senior post at the World Bank and would like-ly accept it before the end of the year and his replacement would be the minister of Labor. Third, preparations were underway for the presidential election in 1956, with speculation running rampant about the probable successor.

They warned me that there would a good deal of uncertainty in top-level government decision-making and how that might further affect project implementation. The director then asked me to advise him of any relevant information that I might pick up at the Ministry of Labor that might affect USOM interests. Bill then briefed me over the lack of progress in project operations at the Ministry of Labor. He had met periodically with the two in-country specialists, Josh Levine and Tom Walsh, and warned me that they were frustrated by the lack of support they felt they were receiving. He urged me to talk with them as soon as possible and get their perspective.

The Ministry Program

The following morning I met with Josh and Tom at the USOM. They described how difficult it had been for the last several weeks to get anything done. Their requests for appointments with the minister,

Moncho, and Rogelio had not been answered. They recognized that the ministry's personnel and budgetary resources were limited, but they needed indications that the ministry was committed to implementing the manpower project. They wanted a face-to-face meeting with the minister and his key advisers, but neither felt comfortable trying to because of their limited knowledge of Spanish.

As they explained their experience in my absence, I began to wonder if I had made a planning mistake in bringing resident technicians to the mission before their projects had been designed and were ready for implementation. Perhaps I should have scheduled short-term consultants to work with ministry officials in designing the manpower program and training Salvadoran technical staff in the U.S. and Puerto Rico before bringing on board full-time advisors. I questioned my original perception that, without U.S. specialists in-country working with senior ministry officials on the design and scope of the manpower project, interest in the project would wane and support would peter out.

Our discussion that morning focused on where we were and how to move forward, not the validity of the manpower project. We agreed that the project was the top priority for the ministry and focused on the human and other resources needed to get it operative—both the employment service and worker skills training. I agreed to lay out our concerns and requirements to the minister and vice minister and then, determine how to proceed.

We also recognized that our timeframe was very tight given the impending election. The country had little experience with constitutional changes of power. We heard that, in prior changes of administration, there had been general house cleanings of personnel from ministers to janitors, and Salvadoran technicians and specialized personnel told us for that reason they preferred to work in a *servicio* that assured continuity in program and staff.

Several of our colleagues pointed out that in education, public health, or agriculture programs and projects, the *servicio* was the instrument for insuring continuity since, once an agreement was reached between the two governments to undertake a program or project, they were insulated from local political upheaval. However, in light of the subject matter with its strong political component, neither the USOM nor the ministry had considered creating a *servi-*

cio. Right or wrong, Josh, Tom, and I had to try to get our projects moving with the resources at hand.

I made an appointment to call on the minister the following morning. When I walked into the office, he greeted me with an *abrazo.* He asked about my leave and I asked him about the ministry. Over a cup of strong Salvadoran coffee, I recited the problems that my colleagues and I were facing. Then, he said succinctly, "I want this program to move forward. I want you and Moncho to make it happen. Work with Moncho, and I will approve the measures that he works out with and for you and your colleagues." He gave no indication of any imminent departure or change in ministry policy.

He then called Moncho to join us, and said, "Irving says there are some problems that need to be resolved. The two of you find the solutions. You have my full support." Then, he said almost as an aside, "Irving, you need your own transportation. So, I have assigned a car and driver to you effective immediately. Your driver will pick you up in the morning and take you home at night. During the day he is available for any trip you or your colleagues may need to make. In emergencies during the day we may use them on other ministry business if you won't need them." He gave me another *abrazo* and we were off to Moncho's adjoining office.

Moncho and I spent the next hour reviewing the immediate needs of the manpower project. He promised to allocate additional resources. He then raised some concerns with other aspects of the program. He pointed out that fifteen Salvadoran personnel had already received training in the U.S. or Puerto Rico. In the labor inspection service, he had noted some improvements with several returned trainees having assumed supervisory and training positions; however, two of those trained left the ministry for better paying jobs. A couple of those slated for Puerto Rico grants were graduating from law school and were offered jobs in the labor courts' judicial police system. He then noted that the scope and quality of their statistical series were still not up to desired standards and he felt additional training was necessary.

Before leaving, I returned to the concerns of Josh and Tom; Moncho said that he would help find workable solutions, but did not have the flexibility in the current budget to hire more ministry staff. Then he asked, "Even if I had more funds, where do we find the people? There is no easy answer. You and I knew that when we worked out the program. So, now we will need to create the people we need from the best we can find in the ministry." I said that we might need to look for some additional talent for both activities. Moncho demurred but didn't shut the door.

Josh, Tom, and I met that afternoon, using my new vehicle to go to the USOM office. We had to improvise and use the available personnel and resources. We agreed to look for bright young ministry personnel who might be assigned to work with us, and ask around among our fellow USOM technicians whether they knew of any Salvadorans we might consider.

That night, Ele suggested that I invite the key people in the ministry for a cocktail with Tom and Josh. It would be an opportunity for them to talk out the situation in an informal setting where there were no other distractions. So, I invited Mario Héctor, Rogelio, and Moncho to come over for cocktails the following week. I asked Tom and Josh to bring working plans that spelled out the minimum resources needed.

Unfortunately, one political crisis after another postponed the working cocktail for several weeks. Then we learned that President Osorio had accepted the resignation of the minister of the Economy and appointed Mario Héctor to replace him. Mario Héctor was absorbing the work of his new ministry as well as getting briefed on El Salvador's first five-year development plan, and making sure that there was a manpower component in it. That informal cocktail party never occurred.

Ele

Ele settled back smoothly into life in San Salvador. In the first two years she had engaged in a wide range of activities, including participation in the charitable activities favored by the embassy. In each diplomatic Mission, the ambassador's wife was the head of whatever wives' organization existed and she selected its activities and it was expected that wives would support them. It was also understood that in each husband's annual efficiency report, the attitude and cooperation of the wife were also assessed—and that many promising careers had been aborted by unflattering comments about a wife's participation in "mission projects."

For the first two years, Ele rolled bandages at the Blum Children's Hospital along with all the other American embassy and USOM wives. She was not surprised to see that this maternity and children's hospital, the best in the country, was overcrowded, sometimes with two or three pregnant women in the same bed. Talking with the expectant mothers, often from marginal urban and rural areas, she found that they considered the care they were given in the hospital to be a wonderful luxury.

Ele felt that this was not the most productive contribution that the wives could make and proposed to Ambassador Hill's wife that our assistance be redirected to help new mothers in their communities after they left the hospital. It would be a service that those mothers and their families would concretely see as a contribution from their friends in the U.S. diplomatic community." She had almost convinced Mrs. Hill before the Hills were transferred to Mexico.

After all, she noted, there were no Salvadoran volunteers at the hospital, with their contribution limited to buying tickets for the annual gala that the foreign diplomatic community organized. Ele asked, "Why shouldn't we expect the wealthy Salvadoran ladies to do the work in the hospital and let us develop a new activity to support people in their homes?

One of Ele's most demanding roles was as hostess of parties for our colleagues from the ministry, the U.S. and diplomatic communities, and the private sector. We had almost no entertainment allowance and covered the costs from the monthly paycheck. Ele managed our budget and made certain that there was always a positive balance at the end of the month: her Scottish instincts would have no other outcome. She had a knack for decorating with candles, ceramics, and flower arrangements that made a cocktail or dinner seem special.

She made everybody feel at home. Many of my colleagues from the ministry had never been to a U.S. family home before. Ele met everyone at the door with a smile and greeting that said *"Bienvenido. Ésta es su casa!"* (Welcome. Our house is your house!) She never put on airs and served simple food that she thought people would like. If she knew someone's favorite dish, she served it.

She never balked at my bringing someone to dinner until one

night when, on the spur of moment, I invited a Harvard tax law professor and two anthropologists from Texas to dinner. When we got home, Ele just stared at me. She had let our maid María go out and had planned a dinner for the two of us of Campbell's soup and sandwiches. She had almost no fresh fruit, vegetables, meat, or eggs in the refrigerator.

After she showed the guests into the living room, she asked what they would like to drink while she looked into the pantry to see what we could have for dinner. The anthropologists took tequila and the Harvard man wanted almost pure gin martini. I hustled up the liquor and mixers while Ele surveyed our limited supplies. Ele returned with a choice of canned pork and beans, green peas and rice. With the first drinks in hand, no one felt any pain, and the menu was approved without dissent.

The anthropologists nursed their drinks. The taxman gulped down three martinis in record time. I was running low on ice and the taxman said that he would fetch some from the kitchen where Ele was preparing our feast. As he crossed the dining room, he was aghast to see a huge spider emerge from behind a straw mat that Ele had attached to the wall above the buffet as an adornment. He rushed into the pantry to warn Ele of the menace. She went back with him into the dining room, looked at the spider and said, "Oh, that's Alfredo!" The stunned Harvard professor returned to the living room ready for another martini.

Ele had me set up TV tables in the living room so as not to interrupt our conversation and arrived in due time with our tea cart loaded with casserole bowls, plates, cutlery and paper napkins. She said, "We have oodles." One of the anthropologists said, "Pass the oodles!" We had a great dinner with lively conversation.

Ele also spent hours each week at the Salvador-U.S. Cultural Center studying Spanish. The director knew of her work in the Cultural Center in Mexico and occasionally asked her to lend a hand in an emergency.

One Tuesday when she was finishing Spanish class, the director asked whether she would step in and replace an ill instructor of an English class. Since she was familiar with the text, she agreed. The class, mainly of housewives, was delighted with her and asked that she come back. She filled in a couple of more times in the spring of 1954 before she went to California to save her family farms.

When she returned in July, the director asked her if she would take over a class in the fall. She agreed, provided she could add a personal touch to the course work. She noted that almost all of the students were housewives who were planning trips to the United States. She thought that they would like to know how to deal with salespeople in the stores, how to understand U.S. pricing and sizes and other details of getting around U.S. cities. The director said, "Fine, provided you cover the full assignment in the text first."

Ele conducted a course in the fall of 1954 and the spring of 1955 before we left on home leave. Her course was oversubscribed. When we returned from home leave for our second tour, Ele taught courses until we were transferred in 1957.

Word about Ele Tragen's classes made the rounds at the Deportivo and many of the wives of coffee planters and businessmen enrolled. That helped build a whole new range of contacts for the Tragens and gave us an opportunity to meet socially with some of those well beyond our official and ministry contacts.

One very wealthy lady who attended Ele's classes invited us to dinner at her mansion one evening. We arrived at 9:30 p.m. for a dinner; 9:30 p. m. was the normal time for society dinners to begin. The hostess was still bathing so we went home and returned at 10:30 p.m., as the other guests were arriving. The man who opened the door was someone we hired occasionally for a large cocktail party or dinner. I greeted him by name and asked whether his daughter had recovered from a serious illness. The hostess said to me, "In my house, guests do not converse with the servants." I was taken aback. Then, she added, "Well, that's what I should expect when I invite a communist." She certainly put a dent in my evening but I couldn't leave because Ambassador Hill and his wife had arrived, and a member of the embassy-USOM staff cannot, under protocol, leave before the ambassador leaves or is given permission by the ambassador to leave.

I was rankled by our hostess's words. I had no intention of her classifying me or my work as communist. Ele agreed. I telephoned our hostess and asked if I could call on her to clarify what I was doing and how it benefited her and her family. She agreed to have me come by one day the following week. I received a cool reception until I outlined our program at the ministry, with its focus on manpower development, increasing the workers' earning capability, and building a stronger middle class. She listened very intently and then summed up, "You are building a cushion between me and them. That isn't so bad."

We were never invited to her home again, but her teenaged son overheard the conversation. A short time later, he came to see me at the ministry to get more information about the program. Some years later, I was told that after graduating from university and business school, he became a leader for democratic development in El Salvador before being assassinated (by the far right or left, no one seemed to know).

A New Ambassador

President Eisenhower had appointed Ambassador Hill to Mexico. The change of ambassador is a time of anxiety for the official community in any post. We had been relatively close to the Hills. He had opened a dialogue with the minister of Labor and met with him regularly. He had assigned me the functions of an embassy reporting officer. His departure created a good deal of uncertainty for us.

Before the Hills left in September 1955, they invited us to a small dinner at the embassy. We had never been invited to dine at the embassy before. We had been to receptions and Ele had attended wives' meetings and teas. There were twelve at table, including three Salvadoran couples, the Deputy Chief of Mission (DCM) another embassy couple, and the Tragens. The ambassador toasted us for our help during his tour. Ele and I were lowest on the protocol totem pole and were seated at the center of the table, alongside the youngest Salvadoran couple present, the Roberto Quiñónezes; he was a Stanford graduate and director of the *Cervecería* (a brewery and soft drink plant). We got to know each other as we discussed our experiences at UC Berkeley and Stanford. It also opened the door for me to call on Roberto for advice and help in planning the manpower program.

In November, Thomas Mann was sworn in as the new ambassador. He was a respected career foreign service officer, fluent in Spanish, with extensive experience in Latin America; His last post was DCM in Guatemala following the overthrow of Arbenz. Our colleagues in Guatemala advised that he was an exacting taskmaster, a traditionalist, and conservative with serious questions about the foreign assistance program. No one seemed to know what his interest might be in labor or the labor program. So, it was with some trepidation that we awaited his arrival.

On the Manns' arrival in San Salvador, we accompanied all the official embassy and USOM community to the airport to receive them. There was a brief ceremony on the tarmac as the chief of protocol at the Ministry of Foreign Affairs welcomed them to the country. The official U.S. community waited in the diplomatic reception area. The ambassador and his wife Nancy then greeted us one by one and, when he reached Ele and me, he said that he looked forward to talking with us and had received good reports of our work. Ele looked at me and we both took a deep sigh of relief.

The following week, the ambassador asked me for a briefing on the labor situation and the status of the labor program. I prepared a one-page summary telling him that the labor movement was practically dormant and progress in implementing the labor program was spotty. The interview went very smoothly. The ambassador asked me to continue to report on labor union developments and expressed his personal interest in being kept informed on developments in the labor program, He then asked me to set up a private meeting with the minister, whom he had a special interest in meeting.

I called on the minister on my return from the embassy and arranged for him to meet privately with the ambassador at the residence. I don't know what they talked about or for how long. The ambassador never made an official visit to the ministry as Ambassador Hill had done, but each of them told me from time to time they had developed a mutually beneficial working relationship.

I learned a great deal from Ambassador Mann. He taught me how to write succinct reports: he took the time to go over some of my long-winded papers and reduced them to essentials. It was in one of those sessions that he challenged some of my premises and presumptions. We got into a very heated exchange in which I made some very indiscreet and personal comments. We left that evening on such a sour note that I told Ele on arriving home that I thought we would be asked to leave El Salvador. Instead, the next morning the ambassador called me to his office and calmly restated his views and explained the basis for them—and he was right. He had considered issues that had not entered my thinking. I apologized for my conduct the night before, and he accepted my apology. From that experience forward, whenever the ambassador or any of my colleagues raised questions about my thinking about an issue, I took time to think carefully before reacting.

A New Minister of Labor

For several weeks, following the postponed cocktail at my home, I went to the minister's office to try to talk to him. Neither his secretary nor Rogelio were in their offices. The vice minister and Moncho were also out of the building. No one to talk to! I was getting hot under the collar when I was advised that Mario Héctor Salazar had been sworn in as minister of the Economy and that the vice minister, Fernando Basilio "Nando" Castellanos, had been elevated to be the minister of Labor and Ramón "Moncho" Ávila as vice minister of Labor. Nando retained his political role as president of the PRUD and planned to run both the ministry and the party operations out of the same office. Rogelio Chavez was moving to the Ministry of Economy as the special assistant to his brother-in-law. Now, with whom should I talk?

Christmas season 1955–56 was not a particularly happy time for Josh, Tom, and me. The ministry was closed until the second week in January. Getting an appointment with the new minister wouldn't be easy as the political campaign was heating up and we presumed that he would be more concerned about PRUD candidates than helping us move the projects forward. We met with Bill Schenk at the USOM during the holidays, and agreed that there was little we could do until I met with the minister.

Ele and I met the new minister of the Economy at a Chávez family gathering. We had his mother-in-law's famous *gallo en chicha* and lots of good cheer. I asked Mario Héctor about his new job and expressed my concerns about not having Rogelio and him at the Ministry of Labor. He told me not to worry, that Nando and Moncho were as committed as he and Rogelio to moving the program forward. When I looked around, Mario Hector had slipped out.

It was mid-January before I got an appointment with Nando. He greeted me warmly and said that he was dedicating himself full-time to running the PRUD election campaign and that Moncho would be taking care of labor ministry business. When I started to raise the concerns that my colleagues and I had, he told me to talk to Moncho who, he assured me, would do everything possible to provide the staff and other resources we needed. He called Moncho and asked him to see me as soon as possible. I guess the meeting had lasted ten minutes.

Moncho saw me later that day and I told him that Josh, Tom, and I were frustrated by the lack of response by the ministry. I presented him with two short papers. The first from Josh laid out the personnel, space, and equipment support he needed for the initial phases of creating the employment service. The second from Tom indicated his immediate needs, including ministry counterparts, information from the private sector on their demand for semi-skilled and skilled workers, resources to hire training instructors, and a venue for conducting training courses.

We spent an hour discussing those needs and the limited resources of the ministry. Moncho agreed to seek the funds, space, and personnel needed, but left no doubt about his skepticism that the Budget Office would be supportive. He pointed out that he did not have the access to President Osorio that Mario Hector had and that most high-level attention was now focused on the election.

When I asked if he would sponsor a meeting with private sector business leaders he said no for two reasons: first, the political timing—it would be seen a ploy by the PRUD to win support for its candidate; and, second, he would not convene such a meeting without representation from the labor movement, and there was no legitimate labor organization with whom he could deal. He made it clear that, until after the election, he did not want my colleagues or I to initiate even private conversations with the business sector.

Then I suggested he reopen the dialogue with the Education Ministry on using the vocation schools for the new skills training program and training some instructors in the segmented training process. I offered to include funds in my annual budget to cover the costs of the training instructors from the vocational schools. Moncho said he understood my proposal but was not sure what he could do or when. He told me that his personal relations with the Education minister were not particularly close, but he would try to set up an appointment. He said that in the election environment it might take time to set up such a meeting. When I asked if he had a problem of my making an appointment for Tom to meet with Peter Allenman, the chief of the education *servicio*, Moncho saw no problem in that backdoor approach. Moncho closed the meeting with a promise to carefully review both papers and work with us on a plan to get the manpower activities moving forward. He did provide additional space and a couple of young technicians to work with Josh, but they fell far short of what Josh needed.

When Tom I met with Peter, he was not receptive. He saw the school's purpose as being to train a select group of young students each year to become journeymen in a limited number of vocations, but nothing more. We didn't give up, but went back several times to talk with the director, and he set up an appointment.

From February to June 1956, there was very little movement on either project. We essentially made work. I went on inspections and visited labor ministry-sponsored programs, such as the fishing cooperative in the Gulf of Fonseca, the labor recreation center in Las Palmas, and the seaside vacation facility in La Libertad. Most of the trips were just for the day, leaving at 6:00 a.m. and returning home by late evening.

Nando or Moncho were out on the campaign trail most of the time. All the ministry employees seemed to be political operatives in support of the PRUD candidate, Colonel José María Lemus, a close friend of Osorio's. He had little charisma and was not well known outside of the army. His opponents attacked him as not constitutionally qualified to run since his mother was Honduran by birth, and the Salvadoran Constitution required parents and grandparents of candidates for president be native-born Salvadorans. It was a lackluster campaign, and I cannot vouch for the legitimacy of the outcome. However, Lemus won and took office in September 1956.

We also had to deal with some other changes. Lloyd Prochnow accepted an assignment to help organize the labor statistics program in Pakistan. His replacement was very competent but lacked the enthusiasm that made Lloyd so special to Salvadorans and us.

In addition, several ministry technicians who had been trained in Puerto Rico either graduated from university or found better paying jobs in the private sector, and so we found ourselves training a second cadre.

Early on in that campaign year, Dr. Francisco "Chico" Lima invited me to conduct his course on comparative labor law at the National University for three months while he and his family made a trip to Europe. I was to cover the U.S. Taft-Hartley Law, the Mexican and Chilean labor codes, and the ILO Conventions. I was flattered that he thought my Spanish up to the task, and it gave me an opportunity to size up the class to see whether there were any potential candidates for vacancies at the ministry. I also consulted Moncho, since I knew that Chico was not a supporter of the PRUD and I did not want to become a *cause célèbre* during the campaign; Moncho saw no problem. I taught fifteen classes over three months, and had no difficulties with the students. Several I had seen at the ministry on various occasions but few of them appeared to be good additions to the ministry staff.

In early June, Washington asked me to go to Honduras to assess the prospects for a labor program there. Ambassador Mann and Mission Director Hackney encouraged me to accept the assignment. The minister and Moncho thought it would be useful for us to know what the neighboring country's labor program was. Ele agreed, but her teaching schedule at the Cultural Center had her tied up through July. So I made the trip alone in the second week of July.

The Honduran president and the U.S. ambassador had made the decision to invite me, but my arrival seemed to be a surprise for the labor minister. I suspect that Andy McClellan may have played a behind-the-scenes role. I talked to the small staff of the ministry and found that its principal substantive activity was to propose ILO conventions for the government to adopt. It had little enforcement capability, no labor statistics to speak of, and no staff for handling labor disputes. My briefings indicated that, whenever there was a labor dispute, political pressure was used to induce a settlement.

I also was taken to San Pedro Sula for discussions with business and textile leaders there and to Tela and La Ceiba to meet with leaders of the banana workers union. I also spent a morning at army headquarters to brief senior officers on the Salvador program. We met in the office of General Osvaldo López Arellano, reportedly the most powerful political leader in the country. I was asked a lot of questions after my presentation, but I did not sense much interest.

In my report on the mission, I noted the need for reorganizing the Labor Ministry and designing a new program, and emphasized the lack of interest in such action by the minister. I also expressed my feeling that there would soon be a serious confrontation between the United Fruit Company and its unions. My report did not recommend initiating a labor project.

A postscript: within months of my visit, another military coup in Honduras brought to power a Junta headed by General Osvaldo López Arellano. He was the ruling force in the country for a decade. He did not initiate a labor program. I guess I was not very persuasive.

On my return to San Salvador, the only topic of conversation was the impending inauguration of the new president, José María Lemus, which took place in September. Ele and I attended a reception at the country club, but were not invited to the official ceremonies or the inaugural ball. The president's message called for unity and austerity. Coffee prices were down and income from that crop was the source of 90–95 percent of foreign exchange earnings and tax revenue.

The new cabinet included Ramón "Moncho" Ávila as minister of Labor. Mario Héctor Salazar was named chief justice of the Supreme Court and Rogelio Chávez was appointed an associate justice of the Court.

Josh, Tom, and I were not optimistic that the new budget would include the resources needed to move the program forward. We had another setback when Peter Allemano completed his tour and was replaced by a specialist in primary education who had little interest in vocational training. Then, my close colleague Bill Schenk was transferred to Peru.

As soon as the new cabinet was sworn in, I went back to the minister with the same presentation I made when he became vice minister; I pressed him to act now in the early days of his incumbency. He agreed to consult the president to see how much support he had and what the prospects were for obtaining the necessary funds.

Based on estimates from Josh and Tom, I urged him to recommend an increase in his budget of one million *colones* (US$500,000) and ten new technical staff members.

A Different Agenda

On my return from the minister's office, I received a message from USOM Director Hackney to go to his office at once where I was told of my selection by Washington to attend a high level meeting in Chile on development planning. He had to advise Washington immediately as to my availability and wanted to consult with me before he answered. I said yes. The idea of spending a few days back in Chile was exciting, especially in face of what I considered foot-dragging by the minister.

That evening Ele and I made our respective plans. She was going to South Dakota and Tulare for a month to take care of family farm business. She would leave shortly before my departure for Chile, and would return before Thanksgiving. So, she prepared her letters to the bank in Aberdeen, South Dakota, and to her mother In Tulare. I wrote a couple of letters to our best man, who had returned with Barbara and the children to Chile, and to Augustín Edwards, with whose family I had lived for part of my student year in Santiago.

Ele flew to Aberdeen, met with her farm agent, visited the farm in Claremont and met with her tenant, Mr.Barnes. They looked at the crops, met with USDA specialists, agreed on a farm plan for 1957, and arranged for the sale of the remaining crops and examined the accounts for earlier crop sales. She was delighted with Mr. Barnes' attitude and his accounts. In two days she accomplished what she had thought would take a week. For her efforts, she doubled her mother and grandmother's income over the preceding year.

Then, in Tulare, she fired the ranch agent after finding his records incomplete and hired the Security Pacific Bank as his replacement, sold the cotton crop, met with USDA crop specialists, hired a new farm tenant, consulted the local irrigation district about greater access to canal water, and discussed county tax and other regulations with local officials that might affect the farm. When she returned to San Salvador she had more than doubled her family's California ranch income over the preceding year.

My trip to Chile lasted ten days. I found out very quickly that the real reason for my trip was a possible transfer to replace the labor officer working in Chile, Willis Whited, who was retiring the next year. I was advised that I had a schedule of meetings outside the conference that included the USOM director and assistant director, the assistant director of the Chilean Productivity Center (the Chilean government agency promoting more efficient business practices), and the embassy labor attaché.

The conference focused on sophisticated development theories that had little relevance to the problems I was dealing with in San Salvador. We needed at least a decade of sustained economic progress before any of the subject matter made much practical sense. The lectures covered the rebuilding of Europe and the reviving of public and private institutions there. Very little attention was paid to building new institutions and creating cadres of managers, technicians and skilled workers from the existing pool of unskilled workers. Based on my observation there as a student, Chile was further developed than El Salvador; but I questioned whether the material presented was relevant to its immediate needs.

After the conference ended, Willis briefed me on the apprentice training program he set up with the Chilean Chambers of Industry. He had applied German and U.S. models for on-the-job training for mechanics, carpenters, electricians and metal workers. The apprentices, usually aged fourteen or fifteen, earned 50 percent of the going wage for a journeyman. Each year as the apprentice learned and passed his course work, he would be promoted and his pay increased by 10 percent. At the end of five years, with his apprenticeship certificate in hand, his wage would be that of a journeyman.

On paper, the programs seemed fine. In practice, very few apprentices reached graduation at the end of the training cycle. Willis complained that almost every employer in the program fired the apprentices at the end of the third or fourth year, and then hired a new batch of apprentices to start all over at 50 percent of the base wage. The frustrated apprentices had no certificate or other recognition of their three or four years of learning at a reduced wage, because only at the completion of the apprenticeship did the program award a certificate or other recognition. Willis was bitter at the employers and the apprentices were bitter at the program.

Those results led the Productivity Center to ask Willis to revise the traditional five-year program. I asked Willis why the program did not award some recognition at the end of each year or segment of training. Willis was reluctant to introduce such awards then because they were not part of the approved international apprenticeship practices. He agreed that new approaches were needed, but he rejected their being called apprenticeship.

When I met with the labor attaché, we discussed the labor scene in Chile. I had followed the development of the labor movement in Chile and the pro-Soviet political orientation of the *Central Única de Trabajadores* (CUTCH). I had studied the Labor Code during my studies in 1945–46. We had a wide-ranging discussion about a potential USOM program.

The last two days in Chile, I spent at the USOM, being briefed on the work of the Chilean Productivity Center and meeting with Chilean and U.S. technicians. On my last afternoon, the assistant USOM director, Oliver Sauce, told me that the USOM would be requesting my assignment to Chile when Willis retired in 1957. He asked me to start thinking about how to broaden the labor program to better support the Productivity Center.

I took advantage of those ten days to discuss with Chilean friends the state of affairs. My best man, Fernando Walker, and his wife and mother, gave me a dreary picture of how difficult life was for landed gentry in a period of hyperinflation. Every day the Chilean peso was losing value against the U.S. dollar and that made the inputs Fernando needed to run his sheep farm more expensive. If Ele and I were transferred to Chile, we would be insulated from the problem because we would be paid in dollars.

From Augustín "Doonie" Edwards, who had become the publisher of the premier newspaper of Chile, *El Mercurio*, I heard the plans of the Chilean Liberal and Conservative Parties to back a single candidate for the next presidential election, either Hernán or Jorge Alessandri. Some young lawyers with whom I had studied at the University of Chile Law School told me about the emerging leftist coalition to back Salvador Allende and the equivocal position of the Christian Democratic Party. Their expectation was that the retiring president would support Allende.

On my flight back to San Salvador, my mind was full of conflicting thoughts. I really didn't want to leave the labor program in El Salvador, but I was also intrigued by the new challenges in Chile.

The Remaining Months

As I settled back into my routine, the center of attention was on how slowly President Lemus was getting his team up and running.

Moncho Ávila as labor minister advised me that he expected presidential support for the manpower program. He was now the only member of the original senior ministerial team still on the job. Fernando Basilio "Nando" Castellanos (the former minister) was not appointed to a senior position; he had been much criticized for his direction of the PRUD during the recent campaign, but he held onto his post as president of the party. Mario Héctor, chief justice of the Supreme Court, and Rogelio, as an associate justice, were pretty well isolated from policy making and told me that they felt it inappropriate to overtly help Moncho move the program forward.

Shortly after my return, the minister asked me to work with him on a request to the Salvadoran Budget Office for funds for the manpower project for the next three years. In preparing the document, Moncho was cautiously optimistic, but he reminded me that he did not enjoy the same relationship with Lemus that Mario Héctor had with Osorio.

At the USOM, the departure of Bill Schenk limited my ability to make things happen there, even though I had an excellent relationship with the director, but he was not a hands-on manager and left those chores to his immediate staff, who were more attuned to the needs of the *servicios* than to mine. The *servicios* could plan two or three years of execution with commitments by both governments that assured the flow of funds. My problems with obtaining budget commitments from the government led USOM staff to question the need for additional U.S. budget inputs. It was a vicious circle: I could not use the carrot of assured U.S. support to induce the Salvadoran government to increase its budgetary and personnel commitments.

In December, Moncho made his presentation for funding and was very disappointed when he received no response to the request.

I tried to shield Josh and Tom from the problems and in our weekly meetings urged them to move ahead. I was deeply concerned, especially since I knew that my second tour in country would end in the summer and I was likely to be transferred to Chile. I did not want to leave the consequences to my colleagues and successors.

I had another diversion in mid-January when I was assigned to go to Panama to advise the minister of Labor on the possible reorganization of her ministry. The minister was Cecilia Remón, the widow of assassinated President José Antonio Remón, the populist National Guard leader who swept to the presidency on a wave of anti-Yankee sentiments. Since its independence in 1903, Panama had been ruled by a succession of presidents from its first families. Remón broke that train. He was assassinated by gunmen in 1955 at the local horseracing track, rumor had it, over a busted drug deal. After his death, his widow had become a major player on the political scene, and speculation was high that she would run for president at the next election. So, when she approached U.S. Ambassador Harrington for assistance in reorganizing her ministry, he asked Washington for help. I got the call.

February was to be my month in Panama. Ele's classes didn't start until March, so she agreed to join me in mid-February for her first visit to that country. Word got around quickly that I was going to Panama. So I sat down with Josh and Tom to tell them how concerned I was with the situation at the ministry, and found out that they were already aware. Their Salvadoran co-workers had been keeping them informed about their own concerns and the brick walls they had been running into since the Lemus administration had been inaugurated. Before I left, I met with Moncho and urged him to continue to press for the resources needed to move the manpower project forward.

On my arrival in Panama, Ambassador Harrington briefed me on the assignment and the political situation in country. The next morning I met the minister. She told me that she was the "tri-minister:" Health, Labor, and Social Security. She called them the centers of government that served the people as she pointed to the piles of papers surrounding her. She had a USOM adviser working with her to improve the operations of the health service, and she wanted me to provide her with a blueprint for improving her labor unit.

She gave me *carte blanche* to look into every aspect of its program and report back to her by the last week of February so that she could recast her budget request for the next fiscal year to reflect the changes, additions, or new directions that I propose. She turned me over to her director of Labor. I didn't see her again until my last day in Panama when I presented my written recommendations.

What I found was a shell of a ministry. The labor legislation was minimal and few labor standards—wages and hours, industrial safety, and hygiene—were in place. It nominally had a labor inspection service, a labor statistics section, and some other units. I spent the first week doing desk audits of key jobs and reading about the history and economy of Panama. I found one of its important activities was the issuance of ninety-day permits for entertainers to perform in Panama, for which the ministry received a fee from each artist and a fee from the establishment employing them.

Panama was not like any other country in Latin America. Historically, it had been a trading hub for transshipping the gold and silver of Peru to Spain and Spanish products to the colonies of South America. Its population was repeatedly decimated by yellow fever until the building of the Canal and U.S. efforts to wipe out the mosquitoes carrying the virus. Panama had been a province of Colombia until its independence in 1903 when the U.S. fleet prevented the Colombians from suppressing the rebellion.

In 1957, it was a country of a million people, most of whom lived along the path of the Panama Canal. Commerce and services, linked to Canal operations and chandlery services for ships, dominated the country's economy, with almost no significant industrial, manufacturing, or mining operations. Only in Chiriquí and Bocas del Toro Provinces were there significant agricultural (bananas) and cattle raising operations. The primary sources of income to finance Panama's budget came from an annual payment from the U.S. for the use of the Canal Zone and various use and sales taxes.

By the time Ele arrived in the middle of the second week, I was scratching my head trying to shape a report. So, I was very pleased to have someone to talk to.

Ele had a problem of her own to deal with. Right after I left El Salvador, the wife of the Italian ambassador invited Ele to tea and asked her to deliver a package to a member of the Italian Embassy in Panama City. Since there were rumors of Italian involvement in the heroin trade in Central America, Ele asked what was in the package. The ambassador's wife showed her a skirt with large pleats drawn together in a series of small knots large enough to hold small packets of something or other. Ele declined but the wife insisted and delivered the package to Ele at the airport. Ele had no alternative but to bring it with her.

We reported our concerns to the embassy security officer, and he raised a delicate political problem. The U.S. and Italian Embassies were working closely together on tracking heroin shipments in the region and wanted to avoid a possible confrontation. Ele proposed the solution. She would deliver the package not to the officer whose name she had been given but to the Italian ambassador's wife. She would ask Artie Souza, our friend from I House, to accompany her to the Italian Embassy, ask to see the ambassador's wife and innocently deliver the package. If it contained any prohibited item—either dirty money or narcotics—the Italians would find it out for themselves. That is what happened, and the Italian ambassador to El Salvador was recalled by his government within weeks of the incident.

Ele had a great time in Panama City; she rode the brightly painted buses, or *chivas*, all over the city and its outskirts, and was often the only *gringa* on the vehicle. She talked to people about life and living conditions, and found a pervading love-hate relationship with the United States. She told me each night about her adventures and the kindness of the people who would help her out if she got lost exploring different areas of the city. While my USOM colleagues were concerned that Ele would get into trouble, she was never worried.

In the third week, I wrote a detailed plan for reorganizing the labor inspection service, strengthening the labor statistics service, and revising the activities of other offices. I did not include a section on manpower because the situation was so different from the one in El Salvador. The Canal administration had been training a skilled work force for generations.

My last Friday in Panama, while drafting the report, I found that I needed some additional information at the ministry. So I arranged for a car to take me to the office even though it was closed to the public on Fridays (since that was the day when applications by entertainers were reviewed). All of the office doors were shut tight, while the labor inspectors interviewed each entertainer one at a time and each entertainer provided intimate personal demonstrations of their skills. I quietly picked up the data I needed and left the inspectors to do their job.

I delivered my report to the minister the following Tuesday afternoon. She listened very carefully, and went over the organization charts and description of duties. She asked penetrating questions and thanked me. She resigned from office shortly thereafter, and I never knew if any of my recommendations were acted on.

The last few months in El Salvador were frustrating. Nothing seemed to move on the manpower front. I ran a training program for labor inspectors. The labor statistics adviser made his annual visit to evaluate progress and select an additional trainee to go to Washington. I visited the regional offices in San Miguel and Santa Ana. This time I did not stay at local hotels but in the homes of people we had befriended over the four years. Wherever I went in the Republic, I had friends who seemed pleased to offer their hospitality.

However, I was marking time. Instead of the excitement of opening an employment office or setting up job training courses, I was waiting for the minister to tell Josh, Tom, and me that the government was ready to provide the resources needed to move forward. I found that even getting an appointment with the minister was not easy. Moncho seemed harried by the political environment and, as he later told me, his isolation from the decision-making process. And while he promoted talented ministry personnel to be his aides, they did not have the savvy and connections that distinguished Moncho and Rogelio when they were Mario Hector's aides.

I don't believe that I understood at the time how complicated a job Moncho found himself in. He was directing a ministry in which his boss, the president of El Salvador, was showing little or no interest. Moncho wanted to implement the manpower program that he and I had worked so intently to shape and get started. Only on the eve of my departure from San Salvador did he tell me how disappointed he was that he could not follow through.

It was early June when I received a letter from Washington advising me that the paperwork was being processed for a transfer to Chile, but that it might take a few months. Ele and I were to take home leave and plan to return to El Salvador while the papers were processed. We made our plans accordingly.

12

Europe and On to Chile

A s we prepared for our second home leave, Ele reminded me that we had not been to Europe yet and that, since our finances were on a more solid basis, she would like to take advantage of a Sabena Airline deal of a land tour lasting eighteen days and visiting twelve countries: England, Netherlands, Belgium, Luxembourg, Germany, Switzerland, Liechtenstein, Austria, Italy, San Marino, Monaco, and France. The price was right and we had enough annual leave, plus our home leave, to visit Europe as well as our families in California. When I queried the ambassador, USOM Director Hackney, and Harold Walker in Washington, they all said, "Go for it!"

Ele found a spectacular air package from El Salvador via KLM from San José, Costa Rica to London and back to Washington from Brussels that cost almost the same as the regular airfare from San Salvador to Washington. However, the USOM administrative officer said that he had to route us to Washington, no exceptions. This was the same bureaucrat who had forced us to ask Jorge Molina to leave our home when he was in need of a place to live. The result was that we had to buy a separate, and much more expensive, round-trip from Washington to London. I later learned that the State Department routinely authorized such adjustments in travel plans, provided the staff member paid any additional cost.

In Washington, Harold Walker had lined up a full program, with visits to senior officials of the International Cooperation Agency (ICA), State Department, the Department of Labor, and the AFL-CIO. But first we had to pass our medicals. Ele had no problem, but my X-rays found a suspicious abnormality on the pancreas. I was told that additional tests were needed and that those tests could only be made at the Bethesda Naval Medical Center and would require a week's internment. I explained that we had purchased our tickets for Europe and the director of State Medical Services agreed that we could go to Europe before my checking into Bethesda.

Our future was up in the air while I made my rounds. ICA and the Department of Labor advised that USOM Chile had agreed to my replacing Willis and asked me to develop a new labor program. At the State Department, Ben Stephansky, who had replaced John Fishburne as the Latin American labor adviser, briefed me on the labor movement and the labor conditions in Chile. He urged me to work closely with the embassy labor attaché in developing a trade union training program that combined the resources of State and ICA.

On Thursday, Harold Walker accompanied me to a meeting with Serafino Romualdi at the AFL-CIO headquarters on 16th Street. After briefing me on AFL-CIO relations with the Chilean labor movement, he took me to meet the president of the AFL-CIO, George Meany, whose office was just across Lafayette Square from the White House. Mr. Meany talked of his concerns about the growing communist influence in Latin American labor and of his commitment to use the resources of the American Labor Movement to counter it. He wished me well and offered his support. I was flabbergasted!

Friday afternoon, hours before we were to leave for Europe, the chief of the ICA Labor Division met with me and confirmed that I was to be assigned to Chile just as soon as medical clearance was received. So, despite concerns about my pancreas, Ele and I left for Europe with the assurance that we would have a paycheck for the next couple of years, barring some catastrophic medical problem.

Also during that week in Washington, I was fitted for a new and more powerful Zenith hearing aid. One feature that was especially important was that it facilitated my use of the telephone, and for the first time in nearly twenty years I was able to use that tool of modern society with some degree of competence.

Washington to New York to London! Our first flight across the Atlantic! We flew all night and landed at Manchester where my uncle Morris (my father's older brother) and his second wife Sophie met us at the airport. It was a partly sunny day in early September—and my aunt told us that this was their summer. We later boarded a British Airways plane for the flight to London where we were met by the Sabena tour director, a German lady still recovering emotionally from the devastation of World War II. We stayed in the Prince of Wales Hotel in Kensington—and what an interesting maze it was! The hotel was made up of series of adjacent town houses connected by hallways on each floor cut through common walls between houses, with stairs installed to accommodate floors not always on the same level. Modest but comfortable!

That night, at a typical English roast beef dinner, we met the thirty people who were to be our companions for the next eighteen days. They were from all over the United States, most were older than Ele and me. A few of the men had been to Europe as GIs, but the rest were first-time visitors like us. We were tired from the flight but eager to begin the adventure. Early to bed! And that is when we had our first introduction to English toilet paper, Silver Silk, which Ele henceforth referred to as "British sandpaper." Our first night also introduced us to the then British custom of turning on the electricity by placing a metal slug given us by the hotel management into a device outside our bedroom. We stayed at the Prince of Wales several times in future years and delighted in its capacity to amuse us.

Our tour around London showed that many scars of the German bombing were still to be healed. The city was gray and smoggy, but we loved seeing the sights and getting a taste of the city where Shakespeare and Dickens lived and wrote. Hyde Park and Buckingham Palace, the Houses of Parliament, the city, the Strand, Drury Lane and the Flower Market, Fortnum & Masons, and Kew Gardens whirled before us. Ele scolded me for complaining that we didn't have the opportunity to see more than the exterior of the British Museum or the Tate Gallery and just tootled past Trafalgar Square without a walk through Soho.

Then we were off to Amsterdam. We had the canal tour, a visit to the flower market, an hour or so at the Rijksmuseum, and a drive to the Royal Palace at The Hague. I kept complaining about the organization of the tour and its scheduling. Ele read me the riot act. She said, "We are on vacation. You are on Sabena's tour. Sit back, shut up, and enjoy it. You are not responsible for anything, so relax." And I did, from that moment forward.

Then began an array of new experiences as we bused down to Cologne and Bonn, took the Rhine steamer to Heidelberg past the Lorelei, the Romantic Road to Rothenberg, and on to Lake Constance. My one bout with upset stomach befell me on the trip en route to Lake Constance, and on arrival, I ran to the rest room. It was a series of stools in a stall-less open room, with Brunhilde seated at the head of the class, watching the captive users. My demands were so pressing that I just took the stool she assigned me, humbly took the small amount of TP that she offered me and paid her for the use of the facilities. I was never less modest in my life.

Then we moved on to picturesque Lucerne and Interlaken with incredible vistas on a wonderful sunny day. The next day we were in Vaduz where the prince of Liechtenstein himself greeted and escorted us through his shop of souvenirs from all over Western Europe. On we drove to Innsbruck and through the Brenner Pass to Venice, with which we fell in love at first sight. We enjoyed every gondola and vaporetto ride around the Grand Canal and through the lesser waterways almost as much as strolling through St. Marks Square and the Doge's Palace. In 1957, there weren't tens of thousands of tourists at every turn, so we could window-shop at leisure and chat with the not-so-busy shop owners.

Two days later, we were en route to Rome through Siena and Assisi; we were enchanted with the palace and winding cobblestone streets of Siena! Then we had two days in Rome where we stayed in a beautiful, but rundown hotel next to the Pantheon—now a five star luxury facility that I can't afford. On the first day, we toured from the Forum to the Vatican, climbed the Spanish Steps, and enjoyed the Borghese Gardens. The second day we took the train to Naples to visit a friend, who had been transferred from San Salvador to the Consulate there; her apartment was on a hill overlooking the Bay of Naples—and with such a view who needed food?

Then we were in Florence absorbing the excitement of the Ponte Vecchio and the incredible art works and sheer beauty of the museums and palaces. The opulence of the palaces contrasted sharply with the evidence of hard times and poverty we saw on the streets outside of the city center; we saw the causes for the appeal of the far left in Tuscan politics. All too soon we were back on our bus, racing through San Remo and the Italian Riviera, before spending a day in Monaco where Ele and I became bon vivant gamblers, losing all of $10 apiece on the roulette wheel! Next came a day in Cannes and Nice among the not so affluent international society of the 1950s, but we loved walking the streets we had seen in Cary Grant movies. Then we turned north to Avignon, the charming city that once hosted the Papacy in exile, sped through Lyons, and stopped for lunch in a small farming town, where I ate the best meal I can remember: country ham in a gruyere sauce.

In Paris, we stayed at the sprawling commercial Hotel République on the Place de la République, which was far from the elite Place de la Concorde. We toured the city for two days, taking in all the monumental buildings and boulevards, the Louvre, the Sacré-Cœur, the Eiffel Tower, and the Left Bank. Ele and I walked along the Seine by day and took in the revues at El Lido and Moulin Rouge by night. Those statuesque showgirls were unlike any either of us had seen before! Touring Paris in those dreary post-war days was far from the esthetic delights that make it the City of Lights today. There was grime and poverty at almost every corner. It had a feel of sadness amid its faded beauty and elegance.

Our final bus ride took us to Luxembourg and Brussels. Our tour ended at the Grande Place with a farewell dinner at one of those incredible bistros on a side street. Our fellow travelers took off for the States while we stayed another week in Belgium and Holland. We took the train to Bruges and walked its lovely red brick streets before returning to Amsterdam, where we explored the canals and byways and took train and tram rides to explore other parts of the country, such as Rotterdam from whence my mother's grandfather had migrated to San Francisco. Our last night we feasted at the famous Indonesian restaurant called Bali.

California

When we boarded Sabena for the trip back to New York, we were two very satisfied little kids who wanted to go back for more. We dreamed of an assignment to Europe that would allow us lots of time to savor more of the Old World.

When we arrived in New York, Ele went on to San Francisco to visit for a week or so with my parents while I checked into the Naval Hospital for my tests. I was given a room on the executive floor that I shared with another foreign service officer, much older than I; he had been diagnosed with anal cancer. I had very little time with my roommate as the hospital had me scheduled for one test after another. Never has my poor body been subjected to a more thorough investigation, the low point occurring when I was strapped nude into an examining contraption and my rear end hoisted toward the ceiling and my head toward the floor. Oh, what an experience!

After five days, the chief physician on my case advised me that there was nothing wrong with my pancreas—perhaps a shadow had distorted the X-ray. He released me and told me that I could leave the hospital as soon as I had my bag packed. Using my new Zenith hearing aid, I called Harold Walker at ICA and asked him if I needed to check in. He said no, and we agreed that I should catch the next available plane to San Francisco. He said that he would call Ele for me and tell her my plans. I caught a shuttle to downtown Washington, and went straight to the Capitol Hilton Hotel where United had its downtown office, rushed in through a side door and almost knocked down Queen Elizabeth II of England as she and Prince Philip came down the stairway after a lunch in her honor. How security has changed in our lifetime!

United had a seat available on its flight that afternoon and arranged for me to take the next bus to National Airport. I called Ele and my parents. They said my brother-in-law would meet me at the airport in San Francisco and take me to my parents' flat.

This was not a happy time for my family. My sister Jackie had died the year before. My father had become afflicted with Parkinson's disease. With our new assignment abroad, we sensed that this might be our last visit with both my parents. Aunty Paula had moved to my brother-in-law's to take care of my niece and nephew. Mother tried to make it as festive a week as she could before we flew down to Tulare for a week there. Mother had all her friends to dinner. We had an elegant lunch at the Stanford Court Apartments where we reminisced with Uncle Mo and Aunt Tillie Harris about their visit with us in Mexico. We also saw I House friends at a dinner in our honor at one of San Francisco Chinatown's most renowned

Chinese restaurants that I House friends, Rene and Randy Sui, had purchased. Jean and Carlos Bee came down from Sacramento: Carlos was then the Speaker *preterm* of the California Assembly. But, our primary attention was to my parents, seeing how difficult life had become for them.

My father died before I was to see him again. Rene and Randy died in a plane crash over the Pacific en route to his family home in Tahiti. And it was our last visit with my cousins, Mo and Tillie Harris. In many ways, it was like the closing chapter of my San Francisco life.

We spent the following week in Tulare, with one round of dinners after another. Ele's mother's friends made us very welcome, as did Mimi and Buzz Hoffman. We spent a day in the nearby town of Hanford with Ele's cousin, Jim Leonard, his wife Jean, and their two boys; Jim had substituted for Ele's late father at our wedding. The week went by very fast. Ele stayed on for another couple of weeks to take care of farm business, including a fast trip to Aberdeen, South Dakota.

While we were in Tulare, Harold Walker called to advise that we were to return to El Salvador and await orders to proceed to Chile. The medical clearance had just been received but there had not been enough time for ICA Personnel to prepare the necessary papers for our transfer. He thought that it would be another couple of weeks before the orders could be cut and cleared through the security system.

Farewell, Dear Salvador

I returned to El Salvador alone and discovered the country very uneasy. President Lemus was even more unpopular with his fellow military officers and the PRUD party than when we left on vacation. The ministry was at a standstill. Moncho told us that he was as frustrated as Josh and Tom. At USOM, we also had a major shakeup. With the Schenks in Peru, a new senior staff, not particularly of his choice, now surrounded Director Hackney.

Ele and I had been extremely fortunate. As the old saying goes, timing is everything. It is so important to act when the circumstances are favorable. In foreign assistance, the ultimate decision rests with the host government. One can propose and advise, but it is up to those with whom you are working to take or not take action. In late 1957, El Salvador was, unfortunately, in the throes of a pre-coup that would paralyze decision-making and undo many of the forward steps taken in the preceding years. Lemus was turned out shortly after we were transferred to Chile. The new generals had different priorities. Much of what we had been helping to build fell by the wayside, but most of the people we had trained stayed active in Salvadoran life, and many remained friends during their lifetimes.

Ele returned in early October 1957. We received orders to go to Chile later that month. We packed up with considerable sadness because we did appreciate the country and its people. We had been from the Ahuachapán border with Guatemala to the Gulf of Fonseca, from La Palma to La Libertad, from Lake Ocotepeque to Lake Suchtitlán. There was no Department in the country we had not visited and worked in. We had been to coffee, sugar, and cotton plantations, and had visited most of the manufacturing and processing plants. We had been present when the new tourist hotel was inaugurated on Cerro Verde and saw the eruptions of the Izalco volcano suddenly come to an end, after hundreds of year being known as the "the lighthouse of the Pacific." Above all, we had made friends throughout the country and felt that we had made a contribution to its development.

Our travel orders read, "Proceed to Santiago, Chile via Panama as soon as possible. Your furniture will be sent to storage in New Orleans since the USOM/Chile will provide you with basic furniture for a two-bedroom house." Packing up was a difficult chore, of which Ele took full charge, Ele separated out about 1,500 pounds of linens, lamps, decorations and other items to go south with us. We sent about 3,000 pounds of our Mexican furniture to storage. Our car would be shipped separately and would reach Santiago by Christmas.

Salvadoran friends, the embassy, and the USOM all gave us going-away parties. Our final farewell was hosted by the minister of Labor, the chief justice of the Supreme Court and the president of the PRUD. They made all the arrangements, but forgot to tell us. Mario Héctor arrived at 9:30 p.m. on the night before our departure for Chile, to find that we were in bed. Josefina roused us and we dressed in a flurry. We were given a large party at the Club Salvadoran, with all of the colleagues with whom we had worked for more than four years. The club was as full as it had been when we attended the British ambassador's celebration of Elizabeth II's coronation. Our farewell was a truly bittersweet occasion.

13

Chile: A Different Experience

On our arrival in Santiago, we were met by the USOM administrative officer and taken to a small suite in the Hotel Santa Lucía in downtown Santiago. It was centrally located at San Antonio and Huérfanos Streets, just two blocks from the USOM office and convenient to all the theaters, shops, government offices, and good restaurants. But, like all the buildings in the center of the city, it was covered in coal dust. The city was grimy and all our white effects soon took on a grey pallor.

While I checked into work, Ele made protocol calls on the wives of the ambassador, the USOM director, and senior embassy and USOM officials. Then, with the USOM housing clerk and the wife of our best man, Barbara Walker, she started to search for a house or apartment as our new home away from home.

We knew that Chile was in the depths of the worst inflation in its history. We thought our dollars would go a long way, but there were no houses on the market that we could afford on our housing allowance. All the prospective landlords demanded payment in dollars, not in Chilean pesos. The houses in our price range were so rundown that we could not afford to repair them. Some had broken sinks and bathtubs; others had kitchens that needed total overhauls. Landlords were so strapped for cash that they could not make the essential repairs. One of the few that we thought had potential had been robbed four times in two years when occupied by a recently transferred embassy family. After several frustrating weeks, she had me accompany her on visits to the some of the most promising in reputable residential areas of the city, and we agreed that there was not one available that we would enjoy living in.

After three months of frustration, Ele proposed that we rent an available suite on the sixth floor of the Hotel Santa Lucía, three floors above our temporary quarters. The building was modern, with elevator service. Frankly, the space was a bit cramped and drab: it was painted an off-white that had taken on a grayish tint from the coal smoke, but it was a better deal than any of the houses or apartments we had seen. It had none of the grace or charm of our homes in El Salvador, but we signed a contract for one year, renewable for a second year, to be paid in pesos, at the dollar equivalent of $600 a month. It was unfurnished, with carpeting and drapes, and consisted of a living room, dining room, two bedrooms, two baths, and a kitchen. The hotel threw in maid service and other amenities. It was within our allowance, and the mission provided us with the basic furniture from its warehouse. The hotel management arranged for a garage three blocks away that would cost about a dollar a day. We were settled, but without the clean air of San Salvador—and Josefina.

Our apartment was not really designed for entertaining. The living room and dining room were box-like 9' x 12' areas with smallish windows at one end. The kitchen was a galley with an old-fashioned gas stove and an oven that functioned in fits and starts. We had coal heating and no air-conditioning. Santiago's climate was usually temperate, very much like Los Angeles; but there were spells of 100 degree weather in the summer when the apartment, with no cross-ventilation, became stifling.

The atmosphere in Santiago from the outset was one of stress, as was evident from our discussions with Chilean friends and colleagues. The topic of conversation was inflation and the gyrations in peso prices for everything they used in their daily lives. Prices for food staples such as milk, bread, and vegetables varied each day in tandem with the declining value of the Chilean peso against the U.S. dollar. Meat, poultry, and fish were extremely costly, in peso terms. One week, a can of Carnation evaporated milk cost us 20 percent more in Chilean pesos on Friday than it had on Monday. For those of us who were paid in dollars, we didn't feel the pain of our Chilean colleagues and friends since the Chilean pesos declined in value to the dollar as sharply as prices rose.

As a result, we found that our many of our friends, like my best man and his family, kept solvent by playing the exchange game, converting pesos into dollars, borrowing in pesos and repaying the peso loans with the profit made on the rise in the value of the dollar against the peso. The impact of inflation permeated every dimension of civic life throughout our stay in Chile and we felt the pain and uncertainty that it inflicted on the people with whom we lived and worked. That stress colored our reaction to this tour of duty.

Getting Started on the Job

My first weeks on the job were spent getting oriented to an entirely new work environment. My office was in the USOM headquarters, not the Ministry of Labor. My assignment was under the agreement between the government of Chile and the U.S. government to support the Chilean Productivity Center. My line of command was to the director of the center, but my immediate supervisor was the USOM director. I had no direct connection with the Chilean ministry of Labor. The minister had a representative on the board of the Productivity Center, but was not considered a significant policy maker. How different from my relationship with the minister in El Salvador!

On day one in the office, I met with the assistant USOM director, Oliver "Ollie" Sause. He reiterated many of the points he had made during my 1956 visit. He emphasized that he expected me to help the mission find new approaches to overcoming manpower and labor bottlenecks that were impeding industrial productivity and long-term socioeconomic development. He told me to take the next few weeks to study the labor situation and become acquainted with the Productivity Center, and to propose a new program to replace the existing apprenticeship project.

Early on, I requested an appointment with the minister of Labor. I wanted to develop a working relationship with ministry officials and offer to coordinate my activities with its programs. I was received by the director general, the highest-ranking career official in the ministry. He quickly made it clear that the ministry received its external assistance from the International Labor Organization (ILO) and had not requested any from the United States. There was a definite anti-U.S. tinge to the discussion. It ended with a comment that my assignment was part of the development work of the Productivity Center, not that of the Ministry of Labor. Clearly my relations with the ministry would be minimal.

So, in preparing my work plan, I focused on the Chilean development strategy and the labor situation in the country. I received briefings from key managers of the Productivity Center on the Chilean development strategy and programs. I read legislation, policy papers, and reports on technical services available to Chilean enterprises, especially in manufacturing. I met with economists and technicians at the Chilean Development Corporation (CORFO) and the Productivity Center. I was impressed by the sophistication and quantity of CORFO and Productivity Center economists and technicians. In Chile there were scores, while in El Salvador there had been only a handful; if the Salvadoran Ministry of Labor had been blessed with half a dozen of them, the manpower program would have readily been implemented.

Chile had a state-directed economic strategy similar to the strategy popular in much of Western Europe and the USSR. The centerpiece of that strategy was import substitution, with a goal of economic self-sufficiency through in-country production of the agricultural and manufacturing products that Chile needed for domestic consumption. CORFO was created to expand and diversify the economy, not to increase the efficiency and profitability of those mining, industrial, and agricultural sectors in which Chile had a natural advantage.

In those initial discussions with CORFO managers, I sensed that profitability of operations seemed to have a lower priority than creating jobs for the increasingly urbanized Chilean population. The mission of the Productivity Center was to support CORFO by providing technical services to Chile's business sector (especially manufacturing), to improve output, raise productivity, and improve profit margins. In answer to my questions, I found that little attention had been given to manpower or labor dimensions of the equation.

To finance this strategy and program, Chile heavily taxed exports, including copper and other traditional mineral and agricultural products that were the lifeblood of the economy. The government placed high tariffs on imports to protect infant industries.

Most of the revenues from export taxes and tariffs were channeled to CORFO, which provided loans and other capital support to the new import substitution enterprises

As I read scores of papers on plans for new industries, including basic industries like steel mills and industrial plants such as automobile factories, I thought that many did not make economic sense, and would require ever greater inputs of increasingly scarce government revenues and declining foreign exchange earnings to support industrial projects with little promise of long-term profitability.

I discussed my conclusions with colleagues in the USOM and other U.S. economists working in Chile, including Sy Rottenberg from the University of Chicago Economics Department, one of Milton Friedman's "Chicago boys" advising at Catholic University, and Joe Grunwald from the Economics Department of Arthur Burns at Columbia University, who was a faculty adviser at the University of Chile. They were critical of the import substitution strategy and pointed out that in practice, few of the new infant industries had achieved the necessary economy of scale to compete outside their highly protected home market. They saw the ever-higher protective tariffs as the trigger for the rising prices for goods and services in the Chilean market. Coupled with the post-World War II decline in commodity prices for raw materials, they saw Chile "wasting" its declining foreign exchange earnings on keeping inefficient infant industries going, and deepening the terrible inflation that the Chilean people were suffering. They felt that reforming the Chilean development model took priority over manpower and training programs.

In my conversations with most industrialists and businessmen, I heard criticism of some government policies mixed with support for CORFO policies and high protective tariffs. Many had views diametrically opposed to those of the U.S. economists working with the two principal universities of the country. They usually described a paternalistic structure in their relationship with their work force; they generally supported government-mandated social benefits in lieu of wage increases; they gave little pririty to improving worker productivity.

I also consulted economists at the UN Economic Commission

for Latin America (ECLA in English and CEPAL in Spanish), which was headquartered in Santiago. Its director, Dr. Raul Prebisch, was a staunch supporter of the Chilean strategy and advocate of import substitution. He and his top aides, economists Enrique Iglesias of Uruguay (later president of the Inter-American Development Bank) and Professor David Kaplan of Canada, indicated concern about the limited attention being given to manpower planning in the Chilean developing programs.

Paralleling my study of the Chilean development strategy, I read papers on the Chilean labor movement and labor-management relations. Daily I scanned several Chilean newspapers and technical publications for articles about labor and labor-management relations. I paid special attention to the monthly issue of *Topaze*, the scathing political journal that used satire and humor to report on the political scene. Nothing like *Topaze* existed in other Latin American countries. The most insightful were the studies of Latin American labor movements and labor-management relations by Professor Robert J. Alexander of Rutgers University.

I also delved into the Chilean Labor Code to identify provisions relevant to productivity and labor-management relations. Promulgated in 1923, it drew on provisions in Swedish, Australian, and German legislation. At that time it was deemed so radical and pro-labor that it led to the ouster of an elected president, Arturo Alessandri Palma—one of the very few such incidents in the life of the Chilean Republic. Unlike most other countries of Latin America, from the time of its independence from Spain, Chile had had a tradition of constitutional transfer of power through the election process. Its one dictator in the mid-1920s, General Ibáñez, who replaced Alessandri, was himself deposed by a peaceful revolution after a month-long civil strike. In 1952 the same General won the national election and was then the sitting president.

The provisions of the Labor Code applied to the service, industrial, and mining sectors—not to agricultural workers. It established norms for labor standards, including wages, hours, and working conditions. It empowered government to deal with labor disputes and regulate strikes and lockouts; it also gave workers the right to strike, under prescribed rules and procedures. It created labor courts to resolve worker grievances, and decisions were on a case-by-case basis. Its provisions made it difficult to fire non-productive or even dishonest workers.

The Code set up a class-divided labor force, with separate rights and benefits for white-collar employees and blue-collar workers. White-collar employees were paid monthly, including Sunday pay. Blue-collar workers received a daily wage and paid for Sundays only if they had worked the other six days. Social security, retirement benefits, and other fringe benefits were substantially different for employees and workers. In addition, labor and social legislation enacted in the 1940s under Popular Front leftist governments had provided benefits for blue-collar workers that often exceeded their wages. For example, each new child brought an increase in benefits paid for by the State. Almost every industry had a separate pension plan, subsidized by the State—even the jockeys at the Santiago racetrack had their own separate plan.

Moreover, since the Labor Code preceded Chile's development planning, it was silent on the role that trade unions could lawfully play in the development process. None of the development policy papers paid serious attention to organized labor in policymaking or implementation of plans. In this environment, designing incentive systems to encourage greater worker productivity and higher wages was a major challenge.

While the Labor Code gave the employees and workers the right to unionize, white-collar and blue-collar employees could not join the same union. In the same company or industry, the separate employee and worker unions could form federations to bargain with employers. Payment of union dues was authorized only for local unions and lawfully established federations. In practice, there was little evidence of dues paying and the sources of local union funding were not always identifiable.

The formation of a confederation of unions from different sectors was not authorized. In spite of this provision, several confederations had in fact existed for decades. The most important in the 1950s was the *Central Única de Trabajadores de Chile* (CUTCH). While not recognized legally, it *de facto* acted politically in the name of labor. Since the authorized federations and unions were denied the right to fund central labor organizations outside their specific industry, how did CUTCH or any other confederation maintain itself? Funding came from political parties that subsidized CUTCH salaries and operations and made it a politically partisan institution—an advocate for its primary funders.

From the early 1930s, the major funders had been the parties of the left, the Communists, Socialists, and to a lesser extent, the centrist Radical Socialists. The right center Liberal Party had been a lukewarm player. After World War II, the Christian Democrats, supported by their friends in Germany and Belgium, joined the process.

The history of the Chilean labor movement was intricately interwoven with Chilean political developments. The CUTCH had emerged under the Popular Front government in the 1940s. Its influence waned in the late 1940s after Chile passed the Law for the Defense of Democracy, following a failed Communist coup staged at about the same time that the Communists overthrew the Beneš government in Czechoslovakia. Under the Defense of Democracy Law, the Communist Party and other leftist parties complicit in the plot had been outlawed and their leaders arrested and detained in the desert areas of the north and frigid Patagonia in the south.

The outlawed parties went underground and quickly rebuilt their bases around the country through "patriotic" collections of funds in theaters and at public gatherings to help their "persecuted" fellow Chileans "exiled" inside the country. Chilean sources told me that only part of the money collected reached the "persecuted" and a good deal was invested by the Chilean Communist Party in a network of movie theaters, bus lines, and print shops from Punta Arenas on the Straits of Magellan to Arica on the northern border with Peru.

When my assignment began in 1957, the Communist Party was the most potent force in the labor movement. The discipline of its membership and the resources available from within Chile and from the Soviet Bloc gave it a decided advantage over the socialist, radical, and Christian democratic factions. In the CUTCH, the rhetoric was anti-capitalist and anti-U.S. One notable exception occurred when Secretary General Clotario Blest made an impassioned attack on the USSR for its brutal repression of the freedom fight of the Hungarian people; he was quickly silenced because, as one of his socialist colleagues told me, "How could he bite the hand that feeds him?"

In those first few weeks in Chile, through colleagues I knew from law school, I attempted to talk to non-communist CUTCH leaders, including Secretary General Blest, at CUTCH headquarters. I met several Socialists and Christian Democrats, whose bite in private was less vicious than their public pronouncements. When I raised trade union, manpower, and other bread-and-butter issues, they seldom appeared interested or knowledgeable, but they were experts on the political party landscape.

In addition to the CUTCH, there were several other labor confederations. The CNT (the National Confederation of Labor) was affiliated with ORIT (Inter-American Regional Labor Organization) and supported by the AFL-CIO. CNT members were primarily white-collar employees, with only a handful of blue-collar workers and almost no presence in the powerful copper mining unions. Its leaders were not well known by the Chilean political establishment and seldom received significant attention in the press. The CNT leaders gave me their ideas about political developments but expressed little interest in programs that did not relate to their white-collar members.

I also tried to get a cross section of political views from personal friends and colleagues who belonged to different political parties from right to left. Almost all were deeply concerned about government policies and the direction of the Chilean economy. We discussed the development strategy and programs, but only one shared my concerns about the role of labor in the development process. That was a Christian Democratic lawyer, Guillermo "Willy" Thayer. He believed the Labor Code needed to be replaced by one that related labor to the development process and depoliticized the labor movement. Willy was a close adviser of the leader of the Christian Democratic Party, Eduardo Frei, and became minister of Labor on Frei's election in 1962 as president of Chile.

The disparity of views led me to consider designing a program to work with Chilean institutions that could assess the situation and conditions in the country and gradually introduce the labor and manpower reforms needed to support economic and social development, provide incentives for workers to raise their productivity and earning power, and promote trade unionism independent of political parties. I was convinced that achieving such objectives could not be done by the U.S. or any other external aid agency, but only by Chileans themselves.

While I discussed those perceptions with colleagues in the USOM and embassy, my constant sounding board was Ele. I discussed with her almost every evening the developments during the day. She raised many questions and frequently challenged my tentative conclusions or approaches. Occasionally she accompanied me on an interview or joined in the discussions. She also met many of the people with whom I was working. Her judgments and perceptions of people and prospects were usually astute and raised aspects that I had not considered. The design of my proposal to the USOM contained a lot of Ele in it.

The Program

In early April 1958, I submitted a program proposal that proposed three lines of action aimed at enabling Chileans to diagnose their labor problems in the context of their development strategy and to take actions to deal with them. The first line of action was aimed at dealing with the more critical labor-related components of the development process by helping Chilean policy makers understand the dynamics of the labor market, the effectiveness of the Labor Code in supporting economic development, and the role of organized labor in it. To meet that objective, I proposed the creation of a Center of Labor-Management Relations at the University of Chile (UCh), with academic and research assistance from a U.S. university.

The second was a long-term approach to upgrading the skills and productivity of the labor force. The objective was to help Chile create more vertical mobility by opening the path for workers to acquire higher skills, even university or equivalent degrees, as their skills warranted. For that objective, I proposed that the U.S. support two Chilean university programs: the first, with the *Universidad Técnica del Estado* (UTE) on worker skills training, and the second with the *Universidad de Santa María* (USM) to create the first Ph.D. engineering program in Chile.

The third was a long-term effort to acquaint labor leaders in Chile with the structure and operations of the U.S. labor movement and to offer them training in how to improve union operations and conduct labor-management relations aimed at raising the income and standard of living of their members. This line of action would be coordinated with the labor attaché at the U.S. Embassy.

In my presentation, I outlined preliminary discussions with UCh, UTE, and USM. On receiving my proposal, USOM consulted the director of the Productivity Center as well as USOM and embassy staff. After some minor substantive and procedural changes, USOM submitted it to Washington as the new USOM/Chile labor program. It was approved by ICA, the U.S. Department of Labor, and the State Department's Latin American regional labor officer. ICA and the Department of Labor agreed to sound out possible U.S. university partners, but made it clear that the critical issue would be the commitment of the Chilean host universities. The labor leader training component was discussed with Serafino Romualdi at the AFL-CIO, and Serafino offered his cooperation.

With the approval of the program, I began negotiations with the UCh Economics Faculty on the creation of the Labor-Management Relations Center. Based on its positive contract relationship with Columbia University, the Dean was favorably disposed to work with me. I had similar discussions with the Catholic University, but in spite of some expressed interest, I doubted whether it would be able to take on another contract. I also contacted the *Universidad de Concepción*, and the *Universidad Austral* in Valdivia, but budget deficits and limited regional faculties made them very iffy prospects.

The dean appointed one of his aides to negotiate an agreement to create an autonomous Center for Industrial and Labor Relations that would undertake in-depth studies of the labor market, labor-management relations, and the efficacy of the Labor Code. Our negotiations were wide-ranging and often very political as my counterpart's political views on capitalism and labor-management relations had a socialist tinge.

Our proposal spelled out the terms and conditions for a cooperative agreement with a major U.S. university to advise on creation of the first Institute of Industrial and Labor Relations in Latin America. The U.S. university would assign one full-time faculty member to be resident in Chile during the life of the agreement and he would advise the Chilean director on the design of a graduate level course of study and the development of a research program on labor and labor-management conditions in Chile. The director in consultation with the U.S. university adviser, would nominate a number of Chilean graduate fellows to pursue advanced degree studies in industrial and labor relations at the U.S. university; and, on receiving a degree, be guaranteed a UCh faculty position. I recognized that it might take several years for the Institute to become an effective influence for change, but the first step had been taken to create a Chilean institution capable of analyzing labor market, labor-management relations and the union movement, and identifying measures needed to make them more responsive to Chile's development plans.

On the second line of action, I negotiated directly with the UTE rector. Thanks to an UCh law school colleague, I met the rector and we established a good working relationship. UTE had been created to consolidate all worker and technical training, from high school vocational education to advanced degrees for technicians and engineers. It operated schools and training centers in almost every Chilean city.

The rector and his advisers were interested in overhauling traditional vocational education courses and broadening their scope from the classroom to the factory floor. They wanted UTE to become the national center for preparing a new generation of technicians and workers for a developing Chile. They were interested in setting up new technical training classes for already employed workers to improve their skills and qualify them as specialists, technicians, or journeymen. They said their goal was to build a training system that would allow even the most humble worker to aspire to obtaining a degree—if not a university degree, one that would be valuable enough in the workplace to ensure its holder the income of a technical specialist.

The rector cautioned that UTE was underfunded and was staffed largely by Marxist-oriented traditional vocational educators and that cooperation with a U.S. university financed by the U.S. government would be a hard sell to his faculty.

I mentioned my initial discussions with the UTE rector to "Doonie" Edwards, who was chairman of the board of trustees of USM in Valparaíso. USM was reputed to be the best engineering

school in Chile, with an international faculty. It had already established a master's program. Doonie told me that the rector and he
were interested in establishing the first engineering PhD program
in Chile.

When Washington indicated its approval of the university-to-university approach, I began working with both UTE and
USM on the framework for separate agreements aimed at improving worker skill training in Chile.

At the same time, ICA/Washington and the U.S. Department of
Labor identified two interested U.S. university partners: the New
York State School of Industrial and Labor Relations at Cornell University to work with UCh, and the University of Pittsburgh School
of Engineering to work with UTE and USM. Washington arranged
for representatives of both Universities to visit Chile for an examination of the prospects. My job was to set up the meetings, arrange
the agenda, and facilitate negotiations.

The first to arrive was Dr. Henry Landsburg of Cornell, a specialist in international labor affairs with a solid working knowledge
of Spanish. UCh and Cornell reached agreement on the scope and
terms of the university-to-university contract in almost record time.
UCh readily provided the space and staff for the Center and allocated the necessary funds; Cornell was eager to provide the adviser
and graduate training at Ithaca. The first line of action was underway.

Shortly thereafter, Dr. Ray Fitterer, dean of engineering at the
University of Pittsburgh, asked that I travel to Pittsburgh to discuss
the proposal. Ele scheduled her annual farm visit so that she could
accompany me to Pittsburgh. We had several days of extensive discussions. Dr. Fitterer was primarily interested in the doctoral program, and some of his staff were enthusiastic about repeating an
experience that the university had in eastern Pennsylvania with a
successful program for upgrading worker job skills. After several
days of in-depth discussions, Ray and a senior member of the faculty agreed to come to Chile to meet with officials of both Chilean
universities. Let me add that Ele helped me by talking up the project with the dean's wife—and the wives of the dean and his advisor
accompanied them in their visit to Chile.

Dr. Fitterer's meetings at USM went like clockwork. The discussions were in English. The USM German-educated faculty had "serious concerns about the competence of Pittsburgh." Those concerns were dispelled during rigorous technical discussions in which Dr. Fitterer displayed the breadth and depth of his faculty and program. By the afternoon, the rector and the dean were drafting an outline for their cooperation and considering faculty members from Pittsburgh who might cooperate with the rector in formulating the Chilean PhD program. At dinner, they discussed which USM faculty members might be candidates for Ph.D. training in Pittsburgh.

At UTE, the discussions were more complicated. Dr. Fitterer's assistant, who directed the eastern Pennsylvania project, made a slide presentation that impressed the rector and his senior staff. There was a language barrier since the Pittsburgh professor spoke no Spanish and the rector and his aides spoke little English; I spent most of the session as the interpreter. In spite of the problems, we were able to negotiate the terms of an agreement. It was clear that UTE had budgetary issues, but they were manageable if the rector could induce the faculty to cooperate. Pittsburgh also had concerns about the number of Spanish-speaking advisors it could provide. However, they decided to sign the university-to-university agreement and try to work out the problems as the program developed.

Ele was the hostess who introduced the two Pittsburgh wives to Santiago and Valparaíso. She showed them the sights and took them shopping. They in turn invited us back to Pittsburgh. The following week we got the go ahead. The second line of action was in place.

To implement the third line of action, Labor Leadership Training, I worked closely with Norman Pearson, the labor attaché. The objective was to promote free trade unions and improve labor-management relations by informing Chilean union leaders (including officials of the CUTCH and CNT) about the U.S. labor movement, U.S. labor-management relations, and free trade unionism through visits to the U.S. and education programs in Chile.

The *modus operandi* was for Norman and me to prepare an annual list of possible candidates and specify the specialized training program that he and I proposed. The U.S. Department of Labor would then design and conduct special programs for Chilean labor leaders during their stay in the United States. Washington enthusiastically agreed to it. So, by the end of 1958, the third plan of action was in place.

Our Life in Chile

Chile is one of the most beautiful countries in the world. It is very much like California. We had many good friends and we had an adequate dollar income for living comfortably. From every material aspect, it should have one of the most satisfying posts in which we were to serve. However, it turned out to be a bittersweet experience.

The primary villain was inflation and what inflation can do to people. We could not escape from its reality, as it was the ever-present concern of our Chilean friends. If we invited colleagues from my law school days, many would decline because they could not reciprocate. Ele never wished to put them in an uncomfortable position, and had a sixth sense about what was happening. She would tell me at night that her dealings with many Chileans, whether in the market or in social settings, were not as direct and upfront as the Salvadorans had been, and she attributed that to the impact of inflation on their lives. Unlike in El Salvador, we found it difficult to make new friendships.

The second villain was the smoke. Santiago is situated at the foot of the Andes in the Mapocho River Valley. It is a beautiful setting, but in the 1950s, it was a dirty compact city, with fairly narrow, traffic-clogged streets—especially in the city center where we lived. Many of the buildings were cement blocks that varied little in design and all had the same gray sheen to their exteriors caused by the ever-present coal smoke pouring from the city's chimneys. None had been scrubbed for years. The smoke cast a pall on Ele's spirits and obviously affected mine.

A stranger would hardly be able to tell that Ele wasn't having the time of her life. She was always smiling on the outside, and always joined in the activities of the mission wives as organized by the ambassador's wife. She was active in the local diplomatic wives' club, the *Damas Diplomáticas*. She participated in the Chilean Flower Arranging Club, and even won first prize for one of her Japanese-style arrangements, the only prize won by a non-Chilean contestant. She pitched in when we were asked to help at the Fourth of July reception at the embassy, and helped plan charity events sponsored by the embassy and USOM wives. But she was never as happy as she had been in El Salvador.

An important aspect of our job was entertaining. Ele enjoyed giving parties, especially small dinners. We tried inviting Chilean and U.S. friends to dinner at our smallish apartment, often with less than desirable results. Ele could never be sure of the results of the old gas stove: fallen soufflés, undercooked legs of lamb and other tragedies spoiled her efforts. We didn't mind that Ele was cook and bartender and that I served and washed the dishes, although we did miss Josefina. We became frustrated with our kitchen equipment and began ordering meals from the hotel dining room and other cafés near our apartment, again with very uneven results.

After the first few months, we stopped giving dinner parties and instead, occasionally invited friends for a cocktail and dinner at a nearby restaurant. Sometimes Ele and a few ladies would go to the Waldorf café where they sipped their afternoon tea to the accompaniment of Yasha on his gypsy violin. But we soon found that Chilean friends were uncomfortable with invitations because, under the pressure of inflation, they could not reciprocate.

Much of our social life came from invitations from colleagues in the USOM and the embassy, often several cocktails or dinners per week. Most of them were in the Providencia area, just a few minutes away from the center of town. Frequently, the cocktails were over by 8:00 or 9:00 p.m., which was usually the time for dinner in Santiago. Those evenings, on returning from cocktails, we would park our car and, as we walked to our apartment three blocks away, decide where we might grab a bite to eat before going to one of the scores of elegant movie houses that abounded in the center of town. Since you could buy your seats in advance, we would choose our movie and buy our tickets before eating.

Occasionally, we would just go down the street from our apartment to the scandalous Bim Bam Boom Theater. It had a live stage show that consisted of a chorus line of the most inept dancers one could imagine—sort of like "Guy and Gals"—with the performers arranging their dates with the guys in the audience as they misstepped and grinded through their numbers. Between the dance routines, there were comedy sketches, a bit off-color, but full of political innuendo. The language used in the skits was street slang, with *double entendres* that told us a lot about what was going on in Chilean politics. We could understand enough of the dialogue to make the rest of the show tolerable.

On a higher note, we were only a block from the National Theater, where there was a succession of plays, symphonies, ballets, operas, and other entertainment from April through November. We tried to take in a ballet whenever possible. Since I could not hear violins or sopranos, we seldom went to musical events. But we did see *Carmina Burana* and *The Green Table*, directed by the composer Carl Orff who we came to know since he was living in Chile at the time.

Ele had often remarked how much she enjoyed the market in Santa Tecla in El Salvador and the friendships she developed with the market ladies. It was quite different in Santiago! She did most of our fruit and vegetable shopping in the Central Market by the Mapocho River, a few blocks from our apartment. Ele did not feel the same warmth there that she had in Santa Tecla. She found it difficult to make friends with the market women even though she usually saw them once a week. Because of her coloring and accent, the market ladies thought she was German, and would tell her how much they disliked the United States in general, and their U.S. customers in particular. Ele never felt comfortable or safe there.

Then, we had a theft at the apartment in the Santa Lucía. It was quite different from the one in San Salvador. It was by someone we had trusted: an employee of the hotel. He had discovered my stamp collection in a locked box on a shelf in a closet. He found the key while looking through my dresser drawer and then stole only a few of stamps each time he cleaned the apartment—some of my valuable U.S. and Canadian stamps. He sold them to the philatelist's store down the street. I noticed one night in the store window a set of scarce 1900 Canadian stamps at bargain prices; I had those stamps in my collection. I just smiled until I got home and realized that they were mine. When I ran back to the shop, the stamps had been sold. The hotel management was solicitous. The young man was fired. But, thereafter Ele and I were always on our guard when the cleaning staff was in the apartment.

Those experiences were balanced by our Chilean friends, like "Doonie" Edwards. By the time Ele and I arrived in Chile, Doonie had married Malu San Fuentes and we were frequent guests in their home. In addition, Doonie's office was a few blocks from our apartment, and many an evening he would drop in for a cocktail before going home or on to another commitment. Ele, Doonie, and I discussed every political, social, and economic event on the local and international scene. We enjoyed challenging him on economic and social problems that beset Chile, but we never left upset with each other or discussed those interludes with anyone else. As Malu once commented, Doonie felt that we would respect his privacy. And we knew that he would respect ours.

Two other good friends with whom we spent many a happy evening were Chita Montealegre de Cohn and her daughter, Nancy. In 1945, I had met Nancy through my best man's mother. When her then beau, Arturo Allesandri Besa, was on a European trip with his parents in mid-1946, I escorted her to many social events and enjoyed the friendship of her family. Nancy's sister, Felicia Montealegre, married Leonard Bernstein after a brief Broadway career. Chita and Felicia had been my tourist guides in New York in the autumn of 1946 after completing my law school year in Chile. When we arrived in Chile, Nancy had married Arturo. Nancy's other sister, Madeline, had returned to Chile. Many an evening, when Chita was alone, she would call Ele and they would chat about Felicia in New York and Nancy and Arturo on the campaign trail for Arturo's uncle (Jorge Allesandri, who was running for the Presidency of Chile). Jorge Allessandri Rodríguez's opponent was then Senator Salvador Allende.

In 1958 on the night of the presidential elections, we were invited to Chita's for an election evening dinner. The polls closed at six, and at that precise minute Santiago was shaken by a 6.8 intensity earthquake. Ele and I were veterans of quakes and survived the minute-long shaking quite well. We arrived at Chita's on time for dinner, at about 7:30 p.m. She greeted us at the door and announced that Arturo and Nancy had been called to his uncle's home since it appeared that Jorge Allesandri was winning the election. Then she smiled and said, "You know that the quake we felt at six o'clock was really don Arturo Allesandri Palma (three-time president of

Chile) turning over in his grave at the thought that his son Jorge was about to be elected!" Chita's recipe for happiness was always a good laugh.

In 1959, our I House friends from Mexico were assigned to Chile: Carlos Quintana and his wife Lulu. Carlos had been appointed director of ECLA, replacing Dr. Prebisch. Although they were very busy people, they invited us to their home on several occasions, and the high point of those evenings would be when Lulu danced traditional noble hulas of her native Hawaii. Her noble blood endowed her with grace and elegance in telling a story of her people.

Our closest friends were my best man Fernando Walker and his wife Barbara. We spent many evenings with them and on several occasions they invited us to his sheep ranch near San Pedro. On our first trip to the ranch, we saw black geraniums for the first time. The ranch house was originally built in the eighteenth century and Fernando added a modern wing with twentieth century conveniences. He spent five days a week there trying to upgrade its productivity by introducing new pasturage and better livestock management. Inflation sapped his financial resources and kept him constantly on edge as he engaged in the dollar-peso loan game.

Ele was intrigued by the uniqueness of the ranch and immediately saw the possibilities of Fernando's using the property as a getaway experience for wealthy Europeans and Americans. So, she suggested that, in view of his inflation induced financial problems, he consider contacting a U.S. tourist organization, but Fernando could not see beyond his immediate cash flow problems.

We also were able to get out of the smoke by travelling around Chile. We made short visits to the Chilean resorts at Pucón and Villarica, with their majestic volcanoes and deep blue lakes. We took weekend trips to the Central Valley of Chile. But more frequently we were invited to friend's homes outside the city.

The only long trips we took were to the Chilean-Argentine lake region and to Buenos Aires. For Christmas 1958, we treated ourselves to a vacation in the south of Chile. We took the Flecha, Chile's high-speed rail service, to Puerto Varas on Lake Llanquehue. The hotel in Puerto Varas sat across the lake from the majestic Osorno volcano. Built by British railways builders, no hotel room window had a view of the incredibly beautiful lake or the perfect snow-capped cone of the volcano. Ele and I lingered long in the dining room to absorb the beauty of the view before returning to our room with its view of the railroad tracks. The following day, we crossed to Todos los Santos Lake, drove past the Tronador Glacier, and sailed across Lake Nahuel Huapi to Bariloche, Argentina.

We spent a week at the delightfully intimate Hotel Tunquelén. The hotel was run by a Viennese chef who loved to cook and eat. We spent nearly a week excited by every excursion into the dining room. Our first lunch brought us face to face with a buffet table heaped with seafood and salads. We thought it was lunch—but, no, it was only the appetizers! We were brought a menu at our table for several more courses. And the appropriate wine was served with each course. Seven days of epicurean delight!

In the hotel dining room, we met some fascinating Argentines who told us tales about life under the Perón regime—none of them very favorable to the ex-dictator! We learned that the hotel had been built by Perón during his presidency to house his teenage dates whenever he came to relax at the lake. Ele and I wondered what the walls in our room could say if they could talk!

We took daylong excursions into Bariloche, and its artisan shops with their Bavarian flavor. One afternoon we took, an elegant and very English high tea, at the imposing Hotel Llao Llao with its great sward of green running to the lake and the magnificent Andes in the distance.

A few months later, we paid our first visit to Buenos Aires and stayed at the charming European-style Gran Hotel Dorá, which had been recommended by Chilean friends. For over forty years since, we stayed there every time we visited Buenos Aires. It is around the corner from the walking street that leads to Avenida Florida and is surrounded by elegant leather shops. We loved Buenos Aires from first sight, its urban plan, its cultural centers, the parks and the restaurants, especially the scores of neighborhood Italian pasta cafes.

Ele also took a couple of trips with friends by herself. In July 1958, in Chile's prime ski season, with the wife of a USOM colleague, she went to the country's most prestigious ski resort, Portillo. She returned totally refreshed, without even having donned a pair of skis. She told me that the evenings at the fireplace with all those international skiers was enough exercise for her.

In 1958, Ele made her annual farm trip to South Dakota and California. She stayed much longer than she had when we were in El Salvador and really was not eager to return. She wrote me that problems kept arising that needed her attention or that she wanted more time with her 97-year-old grandmother. It was nearly Christmas before she returned to Santiago.

It was several months later that Ele suffered her most devastating experience in Chile. It occurred in May 1959. She had been feeling ill and went to the physician recommended by the embassy. When she returned from the examination, she was in tears. The doctor told her that she had stomach cancer and that he would have to operate immediately. She wanted a second opinion from her California family physician. After a very tense discussion, I called the USOM administrative officer to make arrangements for her to fly to California on the next available plane. We called Ele's mother once we got the flight information and the next day she was en route home.

The Chilean doctor's diagnosis came just a week after Ele's beloved grandmother passed away and Ele was still grieving. The morning that her grandmother died, the phone rang at our apartment in Santiago at about 6:30 in the morning (3:30 a.m. California time). Ele said, "I'll get it. It's my mother calling to tell me that Grandmother passed away. Grandmother visited me a couple of hours ago to say goodbye." Ele had elected not to go to her grandmother's funeral.

When she arrived in Tulare, her family physician, Dr. Eugene Mathias (the brother of the renowned Olympic decathlon champion, Bob Mathias) ordered a series of blood tests and x-rays. The technician who did the tests had just returned from two years at Gorgas Hospital in the Canal Zone. His report was that there was no evidence of cancer, but that she was suffering from amoebas. Amoebic dysentery was endemic to Chile, especially from unwashed strawberries and lettuce. No surprise! That diagnosis was confirmed by a second series of tests. Ele wrote me that she didn't want to return to Chile.

Implementing the Labor Program

From late 1958 through February 1960, my primary job was monitoring the performance under the two university contracts and managing the trade union leadership training activity. I developed no new initiatives.

The Institute of Industrial and Labor Relations at the University of Chile developed without a hitch. Professor James "Jim" Morris came down to Chile from Cornell as soon as the university-to-university contract was signed. He was flexible enough to adjust to the politics and economic reality of UCh and effectively designed the curriculum and set up the research and publications activities. He convinced UCh to adopt Cornell's criteria for selecting promising graduate Chilean students for the Master's degree program there. Course work began on schedule and a series of research projects on labor-management relations and the union movement in Chile was initiated in the first year. The research allowed Chileans to analyze the role of labor in development, the need for changes in the Labor Code, and measures to improve labor management relations and raise labor productivity, worker income, and living standards.

I had hoped that by the mid-1960s, the studies at the center would demonstrate the need for a total revision of the Labor Code. However, that occurred before the influence of the institute was felt. In 1962, Willie Thayer as President Frei's minister of Labor, did the job. During my last year in Chile, Willie and I spent many hours discussing revisions needed in the Labor Code, such as (1) the elimination of distinctions between workers and employees, (2) the definition of procedures to facilitate direct labor-management negotiations on working conditions and resolution of plant disputes that defined the role of government as the neutral mediator in the event the parties reached an impasse and (3) rules and regulations that nurtured the development of independent labor movement capable of financing its own activities. Willie incorporated those concepts in a revised Labor Code.

In 1959, I wrote a series of articles for the *Journal of Social and Political Thought* of the University of Chile in my not-too-professional Spanish on what I perceived to be the role of a labor ministry in a developing country. In preparing them I discussed my views with

Willie as well as Chileans in the Productivity Center. The articles created a stir in 1959 and were cited by several political commentaries as thoughtful and necessary contributions. Whether they contributed to reforms, I do not know.

In the second line of action, the efforts to improve worker skills training were only partly successful. The doctoral program at USM was successfully installed and the faculty trained at Pittsburgh. The plan for worker skills training at UTE was sabotaged before it could start.

The University of Pittsburgh and USM worked closely together in spite of initial differences in philosophy and orientation. Both developed a strong respect for each other. Pittsburgh advised on the curriculum for the doctoral program and the criteria for selecting doctoral candidates for the program at Pittsburgh. I met almost monthly with representatives of the two faculties and cannot recall a single issue that was not worked out amicably.

On the other hand, the project with UTE faced opposition from the faculty from the day the rector announced the agreement. We were aware that under the university's charter, the new program required faculty approval and that many faculty members were Marxists and anti-U.S. However, the rector felt he could persuade the majority to join him in developing new approaches for upgrading worker skills and that, on becoming acquainted with Pittsburgh's experience with innovative training programs, opportunity would win over ideology.

He and his immediate circle of advisers lobbied the faculty, especially key instructors and union leaders, to approve the agreement with Pittsburgh as the vehicle for enabling the UTE to offer better access to education for the average Chilean worker and to better prepare them for higher-paying, skilled jobs. He occasionally invited me to join him in some of those efforts.

At the same time, selected faculty members worked with Pitt in designing a series of short-term courses to demonstrate the effectiveness of a step-by-step method in moving unskilled workers to semi-skilled in just a few months. Pitt also worked with UTE on a plan to accelerate training for semi-skilled workers to reach journeyman and master's status. UTE certificates were to be awarded to workers who passed each skill segment and UTE planned a campaign to encourage employers to increase compensation for workers who earned certificates.

In spite of those efforts, when the rector asked for faculty approval, he faced a solid wall of opposition, largely on ideological grounds. The rector was outmaneuvered in spite of political support from a substantial portion of faculty and the Chilean government. Within six months, the Pitt adviser returned to the U.S. very frustrated. UTE and Pitt canceled the agreement.

On the third line of action, union leadership training, the results were disappointing. With the Chilean labor movement dominated by political parties, there were few unions or union leaders with experience or interest in U.S. bread-and-butter unionism. They looked to the government to enact social legislation to provide benefits, not negotiating with management on earnings and working conditions. There was more interest in political action than activity at the company or plant level. Nonetheless I studied the structure and operations of various federations and local unions in different sectors of the economy and in different localities throughout the country.

I talked with union leaders of CUTCH-affiliated federations and local unions, as well as the CNT and other independent unions. The CNT gave me detailed information on white-collar organizations and their bargaining strategies. Blue-collar unions were often one-man operations. I found that many legally recognized local unions were largely inoperative, sometimes because the union leaders, of various political stripes, were on a special employer payroll to "keep the peace." It was never easy to talk to union leaders because they had a strong anti-U.S. bias, much of it linked to grassroots emotional opposition to the power of the large U.S. multinational companies like Anaconda and Kennecott Copper that owned and managed copper and other mineral exports. I can still hear the replies of many Chilean labor leaders that only a political revolution à la Third International could redeem the true rights of the proletariat.

To facilitate contacts with labor leaders, I participated in seminars at various universities and civic organizations. At one at the Centro Bellarmino, a Jesuit-run institution, I met Father Rogelio Vekemann, the Belgian-born Jesuit priest who was a proponent of the new social doctrine of the Catholic Church. We spent many hours analyzing social organizations in Chile, including labor unions, as well as liberation philosophy. We often disagreed, but we respected each other's *bona fides* and intentions. At the Centro, I met many young professionals and labor leaders who were drawn to Rogelio by his leadership and thinking.

In all my contacts with non-Communist CUTCH leaders, it was evident that they had a skewed picture of the United States. Few, if any, had ever physically been to our country. They knew little about our political system or labor movement, except the information provided by Marxist sources. They also had little trust in their own government for its uneven enforcement of the Law for the Defense of Democracy. But, almost to a man, they expressed as much distrust of the Communists as they did of the "imperialists" (i.e., the U.S.). They complained about the high-handed tactics the Communists had used to undermine them and their respective political parties.

Based on these experiences, I worked with the labor attaché to design a union leadership program that had clear political objectives: first, to build a bridgehead inside the CUTCH for better understanding of and relations with the U.S. labor movement, and second, to build ties between the U.S. and Chilean union movements aimed at moderating, if not reversing the Chilean's anti-U.S. position in the Cold War. Norman and I knew that the odds were not favorable, but we believed that exposure to the U.S. and the dynamism of the U.S. economy and society was the most promising path to promoting change in the Chilean labor movement.

To implement the effort, we knew that we would have to use USOM funds. The State Department's leadership grant program to acquaint Chileans with the U.S. and our institutions was limited to a handful each year. Our plan called for as many as twenty a year. The labor attaché had used USOM grants in prior years to send a few CNT leaders to the U.S. for trade union training sponsored by the AFL-CIO, but not leaders of the CUTCH. We also recognized that the stipend of USOM grants were substantially less than those of State Department leadership programs and that ICA could not provide the high level treatment provided under the State leadership grant. When we submitted our proposal to Washington, we got a green light for using USOM money for the special training grants for Socialist and Christian Democratic CUTCH officers as part of the third line of action.

With that authorization, Norman and I widened our circle of contacts with labor leaders, except known Communists. Norman met with the Christian Democratic union leaders at Chuquicamata, the most important copper mine in Chile. I arranged to visit the coal miners at their headquarters in Lota, known as the "Little Kremlin." The union leaders agreed to meet me not in Lota but in the neighboring city, Concepción. After a long discussion, I was escorted by a union leader to the mine that ran seven kilometers under the Pacific Ocean, in order to show me the primitive working conditions under which his members worked.

Norman visited union leaders in the Central Valley, including those at the Teniente Copper Mine. I traveled to Vaparaíso, Concepción, Valdivia, and other cities in Southern Chile. Norman arranged for us to visit management and labor at the oil fields in Tierra del Fuego run by the Chilean government corporation, ENAP. During our visit to ENAP, we spent a couple of days in Punta Arenas on the Straits of Magellan. The first day after our arrival, we walked along the waterfront and found a tower to climb to get a better view for taking some pictures of the Straits. Chilean guards thought that we acted suspiciously and arrested us as Argentine spies. We spent an hour under detention until Chilean Navy officers arrived, reviewed our passports, established our bona fides and returned our cameras but confiscated the film. The following day, we flew in a bi-motor ENAP plane to operations in Tierra del Fuego and talked to managers and union leaders at ENAP headquarters set in a comfortable middle-class suburban community.

Our efforts to develop contacts with the unions were strongly supported by Ambassador Howe, and he invited union leaders to embassy receptions. He also arranged to have the U.S. Navy invite about twenty CUTCH and CNT labor leaders to go aboard the aircraft carrier USS Ranger on its redeployment into the Pacific; it came around Cape Horn, since it was too wide to pass through the Panama Canal. The carrier was too large to enter Valparaíso Harbor and had to anchor at sea. After we boarded, bad weather prevented us from disembarking by barge or helicopter. So, the U.S. Navy treated the Chilean labor leaders like VIPs and bedded them down for the night. A special officers' mess was set up and the food was first-class. Several bilingual U.S. seamen gave them guided tours around the ship. I had the "privilege" of doing the simultaneous interpretation for the movie *East of Eden* as part of their entertainment. The union leaders were frankly delighted with the visit, and even those of the CUTCH became openly friendlier.

When a number of the socialist leaders began to meet with us and opened discussion of Chilean and international economic and social issues, Norman and I thought the time was ripe to invite them to the States. We queried Washington if this could be our first special "training" program using USOM funds. When we were authorized to proceed, we organized "the training program" for some ten senior CUTCH socialist and independent officers.

Norman and I sent detailed information to Washington on those carefully selected leaders. We spelled out the purposes of the proposed training and received assurances that a "special course" would be set up. With the ambassador's support, we ran security checks before we approached the candidates, vetted their names with the AFL-CIO, and received assurances from Serafino Romualdi that they would be well-received. Even so, Norman and I—and our bosses—knew we were taking a calculated risk. We knew that in the Cold War setting, the Chileans were frankly skeptical. We conveyed this to Washington in carefully crafted messages, and called on our Washington support teams to take special care of the participants.

Norman and I accompanied them and their family members to the airport and we gave them a warm send-off in early summer 1959.

Four days later I received a call from Harold Walker in Washington, advising that there was a major crisis with the Chileans and that I was to book a flight that very day to try to quell "an uprising." The ten leaders had threatened to leave the U.S. immediately. I packed a bag and flew up that night. The following morning in Washington the director of the ICA labor office instructed me to straighten out the mess and sent me, with Harold Walker, to the Labor Department. On the way, Harold advised me that the management of the program had been turned over to the Labor Department after a detailed briefing on its special circumstances.

Within minutes we were in the office of George Cabot Lodge, then assistant secretary for International Labor Affairs, who called in the manager for the program. He was a retired union leader who spoke very little Spanish. We were reminded that Congress had set limits on what ICA could allocate for each training course, including the per diem of each trainee and administrative expenses. The program manager reported that those limits prevented the Department of Labor from putting together the high-level "training program" that Norman and I had requested. Asked why they had not so advised us, the answer was very bureaucratic, "We needed the funds from this project to keep our contract staff on board. We didn't bother you with the details because we expected the participants to go along."

Assistant Secretary Lodge had not been briefed about the group nor asked for his support. He also was informed that no effort had been made to contact Serafino Romualdi or obtain an AFL-CIO contribution. He was then advised that the group had been handled like mid-level government trainees and provided living accommodations in non-air conditioned boarding houses in downtown Washington, with three or four to a room to save money (even though it was mid-summer and very hot and humid). They were using public transportation as they moved from appointment to appointment with the escort officer paying their fares.

Assistant Secretary Lodge was visibly upset and took action to salvage the situation. He personally called friends to provide air-conditioned rooms in a well-known Washington downtown hotel at rates within the per diem. He also obtained the full-time use of a government vehicle. New guidelines were given to the escort officer. Then, the assistant secretary and I met with the Chileans, who agreed to complete the "training." I spent two days accompanying them on visits, including their call on Serafino Romualdi and Andrew McLellan, who hosted a lunch at AFL-CIO headquarters. But the damage had been done. The participants ignored us on their return to Chile. We were never able to interest another group of CUTCH leaders, whether Socialist, Christian Democratic, or Independent, to visit the United States. We did send lower-level union officials of the CNT and other marginal union groups to the U.S. for trade union leadership training.

Had Norman and I been alerted to the bureaucratic reality, we would have consulted George Lodge and Ben Stephansky before organizing the CUTCH team. We had taken for granted that, given the information we had provided, our Washington backstop offices would have designed a special package within the policy and financial limitations set by Congress.

The one positive result of my emergency trip was an invitation to dinner at Serafino Romualdi's house, where I met some of the great Latin American democratic leaders of the first half of the twentieth century: Luis Muñoz Marín, the former Governor of Puerto Rico and leader of the Commonwealth Movement; José Figueres, the former and future president of Costa Rica; and Juan Bosch, the leader of the movement in the Dominican Republic to overthrow Dictator Trujillo. The fourth guest, Rómulo Betancourt, could not stay over in Washington because of his campaign for the Presidency of Venezuela following the overthrow of the Pérez Jiménez dictatorship. All of these distinguished Latin Americans had received assistance from the AFL-CIO at critical points in their careers and during their exiles.

To be in such illustrious company nearly blew me away. During the evening we discussed the crisis that had precipitated my visit. They proposed that Serafino consider having the AFL-CIO develop a union leadership center in Washington and ensure the proper treatment of such visitors. I did a lot of listening as they discussed the political scene in the hemisphere and the outlook for democratic governments to replace the formidable array of dictatorships still in power in many Latin American countries.

We're Being Transferred

Before I left Washington, the State Department regional labor advisor Ben Stephansky asked me to join him for lunch. He advised me that, on my trip back to Santiago, I was to spend several days in Lima on consultation with the USOM labor adviser on employment services, Bob Ray. However, the real reason for my stopover was that I was being considered for an early transfer from Chile to serve as labor attaché in Peru. Ben advised me that he had signed off on the papers and that he was reasonably certain that State personnel would approve my appointment.

During those difficult weeks in Washington, I telephoned Ele in California almost every day. She was much better and the debilitating effects of amoebic dysentery had passed. She told me that she arranged to sell the cotton crop and was planning to go shortly to South Dakota. When I told her about my conversation with Ben, she agreed to return to Chile in the near future.

So, I was not surprised when Harold Walker told me that my travel orders had been amended to include a week in Lima to consult with the USOM advisor on the employment service project. Harold said that his office wanted me to push the Productivity Center to sponsor a similar project in Chile.

The schedule in Lima included in-depth discussions with Bob Ray and the Peruvian chief of the employment services project, Dr. Insua, appointments at the embassy with political and economic units, and a call on Ambassador Achilles. This was still a sticky political time in Peru. The military dictatorship of Odría was coming to an end. The leader of the opposition APRA Party, Víctor Haya de la Torre, was still in asylum at the Colombian Embassy. Serafino Romualdi, a longtime friend of the APRA leader, had set up a training center for Peruvian labor leaders, most of them APRA members. I also spent some time at the labor leader training center. No one mentioned a possible transfer to Lima, but all of us knew that I was being looked over.

I left Lima with an understanding with Bob Ray and the USOM director that, if the Chilean Productivity Center indicated any interest in sponsoring an employment service, Bob would be available to come down to Santiago on consultation. The embassy also advised me that, if the ambassador had any further questions, he would ask me to return. I left Lima expecting to return as labor attaché after home leave.

When I returned to Santiago, I was in limbo for a couple of weeks and then the bureaucratic wheels turned in Washington. I was officially advised that I had been qualified by the State Department to serve as a labor attaché and that the background and security investigations were underway. I should expect to be assigned to Lima, but the process could take several months. As a temporary arrangement, State and ICA had agreed that I should take home leave in early 1960 on the ICA payroll, with tentative orders to return to Santiago. That meant that, after home leave, I was to return to Santiago to pack up our household effects while Ele would proceed directly to our new post, probably Lima.

I immediately called Ele in Tulare to tell her the news. She had completed the farm business. She had now been amoeba-free for several weeks. Her response was that she would return to Chile as soon as Dr. Matthias had given her one more checkup. She seemed excited. She said the timing was right and she had time to say her goodbyes to our Chilean friends and embassy-USOM colleagues. Our two and a half year tour had been challenging, but it had given us an opportunity to meet some fascinating people and to get to know an incredibly beautiful country.

On Ele's return, we began making plans for our probable transfer in February 1960. December, January, and February is summer time in Chile. Many professionals leave Santiago for the seashore or skiing in northern climes, and we had expected that our last couple of months would be relatively free of social events. But that was not the case. When we told our Chilean friends and U.S. colleagues that we were probably being transferred, we were honored at receptions by our colleagues at the University of Chile, the University of Santa María, and the *Universidad Técnica del Estado* (UTE). Ele was honored at a tea by the *Damas Diplomaticas* for her voluntary work on several projects. A special moment among those farewell parties was the dinner at Chita Montealegre de Cohn's house at which the first recording of her son-in-law's Broadway classic *West Side Story* was played in Chile.

In January we invited a group of friends for one last dinner at the Waldorf. We had pisco sours at our apartment before walking down to the Waldorf Café on Ahumada Street, where we dined on Chilean specialties like abalone, sea urchins, and *corvina* (sea bass), while Sasha with his gypsy violin played *Fascination* over and over again for the ladies. We also took a few friends one afternoon to tea at one of Santiago's famous sandwich shops that featured specialties named after famous Chilean personalities. We edged our way to the crowded counter and let our guests order their own *Barros Jarpa*, delicious grilled beef treats with garnishes on a special bun. We found that drinking pisco sours and eating sandwiches from our neighboring lunch counter provided us a comfortable environment in which to say thanks to many Chilean and U.S. friends.

In those last few weeks, Ele and I also made a few short trips outside of the city. Chile's natural beauty—the snow-capped volcanoes, the indomitable Andes, the rugged coast, and the fertile valleys—left its mark on us. One weekend we spent at in Viña del Mar and, when we entered the casino, she saw a fabulous Matta painting on display with an asking price of US$500—oh, how we wished we had US$500 in cash on that day before the credit card era.

One last official event absorbed us before our departure: the state visit of President Eisenhower to Chile in February 1960. Chilean President Jorge Allesandri pulled out all the stops, from the welcoming parade to the *Moneda* (the Chilean White House) to the state dinner and Eisenhower's speech to the Chilean Congress. Ele and I were invited by Ambassador Howe to the reception at the embassy at which we were addressed informally by President Eisenhower. We were at a farewell party given by USOM colleagues when the U.S. president addressed the Chilean Congress. Our festivities stopped while we watched Chilean TV coverage of Eisenhower's powerful statement of U.S. support for Latin American and Chilean development and spelled out the U.S. objectives in the Cold War. We later learned that, after his initial meeting with President Allesandri, President Eisenhower rewrote his address and that his aide and interpreter, General Vernon Walters, was translating it paragraph by paragraph for the official Chilean government interpreter as the president was speaking. The warm reception of the Chilean people exceeded everyone's expectations.

We expected to be transferred and have movers pack up our household and personal effects for delivery at our new post. Then our orders, which arrived in mid-January, called for home leave and return to Santiago. Ele and I decided that we wanted to try our first sea voyage: the Grace Line had a twenty-one day cruise to New York, through the Panama Canal, sailing in mid-February and arriving in New York in early March. We got clearance to go by ship.

Ele decided that, going by boat and knowing that we were to be transferred, we ought to take all of our clothing with us. That amounted to seventeen bags! Yes, seventeen pieces of luggage! Santiago to Valparaíso was no great problem, because the USOM would take us to the ship. And I didn't think beyond that. Twenty-one days aboard ship, no problem. I should have remembered that, on arriving in New York, we were going to spend a week with our old friends from Mexico, Perrie and Ed Beyer, in their new home in Norwalk, Connecticut before going on to Washington, D.C., and then California, before going on to our next post.

14

On to Peru?

Leaving Chile in mid-February 1960 was a nail biter. The Grace liner was in port at Valparaíso, but the longshoreman called a strike. For two days, we were told that our being able to board was iffy. Then about noon of the day that ship was scheduled to sail, the administrative officer called to tell us that, even though the strike was still in effect, an arrangement had been made with the longshoreman to load the Grace liner so that it could sail before midnight. "Pack your bags. I'll pick you up at 3:00 p.m. so that we will be at the port in plenty of time for the planned departure at midnight."

So we put the last of our clothes into the one bag we had left open. The other sixteen bags contained shoes, hats, formals, dresses and suits. Some cases were small and a couple quite large, but all were bulky and heavy—there were no fabric cases on wheels in those days. And there were still several footlockers in the apartment for packing up our household effects when the transfer orders were issued.

The trip to the coast went right on schedule. We were permitted to cross the picket line and go on board well in advance of sailing. We were shown to our cabin and had a farewell party with the administrative officer drinking the Grace Line's excellent French champagne. A delicious late supper was brought to our cabin.

The first morning at sea, we explored our home for the twenty-three day trip to New York via the Panama Canal. The ship had about a hundred passengers, but its primary purpose was to carry freight to and from Latin America. The Grace Line had started as a Peruvian enterprise to take guano from the islands off the Peruvian coast to the world market as a highly desired fertilizer, almost a century before the advent of chemical fertilizers. The leaders of the Grace Company knew the South American market well, and were fully attuned to the political intrigues that roiled the countries of the west coast of South America.

Our captain invited all the passengers to join him for a cocktail that first evening. He told us that the strike in Valparaíso had put us behind schedule and that he would have to make up time by skipping some ports. He promised to make up for the skipped ports by providing special services and on-board entertainment. The ship was not like the current tourist extravaganzas that have an activities director surrounded by staff specialists. The captain selected Ele as someone who could help him with the on-board entertainment, and during the cocktail party, he and the purser asked her if she would help him with ideas for special services and entertainment, and of course she did.

Over the next two weeks we had a wonderful time. The weather was warm and the seas calm. We missed the excursions scheduled for Antofagasta and Mollendo, but enjoyed Chilean wine and Peruvian pisco sours to compensate for our being confined to ship while in port. When we arrived in Callao, the port of Lima, we were told that our stay would be limited to one day, not the two promised in the brochure. As compensation, Grace organized one of the most comprehensive tours of palaces, museums, and historical sites that one could hope for, followed by an extravagant lunch at the Lima Country Club. Lima was an elegant city with its colonial core around the Plaza de Armas and Moorish style second-story balconies. The rural-to-urban migration that drew millions of highland poor to the city had just started, and the chicken-coop huts on the dunes surrounding Lima had just begun to sprout up. We were given a special reception at the *Alcadía* (City Hall) and a VIP tour of its elegant high-ceilinged corridors and formal rooms. We marveled at the floor-to-ceiling mirrors and the portraits of Spanish viceroys and Republican leaders who had worked there. It was a memorable excursion since at the next series of ports, Trujillo, Esmeralda, and Buena Ventura, we were permitted only short shore excursions while cargo was unloaded and loaded. We didn't mind because transiting the Panama Canal was our great expectation.

The trip up the west coast of South America gave us a chance to talk out a series of problems that had festered for some time. I doubt that any married couple lives without issues, and ours had multiplied over the nearly three years since leaving El Salvador. We both had lost loved ones whose deaths had saddened us. Ele's grandmother had been a central element of Ele's life and her demise had left a major gap in her emotional wellbeing. My sister had passed and my father had fallen victim to Parkinson's disease. Neither of us had had time to grieve, much less share the impact of those losses until we were aboard ship. Ele had felt left out of decisions I was making on the job that affected her own life and ambitions. I felt that Ele had become so preoccupied with her family's economic affairs that she was ignoring my frustrations on the job. Both of us needed to be reconciled to the fact that we had not been blessed with children and that our married life was now built solely on our relationship with each other.

Those were difficult matters to deal with. Ele opened the dialogue that was sometimes bitter, sometimes bittersweet. But our love for each other led us through the minefields. We never went to bed angry, and we strengthened the base for our marriage that lasted until Ele's death. What surprised me was how little we did not agree on. I had been afraid to talk out my frustrations with the job, and she had been equally concerned about my feelings about the time she was devoting to her family.

By the time we were approaching Panama, we had recommitted to each other. Ele told me her thoughts about my job and that she was equally excited by the development process and our working as innovators and advisers in the process. She, like me, was frustrated with short-term local political considerations overriding sound long-term problem solving. She, like me, wanted to see whether working from the embassy instead of an aid agency would give us greater leverage for influencing decisions by governments and business and labor leaders. In turn, I made clear that I shared her concerns over our mothers' wellbeing and readily agreed to Ele's assuming responsibility for managing her mother's assets. And we agreed that we would respond equally if my mother called for help.

With our recommitment to each other, we made our first crossing through the Panama Canal. The captain invited us to dine with him the night before we reached the Canal entrance. He told us that he was always excited about this leg of the trip, and gave us tips about where aboard ship to stand to get the best view of the passage. We were up bright and early as the ship moved toward the Gatún Locks at the Pacific gateway. We craned our necks to watch the entrance into the gates and the rush of water into the closed compartment that lifted the ship three times up to the level of Gatún Lake through which the ship steamed toward the Miraflores Locks and down again to the level of the Atlantic Ocean. Ele and I joined our fellow passengers in admiration for the engineering marvel that our countrymen had designed and built. We went through the Canal several more times in our lives and the thrill never faded.

After leaving Panama, the captain announced that all the planned Caribbean ports of call had to be canceled in order to get the cargo to New York on time. Instead of ports, we were provided free drinks all the way to the Big Apple. It was now early March and the Caribbean, after being calm for a couple of days, became a monster. We ran into a nor'easter of terrible intensity that lasted for two days. Those were the days before the ships had stabilizers that minimized the impact of the storm. Our ship jerked, heaved, and pitched through the not-blue Caribbean into the equally unruly Atlantic.

Ele just did fine. She was up every morning, never missed a meal and enjoyed much of the ship by herself. The captain later told me that only four other passengers took meals in the dining room during those thirty-six hours and that Ele and he had become good friends as they ate the cold meals that were served to minimize the threat of fire on board. In my case, I was confined to bed since I couldn't find my equilibrium. I didn't lose my appetite and eagerly ate the sandwiches and beverages that the steward brought me. But to get across the room, I had to go on all fours: standing up just tipped me over as the ship lurched in one direction or another. It was on the morning of the third day that the captain announced that the storm was behind us and that we would have relatively smooth sailing into New York harbor.

The captain hosted an elegant party our last night at sea. Ele had her hair done and wore a green ball gown. The captain invited us to dine at his table and he danced his only dance that night with Ele before he went to the bridge to supervise our arrival.

The next morning we arrived in an ice storm. We passed the Statue of Liberty in freezing weather: gray, cold, and sleeting! Looking out of our porthole, Ele changed her planned outfit to anything warm she could readily find. She put on old woolen clothes, ski stockings with a tear in them, socks and Keds, a Russian-style scarf over her head and an old black wool coat to round out a very un-chic outfit. I had on my warmest wool slacks, a flannel shirt, a heavy alpaca sweater and a heavy topcoat and woolen cap. We looked as if we had just arrived in steerage from the old country.

New York was not our destination that March day. It was Norwalk, Connecticut. We had been invited to spend a few days with our friends from the Mexican years, Perrie and Ed Beyer. Ed had been transferred by his employer, Almy Dewey Chemical, to its home office. Their instructions were to take a taxi from the dock to Grand Central Station, board the train to Norwalk and take a taxi to their home.

So, our carefully drawn-up plan was to have Ele arrange for a taxi while I cleared the bags through customs and delivered them to the taxi. All seventeen of them! I duly went to the customs area, identified the bags and had them cleared by U.S. Customs. I had a porter take them to the taxi stand where I found Ele waiting. She not only had secured a taxi but had contracted it to take us all the way to our destination.

On leaving the ship, she was approached by a New York City cabbie who asked her, "Lady, where ya going?" She demurely replied, "Norwalk, Connecticut, via Grand Central Station." She laid out our plan. He replied, "Lady, I can take ya there directly—no need to go by train."

Ele then asked, "How much will that be?" He pulled out his fare book and reported, "Thirty-one dollars." To which she replied, "Oh, that's too just too much!" I suspect that seeing her in her steerage outfit, he took pity and began to negotiate. Ele applied all the wiles she has learned in Latin American markets and bargained him down to twenty-five dollars! He brought around his cab, which was a Nash Ambassador, hardly big enough to accommodate us, much less our seventeen bags.

We spent twenty minutes stowing the bags, including a couple under our legs in the back seat. He cursed under his breath all the time, and made several unkind New York-style comments as the bags were loaded. But a deal was a deal, and Ele insisted that he respect it. So, off we went to the Parkway and on to Norwich. I could see him grumbling in the mirror. Ele was on her most lady-like behavior and just smiled as the miles flew past.

Finally we reached Norwalk, and the cabbie asked for directions. He found that the address was on the outskirts of the city, almost in Darien. As we approached our friends' home, he let out an unkind expletive. As we entered the driveway of an elegant house set on a multi-acre estate, Ele countered, "Just for that, no tip."

I helped the cabbie unload the bags and paid him his twenty-five dollars, plus a five-dollar tip for which Ele smilingly rebuked me. When our hostess opened the door, her first comment was that she hadn't expected us for another couple of hours. When Ele described what had happened, the three of us sat down and chuckled. Ele had outwitted a New York taxi driver!

The house in which we had the honor to stay had been purchased by the Beyers from the great New York theater star, Mary Martin. It was a wonderfully gracious and comfortable home, surrounded by four acres of lovely gardens. We had several days of just plain fun and good living as we caught up on each other's lives since we left Mexico. Ed took us on short trips around the Connecticut countryside and we came to appreciate the allure of the Nutmeg state for so many New Yorkers. The memory of that wonderfully restful and friendly interlude was one that Ele and I fondly cherished all our lives, even though our links to the Beyers over the years were limited to annual Christmas greetings.

Fortunately, when I called Harold Walker in the ICA/Washington office, he arranged authorization for us to send most of the seventeen bags by rail express directly to Tulare. So, when we left Norwalk for Washington five days later, we only had four suitcases with us, which I could handle by myself.

Consultations were very confusing. For three days, I was never sure whether I was still with ICA or being hired by the State Department. That question rested on the decision by the medical branch as to whether I would be granted a waiver of my hearing loss. That decision would determine whether we were headed back to Chile, or on to Peru or Venezuela. Because of the delay with the medical clearance, State and ICA had not been able to work out all the details and the security clearances.

I had my medical exam on the second day of my consultation. After extensive hearing tests, the director of the medical branch said that he was willing to grant a waiver for a two-year assignment as labor attaché. So, the first question had finally been resolved and State advised me that I would be brought on board as soon as the papers were processed.

The second question was then decided by Ben Stephansky. State's priority was that I be assigned to Venezuela, not Peru. The 1959 election had narrowly elected Rómulo Betancourt as the new Venezuelan president. He was our ally and was under siege from Cuba's Fidel Castro on the left and the long-time Dominican dictator Rafael Leónidas Trujillo on the right. Both had allies in the Venezuelan military. The labor movement was a critical component of Betancourt's support, and the excellent labor attaché, Herb Baker, was being reassigned after four years at post. So, after having received days of briefing on Peru, I was given a cram course on Venezuela. At the same time, ICA was still planning my transfer to Peru. So, when Ele and I left Washington at the end of the week, we had ICA orders to move to Lima from Santiago.

Our home leave in California was not a happy one. We went first to San Francisco where we stayed at a downtown hotel because my father had become so ill with Parkinson's that he required my mother's full-time attention. My Aunty Paula had moved down the Peninsula to housekeep for my brother-in-law and to take care of my niece Lynne and nephew Gary. Ele and I felt that there was little we could do to help. Mother loved having us to dinner and seeing her grandchildren and us at the table, but we realized how wearing it was on my parents, especially my father, who had always been so fastidious and was now beset by constant shaking. Mother would say, "Tell me all about Chile," but then run off to take care of my dad. Our only family outing we had during that home leave was to Fisherman's Wharf, but Dad became so upset that we had to cut it short.

After we arrived in Tulare, we were greeted by a phone call

from the State Department that the medical clearance had been received, that the security clearance should be ready by mid-April, and that I should be on State's payroll by May 1. The voice said, "You are now officially assigned to Venezuela. The ambassador expects you by early June." That meant that we could enjoy four weeks of home leave.

Although Ele had been home for medical treatment since her grandmother had died, these few weeks were a trying emotional experience for her. She missed her grandmother and tended to keep her feelings to herself. But at night, I could feel her sob quietly and she would tell me how much her grandmother had influenced her life.

Much of our time in Tulare was absorbed by farm business. Ele had taken charge of the family finances. She was all business as she sat down with her mother and me to spell out how she planned to manage the farms. She asked me to prepare new contracts for both farms and laid out the terms and conditions she wanted. She talked to her two agents and laid out the conditions she wanted them to follow in overseeing the properties. When she confirmed the veracity of rumors that the current tenant in Pixley had run up large debts around town and had been seen gambling at the local tavern. Ele read him the riot act and told him that if he didn't change his behavior, she would abrogate the lease. His response was downright unpleasant. When she called our Tulare lawyer, he advised us that the tenant had left town. After consulting a few friends, she was introduced to Neal Westbrook, who agreed to take over the farm even that late in the season. He signed the new contract that I drafted. As long as we owned the ranch, he and his son rented the land and provided a good return for Ele and her family.

About May 1, a call from Washington brought me back to earth. State could not issue my orders until I was checked out by ICA. Since there was ICA furniture in the apartment in Santiago and I was leaving ICA, I would have to return to Santiago to settle my account with USOM and then return to Tulare. Then, State would issue orders for me to come to Washington for my swearing in as a foreign service reserve officer before proceeding to Caracas by early June.

ICA issued me a round-trip ticket to Santiago and I arrived in time to experience one of the worst earthquakes ever recorded; the 9.1 quake centered near Valdivia that rocked Santiago into numbness. As I went through the checkout process for the next three days, we had a chain of aftershocks and constant concern about what the next few minutes might bring. The pictures in *El Mercurio* of the devastation were harrowing.

Several days after my return to Tulare, the State Department personnel office called to advise that all the paper work had been completed and that tickets had been issued for Ele and me to come to Washington on June 1. We received the documents by mail a day or two later and they read, "Consultation and assignment to the U.S. Embassy Caracas, Venezuela." We were never assigned to Peru.

15

Venezuela:
A Challenging Assignment

The few days in Washington prior to our departure for Venezuela flew by. I was sworn in as a foreign service reserve officer. We had our pictures taken and filled out forms for our first diplomatic passports. Then, I attended a background lecture on the Foreign Service, at which it was suggested that I needed additional diplomatic clothing for my new status in life. So, I went to a second-hand store and acquired a white tie and tails, a morning suit, and some other items, each of which I wore at most three or four times in the next thirty-five years.

Most of my briefings were on the current political, economic, and labor situation in Venezuela. I read "top secret" reports on the efforts by Castro and Soviet agents on the left and by dictator Trujillo of the Dominican Republic on the right to destabilize the new popularly-elected government of Rómulo Betancourt, including Trujillo's day earlier attempt to kill Betancourt by placing a bomb in the presidential limo.

Ele and I lunched at the AFL-CIO headquarters with Serafino Romualdi and Andy McLellan, now Serafino's deputy after completing his assignment in Central America. They told us that they had advised President Betancourt of our assignment and of their endorsement of our selection. This carried great weight since AFL-CIO had provided financial support for Betancourt during his years of exile in Costa Rica, 1947–1958.

We crammed in dinners with old friends and Ele did some last minute shopping for household items, since my briefings stressed that Caracas was then one of the most expensive cities in Latin America and that our cost of living allowance would not cover the excessive prices charged there.

Our Introduction to Venezuela

In early June we arrived at La Guaira, the airport of Caracas and were met by the chief of the political section of the embassy, my new boss and his wife (Jack and Perky Cates), and Ralph Scarritt (the embassy's executive officer). We were escorted through the diplomatic lounge to an embassy station wagon that sped us up the superhighway to our hotel not far from the embassy.

Getting oriented to our new post began that very night. The Cates had us to dinner at their house. My two colleagues from the political section attended: Sam Moskowitz and his wife Shirley, and Bob Cox and his wife Eileen. Sam, the deputy, was a retired marine—a no-nonsense officer who never took anything at face value. Bob Cox was the junior political officer who had a probing mind and astute political judgment. They and their wives became part of our official and personal life for many years beyond Caracas.

They spelled out the importance that Venezuela and its petroleum played in our Cold War strategy and the importance of a friendly stable government. Then they painted a picture of the uneasy political relationship of the Betancourt administration and the military that had run the country unchallenged for most of Venezuela's history. They detailed plots by generals and admirals to overthrow the civilian government and of Fidel Castro's manipulations to stir up trouble among the regime's enemies on the left.

They also described the difficulties Betancourt was facing in working with us. He had barely won the presidential election in 1959 over populist Vice Admiral Wolfgang Larrazábal who had been handpicked by pro-Castro factions for his radical anti-U.S. stands. Popular support for the U.S. was not even lukewarm since we were seen to have supported the deposed dictator Pérez Jiménez (PJ) for his anti-Communist stance internationally. They went over the angry confrontation in 1958 of Vice President Nixon with the students at the Central University after PJ's fall. Jack Cates added that PJ's international stance masked his domestic alliance with the Communists, who fed him intelligence about democratic opposition groups.

The following day, I was welcomed by Ambassador Ned Sparks and the deputy chief of mission, Allan Stewart. They focused on the critical role of Venezuela in inter-American affairs. They laid out the challenges before me, including the skepticism of the Venezuela labor leaders about U.S. intentions after years of strong support for PJ, their nemesis. Many of them had been betrayed by Communist collaborators of PJ and had been imprisoned while the U.S. was praising his strident anti-Communism in the Cold War and welcomed his support in opposing Soviet and Peronist actions in the Western Hemisphere.

That afternoon, I met my colleagues in the economic section led by Carl Norden, who laid out the current economic difficulties that oil-rich Venezuela was facing. The siphoning off of oil money through rampant corruption made the government of Venezuela much less opulent than I had expected, and they painted a bleak picture of the resources immediately available to the Betancourt administration for dealing with pressing infrastructure and social demands.

The following day, Sam Moskowitz took me to the headquarters of the Venezuelan Confederation of Labor (CTV), and introduced me to the CTV President González Navarro and the senior officers who had just won a hot election, defeating a Communist-supported slate, reportedly financed with Cuban monies and resources. González Navarro was quite frank about the threat posed by Castro supporters. That theme was repeated when later that day I met with Tovar, the leader of the Petroleum Workers Federation (FEDEPET-ROL) and his right hand man, Secretary General Manuel Peñalver. Manuel later told me that Serafino Romualdi, who had provided AFL-CIO support to them and their families during the dictatorship, phoned President Betancourt, CTV President González Navarro, and Manuel Peñalver on my behalf, and prepared the way for their trusting and working with me.

While I was getting my feet wet at the CTV, Perky Cates took Ele house hunting. In a couple of days, they found an apartment on Plaza Altamira, in the Cadore building, that became our home for our stay in Caracas. The third story apartment had been vacant since a PJ insider skipped the country and the owner found himself in a difficult cash flow situation. Perky and Ele talked him into accepting a rent within our embassy allowance; he accepted once the embassy agreed to pay him in U.S. dollars, not Venezuelan bolivars.

We were delighted with the three-bedroom apartment over-looking the Plaza. The Cadore had only five apartments, one per floor. Our apartment had a large living room/dining room, a moving glass door in the living room that made it seem like a large open balcony or could be closed off to be a more formal room. Its three bedrooms, two baths, large modern kitchen, laundry room and maid's room were bright and airy. It was not air-conditioned, but it was oriented to catch the prevailing breezes; with Caracas's delightful temperate climate, we lived as comfortably without air conditioning as we had in San Salvador. And the air had none of the coal pollution that had permeated our apartment in Santiago. Located only a couple of blocks from the chancery where I was to work and around the corner from Perky's house, it was as if we had ordered it.

The embassy requested Washington to send our household effects from storage outside New Orleans to Caracas. The effects had weighed about 3,000 lbs. when they left El Salvador on our assignment to Chile. The only additions were a refrigerator, stove, and washing machine from Sears that Ele had ordered—about 200 lbs. more weight.

Our household effects were loaded aboard a ship from New Orleans. The Department of State shipping agent sent me a bill via the executive office of the embassy for excess weight above the maximum of 12,000 lbs. allowed under state department regulations. Ele and I were flabbergasted: how did 3,200 lbs. balloon into more than 12,000?

Fortunately, on our arrival in Caracas, we had been contacted by an old friend, Ed Colson, who had been our insurance agent in Washington, D.C. and had taken a job with an American insurance company in Venezuela. We called Ed, and he agreed to go with Ele to the dock when the ship arrived and supervise the weighing of our effects as they were off-loaded. When they located the lift van with our effects and weighed it, the weight was about 3,500 lbs., including the lift van. Ed had the port master certify the weight. We were off the hook.

The executive officer of the embassy reported back to the State Department and an investigation was opened. It turned out that there had been some shenanigans in New Orleans for some time, and the local agent had on several occasions slipped through invoices charging the department for the weight of the truck as well as the personal effects. Ele and Ed had not only saved us a peck of money, they also saved the department money and embarrassment.

Our household goods arrived intact and Ele supervised their arrangement in our apartment. Once we were settled, we decided not to have a live-in maid. Ele felt safe living on the third floor of an apartment building with only five apartments, and we had a full-time live-in building superintendent. Within days, Ele learned that the "super" was a jack-of-all-trades and was available to help whenever needed. In addition, the cost of a live-in or daily maid was too high for our budget. When Ele told Perky of our decision, she told us of a Latvian refugee lady who was available to cook and clean up for dinners and parties; and she thought that lady would serve us well whenever we needed help. So, between the "super" and our Latvian lady, all of our household service needs could be met.

Ele and I made all the protocol calls. We dropped cards on our embassy colleagues, the Venezuelan government officials with whom my job required on-going contact, and officers at other embassies whose assignments were similar to mine. We were settled in our new home in less than six weeks. We were comfortable and pleased.

Labor Attaché

The first three months were spent getting acquainted with the fourth Latin American country to which we had been assigned. Venezuela was very different in feel and activity than the other three. Even the spoken language was different, with much more of a Cuban-Caribbean rhythm to the speech, fast-talking, and rich with local slang. Urban life was very different from Chile and Mexico. Caracas did not have a central downtown and was decentralized, more like Los Angeles. The colonial flavor of Mexico was missing, and the civic spirit of Chile was not apparent. The contrasts in wealth and poverty were manifest everywhere, with luxurious buildings in a valley surrounded by hills covered with squatter shacks without water or sewerage but connected to the city's electric system, often by pirated power lines.

Caracas was a modern city with freeways and shopping centers. The census identified about 40 percent of the country's population of 7,600,000 was living in or around Caracas. The data on income distribution showed only a small de facto middle class, many of whom were foreign-born. The allure of better jobs, especially in construction, continued to draw poverty-stricken rural families to the city. The expectations of this large, mainly unskilled new urban population represented an enormous challenge to the new government—from providing sanitation and education to employment and a food supply.

In those early months, I read papers on the government's political, economic, and social objectives and the problems that government and labor officials were facing. I studied the labor movement, its structure and operations and its role in the decision-making process on which my predecessor Herb Baker left me a wealth of information. I concentrated on building personal relationships with labor leaders and hearing from them their experience under the PJ dictatorship and on understanding the relationship between the labor movement and Venezuela's key political parties: the Christian Democrat COPEI, the Castro-leaning URD, and President Betancourt's AD.

In pre-colonial days, it was not the seat of a significant indigenous civilization, such as the Aztecs, the Incas, or the Mayas. After the Spanish conquest, it was set up as a Province of the Vice Royalty of New Granada and was governed from Bogotá, and the provincial power was in the hands of the Spanish grandees. It did not have the mother lode of silver and gold that blessed Peru and Mexico. Spain distributed the land in large grants to favorites of the Court of Spain as feudal estates.

Sparsely populated, black slaves were imported to work the feudal estates. Its soils, leached by tropical rainfalls, could not sustain large-scale production of field crops like wheat, corn, cotton, or sugar cane. In the highlands it could raise coffee and on the coastal plain, some cacao. Its lands were most suited to cattle raising, but transporting meat over colonial roads was a perilous occupation.

The Liberator, Simón Bolívar, had been born to one of the great land-owning families of the province and reared in Caracas and Spain. When his dream of a Gran Colombia—the union of Ecuador, Colombia, and Venezuela as the anchor of the United States of South America—was frustrated, Venezuela became an independent state, one of the poorest in Latin America. Most of the population, largely illiterate mestizos, was either tied to the large estates or were small subsistence farmers on not too fertile land, cultivating at best one crop a year.

The discovery of oil changed the economic base of the country overnight and made it rich. But the extractive industry benefited few of the three to four million subsistence farmers. Instead, it bred a new moneyed class that sat atop a structurally skewed political and social ladder. That led Dr. Arturo Uslar Pietri, one of Venezuela's premier political scholars of the twentieth century, to comment: "We fell out of palm trees into Cadillacs."

Oil was discovered in commercially viable quantities during the dictatorship of Juan Vicente Gómez, who dealt astutely with the big oil companies in granting concessions and assuring a flow of revenues for his coffers. Some of that revenue went into building Caracas and other Venezuelan infrastructure, but a great deal went into the pockets of Gomez, his cohorts, and the military. Juan Vicente Gómez and subsequent governments through the PJ dictatorship did little to educate and prepare the people so that they could share in the new oil economy and transform their socioeconomic lot.

From the founding of the Republic in the 1820s to 1945, the government had been run by a succession of *caudillos*, military strong men who vied for power through the use of force. One general followed another to power in the nineteenth century. In 1905, Juan Vicente Gómez, a shrewd indigenous leader from the Andean highlands, seized power in a bloody revolution and ran a one-man government until his death in 1935. The stories of his wiles are many and varied.

Juan Vicente Gómez dealt ruthlessly with any internal opposition, and periodically announced his own death. When his death was widely reported in the newspapers in the mid-1920s, the news was received with jubilation by the people, especially among the students of Central University. When he reappeared a few days later he rounded up his once jubilant opponents and dropped them into the shark-infested waters of the Caribbean. When he did finally die in December 1935, no one believed the news and waited for weeks before responding to the end of an era. The date of his death is still debated, since the date on his death certificate is December 26, the same day a century earlier on which the Great Liberator Simón Bolívar had died.

Modern Venezuelan political life took shape in the later years of the dictatorship. In 1928, at the Central University, a trio of political leaders emerged: Rómulo Betancourt, Jovito Villalba, and Rafael Caldera. All three had been formed in the same crucible and knew each other from university days. Jovito was the great silver-toned orator who could arouse the people. Rafael was the Christian humanist. Rómulo was the organizer, and at first the dedicated Communist. When Gómez died, it was those three leaders who confronted the successor military regime and fought for reform and a popularly-elected government.

The only other political party that was created underground during the Gómez dictatorship was the Communist Party of Venezuela. It was founded in the 1920s by intellectuals who found Marxism an ideological alternative to the dictatorship, and one that was ostensibly directed to overcoming the poverty and underdevelopment of the country. The Party was cultivated from above, not from a proletarian base, and was led for two decades by wealthy converts. Rómulo Betancourt, had been a Communist Party member in his university days, but by 1935 had found that the doctrine and its apparatus were inconsistent with his vision for a Venezuela with open political, economic, and social systems. He became a pragmatist, not an ideologue.

After the death of Juan Vicente Gómez, Venezuela was governed by a succession of military juntas until 1945. By 1935, Betancourt organized with Jovito Villalba a new political party called Acción Democrática (AD). For reasons that appeared as much personal as political, Jovito was unable to share power and, when Betancourt by dint of his organizational skills took control of AD, Jovito formed his own party, the URD. Rafael Caldera had always been immersed in the Catholic social movement and spearheaded the creation of his own Catholic Party, COPEI. In 1945, after a coup by younger officers, Betancourt was installed as president.

In 1947, the first contested presidential election in Venezuela history took place. AD, COPEI, and URD competed. AD won the election and one of Venezuela's most famous and respected men of letters, the novelist Rómulo Gallegos, became president. His administration lasted about a year before the military staged a coup, deposed him, and forced him and his supporters, including Betancourt, into exile.

General Marco Pérez Jiménez, known as PJ, took over. During his ten-year regime, PJ used the Communists tactically to identify and dispose of his political enemies. In turn, he gave them free rein to install their allies in key positions in unions and rural and urban social organizations. AD and COPEI labor leaders told me first-hand the stories of betrayal and imprisonment they had suffered as a result of Communist moles who kept special police units informed of their activities and forced them to live underground, away from families and friends. I could feel the hatred that these labor leaders felt for the Communists and their determination to root them out of the union movement.

From my first meeting with CTV leaders, I recognized that the CTV, like the CUTCH in Chile, was an essentially political organization. The leadership was elected, but the elections were run by the political parties. The AD, with the money from government coffers, was the predominate force. President Betancourt had trusted lieutenants in key positions—and those lieutenants were also senior AD party members. COPEI, as the junior partner in the administration, was also the junior partner in the CTV. A few posts were "given" to URD as window dressing, but the URD incumbents rarely participated in policy making.

This reality led me to complement my relationship with CTV leaders with key labor policy officials in AD, COPEI, and URD. In AD, most of the policy makers were also key leaders of the CTV and FEDEPETROL. In URD, it was the party leader, Dr. Jovito Villalba who ran the party as a one-man operation; when I approached him, he politely advised me that he dealt only with the ambassador and the DCM.

One of President Betancourt's most trusted advisers on labor matters was Manuel Peñalver. While he was always professional in his dealings with me, he helped me understand the inner workings of the CTV and FEDEPETROL.

The top COPEI policy maker on labor and social issues was Dr.

Arístides Calvani, one of Dr. Rafael Caldera's closest advisors and political strategists. He was also a leader of the Christian Democratic political movement in Latin America. Willie Thayer, my friend in Chile arranged for me to meet Dr. Calvani, who gave me a comprehensive briefing on social development in the country as well as the power balance in the labor movement. Through him, I met Dr. Rafael Caldera, the leader of COPEI, and all of the senior COPEI leaders.

In my orientation, the embassy also arranged for me to meet business leaders. One of the first was Dr. Carlos Lander, the vice president of Creole Petroleum (a subsidiary of Standard Oil of New Jersey). He was the manager of labor-management and government relations and chief negotiator with FEDEPETROL, and is credited with Creole's decision to support the families of union leaders after the PJ dictatorship had declared them outlaws. After reviewing the development of the oil industry and the impact of the industry on Venezuelan development, he outlined the social and political turmoil that followed the death of Juan Vicente Gómez, the impact of PJ, and the rationale for Creole's commitment to a constitutional political system. He stressed the importance of an effective public sector to the stability of the petroleum industry, and the role that the oil industry should play in contributing to the economic diversification of his country and preparing a new generation of Venezuelan technicians capable of diversifying the economy. He called the unions an integral part of democratizing the country.

Dr. Lander's orientation rang true. The Venezuela I came to know had very limited experience with democratic government and very few civic institutions. It was an oil-rich economy without the economic, social, and political institutions for building a viable diversified economy and spreading the oil wealth throughout the body politic. That is why President Betancourt defined his objective as *"Sembrar el Petroleo,"* that is, investing the income from oil in development of the people.

Oil was selling at one to two dollars a barrel, and the price gyrated on world markets. The government had no significant source of revenue other than its taxes on oil exports for financing long-term economic diversification plans or sustained social and education programs. Betancourt's predecessors had spent much of the country's oil income on expensive, ill-conceived projects or siphoned it off in graft. A prime example was PJ's spending tens of millions of dollars to irrigate a region of Carabobo State with the intention of cultivating a variety of row crops and vegetables that the country was importing. He gave land to some cronies as well as landless peasants. However, no soil or other technical studies were made and the irrigated land could not sustain production for more than a year or two. Most of the small farmers failed and migrated to the cities. Much of the land reverted to raising cattle. The cement plants owned by PJ associates made millions for building the canals, and the government acquired large external foreign debts.

Other projects were for urban development, largely in and around Caracas: broad avenues, infrastructure for utilities and services, and government buildings. Millions were also spent on multi-storied super-blocks to replace the slums mushrooming around the burgeoning cities, especially Caracas. Unfortunately, the rural people transplanted into the buildings were given no preparation for living in such edifices and turned many of them into eyesores. The cement plants owned by PJ associates once again made fortunes; the government acquired additional foreign indebtedness.

Above all, unlike Mexico and Chile, Venezuela did not have a cadre of economists and technicians to analyze, design, and administer cost effective programs and plans of action. Betancourt's predecessors had not invested in building the skills and knowledge base of the people, so he now had to begin a comprehensive educational and training process that might well take two or three generations to show their effectiveness.

In his term as interim president 1945–47, Betancourt recognized the shortage of professional and skilled workers and opened the doors to large-scale immigration by holocaust victims, war-weary southern Europeans, and ambitious Latin Americans. Tens of thousands of workers, farmers, and businessmen emigrated from Europe. Engineers and technicians from Chile and Bolivia were drawn by the high salaries offered by government and oil companies. This injection of people stimulated small industries and businesses throughout the country, but few of the immigrants had the experience or training to provide the entrepreneurial and planning skills needed to transform the economy and fill the gap.

Whatever policies and programs President Betancourt adopted, he had to deal with the institutionalized graft that permeated the public sector. Political life after independence from Spain was run by caudillos and required special favors for their inner circle to get anything done—in other words, pay-offs for "favors." When the petroleum era began, Juan Vicente Gómez and the generals established a system that required special government permits or licenses for the oil companies to conduct their business. Whether the oil economy produced it or whether it was a historical legacy, every businessman I met seemed to have a story to tell about getting a permit or license. Everything cost something. Every license, permit, and administrative action seemed to require an extra "gratuity" for moving a piece of paper through the maze. Procedures seemed to change overnight, and each change seemed to mean that more hands were outstretched. The specter of pay-offs made almost everyone skeptical of the government's capability to perform.

President Betancourt

Ele and I had been at post for nearly three months when DCM Allan Stewart called me up to his office to tell me that President Betancourt had invited Ele and me to his home for a drink. Very unusual indeed for a president to invite a mid-level embassy officer to a meeting, much less to his home! Allan Stewart escorted us to the modest private residence where the president lived, not to Miraflores Palace, the Venezuelan White House. The Stewarts had known the Betancourts for many years, from the time when the president had lived in exile in Costa Rica. Allan had been one of the few newspapermen who had befriended him at that time.

In a very informal setting, we were taken to a study by the president's secretary, Edilberto Moreno, where the president was working. Our first reaction was to gasp at the sight of the red raw hands that had been so badly burned by the explosion when Trujillo tried to kill him shortly before our arrival. Neither one of us was prepared for those blood red hands nor the pain etched so deeply on his face. Ele, generally very poised in such situations, started to tear up. The president and the DCM reminisced a bit and discussed some item of immediate concern. Then the president mentioned that Serafino Romualdi had written him about Ele and me and said how important a factor Serafino's comments had been in my reception by AD and COPEI. He then turned to the political importance he attributed to AD and COPEI taking back control of the some 1,500 union locals throughout the country that PJ had allowed the Communists to take over. There would be local elections throughout 1960–61 and the Communists who had entrenched themselves during the PJ regime had to be displaced. He mused that Castro had now joined Trujillo as his adversary and that he was prepared to combat Castro's potential allies in the Venezuelan Communist Party if necessary. He identified two or three of his most trusted allies in the labor movement and told us that, if we ever needed to consult him, one of those men would be able to reach him expeditiously. He advised me not to make quick judgments about the labor leaders, to get to know them as people and appreciate what they had lived through. The drink lasted only a few minutes, but the president's face and burned hands were engraved in our memory.

The Work

By September 1960, Ele and I fell into a routine. I spent more and more time at the CTV and FEDEPETROL working with the labor leaders. I usually went from the embassy to the union headquarters by cab. One of the AD leaders introduced me to a cab driver who was a party stalwart, and he (Luis) was the one I called to drive me around, day or night. I met state and local union leaders as well as the national leadership, and was often invited to observe local union meetings.

I also talked to U.S. and Venezuelan businessmen to hear their views of the situation in Venezuela and their appraisals of relations with the unions and the leadership. Especially important were my conversations with the executives of the major oil companies on their relations with FEDEPETROL, and procedures for resolving on-the-job disputes and grievances. I received a ton of information about problems and a score of different opinions about the Betancourt government and the labor movement. A few longed for the good old days with PJ, when "an appropriate expression of goodwill would make a problem just disappear."

By September, I was invited regularly to attend meetings at the CTV and member confederations. The AD national officers of the sugar workers union invited me to sit in at a series of union meetings in the State of Carabobo where locals had recently been recouped from the Communists. I listened to sugar workers describe how PJ strong-arm pressure got communist union leaders into office, and how those leaders betrayed AD members and sympathizers to PJ's secret police. The COPEI union leaders introduced me to local teachers' unions in Caracas and Mérida where, under the dictatorship, being a Christian Democrat had blacklisted them from running for union offices. The AD leader of the construction workers took me to union locals in Miranda and Puerto Cruz where supporters of Fidel Castro, who had been PJ henchmen, were still in control. The president of FEDEPETROL invited me to attend a meeting of his executive committee. I was being given first-hand experience with the Venezuelan labor movement from the bottom up and the top down.

On each of these visits, I observed political party politics at work. The union leaders set the agenda to support party interests. The meetings always included discussions of plant conditions and grievances, but also always with a partisan political party orientation and credit to the Party for resolving specific plant issues. The meetings were run without any specific rules of order and often broke down in confrontations over partisan political issues. Little attention was given to union finances or services for members. It seemed to me that many of the meetings I attended were political rallies, not union meetings.

By my sixth month in country, I became convinced that to do my job I had to go beyond reporting on the labor situation. I saw the need to help strengthen the democratically oriented labor movement and support the building of its institutional capability to overcome the very real threat posed by the Communists and their pro-Castro allies. The CTV lacked many of the tools and systems needed to be an effective, long-term representative of Venezuelan workers and their aspirations.

This conclusion led me to propose that the embassy consider an action plan to support the development of free trade unionism. No matter how pro-democratic AD or COPEI leadership appeared to be in 1960, so long as they remained primarily political partisans, it would remain susceptible to enticements by political groups from Fidel Castro to Juan Perón, from Communist to fascist. U.S. interests in the Cold War lay in a democratic Venezuelan ally with a trade union movement allied to the free world labor movement.

Specifically I proposed to the ambassador that the embassy authorize me to add an education dimension to my job: first, sending selected labor leaders to the U.S. for training in the direction and management of national and local unions; and second, the preparation in country of educational materials on union operations and services for union officers and rank-and-file members.

Under the second line of action, I proposed to provide national, regional, and local union leaders with a steady flow of information and materials that would help them better manage the unions, improve their oversight of the resources they managed, and provide information on the services their unions could offer the rank-and-file. The Venezuelans had to decide what worked best for them, but they had almost no information about U.S. and Western European union movements or the potential advantages of union membership,. The ambassador approved my proposal.

For the preparation of information materials and their distribution, the United States Information Service (USIA) assigned Art Diggle, a talented professional with labor experience, to work with me. We contacted Serafino Romualdi at the AFL-CIO and the U.S. Department of Labor for relevant materials.

In late 1960 I drafted the first pamphlet. Art and I played around for several days with the name until we agreed to call it "*Carta Obrera*" (A Letter to Workers). The first *Carta* dealt with union management and workers' rights and responsibilities, the structure and governance systems, the role of membership committees in shaping union policies, and the responsibilities of union leaders to represent the members, especially in collective bargaining.

Each month through 1961, we put together another *Carta Obrera* and distributed it throughout the union movement in Venezuela. I drafted the text in English, drawing on my experiences in Mexico, Central America, Peru, and Chile, as well as Venezuela, to deal with the real problems that workers and unions were facing. Art made sure that the concepts and language were clear for easy reading by rank-and-file union members. A translator put the text into the vernacular Spanish used by workers throughout the country. The translator, Art, and I reviewed every word in the text to make sure the right words were used in the right places. Then Art added drawings to liven up the text.

During 1961, we covered a wide variety of subjects: union finances and the importance of membership dues; worker education and the importance of informed union membership to democratic governance; the rights and responsibilities of unions; the planning of union meetings; the role and responsibilities of shop stewards; the need for and importance of socioeconomic studies for union planning and labor-management relations; rural and urban cooperatives; union bookkeeping and membership rights to review the accounts; and press and public relations. We also obtained pamphlets in Spanish from the U.S. Department of Labor on worker safety and safe working conditions that were distributed not merely to unions but also to companies and businesses.

The *Carta Obrera* found an audience outside of Venezuela. Art began receiving requests from U.S. Embassies around Latin America and from unions from Chile to Mexico. That led USIA and AID (the Agency for International Development that in the Kennedy years replaced the ICA) to prepare a compendium of the various *Cartas* and distribute it hemisphere-wide. Indeed, the *Carta Obrera* was the first systematic effort to disseminate operational trade union information in Spanish to rank-and-file workers in Latin America. For at least two decades, *Cartas* were used in union training programs in a number of countries, including the United States.

The first six months in Venezuela had been productive and rewarding. Not only had I developed a rapport with the labor leaders, but also Ele had developed a circle of friends in the Venezuelan labor and business community. I took Ele to various social events sponsored by the CTV and FEDEPETROL. My bringing Ele led several labor leaders to bring their wives. The wives of the petroleum union leaders told Ele that Creole Oil had continued to pay them the salaries of their spouses while they were fugitives or imprisoned in the PJ era. Ele also made friends with wives of Venezuelan and American oil executives and businessmen. That led to social occasions where I met their husbands in social settings where the executives talked quietly about doing business, including graft, and working with unions in order to keep them in business; those conversations were often very different from formal discussions in an embassy office.

1960 was not a quiet year. Far from it: we lived through street riots and several coup attempts in our first six months in country! It was personal relationships with key labor leaders that led them to alert me of rumors of possible coup attempts and of their steps to mobilize workers in support of the government.

One coup attempt came very close to home. It was masterminded by the occupant of the penthouse in the building in which we lived. He amassed weapons in the penthouse and in a ground floor storage area for a coup, but loose lips gave away the plot before he could move. Ele watched while the National Police arrived and took him off to jail. Ele regaled us for weeks with her descriptions of the raid, the lock down of our building, and the seizure of arms and ammo.

The Central University was a hot bed of pro-Castro activities. Its leader was Douglas Bravo. A meeting with him was arranged by my colleague, Bob Cox, through a graduate student at the University, Ann Brownell, the daughter of former U.S. Attorney General Herbert Brownell. Ann was a politically astute advocate of U.S. interests who engaged her fellow students, including Douglas, in substantive discussions. One afternoon, Ann invited Bob and me to meet with a couple of her Venezuelan classmates, one of whom was Douglas. We had a rip-roaring discussion about U.S. imperialism, the revolutionary role of Fidel Castro, and their conviction that Venezuela needed a Castro-like revolution. I don't think we changed his views because several months later, he led a student faction into the Mountains of Lara as part of the Castro-backed insurrection to overthrow Betancourt.

The ferment at the Central University continued throughout our tour. Pro-Castro elements took charge of the student body and embassy personnel were instructed not to enter the campus. The only other occasion we entered the campus was to attend a performance by José Greco and his famous troupe of dancers in the fall of 1960. While we were being entertained upstairs by the stamping and *olés* of the company, Douglas was directing the removal of weapons from the basement to the Mountains of Lara.

The threat posed by the Soviet bloc and Castro led to the assignment of a Soviet specialist, Nathaniel Davis, to replace Sam Moskowitz in the fall of 1960. Nat's perception of USSR strategy and tactics helped us understand the dynamics underlying the threat to the Betancourt government. He became an especially important new component of the embassy staff, and he and his wife Elizabeth became lifelong friends.

Venezuela and the United States

To almost all Venezuelans in the fall of 1960, the presidential election between Kennedy and Nixon was of immediate interest. The government and most of the political parties were pro-Kennedy. The Nixon visit in 1958 had not gone well, and many suspected that he would favor PJ's return.

On election night at the chancery, the U.S. Information Service erected a large board to display the election returns. This, of course, was before the instant communications that encircle the globe today. All of us working at the embassy greeted the hundreds of Venezuelans, including many important national political and business leaders, who came to watch the returns. Receiving real time wire reports from the U.S. was a unique experience for Venezuelans who had just held their second contested election in over 140 years of independence. There was no disguising the joy among the Venezuelans when the election of Kennedy was predicted. Jovito Villalba, head of URD, while professedly pro-Castro, left the chancery smiling.

Kennedy's election was well received by the CTV who speculated about his policy toward Castro. The ascendency of the Communist Party and the detention of democratic labor leaders in Cuba concerned them deeply. They believed that their support of the democratic labor leaders in Cuba led the Castro supporters in Venezuela to accelerate and expand their efforts to subvert and overthrow the Betancourt regime. They alerted me to several threatened coups—and there was about one per month in the first six months we were in country. None of the threats proved idle. Jack Cates, my boss in the embassy political section, usually had impeccable contacts and would look at me and say, "Yes, I already know."

Following Kennedy's election, CTV seemed to be more friendly. The leaders told me that they expected the anti-Castro position of the AFL-CIO would become official U.S. policy once Kennedy was inaugurated. They were much more comfortable with having us as an ally.

One evening a couple of weeks after the election, I received a surprise invitation to observe a critical election at a powerful construction worker local in Petare; the union had been under Communist control for several years. They wanted me to report the seriousness of their efforts to displace the Commie leadership. I watched while they urged the membership to recognize the danger of a dictatorship like that emerging in Cuba, reject the communists and commit the union to democratic principles. I observed the carefully orchestrated work in the aisles by both sides to line up votes, and I was surprised that no one took notice of my presence. Unlike the CTES organizing meeting in San Salvador, I watched AD and COPEI activists take charge and outmaneuver their opponents. I had no doubt that government resources were being channeled into the effort. That evening's organizational planning was repeated in more than a thousand other urban and rural union locals around Venezuela, and I duly reported on each one.

Shortly after the election, CTV leaders invited Ele and me to join a group of them and their wives for a long weekend on the beautiful island of Santa Margarita. We had leisurely days on the beach during which we talked a lot of politics and, in the evenings, we were regaled with stories of pirates of the Old Spanish Main and modern day smugglers who outwitted even the shrewdest customs agents. We also heard tales of the torture and imprisonment that many of the CTV leaders had suffered under PJ and the hardships of their impoverished families.

Life in Caracas

Living in Caracas was expensive. Almost all of the food supply was imported. There were some locally produced fruits and vegetables available in the markets, but the prices were skewed to the petroleum economy. The embassy had a commissary at which we could purchase canned goods, liquor, and cigarettes, and occasionally some special meats flown in from Miami or Panama.

Ele set up a budget from the very beginning. Yes, we had an allowance for the higher cost of living in Caracas. Yes, we had a rental allowance. No, we did not have enough income to consider the luxury items available in the smart shops in the more opulent zones of the city like Las Mercedes.

Ele enshrined the principle that one must live within one's means and that some money must be saved from each paycheck. In our case, the paycheck was deposited in our Bank of America account and Ele told me how much money we had available each month to spend. The balance she deposited in savings accounts or occasionally in the purchase of a blue chip stock, usually ten to fifteen shares at a time, spreading the risk over a number of companies. She and I had been reared in the Depression, and like most Depression children, we always tried to minimize the risk.

In Caracas, our source of news, besides the local press, were the Miami Herald and the Sunday New York Times that arrived only a day or two late. Short wave radios provided us some U.S. and international news, and we depended on our embassy to make sure that we didn't miss an important piece of political or economic news. Evenings with our friends were full of discussions about the business environment in Caracas and New York.

Most of our social life was with embassy colleagues and business friends. The diplomatic whirl was quite different than in our previous posts. It was mainly for the more senior officers. We were invited to National Days at many Embassies, but the diplomatic list was extensive, entertaining was expensive, and invitations were sparse. The embassy also included us in special outings, like a weekend visit to the estate of industrialist Eugenio Mendoza, where we had a series of frank discussions about the economic, political, and social problems facing Venezuela. Mr. Mendoza had created a foundation dedicated to supporting education and finding solutions to pressing economic and social problems facing the country, especially the needs of lower income rural and urban families.

We also participated in the activities at the Venezuela-U.S. Cultural Center that frequently honored Venezuelan and U.S. authors and composers. There were extraordinary evenings of Venezuelan music that featured the guitar and harp. Then there was an evening with the great Venezuelan novelist and ex-President Rómulo

Gallegos, who talked of his life and the inspiration for several of his internationally acclaimed works. And there was the afternoon with William Faulkner, who talked with us about life in Mississippi and the origins of his Nobel Prize winning literature. His daughter lived in Caracas and she invited Ele and me to an informal evening at home with her father and family.

We also regularly attended performances of the *Ballet Folklórico*, and their traditional dances of the country, some of Spanish origin, some brought by the African slaves, and some adapted from the indigenous pre-colonial peoples. Ele and I often ended up on stage attempting to follow directions and move to the rhythm. We were invited by CTV officers to attend performances of the *Teatro Obrero* (Worker's Theater), an organization created during the PJ dictatorship to put on free plays and musical events for workers and low-income families around the country. An annual event was the production of the American Theater, a little theater group supported by the English-speaking population in the country. The expatriates had constructed an elegant modern theater at which once or twice a year a Broadway-style show was staged, with actors and stage sets that met high professional standards. Ele was interested in trying out for the next production until security concerns ruled that out.

Even with those social opportunities, Caracas was primarily a working post for us. If I had an assignment, dinners or other outings were set aside. Many an evening, I would have a quick bite, leave Ele at home and go out on labor attaché business. Sometimes, left alone, Ele would be invited to dine by embassy colleagues or with Marsha Schor, the wife of an executive of the United Merchants and Manufacturers Company (UMM), whose apartment house backed up to ours. Whenever Marsha learned that Ele was alone, she would add another place at the table. Marsha was an artist—a very good one, and her interest in the arts gave Ele a welcome respite from the pressures of the job. With Marsha and her husband David, we spent many weekends relaxing at the coast or the country club. Through the Schors, we met most of the U.S. and Canadian textile executives working in Venezuela, and I got earfuls about how businesses were run and how they dealt with government officials and union leaders.

Near Christmas 1960, we joined embassy friends on a weekend visit to Angel Falls, one of the most beautiful natural sites in the world. Ele and I were not made for rustic living and mosquitos, but we were thoroughly fascinated by the beauty of the Falls and the surrounding jungle terrain.

From Elation to Pain

1961 started with great promise and turned out to become one of the most difficult years of Ele's and my life.

Ele and I decided that we wanted to host a special evening for CTV leaders at which we could introduce them to the ambassador, our embassy colleagues, and some U.S. business contacts. Ele emphasized that the evening should be a special party in which all were made to feel invited guests, not business acquaintances. Our apartment could not hold more than fifteen to twenty people, and we were thinking of inviting up to fifty. As she explored possible venues, she found that we could use the Venezuela-U.S. Cultural Center for an evening, only paying the cost of cleaning up. We had a small entertainment allowance for the year, about $200, and we decided to use it all on that party, if necessary.

We carefully thought about an appropriate occasion, and Ele pointed out that all the Venezuelans she had met were high on President Franklin D. Roosevelt and his Good Neighbor Policy. So, we chose FDR's birthday, January 30, 1961, as the date for a celebration of U.S.-Venezuelan friendship and U.S. support for the development of free trade labor union movement in our host country. At Ele's suggestion, I contacted Serafino Romualdi and he arranged for a special message from Eleanor Roosevelt to the workers of Venezuela. Ele contacted Jim Graham, a new friend at USIA, who played the accordion and called square dances. He agreed to join us for the evening. Ele got the full cooperation and help of the wives in our political section: Perky Cates, Elizabeth Davis, Eileen Cox, and Ele made hundreds of delicate sandwiches and other finger food. We put together a bar with supplies from the embassy commissary and hired a bartender. And we put on quite a fiesta!

We invited all the senior CTV and FEDEPEROL union leaders and their wives, an equal number of American businessmen and oil company executives, the ambassador, and senior embassy officers and their wives. The evening began quietly until the ambassador and Mrs. Sparks arrived. Then, I read the letter from Eleanor Roosevelt and delivered the original to the president of the CTV. The effect was electric. Jim Graham then organized and called a square dance, and everyone participated—union leaders partnering with wives of industrialists, and Mrs. Sparks with a labor leader. After two or three dances in which everyone seemed to be having a good time, several CTV leaders slipped out. Ele and I were perplexed. But they returned shortly with their own guitars, sax, clarinet, and other instruments and played Venezuelan popular music to which the rest of us danced until it was closing time at the Center.

We had a great evening, one that has lingered in my memory and that of my Venezuelan friends for many years. On subsequent trips to Venezuela, American and Venezuelan friends reminded me of that very special evening. Every time I invited CTV or other labor leaders to a cocktail at my apartment after that night, many of their wives also came in hope of another evening with Jim Graham and the square dance. In fact, Jim did agree to call two more square dances at our apartment that year: one for labor leaders and their wives and the other for some petroleum and business management friends. When Jim wasn't there, Ele held court with the wives in the study while I had drinks with their spouses in the living room.

The election of President Kennedy brought changes to the embassy. In April Ambassador Sparks was transferred to Uruguay in time to host the U.S. delegation to the special meeting of the Inter-American Economic and Social Council that created the Alliance for Progress. He was succeeded by Teodoro Moscoso of Puerto Rico, the architect of Operation Bootstrap and longtime friend of President Betancourt. Jack Cates was reassigned to the U.S. Mission to the United Nations and was replaced by Ted Long. Bob Cox was transferred to Washington, and his replacement was Peter Lord. Except for DCM Allan Stewart, the leadership of the embassy had been renovated.

April was also the month in which the ill-fated Bay of Pigs occurred. The CIA-planned and managed invasion of Cuba also triggered an upsurge of violence within Venezuela. Pro-Castro forces called Betancourt "the enemy" and set out to topple his government. There was no doubt in my discussions with CTV leaders that they would have welcomed U.S. success in overthrowing Fidel and his totalitarian regime. They were in daily contact with their democratic friends in the Cuban labor movement who had fought Bautista and the leadership of the Cuban Labor Confederation (CTC) under Eusebio Mujal, which had accommodated to Bautista. The Cuban democratic leaders feared for their lives and the safety of their families as they were systematically barred from taking part in union activities or arrested for "anti-social" behavior. CTV leaders became actively engaged in helping their friends leave Cuba. They introduced them to me, and I helped many of them and their families obtain visas to immigrate to the United States.

Violence erupted on the streets of Caracas and other major cities. The revolutionaries announced a plan for killing a policeman a day, usually by a hit-and-run shooter on a motorcycle gunning down a single officer on patrol. The Central University was the center of anti-Betancourt and anti-U.S. agitation. The situation was made worse by the failure at the Bay of Pigs and the emotional lift to the pro-Soviet sentiment of the students and their supporters. I remember the words, "First, Sputnik! Now the Bay of Pigs! The West is all through." It taught me not to undertake adventures that were not designed to bring clear-cut victories.

Douglas Bravo led his brigade into the Lara Mountains to wage a mirror-image campaign of Fidel's in Cuba. As they broadcast on clandestine radio, "the Mountains of Lara are our Sierra Madre, from which we have launched a crusade to replace the bourgeoisie and its government." The rebels confronted the Venezuelan Armed Forces as they entrenched themselves in the mountains. They kept in close touch with their urban allies and took every opportunity to create disorder and disrupt the normal flow of city life. They aimed to foment urban unrest as the second prong of their Revolution.

New safety and security regulations were set in place by the government and the embassy. My freedom of movement was somewhat curtailed. Ele had always been the primary driver in our family, and she and I were given safety instructions about how and where to drive. My frequent visits at night to unions around the city were carefully planned, and I took taxis only with carefully screened drivers.

In late May, our new ambassador arrived. Teodoro Moscoso had been handpicked by President Kennedy to work with President Betancourt in accelerating his economic development plans. Security was very tight when the senior embassy staff joined Venezuela's chief of protocol in welcoming him. The ambassador presented his credentials to President Betancourt almost immediately and the ambassador was in business.

At his first country team meeting, he gave the embassy staff an assignment: to tell him tersely and factually what the real situation in Venezuela was. He specifically tasked Bob Cox and me with preparing an analysis of government operations and the situation of the labor movement. I prepared my section in a day or two, and Bob incorporated it into the final document. We wrote as candidly as we could about the progress and problems, including very frank statements about graft, inefficiencies, and nefarious influences that permeated the public administration and the political system—the challenges that we believed Betancourt had to deal with, and that our ambassador had to be aware of in his relationship with the president.

The paper was classified "For Official Use Only." We vetted it with our boss Jack Cates and the chief of the economics unit before sending it to the ambassador. He placed it in his immediate reading file and tucked it into his briefcase for reading at home that night, along with a number of other secret and highly classified dispatches about military and intelligence matters.

As the ambassador was leaving the chancery en route to his residence, he ran into the cultural attaché who told him about a new exhibit at the Architecture School of the Central University that USIA had arranged, but he did not advise the newly arrived ambassador that embassy officers had been instructed to avoid entering the campus for security reasons.

The ambassador took up the invitation and they went in the ambassador's car. When they arrived at the Architecture School, they went right up to see the exhibit, leaving the car unguarded and the ambassador's briefcase inside the car. Word spread quickly around the campus that the ambassador's car was parked in front of the Architecture School. An anti-U.S., pro-Castro mob formed, chased the chauffeur away, took charge of the briefcase, and burned the car. The ambassador was rescued by Venezuelan authorities, but the briefcase with his papers was on its way to Havana.

Our first concern, of course, was for the welfare and safety of the ambassador. Clearly upset, he called a senior staff meeting the next morning and expressed his regrets for having created the incident. He told us that President Betancourt had called him to express his government's concern and underlined the need for embassy personnel, and indeed all U.S. citizens, to avoid going onto the university campus under the present circumstances.

Then, a few days later came the bombshell. Radio Havana started to read excerpts from the documents found in the ambassador's briefcase, including passages from Bob's and my paper. That night about 3:00 a.m., our phone rang at home: it was the first of nightly threats against Ele's life, and the language was harsh, laced with epithets and nasty words. I called the Marine Guards to report the call. That call was repeated for several days before the embassy security officer, Jim Ellis told us to keep the phone off the hook after we went to bed. Fortunately, he and his wife Ruth had moved into the apartment on the second floor just beneath us, and at night he became my link to the embassy in case of any emergency.

Well, I became the center of controversy. Some senators who heard the excerpts from Radio Havana and then read them in each and every newspaper in Venezuela called for my expulsion for "interfering in the internal affairs" of Venezuela. Ambassador Moscoso met with the president and gave him a summary of the Cox-Tragen paper as well as of other documents now in hands of Fidel. President Betancourt told the ambassador that he agreed with the appraisal that Bob and I made, but regretted that the document had not stayed within the confines of the embassy. He also instructed me to stay out of sight for a while. Bob didn't present a serious problem because he was being transferred to the State Department in Washington and was practically on his way out of the country. The same was true for Jack Cates, who was being reassigned to the U.S. Mission to the UN in New York.

So, Ele and I, with the support of the CTV leaders and Creole Oil, spent the next several weeks visiting oil centers from Maracaibo to Caripito. We visited almost every major oil installation in the country. Sometimes we flew in Creole planes, but mainly we drove, with Ele doing most of driving. We met with local union and management officials, had private meetings with state governors and inspected living conditions at the oil camps.

Then, things seemed to have quieted down. The storm seemed to be abating as we approached the special meeting of the Inter-American Economic and Social Council in Punta del Este, Uruguay in late July. But, at the opening session, Che Guevara took the floor to read, word for word, line by line, the full text of the Cox-Tragen paper. As the U.S. ambassador in Uruguay, Ned Sparks, told me some years later, U.S. Secretary of State Dean Rusk turned to him and asked, "Is this a forgery?" To which he replied, "No. This is no forgery. Both men worked for me and I know their thinking process and writing style. The paper is theirs. Besides, it is an accurate, objective analysis of the situation that Betancourt is facing."

The following morning I was back on the front page of every newspaper in Venezuela. President Betancourt called Ambassador Moscoso to express his displeasure with language used in the paper. He said that the tone and phrasing was an embarrassment, but reiterated that he could not quarrel with the contents. He told the ambassador to keep me at home for the next several days while the affair played out. In his press interview, the president condemned the Venezuelan students for sending the briefcase and its contents to Havana and regretted that the immunity of diplomatic correspondence had not been respected. His final comment was that, if he were in a similar situation, he would have expected his staff to keep him as well-informed as Ambassador Moscoso had been.

The ambassador called me to his office and expressed his regret for the stress that Ele and I were under. He told me that he and the rest of the embassy staff supported us. He instructed me to work inside the embassy for a while and cancel outside appointments. Ele and I attended some official functions and a few dinners hosted by embassy and personal friends. But for about a month, my routine was home to chancery, work at my desk and then home. Someone usually picked us up to go to a cocktail or dinner—we did not use our own car.

In about a week the public outcry had subsided and new rumors of coups attracted the attention of the columnists and politicians. My hour seemed to have passed for everyone but Ele and me.

My relationship with the labor leaders never returned to the same close level that existed prior to the briefcase incident. I felt that many of the AD labor leaders did not level with me for fear that my reporting on their activities might fall into the wrong hands. Only one, Manuel Peñalver, continued to talk frankly with me—and I knew that was because he was close to President Betancourt and the president had told him to "take care of Tragen."

With the Christian Democratic COPEI leaders, I experienced a different reaction. Party leader Rafael Caldera and his principal labor advisor, Arístides Calvani, invited me to discuss the labor and social situation in Venezuela, including a weekend retreat in the mountain town of Los Teques. I was invited to join working sessions with Vatican representative Monsignor Ligutti about CO-PEI's plans for broadening the appeal of its programs to farmers and workers through their participation in formulating policies and strengthening grass-roots organizations, such as trade unions, youth groups, and cooperatives. I also sat in on private discussions with Monsignor Ligutti, Rafael Caldera, and Arístides Calvani in which they analyzed the status of Christian Democratic parties in Latin America and their concern about the vestiges of Peronism and the message of "liberation theology," especially in Argentina, Brazil, and Chile. While charting a central role for the Catholic Church and COPEI, they were exploring how to build bridges to non-Catholics for a broader popular base.

My last nine months in Venezuela were dedicated primarily to working with Art Diggle on the *Cartas Obreras*, trying to publish a new edition every four to six weeks, and reporting on developments in an uneasy labor movement. Ele and I made no additional trips around Venezuela, postponing our planned visit to the Andean region around Mérida; and Ele chose to cancel her farm trip in 1961 to be with me. Our travel was confined to an occasional weekend to the coast with our friends the Schors, always traveling in their car.

High-level Visitors

During the last year in Caracas, perhaps more important than my day job at the embassy were my assignments to support high-level fact-finding missions by senior Washington officials, Congressional teams, and even President Kennedy himself. In 1961, after the failure of the Bay of Pigs, the growing rift between Washington and Havana and the creation of the Alliance for Progress, Caracas became a prime destination.

One of the first high-level visitors was Prince Philip, Duke of Edinburgh. He was on a State visit, with pomp and circumstance. Ele's and my involvement was limited. My counterpart at the British Embassy consulted me as he prepared briefing papers and we were invited to the state reception at Miraflores Palace. For the reception, we dressed to the nines; I even wore my white tie and tails for the second time in my career. Prince Philip chatted with us for a few minutes.

The Washington visitors required special preparations. The ambassador designated the embassy officers who were to work with and take care of congressional delegations and senior administration officials. I usually participated in briefings and occasionally would escort a group to meetings with labor leaders or government officials.

The first high-level visitors I escorted were a subcommittee of the Senate Government Operations Committee, headed by Senator Gale McGee of Wyoming. It was reviewing reports of corruption in government operations and the impact on the oil market. Petroleum was selling at less than a dollar a barrel, if memory serves. I accompanied them to meetings with the minister of Labor and the head of the Development Corporation. Both officials spoke English and my role was merely to accompany the congressmen and take some notes. I vividly recall the dilemma defined by the development minister when he laid out the government's frustration with the inability to move forward infrastructure and housing projects to create employment and counter social unrest because of the fluctuating price of oil. He asked, "How can we combat Castro Communism when the fluctuating price of oil prevents the government from being sure of long-term income to finance critical programs?"

Then came a visit from Senator John Tunney of California and Teddy Kennedy, brother of President Kennedy, to review the status of rural development and land reform. My colleague, Nathaniel Davis, was their control officer and took them on visits to land reform projects near Caracas. My contact was their technical adviser, Dr. John Plank, then a professor of political science at the University of Connecticut, whom we had known as leader of the American Friends group at *Sitio del Niño* in El Salvador. He invited me to brief the team on the status of the labor movement and rural labor conditions.

U.S. Ambassador to the United Nations Adlai E. Stevenson, two-time presidential candidate, came to coordinate U.S. and Venezuelan positions on Fidel Castro in the United Nations. My only interaction with him was at the country team briefing on the situation in Venezuela. I spelled out the support given by CTV leaders to anti-Castro labor leaders and the efforts they made to bring the dissidents to Venezuela.

Ambassador Stevenson's visit had special meaning for my colleagues in the political section and me, because our boss, Jack Cates, had been transferred to his staff. Jack had left a few weeks before the visit and all of us in political section had given him a farewell party, the highpoint of which was a parody written by Ele, Eileen Cox, and Jack's wife Perky called *This is Your Life, Jack Cates*. We all laughed together with Jack as we recreated his life as a student at Yale, his personal peccadillos, and his proclivity for receiving security citations from the marine guards. Jack knew all the key players in the Venezuelan political scene and often received tips on planned coups hours before the CIA or the military attachés. Whenever he did, he would go to the embassy, prepare a dispatch on what had happened and who the plotters were, and depart without securing the safe in our political section. He scooped everyone, but ended up getting a reprimand for his security breach. We gave him the text of *This is Your Life Jack Cates* as one of his going-away presents. In years to come, every time we saw Jack he would throw his arms around Ele and tell her how much he had enjoyed the evening.

The Cates' replacements were Ted and Phyllis Long. Ted was a Cold War veteran, having served in Western Europe and was a specialist on Soviet political strategy and tactics. Clearly our primary strategic interest in Venezuela had expanded beyond oil and inter-American affairs to the core issues of the Cold War and the apparent threat posed by Castro.

Shortly after Ted Long's arrival came a high-level visit by the

Senate Foreign Relations Committee, headed by Senator John Sparkman of Alabama. I accompanied them on a visit to the CTV for a meeting with CTV President González Navarro and senior AD and COPEI leaders. I did the interpreting. González Navarro laid out in detail the power struggle in the labor movement between the AD and COPEI as the democratic force against Castro Communists. He tied Communist strength in Venezuelan unions to the alliance with the ex-dictator PJ and advocated close U.S.-Venezuelan labor cooperation to fight for a free labor movement in Cuba and to combat Fidel's effort to penetrate labor unions in the rest of Latin America and the Caribbean.

Throughout the presentation by González Navarro, Senator Sparkman's eyes were closed, and I was worried that the Senator had fallen asleep, for it was a hot day and there was no air conditioning in the room. When the CTV president completed his presentation, Senator Sparkman opened his eyes and began a stream of questions touching on almost every point that the CTV leaders had made. He and his colleagues turned to the other labor leaders present to verify that they indeed, despite party affiliation, were in agreement with the CTV president. Other questions raised by the senators indicated that they had listened and that they supported democratic development in Latin America. The senators' questions and comments made it very clear to the CTV officers that they shared CTV concerns about developments in Cuba and about Castro's efforts to subvert the Betancourt regime. The meeting ran nearly an hour over the time scheduled, and a call from the embassy reminded Senator Sparkman that he was due for a lunch with the Speaker of the House, Dr. Rafael Caldera.

Another congressional visit was by the Latin American Subcommittee of the House of Representatives, led by Subcommittee Chair Armistead Selden, Jr. of Alabama and included the ranking Democrat, Dante Fascell of Florida. Ele and I were asked to host a breakfast at our apartment with the key AD and COPEI leaders of the CTV. Breakfast meetings were difficult to set up, but the congressmen wanted to meet the labor leaders in a non-work setting. I invited fifteen, some of whom were black, some of whom were mestizo, and some of whom were Caucasian. Ele set up two tables for our twenty expected guests and arranged a buffet to minimize interruption of the discussions. The subcommittee brought its staff chief, Ricky Bennett, a knowledgeable and vivacious bilingual professional.

The labor leaders arrived a few minutes prior to the arrival of the congressional group. We were talking informally when the congressmen arrived. I noted a surprised look on Congressman Selden's face, and an immediate reaction by Congressman Fascell. He moved over to the black union leaders and took them with Ricky to the second table and motioned to me to seat Congressman Selden and the remaining labor leaders at the other table where I ended up as the interpreter. This was 1961 and, as Congressman Fascell later told me, his colleague from Alabama was not accustomed to eating at the same table with black people. Dante Fascell became a friend for life from that moment in which he averted an unpleasant scene, and no Venezuelan was unattended or offended. The breakfast was a success, and all the labor leaders left with strong praise for the interest and knowledge of the U.S. congressmen.

Another visitor for whom I was the embassy liaison was Jimmy Yen. Jimmy was sent to Venezuela by the Rockefeller brothers to see if he could help the Betancourt administration reorient its land reform and resettlement program. Betancourt sought to place substantial numbers of landless and tenant farmers on farms of their own, perhaps even luring some recent rural-to-urban migrants out of the cities back to farms of their own. PJ had built extensive irrigation networks that had not triggered the substantial increase in agricultural production that its sponsors had predicted, partly because of the poor mineral content of the soil and partly because there had been inadequate provision of technical support required by the newly settled farmers with little experience managing farms. The National Agrarian Institute (IAN) was responsible for managing the agrarian reform and resettlement projects, and the Rockefeller brothers, closely associated with Creole Petroleum and with their large financial stake in Venezuela, arranged for Jimmy to advise the government and IAN.

Allan Stewart, the DCM, introduced me to Jimmy and asked me to help him in any way possible. Jimmy was something special. He was from one of the great Mandarin families of China. During World War I, when he was studying at Yale, he volunteered to go to

France to serve as interpreter and letter writer for the tens of thousands of illiterate coolies who were brought to the Western Front to dig ditches and perform other manual labor. Jimmy decided to teach the coolies to read, and designed a system based on about two hundred and fifty characters to facilitate the process. He taught thousands to read and write.

On returning to Yale, he prepared himself to be a teacher and attack the problem of illiteracy in his homeland. Before returning to China, he married Alice, the daughter of a Presbyterian minister in Oakland, California. From Beijing, Alice and he organized the "back to village" movement to educate the peasants. They recruited scores of other Mandarin colleagues to participate in the movement. Alice and he, and all their fellow members, moved into villages to teach. After five years, Jimmy and his colleagues found that the program had not achieved the desired results. As Jimmy told me, "One day my prize student came to me and said, 'Master, I have learned to read and write but I make less from my labors than my neighbor who has never studied with you. So, I must give up my studies to spend more time working and earning income to improve my family's conditions.' So, Alice and I returned to Beijing and designed a new approach to helping villagers not only read and write but also earn money and raise living standards."

The new program was called Rural Reconstruction. It was based on four integrated steps: livelihood, education, public health, and self-government. Jimmy knew that for the peasant, the first priority was to earn a living. So, the first phase of Rural Reconstruction was to work with farmers to increase production and marketing of crops. As the peasant became acquainted with fertilizers and other inputs as well with the market place, he had to read instructions and reports. So, education became a necessary part of the peasant's life and he could then see the importance education would play in the lives of his children. Once you better educate and train your family, especially your children, health becomes a more important concern. And once you have built up the farm and the family, your relations with your neighbors take on new dimensions so that you must learn to work together to ensure that your village has essential services required to sustain your and the other village families.

The work in Northern and Central China had begun to have

positive effects when the Japanese invasion occurred and Chiang Kai-shek's nationalists took control of China. Chiang saw Jimmy's movement as a threat to his concept of centralized power and forced Alice and Jimmy to leave China. The Rockefeller Foundation had been following his work in China and recommended Jimmy to the dynamic young reformist president of the Philippines, Ramón Magsaysay. Jimmy was hired by Magsaysay to develop a nation-wide community program based on his four steps. After Magsaysay's tragic death, Jimmy had to leave the Philippines and the Rockefeller Foundation hired him as a consultant.

Jimmy and Alice became our friends during their stay in Venezuela. Ele and I accompanied them on visits to various land resettlement projects in the country. I usually coordinated their visits with Daniel Carias, the president of the Sugar Workers Union or some other CTV officer. Jimmy was trying to train a cadre of IAN technicians in the design and application of the Rural Reconstruction program. The critical problem was that the poor quality of the soil impeded efforts to improve production and farmer income. The experiment was frustrated not by concept or leadership, but by Mother Nature.

The culminating event of my tour in Venezuela was the state visit of President Kennedy in December 1961. Ted Long was assigned to work with the White House and the secret service advance team. Once or twice I accompanied Ted to Miraflores Palace for discussions of timing and sites to be visited. Ted made almost all of the field visits and inspections of the key sites where speeches were to be delivered.

One day when Ted had a conflicting commitment, he assigned me to accompany the White House team and the secret service detail for a visit to a rural community that I had come to know on visits with Jimmy Yen and CTV leader Daniel Carias. President Betancourt had proposed that the two presidents, accompanied by the First Ladies, visit that agrarian reform project and deliver major addresses there. President Kennedy agreed and the Secret Service had to case it out and interview community leaders.

When I arrived at the embassy, I met Richard Goodwin and two secret service agents whom I was to accompany. Our trip was by helicopter, a duplicate of the one the two presidents and their wives would use. I was assigned to play the role of President Kennedy as secret service agents analyzed the potential dangers that the official party might face. I also interpreted for them as they interviewed community leaders at the site. We inspected the availability of bathroom facilities since they might be needed during the visit. I took Mr. Goodwin to a small house that had inside plumbing. I said hello to the owner of the house whom I had met on an earlier visit. I asked whether Mr. Goodwin could look over the house, especially the bathroom. He said, "Of course." When he opened the door to the bathroom, a photo of Teddy Kennedy smiled out at us. The owner said quietly, "This is the Kennedy room. Mr. Teddy used it when he visited here." If memory serves, I believe that the president did, too—even though I was not in the community when the actual visit took place. His picture was alongside his brother's the next time I visited the house.

On the way back to Caracas, Mr. Goodwin asked me whether I was interested in being assigned to Washington. He told me that my name was under consideration for a senior position in the Alliance for Progress. I was surprised and mentioned it to Ele before we went to the embassy that night for a reception in honor of Mr. Goodwin.

About a week later, I received orders to report to Washington for consultation. On my arrival at National Airport (now Reagan), I was met by my old friend and colleague, Harold Walker. He took me to his home where he and his lovely wife Elizabeth put me up for the week. Harold told me that he wasn't in on the reason for the consultation, but that I would be meeting people at the White House, the Department of Labor and AFL-CIO as well as at State. He also said that the Office of the Regional Labor Adviser for the Western Hemisphere had not been filled since its former occupant, Ben Stephansky, had been appointed U.S. ambassador to Bolivia. We speculated over dinner.

My first appointment the following morning was with an aide to Richard Goodwin, who told me that I was under consideration for the regional labor position. He also said that in order to implement the Alliance for Progress, discussions were underway to integrate the Latin American areas of the State Department and the newly established Agency for International Development (AID) that replaced ICA. I was given a schedule and advised that Harold had access to vehicles to get me to appointments.

I can't remember the order of the appointments but they included Mr. Goodwin and Ralph Dungan at the White House. I saw Daniel Patrick Moynihan, then assistant secretary of labor for International Labor Relations. I met with Serafino Romualdi and Andy McClellan, followed by lunch with AFL-CIO President George Meany. I also met Victor Reuther, who had been the international secretary of the CIO before the merger with the AFL. I met Ambassador Robert Woodward, who was assistant secretary of state for American Republics Area (ARA), followed by an interview with someone in AID at Director David Bell's office. My last meeting before going back to Caracas was with Assistant Secretary Woodward, who advised me that I was the leading candidate to fill the regional labor adviser vacancy.

He also told me that, back in Venezuela, a plastic bomb had gone off in the men's room at the chancery, just outside the ambassador's office, but there were no casualties and the damage was apparently limited. His secretary called Ele for me, but there was no answer at our home. That evening, Ele called me at the Walkers to tell me that she was fine. Marcia Schor, when she heard the report about the bomb, had moved Ele over to the Schors' apartment and would keep her there until I returned on Sunday.

Marcia had reason to be concerned about Ele. A few weeks before, the wife of the personnel director of the Mene Grande Oil Company, the Venezuelan subsidiary of Gulf Oil, had been kidnapped with her daughter before being released on the outskirts of Caracas. The kidnappers told her that they had picked up the wrong person, and that the real target was Ele. You see, the Mene Grande family lived in the apartment above us, and drove a white Plymouth, as did we. We parked next to each other in the parking garage. However, the Mene Grande wife had a daughter, whom she had just picked up at school, and the kidnappers knew that Ele and I had no children. When the "chief" kidnapper rendezvoused with his colleagues on the outskirts and found that their captive had a daughter, he knew that they had made a mistake. When the embassy was advised of the kidnapping, Ele and I were moved to the home of another embassy family for several days until the security officer felt it was safe for us to return to our apartment. A bit of irony is that U.S. government policy is to refuse to pay ransom for the release of a kidnapped embassy official or dependent. I suspect that Mene Grande would have. I think the kidnappers knew that, and so money was not the motive.

President Kennedy and the First Lady made their state visit in early December. Caracas was like an armed camp, with Venezuelan soldiers and marines stationed at strategic points throughout the city and on the roofs of the houses near and around the embassy where the Kennedys were staying. The weather turned cool and rainy. The visit went off without a hitch. However, the Secret Service was given a real scare when President Betancourt led President Kennedy off the platform in the rural community to shake hands with the *campesinos* assembled to hear the presidents speak. That was not included in the program, and the Secret Service couldn't cover President Kennedy and the First Lady as they mingled with the people. The two presidents worked the crowd with enthusiasm and political skill, and the people responded with equal enthusiasm. After the state dinner that evening, the president met with the embassy staff and thanked each of us for our efforts.

On his return to Washington, President Kennedy formally nominated Ambassador Moscoso to be the coordinator of the Alliance for Progress. He had stayed on for the presidential visit and left before Christmas for Washington. In late January, an announcement was made in Washington that the Latin American country and substantive offices of State and AID were being merged. In February, I was advised that I would be transferred to Washington within sixty days to head up the combined Labor and Social Development Office for Latin America and report to the assistant secretary of state and the coordinator of the Alliance for Progress. I was authorized to make the trip by ship and we were booked on the Grace Line Santa Rosa from La Guaira to Baltimore.

Allan Stewart was quickly confirmed as the new ambassador to Venezuela to replace Ted Moscoso, and a replacement for me was requested. The last weeks in Caracas flew by as we said our goodbyes and packed our household effects for the move to Washington. Elizabeth and Nat Davis put us up at their home for the last few days. It was only a few weeks later that Nat and Elizabeth also left

Caracas, as Nat was named political adviser to Sargent Shriver in the newly created Peace Corps.

The night before we left, Ambassador Stewart picked Ele and me up for a surprise farewell party. He drove us to the AD Social Club where we were met by all of the leaders of the CTV and the AD and COPEI members of the Venezuelan Congress. We were hardly seated when President Betancourt and House Speaker Rafael Cordero arrived. It was a farewell never to be forgotten! They presented me with a copy of the Venezuelan Constitution of 1959 signed by all the AD and COPEI signatories. The president spent an hour with us, and thanked me on behalf of the government and the CTV for my efforts. As he was leaving, he said that he knew that I prized *Cantaclaro* and *Doña Bárbara*, two of the most famous novels of Rómulo Gallegos, the most heralded Venezuelan author and first elected president of the country. He then presented us with signed copies of both books. A warm *abrazo* for Ele and me—and the president departed. Allan Stewart then gave me his signed photograph, which reads, "To the best Labor Attaché I have ever worked with."

PART III

THE ALLIANCE YEARS, 1962–1977

16

The Alliance for Progress,
Washington, D.C.

Ele and I were returning to Washington as the Cold War was
heating up in the Western Hemisphere. U.S. interests were
threatened by Fidel Castro and his adherence to the Soviet bloc.

Post-World War II Latin America was in the throes of political,
economic, and social transition. The traditional feudal order and
mercantilist economic system were disintegrating. While most of
its 150,000,000 people lived in rural areas, the rural-to-urban migration had begun. Military caudillos who governed many of the
countries were challenged by reformers. The region was seething
with social unrest. Those conditions offered unique opportunities
for political upheaval, and the U.S. was determined to take action
to prevent its Cold War adversaries from moving in.

The U.S. Cold War strategy, designed by Secretary of State
George Marshall in the late 1940s, was to cement the twenty Republics of Latin America and the Caribbean to the West through
the Inter-American Treaty of Reciprocal Assistance (known as the
Rio Treaty), signed in 1947, that established collective security and
stipulated that an attack on one member state was an attack on all.
The same principle was enshrined in Article 28 of the 1948 Charter
of the Organization of American States: "Every act of aggression
by a State against the territorial integrity or the inviolability of the
territory or against the sovereignty or political independence of
an American State shall be an act of aggression against the other
American States." To reinforce that political and military alliance,
the U.S. agreed to provide economic and social assistance for economic development. In 1959, the Eisenhower administration agreed
to participate in the formation of the Inter-American Development

Bank (IDB) and then established the $500,000,000 Social Progress Trust Fund, which it entrusted the IDB to administer.

That strategy came under attack in 1959 when Fidel Castro took power in Cuba and embraced the Soviet Union and pro-communist revolutionary groups in several neighboring countries. After the CIA- directed Bay of Pigs invasion of Cuba failed to overthrow Fidel, President Kennedy called for an Alliance for Progress (AFP) in the western hemisphere—an economic and technical cooperation program to promote democracy, economic growth, and improved social conditions. It was modeled on the Marshall Plan that had revived Western Europe in the late 1940s and the 1950s. In August 1961, at Punta del Este, Latin America and the U.S. adopted the AFP. The U.S. pledged 20 billion dollars of public and private sector aid over the next decade and the Latin American countries committed themselves to political, economic, and social reforms needed to facilitate their development. The goal was to achieve a 2.5 percent annual growth rate, significant increases in employment, improved education and health systems, agrarian reform, progressive tax structures, and greater social justice. This was the meeting at which Che Guevara read aloud the Cox-Tragen paper on Venezuela.

To implement the AFP, President Kennedy integrated the Latin American bureaus of the State Department and the Agency for International Development (AID), merging the political, economic, and technical assistance resources of the U.S. government to achieve AFP goals and thwart any further inroads in the Americas by the Soviet Bloc. My job in the combined bureau was as regional labor advisor and chief of the Social Development Division.

Return to Washington

The move from Caracas to Washington was seamless. The Department authorized us to return by ship; that gave us an interlude of sun and relaxation after the tensions of the past several months in Caracas. We enjoyed ports of call like good tourists and arrived in Baltimore ready for the new challenge. My colleague and friend, Harold Walker, and his wife Elizabeth met us at dockside and drove us to a furnished apartment in Upper Georgetown that they had located and stocked with food and household supplies to tide us over for the next few days. On the drive back to Washington, Harold fed us the latest news on the bureaucratic front and briefed us on AFL-CIO's expectations from the Alliance.

I reported to work the following morning and Ele began the search for permanent quarters for us. On the trip up, we discussed in detail where we wanted to live. We decided not to live in suburbs and spend hours every day commuting to and from work. We had no children and the prospects of our becoming parents were not promising. Our choice was to buy a two or three bedroom house in the Northwest area. Ele, in her usual practical manner, had said, "Let's wait and see what is available."

While I got acclimated to the new position, she systematically scoured Northwest Washington. Each night when I got home around seven o'clock, we would have a drink as she reported on her adventures with real estate agents. She thought that most of the houses were either too large or too expensive for our pocket book. Ele refused to take on debt, and house cleaning was not on her priority list.

In the third week, she found the Towers on Cathedral Avenue, a large apartment complex of two fourteen-story towers that had a one-bedroom vacancy on the tenth floor of the East Tower at a rent comfortably within Ele's budget. It consisted of a large living/dining room, a galley-like kitchen, and a large bedroom and bath, and lots of closets, in all, about 1,000 square feet. It also had an Olympic-sized swimming pool in the park area between the two towers, a gourmet restaurant, its own weekday bus service from 7:00 a.m. to 7:00 p.m. to downtown Washington, and a well-trained maintenance staff that serviced the apartments. The rental manager and Ele hit it off, and the manager agreed to hold off showing the vacant unit to anyone else until Saturday when I was not scheduled to work.

My reaction was that it would not meet our needs! I had visions of our living the same sort of social life we had enjoyed in El Salvador, Chile, and Venezuela. Before we went to bed, she persuaded me to agree to visit the Towers on Saturday morning.

On Saturday morning, the rental manager showed us the unit, which was light, airy, and spacious. Ele described how she would arrange the furniture and how each piece would be placed. We would need to buy a few rugs since there were hardwood floors, and she said quite casually that she had found just the right living room and area rugs, drapes, and other items the day before on sale at the Hecht Company. I was trapped and I knew it!

We signed a one-year lease and headed downtown to Hecht's. As we left the rental office, Ele produced a bus schedule and told me that in ten minutes a bus would be arriving to take us downtown, then we would have lunch at the National Gallery before taking another bus back to our temporary apartment. I never regretted that Ele had taken charge and found the Towers. We spent all our remaining years in Washington residing there, and made lifelong friends.

For Ele, the Towers was a welcome place to live. During that tour, I went to work at 7:00 a.m. five or six days a week, and got home no earlier than 7:00 p.m. Ele was by herself most of the time. She found neighbors she liked and with whom she could discuss the political and economic issues of the day. She had her Washington Post every day and the New York Times on Sundays to keep abreast of events. The Towers bus to downtown Washington gave her a comfortable schedule for getting around. She built a social life with people in the building since so many of our colleagues at the State Department, with families, lived in different directions, some in the Virginia suburbs and others in Maryland. Getting together with many of those friends usually required long-term planning and a choice of dates that did not conflict with their family commitments and demanding jobs. Living in the Towers offered Ele an opportunity to use her time effectively in her own way.

My Position

My first day at the State Department started out routinely. I presented myself to the personnel office where I was advised that the medical branch had determined that I no longer needed a waiver for my hearing loss and was asked to sign the transfer papers as a Foreign Service reserve officer. After I was given a short orientation course on the Foreign Service and the lay-out of the State Department building, I was instructed to report to the administrative officer for the State/AID Bureau for Inter-American Affairs, Mel Spector.

When I arrived at his third floor office, I was awed by the activity as people rushed in with a seemingly unending flow of papers with demands for his immediate attention. Mel did not keep me waiting for long and then he took an hour to brief me on the fluid situation in the newly formed joint State and AID Bureau. He spelled out the tensions that had arisen when two groups of officers from organizations of different cultures were merged. The State Department officers were schooled in policy and analysis, while those from AID wanted action now to deal with urgent operating problems. State was a career system with slow advancement in grade and salary while AID paid higher salaries to attract needed technicians for project planning and implementation. Mel told me that tensions were abating as AID and State officers learned to work together in analyzing policy and operations to achieve U.S. foreign policy objectives.

Mel further explained that there was confusion about lines of authority in both State and AID. When President Kennedy created the Alliance for Progress and named Ambassador Moscoso as the coordinator, he did not give Moscoso the autonomy that he invested in his brother-in-law Sargent Shriver as head of the Peace Corps. Ted was to run the Alliance, but report not to the White House, but to both the secretary of State and the administrator of AID—two bosses with different agendas and bureaucracies.

Mel took me down the hall to see Richard Goodwin, the acting assistant secretary of State, and Ambassador Moscoso. Their offices were mad houses, with the people rushing around, reams of paper piled on the desks, and lots of loud talking in surrounding corridors. I think Mr. Goodwin said, "Good to see you again. Get settled. We'll talk later." Moscoso gave me a firm handshake as he ran out for an appointment, with an entourage in tow.

Mel then ushered me up a corridor, around a corner to an interior hallway far from the nerve center, and opened the door to an office that had my name on it. "This," he said, "is the office of the state regional labor advisor and the chief of the Latin American Social Development Division." He opened the door and I met my staff: Harold Walker and my secretary, Becky Scroggs, both on the AID payroll. Mel explained that AID had more money than State, so my State position would be funded by AID for the time being.

Harold I knew well from my AID assignments. Becky was a career secretary from North Carolina—a crackerjack with superior secretarial and administrative skills.

After Mel left, Harold, Becky, and I went to lunch in the State Department cafeteria where they briefed me on the tensions and friction that existed between the AID worldwide offices and the "autonomous" Latin American Bureau. AID, headed worldwide by David Bell, directed the worldwide foreign assistance program, with one of his regional directors, Ambassador Moscoso, assigned the specific responsibility of implementing the Alliance for Progress (AFP) without a presidential directive spelling out the relationship between the two. Bell considered himself Moscoso's boss, while Moscoso considered that he was the head of an autonomous office. That conflict affected me directly since the AID Central Labor Office expected to direct the AID aspects of my work—and Moscoso had said no.

He also described a tug-of-war at the AFL-CIO between Bill Doherty, Victor Reuther, and Serafino Romualdi for control of labor policy for Latin America. Bill Doherty, the son of the president of the powerful Postal Workers Union, had been directing a labor-training program in Brazil independently of the Peruvian center created by Serafino. Victor, the brother of AFL-CIO Vice President Walter Reuther was maneuvering to become the director of international affairs for the AFL-CIO and sought to reorient its worldwide labor strategy and operations.

Harold then informed me of tensions with the Department of Labor. One of the president's inner circle, Daniel Patrick Moynihan, had been named to replace George Cabot Lodge as the assistant secretary of Labor for International Labor Affairs. Harold's friends at the Labor Department had alerted him to Moynihan's intention of playing a major role in formulating international labor policy and overseeing activities at State and AID.

That was enough for my first day. I briefed Ele that evening over scotch and soda.

The next day, Becky walked me around to each one of the State-AID offices and introduced me to secretaries and clerks, most of whom had been reassigned from AID and State to this new hybrid animal. People on the AID payroll were working side-by-side with people from State. Many were visibly upset and complained that lines of authority were not clear. The "them" and "those" of a few weeks earlier were still in the process of becoming a "we."

Becky then set up appointments for me to meet those with whom I was to work. The first was with the assistant secretary of State, followed by Ambassador Moscoso, the international labor adviser to the secretary of state, the director of the AID Labor Affairs Office and then the office directors of the new AFP Bureau. My predecessor as regional labor adviser looked to the adviser of the secretary of state for policy guidance on labor matters and to the assistant secretary for area and country direction.

That day, Richard Goodwin, the acting assistant secretary of state, met with me. He told me that Ambassador Edwin Martin would be named assistant secretary and advised me not make appointments with aides in the assistant secretary's office until Martin took over because there would be front office personnel changes. He urged me to get acquainted with Moscoso's team. He also instructed me to inform Ralph Dungan at the White House that I was on board.

After I left Goodwin's office, I learned that a few weeks earlier, on a Saturday afternoon, after the then Assistant Secretary Robert Woodward had left his office, crews came in and removed all his personal effects and replaced them with Goodwin's. The ensuing uproar over the event caused the president to drop his plans to name Goodwin as assistant secretary.

Later that day, I met with the AID director of Labor Programs who told me that he was not at all happy with the concept of "the autonomy of the Latin American Bureau." I promised him that, through Harold Walker, I would keep him fully informed about all relevant developments in the Western Hemisphere and consult with him on proposals for labor projects in the region.

The following day, about 7:30 a.m. before he got swept up in his routine of meetings and appointments, I stuck my head into Ted Moscoso's office and asked whether he had any advice for me. He gave me a green light to meet his key senior staff. So, that morning, Becky set up an appointment with Marvin Weisman, the Director of Institutional Development, in whose office my division was located on the organization chart. I would ask his assistance in meeting Moscoso's inner circle: Ray Sternfeld, the Director of Programming; Phil Glaessner, the Director of Development Lending; and Bill Rogers, the AFP Legal Advisor. My first meeting with Marvin Weisman went well. We developed an easy and close relationship from day one. He was the only senior officer around Moscoso who had actual field experience in Latin America. His field was public administration, and he had worked with Ray Sternfeld in the Bureau of the Budget before an assignment to Chile. We compared our experience in Latin American and had similar perceptions of the challenges facing the Alliance, especially the dearth of viable, efficient public and private institutions throughout the region.

We also discussed the inherent difficulties in my job as a State Department labor policy adviser and as an AID program manager. We reached an understanding that I looked to State, not him, for policy direction on labor policy issues, advice to labor attachés, and relations with trade unions. On labor and social projects for the Latin American region, we agreed that I considered him my immediate supervisor. I also alerted him to possible White House interest in the regional labor program.

Marvin took charge of my meeting the rest of Moscoso team. He asked his secretary to make appointments with Bill Rogers and Phil Glaessner. As for Ray Sternfeld, he just walked me around the corner, entered his office and said, "Ray, meet Irv. You two need to talk soon." Ray gave me an appointment for the following day.

Ray was from the Bureau of the Budget where he had been a specialist on foreign assistance programs, including the Marshall Plan, Point Four, and IIAA. He had no field experience except for investigating "problem" projects. He was known for his analytical skill and managerial capabilities, with an expert eye for identifying inadequacies and lacunae in programs and projects. My colleagues told me that he was the man to be convinced before a program or project could move forward.

Ray briefed me on criteria and procedures for the preparation and approval of projects that either strengthened public sector capability to plan and implement programs or improved tax revenues and foreign exchange earnings. He gave priority to comprehensive sectoral programs in agriculture, industrial development, and education over individual projects because they offered greater promise of achieving the objectives set forth in the Charter of Punta del Este. He also made clear that, while he was concerned about Communist influence in Latin American labor movements, he was skeptical about manpower, skills training, and labor union projects. He also understood that my job had two dimensions and that he did not play a role in my State Department reporting functions or my office's relations with the Embassies.

He stressed the need for moving money into Latin America as expeditiously as possible. He described how that was done under the Marshall Plan through program loan and reported that the AFP was testing the effectiveness of program lending with Brazil, Chile and Colombia. Under program loan, the U.S. government and the host government would agree on a number of macroeconomic and sectoral objectives to be reached during the fiscal year and the U.S. would then make a global loan to assist the government in meeting those objectives.

He also told me that *servicios* were to be phased out. I was surprised because I had seen them as an effective vehicle for introducing new government programs and for insuring the continuity of qualified staff in public sector agencies. He said his experience in the Bureau of the Budget had demonstrated that the mechanism impeded effective oversight of the use of funds, that the *servicio* programs were not innovative and tended to get struck in given project operations, and that host governments were not incorporating the funding of established programs into the national budgets as contemplated under the *servicio* agreements. In addition, he said that many Latin American political leaders had complained about the *servicios'* autonomous status and cited them as impediments to developing more comprehensive government programs; those critics advocated direct monetary grants to their governments, which would allow them to choose within their own budgetary process which activities to fund.

Joining us at the interview was one of Ray's program economists, Chilean born John Elac. From his comments, I felt that he shared my concerns about the different stages of development in Latin America when compared to the developed, but war ravaged countries of Western Europe. I questioned the capability of Latin American political, economic and social institutions to implement complex development projects and the absence of technical and skilled work force needed to design and implement the process. I argued that the first priority of the AFP should be to help countries build the framework for a modern state, create a viable economic base and train people at all levels to do the required jobs.

My next appointment that morning was with Bill Rogers, the astute lawyer from the Washington firm of Fortas, Arnold & Porter; he had worked with Ambassador Moscoso in Operation Bootstrap in Puerto Rico and subsequently represented major U.S. corporations in negotiations and litigation in Latin America. He had a firm grasp of the political and policy issues with which the AFP was dealing, but little operational experience in addressing development problems. I admired his ability to define succinctly the crux of a situation or problem. He covered some very thorny issues with a precision that readily gained my confidence. He understood the complications of my job and assured me that he was there to help.

When I returned to my office, Becky told me that Ralph Dungan's secretary from the White House had called and asked that I be at his office at 1:30 p.m. That was my first official visit to the White House, and to an office just around the corner from the Oval Office itself!

I remember my trepidation that afternoon when I appeared at the back gate of the White House, introduced myself to the guard and was escorted to Mr. Dungan's office. His first question was, "Why didn't you call me the first day you reported for duty?" I said that I hadn't understood the priority. He just smiled and said, "Irv, you have a major job to perform in the next few weeks. You are to negotiate a contract with the AFL-CIO to create a hemisphere-wide labor-training program to support free trade unions. The president wants the agreement in place by summer. Keep me informed of progress and problems."

As I left his office, I almost bumped into his next appointment. Mr. Dungan said, "Irv, meet Cord Meyer if you haven't met him before." Well, I had heard of Cord Meyer. Some of my colleagues in Chile and Venezuela had told me that he was "Mr. Hush Hush," CIA Chief of Special Operations. We nodded and I left.

As soon as I reached my office, I called Serafino Romualdi, and we set the following Monday for me to spend the day at his office, working on a draft agreement between AID and the AFL-CIO.

It was not until several days later that I finally met with Philip Glaessner, the Director of Capital Development, AFP's chief loan officer. A veteran of the Marshall Plan, he was an expert on loan programs He and his staff designed an autonomous AFP loan process independent of that of AID for the rest of the world. He supervised loan officers assigned to the various AFP countries. I was briefed on the criteria for making and approving loans and the critical inputs needed for justifying a loan. I also learned that the Capital Development Office, like the Program Office, had little interest in social development, manpower, and trade union programs.

American Institute for Free Labor Development (AIFLD)

Most of April and May was spent with Serafino Romualdi and Andy McClellan negotiating line by line an agreement to create an inter-American labor leader training program. The purpose was to counter communist efforts to take over union movements in the region by providing Latin American unions with the leadership, skills, and programs to attract worker support.

Serafino had spent many years perfecting the design of a center based in Latin America and operated by Latin American leaders trained by U.S. trade unionists. He saw the process in two steps: (1) a teacher training activity by U.S. instructors preparing Latin Americans to be future teachers and (2) adapting the U.S. bread-and-butter union model to the Latin American milieu, including union management, labor-management relations, and services for the members. He proposed a training base in Mexico, a formal link between the training base and the International Confederation of Free Trade Unions (ICFTU) and its regional affiliate, the Inter-American Regional Workers' Organization (ORIT). His timeline was for a ten– to twenty–year project that included technical assistance by the Mexico center to union movements throughout Latin America. He understood the history of political party involvement in union affairs in Latin America, including "subsidies" for union leaders paid by political parties, governments, and some employers, and had some ideas about how to displace them over time. He also agreed to reaching out to the Christian Democrat and other non-Communist labor unions not affiliated with ICFTU and ORIT. Molding those ideas and considerations into an operational plan that met U.S. political objectives and AID's project norms and format took a lot of detailed work and careful wording. The negotiations were slow.

The agreement being negotiated was for a non-repayable regional grant to the AFL-CIO. AID had extensive substantive and procedural requirements for such an agreement. And, regional funds were limited. About 85 percent of the AFP funds were allotted to country programs, that is, funds designated to each eligible country for the in-country program. The remaining 15 percent was available to the Washington office to finance regional projects. A regional project could be justified if it was to test an experimental approach to dealing with a given development problem that existed in various countries or a service to the missions that could be provided more effectively or economically regionally than in country programs. I was designing a regional service available to all countries.

As I started the negotiations, I met resistance from the Program Office, which advised me that no regional funds would be allocated for a labor leader training activity of any kind. It was argued that if individual countries wanted such a project, it could be included in that country's annual program. It took a high-level intervention from the White House to Ambassador Moscoso to overcome the reluctance of the Program Office. It was only then that I received a go-ahead to put the proposal into the project approval process.

Just as I thought we had reached an understanding, I received a call to go urgently to Ralph Dungan's office. I briefed him on what we had negotiated and where we stood. He then informed me that I would have to begin again, because there had been a major policy decision by the AFL-CIO that Bill Doherty, not Serafino, would be in charge of the labor leader training program, and that Bill had a totally different approach from Serafino's. So, back to square one of a very difficult negotiation that often had me back in Ralph Dungan's office to explain why Bill and I could not agree on a provision or procedure. Bill wanted a simple agreement under which AID would turn funds over to him and let him design and run the program. I told him that was not permitted under the Congressional mandate given to AID. He went over my head to Ambassador Moscoso where Bill was told that AID required a detailed operational plan before money could be allocated. On his appeal to Ralph, he was given the same message.

June and July were spent in long, difficult sessions on Bill's proposal to set up a training center in Washington, D.C to be called the American Institute for Free Labor Development (AIFLD). Its program was AFL-CIO designed and delivered. Its courses, while similar to those outlined by Serafino, were to be taught by U.S. instructors. The selection of labor leaders for training was an AIFLD process in which AID participation was limited to obtaining security clearances. When I raised the need to broaden the base of labor support for the free trade union movement by reaching out to Christian Democratic and other non-communist unions not affiliated with the ICFTU and ORIT, Bill rejected the language worked out with Serafino, and said that was a policy question that AIFLD would consider at the proper time. Several other substantive issues that had been worked out with Serafino were not included in Bill's plans.

In early August, I presented the AIFLD regional project proposal for approval. It described the structure of AIFLD, the training courses, the curriculum, the number of instructors and criteria for selection of trainees, the number of courses per year, the number of Latin American trainees to be invited to each course, the relationship of the regional project to country programs and the inputs expected from the AFL-CIO to support AIFLD. I don't remember which item Bill believed he had not agreed to, but I was summoned to Ralph Dungan's office for a meeting with Bill, where we went over the document, changed a few words and I was authorized to proceed. As I left Mr. Dungan's office, I ran into Cord Myer, who invited me to lunch.

The draft agreement was quickly approved. In September 1962, at a meeting in the office of AFL-CIO President George Meany, the Regional Agreement was signed, Mr. Meany announced that Bill Doherty would be the Director of AIFLD. Serafino did not hide his disappointment. I was named AID liaison with AIFLD and delegated to my colleague, Harold Walker, the job to keep up with developments and monitor compliance with the conditions of the

Agreement.

No one in the Latin American Labor Office or the Social Development Division was surprised about eighteen months later when the New York Times and the Washington Post published reports that the Bill Doherty's work in Brazil had been a CIA clandestine operation and that AIFLD had been originally planned as a CIA operation. It was speculated that someone at the White House or the AFL-CIO learned about the CIA plan and sabotaged it by announcing that it would be an Alliance for Progress initiative. Maybe that's why I usually ran into Cord Meyer as I left Ralph Dungan's office. At any rate, AIFLD is still operating as an AID regional project.

The Alliance

While I was negotiating the AIFLD contract, Edwin Martin was named assistant secretary of State for Inter-American Affairs. He was a well-respected economist who was well-ground in labor affairs. It was not until mid-May that I was able to talk with him one-on-one even though I attended his staff meetings. He understood the threat that Cuban and Soviet infiltration posed to the West and of the importance of both solid intelligence about the situation in each country in Latin America and positive action under the Alliance to strengthen free trade unionism. His orientation helped me understand the comprehensive strategy that the Alliance for Progress embodied for linking Latin America to the West in the Cold War through a partnership for political, economic and social development.

The Agreement reached at Punto del Este spelled out the development goals and the obligations of the parties to achieve them. To coordinate U.S. actions to support those goals, President Kennedy merged the Latin American bureaus of State and AID. The combined operation provided the machinery for an integrated political, economic and social analysis of conditions in each country that would enable the definition and implementation of short and long term actions to deal with priority issues. Resources from both agencies would be used to design and evaluate courses of action. At the country level, each Ambassador headed a Country Team that would assess country conditions and oversee the execution of program operations.

My briefings by the U.S. leadership of the Alliance all fell into place as I understood the overall strategy. I saw my specific role as the monitor of labor movements in Latin America, who was to alert the assistant secretary and the AFP Coordinator to emerging problems and to propose actions that could minimize social unrest through improved working and living conditions and the participation of people in the development process.

Ele's Decision

During the first few months in Washington, Ele rested after the ordeal of the last several months in Caracas. Then came Memorial Day when the swimming pool opened, and she developed a wonderful circle of friends with whom she spent many afternoons swimming and talking. There were young U.S. professionals, Pentagon officers, officials of international agencies, diplomats, and even the lady from Alabama Dorothy Bush, then secretary of the Democratic Party, who read the roll call at the National Convention. At the center of the group were Faye and Frank Sherry, he a patent attorney and she a distinguished artist. Senator and Mrs. Long of Missouri were frequent participants (their daughter had married John Dean of Watergate fame when he was lifeguard at our pool the year before). It was like living on a trans-Atlantic liner.

By the time the pool closed on Labor Day, Ele was over rehab and wanted something to do. She was invited to lunch with Gertrude Schermerhorn, Olive Clapper, and her old bosses at the U.S. Department of Labor, and they offered her the old job back. When I arrived home that Friday night, Ele was very excited. She wanted to take the offer, but had decided to discuss it with me first. I was not sure that she ought to take it. In fact, based on her superb job with the farms, I was hoping that Ele would become the investment manager for our family.

Well, we had the worst argument of our married life that ran through Sunday night. Lots of shouting and quite a few tears! Friday night was the first night of our married life when we went to bed mad at each other. Saturday, I went shopping alone, because she was so upset. Saturday afternoon I asked her if she would post-

pone her decision while she explored the stock market and investments. She was somewhat mollified. We had a pleasant dinner and
an amicable goodnight kiss. Sunday afternoon she proposed a one-
month delay in responding to the job offer while she investigated.

The following day, Ele went down to the office of a Washington
brokerage firm to investigate. She was introduced to Jim Staggs, the
broker of the day, that is, the broker assigned to meet potential new
clients or answer questions that non-clients might raise. Ele and Jim
spoke for hours. Ele laid out what she wanted to learn about the
stock market. He asked about her experience. When she told him
of her work at Allied Youth on teenage drinking, Jim confessed that
he was an alcoholic. He offered to teach Ele the market if she would
help him kick the habit. An agreement was struck.

For the next several months, Jim taught her the market. She
read every available piece of literature on the stock market, business cycles, rating of stocks and bonds, annual reports, practices
of brokerage houses, and creating diversified investment packages.
Whenever Jim had the urge to drink, he would call her and they
would be on the phone for hours. Ele had the patience of Job, but
she knew that only he could make that critical decision to say "no."

She also contacted other brokerage offices to round out her
learning process. At one she ran into Ken Cosby, the son-in-law of
our old friend from Mexico, Josephine Littlejohn. He was as helpful
to her as Jim.

Ele never again raised the question of going back to work at the
Department of Labor. She loved the challenges of the stock market and the analytical work required to evaluate and make investments. In 1962, she took over the management of not only our stock
holdings but our other assets, as skimpy as they were. She built our
financial base.

Labor Advisor and Division Chief

While AIFLD was my primary activity for my first six months on
the job, I also had two other functions to carry out: first, as the regional labor adviser for the inter-American region, and second, as
chief of the newly formed Division of Social Development. The first
was a traditional State Department analytical and advisory posi-

tion. The second was to advise AID missions in twenty countries on planning and implementing social action projects.

My daily routine began about 7:30 a.m. with reading the dispatches from labor attachés and embassy labor officers about happenings in their respective countries and identifying those that should be brought to the attention of the assistant secretary, the worldwide Labor Advisor, the AID Labor Office and/or the Coordinator of the AFP. I attended staff meetings of the assistant secretary to keep him abreast of regional labor developments and make sure that I was in turn aware of other events that might affect my job.

The number of dispatches per day varied greatly; sometimes my entire morning would be dedicated to prepare a synthesis of reports, with recommendations for appropriate policy guidance to the embassy. Sometimes, I would find the information important for a jigsaw of events, like a wave of violent actions or strikes that were similar to those in neighboring countries, many with operational patterns that bore the footprint of Castro or the Communist-led WFTU. Sometimes the information would raise questions that required further elaboration from the embassy or background information from the Intelligence Office of the State Department or the Office of International Labor Affairs of the Department of Labor (OILA), Sometimes, calls came from the CIA for clarification about a dispatch or my take on its significance.

The most time-consuming part of my job turned out to the formulation of the social development program. The DSD was one of five divisions in the Office of Institutional Development, the others being: Rural Development (formerly Agriculture), Public Health, Public Administration, and Urban and Industrial Development. There had been no similar activity in predecessor inter-American aid agencies and what its scope should be was unclear.

The heads of the divisions came together once or twice a week at staff meetings chaired by Marvin Weisman. Through 1962, my relations with the other divisions were limited. While I met my fellow directors and was briefed on their activities, I concentrated on AIFLD, my State functions and weighing the potential role of the DSD.

In considering the options for a DSD program, I analyzed the program presentations from the AID Country Missions. Most were concentrated in agriculture, education and public health, following the traditional pattern of the IIAA. Only in a few countries—Argentina, Brazil, Chile, Colombia, and Mexico—were there sector programs or urban and industrial development projects. Several had social activities in public health and agriculture projects such as training health workers in rural communities, organizing mothers' groups to improve nutrition, and/or support for rural credit unions or marketing cooperatives. Almost none of the education projects had components that dealt with the school as a community catalyst for change or providing night courses. The proposed programs reflected that the Missions, which had been set up to transfer technology, were not staffed to deal with the macro development objectives of the AFP.

Each country presentation highlighted multiple socioeconomic problems each country faced, including the lack of political maturity, the weakness of institutional, physical, and financial infrastructure, or the shortage of trained specialists and technicians to deal with problems of transition. Some cited burgeoning rural-to-urban migration, lack of social cohesion, and widespread rural or urban poverty. Few had projects that addressed those key problems. I raised with Marvin Weisman and Ray Sternfeld my concern about the absence of projects to deal with rural-to-urban migration and burgeoning urban slums that were potent threats to achieving the objectives of the AFP and most vulnerable to Cuban and Soviet infiltration. I proposed that the SDS concentrate its efforts on new approaches to dealing with those problems and asked for a couple of experienced brains to help us think through what might be done and how to introduce appropriate steps for incorporating them into country planning.

I was authorized to hire two consultants. One was Ann Brownell, whom I had known in Venezuela and the other, Csanad Toth, a Hungarian urban planner who was a student leader in the 1956 uprising in his home country. Ann concentrated on the rural sector and Csanad on the urban. In late 1962, I was authorized to contract another, Frank Gannon, an experienced manager of Catholic social programs in Central America and a former New England teamster union leader. Frank also backed up Harold Walker in monitoring the rapidly growing AIFLD program.

As we formulated the SDS program, I periodically consulted two of the principal congressional supporters of the AFP: Dante Fascell of Florida, then ranking Democrat on the House Foreign Affairs Committee, and his Republican counterpart, Bradford Morse of Massachusetts. Both had special interest in social development and made significant inputs into our thinking.

While we were getting underway, two Cooperative Specialists not in my division, Al Marble and Bob Bonham, presented a multi-country social development initiative that offered promise for helping lower income rural and urban people. With the support of the US Cooperative movement, they proposed the creation of an Inter-American Cooperative Bank to provide greater liquidity for credit unions and other grassroots cooperatives throughout Latin America. Its existence could provide a source of funding for grassroots projects that Ann, Csanad, and Frank might identify. We didn't call it micro-finance then, but that was the purpose. Those of us who knew about the "Penny Foundation" (*La Fundación del Centavo*) in Guatemala and its work in helping small communities finance small water projects, bridges, and other community improvement projects found the prospect of a cooperative bank promising. My colleagues and I were disappointed the proposal was not approved by the AFP Loan Committee; its message seemed to be that AFP loans should be government-to-government.

While we were still considering the long term focus for the DSD, some promising project opportunities arose. For example, after the AIFLD agreement was signed, I was invited to join Ambassador Moscoso and Ray Sternfeld on a visit to Central America. Our first stop was in Guatemala where we met with Henry "Hank" Duflan, the director of ROCAP (the Regional Office for Central America and Panama) and undersecretary of Defense in the Eisenhower administration. President Kennedy created ROCAP as a multi-country mission to support Central American economic integration. In his briefing, Hank raised the need for training a new generation of grassroots rural people in the use of modern facilities, equipment and services available to raise agricultural production and improve living conditions in their communities, as an initial step in moderating the accelerating rural-to-urban migration in the region. When I returned to Washington, I asked Ann Brownell to see if she could design a responsive project and she did: the Central American Rural Community Leadership Program that Hank approved.

Ann found a capable partner in Father Toomey of New Orleans' Loyola University and negotiated a program to train young community leaders and acquaint them with the means for their communities to access government and private sector facilities, equipment, and services. The course included information on accounting, marketing crops, community organization, and managing small businesses, including cooperatives. Father Toomey enlisted the cooperation of Landívar University in Guatemala City, a Jesuit center whose core curriculum was agronomy and rural development. The course provided sixty days training at Loyola, followed by a month at Landívar. It was planned that once established the program would be conducted at Landívar to reduce costs and be identified as a Central American program.

The design of another project for northern Brazil was proposed by the Consul General in Recife, Ed Rowell. This was the time of great unrest in the northeast Brazil, with farm invasions led by Francisco Julião, and the heyday of liberation theology that some called "Communism with Christ". No area of Latin America seemed more attuned to Castro's message of Revolution than this poverty-stricken area. Over a long weekend, Ed and I discussed the need for social change in the region and the contrast between the still feudal system of the Northeast and emerging capital formation structures of the more developed area of São Paolo and Porto Alegre. We also talked with priests whom I had met at the Centro Bellarmino in Santiago, Chile about their views of the situation. When I returned to Washington, I asked Csanad, based on his experience in Hungary, to develop a framework for possible projects to discuss with the Consul General.

A third proposal arose from a trip to Bogotá and Lima that I made primarily on my State Department trade union agenda. Colombia was emerging from a decade of violent Civil War typified by horrendous acts of revenge by Conservative Party adherents against Liberal Party followers and vice versa. Rural life had been disrupted and people fled to the cities for safety. I was struck by the population growth in Bogotá since my last visit and the sense of insecurity one felt in the downtown areas, where gangs of children were living on the streets and spreading an aura of violence. The ambassador advised me that city services and police were overwhelmed and asked me to think about what might be done. On my return, I asked Ann to consider possible approaches to redeeming those young people.

In Lima, the Odría military dictatorship had been replaced by a democratically elected government. Here, tens of thousands of poor indigenous people were pouring into Lima from the Andean highlands. Lima had been an elegant colonial city known for its parks, plazas and stately buildings. Now, its colonial glories were being inundated by people living in chicken coops in the desert surrounding the city. Communities without basic services or sanitation had already doubled or even tripled in size. Jobs and opportunities for these new residents were a political concern to the embassy but not the subject of project plans by the USAID. I recommended to Marvin that he send a team to work with the Mission on a urban development plan, with a strong social development component.

The Inter-American Arena

In May 1962, at the second meeting of Economic Ministers on the Alliance held in Buenos Aires, it was decided, among other things, to create a task force on social development, which was to prepare a policy statement and plan of action for consideration at the third meeting to be held in October 1963 in São Paolo. After the meeting I was appointed the principal U.S. member of the task force to prepare the policy statement and instructed to contact Dr. Theo Crevenna at the Organization of American States (OAS) who was the secretary of the task force.

At my first meeting with Theo, he indicated how difficult it was merely to define social development, much less a course of action. To many Latin American delegations, it was essentially education. To others, it was social programs by governments to service people. To a few, it meant helping the people to mobilize resources, both human and material, to help themselves. To some economists, it seemed just a bad word. In this milieu of disaccord, he scheduled inter-country drafting sessions in Washington in the fall, looking to present a consensus paper in January 1963 to the third meeting of Economic Ministers in Buenos Aires.

The task force met several times in the fall but made very little headway. Military governments wanted no talk of popular participation or grassroots programs that might give their opponents a pretext for demanding more voice in governing. Almost all of the countries vetoed proposals to increase social services since their treasuries were already short of resources and their tax structures and collection systems were so ineffective. Every time a new social service was proposed in the draft paper, the Latin American members of the task force called on the U.S. to provide grant funds to cover the cost.

Preparing for the trip to Buenos Aires, I obtained permission from Ambassador Moscoso and Ray Sternfeld to have Ele accompany me. As the only U.S. member of the task force, I needed her to be with me to make sure that I heard everything being discussed around the table. I offered to cover all her expenses and they gave me their approval.

While I was engaged in the negotiations, Ele had been on her annual farm trip. She had taken a briefcase full of data on crop and marketing conditions in South Dakota and California that she accumulated from consultations at the U.S. Department of Agriculture. She decided to travel by Greyhound bus: however, the bus trip didn't turn out to be as easy or comfortable as she had expected. The service had deteriorated substantially since her mother, grandmother, and she made their 1939 trip to the two Worlds' Fairs in New York and San Francisco.

Other than an incident in Chicago, the trip went well. The president of Railway Telegraphers Union, Bob Coutts, a friend whom we met through my colleague Harold Walker, invited her to be his guest for a couple of days en route to the South Dakota farm. On her arrival, while she was telephoning to advise him of her arrival, a sneak thief tried to steal her purse. Ele laid down the phone, grabbed the man's shirt, screamed "Police!," pinned him against the phone booth, and kneed him in the crotch. The police led the young man away while Ele continued her call to Bob. When Ele left two days later, Bob and a couple of his union executives accompanied her to the bus and waited until she was on her way.

The rest of the trip went extremely well. In Aberdeen, she and her tenant spent three days together reviewing the land and the accounts and arranging to sell the fall crops, an additional tree program to protect the topsoil, and other improvements to hold water. At dinner the last evening, her tenant suggested that they work together without a farm agent and move from a share cropping arrangement to an annual cash rent payable at the beginning of the year, offering an annual rent substantially higher than the sharecropping arrangement.

In Tulare, she inspected the ranch and supervised the sale of the crops. The output was substantially better than prior years. She also found that her Pixley tenant preferred a similar arrangement to that offered in South Dakota. So, she converted both farms to the new direct relationship and an annual rent.

On her return from the farm trip, I invited her to join me at the meeting in Buenos Aires. She proposed visiting Colombia, Peru, Bolivia, and Paraguay en route to Buenos Aires. Pan Am had no problem accommodating the stopovers for the same fare as Washington–Buenos Aires–Washington. So, we made plans for the trip in mid-January 1963.

Shortly after I bought the ticket, Theo determined that we were not close enough to a consensus to produce a draft paper. It was decided to cancel task force participation at Buenos Aires and continue its work in Washington in early March.

In the meantime, the ambassadors in Venezuela, Peru, and Bolivia requested that, in my capacity of regional labor adviser, I consult with them on various in-country labor problems. Assistant Secretary Martin instructed me to go to the countries as soon as possible and authorized me to travel in January 1963. With Pan Am's help, Ele's trip was rescheduled so she could meet me in Bolivia. Her new itinerary included Guadeloupe, Barranquilla, Bogotá, Lima—Macchu Picchu, La Paz, Asunción, and Buenos Aires. She left several days before me.

I worked on some thorny issues in my three stops; almost all had both State and AID dimensions. I met many government officials, labor leaders, and a few Cuban refugees and made extensive notes for discussion with the assistant secretary and Ambassador Moscoso on my return to Washington.

Ele had a wonderful time savoring the art and culture of the places she visited. The high point was her visit to Cuzco and Macchu Picchu with its unique beauty and extraordinary vistas. She took the train from Cuzco to Puno and a boat across Lake Titicaca to La Paz where I met her at the train station. She regaled me with the description of her train and boat ride across the Lake. A storm broke as her train approached Puno about 10:00 p.m., with the passengers rushed under umbrellas to the *Esmeralda*, the passenger ferry that in the late nineteenth century had been brought up in sections from a Pacific port to the *altiplano* at 12,000 feet. Each of the passengers was assigned a berth and advised that dinner was being served in the dining room. The passengers in rain gear were seated at small tables, as waiters in formal dress and gloves, their feet splashing through rain-swept floors, served a four-course dinner. She recounted the elegance of her server, his gloved fingers holding her soup bowl while maneuvering to avoid the pitch and roll of the ship in the rain engulfed the dining room. In spite of her concerns, the captain assured his guests that the *Esmeralda* had survived more hazardous storms.

During my consultation in La Paz, we were the guests of the AID director, Alex Firfer and his wife Amy. Most of my work was with the U.S. Ambassador Ben Stephansky, my predecessor as regional labor advisor. He briefed me on labor union developments and involved me in discussions with labor leaders, including Bolivia's then Vice President Juan Lechín who was also leader of the Bolivisan Confederation of Labor (CTB). Alex also introduced us to social development components of the AID program, including plans for a national community development program, in which AID would train community workers in rural communities to help their fellow *campesinos* deal with local economic and social problems. It had many components of Jimmy Yen's program. We took trips across the *altiplano* to see conditions in various rural villages. At one village, we ran into some *Aymara* farmers (the traditional indigenous people of the *altiplano*) who were celebrating some feast day and feeling no pain; they approached Alex and offered to trade their women for Amy. We rushed back to the official car and were several kilometers away before slowing down.

Inter-American Meeting of Ministers of Labor

Soon after I returned from Bolivia, I was advised that the first meeting of Labor Ministers of the OAS member states had been convoked for May in Bogotá, Colombia. I was instructed to prepare the briefing book for U.S. Secretary of Labor Willard Wirtz and Assistant Secretary of Labor Daniel Patrick "Pat" Moynihan. I met with Pat and we arranged a timeline for reviewing the documents, drafting the briefing book and briefing the secretary. As it turned out, Pat had a conflicting commitment with the International Labor Organization (ILO) in Geneva and only I accompanied the secretary.

After obtaining all the documents and a list of anticipated participants, I drafted briefing papers on each item, with proposed positions for the U.S. to take on each issue, and bio sketches on each of the participants, including some personal notes on those ministers I had already met or worked with. I also added a special briefing paper on issues I thought might arise that could cause some problems for the secretary. One special item was a probable host country (Colombia) initiative to ask the ministers to call for inter-American action to compensate coffee workers for lost wages because of the low world price. To that paper, I attached statistical data that showed that only large wealthier growers actually employed substantial numbers of farm workers and that those wages had remained constant for many years, demonstrating little connection between world prices for coffee and the wages paid farm laborers. The data also showed that most small coffee planters did their own picking no matter what the price.

I finally met Secretary Wirtz a day or two before we departed for Bogotá. He decided not to take anyone from his own staff, so the U.S. delegation was just the two of us, plus the labor officer at the embassy. We flew in an official U.S. government plane that President Kennedy authorized. During the three days in Bogotá, I was almost constantly at Secretary Wirtz's side, as his interpreter, his analyst, and his adviser. I arranged meetings with key ministers, many of whom I already knew; the meetings were cordial and non-confrontational. When the Colombian government, led by Finance Minister Carlos Sanz de Santamaría, proposed a resolution to recommend the creation of a special inter-American fund to relieve the burden of low coffee prices on Colombia farm workers, Secretary Wirtz had his answer ready. The other ministers from Mexico to Chile backed him up.

On our return from Bogotá, I prepared the first draft of Secretary Wirtz's report to President Kennedy and Secretary of State Dean Rusk. A few days later, I was asked to go to Secretary Rusk's office—my first visit to the inner sanctum. Secretary Wirtz had called the secretary of state to report on the meeting and thanked him for assigning me as his advisor. The special assistant to the secretary informed me that the Secretary Rusk asked him to tell me of Secretary Wirtz's call and his appreciation for my work.

Two days later, the deputy to the labor advisor to Secretary Rusk invited me to lunch in the Secretary of State's Eighth Floor Executive Dining Room. Another first for me! The deputy told me that he was about to be reassigned overseas and that Secretary Rusk had asked him to talk to me as potential candidate to replace him.

The conversation went very well. He described his relationship with the Labor Advisor, with Pat Moynihan at the Department of Labor and the regional labor advisors for Europe and Asia. He asked me about my job and my priorities. He detailed his recent trips abroad, including three that were annual events: two to Geneva to attend International Labor Organization sessions, and the annual convention of the ICFTU (International Confederation of Free Trade Unions.) He also informed me about recent trips to Tokyo, London and Stockholm to coordinate inter-country Cold War strategy and tactics to combat the Soviet-bloc World Federation of Trade Unions (WFTU). When we left the table, he said that he was prepared to recommend me to replace him and gave me two weeks to let him know my decision.

A couple of days later, Marvin Weisman called me to his office. He advised me that Ambassador Moscoso, Bill Rogers, and Ray Sternfeld had authorized him to create a new post: Deputy Director of the Office of Institutional Development. Marvin wanted to refocus the office on sectoral planning, instead of project support. He noted that only I had focused my division on Alliance priorities and sectoral planning. He wanted me to work with the other division directors to refocus their efforts.

We then had our first in-depth discussion about the work of the

office. We saw the Office of Institutional Development as the vehicle for helping each country plan and implement programs that
responded to the priorities of the Alliance to build and strengthen
key institutions critical for promoting sustained growth. The professionals in each sector—rural development, education, health,
urban development, and social development—had to be prepared
to analyze and evaluate plans and programs in each country in
light of goals. They would need to advise on their viability and,
where feasible, to recommend the sequence of actions and inputs
to achieve AFP objectives. To play such a role, the office needed to
reorient its staff and engage them in the process.

That conversation went on for a couple of days as we discussed
what he expected his deputy to do and his relationship with the
division directors. We talked a good deal about the challenge of
introducing the concept to technical officers who for almost all of
their careers had worked in projects and were not encouraged to
think about the relationship of one project to another.

I faced a wonderful dilemma: the choice of one of two very
distinct career opportunities. I talked over the choice with only
two people: Mel Spector, the regional administrative director who
knew more about State Department operations than anyone else I
knew, and Ele, my partner who knew me better than anyone else.
For a week, I weighed the options and talked them out every night
with Ele until I felt comfortable about making a choice.

17

Office of Institutional Development

My memory sometimes plays tricks on me, but I believe that it was late May or early June 1963 that I was named deputy to the director of the Office of Institutional Development. I physically moved from my niche on a dimly lit back hall of the third floor to one close to the wide airy front corridor. Now, why did I choose to remain with the Alliance for Progress rather than take the post on the Seventh Floor of the State Department, in the office of a senior adviser to the secretary of state?

The primary factor was my interest in inter-American affairs and my conviction that the Alliance for Progress (AFP) was a sound long-term policy for building optimum relations between the U.S. and Latin America. The Cuban Missile Crisis made me aware of the immediate threat to that relationship. While my office was not immediately involved in it, the event redoubled my determination to make the AFP an effective vehicle for preventing further Cuban and Soviet intrusions into the region. Ele played the key role in my making that decision by reminding that my experience in the various Latin American countries would be better used in the AFP.

The final factor in making the decision was my conviction that achieving the political, economic, and social goals of the AFP, with expanding employment opportunities and rising living standards, was the best defense against communism. In addition, my years of association with the AFL-CIO, including the negotiation of the AIFLD agreement, assured me that the AFL-CIO, with or without State Department support, would spearhead necessary action to counter any intrusion by the Cubans or Soviets into the labor movements of the region.

I was intrigued by the opportunity that I perceived the AFP presented for development in Latin America. I doubted that the Marshall Plan blueprint would work in Latin America since it essentially injected financial and technical resources to revive institutions devastated by two World Wars and restored its economic system and put its unemployed skilled workers back to work. Latin America, and most of the Third World, was in the initial stage of socio-economic change, rural-to-urban migration and capital formation. They lacked the sophisticated public and private institutions and trained work force that evolved in Europe over centuries.

The challenge offered in the AFP job was compelling. I was to work with Marvin in reshaping the Office of Institutional Development to (1) analyze country by country, sector by sector, the critical obstacles to attaining the political, economic, and social goals set by the AFP and (2) provide information to USAID missions in each country on the most effective plans of actions in each sector that they could use to advise host governments on building and strengthening public and private institutions and helping those institutions design and implement priority programs.

My field experience had demonstrated that there were no quick fixes and it takes well-planned, timely, and sustained effort to build public and private institutions and to help them become effective. Finding the right policies and programs does not occur overnight, and there certainly will be periods of trial and error. Training and installing a competent work force is an exacting process that takes even longer. All of this takes money, and building up revenue requires effective collection systems—no small task in counties beset by widespread corruption.

I perceived a process that would require a generation or two of hemispheric cooperation. I saw the first ten years as building physical, institutional, and human infrastructure to serve as the base for accelerated development in the second decade. I recognized that such a long-term approach would be a hard sell to senior levels of the government and Congress who looked for immediate results. But, I felt it was worth a try.

The New Office and a Phone Call

My new office was part of a three-room suite: Marvin Weisman's large office that also served as our conference area, a room opening onto the corridor in which our two secretaries were housed, and my smaller office. Becky Scroggs was promoted to be my secretary and helped make my transition as easy as possible.

My job description said that I was to coordinate the work of the five divisions, supervise their review of country and regional programs and projects, oversee their advisory services to country missions, and clear their recommendations on personnel assignments and other support for AID missions. I also presided over the internal office review of proposed regional and country grant projects before their presentation for approval by the Project Review Committee chaired by the coordinator. I also kept my old duties as Latin American regional labor adviser until the State Department could assign a replacement. The job kept me busy seven days a week, and I had a ball.

My first weeks were a blur of briefings and meetings. Every morning at 8:00 a.m., Marvin and I discussed the agenda and items to raise at the senior staff meetings with the assistant secretary and the coordinator. Each day I met with a different division chief and reviewed issues that had arisen in Latin American projects. I met with Ray Sternfeld's staff to understand the criteria used in reviewing country proposals. Marvin introduced me to senior AID officers. Then, he took me to New York to meet key non-government partners like Frank Pace of the Senior Service Corps, David Rockefeller at the Council of Americas in New York, and J. Peter Grace of the AFP Business Advisory Group. Ambassador Moscoso invited me to a lunch with the Advisory Committee of University Presidents, which included President Grayson Kirk of Columbia University, John Hannah of Michigan State, and Clark Kerr of California. Sternfeld took me to meet with the president of the Inter-American Development Bank, Enrique Herrera, whom I had known in Chile. I attended a meeting of the Business Advisory Group headed by John Gallagher of Sears and Edward Marcus of Neiman Marcus. Within a month, I was representing Marvin at meetings whenever he had other commitments.

Toward the end of the month, Marvin took me to the quarterly meeting with the National Association of Public and Land-Grant Universities at its Washington offices to review progress and problems related to their AID financed projects with Latin American universities. It was a lengthy meeting running much longer than anticipated. We still had not completed discussions on several possible new contracts when the meeting adjourned. I was given the assignment of working with the secretary of the association in drafting an *aide memoire* on our conclusions, with recommendations for action by the coordinator and the president of the Association. When we broke up after 6:00 p.m., the secretary agreed to call me early the next morning to work on the text, alerting that he might call as early as 7:30 a.m.

Early next morning, I was at my desk, writing out a summary of the land-grant meeting and waiting for the secretary's call when the phone rang shortly after 7:30 a.m. I picked up the phone, and the voice on the other end said, "This is the president." And I responded, "Of what?" It seemed an eternity before President John Fitzgerald Kennedy came down off the ceiling of the Oval Office as he told me off.

I think that I blubbered that I had never received a call from the president before and some other lame excuse. He then asked my name and told me that he wanted information urgently about the action AID had taken on a proposal for an AID-Heifer Program to distribute livestock to subsistence farmers in selected Caribbean countries that he had referred to AID a couple of weeks earlier. He said that he wanted to know why no one in AID had responded to him or sent him a plan of action. He then succinctly said that he wanted action "right now." I promised him an answer ASAP. He said, "Fine," and hung up.

I had no sooner put down the phone than someone from the office of AID Administrator David Bell was inquiring, "What did you talk to the president about?" I assured the voice at the other end that I had not initiated the call and that the president had asked about the Heifer Project in the Caribbean. I was chided for talking to the president and told that all calls from the president should be channeled to Mr. Bell's office. I thought, "Good luck, man, if you ever receive a direct call from the president and he is on the line!"

Since, most of the English-speaking Caribbean countries were still British colonies and were not parties to the Alliance for Progress, projects involving them were handled by Central AID, not by the AFP. I asked the voice on the other end of the line if his AID office knew anything about the president's memo. After a pause, he said he would look into it at once. It turned out that some middle-level officials had doubts about the proposal and sat on the president's memo. It took several phone calls and intricate bureaucratic maneuvering before the president got his answer later that morning. Mr. Bell and Ambassador Moscoso presented a proposal that included activities in Caribbean countries—both British colonies and AFP members. The Heifer Program marched forward—and it was a good one. The project accomplished what the president foresaw: a better supply of food for small farmers and an additional source of income for many of them.

The president's phone call also elicited inquiries from Assistant Secretary of State Ed Martin's office and from Ambassador Moscoso's before Marvin arrived at 8:30 a.m. The Land-Grant Association call came about 10:00 a.m. My moment in the spotlight faded quickly and by lunchtime, I was free to complete the *aide memoire* on the preceding day's meeting.

Learning the New Job

For the next two months, I met with the division chiefs and technicians on the country and regional projects they backstopped. One day we might be analyzing the deficiencies of elementary education in Colombia and the next, constraints on agricultural production in Guatemala, followed by problems posed by accelerating rural-to-urban migration and the increasingly restive unemployed in the growing urban centers of Brazil and Peru. Each review raised questions about the capacity of host government institutions to reach goals set for the project and the impact of rising populations on the institutions. Each project was unique, because each country was different, and each project action had to be relevant to the reality of that country. There were no easy solutions.

I had not known many of my fellow office members previously. I had worked in a unique slot in the office, more politically oriented than technical. I had been viewed primarily as the state department regional labor officer, and labor was not a popular subject with most of the technical officers. As I came to know the technical staff, I found that many had worked with IIAA and their field experience was in *servicios*. Most were project-oriented and had little experience with sector analysis and planning. They viewed their job as backstopping their colleagues in the field, not looking at the broader range of sector issues that the AFP raised.

Step one in the process of change that Marvin laid out was to broaden the outlook of our current staff and expose them to new ideas and new approaches. When we began discussing the new approach with them, we found several in rural development, education, social development, and cooperatives who shared our concerns; but they saw their jobs as back stoppers of field proposals in the IIAA tradition. They were interested in new ideas, but wary of changing the way they had done business for almost two decades. Marvin and I encouraged them to look at their jobs as advisers to the USAIDs, not merely field support staff. Marvin also brought in some fresh blood. Tony Granger was appointed chief of the education division. An educational planner from Philadelphia, he had experience in broadening the role of traditional educational systems and reaching out to marginal urban and rural groups often ignored under traditional models. He knew little about Latin America on arrival and had to acquaint himself with the field programs and technicians as well as his Washington staff.

He also contracted Dr. Edgar Berman of Johns Hopkins University to help refocus the traditional public health programs. Dr. Berman was a specialist in family planning. He understood that the burgeoning population growth in the region was creating strains on the already overburdened education and health systems and on the capability of governments to provide essential public services. The population growth rate in many countries exceeded 3 percent, and the average age of the population in most was under fifteen.

By the end of my first month on the job, I proposed a plan for re-orienting the work of the staff to sectoral analysis through an on-the-job training plan that included the design of comprehensive sectoral programs to meet AFP objectives, the identification of priority actions needed in each sector, and the analysis of field requests. It was a practical exercise to focus them on AFP objectives and help them identify critical gaps in each country's programs.

To help in this training process, we invited specialists from the AFP program office, the World Bank, Pan American Sanitary Bureau, AIFLD, the U.S. cooperative movement, and subject matter specialists to describe their experience with sectoral analysis. Congressmen Dante Fascell and Brad Morse briefed the staff on the new directions they expected the AFP to take, especially focusing on measures to incorporate marginal rural and urban populations into the development process.

In the second month, I set up a systematic review of field projects, starting with the rural development division. It backstopped projects in all countries except Argentina and Mexico. Almost all involved technical assistance in agriculture, in the *servicio* tradition. They aimed at increasing agricultural output through research stations and extension systems. A few included some elements of farm credit and marketing. Some described land tenure patterns and a few identified obstacles to implementing modern agricultural technology. Almost all reported the local ministry lacked technical depth, especially in planning. Some missions reported on farm credit, usually noting limited access for small farmers and onerous collateral requirements. A few included analysis of marketing conditions, which were usually primitive and controlled by large landowners. Farm services such as machinery and fertilizer were keyed to the needs of large landowners; government efforts to provide such services to small farmers were deemed inefficient, politically-driven, and often rife with corruption.

The second review was with the education division. Projects existed in all countries except Argentina and Mexico and they were carried out through *servicios*, with annual budgets of about one million dollars. In the IIAA tradition, many projects still emphasized vocational education and literacy. In recent years, the emphasis in most countries shifted to teacher training and curriculum development, primarily for public elementary schools.

The country reports pointed out that, while universal public education through the twelfth grade was the pledged in almost every constitution in the region, the reality was far from the ideal. Few countries had an adequate tax base to sustain even the system in place. Physical facilities were often described as inadequate even in capital cities. Rural schools in many countries did not exist beyond the third grade. Trained teachers were in short supply, and salaries were minimal. The quality of education in urban public schools was considered inferior to that of parochial schools. Some missions reported difficulties with some teachers who were Marxist and resisted working with U.S. advisers.

In our discussion of the sector, I was told that for years, the IIAA and its successors (FOA and ICA) had tried to develop longer-term plans to attack critical bottlenecks in the public education systems, but were usually frustrated by lack of financial and technical resources. Dealing with core problems required capital funding and/or systemic reforms beyond the classroom.

In additional to the country education programs, there were several regional projects. One funded textbooks in reading, mathematics, and science for the first through sixth grades for the Central American countries; the texts were drafted by a multinational team, but the product was not widely used because of xenophobic differences—each country now wanted funds to write its own adaptation in its own vernacular and historical setting. A second was a regional project for Peru, Colombia, and Brazil that experimented with the use of filmed courses to deliver education to rural areas where qualified teachers were in short supply, but the results were mixed. The third was a regional project with selected U.S. universities and teacher colleges to advise countries on evaluating country education systems.

The third review was with the public health division. Public health had been the largest and most important program area of the IIAA. Since World War II, health *servicios* provided about one million dollars annually in technical assistance to each of the Latin American countries for projects that included control of contagious diseases, building public health facilities, developing rural health centers, installing latrines, and improving water supplies. The program pioneered the creation of rural health posts and the training of community health workers in almost every country of the region and supported the first rural community projects that involved women and families. The health *servicios* provided professional training to thousands of doctors, nurses, and technicians;

and schools of medicine and nursing received aid in course design and equipment.

The review started with an analysis of health services throughout the region and revealed that health services in most countries had achieved accepted international standards, that death rates since World War II were substantially reduced, and that the population growth rates in most exceeded 3 percent per annum. The current project mix showed an emphasis on maternal and child health, community clinics, health education, and community health centers. There were no proposals dealing with family planning. Many of the missions noted that ministries had trouble matching U.S. *servicio* funding because large segments of their budgets were earmarked for the operation of hospitals in urban centers. Several also pointed out that funds from payments into their social security systems were used to build and equip large hospitals for social security beneficiaries but had insufficient income to operate them effectively.

Many missions requested funds to improve the quality and availability of safe water supplies in both rural and urban areas to combat water-borne diseases in the public water supplies. Under the AFP, a priority was given to loan funding such projects, including necessary technical assistance. So, it was necessary to orient the division staff on how to handle those requests and help them develop contacts with loan officers in the Bureau, the World Bank, and the Inter-American Development Bank.

The fourth review session was with the social development division and the cooperative specialists from the urban and industrial development division, which was still being formed. Few country programs contained projects related to either division. Several identified lack of skilled manpower as an obstacle to development, but none proposed relevant projects other than traditional vocational education. In social development, there were a handful of projects including: (1) the Cornell-Chile and Pittsburgh-Santa Maria projects that I had initiated had achieved their objectives, and they were phasing out; (2) the employment service in Peru; (3) the incipient Central American rural leadership project with Loyola of the South; and (4) AIFLD. With the creation of AIFLD, funds were no longer included in country budgets for labor leader training. In our discussion, the staff favored integrating social development components into relevant rural development, education, health, and urban development programs, rather than setting up separate projects.

Almost all of the projects backstopped by the cooperative specialists were regional and involved funding of technical assistance by the U.S. cooperative movement to Latin American cooperatives. By far the most active in a score of counties was the U.S. Credit Union Association (CUNA). Other projects included a rural electric cooperative in Nicaragua, farm marketing cooperatives in a few countries, and a housing cooperative in Panama. Projects with CUNA and the Cooperative League of the U.S.A. provided training for cooperative leaders in both urban and rural areas. The cooperative specialists were working on a new proposal for funding a hemisphere-wide cooperative financial mechanism.

The last specialist with whom I met was Public Administration Adviser Hiram (Hi) Phillips, the dean of public administration advisers in Latin America. Hi and his colleagues were advisers to the other divisions on public administration. They worked with *servicios* to advise ministries throughout Latin America on measures to overcome operational bottlenecks and strengthen management. Hi had taken a sabbatical to write a book on institutional development and the urgent need to improve public administration and create a professional career civil service. He spelled out the norms for good management systems and practices, the principles for project planning and implementation, and measures to control corruption. He understood sectoral analysis and planning and fully supported Marvin's initiative to reorient the work of the office. Our discussion was substantially different from that with other divisions.

The discussion with Hi had less to do with specific country or ministry problems than an overview of the capability of governments in Latin America to implement AFP programs. He emphasized that the weaknesses throughout the region were systematic, but that they had to be dealt with in the context of the country in which they arose. Hi led me through an examination, country by country, of the public service and the options that were available for improvement—especially in critical areas like public finance, national planning, education, agriculture, and public health. Hi emphasized that solutions had to be country-specific and required top-level national leadership to take place. For example, Costa Rica was a multiparty democracy in which at each change of administration in every ministry almost everyone from the minister to the doorman was changed—including most of the trained technicians. In entrenched autocratic and military regimes such as Guatemala, Paraguay, and Haiti, national leaders resisted any attempt to decentralize control or empower effective administrators.

We also spent considerable time analyzing government revenues and the capability of governments to finance road, power, airport, and seaport infrastructure projects as well as agricultural, educational, public health, and other essential programs. All are critical components of economic growth and provide critical services to the people; assuring a steady in-flow of funds was essential. Most countries relied heavily on export taxes on oil, minerals, and other commodities, with income and sales taxes providing only a small portion of government revenue. Very few had efficient tax collection systems, and evasion was widespread, sometimes facilitated by pay-offs to the tax collectors. He pointed out that the revenue data we used was often unreliable and spotty, usually biased toward the high side. Some statistics were compiled by public health, education, or agriculture technicians for the purpose of justifying the foreign assistance. He recommended that the AFP place a high priority on improving the quality of fiscal data and establish norms and procedures for compiling, preparing, and issuing information on financial and budgetary reports.

Reality Steps In

Through this in-depth review process, I became aware of the constraints of creating the office that Marvin and I envisioned. The staff was much smaller than I had anticipated, and only a few really understood the concept of sectoral analysis. Many just didn't want to change the old way of doing business. In addition, in the review of field projects, it became clear that most of our field technicians were subject matter specialists not trained to help their host country counterparts conduct the studies and analyses required for sectoral planning. As I studied the budget and the instructions for preparing the next one, it was clear that the chances of obtaining additional personnel for the divisions were very slight.

I began to realize that the office was not as high on the totem pole as I had thought. AFL-CIO had a lot of top-level political pressure to move the AIFLD project through the system. Other office initiatives had not fared as well. The power of decision lay not within the office, but with those who controlled the money. Many were veterans of the Marshall Plan, accustomed to working with sophisticated host country agencies and unreceptive to arguments about difficulties in gearing up country capabilities. It was difficult for veterans of Europe to realize that most of our Latin American counterparts did not have the training or experience of their former European associates.

These differences were accentuated in the loan approval process. Their objective was to disburse money and they did not look kindly on our explanations. Our office chief was a member of the loan approval committee. Before each meeting, our office held an internal review of the proposal and prepared a position paper on the problems we could identify. On almost every one, we raised questions about the administrative capability to administer the loan and often on its ability to repay. Most of those technical problems were massaged and treated with band-aids, with limited attention to building the institutions and training the host country administrators before approving the loan.

Our concern about building institutions and training host country personnel led many to oppose phasing out the *servicios* as the senior leadership of the Alliance planned. Many, including Hi Phillips and me, believed that the *servicios* could be reorganized so as to fill the institution-building gap. We raised with senior officials the possibility of using the *servicio* during the life of the Alliance to train and supervise the technical staff in each country that was needed to plan and implement sectoral projects in agriculture, education, public health, and other key sectors—in short, to use the *servicio* to help each country build institutional capability to provide a flow of key projects to improve the chances of meeting Alliance objectives. We argued that such *servicios* could concentrate and protect the most effective technicians in each country and assure them the income and job security needed to build a viable in-country base for Alliance programming. None of the Alliance senior staff, including Marvin, was enthused by the proposal. In retrospect, I wish that I had tried harder because, as Ray Sternfeld said so often then and over the fifteen years during which he served as vice president of the Inter-American Development Bank, "Money is chasing projects, not projects chasing money."

We also suggested using the program loan mechanism to improve the public administration and program development capabilities of Brazil, Chile, and Colombia. The office played no direct role in drafting and negotiating those loans. The primary focus was on macroeconomic performance gauged mainly by impact on GDP, GNP, and tax revenues, less on sectoral goals that concerned the office. However, with the program loans, there were allocations for education, agriculture, public health, and industrial development; those of us in institutional development were not normally consulted about sectoral goals to be met or programs to be carried out. In addition, the office did not participate in the annual evaluation of performance.

By the end of 1963, I was not sure that I had made the right choice in accepting Marvin's offer to be deputy office director.

The Inter-American Economic and Social Council

Marvin assigned me the job of representing Institutional Development at the planning and technical level meetings set up to prepare the U.S. positions for the Third Meeting of the Inter-American Economic and Social Council (IA-ECOSOC), which was scheduled for September 1963 in São Paolo, Brazil. This brought me into contact with Governor Averell Harriman, Attorney General Robert Kennedy, and Walt Rostow. Governor Harriman presided over the State/ AID meetings and my friend John Elac often sat at his side, advising him on agenda items. In the initial meetings, I was in the back row, but by August, I was often seated at the long table. I seldom entered discussions because I could only hear or lip-read a few of the participants. But apparently my comments caught the attention of one or two of the participants because I was often called to private meetings with the principals to elaborate on a question or comment.

After one of the meetings, Walt Rostow, who was head of the State Department Policy Planning Council and renowned author of *Stages of Economic Growth: A Non-Communist Manifesto*, called me to his office. We had a lengthy conversation about the situation in several key countries. Following that meeting, he called me several more times when he was weighing possible U.S. options on key issues to be discussed at the meeting.

Walt, a European expert, was keen to absorb information about Latin America. In our discussions, we contrasted the political, economic, and social conditions in Latin America, country by country, with those in Western Europe. He had a scholar's patience that was not always apparent in the discussions with other State and AID colleagues as he analyzed complex and penetrating questions related to defining different positions the U.S. might take on each agenda item. Walt Rostow was a stern taskmaster, and when he felt that I had missed an important consideration, he quickly let me know.

In August, I was advised that I would be a member of the U.S. delegation to the IA-ECOSOC and would work with John Elac on the technical committee dedicated to social development. I helped draft policy papers for the U.S. position and participated in some of the briefings for Secretary Rusk, Governor Harriman, and Walt Rostow.

The first year of the Alliance had not progressed well. The quality and quantity of proposals submitted by the Latin American governments were not impressive. The criteria for preparing and evaluating proposals were ill-defined. The U.S. government found itself in the middle. The Latin Americans wanted the money to flow, and the U.S. couldn't justify providing it. There was concern that the low disbursement of funds would raise questions with Congress the following year when additional funding requests would be submitted. In the ensuing high-level discussions, a proposal took shape to create a multinational body to help countries prepare and present development projects.

While I played no role in the decision-making process, I worked on papers that were integrated into the U.S. proposal to create the Inter-American Committee for the Alliance for Progress (CIAP) as that multilateral body. Its creation became the centerpiece of the meeting in São Paolo. A high-powered delegation headed by

Averell Harriman was to present it.

One of my assignments as a member of the U.S. delegation was to report on the progress of the OAS staff, under the direction of Walter Sedwitz, in advising member states. His staff was made up of talented young Latin American economists who were learning on the job. Only a few had prior experience in planning or implementing national development programs. Most of them had been trained in European and U.S. universities, and a few had gained their initial experience working in the United Nations Economic Commission for Latin America (ECLA) and had been trained by its long-time leader, Dr. Raul Prebisch of Argentina. Like most Latin American economists and intellectuals of the era, they tended toward Marxist precepts of state control of the development process and state ownership of the basic means of production.

This assignment also brought me into contact with delegates from Latin American member states with whom I discussed their expectations from the Alliance and the forthcoming ECOSOC meeting, I found that most of those from the larger Latin American governments respected Dr. Prebisch and favored him to lead the Alliance. However, the United States and one or two other governments viewed him with suspicion because he was not deemed to be a market economist and advocated state-directed development and import substitution. However, I found that many of his detractors, especially from my own government, had never really talked in depth with Dr. Prebisch or analyzed his papers. I had met Dr. Prebisch when I was assigned to Chile found him much more pragmatic than the doctrinaire figure so many of my U.S. colleagues seemed to believe he was.

I reported back to Walt Rostow and Ambassador Moscoso the reactions that I received from my Latin American colleagues. I urged Dr. Rostow to talk with Dr. Prebisch and make up his own mind before making a decision. I also felt that, in the current circumstances, Dr. Prebisch could well be the best man to convince Latin American governments to undertake the critical reforms required to move the Alliance forward. Walt did not react to my suggestion. I found out later that our government had already reached an agreement with Colombia to support its finance minister, Carlos Sanz de Santamaría, to head the Inter-American Committee on the

Alliance for Progress (CIAP).

The São Paolo meeting lasted two weeks. The first week was at the technical level and was headed by Ambassador Moscoso and Bill Rogers. My specific assignment was to help shape the social agenda for the ministers to consider and, as required, to explain the role of the proposed CIAP. I was designated occupant of the U.S. chair in the social development subcommittee and was to represent the U.S. government on drafting groups to prepare the documents for consideration at the ministerial session during the second week. My colleague John Elac was my companion at the table. When my subcommittee was not in session, I joined Ray Sternfeld and John Elac at the meetings of subcommittee on economic affairs.

Bill Rogers took on the central task of selling CIAP to the chiefs of delegations. He met with Ray Sternfeld, John Elac, and me the first thing every morning and oriented us to the work of the day, including meeting with key members of vacillating delegations. Ambassador Moscoso then chaired the delegation at a working session where we gave feedback on our conversations and reviewed the issues we felt would arise in the sessions scheduled that day.

In my subcommittee, the initial statement by various governments revealed substantial distrust of U.S. intentions. The meetings were tense and fraught with controversy. Few had any clear concept of social development. Most were advocating large-scale health and education projects that were not well-defined and would cost millions. Some advocated, "Give us the money because we know how to spend it to solve our own problems." Suspicion of CIAP was high, and the influence of Fidel Castro was evident in several delegations, especially the Brazilian.

One of the major issues raised repeatedly by the Latin American delegations was their perception of the low rate of disbursements. This anti-U.S. accusation in the corridors and on the floor was fanned by the host delegation, Brazil. Its leftist president João Goulart was believed by some in the U.S. delegation to be actively supporting Castro's interests and seeking to undermine any U.S. initiative.

Each evening, John Elac would set up dinners with key Latin American delegates, including Miguel de la Madrid of Mexico (later president of Mexico), Celso Furtado of Brazil, Enrique Iglesias of Uruguay (later president of the Inter-American Development Bank), Enrique García (later president of the Andean Development Corporation), and José Gumucio of Bolivia. We tried to allay their concerns and present CIAP as a genuine U.S. effort to multi-lateralize the Alliance and help countries improve their capability to access funds. We laid out the U.S. concern over the limited number of solid projects being presented for funding and the inability of officials in many countries to "absorb and apply" the criteria and discipline for preparing proposals—this was the other side of the complaint by the Latin Americans. We also pointed out that many project proposals were not consistent with AFP priorities; many lacked precision in objectives, proposed courses of action and/or criteria for measuring impact or progress. We explained that, since there was no inter-American machinery in place to define criteria and procedures as guidelines for the countries to follow, it had fallen on the U.S. to be the taskmaster. CIAP, a multilateral entity, would replace the U.S. in this role. We also identified CIAP as the mechanism that many Latin American delegates had called for to help countries build planning and operational competence. Under CIAP, specialized missions would be sent to countries to help national technicians prepare their development plans and project proposals that would be presented for CIAP review and appraisal.

The U.S. delegation at the ministerial meeting was headed by Averell Harriman and a high-powered group of financial and development specialists. The president of Brazil, João (Jango) Goulart, opened the meeting. His development minister, Celso Furtado, long-time associate and friend of Dr. Prebisch, sat next to him. The tension in the room during his presentation was high. He made a strong pitch for a more flexible funding plan and emphasized the importance of Latin American leadership for the Alliance.

The U.S. delegation was not pleased with the opening statement, and friction between the U.S. and Brazil was the topic running around the corridors after the speech. Governor Harriman introduced the proposal to create CIAP and left São Paolo after the presentation. Speculation ran high about the governor's abrupt departure. But the delegation was focused on obtaining approval for CIAP and the appointment of Dr. Carlos Sanz de Santamaría of Colombia to be its first chairperson.

For the first couple of days, senior members of the U.S. delegation met privately with each delegation chief, usually the economic minister, and garnered support for CIAP. When the resolution to create it was brought to the floor, Brazil did not oppose and it sailed through. CIAP was established for ten years to plan, oversee, evaluate, and implement the Alliance for Progress.

The selection of the chairman was fought in the corridors. There was a sharp and bitter division over Prebisch and Sanz de Santamaría. The U.S. used its political and financial muscle to win over delegations to support Sanz de Santamaría. I remember reminding some delegates that the U.S. had established our *bona fides* by pledging some US$1.4 billion a year for ten years, and creating the Social Progress Trust Fund (SPTF) of US$525 million that we turned over to the newly established IDB to administer. Late on the third day, a friend in the Chilean delegation told me that the pro-Prebisch countries had surveyed the other delegations and found that the U.S. and Colombia had lined up fourteen votes, and that Dr. Prebisch's name would not be placed in nomination. So, Dr. Sanz de Santamaría was the only candidate and was elected by acclamation.

Resentment over that election lingered among the larger Latin American countries. It became more strident when CIAP did not live up to U.S. expectations. By the late 1960s and early 1970s, CIAP had become a largely unproductive annual exercise indulged in for smaller countries, and it was allowed to lapse in 1973. At its demise, one heard the same lament in Washington that I had heard at the ECOSOC meeting in São Paolo: performance by the Latin American countries had not met the expectations of the United States, and the Latin American countries were unhappy with the strings and controls that the U.S. placed on the expenditure of funds. I felt then and still do that one of the greatest flaws of CIAP was the choice of its chair. I wondered what would have happened if Dr. Prebisch had been in charge.

When we returned to Washington in late October. I got a call from Bill Rogers to accompany him to a debriefing at the White House. We met with NSC staff and Ralph Dungan. When we finished, I was advised that a colleague, Jim Boren (who later founded the Partners of the Americas and the Association of Professional Bureaucrats), and I had been selected to discuss the result of São

Paolo on a CBS talk show on November 23 at 1:00 p.m.

Jim and I arrived at the CBS studio on Connecticut Avenue at 1:00 and learned that President Kennedy had been shot, and that the talk show had been canceled. We walked back to the State Department in shock. When I reached my office, I was told that Pat Moynihan had called and wanted to see me. Jim drove me to the Department of Labor and we shared an hour of disbelief and grief with Pat. The Alliance for Progress changed the day the president was killed.

No Social Life That Summer

My only field assignment in the spring of 1963 had been to Mexico, and I was able to take Ele with me. Most of my work was in Mexico City and that allowed us to visit and marvel at the newly opened Mexican Museum of Anthropology. She also joined me when I inspected the work of the Mexican Institute of Rehabilitation in whose creation and development USAID technical adviser David Amato had played a significant role. David accompanied us on visits to facilities in Guanajuto, San Miguel Allende, and Guadalajara. For almost two weeks, we spent almost every day together.

After our return from Mexico, Ele and I had very little time together except for an occasional Saturday afternoon or Sunday. During the excessive heat and humidity of that summer, with my absorption with the ECOSOC meeting, she essentially made her own plans. Her only regular excursions out of the Towers that terrible summer were to enhance her knowledge of investments. She practically earned an MBA that summer on the workings of the New York Stock Exchange and the role of the Securities and Exchange Commission (SEC). She learned the rules and regulations and how to read the tape. She was introduced to Granville and market cycles. She mastered how to work with a broker, and to beware of phone calls to "buy" stocks.

One special treat that summer was a series of invitations by Dorothy Guthrie at the Smithsonian to attend the opening of the new jade collection (of which Dorothy was the curator) and the behind-the-scenes world of the Smithsonian collection of jewels. Dorothy arranged for her to visit the about-to-be-opened Museum of

American History and Ele acquainted Dorothy with our visit that summer to the recently opened Mexican Museum of Anthropology in Cuauhtémoc Park and induced the Guthries to visit it the following year.

During that long summer Ele began working on notes for a book on El Salvador that she planned to call *Mañana Was Yesterday*. She would regale me when I got home late from the office with ideas that she had brought together during the day as adventures of her heroine, Leona. Her enthusiasm usually overcame my tensions and got to thinking about more than the trials of the day.

By late August, she began planning for her annual farm trip. We tried to coordinate the dates so that she would be away while I was scheduled to be in São Paolo. This year she abandoned any plans for taking the bus and instead arranged to fly to Aberdeen, South Dakota, and then on to Tulare. No more transits through the Greyhound depot in Chicago! Her plans called for a week in South Dakota and a month in Tulare. She would leave in late September and return by early November, about the time I was scheduled to return from São Paolo.

Her trip went very well. The income from both the South Dakota farm and the Pixley ranch had beat expectations and her workload had declined thanks to the effectiveness of the tenants she had selected. She had ample time to spend with her mother and friends in Tulare. When we reunited in Washington, she told me that it was the most restful farm trip she had ever experienced.

18

Director of Institutional Development

The assassination of President Kennedy spawned uncertainty and change in the Alliance for Progress. In December 1963 when Marvin Weisman, my boss, was chosen to be the AID mission director in Guatemala, Ambassador Moscoso and Assistant Secretary of State Martin asked me to replace him as director of the Office of Institutional Development. In early 1964, I was sworn in. I participated in the daily staff meeting of the coordinator, not those of the assistant secretary, as I was no longer the regional labor adviser. As Latin American labor advisor, I was replaced by career foreign service officer Dan Montenegro.

My new job included not only the direction of the Office of Institutional Development (OID), but also becoming a senior member of AID liaison group for CIAP. Ambassador Moscoso, as the U.S. coordinator of the Alliance, was the U.S. representative; Ray Sternfeld was his deputy, and I was next in line. I was also given liaison assignments to regularly brief senators and congressmen and their staffs on Alliance developments.

The first few months of 1964 were a time of rumor and concern. My new office and its conference table were the site of many tense meetings, quite a few provoked by changes in Alliance leadership. First, I learned of the departure of my contacts at the White House, especially Ralph Dungan, who had guided me through several rough patches. Then came changes in the Alliance itself. By spring, Ambassador Moscoso resigned and returned to Puerto Rico. Ed Martin was named Ambassador to Argentina. Thomas Mann, the ambassador for whom I worked in El Salvador, was appointed both assistant secretary of state for American Republic Affairs and coordinator of the Alliance for Progress, and Bill Rogers as the deputy coordinator.

Ambassador Mann took over the suite of offices that Moscoso had occupied and brought in career foreign service officers to key staff posts. He put his stamp on the program and its operations. As one colleague observed, "He brought the Alliance down to earth." His focus was less on the ideals and vision of the Alliance, but on the specifics of implementing the program in the context of the contemporary political, economic, and social reality of each participating country. His emphasis and style contrasted sharply with the aura of excitement and spirit of innovation that had marked the Kennedy days. While Sternfeld remained as program director and Phil Glaessner as loan director, many of the Marshall Plan veterans in senior posts departed. Talented members of my office staff left to pursue other career opportunities.

While those developments made my job more difficult, I was determined to move forward. I now had a chair at the coordinator's policy table and was hopeful that I could convert the office into a think tank and induce the AFP coordinator to consider a more realistic time frame for achieving AFP objectives.

A momentous career development also came to pass. Ambassador Mann proposed that I be integrated into the Foreign Service; he had Mel Spector shepherd the paperwork through the state personnel system. In 1964, I moved from the Foreign Service Reserve into the career system as an FSO-2, which at that time was the second highest grade in the career Foreign Service.

Office Operations

During the six months that I had served as Marvin Weisman's deputy, I worked with the staff on a daily basis. I came to know all the professional and clerical staff, and recognized their strengths and their limitations. I knew the workload and understood priorities. So there were no great expectations on assuming direction of the office. I asked my colleague Hi Philips, to be the deputy office director. As of January 1, 1964, the office consisted of five operating divisions: rural development (formerly agriculture), education, public health, social development, and public administration.

Most divisions consisted of two to four technicians and one or two clerk-stenographers. Most of the technicians were on rotation from field assignments and expected to be reassigned overseas in two to three years.

As I pointed out earlier, the primary work of the divisions until the AFP had been to backstop field operations and that the AFP leadership expected the office to play a different role—to evaluate program and project proposals to ascertain how they contributed to achieving AFP goals. My experience as deputy office director had illustrated how difficult it was to make the change. Hi and I believed that we should continue to broaden the work of the office to meet AFP objectives and we set that as our goal.

Our workload was heavy. We began our day about 7:30 a.m. and met daily right after the coordinator's staff meeting to firm up plans for the day. We divided up the front office workload. I attended almost all the loan and grant approval meetings with the deputy coordinator and the CIAP and inter-American meetings from which Hi excused himself because he felt his Spanish was too limited. Hi took charge of operating the office. He prepared the agenda and frequently conducted weekly reviews of activities with each of the divisions. He also supervised the preparation of office position papers on proposed grants and loans.

Hi and I *de facto* abolished the urban and industrial development division after several months of fruitless efforts to recruit staff. We decided to backstop its four projects from our office. Three were related to the creation of business schools in specific countries; the USAID missions in each country supported their operations and only called on the office when a special problem might arise. They included the Harvard Business School initiative to create a business school for Central America and Panama, INCAE; the planned Stanford Business School project for building the Peruvian Business School in Lima; the Columbia University project with the University of Buenos Aires in economics and business administration.

The fourth was to develop markets for artisan handicrafts from the region, an initiative of the AFP Business Advisory Group. In the Johnson administration, the president's brother-in-law, Anthony Taylor, was appointed the artisan handicraft advisor to the Alliance and was assigned to run the project. His physical office was somewhere in the West Wing. I only met him once, at a tea hosted by the First Lady at the White House. When I was contacted by AID Administrator Bell's office about a TV report that Mr. Taylor had accompanied the president on a state visit and was introduced as the Alliance artisan handicraft adviser, I replied that I had not been requested to sign a travel order and that we did not receive reports on his activities. The project was terminated in the mid-1960s because Latin American artisan production could not uniformly meet U.S. demand and quality standards.

By way of a postscript, the Harvard and Stanford Business School achieved the desired results. INCAE, now functioning in Costa Rica and the Peruvian Business School have produced several generations of business executives. The Buenos Aires project was aborted by Peronist opposition to cooperating with a U.S. university; nonetheless, a number of Argentine economists received post-graduate training at Columbia; one graduate, Luis May, became the minister of Economy in the Onganía regime (1969–70), and championed economic reform and pro-market economic policies.

Hi and I tried to convene a second meeting of U.S. university presidents and rectors from Latin American universities. The first meeting had been an initiative of the Kennedy White House, and the president invited a group of U.S. university presidents to meet with rectors of key Latin American universities in Rio de Janeiro to discuss measures for promoting inter-American cooperation in higher education. The education division prepared the background papers and I accompanied Marvin to the meeting and served as its secretary and informal interpreter. President Grayson Kirk of Columbia University, John Hannah of Michigan State, Father Theodore Hesburgh of Notre Dame, and Clark Kerr of the University of California were among the U.S. participants. At the meeting, I noted a language barrier since few U.S. participants spoke Spanish or Portuguese fluently and an equally small number of the Latin Americans were comfortable speaking English. They found areas of common interest but had difficulty explaining their quite different approaches to university organization and operations. General agreements were reached on working together and the Office of Institutional Development was tasked with preparing the agenda for a second meeting to be held in the United States. John Hannah offered Michigan State as a possible site.

When I tried to convene that second meeting after the assassination of President Kennedy, I was unable to find anyone to interest President Johnson in issuing the invitation to university presidents or in requesting U.S. ambassadors to whet the interest of Latin American rectors. The meeting never took place.

Sectoral Planning

Hi and I decided to stop preaching about sectoral planning and, instead, present practical information to the technical staff on its utility in their backstopping of the field programs. To do this, we presented case studies of shortfalls in projects and asked penetrating questions about project operations that would require them to identify lacunas in the projects they were backstopping and encourage them to identify new component activities to improve the effectiveness of the projects.

Hi took the leadership in working with the divisions. He developed a list of questions for the technicians to answer in responding to field requests that included information about assistance being provided by other donors. Each week he met with each division and asked technicians to report on progress and problems in the projects they were backstopping. Several weeks into the process, he was pleased that the heads of the education and rural development divisions reported that their staffs were suggesting changes in some country programs and proposing a better mix or sequence of project activities to meet AFP objectives.

In those meetings, one problem raised by almost all those backstopping projects was the deficiencies of host government agencies in administering projects, from planning to implementation. They reported that the field technicians were requesting assistance in advising host government officials on how to better plan or implement the project. Hi helped our staff prepare relevant questions for field technicians to answer in the process of pinpointing specific administrative problems.

Hi's meetings with the health division guided it to looking beyond the traditional public health projects to focus on population, family planning, and post-natal care. He supervised the collection of information on health programs in each Latin American country including the prior U.S. projects, those managed by the World Health Organization/Pan American Sanitary Bureau, and those financed by international lending agencies. It was our first effort to build a comprehensive data base on health programs as a tool for determining what future health sectoral priorities should be. This was before the era of computers and instant access to such data.

The approach Hi and I used in our meetings with the divisions was to encourage our technical specialists to propose innovative approaches to solving problems in their respective areas of expertise and then provide them a forum for highlighting them. One I remember clearly was a presentation by an agronomist who added the AFP objective of increasing farmer income to the traditional IIAA objective of increasing farm output. He identified marketing as a decisive factor in achieving both objectives after analyzing projects from various countries. He found that, even with improved seed, fertilizer, insecticides, and advanced growing practices and a bountiful crop, the impact on farmer income was minimal if good access to market was not provided. He pointed out that in his extensive field experience, most farmers in Latin America had limited access to information on market conditions and marketing techniques. One specific example he presented was the project in the Yungas of Bolivia in the late 1950s that was designed to reduce the production of coca leaf. Farmers were given improved seed, fertilizer, insecticide, and low interest credit to produce tomatoes, and they had a bumper crop. However, the annual rains started just as the crop was being harvested and the only road up the mountain to La Paz was washed out. He asked, "What do the farmers do with tons of ripe tomatoes? Why didn't someone think about the marketing before starting the project?" The impact of his paper was immediate. We distributed it to all the field missions and many incorporated it into their project planning. Marketing was incorporated into each project proposed from the field, and presentations without it were returned to the field mission for its inclusion.

Another approach we used was to promote the interaction among technicians in different divisions. We sparked discussions between education and agricultural technicians about the potential benefits of cooperation between rural schools and farm extension services. We learned that up to that time, never the twain had met.

The Job and Me

My schedule began with an early morning staff meeting with the deputy coordinator before his meeting with Ambassador Mann. Then I would brief Hi and the division chiefs on major issues under discussion. Once a week Hi and I would review the weekly calendar of meetings to consider funding of new projects and schedule internal office review sessions on proposals under consideration. Hi briefed me on problems that had arisen in project implementation and his proposed actions to deal with them. We would also go over his plans for project reviews with the division chiefs during the week and identify any special matters that required immediate attention, and recommend the meetings that he felt I should attend.

My weekly schedule included participation in the meetings of the AFP organs that approved funding requests. Preparing for those meeting required hours of preparatory work to analyze and understand each proposal. It also included preparation for periodic meetings with key organizations contracted to provide services for the Alliance program, such as, the Land-Grant College Association, national cooperative organizations such the Credit Union National Association (CUNA) and the Cooperative League of the USA (CLUSA), and AIFLD.

The schedule left little time for Ele and me to be together. I was often so tired when I got home that I could hardly do more than flop into bed. Trying to insure I didn't miss the flow of discussion, especially at meetings outside the office put a heavy strain on my hearing and kept me constantly on edge. I often waited until I could read an *aide memoire* after the session before I substantively responded to a proposal.

The increased workload also meant that I could no longer do justice to my course on Latin American labor movements at American University that I had taught for three semesters. In the spring of 1964, I proposed that Daniel Montenegro, my successor as regional labor advisor for Latin America, be appointed in my place. Dan assumed the lectureship, and the course was renewed annually until his retirement in the late 1960s.

Relations with Central Aid

When I took up my new job, Bill Rogers' instructions were that I operate an autonomous office and not look to the central AID offices for policy or technical direction. Ray Sternfeld counseled me that, since the executive order establishing the Alliance was not very explicit about that autonomy, I should act as independently as possible without offending my colleagues in central AID.

The worldwide AID director of institutional development was Dr. Leona Baumgartner, an eminent expert on population and family planning. Within a week of my assuming the directorship, I was called to her office to explain what Dr. Edgar Berman, the regional consultant on family planning, was doing. Contacts in the Vatican had advised her that he had visited the Pope, that the visit had not been cleared with her, and that she was not sure Dr. Berman and she were on the same wavelength. She raised serious concerns about the Alliance efforts, and insisted that Dr. Berman's work be supervised by and coordinated with her office.

I immediately consulted Bill Rogers, who advised me to set up an interview between Dr. Baumgartner and Dr. Berman but to make clear to Dr. Baumgartner that, while the Alliance wished to coordinate with her and keep her fully informed, our program was operating under its own policies and procedures. A very neat balancing act!

Even though prevailing on Dr. Berman to meet with Dr. Baumgartner was not easy, the meeting went quite smoothly—two professionals discussing the problem and agreeing substantially on the appropriate approach and the need for care and discretion in order not to open a Pandora's box, especially with the powerful Catholic Church in Latin America. Dr. Berman told her that Pope John XXIII had met with him and talked of responsible parenthood and the importance he placed on educating the young. The meeting ended with Dr. Berman agreeing to keep Dr. Baumgartner informed, but he certainly did not agree to her prior approval of his activities. Clearly, I was in middle if and when issues might arise.

Dr. Baumgartner and her public health chief, Dr. Lee, a renowned public health specialist, also asked me to explain the AFP health program. I told them of our concern over the population explosion in the region and that, with the average age in Latin America of about fifteen, our emphasis had to be on education and increasing family income, especially for the growing numbers of urban poor. I suggested that we needed new approaches to providing sanitation and better health for those new urban population centers. After a lengthy discussion, Dr. Lee agreed to support our program focus.

In dealing with central AID, I had to keep a reasonable equilibrium. Indeed, as I talked to central AID programmers and subject matter specialists, I often found quite different perceptions of the development problem depending on their field experience. Those from the Marshall Plan and work in Japan had very different perception of priority and needs from those whose experience was in Southeast Asia, the Indian sub-continent, and the Middle East. Those interactions made clear how important it was to avoid generalizations about how to provide assistance. The conditions in each country varied substantially: one size certainly did not fit all.

I did not discourage the professionals in my office from building working relationships with their counterparts in central AID and other regional Bureaus and consulting with them when they deemed it beneficial. All of us needed to understand the development experiences outside Latin America and learn what projects were effective and what projects did not work out in different settings and why. The cumulative experience illustrated the need for carefully designed projects to respond to the special needs of each developing country.

I also found great interest in other regional bureaus with AFP programs, especially projects in rural development, teacher training, cooperatives and leadership training. I arranged briefings for directors and program officers in several AID regional bureaus. After one of them, Frances Johnson, the program director for the Near East Bureau laid out problems that field technicians in the Near East and South Asia were facing in introducing advanced agricultural and education systems. She introduced me to Dana Reynolds, an agricultural specialist who had served in Afghanistan, Pakistan, Iraq, and Iran. They described their frustration with trying to introduce new farm practices to tribesmen and small farmers in those countries. They found receptivity to new ideas among young people, only to have the people they helped find themselves ostracized by the tribal elders and religious leaders who rejected any change in existing practices. They asked me to join an inter-regional task force to explore ways to overcome those obstacles. It became one of my extra-curricular activities.

Our task force met with Middle Eastern specialists at the Johns Hopkins School of International Studies, the World Bank, and UNDP. All had faced similar problems, and several pointed out that their counterparts in national governments experienced similar problems. The task force sought to identify alternative approaches to gaining the confidence and support of local and tribal leaders. Frances Johnson years later told me that the problem persisted and that it would take much more time to build the working relationships that Dana and she had hoped for. Press reports from Iraq and Afghanistan today indicate that the problem still persists.

Another central AID officer, Ted Owens, was especially interested in the AFP. He had made case studies on development experiences in various countries, and reached the conclusion that development is a political process that utilizes economic, social, institutional, and psychological tools to achieve its objectives. He found that every one of his country case studies illustrated that success or failure depended on the political leadership and commitment in the country. He found that external aid, including substantial flows of funds, was only productive if the host government had the political will and capability to move forward.

It was a difficult message for many AID technicians and economists to accept, but it made sense to me based on my field experience. Top-level political support, not merely ministers but presidents, had been essential to so many projects on which I had worked. Ted's message was that the AID Missions had to involve presidents, prime ministers and key political leaders—including tribal elders in some countries—and that access to such leaders in each country is through the U.S. Ambassador. It is he, not the USAID mission chief, who deals directly with presidents or prime ministers. That made the experiences under AFP of special interest to him.

Ted noted that in his experience in several countries the ambassadors and mission directors did not have a close working relationship, with the result that ambassadors tended to downgrade the importance of U.S. economic aid vis a vis military assistance and other political arrangements. He speculated that the AFP merger of State and AID would systemically involve ambassadors in the work of AID and give development aid a high priority on the ambassador's agenda in his dealings at the highest levels of government.

Relations with Congress

Another recurring dimension of the job brought me into contact on a regular basis with members of congress from both major parties. Bill Rogers as deputy coordinator managed relations with congress and cleared all our contacts. Ray Sternfeld was the key man on budget presentations. I occasionally participated in congressional hearings, always as a back-up to Bill or Ray. I also accompanied Bill on calls to various senators and congressmen when he so requested.

More frequently as office director I received requests for information on a program or project. On receiving a verbal or written request, I prepared a draft response that I submitted to Bill for his okay. Occasionally I would get a request from Bill to set up an appointment to see a congressman in person to provide him with the requested information.

One of the most frequent questions we received from members of congress dealt with the depth of support in the Latin American countries for development in general and for the AFP in particular. Just as often I was asked what actions we were taking to mobilize support for the Alliance from non-Communist political parties in each of the countries. Congressmen stressed the importance they attributed to strong in-country political support, and suggested that a major role for the U.S. should be to help strengthen and unite the non-Communist political parties.

The response in 1964 was that the AFP was designed as a cooperative program of economic and social development and that our objective was to support the conditions necessary for sustaining multiparty democracies. The U.S. had to avoid actions that might be misread as U.S. interference in the internal affairs of the Latin American partners. I suggested that the CIAP process would provide an inter-American multilateral forum for promoting internal political reforms, strengthening the judiciary, and installing effective checks and balances. The U.S. would work through CIAP, a multilateral body in which each government had a voice, to call on governments to tackle critical political, economic, and social reforms in their annual presentations and to monitor government actions.

When congressmen questioned me about the population explosion, rural-to-urban migration, social change resulting from rapid urbanization, and low levels of education, we inevitably discussed domestic political obstacles in each country that made progress difficult. I tried to place what was happening in a long-term context; however, the congressmen reminded me that the AFP had only ten years to prove itself. And, several pointed out, the attention span of congress is much shorter and that they want results quickly.

Some members of congress had little interest in the Alliance. Getting their attention depended on their constituents' interest. That led Jim Boren, after serving as deputy director of the AID Mission in Peru, to propose creating the "Partners of the Alliance" to complement public programs with private sector organizations based in each of the fifty states. His objective was to have each state organization partner with a similar private group in a designated Latin American country or region of a country and that the partners jointly design, fund, and execute projects with a counterpart body in the host country or region.

In 1964, Jim got a green light to begin the program. In those early days, we talked regularly as he designed the ground rules and forged the first partnerships. His enthusiasm and endless energy created an enduring legacy of the Alliance for Progress. Today, his initiative lives on as the Partners of the Americas. And I benefited in my next post, Bolivia, where I had three partnerships: Utah in the Altiplano of Bolivia, North Carolina in Cochabamba Valley, and Arkansas in the Santa Cruz area.

In 1964 and 1965, I was invited by both the Republican and Democrat National Women's Clubs to participate in discussions with congressmen on the Alliance. On one such evening at the Democratic Women's Club, Representative Donald Fraser of Minnesota expressed the impatience of his fellow legislators with the pace of Alliance achievements. I remember trying to draw the contrast between reconstruction in Europe and development in Latin America, especially the maturity of the political systems.

Congressman Bradford Morse, later director of the United Nations Development Program, and I made a lengthy presentation at the Republican National Women's Club about progress in Latin America. I emphasized the need for time and how important it was that the leaders in the host countries take ownership of the process. Castro and Cuba were major topics of discussion, and I contrasted the differences between the democratic development objectives of the Alliance for Progress and the emergence of a one-party political system in Cuba.

A congressman with whom I was able to work with closely and consistently was Dante Fascell of Florida. He knew Latin America well and was committed to the Alliance and wanted more attention given to the human dimensions of the development process. He felt that there should be a reasonable balance between major loans to governments and grants for people-directed projects. He expressed frustration that the projects being funded had so little immediate impact on the lives of people. After one meeting, he asked me to work with the staff director of the House Inter-American Affairs Subcommittee, Rickie Bennett, to include language in an authorization bill to ensure adequate attention to social development and participation by the people. Much of the language we worked out became the basis for Congressman Fascell's initiative to create the Inter-American Social Development Institute (ISDI) in the late 1960s. ISDI was renamed the Inter-American Foundation (IAF) in 1971.

Inter-American Committee on the Alliance for Progress (CIAP)

The expectations of CIAP in Washington were enormous. It was to be the mechanism that guided countries in the preparation of their annual and long-range development plans. It was the forum at which those plans and component projects were to be analyzed and endorsed. On approval, CIAP was to help the member countries find financing by multilateral agencies and more developed governments.

The months after its creation at the São Paolo meeting and the appointment of Carlos Sanz de Santamaría of Colombia as its chair were devoted to organizing a staff and defining operating procedures. Walter Sedwitz was retained as the chief operational officer for CIAP, and it really fell on his shoulders to get the operation up and running. He needed to recruit a bilingual, sophisticated technical staff of economists and other development specialists. He also had to define norms and procedures that met the standards of the international lending community, especially the World Bank, IDB, and the U.S. government. He had six months to do the job.

In building a staff, Walter had to avoid stripping governments of their small supply of national planners. He was offering internationally competitive salaries to nationals who sometimes worried about their government's ability to meet the next payroll. Walter could look for help from the Latin American economists working in Washington at the IDB, then in its infancy, the World Bank, and the IMF. However, few of them were prepared to risk career assignments to work on a precarious venture. Few had much confidence in Sanz de Santamaría, and many believed placing CIAP under the OAS had been a mistake.

Walter was able to bring together an essentially green crew of economists, almost none of whom had prior experience in drawing up development plans or managing development programs. But they were sharp and eager. He had to train them almost overnight to go to countries with instructions on how to prepare country reports, put together country reporting systems, and design programs attractive to international financing entities. The job was monumental when one surveyed the limited number of national planners that were in place in the various countries. The larger countries like Mexico, Brazil, Chile, and Argentina were reluctant to subject themselves to the CIAP process—some out of principle, others because they were adherents of Raúl Prebisch. I found only Colombia was enthusiastic and supportive—I suspect that was because Sanz de Santamaría was Colombian.

CIAP had a deadline to set up its first cycle of country reviews by the fall and to make a progress report to the 1964 meeting of the Inter-American Economic and Social Council (ECOSOC) scheduled for May in Lima.

As office director, a substantial portion of my time was spent working on CIAP. In day-to-day relations with CIAP, Sternfeld was the chief U.S. spokesman and I was his deputy. I participated in policy sessions at which the U.S. reaction to national development plans presented to CIAP by Latin American governments was formulated and I attended CIAP reviews of those plans as part of Ray Sternfeld's team.

I spent at least half a day each week at CIAP headquarters. I attended planning and policy meetings. I talked to the delegates from all the Alliance countries. I listened to the concerns of Venezuela because it was deemed to be too "wealthy" to be a recipient of financial support under the Alliance. I was aware of the confusion of the smaller countries about how to prepare country presentations with little technical competence in their governments. Nonetheless I was more optimistic than many of my U.S. colleagues—I was optimistic because I wanted it to work.

For the ECOSOC meeting Ambassador Mann was named chief of the U.S. delegation. The delegation did not have any of the glamour of the year before when Governor Harriman was its chief. This year there was no White House or Treasury representation. We had no planning sessions with Walt Rostow. All our preliminary meetings were conducted by Ambassador Mann and Bill Rogers.

I was sent to Lima as part of the advance party. I was also tasked with checking on some serious problems that had arisen in implementing projects in Colombia, Ecuador, and Peru before the meeting. In all, I was away from Washington for nearly six weeks.

The meeting itself was very pedestrian. There were no major policy issues to consider. The discussions revolved around the progress of CIAP and the start of the country review process. Sanz de Santamaría was the central figure. The Latin American delegations like the U.S. did not have senior political representation. Some were headed by ministers of the Economy or Planning, while others were headed by the country's permanent representative to the OAS, and not by a cabinet minister. The excitement that marked São Paolo was gone. It was clear that we were settling into a groove, rather than taking additional actions to strengthen the Alliance. All of our chips were on CIAP and Sanz de Santamaría.

Ele

This assignment put a great strain on our personal relationship. I was gone six days a week from early morning to late evening. Occasionally I could get a half-day off on Saturday so that we could lunch at the National Gallery or see a play at the National Theater. She never complained, but I think that I was so absorbed in the job that I would have probably missed any signs that she may have given me.

The only real time we had together was over the Christmas holidays. We joined the Guthries on a trip to Williamsburg—our second. The weather was cold but clear, so we could walk through the exhibits and enjoy once again the artisan skills of the early English settlers. We had Christmas Eve again at the Inn and savored the delightful presents that the Inn bestowed on its guests that Christmas.

The week between Christmas and New Year's was mild and we enjoyed days in downtown Washington and at the Smithsonian. On New Year's Eve we joined the Guthries for dinner and a movie—and the sleet rained down on us when we made our way home. New Year's Day we watched football at home before dinner and bridge with our neighbors, Faye and Frank Sherry. We looked out the window as the sleety rain continued, delighted that we did not have to go out onto the treacherous streets.

Ele had come to dislike winter in Washington very much. She avoided leaving the apartment during the raw cold weather and the icy streets of January and February. So I had to do all the marketing by myself during those months, usually Sunday morning; I had a cart that I would pull up the hill to the Giant on Wisconsin and load it up for the week. Ele would read the Washington Post and New York Times while I made the excursion. She would tell me what articles I might find interesting.

It was not until March that Ele was ready to face the world. Then she spent the days with her brokers and bought stocks, usually no more than ten shares at a time, because our budget couldn't afford much more, but she held on to them—she was no trader.

Ele and my secretary Becky Scroggs became good friends. Becky would call her whenever I was delayed in the afternoon and let her know that I would be late for dinner. Becky would also give

Ele any significant news about a birthday or other event of interest. That led to Ele coming down to the State Department quite often to help Becky with a party for the birthday of an office member and other important office events. They put on a special party the day I became a full-fledged Foreign Service officer. When I got the word that a date was set for my swearing in, Becky informed Ele. There was no hoopla in the swearing in, just a clerk very unglamorously handing me papers to sign and administering the oath. When Mel Spector and I returned to my office, Becky and Ele had a festive party to which most of the AFP staff—State and AID—were invited. How they smuggled the champagne into the building remains a state secret.

Our social life was very sparse. Ele had occasional lunches with old friends from the Department of Labor, but mainly it was not an exciting routine. The high point that summer was a pool party one weekend with our former colleagues from Caracas, Elizabeth and Nat Davis, who was working with Sargent Shriver at the Peace Corps, and Eileen and Bob Cox, who was then assigned to the White House. We did not even have time to play bridge or go to the Eastern Shore. All I remember was the pile of work that never seemed to stop flowing to and across my desk. Thank the good Lord, I had Hi Phillips to route most of it to.

Another Change Is Impending

When I returned from the IA/ECOSOC meeting in Lima, I spent a couple of days with Ele just relaxing and enjoying the pool. All of the discussion revolved around the presidential election in November. There were lots of Rockefeller and Johnson supporters, but very few Goldwaterites. There was very little interest in the Alliance, unlike the year before when I had returned from São Paolo. The discussions were all about civil rights and Vietnam. There was a new political climate in the city as LBJ put his stamp on government operations. Kennedy was passé, as was attention to Latin America and the Alliance.

When I returned to the office, I found a changed environment. The departure of Moscoso had been followed by that of Deputy Assistant Secretary for Economic Affairs Tony Solomon. His replacement was a state department economic officer who had neither the prestige nor commitment to the Alliance of his predecessor. In addition, Ambassador Mann had set in place new procedures and approval processes much more in traditional state department mode than the freewheeling, corner-cutting, gung-ho rhythm of the Moscoso years.

Hi Phillips briefed me on the new routine and significant changes that he felt indicated the Alliance was no longer a priority of the administration. He called my attention to the appointment of Ellsworth Bunker as U.S. representative to the OAS and noted that many policy questions formerly handled by the coordinator were being referred to the ambassador. Hi sensed that Ambassador Mann was more concerned about traditional U.S. political and economic interests in Latin America than the Alliance or CIAP, and had turned to Ambassador Bunker to deal with them. Hi worried about the relationship between Ambassador Mann and Bill Rogers, which didn't surprise me because it had not been close during the Lima ECOSOC meeting.

As I settled back into the office routine, my primary source of official news was Ray Sternfeld, who cued me in on changes in the front office and shifts in operating tactics. Most of my time was spent on discussions with division chiefs and specialists on regional and country programs and projects.

One of the first major changes in operating procedures grew out of our support of CIAP. The office was advised that we were to hold off informing countries about loan and grant approvals until the CIAP review for that country was completed. We planned to announce our package of support in the donor meetings following the reviews. So, we were giving priority in our internal review process for those countries first in line for CIAP presentations.

We tried to maintain a sense of normalcy. But rumors about the role of CIAP abounded that made it difficult to keep people motivated about our internal project review process. A technician would report that he heard from a reliable source that, in CIAP reviews, countries could reopen the negotiation of projects already in the approval process. Another heard that final decisions on projects would be made by CIAP—even on those already approved by the U.S. government. Those rumors complicated in-country negotiations and sapped the interest of the office staff in critiquing loan and grant proposals under consideration for AFP financing. It was early August that we finally got word from Ambassador Mann and Bill Rogers that the U.S. government had never considered submitting AID projects to CIAP review and that U.S. loan and grant approval criteria and procedures would remain unchanged. The only question being considered had been the timing for announcing grants and loans.

Throughout those sweltering months, I would walk at least once a week over to the CIAP offices for briefings by Carlos Sanz de Santamaría. Occasionally I accompanied Ambassador Bunker and Bill Rogers to policy level discussions. Walter Sedwitz outlined the scope of the national plans he expected from the member states and briefed us on the country visits his team had been making to help in their preparation and presentation There was an aura of expectation.

The country presentations finally began in early October and were scheduled to last one week per country. The opening session of each country presentation was attended by Ambassador Bunker, Ray Sternfeld, and me. During the week-long hearing, our program, loan and technical officers carefully followed each detail of each country's presentation and their requests for financial and technical assistance. Ray and I usually attended discussions on critical issues and the closing session.

The presentations were pedestrian at best. The questions by the CIAP staff were often superficial, and I got the impression that CIAP was more concerned with the reaction of the government making the presentation than with the substance and quality of the national plan. Few of the countries had put together comprehensive documents, and many of those initial presentations were disjointed and lacked appropriate data to support conclusions and requests for financial and technical support. As I recall, not one included commitments to undertake policy or economic reforms called for under the AFP. The presentations displayed each country's lack of planning experience, institutional maturity, and seasoned planners.

The reactions by the larger countries indicated that they were not impressed by the technical qualifications of Sanz de Santamaría or Walter Sedwitz. The small countries seemed overawed by the process; but in the end only supplied shopping lists of projects they wanted funded. Even submissions by countries like Colombia and Chile provided minimal information for making sound judgments on their fiscal and monetary situation, much less identifying priorities for program and project loans and grants. The aura blew away all too fast.

Walter Sedwitz identified the problems as clearly as anyone and suggested the need for greater in-country work by his economists and technical staff in the preparation of the next round of country presentations. To work intensively with twenty countries would be a huge undertaking.

I felt then as I do today that CIAP was an excellent concept. Once again, the problem was not the concept, but the capability of the Latin American countries at their individual stages of development to prepare the information needed for CIAP to do the job expected of it. I suggested to Ray Sternfeld that CIAP needed at least three or four years of intensive work with each country to prepare the economists and other technicians needed to develop sound national plans and sectoral studies. For this to happen, CIAP needed commitments by countries to build such staffs, give them career protection, and ensure their autonomy—an adaptation of the *servicio* concept to the inter-American system. I also suggested that CIAP might need additional grant funds from the U.S. to finance such an operation. Ray did not feel that such a proposal would fly, so I didn't pursue the idea.

As November approached, the U.S. political campaign seemed to overwhelm all other aspects of our bureaucratic life. The office was riveted as the election unfolded on television. LBJ's election reassured our Alliance office and we awaited a new White House initiative to revive its spirit and commitment.

In late November, Mel Spector accompanied me to a meeting with Ambassador Mann and Bill Rogers. Ambassador Mann said very simply: we want you to go to Bolivia as AID Mission Director. Alex Firfer was completing his second two-year tour in the altitude and was to be transferred in June. Bill Rogers added that Bolivia had the largest loan and grant portfolio in Latin America, still received budget support, and was one of the largest recipients of PL 480 wheat. He said, "We believe that you can handle the job and want you to give us your answer as soon as possible."

That night Ele and I reviewed our situation. Ele had been to Bolivia in 1963 and liked the Altiplano. We had actually stayed in the director's house. The altitude had no negative effect on our health during the visits. She smiled and said, "Yes, I would love to go to Bolivia."

The next morning I poked my head into Ambassador Mann's office and gave him my reply before going down the corridor to report to Mel Spector. I would leave Institutional Development by March 31, begin orientation for my new assignment in early April, and depart for post in early May to allow a short overlap with Alex before he moved to his new post, the Dominican Republic. The timing was crucial because the deputy director, Jack Edison, would be departing post for a new assignment in August. With the short overlap, I could be settled in the job before Jack departed.

Leveo Sanchez was named to replace me as office director. I had worked with his mother, Victoria Sanchez, in Central America in the mid-1950s when she was the prime mover of the multi-country textbook project for elementary schools. Leveo and I were to have a two-week overlap.

Ele and I had a wonderful Christmas with the Guthries and the Sherrys. We also received an invitation from Fran Howard to a pre-Inaugural family get-together with her brother—Hubert H. Humphrey, the newly elected vice president of the United States. I took two weeks off so that we could relax and talk, as we had not for nearly a year.

Then, in January 1965 came a *coup d'état* in Bolivia. President Paz Estenssoro had been elected to a second term the preceding November and the expectation had been that I would continue to work with Planning Minister Gumucio and his staff in moving the agreed upon development program forward. Now our plans were on hold while the new government took shape. Two generals, Ovando of the army and Barrientos of the air force, assumed power jointly as co-presidents. Ambassador Douglas Henderson put my appointment on hold while the situation clarified. By late February, he gave the green light for me to arrive in May.

When the assignment was back on track, Ele proposed that we take another vacation to Europe over Easter, spending three weeks together in Spain before she took another month on a Eurail pass wandering over Western Europe. I checked with Ambassador

Mann, Bill Rogers, and Mel Spector who gave us the green light. Mel even arranged for the State Department travel office to help Ele with the reservations from Pan American Airways for flights and in obtaining Eurail passes.

Mel Spector arranged for Ele and me to take our physical exams in early March. Both of us passed the altitude test and I was given medical clearance without a waiver. As the State medical officer told me, "You already have served in four posts and shown that you can handle the challenges to your hearing." By the way, I bought a new advanced Zenith that helped me better understand conversation.

Mel Spector arranged for a swearing-in ceremony as soon as he received the security and medical clearances. It was a memorable occasion in the large entrance chamber to the suite of the administrator of AID, formerly that of the secretary of state. Bill Rogers administered the oath of office, with Ele standing next to me. The room was packed with friends and colleagues, including Ambassador Mann, Congressmen Fascell and Morse, Frances Howard, and the newly named ambassador of Bolivia to the United States, Julio Sanjinés. A new chapter in our lives was beginning.

Europe to Bolivia

A monkey wrench was thrown into our plans when an attempted revolution led by Juan Bosch broke out in the Dominican Republic, reputedly with help from Fidel Castro. The Johnson administration moved quickly to help the Dominican government squash it. That led to my assignment to an emergency task force that affected our vacation plans. I would have only eighteen days off instead of nearly a month.

When I told Ele of my assignment to the emergency task force, she was very upset. She said that I had practically abandoned her for a year, and now she would have to put off a vacation she wanted us to share. After many harsh words, we agreed that she would leave for Spain on April 2, the day after her birthday as we had planned, and that I would join her in Madrid twelve days later when my emergency assignment ended just before Easter.

Although she was apprehensive about going alone to Madrid,

her trip was uneventful. When she arrived at Barajas Airport, she went to the Spanish tourist office to book a hotel, because when we had changed our plans, we had canceled our hotel reservations. The Spanish clerk responded that there were no available hotel rooms over the Easter holiday. When asked how long she needed a room, Ele replied, "Three to four weeks." The clerk then offered her an apartment at the Plaza Hotel for thirty days. Ele swallowed hard, and asked what the rate would be. The clerk replied, "$10 a day." Ele said, "That would be fine." She gave the clerk fifteen twenty-dollar travelers' checks, and received a receipt and instructions. She walked out of the airport into a taxi that took her to the renowned Plaza Hotel.

On arrival she was escorted to a two-bedroom, two-bath suite, with a living room, kitchen, and all the conveniences one could ask for. The hotel maid who came in to check the apartment asked Ele if she could be of service. Ele asked her about a beauty shop to get her hair done, and about seeing Madrid. The maid had a sister who ran a beauty shop around the corner, and a brother who ran a tour bus company. The maid took Ele to the beauty parlor and then to meet her brother. She scheduled tours to the various sights of Madrid, as well as the Prado and the Royal Palace. Franco was still in power and the Palace was almost like a museum. Her new friend gave her tips on places to eat well and reasonably and went with her to a store for bread, eggs, fruit, and other essentials. Ele had a ball.

Then she asked the maid about getting out of Madrid during Holy Week. The next morning, she told Ele that her brother was driving a Spanish-speaking tour to southern Spain for a five-day visit to the ceremonies in Sevilla, Córdoba, and Granada. He had just one seat left on the bus. "How much?" asked Ele. "$12 a day including hotel and meals." "When are we leaving?" replied Ele. "Tomorrow morning," replied her new friend.

Ele told me later that the tour was far better than the expensive Meliá tour that we took for the first week of my stay in Spain. She stayed in small Spanish hotels, which had comfortable beds, with bathrooms down the hall, and lovely Spanish ladies as roommates. Ele saw the processions in all three cities, participated in the medieval church services, had aperitifs at fashionable sidewalk cafes, and loved every moment with her fellow passengers. In Sevilla, she and the other passengers went to the *Patio Andaluz* nightclub for gypsy music and dancing. She made friends with the owner and some of the staff—enough to get me a royal welcome and free drinks when I visited there the following week.

Ele returned to Madrid the night before I arrived in Spain. She sent word that we were staying at the Plaza Hotel Apartment, not the hotel itself. When I arrived there, the maid was waiting for me since Ele was getting her hair done. What a treat the apartment was! I bathed and crawled into bed for a nap. When Ele returned, I had never seen her happier.

She arranged for us to tour Madrid with the maid's brother in his private car. Starting from the Puerta del Sol, we drove to the Prado and along Madrid's gracious avenues, before visiting Escorial and other sites in the suburbs. On our way back to the city, Ele and I discussed our forthcoming two weeks. The day after next, we were heading to southern Spain on a Meliá five-star tour to Marbella via Toledo, Granada, Córdoba, Sevilla, and Jerez. But we weren't sure what to do the second week of our stay in Spain. Ele asked our driver whether he would be available, and he said he would be pleased to drive us wherever we wanted to go. Ele asked, "How much?" He replied, "Ten U.S. dollars per day with car plus expenses." So, we sat down with Pablo and worked out a seven-day itinerary from Madrid through Estremadura to Lisbon and back to Madrid via Salamanca, Ávila, and Segovia.

I thoroughly enjoyed the Meliá Tour and the accommodations. Ele compared it to her own tour and complained that it was too expensive and lacked the flavor of being with Spaniards. She conceded that the hotels were more modern and elegant, but the food was no better. She commented that our English-speaking guides knew less about the sights we visited than her fellow passengers on the Spanish tour, and that our fellow U.S. passengers were not as much fun as her cohorts on the earlier tour. We did agree that one of the high points of the Meliá tour was our stop at Aranjuez for white asparagus and *vino blanco*. Toledo fascinated us with its medieval castle and El Greco presence, but it was Andalucía that captured our hearts. We saw the Costa del Sol and enjoyed its warm waters. We drank sherry in Jerez and spent three consecutive evenings at the *Patio Andaluz*, even dancing with the gypsy entertainers. We walked the gardens of the Alhambra at sundown and reminded ourselves of the tales that we had read by Washington Irving. We marveled at the mosque turned church in Córdoba and remembered that in the Middle Ages, this had been one of the great centers of learning and research. Madrid seemed anti-climactic when we returned to the Plaza.

We had another day in Madrid walking the tree-lined streets and riding a bus to a neighborhood whose name caught our fancy. Then, we started out with Pablo to experience a totally different part of Spain before crossing into Portugal. With a flavor totally different from Andalucía, Estremadura and its somber aura and arid mountains led us to appreciate why so many of its sons in the sixteenth century had made their way to the New World as *conquistadores* and seldom looked back. We spent the first night in Trujillo at a not too comfortable hotel in the center of town and walked streets where legend said Cortés and Pizarro once strode. It had none of the colors or flowers of Andalucía.

Lisbon was a pleasant interlude. We found a comfortable modern hotel with colorful tiles in the entrance, and delightful staff whose Portuguese was alien to my ears. How different the accent in southern Brazil to the tones of the Lisbon natives! We spent two days visiting the harbor and the great buildings that bear witness to the Golden Age of Portuguese exploration, of Prince Henry the Navigator and the voyages of Bartolomeu Dias and Vasco da Gama opening up India. We crossed the Tagus River Bridge to explore southern fishing villages and eat just-caught fish in open-air family restaurants overlooking the Atlantic. Our second night we found a small café near the hotel where we listened to the haunting tones of the *fado*.

Then we turned north along the coast to Estoril, Nazare, and Coimbra. We stopped at all the churches that the guidebooks mentioned and wandered down to see the fishing nets on the beach at Nazare. We spent the late afternoon at the University of Coimbra, the Oxford of Portugal. As we wandered around the campus, we met an elderly professor who welcomed us and took us to the elegant red, green, and gold lacquered King John Library, where he showed us a copy of the 1386 Treaty of Windsor with Great Britain, the oldest treaty of friendship in the Western World. As he walked us back to our small hotel, we passed a student wearing one of the black silk shawls that we had seen on all the male students. The professor smiled and commented that the student must be a great Casanova. I asked why. He replied, "Each notch that he has cut on his shawl is for a conquest, and he has quite a few."

From Coimbra we reentered Spain and spent the next night in Salamanca, visiting the university, the cathedral, and the home of Cervantes. Then we wended our way back to Madrid through Segovia and its great Roman aqueduct, and Ávila with its magnificent medieval walls and shrine to St. Teresa. On the last day in Madrid, we prepared for our flight to Brussels, with lots of tension about how to get back the souvenirs we had accumulated. Ele planned to take only one bag with her on her Eurail adventure, which left me with three bags to get back to Washington—and I did not want to pay excess baggage. Then, too, Ele had purchased a painting before my arrival. It was a superb abstract by a young painter influenced by Picasso. With the two of us we had no problem on the flight to Brussels, but my concern was getting everything home by myself.

We had two nights in Brussels. The first afternoon we toured the *Grande Place* and ate at a fabulous café on a side street. The second day, we took the train to Bruges, went on a canal ride and walked once again through that living museum. On the third day, I took Ele to the rail station and helped her board a train to Salzburg. Her two weeks in Spain had shown her that she was perfectly able to get around by herself. A hug and kiss, and she was off.

I spent the time until I left for the airport fretting about my three bags and the painting. When I got to the Pan Am counter, the attendant checked two bags and smiled. There was no overweight charge. I carried the painting and the third bag on board with me without a problem. I was really annoyed with myself for upsetting Ele with my fretting.

Back in Washington, I had three days of briefings on recent political and economic developments in Bolivia. I worried about Ele alone in Europe, but I really did not have to—she was enjoying every minute of it.

She had two glorious days in Salzburg. When she arrived, she went to the Austrian tourist office and arranged for a room at the Elefant Hotel on the main street for three dollars a night. She spent her two days absorbed by the fabulous shops and Mozart. Then she took a train over to Vienna, just emerging as a free city again after the occupation by the Four Powers following World War II; she was able to obtain a room at a fashionable pension near St. Stephen's Cathedral for less than five dollars a day. Then, she took the train across West Germany, stopping at Munich, Heidelberg, and Cologne before moving on to Copenhagen, Stockholm, Oslo, and Bergen. She never paid more than ten dollars a night for good lodgings, often with meals included. Her favorite experience was the Tivoli Gardens in Copenhagen, where she spent an afternoon walking around and watching the Danes enjoy themselves. Another special memory was staying at the Royal Viking Hotel in Oslo, where she paid three dollars a day with breakfast included—a breakfast, she said, that "filled me for the day." She described the petite bathroom as one where you could sit on the toilet and take your shower at the same time. Ele and I stayed there thirty years later at a hundred and fifty dollars a day. After Bergen, she made her way back to Brussels. Pan Am flew her safely home after I had departed for La Paz.

Before joining me in Bolivia, Ele stopped off in Aberdeen, South Dakota, to make certain that all was well with the farm and then visited my mother in San Francisco and her mother in Tulare, to make sure that our families were in good shape.

19

Bolivia

The Bolivian AID program was one of the largest in the hemisphere, with hundreds of millions of dollars in project funding and a technical staff of over two hundred fifty economic and technical advisers. Bolivia was in the initial stages of its political, economic, and social evolution.

Ele was excited about the assignment. In the 1963 visit, she was attracted by its unique beauty and its handicrafts. She knew the house in Calacoto in which she was to live and had been charmed by it. It was a Mediterranean style two-story modern house, with an acre of garden off its side terrace. It sat in a valley at 11,800 feet, down the hill from the heart of La Paz at 12,600 feet. It had an elegant living room larger than our 1,000 square foot apartment in Washington, D.C., with French doors opening onto a large terrace above the garden. When the landlord fled Bolivia to live in London after the revolution of 1952, the U.S. government rented the home with all the furnishings. Since the house was furnished, we only needed to send down personal effects, household linens, and items for decoration. All the rest of our furniture was stored in a Washington area warehouse.

When I got back to Washington after our trip to Spain and Portugal, my first stop was at Bill Rogers' office. He looked up at me and asked, "How soon can you leave?" I said, "As soon as you want me there." His answer was, "Next week." I flew to Bolivia three days later. Ele joined me six weeks later.

The Country

Bolivia is one of the most captivating countries in the hemisphere. It is landlocked in the heart of South America, just south of the equator, and includes the high Andes, lush Andean valleys, and the rich eastern and northern lowlands that form part of the Amazon Plain on the north and the Gran Chaco to the east. It is a series of different ecological and ethnic enclaves. Its high Andean west is the home of the Aymara nation, a people with their own language and lore who expelled the Incas from the land surrounding the highest navigable lake in the world, Lake Titicaca. The Incas conquered surrounding indigenous populations, converted them into subjects of their empire, and extended the Quechua language all the way to the northernmost provinces of modern day Argentina, but the Aymara remained fiercely independent.

When the Spanish conquered the Inca Empire and pushed on to the high Andean plateau that is now Bolivia, they found the source of much of the Incas' gold and silver in one mountain, Cerro Bolivar—called Cerro Rico in colonial times. It had been worked for centuries by the indigenous people. Its gold and silver financed Spanish grandeur for over three centuries and made Potosí, the city that sits at its base, the largest urban area in the Americas for two centuries. It was the home of the first mint in the New World, and the economic center of Spanish America. Some of the wealthiest *conquistadores* made their fortunes there and built great edifices, elegant cathedrals, public buildings, and the renowned Potosí School of colonial art that rivaled Quito, Lima, and Mexico City as the cultural center of Latin America. Cerro Rico is said to have produced enough gold and silver for the Spanish Crown to build a bridge nine feet high and nine feet wide around the equator.

Living in the high altitude of Potosí, over 14,000 feet, was difficult for the wealthy Spaniards. When they found a lush semi-tropical valley in Sucre, over a ridge of the Andes, they moved their families and built estates there. Sucre became the seat of government (*Capitanía General*) for the province, under the Vice Royalty of Peru, headquartered on the Pacific coast in Lima. Sucre was endowed with executive and judicial powers to govern all the way to the Atlantic coast of what today is Argentina, whose primary interest for Spain was its farm products for Potosí, Sucre, and the mines.

The gold and silver of Cerro Rico was minted into bars and coins at the mint in Potosí and transported by llama and burro trains over the Andes to the Peruvian ports of Mollendo and Callao, for transport to Spain. Midway to the Pacific the caravans rested and refurbished their supplies at a way station, La Paz, at the edge of the Aymara homeland. Over centuries, Aymara La Paz grew and competed with Sucre for control over the right to govern the province.

It was from the crest of Cerro Rico that the Great Liberator Simón Bolivar declared Upper Peru an independent nation, and the local leaders called it Bolivia in his honor. Independence did not, however, lead to a change in the economic and social system. The powerful creole families replaced the Spanish Crown but retained the feudal system and their control over the mining sector. Civil wars by factions of the powerful families spawned as many presidents as years of independence up to 1952. One famous Cochabamba Valley caudillo, President Melgarejo of Tarata, declared war on Germany when he learned of its invasion of France in 1870; he is said to have led his army from Cochabamba over the eastern ridge of the Andes and, after several weeks, called in an aide to ask, "How much longer before we get to France?"

Bolivia lost a third of its territory in the nineteenth century, including its seacoast to Chile in the 1870 War of the Pacific, and a vast area of its Amazon interior to Brazil for navigation rights through a tributary of the Amazon to the Atlantic—unfortunately, the rapids on that river are so formidable and dangerous that they are still deemed unfit for shipping.

Bolivia is divided into three primary geographic regions whose interconnection is impeded by one range of the Andes after another. For some regions, the airplane is the primary means for connecting to the others. The occidental region is the Altiplano, at 11,000 to 14,000 feet, surrounded by majestic peaks reaching 24,000 feet. The second, in the center of the country, encompasses the high valleys of the Andes, including the lush valleys of Cochabamba, Sucre, and Tarija. The eastern third is made up of lowlands that stretch to the Amazon on the north and to the Chaco on the east.

Not only is the topography of each region substantially different, but the mindset of the population in each region defies comparison. The Altiplano is essentially Aymara: its harsh environment has created a stoic and fierce people who defied the Incas; they were put into feudal bondage by the Spaniards in mines and farms for four centuries but never lost their own identity and distrust of the non-Aymara.

The high valleys are like eternal spring and with soils suited for agriculture. Its people speak Quechua and were part of the Inca Empire before the Spaniards arrived, and more readily fit into the feudal agriculture system installed by Spain. There was little to attract Spain to the eastern lowlands so the Crown gave large land grants for cattle ranching where, like the "Old West," the inhabitants learned to do for themselves and developed an economy, society, and spirit of independence different from the rest of the country.

The three regions fought each other throughout Bolivia's history to protect their regional identity and interests. In the early years of the twentieth century, a civil war between the High Andean Valleys and the Altiplano was won by the Altiplano. The seat of power shifted from the traditional capital of Sucre to La Paz. The terms of the settlement left the official capital, with the Supreme Court, in Sucre, but moved the executive offices, including the high command of the Army and Navy, to La Paz—with almost all the official positions occupied by victorious La Paz. To this day, Bolivia remains a country with two capital cities.

Since independence, Bolivia has been a poverty-ridden republic with a small elite sustaining the colonial structures of serfdom and forced mine labor. Its population mostly lives on the Altiplano and in the high valleys of the Andes.

Mining has been the backbone of the Bolivian economy, and its primary source of foreign exchange. Gold and silver reserves were almost mined out by Spain, and by the late 1700s, Bolivia declined in importance. However, at the end of the nineteenth century, a shopkeeper named Patiño in the Altiplano region took a deed for a mining property as payment for a bill from one of his customers, and made the great tin strikes at Catavi and Siglo Veinte making Bolivia one of the most important suppliers of tin for the world market.

Tin became king of the Bolivian economy. Three tin barons— Patiño, Hochschild, and Aramaya—emerged as the most important economic and political force in the country. Revenues from tin exports accounted for almost 70 percent of the national treasury and almost all of the country's export earnings. Tin gave Bolivia its significance in both World Wars. Cheap labor and minimum investment in technology kept the tin boom going for a half century. Bolivia exported tin ore, not smelted tin, since the three great tin companies had limited their investment in technology in Bolivia and built their smelters in Europe, primarily Germany. In World War II, when Bolivia agreed to sell all its tin ore to the U.S., a smelter was built in Texas.

In 1952, after a bread shortage in La Paz led to riots, the government was overthrown by the police force, which then abolished the army and navy and placed the defense of the country under police control. Victor Paz Estenssoro, the firebrand leader of the National Revolutionary Movement (MNR), was brought back from exile in Argentina to form a new government. That called for an end to the feudal agriculture system and nationalization of the tin and petroleum industries—with government assuming the central role in national development. The MNR philosophy was national socialist, closer to the fascist model than the communist, but it was anti-U.S., anti-capitalist, and seemingly pro-USSR in those critical years of the emerging Cold War. Washington became deeply concerned that Bolivia was about to ally itself with the USSR.

That year, 1952, turned out to be the start of a social revolution. The peasants chased landlords off their feudal lands and de facto divided up the agricultural estates throughout the country. The government nationalized the tin mines and set up government planning and oversight machinery that had never existed before. When the newly emancipated rural people consumed the food supply, traditional marketing systems broke down. Shortages of food and almost every essential commodity ensued.

Tin mining went into shambles as the MNR placed its supporters on the payrolls. The tin industry went from 12,500 miners producing 25,000 metric tons per year to 25,000 workers producing 12,500 metric tons. Government revenues dwindled since the mines operated at a loss. As there were no tin refineries in country, the government had to negotiate with Patiño and Hochschild for them to buy the ore for processing at their mills on terms they dictated.

Nonetheless, the exuberance of change swept Paz Estenssoro into a unique position in Bolivian history. He was a new liberator of the Bolivian people and quickly consolidated control over the government. Bolivia wrote a new Constitution, with universal suffrage and four-year presidential terms with no reelection of the incumbent.

With each revolutionary step, the U.S. government became more deeply concerned that the MNR would turn pro-Soviet. There was strong Communist influence among the tin miners, more Trotskyite than Stalinist. The national Communist Party was flirting with the MRN. Most of the political, business, and military leaders with whom the U.S. had traditionally dealt went into exile or disappeared. We had to establish new arrangements with the new leaders, about whom we had very conflicting information.

In 1954, to prevent further deterioration, the U.S. made an agreement to help the MNR government with budget support to fill the gap left by the declining revenues from tin, and to provide monetary and technical assistance to help rebuild the economy. It was a period of agitation in which mobs marched periodically on the embassy located in the center of downtown La Paz. One ambassador, Philip Bonsall, told me that during one of those marches, he received a call from the foreign minister, who asked, "Are you and your staff all right, sir?" When the ambassador replied, "Yes," the foreign minister asked, "Is there anything that I can do for you?" The ambassador said, "Well, yes, call off your mob!"

Bolivia became the site of one of the largest U.S. aid programs in the world, including budget support, substantial loans for infrastructure, and technical assistance. My former mentor in Mexico, Merwin Bowen, headed a task force to prepare a blueprint for Bolivian development, which placed great emphasis on the development of the Eastern lowlands and the rehabilitation of the mining industry.

The U.S. engagement in Bolivian development began during World War II as one of the *quid pro quos* for Bolivia's agreement to sell to the U.S. all of its tin ore production. Part of the tin deal included financing the construction of the highway over the Andes from the valley of Cochabamba to Santa Cruz and the eastern plain. In the mid-1950s, we agreed to finance a second route to Santa Cruz from the Cochabamba Valley through the Chapare, and to provide funds and technical assistance for developing the potential of the eastern lowlands. The United States subsidized the creation of agricultural communities made up of Hong Kong and Okinawan colonists. With the West German government and the Inter-American Development Bank (IDB), the U.S. initiated a tripartite plan to rehabilitate the tin mines. Each year, the U.S. supplied millions of dollars of PL 480 wheat to ensure a steady supply of that staple. The U.S. used its influence to encourage the IDB to finance the building of the Santa Isabel power complex in the Cochabamba Valley, and encouraged our European allies to invest in projects all around Bolivia. In addition, the U.S. assembled one of the largest technical assistance missions in the hemisphere to advise the Bolivian government on measures to improve agriculture, education, health services, public administration, banking, and economic planning.

From 1952 to 1965, the MRN won four successive presidential elections. Paz Estenssoro was followed by Hernán Siles Suazo. Paz Estenssoro won a second term in 1960 and, with encouragement from the U.S. government, ran for re-election in the fall of 1964 in spite of the prohibition against re-election. Paz won but the MNR split. That opened the way for a military coup in January 1965 that deposed Paz and the MNR. The longest period of constitutional government in Bolivian history came to an end.

I was arriving to head the U.S. economic development assistance program in the fourth month of a military-led government, with two presidents: Co-Presidents Army General Alfredo Ovando and Air Force General René Barrientos. The MNR leadership was in disarray, with its two ex-presidents in exile.

Understanding the Aid Program

My arrival in La Paz was breathtaking—not only because of the incredible landscape of the airport at 13,600 feet above sea level but also because of the impact of the lack of oxygen. It was a clear, cold day with blue skies arching above the brown expanse of the Altiplano. AID Deputy Director Jack Edison and his wife and USAID Executive Officer Les Gottlieb and his wife met me, rushed me through Immigration and Customs, and headed to the house in Calacoto that I would occupy for the next three plus years. I was met by our house staff of Eduarda, Elsa, and Zenovio. They had lunch ready for us and then the Edisons left me to rest. And Eduarda, the cook, had a cup of coca tea for me to drink to help limit the effects of *soroche* (altitude sickness) and a sleepless night.

The following morning, Jack Edison picked me up and we drove to the USAID office on the fourth floor of the *Banco Popular del Perú* building, across from the Central Bank of Bolivia. My office overlooked the intersection where most anti-Yankee demonstrations took place. The office was quite large, with a sitting area with sofa and chairs to talk with guests and a large conference table for twelve to sixteen participants. One door opened to a foyer office where my secretary and the secretary for the deputy director were stationed. Opposite my entrance door was the door to the deputy director's office. When I needed to talk to the deputy in private, I could just cross the secretaries' area and close the door. A second door opened into the office of the program officer, who kept the records of the progress and problems in each of the mission programs and projects, prepared the annual program presentation to Washington, and drafted periodic program analyses and reports required by my former Washington cohorts.

I met my secretary, Peggy Hook, who became a life-long friend. She and I barely had time to say "hello" when Jack Edison said that Ambassador Douglas Henderson was waiting for me. We took the elevator up to the sixth floor to meet the ambassador and the deputy chief of mission (DCM), Robert Hurwich, whom I had known since he was on the Cuban Desk during the Missile Crisis. We got down to a first name basis very quickly as the ambassador briefed me on the political situation in the country. At post, I always called Douglas Henderson "Mr. Ambassador" because he was the personal representative of the president of the United States. After we left Bolivia, as personal friends, he was Doug, a man I admired for his principles, intelligence, and dedication.

The ambassador described the consolidation of power taking place under the military. All of the ministers were army and air force generals or colonels, with the navy admiral appropriately accommodated. The real power, he opined, was General Barrientos of the air force—the man with charisma and support among the younger officers of the army and air force. The ambassador made no bones about his opposition to the coup that had taken place. He felt that Paz Estenssoro and the MNR had been making good progress in developing the country and felt that the coup was counterproductive. Nonetheless, he emphasized that our job was to work with the Bolivian government and to help the Bolivian people in order to ensure that U.S. interests were protected. He assured me of his full support.

Before I left his office, the ambassador called in Bill Broderick, the economic counselor. The ambassador proposed that Bill replace the departing Jack Edison as assistant USAID director, both to provide continuity and help me through the initial stages of meeting key government officials and understanding the extensive AID program. Bill had one more year left on his assignment to Bolivia, and the timing of his departure would give me time to identify a long-term replacement for Jack. The ambassador, Bob Hurwich, Jack, Bill, and I talked for about a half an hour, and then we all agreed that Bill's replacing Jack made good sense. I agreed to consult Bill Rogers and Ray Sternfeld about this interim arrangement.

On returning to my office, I met with Les Gottlieb, who helped me complete the paperwork required to advise Washington that I had taken up my post as USAID director. He then briefed me on USAID staffing and pending vacancies. Between our U.S. and Bolivian staff, we had a complement of over three hundred. I froze all hires until I could get a feel for the program, and until replacements for key departing officers, including the deputy director and the program officer, were in place at post.

Les then called in our mission controller, Gene Barrett. We went over the financial situation of the mission and the over US$500 million in active projects and in the pipeline. I raised the possibility of having Bill Broderick named the deputy director for the rest of his tour. Both had favorable impressions of Bill and his knowledge and support of the mission. However, they were concerned about the reaction in AID Washington at having a second State Department officer in a senior post in one of the largest missions in Latin America. We agreed that we would talk about the matter later in the week. I was indeed fortunate to have such competent, thoroughly reliable officers to guide me.

The next day, Jack Edison scheduled meetings for me with all of the USAID staff. Bill Broderick joined us. Our first meeting was with Andy Johnson, the about-to-depart program officer, and his two U.S. and two Bolivian assistants. Andy's replacement, John Blumgart, was due to arrive in a few weeks. One of the Bolivian program assistants was Ernesto Wende, who shortly thereafter resigned to become president of the Savings and Loan System of Bolivia. Next I met the regional legal officer, David Lazar, with whom I bonded immediately. His grasp of the problems facing the mission was incisive. I asked David and Bill to stay on with me during the rest of the briefings that Jack set up.

The following morning, Jack, Bill, Dave, and I met with John Edmundson, the chief economist, who was about to return to the University of Utah, his deputy, Jake Merman, and his top Bolivian economist, Jorge Crespo, who later became foreign minister of Bolivia and Bolivian ambassador to the U.S. They briefed us on the country's dismal economic and fiscal condition, highlighting the continuing losses in the tin industry and the projected deficit in the national budget. They impressed me with their understanding of not only the country's situation but of the people who were managing—if not manipulating—the fragile economy. By the end of the third day, it was not the altitude that caused me sleepless nights.

Then we met with the division chiefs and their staff. Our first was with Emerson "Em" Melaven, the chief of the public administration division, who worked directly with the minister of Finance. His staff included specialists in tax administration, banking, civil service, and public administration. Their goal was to help the Bolivian government set up central operating systems and increase tax revenues and to advise the minister on transforming its usual "cronyism" style of doing business to one that impartially served the public interest of the nation.

Raising revenues was a tremendous challenge because the tax base from mining exports and customs duties had been in steady decline for a decade. Revenues from customs appeared to fall each time tariffs and duties were raised. A standard joke at cocktail parties was that the largest union in the country was the smugglers syndicate, who celebrated each time the U.S. forced the government to raise another import duty. Em had an IRS team at work in the

Ministry of Finance and a specialist in finance and banking, Philip Faucett working at the Central Bank. They detailed their work and the obstacles they faced. I arranged for Em to set up appointments with the minister and the president of the Central Bank.

The following week, I met the general who was minister of Finance and his vice minister, Jorge Jordán Ferrufino. They were appreciative of the USAID support and the meeting was cordial. They told me that the Junta government was committed to the administrative reforms proposed by Em's team and was pressing at cabinet meetings for authority to adopt certain aspects of the tax reform package that had been under consideration by Paz Estenssoro at the time of his ouster. As the meeting evolved, it became clear that the vice minister was the policy chief and decision-maker. The minister described the government's fiscal position as "precarious" and asked whether the U.S. would consider a special budget stabilization grant. I assured him that, while no one in Washington was prepared to consider such a request, the USAID would work with him to carry out other aspects of his fiscal agenda. We agreed to meet once a month in the minister's office to deal with all the items that either he or USAID felt needed attention.

Phil Faucett followed up the next week with the president of the Central Bank. The president of the Bank had almost no central banking experience and demonstrated no interest in changing the way the bank operated, which was primarily as just another commercial bank.

Friday afternoon of the first week, I called Les Gottlieb and Gene Barrett to discuss the appointment of Bill Broderick as the deputy director. I proposed that Bill be nominated and David Lazar, the regional legal adviser, be nominated to fill a new post of associate director, with the understanding that David would become deputy on the completion of Bill's assignment. Les and Gene agreed with the proposal, and said it would ensure continuity in mission leadership for the next three years and enhance the cooperation between the embassy and the mission. A few days later Washington approved the proposal.

I ended my first week with a roundtable discussion with the program officer, Andy Johnson; the loan officer, Bill Brister; and the chief Engineer, Chuck Shirley, about the loan portfolio of almost US$500 million in projects. Most of them were dollar loans for roads and infrastructure. USAID also had the largest Bolivian peso account in the Central Bank, over $16 million in U.S. dollars derived from repayments to the U.S. government of Bolivian purchases of PL 480 wheat and other commodities. From that account, the mission financed a variety of projects including school building; loans to the Agricultural, Mining, and Industrial Banks; community water supplies; and some public buildings. The scope of the operation was extensive and many of the projects had operating problems that Chuck Shirley and Bill Brister detailed. After the meeting, Bill, Jack, Dave, and I spent an hour discussing what criteria we needed to establish in considering future requests for U.S. loan funds and what other measures were needed to alleviate the effects on the already stretched Bolivia budget and expanding public debt.

The ambassador and his wife, Dorothy, invited me to a family dinner that Sunday night. We spent the evening discussing the political scene and the relations between the co-presidents. The ambassador told me he had agreed with the co-presidents to meet once a month to review the state of the economy and U.S. government support for the public sector and the budget deficit. The U.S. government had been providing budget support for a decade, but it was to be phased out at the end of 1966. I told the ambassador that I did not favor budget support and believed that there were other more effective ways to assist the government to deal with its fiscal problems. The ambassador smiled—I was on his wavelength.

On Monday of my second week at post, Jack, Bill, David, and I met with Milt Lobell, the rural development chief, and his Bolivian counterpart, who was the departing director of the agricultural *servicio*. Milt also brought in the chief of the Utah State Agricultural Team, Clark Ballard, whose team had just arrived to replace direct-hire U.S. technicians as advisers to the ministry of agriculture. They briefed us on the agricultural research and extension service that had been the focal point of *servicio* activities for more than a decade. They detailed the tensions over PL 480 wheat imports that undersold new varieties of highland wheat being developed by the *servicio's* research program. They advised me that wool production on the Altiplano had collapsed after the 1952 revolution. Milt also gave me a recap of the special program in the Santa Cruz lowlands for field crops and cattle production. Milt had to delay briefing me on the incipient rural community development program because its chief was out of La Paz.

The following morning, we met with Dr. John Holmes on the education program. A former superintendent of schools, he impressed me with his knowledge about the workings of the school system and the quality of the education being provided. He described an underfunded ministry with a herculean task, ranging from reducing the high illiteracy rate among children and adults to building a network of urban public elementary and high schools. Prior to 1952, the only quality education was provided by the church to the elites. In most of Bolivia, he reported that Spanish had to be taught to rural children as a second language, and that educational materials had to be adapted to objects and things that the children could understand—texts that used words like "apple" and "cake" had to be reworked to talk about "corn" or "llamas." He also spelled out a critical shortage of rural schools and trained teachers. In essence, centuries of neglect had to be overcome in a decade or two.

Dr. Holmes described a multidimensional program that included selection of sites for schools being built with USAID loan funds, combined with basic teacher training at one of the few teacher colleges in the country. Teacher training was for both new teachers and those already in the classroom. The mission had a contract with San Jose State University in teacher training and the USAID engineering staff oversaw school construction. Dr. Holmes also advised the minister on systems and procedures to improve the ministry's administrative and accounting practices, including accounting for and controlling expenditures, to replace ones that had allowed school administrators to use funds with little or no supervision. I immediately understood why school administrators were complaining in the press about U.S. intervention into Bolivian sovereign issues.

Following Dr. Holmes, we spent the afternoon with the acting chief of the Public Health Division, who told me that the *servicio* had been phased out by my predecessor, who felt that health programs were of lower priority than education and agriculture. The *servicio* had a record of accomplishments, including upgrading the ministry's structure and operations, broadening its outreach to rural areas, setting up medical posts, and building latrines. Its current program concentrated on providing maternal and child health services in urban areas and on supporting rural clinics across the country. He also advised me that the ministry's budget had been affected severely by the reduction of U.S. budget support.

The final briefing came from the Industrial Development unit, which was the newest area in which the mission had become involved. The unit consisted of three specialists who outlined plans to help companies improve business accounting and management systems and to support the Industrial Bank in identifying small enterprises that could be candidates for loans. They also laid out a not very attractive investment environment, including the complicated procedures for obtaining approval to open businesses or begin private mining operations. They warned me of widespread rumors of graft in obtaining required licenses, especially for mining leases; they explained that, while the mines of the former Big Three tin companies had been nationalized, private companies continued to operate the other mines throughout the country. They also pointed out that Gulf Oil at the time was the only international company engaged in petroleum operations in the eastern lowlands around Santa Cruz, and that Gulf had filed complaints with the embassy about regulatory problems and government oversight.

Early in the first week, Jack Edison laid out for Bill, Dave, and me the status of the tripartite effort to rehabilitate the national tin mining company, COMIBOL. He included two specialists from the U.S. Geological Service who had worked with COMIBOL for over a decade as they mapped Bolivian mineral deposits and reserves. They spelled out a dismal picture of Bolivia's tin prospects and called the reserves no longer adequate to sustain current scale mining operations. They pointed out that situation was made worse by unfavorable marketing contracts with Patiño and Hochschild when the government realized that the only market for the nationalized tin production was the European refineries owned by those two companies. With little understanding of the cost structure of the mines or of the tin market, the government negotiated long-term marketing contracts in the mid-1950s that insulated the two purchasers from increases in the cost of mining the ore. As a result,

COMIBOL losses increased with every increase in ore production while the profits of the two companies grew as international market prices rose.

After that sobering exposure, Jack scheduled a meeting for Bill, Dave, and me with the president of COMIBOL, General Juan Lechín. There were two Juan Lechíns on the political stage: one was the former MNR vice president of the Republic, who had also been president of the Bolivian Labor Confederation (CTB). The other was an army general and the president of COMIBOL. The former, Juan Lechín Oquendo, now in exile, was supposed to have been the MNR candidate for president in 1964 when Paz Estenssoro opted to run for re-election; his split with Paz helped spark the coup that overthrew Paz Estenssoro in January 1965.

Our meeting with the general began with an outline of his views about the outlook for the tin industry and COMIBOL. He expressed the same concerns as the U.S. geological experts about tin ore reserves and the company's financial situation. He proposed that we set up, as soon as feasible, an informal meeting with the German ambassador and the IDB representative to consider additional support for COMIBOL under the Tripartite Plan. General Lechín was as new on his job as was I on mine.

We held it the following week at COMIBOL headquarters, General Lechín advised us that, in spite of extensive investments and cost cutting measures, the profit and loss statement was dismal. The chief of the Tripartite Advisory group reported that miners had once again ripped out most of the technological improvements introduced into the mines and were staging "political" work stoppages to protest plans for changes designed to improve mine safety. The review of tin market conditions projected weakness in world market price for the next year. We left that meeting wondering if we could reasonably expect to save COMIBOL and the tin mines from collapse.

Critical Problems

Before Jack Edison departed, I asked him to brief me on some of the critical problems that he thought required special attention. The first he raised was the unique role that USAID played in the monetary stability of the country since it held US$16 million of local currency. That was more local currency than either the Bolivian Treasury or the Central Bank had available for development projects. The situation had arisen because of Bolivian repayments in local currency for purchases from the U.S. of PL 480 commodities. The terms of sale for PL 480 surplus agricultural commodities provided for forty-year loans, repayable in dollars, at a minimal interest rate. On receipt of the commodities, the Bolivian government could sell them on the local market at established local prices and deposit the proceeds into the PL 480 local currency account. Those repayments could be used for new development loans at market interest rates and for a term set by the two governments. This process could be repeated over and over again for forty years — when the original PL 480 loan must be repaid.

The significance of that account by the early 1960s reached a level that the International Monetary Fund, as part of its annual stabilization agreement with the government of Bolivia, set a limit on the amount that USAID could dispense each year from the PL 480 account. It also became a substitute for the non-existent rediscount window of the Central Bank. Whenever one of the development banks ran out of funds, it did not go to the Central Bank, but put pressure on USAID for an additional tranche funded from the PL 480 account. As a result, a photo of the USAID director appeared almost daily in the press, claiming that he was threatening the existence of some local institution by not approving a loan from the PL 480 account.

A related issue we considered was the criteria for the lending of local currency PL 480 funds. I noted that the current loan portfolio seemed a grab bag of projects. Jack agreed and reminded me of the political environment in which USAID was working, that the only source of local funding for development projects was the PL 480 account and that there had been politics at play each time a loan proposal had been considered. He also alerted me to the special interest of minister of economy in PL 480 purchases and warned me not to set "criteria" that might raise friction with one of our key contacts in the government. The local sales of PL commodities was the only source of discretionary funds for the ministry of economy; those funds were derived from the difference between the FOB price in the U.S. and the higher price in the Bolivian market, with that difference being deposited into the ministry's development account.

The second set of questions discussed with Jack was his perception about the future direction of the USAID program. We were in a country in the first stages of emergence from a feudal social order and dependence on mining revenues. We discussed how USAID should realign its resources to support the government and people, the public and private sectors in directing and moving forward the process of change already under way. We considered whether the current program placed too much emphasis on physical infrastructure and needed to focus more on the needs and role of people in the transformation process.

The third set of issues were raised by Jack and related to the phasing out of budget support. He warned me that it was constant point of tension. Budget support had become a way of life since the mid-1950s. At one time, the U.S. covered as much as 25 percent of government budget expenditures, and we negotiated what sectors of the budget we would support. U.S. money ensured that key programs in agriculture, education, public health, and public works were adequately financed. We had never agreed to fund sectors like public safety, national defense, and general public administration. Ambassador Stephansky and Alex Firfer had a bitter struggle to get President Paz to agree to its phase-out over five-years, and 1966 was to be the last year of payments. He wished me good luck in the final phase-out.

The fourth set of problems related to the demise of the *servicios*. For two decades, most technical service programs of the government had been implemented by the *servicios*. Washington mandated the closing of the Bolivian *servicios* by the end of 1965 and I had to work out the closing down the remaining *servicios* and transferring their remaining projects and personnel to the respective ministries. Once that was completed, the mission had to design requests for USAID project funding for those activities in which the mission had continuing interest. Not only did the transfer mean that political decision-makers of the Bolivian government would take over policy and technical direction of the activities, but also that the technicians and other personnel would be moved from the secure payroll of the *servicio* to the unstable national budget, with a probable reduction in salary and benefits. Those very human and real personal problems for technical staff so long nurtured by USAID were difficult to deal with.

Jack advised me that Bolivian labor law stipulated that whenever there was a substantial change in the terms and conditions of employment, that change was interpreted to be a termination of current employment. On termination, the employee affected becomes entitled to an indemnification of at least three months' wages, with the amount rising based on years of service in the "terminated" post. Jack warned me that, although the mission had negotiated with the government of Bolivia to ensure that each employee was hired by the government, the affected employees had filed a suit in Labor Court for over US$4 million dollars on the grounds that the labor law covered public and private employees. AID legal advisers reached an agreement with the Bolivian government that the U.S. government was not subject to the labor law because of its sovereign immunity and that the Foreign Ministry would take necessary action to have the suit quashed.

Jack raised one final concern with Bill, David, and me: the need for better monitoring of loan projects. With over US$500 million in our active loan portfolio, Jack emphasized that the loan and engineering staff was stretched and that the economic and audit staff was overloaded tracking disbursements of loans by banking institutions and businesses. He urged me to assess our ability to effectively monitor operations and to absorb additional monitoring responsibilities. As we knew only too well, the problems lie in in the details—and no detail was too small to pass over. Bill, Dave, and I agreed that this topic would be on the agenda in our planned weekly sessions not only with the engineering and lending staff but also all the division chiefs and economists.

Meeting with the Co-Presidents

Shortly after the January 1965 coup that ousted Paz Estenssoro, Ambassador Henderson persuaded the co-presidents, Air Force General René Barrientos and Army General Alfredo Ovando Candia, to meet with him regularly in order to resolve political and development issues that could create tensions between our two countries.

Halfway through my first month, the ambassador advised me that the next meeting with the co-presidents had been scheduled and that an agenda agreed upon. He then invited me to work with him in defining the U.S. position on each agenda item.

That meeting took place in the president's office, a few blocks from the embassy. The co-presidents sat at the table facing the ambassador and me. There were three other generals at the table, including the foreign minister and finance minister. We had an extensive agenda, which was addressed point by point. On each issue, a memorandum was prepared on the action needed. The ambassador and Co-President Barrientos did most of the talking. General Ovando spoke on one or two items, especially those related to military measures that the army was taking to bring the erstwhile independent police force under its control. The ambassador objected to those measures, but the general indicated that there was no changing his mind or that of his fellow generals. Before we adjourned, the agenda was agreed on for the next meeting. The key item would be the status of AID support for the Bolivian government, including the end of budget support and the phasing out of the *servicios*.

After the meeting, the ambassador told me about the severe measures taken by the military against the national police force. As I pointed out earlier, after the revolution of 1952, the police had assumed control of security in the country and abolished the army, navy, and air force. During the MNR rule, the police took over all the strategic and tactical aspects of both internal protection of the government and the defense of national territory. USAID had provided technical assistance for training the police and financed a modern police academy for an officer corps for the urban and rural police forces. In the late 1950s, U.S. concern about a Castro-supported insurgency induced the successive MRN regimes to revive the army, navy, and air corps; and the U.S. supplied military missions in country and sent officers for training in the U.S. and Panama.

The ambassador added that, as part of the anti-Castro strategy, the U.S. Defense Department financed civic action programs by the newly re-established military to help rural communities by building bridges, roads, schools, and health posts. The civic action program gave the military access to the rural communities and their recently emancipated populations. Since the government had little money for community improvement projects, to pay rural teachers, or to provide health services, the civic action programs were the only concrete presence of the government in people's lives in many parts of the country. Civic action responded immediately to a community's request and astutely asked no favors in return. That was in stark contrast to the payoffs usually asked by the police and politicians when communities requested assistance. In addition, the peasants who had run off the landlords wanted titles to the lands they occupied and politicians kept them waiting. So, in just five or six years the civic action team won the support of many communities across Bolivia, and those communities did not rise up in defense of Paz Estenssoro when the coup occurred.

It was not until 1963 that Paz Estenssoro saw the threat posed by civic action and then he asked USAID to help the government develop a counter strategy to regain the support of the rural people. a countrywide community development program. It took over a year to recruit an advisor for the project. Community programming was just beginning when the coup took place.

Settling into the Job

As USAID director, I was a member of the ambassador's country team. Each day I checked with him about country developments and program problems. The country team met formally at least once a week and informally as often as an issue might arise. The meetings took place in the ambassador's office and he made a special effort to facilitate good working relations with the other members of team: DCM Bob Hurwich, U.S. Information Officer Ed Fogler, Peace Corps Director Bill Purcell, Political Officer Chuck Grover, Economic Counselor Bill Broderick, the military attachés, and the CIA station chief. All of them invited me to briefings and provided me with insights on the key players in the current government.

Directing the work of the USAID entailed a succession of meetings. One morning each week, Bill, David, and I met with the controller and the executive officer to deal with problems they believed needed our attention. On alternate days we met with the program and loan officers to review special problems. Often I had appointments out of the building with ministers and other Bolivian officials. My schedule in the afternoon was dedicated to detailed briefings on progress on loan and grant projects. Each week I spent an afternoon with a division chief and his key U.S. and Bolivian technicians in meetings that lasted as long as the agenda required.

While I was getting acquainted with the extensive USAID program, I learned two important lessons about being the USAID director in Bolivia. The first was that I had to be extremely careful about what I said, even casually, because what the USAID director said and did made the news. At receptions or in the hallway I would be asked about some issue, and later I would find my opinion on the front page of a newspaper. The director was the center of attention because he was perceived in La Paz as the moneyman. I almost put my foot in my mouth in a couple of situations.

The second lesson was to be patient with communications. There was only one landline over the Andes to keep us in touch with Washington. All of our secure correspondence went over that line—so unlike today's satellite connections and computers, tweets, and cell phones. When we needed Washington's authorization to take an action, we had to wait not only for the usual clearance process in the Department of State and AID, but also deal with the vagaries of the landline. I had been trained to wait for instructions, but here when the line was out and we needed to act, I consulted with the ambassador and took action.

Another dimension to our communications problem was that the La Paz telephone system was not state of the art either. It had old-fashioned switchboards and frequent interruptions in service because of equipment failures. It was government-run and operated on a tight budget. In Calacoto where our residence was located, we had a manually operated switchboard and had to call the operator to get a line up to the city. Both Ele and I suspected that someone was listening in on our calls most of the time, and we were very careful about what we said. Paralleling the public telephone system, the embassy had a short wave network tying together the senior staff with the Marine Corps guard on permanent duty at the chancery. Over the next three years, that network had to be used on several occasions.

Ele's Arrival

In the middle of the second month, Ele arrived after completing her European tour and farm and family business. She made a return visit to Washington to deal with a tax problem that had arisen with the District of Columbia related to our temporary residence during our assignment to the State Department.

Learning she was in Washington, the ambassador asked her to help get approval for a request that he had made to the State Department to authorize the shipment by air of household effects for all U.S. personnel assigned to Bolivia, instead of by the longer, more costly, and dangerous sea/rail route through Peru or Chile. The embassy had sent data to Washington showing how much more economical and expeditious was shipment by air. Nonetheless, rules are rules and changing them is frowned on.

Ele went every morning to the desk of the person responsible for approving a revision of the rules. She detailed one horror story after another of the thefts that had occurred using the sea/rail route that the ambassador and the USAID executive officer fed her. The latest befell the USAID chief engineer on his transfer from Thailand to Bolivia; his household effects arrived in La Paz in exactly the same crates and weight as they had left Bangkok, but the family goods had been replaced en route with Peruvian rocks. The cost to the department for replacing the effects was in excess of $10,000. Ele not only estimated the cost but also added in the agony of the loss to the family. She presented to the state officer a list of her estimates of the cost of the losses as well as a lecture on the impact on morale at the post. That day, the rule was changed and the ambassador, who had not yet met Ele, sent her a thank you for her efforts. She had made a close friend before she ever arrived at post.

She adapted quickly to the altitude because she had low blood pressure, that minimized the effects of *soroche* (high altitude disease), and she was up and running from day one. From our prior assignments and her impressions on the 1963 visit, she expected the post would be demanding and our job very challenging. The ambassador and his wife, Dorothy, reinforced her expectations when they had us to a family dinner the night after Ele's arrival. Dorothy talked to us about life in La Paz, altitude problems, and morale.

She introduced her to the activities of U.S. Embassy Wives Organization and *Damas Diplomaticas*, which brought together spouses from all the Embassies in La Paz. While we technically were not on the diplomatic list, because of my post, Ele was expected to be an active participant. Dorothy said that, while we were not required to "drop cards" (formally introduce ourselves) on the wives of other ambassadors, she urged Ele to do so because of my position. Following the family dinner, Dorothy had a tea to introduce Ele to the embassy wives, including the wives of the military attachés and the CIA station chief. Ele dropped her card on each of them before the tea, so that all of the formalities were complied with.

Ele in turn had a reception for all the wives of USAID members. We had a large number of Mormon families in the mission, and to ensure that they would not be offended, the reception was more like an ice cream social than a cocktail party. Our cook, Eduarda, was a veteran of ten years of working for mission directors and knew how to bake cakes and make ice cream. Coupled with the raspberries that grew in our Calacoto garden, an ice cream social was a success.

Once word got around that Ele had arrived, we received invitations for cocktails and dinner almost every night of the week. Many were official functions that we had to attend and many were from our embassy and USAID colleagues, most of whom became friends. One of our challenges was to make people understand that we could not accept all invitations, no matter how much we might have wanted to attend. The high altitude was a strain, and both of us needed to rest regularly.

Her running the household had its share of problems. Ele took charge of a staff that had served my three immediate predecessors, and each wife had a different style and often different methods of organizing household chores. Ele had to get to know our staff of four and understand what the ground rules and systems had been in prior years. She knew that the continuity of their employment was evidence of their capability, honesty, and trustworthiness; but she had to determine for herself whether she could work with them and whether their personalities suited her. So, she carefully talked to each of them about their jobs and their expectations as well as ours. They meshed, and the household was humming and happy.

The staff loved parties, especially the cook Eduarda. She looked like a typical *chola* (indigenous lady) and wore the traditional dress of the La Paz region, including the singular bowler hat over her pigtail whenever she left the premises. She knew all of the traditional Bolivian dishes as well as most European and American favorites. She loved to prepare calorie-laden dishes, topped with cream sauces. Her ice cream made Ben & Jerry's seem bland! Ele had to talk to Eduarda about cutting down on the calories without offending her. I don't know exactly what was said, but a very happy Eduarda told me she was going to help me "stay well in the altitude."

Ele and Eduarda always went together to the Central Market to buy fruit, vegetables, and meat. They had little jokes that they shared, like the day that Ele saw three navel oranges that she wanted to buy. The market lady had sold all of her produce, except those three. Ele asked for the price, and the lady said 8 cents each or three for "*dos reales*" (25 cents). Eduarda looked at Ele when Ele said that she would buy all three for 24 cents and the market lady said "No." So, Ele bought one for 8 cents and made other purchases before coming back to the fruit vendor and buying a second for 8 cents. After another sweep around the market, Ele bought the third for 8 cents. When Eduarda told me the story, I commented that the vendor couldn't add; she responded, "Oh, no, I know her and she is smart. She just wasn't ready to lose her post." For the vendor, the market was both her source of income and social life.

Eduarda's sister Elsa was the housemaid, who did all the cleaning. She kept the house spotless even when we had houseguests. Unlike her sister, she dressed in western style clothing and considered herself a city lady. She was very fussy about her appearance and her hairdo. She and Eduarda shared a bedroom, and I can never remember there being a harsh word between them. Elsa was always serious, while Eduarda was usually smiling. Ele decided early on to let Elsa follow her own routine.

Out third staff member was the butler Zenovio. He was a crackerjack in preparing and serving drinks as well as waiting table. He was a nice looking young man who had graduated from elementary school and intelligent enough to get into high school, but had gone into service for financial reasons. His problem was that he enjoyed alcohol, and after most big parties, he would the mix the dregs of all the leftover drinks into a big glass and get himself drunk. Eduarda and Elsa covered for him for almost two years until one day he disgraced himself in front of Eduarda, Elsa, Ele, and me, and had to be dismissed. Ele had long known of the problem and worked with Eduarda and Elsa to help Zenovio. His departure at the beginning of our third year in La Paz was a blow, but we helped him get another chance with an embassy family—and I met him many times when I visited La Paz after our assignment ended.

The fourth member of the staff was Rosendo, the gardener. He lived with his family on his own piece of property a few blocks from our house. He was a good farmer and appeared right at home in the garden. He was primarily an Aymara speaker and frequently Zenovio or Eduarda had to interpret for Ele when she discussed with Rosendo her plans for the nearly one acre garden. There was plenty of land for growing vegetables as well as flowers for the house. Our predecessors had planted some apple and pear trees as well as raspberry brambles along the back walls. There was a mass of pampas grass about halfway through the garden, and Ele decided to plant rows of artichokes, lettuce, broccoli, carrots, and onions on the far side of the pampas grass. We found out that, despite the altitude, the ultraviolet rays, and the cold nights, everything she chose grew very well. For the three years that we lived in Bolivia, we were able to eat vegetables and fruit from our own garden, send baskets to each new family arriving at post, and give birthday treats to embassy, USAID, USIA, and Bolivian friends.

Another inhabitant of the house was the longtime family pet, Diana, a lovable mongrel who adopted Ele the minute she entered the front gate. No one quite knew her age. She had been spayed twice and still bore litters. She lived in the garden and never strayed into the house, but she was waiting for Ele whenever Ele appeared and stayed at her side day or night while she only tolerated me and the other members of the household. Diana chased out any intruders, except when she went into heat—which she did again even after a UN veterinarian adviser had assured us that she was incapable of bearing pups. When she went into heat, she would find the macho with whom she wanted to mate and show him how to smuggle himself through the tree-lined fences into her boudoir.

Ele planned to use the house as a community center for USAID families. Her first proposal was to use it as the setting for monthly meetings of the USAID wives. Until our arrival, the only meetings of wives had been periodically at the ambassador's residence, and the ambassador's wife involved them in charitable and other social activities. Ele wanted to go beyond those activities and expose the wives to the development process underway in Bolivia. Ele approached Mrs. Henderson and won her support for that initiative, provided the embassy wives were also invited.

At the first meeting of the group, Ele encouraged the wives to elect their own officers and plan their own programs and activities. For the three years we were in La Paz, the ladies met regularly, programmed special activities, visited projects, and provided financial and personal support for grassroots activities that excited their interest.

Ele also set up an ice cream social open house on the first Monday of the month to welcome families newly arrived and to say good-bye to those departing. We averaged about forty people per open house, and usually included Bolivian friends, Canadian priests, UN officials, and members of other embassies. We had hosted over fifteen hundred guests at our open houses by the time our tour ended.

Ele coordinated the scheduling of our open houses with Dorothy Henderson so that we did not conflict with her plans. The ambassador had a monthly open house cocktail to meet and say farewell to U.S. and foreign diplomats. We always attended the ambassador's open house, and they ours.

Shortly after Ele arrived, the parish priest for Calacoto, Father Walter from Canada, paid a courtesy call. The two became fast friends and Ele invited him to dinner shortly after their first meeting. He told us of the convent he supervised and of the nuns who had lived a cloistered life there for many years. Their order believed in prayer and isolation. When Father Walter received orders from the Vatican to end the cloistering of the nuns in his parish, he talked to Ele about his dilemma. He had orders from Rome, but the nuns did not want to leave the cloister. Ele suggested that they come to an open house. Father Walter agreed.

Ele tried to make it a special evening. All the nuns save one seemed to enjoy it greatly. They talked to the other guests and discussed the world they were re-entering. The one exception was an elderly nun who had lived in the cloister for over thirty-five years and was clearly uncomfortable leaving her established routine. Ele brought her some cake and ice cream, and she seemed almost upset about partaking of a worldly delight. Father Walter came over to tell her that enjoying the food was not sinful. They left her to herself. Ele peeked over a couple of times and watched her carefully taste and then slowly consume the sweets. She smiled and blessed Ele when she left with her sisters at the end of the evening. I believe that the embassy and USAID families there that night were delighted to have helped Walter and Ele open the nuns to the world of 1965.

Ele was invited to join the *Damas Diplomáticas*. As in most countries, this was a social group that held monthly luncheons or teas and sponsored charitable projects. The membership usually included the wives of the members of the diplomatic corps and the host country social elite. At the first meeting she attended, Ele made her way around the room introducing herself to the members. She met ladies that afternoon who remained friends throughout our tour in Bolivia, and beyond. She was elected president of the *Damas Diplomáticas* in 1966.

One of the ladies present was the wife of the Chinese ambassador. Bolivia recognized Taiwan at the time, and the ambassador's wife was a personal friend of Ele's onetime roommate at International House who was the daughter of the then Chinese consul general in Honolulu. Shortly thereafter, we received an invitation to dine at the embassy. We were surprised to find the embassy was attached to La Paz's most popular Chinese restaurant. The ambassador explained that Taiwan did not have a budget to fund the embassy and many like him had opened businesses to supplement their limited personal wealth. Since the ambassador's wife was a superb chef, she oversaw the operations of the restaurant and its daily menu. The dinner was a spectacular Mandarin feast. Until the ambassador was transferred, we welcomed many an invitation for dinner and frequently took visitors to the restaurant for special evenings out.

A New Look

With the breadth and diversity of activities in the USAID program, it demanded a lot of reading of program documents, economic and social analyses, newspaper and magazine articles, and monthly reports by the various operating units of the mission. It entailed visiting projects in operation throughout the country. On my first visit to Cochabamba and Santa Cruz, I accompanied our chief engineer on inspections of road and other construction projects. I became acquainted with rural development, education, and health projects in the Chapare, Sucre, and Oruro. I was asking lots of questions and wasn't always happy with the answers. I wanted to see and understand the Mission in action.

Seeing first hand field operations was extremely useful in the discussions with the co-presidents. They knew little about project operations and their support staff was weak. Most of the key technicians of the Paz Estenssoro administration had resigned or gone into exile. So it fell on the shoulders of the USAID staff to provide most of the information about USAID assistance and prepare background documents that were used in the meetings with the co-presidents. Those provided a unique mechanism for getting top-level consideration for projects. It also provided a vantage point for understanding the Bolivian power structure and decision-making process.

At one meeting over lunch, the co-presidents advised us of their plans to schedule new elections by the end of the year and that co-president Barrientos would be the candidate for president and General Ovando would retain command of all the armed forces. They also advised us that all of the current ministers who were military officers would be replaced after the election. That provided the ambassador and me with information that permitted us to review the U.S. strategy, including development assistance, before the inauguration of a new administration.

On returning to my office, I proposed to Bill and David that we use the time to reassess the priorities and direction of the US-AID program. Based on my initial briefings and project visits, I was concerned about the number and diversity of our projects, the capability of the government to absorb the assistance and repay infrastructure loans, and the role of the USAID as lender of last resort in the country. I found that Bill and David shared those concerns and interest in taking a fresh look at our program.

We agreed to consider the area in the country where our resources could be best used. We agreed to rethink the priority established in the mid-1950s to concentrate our investments in agriculture to Santa Cruz and the eastern lowlands because that offered more immediate promise of raising the GNP. The results were positive; the Santa Cruz regional authority was well-financed, had a good technical staff and obtained national legislation that gave it a fixed share of the tax on petroleum exports and the power to select its own programs and projects. With ten years' experience and its own technical and engineering staff, we felt that it was capable of doing its own development job.

On the other hand, in the Altiplano and the high Andean valleys where most of the people lived and the social unrest persisted, the socio-economic picture was hardly promising. The mines were playing out. Farm and cattle production were languishing and. since the revolution, there had been a steady, yet still small, migration from rural areas to the city of La Paz, where several thousand people had formed a sprawling community, El Alto, around the airport. The Altiplano people feared living in the lowlands and resisted government programs to resettle them there. They had not forgotten that former governments shipped truckloads of disgruntled miners from the Altiplano to the Chapare to suppress their protests, and had left them pretty much to their own devices in an environment alien to their rocky homeland.

What could be done in the Altiplano was not clear. We needed to study the region and do a lot of thinking. One of the economic reports stated that there were an estimated six million head of sheep on the Altiplano; yet Bolivia imported all of the wool for its small textile industry from Chile, Argentina, and Uruguay. When I asked Bolivian and U.S. economists and agronomists about the anomaly, they reminded me that before the revolution of 1952, the indigenous population was barred from owning sheep and that, when they chased off the old landlords, they divided up the flocks among themselves—and just owning them was a new status symbol. I was also told that a program in the late 1950s to introduce the new owners to sheep shearing had been a failure. Nonetheless, I asked Milt Lobell, the chief of the Rural Development Division, and Clark Ballard, the chief of the Utah State Team to look into the viability of introducing sheep shearing and replacing wool imports with domestic production, not only saving millions of dollars in foreign exchange but also providing income for the Altiplano people and a possible source of tax revenue.

Two weeks later Clark advised me that the prior sheep-shearing effort had been with power shears in an area that had no source of power and proposed that his animal husbandry specialist, Matthews, train a group of Bolivians from the Ministry of Agriculture to use hand shears and conduct a demonstration in a village where there was no record of prior sheep shearing. Milt and I agreed.

Clark and Matthews took the team to the Altiplano village and set up a site for shearing. Clark wisely kept everyone away from the villagers until one lady wandered over to ask what was happening. She was told that, if she allowed the team to shear her sheep, she would be paid five pesos per pound for top grade wool, four pesos for second grade, and two and a half pesos for black wool. She thought for a while and decided to give it a try. She brought over her sheep and they were sheared.

When she was offered the equivalent of US$75, the per capita annual income in the area, she panicked and ran for her husband. He came back berating her in Aymara for being a fool. How could she risk their sheep on such a terrible scheme? He came up to the shearer with blood in his eyes and demanded his sheep back. The shearer said, "Here are your sheep and here is your money."

Dumbfounded the farmer asked, "The sheep are mine?" "Yes," was the reply. "The money is mine? All you want is the wool?" "Yes," again, and a nod of assent.

He took his sheep and money over to his fellow villagers, and the team spent three days shearing every animal in the area. When they had finished, the same lady who had broken the ice asked the team leader if she and her husband could hook a ride to La Paz so that they could use part of their new wealth to purchase a short-wave radio.

The lesson was loud and clear. The *campesinos* were open to new ideas but had to be treated honestly and with respect. Fixed prices and honest, open weighing of wool probably showed the sheep owners that the operation was above-board and merited their support. With that experience, the ministry and Utah State expanded the effort throughout the Altiplano. Within weeks, Ele and I attended sheep-shearing events in several communities of the Altiplano. Utah State wrote up the experience and had it published in the *Readers Digest*.

The same lesson was demonstrated again in August when, in a break in the rainy season, David Lazar and I drove down to the Yungas, the lowland gold placer mining region near La Paz. We went down a primitive road carved out of the mountainside as it dropped from 14,000 feet to nearly sea level. Around many a curve, there was evidence of landslides that had been manually moved off the road surface.

When we got to the Yungas, our first contact was with a priest who had been educated at Notre Dame. When we introduced ourselves, he advised us not to announce our presence because USAID was not well regarded in the area. When we asked why, he told us of a project in the late 1950s that had been used in a presentation in the Office of Institutional Development the preceding year. The priest recounted how the *servicio* spearheaded an effort to replace plantings of coca leaves with vegetables and tomatoes for consumption in La Paz. The first big push was tomato production. The agronomists brought in the right seed, fertilizer, and insecticide for the region. Tomatoes were multiplying throughout the Yungas when the annual tropical rains came early. No one was prepared to deal with the crisis. The packing sheds were inadequate. No tomato canning or catsup making plants had been set up. No alternate plan for moving the crop to market had been devised. The farmers were left with a bumper tomato crop that rotted in the fields, along with debts for the seed, fertilizer, and insecticides. The farmers chased out the agronomists and blamed USAID. Now, the priest continued, the *campesinos* have gone back to reliable coca growing with its traditional marketing system and are still fuming about the ministry and USAID.

David and I talked to a couple of couple of owners of gold placer operations who confirmed the story, and who also told us of the plight of the private mining sector and its dependence on the "goodwill" and timely payments to government officials. David and I well understood their message: since the government owned the mineral and subsurface rights, they paid not only license fees and taxes but also protection to the officials who oversaw their operations.

As we considered the viability of developing a plan of action in the highlands, we consulted two advisers working with the people at the grassroots. One was a Maryknoll brother, Joe Beaugleau, who spearheaded the development of urban and rural credit unions in the Cochabamba Valley. There were few, if any, sources of credit for middle-income people, much less for *campesinos*, to purchase essential household goods. Belonging to credit unions trained the people in the discipline of savings and offered them access to credit they needed to improve their standard of living. Joe believed that popular support for credit unions had grown so rapidly because the members themselves were able to police their own organization and ensure the probity of their managers. The experience in Cochabamba had awakened interest in other areas of the country, and the movement was growing; USAID had agreed to help finance that expansion. When I proposed to Joe that credit unions serve as micro-financing entities for providing credit to *campesinos*, Joe reminded me that credit unions did not lend funds for commercial activities.

The second was Juan Demeure, a Belgian expatriate who was an associate of Father Roger Vekemanns of the Jesuit Centro Bellamino in Santiago, Chile. With the support of the West German Christian Democratic Development Foundation, Misericordia, he built a technical assistance program for *campesinos* in the Cochabamba Valley. He advised them on improved farming practices and organizing cooperatives to purchase seed, fertilizer, and other inputs for upgrading and expanding crop production and for marketing. His programs helped *campesinos* become good farmers.

Any program in the highlands required us to consider the mining sector and our future relationship with COMIBOL. Bill, Dave, and I spent considerable time considering new initiatives to prevent the failure of the Tripartite Mining Program. Restoring COMIBOL to profitability would provide the public sector with critically needed resources to fund long-term development.

While tin prices were improving, COMIBOL deficits month by month were rising because of its marketing contract. In addition, the quality of the ore was declining. The costs of shipping ore to European refineries were rising, and interest rates on thirty-day loans to finance those shipments were astronomical. COMIBOL also faced persistent labor unrest, and that made shipment schedules uncertain. Probably only half of the 24,000 people on the payroll actually worked in mining operations. Measures to raise productivity and enhance worker safety were not only resisted by the miners but were often sabotaged once installed. Efforts to find employment for the surplus workers were fruitless. Without concessions by the Miners Union, COMIBOL's prospects appeared to be dismal.

Through Father Walter of the Catholic parish, arrangements were made for me to meet a Canadian priest in Catavi who had made friends with some of the union leaders. He warned me that they were anti-U.S. and dedicated Trotskyites, but on my insistence, set up a meeting for me with some mine leaders in Oruro. I drove down the paved highway that USAID had designed and financed, and arrived in late afternoon. The priest arranged for a light meal that he hoped would overcome the icy reception that he expected the union leaders to give me. Over the snacks, I asked the miners their opinion of COMIBOL. They said that since the co-presidents took over, they were no longer consulted about policies and plans. When I asked what they thought needed to be done to help the union and the miners, they started a diatribe about imperialism. I just listened until one leader said that the commissaries were never stocked with items that the miners needed, and that the company was trying to cheat them out of the 25 percent bonus to which workers were entitled for working in unsafe conditions. As we talked about their specific grievances, the environment improved substantially. We then had pisco sours and were getting along much better when I made a tremendous mistake. I asked one of the mine union leaders about his interpretation of Trotskyism since Trotsky himself had died over twenty-five years earlier. He exploded all over me, calling me an "imperialist liar." He asserted that the allegation of Trotsky's death was U.S. propaganda and that he had seen Trotsky no more than a month ago in Lima. To my regret, they walked out and never agreed to meet with me again. I was even told that the union would not assure my personal safety if I were to visit Catavi or Siglo Veinte.

The following morning, I discussed the meeting with the ambassador. I asked him if anyone had raised the idea of paying a 28 percent bonus for improved productivity and better conditions. He thought a minute and said, "No." But, he added, "It's too late. The Tripartite Group decided to end its support for COMIBOL. The latest geological reports indicated that the tailings around the mines had a higher tin content than the seams underground. We are instructed to advise COMIBOL that our assistance will end at the end of the year." The ambassador advised the co-presidents and I advised the president of COMIBOL.

Ending assistance to COMIBOL would force the company to lay off more miners and exacerbate unemployment in the mining regions of the Altiplano. That led me to ask the mission economists and the specialists from the U.S. Geological Service to provide me information on two options to help COMIBOL. The first was on the cost of building an international freight airport near the mining area that could permit overnight delivery of ores to refineries instead of the then prevailing thirty-day land-sea shipment routes. The second was on the cost of building a refinery to smelt tin ore on the Altiplano. The studies showed not only a prohibitively high cost to benefit ratio but also an inadequate supply of electricity to operate a freight airport, much less both an airport and a smelter.

One other project initiating operations in the highlands got a careful look: community development. Bill, David, and I looked at its potential for improving the income and living standards of the people. Its objective was to help rural communities identify projects to improve local conditions and then to provide technical and material resources to make a project into a reality. It was a bottom-up effort to involve the people themselves in the development process. USAID supplied the funds to purchase the technical and material inputs required to respond to community initiatives. The Bolivian government supplied the staff and services. As we evaluated this project, we consulted not only with Bolivian Community Development (CD) Director Major Ramirez and his USAID advisers, but also Peace Corps Director Arthur Purcell and his Peace Corps volunteers working on projects in villages of the Altiplano and the high valleys. The program was still in its first phase of training young recruits from the communities, called liaisons, to do the grassroots work of talking to their neighbors in four or five villages on their perceptions of needs for improving living conditions. The liaisons were also being briefed on government services available to help communities in the design and implementation of projects and the procedures for providing that support to the communities that need them.

To get support to the communities, the liaison was to submit the community request to the nearby office, which would forward it for review and approval by the CD office. At that point, hopefully within days of its receipt, the CD office would find the technical and material resources needed to respond to the community's defined priority.

The reports on the prospects for the CD program were mixed. The chief adviser, whose Spanish was very limited, reported that the training of the liaisons was progressing well and that Peace Corps volunteers in many villages were actively supporting the program and had helped him identify candidates for liaison training. His deputy, who was fluent in Spanish, agreed that the training was going well, but warned us of the distrust of the program in most communities he visited. Communities were bitter over unkempt promises by government officials and politicians. We were also told of the *campesinos'* bitterness for not receiving titles for the lands they occupied in 1952 when they chased the landlords off the estates, and they blamed the government and the politicians for the delays.

Another approach I used for assessing the prospects for programs in the highlands was talking to local leaders about their concerns and priorities while attending the inauguration of a school, a road, or a water supply in rural communities. Talking to them was never easy since my Spanish was not their Aymara or Quechua, but I often found that they were skeptical about the government's intentions and how USAID could help them. Another reason that dialogue was difficult was that inaugurations across the Altiplano were often occasions for a community fiesta. The villages were decorated with banners and the local citizenry dressed up in their finest apparel. Whenever I tried to sound out a local official, I found the same reserve that Chuck had reported.

Participating in inaugurations took Ele and me to Cochabamba, Santa Cruz, Chuquisaca, Oruro, Potosí, and the Beni. General Barrientos often invited us to fly with him and members of his entourage on his DC-3 to inaugurations. Whenever it was for a school, then Colonel Hugo Banzer, the minister of education, and his wife Elvira, were members of the party; Hugo Banzer in the 1970s became president of Bolivia. When it was a public works project, the minister of Public Works, who formerly directed the Civic Action Program of the Armed Forces, accompanied the co-president. The co-president was always at the controls of the plane when we approached a community. He would get off the plane first, and there were always a number of ladies holding babies up for him to see, frequently accompanied by shouts of, "Look how wonderful our baby is!" Barrientos was quite a ladies' man and had fathered children all over the Republic.

When Ele didn't join us, the co-president would call me up to the cockpit and we would talk about government affairs and US-AID projects. I was often standing up and holding on for dear life when he made his descent and taxied in. By the time he announced his candidacy for president and resigned the co-presidency, we had established a good working and personal relationship.

I was invited by Co-President Ovando to accompany Colonel Banzer and him to the inauguration of a school in his home Department of Panda. We traveled on the austere DC-3 that he used as army chief. Conversation on the trip was short and terse. Ovando was taciturn and no more inclined to discuss issues on the plane than he was at our working sessions. When he made a comment, it reflected a firm bias for state exercise of power and the superiority of military decision-making to civilian rule. The contrast between the arrival of General Ovando in Pando and Barrientos' arrivals was significant: when Ovando arrived, he was all business. When Barrientos flew in, it was like a fiesta.

My introduction to the formidable terrain of this country was not only by the co-presidents and ministers, but also by USAID Chief Engineer Chuck Shirley, who took me on road inspection trips through various chains of the Andes and over the new highways being built between Cochabamba and Santa Cruz through the Chapare. Everywhere we stopped to talk to the *campesinos*, we found the same reluctance to deal with government. The challenge for the community development program would be to earn the trust of the people it sought to serve.

As 1965 drew to an end, we had a visit by Ray Sternfeld and his bride Marsha en route to a CIAP meeting in Buenos Aires. Bill, David and I talked at length with him about concern about the direction and content of the USAID program. He urged us to make our new thinking the centerpiece of our program presentation in 1966. So, Bill, David, and I redoubled our thinking about what the USAID program and its priorities should be for future years.

Living in La Paz

Life in La Paz was a unique experience. Being so close to the equator, the days are almost uniform throughout the year. Its altitude has an impact on mind and body. If you sunbathe, the ultraviolet rays can cause a bad burn in only minutes. If you have a physical or psychological weakness, the altitude seems to magnify it. If you have a temper, you tend to explode often and violently. If you like to drink, you can become an alcoholic. If you are a workaholic like me, you'd better pace yourself or you will be grinding away twenty-four hours a day.

The uniqueness of the terrain is awesome. Our house sat the base of the great mountain Illimani that the Aymara believe is the navel of the universe. It stretches up to over 23,000 feet with snow on its cap perennially. Every morning as I looked out at Illimani, I watched trains of llamas coming down the mountainside, and Ele told me that their bells were clanging as they passed the house. The *campesinos* with their colorful *lluchus* (multicolored woven llama yarn caps that covered the ears) herded the llamas past the front fence as Diana, the loving house mongrel, barked her greetings.

The daily drive from the residence to my office took only fifteen minutes, but we rose in altitude over eight hundred feet. When I had the luxury of looking out the window on the road up, I would see the moon-like bare rock terrain that stretched across the valley. We were above the tree line and the stretches of bare rock often changed color as the rays of the sun passed over. There was a golf course in the valley and the occasional patches of green seemed to set off even more the beauty of the rock formations.

For the people inhabiting that terrain, Ele and I developed a special affection. We visited fairs and markets on the Altiplano. We attended cultural events in La Paz and neighboring cities. We tried to immerse ourselves in the life of the country. Those we met in the countryside had faces that reflected the strength of a long-suffering people. Their dignity impressed us whenever we were at country fairs and markets. Given their long history of subjugation by the Spaniards and their struggle to retain their own sense of identity, they kept outsiders at arm's length. When we dealt with them, we learned that they were instinctively smart; they had learned how to survive in hostile world and were not prepared to give one the benefit of the doubt. They wanted to see who a person was and what he did before committing themselves.

Wherever we went in Bolivia, we were recognized because we were often on the front page of the newspapers. The breadth and depth of USIA connections with almost every news outlet assured front-page coverage of almost everything USAID. But not all the news was favorable. There was resentment among many columnists over the coup that ousted Paz Estenssoro and they accused the U.S. Embassy, of which USAID was a part, of engineering the event. For me, the most immediate were those news reports that blamed USAID for shortages of lending funds in the three development banks that the U.S. had helped create and finance.

Dealing with businessmen and government officials was a unique experience; they played games with outsiders, and I learned the meaning of the old Andean saying, "There is the right way, the wrong way, and the Bolivian way." You had to figure which game was being played whenever you became involved in a deal or negotiation. And never think that you are outwitting your Bolivian friend or foe! Ele and I loved the challenge.

We frequently went to dinner parties where the guests' primary objective was to find out what the embassy or USAID was planning to do about a particular problem, especially when money was involved. Ele and I had learned to nurse one drink an event, and how to avoid answering direct questions. But the Bolivians were masters at asking questions indirectly. I learned that it was prudent of me to ask the ambassador what gossip he was being fed because often it was false when it related to me or to USAID—and always self-serving to the gossiper.

Being involved in the social circuit was not glamorous. It was hard work standing on your feet at 12,000 feet, often in cold halls. That is the reason that, when Ele planned our monthly Mondays at home, she tried to recreate an old-fashioned ice cream social with a buffet table heaped with cakes, fruit, punch, and ice cream and with plenty of chairs and tables in the large living room-dining room. People could fill their platters and sit down to talk and treated like guests. Ele had said to me very sternly in San Salvador, "When I invite someone to our home, they are our guests, not targets of inquiry. So, treat them as guests." I soon learned that a friend shares information with a friend, often without being asked.

We had many other social events in our residence. We gave small dinner parties and hosted the only black tie supper of our married life. To that black tie event, we had invited twenty couples, including Co-President General Ovando, ten ministers, the ambassador, and senior embassy and AID officers. Co-President Barrientos was in Cochabamba and declined. The afternoon before the dinner right after Ele had arranged tables of eight in the living room/dining room and planned not to light the large fireplace, the central heating unit (just one of four in La Paz) sputtered and died. The technician arrived by five o'clock and had the heating up and running just as the first guests arrived at eight. By the time we sat down to dinner at nine, the house was comfortably warm again. As a postscript, seven of our Bolivian guests became presidents or members of governing Juntas within the next decade.

Ele told me just before Christmas that we would have to slow down the pace of our work and social life. I had been working seven days a week and we had social engagements almost every evening, and often with working lunches thrown in. She wanted one day a week when we were off duty and she wanted that day to be Sunday. She gave the servants the day off and she wanted to be home alone. Eduarda was asked to leave food in the fridge that we could cook whenever we wanted to eat. We had met some couples with whom we could relax—no business, no gossip, and no stress. We ended up spending many of our Sundays for the next couple of years before the fireplace in our cozy study with them, especially Lois and Ed Faison or Ana Rosa and Eli Hill. They became our safety valve after a week of adventures.

Christmas in La Paz was special. Bill Broderick was being transferred back to Washington, and we had a series of farewells. We received confirmation from AID Washington that David Lazar would be the new deputy. We invited all the U.S. embassy and mission staff to an open house. As the time came to toast the Broderick's, David Lazar joined Ele and me in front of the fireplace and capped the evening by presenting the Broderick's with an elegant certificate on parchment, with scripted calligraphy, and then asked me to read it. It proclaimed that Bill was the charter member of the SOBs, the Survivors of Bolivia. During the rest of our stay in La Paz, every departing member, including David and me, became an SOB, an honor that we cherished.

20

Reshaping the Program

January 1966 ended the co-presidency. President Barrientos chose José Adolfo Siles Salinas, head of the small Christian Democratic Party and half-brother of the former MNR President, Hernán Siles Suazo, as his running mate. President Ovando cancelled the monthly meetings and advised that there would be no changes in the cabinet or government policies until the new president was sworn in in August.

With the pending change in government, David Lazar (now the deputy USAID director) and I concentrated on redefining the scope and priorities of the USAID program. An important objective was to end the Bolivian government's continued dependence on U.S. economic aid to sustain its public sector or for funding their most important development banks. Like the ambassador, we did not believe that was in the best policy interest of either government. We knew that, even though an agreement was reached in principle to end that dependence during the last administration of Paz Estenssoro, there had been little success in finding a formula to implement it. We had to learn by experimenting.

The challenges for both governments were great. It had taken a decade for the MNR leadership to become pragmatic, rather than ideological, in its efforts to develop the country. The coup in 1964 had forced many of the civilian officials who had been learning on the job to leave their key government posts. While some of the elements of change were still in place, the military had erased some key advances, especially in development planning.

Preparing the Groundwork

As part of our assessment, David and I made an in-depth review of the ongoing projects and the recommendations by the division chiefs for inclusion in the next budget presentation. USAID was financing a large spectrum of activities and had a staff of almost three hundred. We looked at the relevance of each project, the size of the mission, and our capability to oversee operations and assess performance. David and I reached the conclusion that the mission should set priorities and trim projects and personnel in non-priority areas. Because of the size of our operations and the not-too-incisive quality of the monthly or quarterly progress reports, the mission added a specialist in project evaluation to our staff.

Our starting point was that the USAID program was part of an essentially political process to support the Bolivian government's effort to improve national stability and raise the living standards of the people. Our goal as a mission was to enable the government to develop the capability to make policies and take economic, social, psychological, and other actions to achieve those goals. That meant not only providing advice and training, but more importantly, helping it build fiscal and people-oriented institutions. The ambassador fully supported us.

Then we divided development into six sectors in which US-AID was working: physical infrastructure; financial infrastructure; human resources development, including education and public health; increasing rural and non-agricultural production and job generation; the public sector; and the private sector.

Next we identified what the USAID role should be in each sector. In this analysis, we considered not just what the USAID inputs should be but also those potentially available from other donors such as the Inter-American Development Bank, the World Bank, International Monetary Fund, the United Nations Development Program (UNDP), and other bilateral government agencies.

As I recall, our analysis and discussions reached the following conclusions:

First, in the area of physical infrastructure, USAID had several pending commitments to finance construction for a major highway in the Chapare, farm-to-market roads, and road maintenance. The

U.S. had been the major financer of road construction since World War II when we agreed to build a paved highway over the high Andes, from La Paz, to Cochabamba, and on to Santa Cruz. We concluded that the political fallout from our pulling out of the sector outweighed other considerations. So, we proposed that USAID honor current commitments whenever feasible, and then encourage the Bolivians to look to the IDB and the World Bank for financing further feasibility studies and construction of major future physical infrastructure projects. There had already one successful experience with such a substitution—the Santa Isabel power plant in the Cochabamba area, where USAID financed the preliminary studies on electric power generation in the country and then encouraged the IDB to finance the building. We recognized that such a policy might not be popular with U.S. construction firms since they would have to compete with other firms worldwide to bid on projects funded by the international banks, and that they might well call on members of congress to pressure AID against such a policy.

The second sector was the financial infrastructure. Since the re-election of Paz Estenssoro in 1961, USAID had been advising the Ministry of Finance on formulating and applying responsible fiscal policies, broadening the revenue base, designing and installing workable control and enforcement procedures, and training technical personnel on both fiscal and monetary policy. The IMF also advised the Bolivian government in this sector, trained policy and technical staff, and reviewed annually fiscal and monetary policy that included setting limits on public expenditures and borrowing. The coup had led to an exodus of trained technical advisors, and much of the work of the previous four years had to be repeated all over again.

The role of the Central Bank was confused. My predecessor had brought a first-rate banking advisor, Phil Faucett, to work with the minister of Finance and the president of the Central Bank on monetary policy and restructuring the bank. Phil told us that the Central Bank functioned more like a private commercial institution than a central bank. When I asked Phil about the capability of the Central Bank to handle requests for additional funding by the Agriculture, Mining, or Industrial Banks to ensure their liquidity, he explained that the Bank had no rediscounting facilities and could not provide liquidity relief.

The strengthening of the Central bank was critical to ending the reliance of the Bolivian government and the development banks on USAID as the funder of last resort. In addition, we needed to set a timetable on USAID's being the primary adviser to the Ministry of Finance. Given the immediate problems of the Bolivian government, any abrupt changes could be counter-productive since phasing out budget support and the *servicios* had already caused serious friction. So, we needed a strategy in this critical area that could be carried out jointly with the IMF.

USAID Public Administration Adviser Emerson Melaven, Banking Adviser Phil Fawcett, Mission Economist Jake Meerman, Mission Controller Gene Barrett, David Lazar, and I worked as a team for several weeks in early 1966 to design two lines of action to be carried out over the next five years, with the goal of gradually replacing U.S. bilateral assistance with multilateral support through the IMF and the World Bank. One line of action was for USAID to help the Central Bank develop the tools and trained personnel to set and manage monetary policy as well as install appropriate windows for rediscounting paper from the development banks; repayments of U.S. dollar and local currency loans would be earmarked for financing the rediscount windows. The second was continuing high-level advisory services to the ministry and the training of Bolivian economists and technical specialists in fiscal policy, management of public sector financing, tax policy, and revenue generation. Those efforts would be coordinated with the IMF.

The third sector was human resource development including education, public health, and community development. David Lazar and I did not see education as a social dimension of development, but rather as the keystone for building a more dynamic economy capable of providing jobs and opportunity for the Bolivian people. Our concern was how best to deploy limited resources to extend education and improve the skills of both the urban and rural population.

Since the 1952 revolution, large numbers of rural people were being offered access to education for the first time in Bolivian history. The data at hand on the literacy rate prior to 1952 was suspect, but it indicated that well over 80 percent of the rural population had little or no education—and most of the country's population lived in rural areas. The MNR governments had given a high priority to education, but given its small national budget, there was much more to be done to provide the people with at least a basic education and some of the skills needed for Bolivia's development aspirations.

The government reports we studied showed shortages of trained teachers, physical plants, and budget. We noted that to overcome those deficits the Bolivian government had placed a higher priority on funding for education than the health sector—and USAID agreed. While we recognized the importance of improving people's health, if they did not become better qualified to take advantage of development opportunities, we would be putting the cart before the horse. The assignment of resources between education and public health is always a difficult choice, and we felt that with limited resources over the next few years, the best use of those limited resources would be in education.

Which area of education should be given priority? The USAID senior education advisor, Dr. Holmes, and the senior technical staff of the Ministry of Education defined teacher education and curriculum development as the priorities. USAID had a well-established program with San Jose State University that could provide the technical inputs needed for teacher training and advice on curriculum. Two of the most important teachers colleges in Bolivia already had established ties with San Jose State, and told us they were committed to work with us in organizing and conducting training courses around the country and advising on curriculum, if funding were available. They also told us that, if resources could be provided, they were prepared to substantially increase the number of teachers in training and expand their facilities for science and special subjects.

The most difficult problem was how to increase the budget allocation for the Ministry of Education in the face of very limited government revenues. That would require my lobbying the senior policy makers. A second problem that Dr. Holmes had to deal with was ensuring the cooperation of some not too friendly Marxist professionals directing ministry programs.

At the same time, however, we did not want to phase out support for public health programs. We reviewed proposals by UNDP to support rural health centers and by the World Health Organization, through the Pan American Sanitary Bureau, to provide technical assistance for certain public health projects. We also noted that the government was requesting money to construct new health facilities, but could not give us any assurance that it had the budgetary resources to hire staff or operate the facilities. We did not feel that in the stringent budgetary environment, it made sense to build new facilities, but rather concentrate on upgrading services using the medical clinics and posts already in place. Among the medical programs in operation, we opted to continue support for maternal-child health services.

A major component of the strategy for human resource development was the newly activated national community development program. It had the dual objective of helping communities deal with their priority needs, and nurturing the formation of local leadership. The program was designed to help communities identify their immediate needs and encourage their residents to work together to mobilize the resources needed to carry out projects. In our mission analyses, we anticipated that many of the projects in the communities would involve building schools and medical facilities. We therefore needed to program USAID technical and financial resources to support both building the facilities and training teachers and practical nurses to staff those facilities. We anticipated that the local communities would cover the salaries for teachers and rural health workers since in recent years, whenever the Ministry of Education did not have the budget to finance the salary of a teacher, communities would raise that money and pay the teacher directly.

The fourth sector was increasing production and job creation. Our sector team included David; Rural Development Division Chief Milt Lobell; Ed Faisan, USAID consultant on marketing; Jake Meerman, mission economist; and Dr. Roberts, the economist on the Utah State University agronomy team. We also consulted René Balliván, the president of the Industrial Bank, and two Bolivian ex-mission members: economist Jorge Crespo, who was then head of Grace Co. of Bolivia, and Ernesto Wende, president of the Savings and Loan Bank of Bolivia.

Our goal was to channel future mission investments into projects that would increase farmers' income and create jobs for the growing number of miners whose employment was imperiled by the decline in tin ore production, and the increasing number of urban underemployed and unemployed. The data showed that rural-to-urban migration was accelerating, and that there was a substantial increase in the numbers of young people about to enter the labor force. The impact of the public health programs had led to a decline in infant mortality, and the education system, especially in urban areas, was educating larger numbers of youngsters every year—but there was no evidence of increased job opportunities. Most of the young people looked to the government for a job, and government policy to promote private investment and small industry development was almost non-existent. The words of the longtime Associate Director of the Bureau of Labor Standards Clara Beyer, rang in my ears, "Jobs and income are the critical elements for ensuring social stability while longer term development programs are put in place."

In agriculture, we changed the focus from production *per se* to increasing farm income. We shifted the emphasis of the USAID effort from production in the rich lowland areas where extensive private farming and stock raising had built a solid base for export earnings to the needs of the upper valley and Altiplano farmers whose per capita income, while substantially higher than before the 1952 revolution, was still minimal—probably no more than US$75 to $100 per annum. We wanted to induce small farmers to stay in rural areas by providing them better income and living conditions. The sheep shearing had shown that, properly organized and marketed, sheep's wool, along with llama and alpaca fibers, could offer an immediate source of additional income.

The potato is the staple crop of the highlands. USAID-led research had already found that planting the buds lower in the soil would protect the crop from freezing during the winter. We agreed that one of the major efforts of the Utah State team would be to work with Bolivian research stations to improve potato production and to identify multiple crops, like quinoa, that could be grown profitably on the Altiplano.

To increase farm income, we also asked the industrial team to focus on processing plants and marketing systems for the highland areas, and to support handicraft development in decentralized production centers that could use wool and llama, alpaca, and vicuña fibers of the Altiplano and that would provide additional sources of income for highland farm families. They were also charged with investigating marketing opportunities for crops and artisan hand-icrafts.

David and I kept for ourselves looking for a process that could expedite the granting of titles to land the *campesinos* had occupied since 1952. Politics had held up their issuance and the legal process was arcane and complex. Without settled title, it was almost im-possible to channel loan funds to small farmers for improved pro-duction programs. Without titles, *campesinos* would be much more likely to add to the rural-to-urban migration.

The other priority for the industrial division was to promote new industries for food processing, building supplies, consumer goods, and the service sector. The president of the Industrial Bank offered his assistance in analyzing the possibilities. For example, in La Paz, there were only five gasoline stations and only a hand-ful more throughout the country, all owned by political cronies. There were opportunities for employment in that sector if training were provided for hundreds of youngsters. Another possibility that was identified by the rural development team was the shortage of trained agro-mechanics throughout the country. The mining sec-tor was very complex. The Tripartite aid to the COMIBOL Project had just been terminated and the dismal results hardly justified the investments and expenditures. The oil and gas operations in Santa Cruz were primarily a private sector activity. *La gran minería* (large-scale mining) was controlled and operated by government entities and was losing money. *Minería mediana y pequeña* (medium and small-scale mining) were profitable and were in private hands and mined different minerals such as zinc, lead, gold, and silver. We asked the industrial team to take a new look at the job creation potential in the latter. We asked Jake Meerman and his economists to look again at the potential and problems of trying to build a tin refinery on the Altiplano, including a projection of its probable im-pact on job creation in the mining regions and Oruro.

Then we looked at public services. Since 1952, USAID had ded-icated significant resources to helping the Bolivians improve public services. The *servicios* had trained hundreds of technical and administrative personnel. USAID had invested advisory services and money in building a capability throughout the government to analyze and plan programs and projects, especially in the Ministries of Planning, Finance, Agriculture, Education, and Public Health. By 1964, a professional cadre was emerging.

When the coup occurred in late 1964, most of the MNR-trained officials were fired or sidelined, and many key Bolivian public sector economists and administrators had taken jobs at CIAP, the Inter-American Development Bank, other international organizations, and private entities throughout the hemisphere. Bolivia had no civil service law, and the new government—as had been the practice throughout its history—tossed out the incumbent officials and replaced most of them, from janitor to bureau chief. This was a major obstacle to building a stable public sector technical and administrative staff.

Our analysis focused on the need for some form of civil service system to ensure that the people trained and the administrative systems installed had some hope of continuity beyond the next election. Given the impending change in government, our decision was to delay discussions on this issue until the new administration was in place and we had identified the key officials with whom we could negotiate.

Our next important issue was the role of the private sector in the development process. Bolivia had little or no experience with modern capital formation and depended on foreign investment. Most of its operating capital came from institutions and markets outside of the country.

The Bolivian domestic market was small. The electrical and transportation infrastructures were inadequate. Our industry advisers told us that there were small privately owned textile mills and ore processing and metallurgy plants. The railways, built in the 1880s by a British company, had recently been nationalized and were a museum of early twentieth century technology. The most modern and efficient industrial plants in the country were the privately operated lead and zinc refineries in the Altiplano and the gas and petroleum operation run by Gulf Oil near Santa Cruz in the eastern lowlands. The reputation of Bolivian-made products was not good, and Bolivians themselves invariably chose foreign goods over those made in country. The sad truth was that one of the most profitable businesses was smuggling, and smugglers took kickbacks from Bolivian-manufacturers of nylon hose so that they could be sold as Chilean-made throughout the country.

A critical obstacle to private sector development was the policy and attitude of government. Most of the MNR officials believed in state ownership of the productive sectors of the economy. That same view was vigorously advocated by Socialists, Stalinists, and Trotskyites at the *Universidad Nacional* located just a few blocks from the presidential palace. The military seemed to share that view. In the early 1960s, their experience in governing the country had shown Paz Estenssoro and his talented Planning Minister Gumucio that the Bolivian government alone was not capable of providing the economic development needed to raise incomes and create jobs. They recognized the need for private sector development. They created incentives for private investment and protections for entrepreneurs, including those engaged in petroleum and non-tin mining. The president of the Industrial Bank told us that requests for loans to build and modernize plants had increased dramatically in the early 1960s, but that, after the coup, loan applications had dried up.

We were also advised that, while the private companies were inevitably subject to "pressures" by government regulators, many businesses were not well run. We were told that in mid-1965, in the first course on accounting offered for senior business executives, the consultant—a professor from UCLA—was speechless when the owner of a textile mill asked, "What are fixed costs?" And he was dumbstruck when another asked, "What accounting system should I use for the set of books that I keep for tax purposes?"

After this discussion, David and I determined that our top priority was to influence the highest level of the new government to adopt positive policies to promote private investment. We would continue to provide capital and technical assistance to the Industrial Bank, the credit unions, and the new Savings and Loan Bank, and use them as showcases for the profitability and effectiveness of efficient, up-to-date business operations. We felt that before providing more technical assistance on plant layout, safety, marketing, and management systems, Bolivia needed to define policies and adopt practices that effectively supported private sector development.

Approval of the New Program

By mid-March, I began to write the program presentation for Washington review. David worked closely with me. I would begin a sentence and David would finish it for me. He would raise an issue and I would often find it on my own list of concerns. We involved the ambassador and DCM as well as key members of USAID—especially Emerson "Em" Melaven, and the program officer, John Blumgart; but essentially the document was David's and mine.

Following our analysis, we concluded that we needed another front office position to help David and me oversee program operations. We proposed the creation of an associate director for operations and nominated Em for the post. Em would consider it only if he could also continue to coordinate the public sector division. David and I agreed.

We submitted our revised program and organization chart to Washington for review, and the reception from the senior State and AID staff was very positive. I was given a date in late spring to go to Washington to discuss it with the senior AFP staff and key members of congress.

I spent two weeks responding to in-depth questions about the rationale and program choices. Every component of our new program was examined. As the second week came to a close, I was given a green light to begin negotiating the new program with the in-coming Bolivian government.

I was also routed to New York to talk with business executives, bankers, and foundation leaders with interests in Bolivia. I had lunches in boardrooms and at the Bankers Club.

I returned to La Paz excited about the prospects for the new direction of the USAID Program and Washington's endorsement of it. I anticipated meeting with the key members of the new administration. All the polls and grapevine information said that Barrientos and his running mate, José Adolfo Siles Salinas, would win easily. I had come to know the about-to-be vice president through introductions of Christian Democratic political leaders with whom I had worked on earlier assignments. José Adolfo and his wife Cristina, with their children, would often drop in to say hello on a Sunday afternoon. I saw the odds for a productive relationship with the administration as favorable.

Ele, the Working Partner

Ele kept me informed about the problems and needs of the USAID families, and often proposed changes in USAID procedures to improve services and morale. She saw to it that I did not overlook the human part of my job.

Ele worked with the USAID wives on monthly meetings at our home, which often included special events like a flower show or briefings on the country. At one, the USAID senior mining adviser set up a prototype of a mine in our basement for the ladies to walk through. They met at our house, and Ele provided the refreshments, but the ladies chose their own officers and planned their own programs.

She also lent a hand at the office whenever needed. David and I had a great front office. His secretary, Polly Harris, and mine, Peggy Hook, kept not only the work moving efficiently but also a calendar of all the birthdays and wedding anniversaries of the Bolivian and U.S. staff. Peggy loved to cook, and baked pastries and muffins regularly. When it was a birthday or special celebration, she, Ele, and Polly arranged for cake and coffee. Ele's smile was always there to congratulate and honor one of our colleagues.

Ele and I made a special effort to know our counterparts in the other donor agencies. When the new UN resident representative, Santiago Quijano Caballero and his wife Cristina arrived at post, we held a reception in their honor. When Andrew Beith, the resident representative of the International Monetary Fund (IMF), told us that his bride-to-be, Marianne, was coming to La Paz for the wedding, Ele offered our residence as the site for the wedding reception. Inter-American Bank Representative Briceño and his wife were frequent guests at our home and at USAID parties. When Marcelo Caiolo, the IMF Washington office director, made his annual country review, we had small working dinners at our home.

In January we had our first chance to enjoy the La Paz fair, with its colorful booths of handicrafts. We spent hours reveling in the genius of Bolivian artisans. At the market, we watched artisans weave alpaca and llama cloth, make a variety of ceramic items, and mold Bolivian pewter into jewelry, bowls, and ornamental flatware, using patterns that had been passed down for generations. We were especially fortunate that Daisy Wende, the wife of Ernesto—the ex-USAID economist who became the president of the Savings and Loan Bank—guided us through the aisles of the open-air market. Daisy was a moving force in promoting artisan handicraft development in Bolivia and organized a program to nurture handicraft centers across the country and to market the products. She operated a prestigious shop in La Paz that sold high-quality artisan products.

In 1966, one of our first guests was Frances Howard, the director of AID's worldwide program to cooperate with private voluntary organizations (PVOs). Since Fran was the sister of Vice President Hubert Humphrey, her arrival prompted great interest among the top Bolivian government officials. Fran had planned to stay with us, but because of her rank, she was the guest of the ambassador and his wife at the embassy. Fran's program included high-level protocol calls on President Ovando and the foreign minister. The ambassador hosted a reception, and Ele and I set up an evening with the USAID staff at our residence.

I had urged her to come to Bolivia to help the mission improve its relations with the scores of PVOs (many religiously affiliated) which operated schools, health centers, and other facilities. I was eager to broaden our contacts and explore possible areas of project cooperation. My association with Jim Boren in the creation of the Partners of the Americas had shown me the possibilities of enriching USAID efforts with inputs from PVOs, and I wanted to explore the possibilities of working with those already established in Bolivia.

When Fran agreed to come, I sent invitations to about forty PVOs to meet Fran at my office and discuss with her their programs, interests, and needs. The response was poor, with only a few Protestant groups, Catholic Relief Services, the credit unions, and the Building and Loan Association responding. All of them had already established a relationship with USAID. On the eve of the meeting with Fran, calls were made to each of the PVOs to remind them of the invitation. Most of them wanted no relationship with the U.S. government and expressed little interest in learning what other PVOs were doing in Bolivia. Even those that attended the meeting, while pleased to meet Fran, were reluctant to discuss their activities in the presence of other PVOs. Frankly, it was disheartening.

The high point of the visit was a program of traditional Bolivian dances and pisco sours sponsored by the Ministry of Rural Affairs at which Fran was the guest of honor, along with the ambassador's wife and Ele. We arranged for the PVO leaders to be invited but again few attended. We agreed that any further initiatives with the PVOs at that time were not opportune.

The weekend before Lent, we were invited to join President Ovando and the diplomatic corps to attend the ceremony of the devil dancers in Oruro. Oruro is a mining center on the Altiplano, about one hundred kilometers from La Paz. The devil dancers are to Bolivia what carnival is to Brazil. Carnival is not celebrated in the streets of La Paz as it is Rio. We drove there with Ambassador and Mrs. Henderson, climbed to the second floor of the *Alcaldía* (City Hall), and found our seats on the balcony to watch the thousands of masked dancers as they whirled around the plaza in front of us, circling to the strains of one *huayna* after another for hours on end, as they depicted what was described to us as the victory of the Spaniards in their white masks over the Moors in their black masks. Ele and I thought it more likely that to the Bolivians, it was their opportunity to wage the battle of the indigenous people against the invading Spanish. The elegant embroidery of the costumes, the whirling skirts of the ladies—many, we were told, wore twelve or more petticoats under the skirts—and the intricately carved masks, brightly colored, with a wonderful assortment of horns for the devils, kept us glued to the scene on the plaza below us. We occasionally sampled the Altiplano delicacies that were heaped on the buffet tables at the end of the assembly room, but the dancers were much more alluring than the food. At nightfall, the ambassador led us to pay our respects to the dancers before we headed back to La Paz.

A couple of weeks later, West German Ambassador Mock and his wife invited Ele and me to a dinner to say goodbye to the last in-country manager of the Tripartite COMIBOL program. The ambassador was punctilious about appointments, and the invitation read, "Dinner at 7:00 p.m." Mrs. Mock and the first secretary received Ambassador and Mrs. Henderson, the representative of the Inter-American Development Bank, and the president of COMIBOL, General Lechín and their wives and us at the front door. About 7:10, the ambassador's wife came into the living room quite upset, and told us that she was worried because the ambassador had not returned from a quick trip to the chancery. We sipped our cocktails while the first secretary called around to try to locate the ambassador. When he returned to report that the ambassador had never arrived at the chancery, we all offered to help in the search. Calls to police and hospitals indicated that there had been no reports of accidents. Dinner was delayed while the search continued.

About eight o'clock, the ambassador called to advise that he was being held at the notorious central La Paz criminal jail after being booked for allegedly hitting a pedestrian while driving uphill past the British-Canadian Hospital. The policeman could not read, did not realize that he had arrested the German ambassador, and knew nothing about diplomatic immunity. So, Ambassador Henderson and General Lechín accompanied the German first secretary to the jail to get Ambassador Mock released. He was finally home by nine o'clock and we sat down to dinner at about half past nine.

At dinner, the ambassador gave us a graphic description of his adventure: he was the victim of a scam pulled on many others for quite some time. A policeman and one of his stooges would situate themselves halfway up the hill leading from Calacoto to the center of La Paz and wait for a car climbing slowly up the steep incline. Then the stooge would run out in front the car and get himself hit. The policeman would arrest the driver and impound the car. However, as all good Bolivians knew, an adequate payment to the policeman cleared up the problem, and everyone would go home. Well, the ambassador had changed the script: he insisted on taking the "injured" stooge to the hospital for treatment, and to go to the jail to clear up the accident in the proper legal manner. The hospital reported that the man had not been injured, just skinned his knee. By the time the relief team from the embassy had arrived, the governor of the jail had been summoned and he was apologizing to the ambassador for the inconvenience.

The foreign minister called his apologies to the ambassador the next morning, with the government's assurance that the scam would permanently cease. For several months, there were no reports of anyone being victimized on that stretch of the hill up to the city!

During Lent, we received many invitations to dine at the homes of Bolivian friends and colleagues. One special evening was an invitation to dinner at the Camacho family home. It had special meaning for Ele and me in our relations with top levels of the Bolivian government. Maria Teresa Camacho was a secretary in the USAID capital development office and was about to be engaged to a Marine guard at the embassy, Chuck Hull. The Camacho family included a brother Edgar of the Foreign Ministry (later foreign minister and ambassador to the U.N.); brother-in-law Jorge Jordan Ferrufino, the vice minister of Finance; and half-brother to General Barrientos, Oscar Vega, a rising young economist at the Ministry of Finance. As we sat down to dinner, Mrs. Camacho's sister arrived; she was the wife of the president of Bolivia, General Ovando. That evening not only built lifelong friendships but also facilitated my relationships with senior government officials.

Besides our outings Ele had her own schedule of events at which she met most of the wives of the ambassadors posted to La Paz and many Bolivian socialites. One was Beatriz Lavayen de Horne from Cochabamba. Her family estates were expropriated during the 1952 revolution and as a widow she went into business marketing the produce from the farmers who took over the family lands and investing her profits in urban properties, including Cochabamba's leading hotel. Beatriz was an invaluable ally when the Partners of the America were organized. Jim Boren said that a group in Little Rock, Arkansas had opted to partner with the Cochabamba Valley. Beatriz was a member of the Cochabamba organizing committee. I told her of the great cooperation that had developed between Utah and the Altiplano, and arranged for her to meet with Gary Neeleman when he led the Utah delegation to Bolivia in 1966. Through Beatriz, Arkansas Governor Winthrop Rockefeller was invited to head a delegation to begin discussions on possible areas of cooperation.

The Cochabamba committee moved ahead with its plans for a mid-1966 visit, but Arkansas ran into various hitches in getting its committee together. Governor Rockefeller decided to make the visit anyway in order not to disappoint Cochabamba. We got word from the State Department that the governor and his wife were flying down on their private jet and would spent four days in Bolivia. The ambassador appointed Ele and me to represent him throughout the visit and travel around the country with the Rockefellers.

They arrived in the rainy season and were met by the ambassador, Mrs. Henderson, the chief of Protocol, and the Tragens. They were whisked down the hill in the ambassador's car to a meeting with the president and a lunch that Beatriz had organized with the cream of Bolivian society. We picked the Rockefellers up after lunch and joined them on their jet for the one-hour flight to Cochabamba where an official reception was awaiting us. This was our first flight on an executive jet, and we were overwhelmed with the comfort and services. Jeanette Rockefeller made us at home and Winthrop was full of good cheer.

When we arrived at the hotel, Jeanette took Ele and me aside, and said that Winthrop never carried money with him and that he liked to acquire things. She said that if he liked something, he often would just pick it up and expect someone to send him a bill. She said, "If he does that on this trip, please keep a list of the items and their cost and I will pay you before we leave." We did, and she did.

The arrival in Cochabamba was in a light rain, but all the local dignitaries were there to meet us. That evening, we had a banquet at the hotel owned by Beatriz, at which it was quite clear that most of those attending wanted to get Winthrop to invest in the region. The speeches were like sales pitches, at which the governor smiled and drank another glass of whisky. Ele and I, who had learned to nurse one scotch for the evening, soon found out that Winthrop and Jeanette never turned another one down. As Winthrop told us, he had grown up on the oilrigs of Texas and Venezuela and learning to hold his liquor was one of the rites of passage.

The next day we flew in a DC3 to Sucre, the legal capital of Bolivia, where Governor and Mrs. Rockefeller were met by the president of the Supreme Court, the rector of the university and the mayor of Sucre. We attended a ceremony at the Supreme Court and then at the university where Rockefeller was awarded an honorary degree. At lunch, the Mayor gave him the key to city and invited him to invest in the bright future of that region of Bolivia. By the time we returned to Cochabamba, Winthrop had had enough expressions of interest to turn him off. We had another dinner that night with the incipient Partners group, but it had not done much preparatory work. Beatriz was clearly unhappy with her colleagues, and the Rockefellers graciously excused themselves and went up early in the evening to their suite for their nightcaps.

Early the following morning, Jeanette called me to her suite. A Cochabamba lady with her newborn had broken through the hotel security and rang the doorbell to the suite to tell Jeanette that she was holding Winthrop's new son. I called security to hustle the lady out of the building. Jeanette just smiled and said that it happened all the time!

Later that morning, we broke into two groups. Jeanette, Beatriz, and Ele went on a tour of the Cochabamba Valley while I accompanied the governor on a DC3 flight to the Beni for lunch with a group of cattle barons. Julio Sanjinés, the Bolivian ambassador to Washington, joined us that morning and began a long explanation of the prospects for cattle raising in the Beni. The ambassador praised the governor for his extraordinary development of Winrock Farms in Arkansas. As we approached the great hacienda house and landing strip, the governor turned to me and said, "Did you see the cattle grazing under water?" The ambassador replied that, because of heavy rains, the animals had naturally adapted to grazing under water. The governor just looked out the window.

The house was an elegant, multi-storied Spanish hacienda, made of concrete, adorned with Talavera tile, and composed of large, gracious high-ceilinged rooms, with broad verandas overlooking the river valley. We had drinks while the cattlemen extolled the production and returns on the operations in the Beni. Lunch was an array of barbecued T-bone steaks and whisky. The governor was gracious throughout the lunch and exchanged lots of information about ranching. He asked many questions. When lunch was ending, he said to his host, "I think that you invited the wrong Rockefeller. This is not my kind of ranching. You should have brought Nelson down. He would have probably bought in." The governor snoozed on the way back to Cochabamba.

On our return to Cochabamba, the governor's jet was ready for departure. We flew to La Paz. We said our goodbyes and they returned to Little Rock. The Bolivians had blown an opportunity, and the Arkansas partnership with Cochabamba remained dormant during the rest of my tour.

Throughout the first year in Bolivia, we kept in touch with those MNR leaders who had stayed in Bolivia. The top leadership—Paz Estenssoro, Siles Suazo, labor leader Juan Lechín, and Planning

Minister Gumucio—had gone into exile in neighboring countries or took positions with international and inter-American organizations. But, some like Tony and Goni Sanchez de Lozada stayed in country—Tony in finance and Goni in mid-size mining. I had known their father when he was ambassador to the United States, and once met the brothers at the embassy in Washington.

We also found MNR technical people in some ministries and in the private sector, and tried to include them in gatherings at our house or at USAID events. When they described their experience in the twelve years after the Revolution of 1952, they gave me invaluable insights into what had worked and what had not worked. Indeed, they helped me keep a balanced political perspective on developments in the country.

Easter 1966 was very special because our closest friends, Dorothy and Chet Guthrie, came for a two-week visit. Chet had retired as the deputy archivist of the United States and opened a consulting firm to support AID training programs in fiscal management. I arranged for Chet to consult with David, Em, and our advisory group to the Ministry of Finance. Since Dorothy was the curator of the Jade Exhibit at the Smithsonian, Ele took her to various cultural and artisan handicraft centers.

The only trip we took outside of La Paz was to Lake Titicaca on Palm Sunday. Ele and I had been invited to participate in a program in Copacabana on the lake, and we took a picnic lunch for an alfresco meal on the shores after the program. It was a wonderful, warm day—not a cloud in the sky. We arrived on time to catch the hourly ferry that carried people and cars from the mainland to the *Isla del Sol* on which Copacabana is situated. Bolivian mythology tells us that the *Isla del Sol* is the navel of the universe and that all civilization originated at this sacred place. We all enjoyed the program at the cathedral, especially the little children depicting Jesus' arrival in Jerusalem, complete with palm fronds and a donkey. After I made a thank you speech, we visited various pre-Columbian ruins around the lake, including the Church of St. Peter and St. Paul, with its statues of the Aymara gods of Sun and War, who had been renamed St. Peter and St. Paul. Then we looked for a picnic spot.

The shores of Lake Titicaca are full of glacial scree and rocks, and very few sandy beaches. We finally found a spot, and Chet told my driver how to park the four-wheel drive so as to make it easy for us to leave. The driver took no heed. We had our lunch and at 3:00 p.m., we were ready for the return trip. But when the driver tried to start the car, the wheels were stuck in the rocks and could not build up any traction. It was half past four when we finally pushed the vehicle to a spot where it could gain traction, and we raced across the *Isla del Sol* to the Straits of Taquina to make the last ferry back to the mainland. We arrived just as the last scheduled ferry pulled out, only to be told that we were stuck on the island until Tuesday because the boatmen were having their annual two-day fiesta for the "arrival of Jesus." My driver was devastated; he had lost face!

We found the Bolivian navy headquarters on the island, and asked for help. The Lt. Commander in charge was summoned. He greeted us in colloquial American English, and recognized our plight. He sent his second in command over to the mainland to order a ferry back to take us over. In the meantime, he arranged for some refreshments and showed us around the base, including the sleeping quarters where some of his men were beginning to sleep off the festivities of the day in Copacabana. He said that he had just returned from a year-long internship with the U.S. Navy that had been arranged by the U.S. naval attaché. He had had a great time and couldn't do enough to thank us for the opportunity that had been given him.

It was after 8:00 p.m. when the ferry returned to pick us up. The crew was semi-sober and not happy at all at having been rousted from their fiesta. The commander gave them a stern lecture about their duty to Bolivia's friends, and led us onto the ferry before saying goodnight. On the remaining hour's drive home, my driver never opened his mouth or looked at us. Later that week, at my driver's initiative, he was transferred to the USAID heavy truck unit, and we never talked together again.

The following Monday morning, I had a meeting with the minister of Economy, General Jaime Berdecio, on the terms and conditions for a new PL 480 Agreement. I opened our session with a report on my *Isla del Sol* adventure and my rescue by the Bolivian navy. We both broke into smiles. The meeting went well. General Berdecio contacted General Ovando and advised me that the Bolivian government had no objections to the terms and conditions. As I was leaving, the minister chortled, "The gringos were saved by our navy!"

Installing the New Program

Barrientos's inauguration was a gala event. President Johnson sent Chief Justice and Mrs. Earl Warren to represent him at the ceremony. They were accompanied by the new assistant secretary of state, Jack Hood Vaughn, an old friend. Ele and I were not on the U.S. delegation, but we attended almost all of the festivities, and the chief justice's son, Earl Jr., and his wife were our houseguests.

One of the major concerns was the effect of the altitude on the health of the chief justice and his wife. But they held up extremely well. They did not miss a single event and were coping with the altitude and the pressure of the official commitments better than their son and daughter-in-law. Having the opportunity to spend some time with the chief justice and Mrs. Warren at an embassy dinner was a special delight because one of my first ventures into politics was supporting him when he ran for governor of California for the first time.

It also gave me an opportunity to talk with Jack Vaughn when we went together to an Altiplano village for a special community celebration to honor the new president. We were accompanied by a delegation of newsmen, none of whom had ever been to Bolivia before. Jack already had served in Bolivia and knew the situation of the *campesinos* and their propensity for *fiestas*. There were colorful paper decorations strung on high wires along the route of the president and his official party and the people were in brightly colored holiday dress, which was in stark contrast with the adobe brown of the houses and terrain.

At one of communities, two newsmen, Dick Dudman of the *St. Louis Dispatch* and Jerry O'Leary of the *Washington Star* joined me in visiting the sparsely furnished homes and the primitive living conditions and asked about the poverty around them and the lavish celebration. I tried to explain that "poverty" was relative: twelve years earlier, the people were still living in a feudal system in which they were subjected to the mandates and whims of the landlords, and now they owned the land on which they lived and were beginning to take some control over their lives. Their standard of living was poor by our standards but not necessarily in their eyes. I pointed out that now, in 1966, USAID and all of us could deal with them as individuals, not as chattels of the landlords, and that USAID's challenge was to help the government of Bolivia provide the people with the tools and instruments they needed to progressively raise their standard of living. Jack Vaughn apparently overheard and told me that night at dinner that he agreed with my perceptions of the changes occurring at the grassroots and supported the USAID program.

The following day, it was time for the chief justice to return to Washington on Air Force One. With the Bolivian chief of protocol, Ambassador Henderson, Mrs. Henderson, and other dignitaries, we trouped up to the airport at El Alto, and said our goodbyes to the Warrens, Jack Vaughn, and the newsmen. They boarded the plane. We retired to the diplomatic area of the airport and waited. The low air pressure on the Altiplano prevented the engines of the 707 from starting up, and the controllers at Andrews Air Force Base found it unsafe for the plane to take off. So, after waiting an hour, the chief justice decided to deplane. We loaded up the official cars, and took everyone back down the hill from the airport at 13,600 feet to the embassy at 12,600 feet where Mrs. Henderson put together an impromptu dinner.

Before we brought Earl Warren, Jr. and his wife back to our house at 11,800 feet, I had a chance to talk to Jack Vaughn about coordinating the USAID and Peace Corps Community Development Program in Bolivia in order to optimize our effort to help the *campesinos* help themselves. Jack called over Arthur Pursell, the Peace Corps country director, and asked him his opinion. He said that we had talked for months about our common interest but had not proceeded because of Peace Corps/Washington directives to work independently of USAID. Jack, who had been the Latin American director of the Peace Corps before assuming the post of assistant secretary of state, promised to talk to Sarge Shriver and get back to us as soon as possible.

About 3:00 a.m. the next morning, the emergency embassy telephone rang by my bed to advise us that Air Force One's engines had ignited and that we were to get the Warrens to the airport as soon as possible. Ele and I got everyone up and into the car and streaked up the hill as fast as was safely possible. With quick farewells, the plane took off at about 4:30 a.m. The ambassador told us all to take the day off.

Now, David and I had our work cut out for us. We had to call on all the new ministers and other key officials with whom we were to work. We had a special meeting with our division chiefs and specialists to find out what previous contacts they might have had with the new appointees. None of them was a technocrat and few had had previous high-level government experience. Several were army or air force officers. Two key civilians were Minister of Foreign Affairs Crespo, the father of USAID's former economist Jorge Crespo, and Minister of Finance José Romero Loza, a well-respected businessman.

We scheduled meetings with each minister. David and I went together because we wanted to compare our impressions. We always took the division chief or USAID official who would be working closely with that official. The process took over two weeks and involved at least one hour with each minister. The round included Finance, Economy, Planning, Education, Public Health, Rural Development, Labor, and Public Works. The only holdover that I recall was at Public Works.

What worried David and me were the wide differences in perceptions about problems that we heard from the ministers. Some were outspoken nationalists who were uneasy working with the United States. One or two were Marxist-leaning and showed little interest in assistance from the U.S., except for money. A couple were assigned ministries only because their political party had been promised cabinet posts if they supported Barrientos. There were two ministers whom we found impressive and with whom we thought we could work: one was José Romero Loza in Finance, and the second, General Vilfredo Montalvo in Agriculture. In Education, we hoped that the new minister would also be as insightful and dedicated as his predecessor, Colonel Hugo Banzer, whose new assignment was as military attaché in Washington.

A few weeks after Barrientos took office, I received a phone call at eleven o'clock at night. It was an aide to the president, who said that the president wanted to talk with me and was sending a car.

I hurriedly dressed and was taken to Barrientos' home just a few blocks away. We sipped brandy and discussed some of the trips we had taken together when he was co-president. He also talked about the challenges he was facing and told me that the key member of his cabinet was José Romero Loza, the minister of Finance, and that we should be able to work together. With Jorge Jordán (Barrientos' half-brother) as his vice minister, they would offer a direct channel to him, Barrientos, for any matters that required his attention.

For the next two years, there were several other occasions on which the phone rang late in the evening and a car was sent for me. Sometimes I was never quite sure what the president's purpose was. Sometimes, he would obliquely discuss a problem that bothered him. Other times, he would want me to explain a proposal that USAID was discussing with one of his ministers, especially if it involved rural development and strengthening the capability of rural communities to deal with development needs.

In fact, Romero Loza and Jorge Jordán proved to be the most capable and responsible officials with whom USAID worked. We were able to open a constructive dialogue on almost aspect of the development program. It was with Romero Loza and Jorge Jordán that David and I laid out the new focus for USAID support for Bolivian development. It was with Jorge Jordán (when he was subsequently appointed President of the Central Bank) that the bank was restructured and the first rediscount window opened.

We made a concerted effort to work with the Ministry of Development. In the MNR period, Development Minister Gumucio had been USAID's primary contact in planning and implementing the program. David and I expected that this ministry would continue to serve that role, especially since, under the guidelines and procedures set up by CIAP, it was the Development Ministry that was to prepare the annual development plans from which CIAP would select projects to submit to bilateral and multilateral donor agencies for possible financing. We met with the new minister several times in the first weeks of the new administration and arranged for the USAID economists to continue advising specialists in the ministry. Our economists and veteran ministry officials expressed their disappointment with the new leadership. When I next met with the president, I raised my concern about the Planning Ministry; he nodded and advised me to work with Romero Loza and Jorge Jordán.

So, we turned not to Development Ministry, but Finance to implement the new program. Changing the direction of a USAID program takes time, and time is precious since USAID officers usually spend no more than three to four years at the same post. If a new focus or direction for development assistance is appropriate, there is only a year or two in which to implement it—and half of that time may be lost while counterpart technicians get trained and the host government gets the funding, staff, and other resources in place. Often, there is only one year for actual program implementation before staff changes. Continuity is critical for development programs to take shape and move forward. David and I understood that and dedicated our efforts to making the transition as expeditious as possible.

We met with José Romero Loza and Jorge Jordán twice a month. As we became acquainted, we found that we could discuss frankly both the ministers' problems and the refocusing of the USAID program. Early on, we advised the minister that we wanted to extricate USAID from being the lender of last resort in Bolivia by building up the facilities of the Central Bank to rediscount bank paper.

We also engaged him on specific financial issues such as ending U.S. subsidies for some Bolivian enterprises, like the national airline, Lloyd Aéreo Boliviano. Given the deficit in the Bolivian government's operating budget, we understood the dilemma he faced. In every case, the minister was able to obtain the president's approval to end the subsidy. In the case of the airline, we negotiated as the quid pro quo for ending the operating subsidy a local currency loan to complete construction of the La Paz airport building. Each of those negotiations took precious time.

David and I also met with the minister of the Economy twice a month on economic policy issues. The ministry had a handful of university-trained economists but almost no operating funds except for those generated by the purchase and sale of PL 480 commodities. David and I focused our work with the minister and his staff on formulating policies and programs for expanding private sector investment and job generation.

David and I also met at least once a month with the ministers of Agriculture and Rural Development. USAID Chief of Rural Development Milt Lobell and Utah Team Chief Clark Ballard always accompanied us. The minister of Agriculture, an able, straightforward army general, rapidly became a key player in defining and implementing government policies in this sector. The minister laid out his plans and priorities and we adapted ours to meet his. We deepened that relationship with field trips to inspect agriculture projects, the Okinawan resettlement farms, research stations, processing plants, and farm-to-market roads. Milt and Clark took him on several trips across the Altiplano, Cochabamba, and Chuquisaca where he could compare the relative standard of living of the highland people with that of the farmers in the eastern lowlands. We systematically acquainted him with the reality with which he had to deal and in building bridges between him and his trained technical staff, many of whom were veterans of the former agricultural *servicio*.

The minister's initial commitment was to large-scale agriculture and livestock development in the eastern lowlands. As our relationship grew closer, we were able to focus his attention on the strategic importance of increasing financial and technical resources to improve production and farmer income in the highlands. He was particularly attracted to the community development concept and the prospects of enabling *campesinos* to solve problems for themselves and enlisting their support for ministry plans for increasing production. He shifted ministry support from the large landowners in eastern lowlands to highland projects and authorized the closing of the USAID office in Santa Cruz.

Another minister with whom Dave, Chuck Shirley, the USAID chief engineer, and I met monthly was the minister of Public Works. He had been chief of civic action for the armed forces before the 1964 coup and was a holdover from the co-presidents regime. Working with the USAID was quite different from his prior experience with the U.S. military missions; with us, he had to have plans and budgets before we could consider moving ahead on a proposal; with the U.S. military missions, he just presented proposals and money was made available. During the regime of the co-presidents, Chuck Shirley established a good working relationship with the minister and the ground rules were well understood. We quickly agreed that all previously agreed on projects would proceed on schedule, including the completion of the road linking the Chapare with Santa

Cruz, repairing the main highway over the mountains from Cochabamba to Santa Cruz, and assisting the ministry improve its road maintenance capability.

After our first meeting, we asked the minister to invite the IDB representative to join us. That was our initial effort to encourage the minister to look to the IDB, not to USAID, for funding for future infrastructure projects. By mid-1967, the minister agreed to limit future requests to USAID to farm-to-market roads and highway maintenance.

After an initial meeting, the minister of Education asked that we only meet when issues warranted high-level attention. He proposed that he meet regularly with the division chief, Dr. Holmes, on implementing the education program. I suspect that he was not comfortable having David and me come to the ministry too often because some of his advisers were Marxists. We agreed, and Dr. Holmes negotiated the agreement to provide USAID support for teacher training and curriculum development in urban and rural schools. Dr. Holmes' experience in school administration provided the minister with a special adviser who helped him deal with a myriad of operational issues that plagued the public education system.

The minister of Education was also charged with implementing one of President Barrientos' campaign promises: to build and operate a public elementary school in every community across Bolivia. The minister's construction budget was nil. USAID was the principal source of funds for rural schools, and the new community development program included funds for supporting those communities that gave priority to building a school. In addition the minister had almost no budget for supplies and equipment, and he welcomed a steady stream of supplies and equipment for rural schools organized by the Utah Partners of the Alliance, under the leadership of its chairman, Gary Neeleman.

The discussions with each minister inevitably dealt with the support that could be expected from USAID. We not only considered dollar U.S. loans and dollar-funded technical assistance for major programs and projects, but also explored the use of the local currency PL 480 fund to meet an immediate need or to test an innovative approach. The availability of those local currencies played a critical role in our negotiations with the ministers.

In making arrangements with each minister, David and I would inevitably take into account the presence of graft in Bolivian public life. There was no way USAID could wipe it out, but we made it as difficult as possible to misuse program funds, without compromising our long-term ability to work with the government. Accusing any official publicly would not only inevitably lead to confrontation and probably our expulsion from the country but also complicate our government's ability to work with the current and successor government officials. Problems most often arose in connection with PL 480 local currency funds. USAID was responsible for overseeing the transport to and sale of commodities in country, as well as the accounting for the funds. The USAID controller, Gene Barrett, had auditors on his staff to see that the government of Bolivia complied with the relevant rules and regulations. There is no easy solution to dealing with graft and corruption.

Two serious problems of misuse of PL 480 commodities arose during my years in La Paz. The first was at the port of Arica in Chile where the government of Bolivia had bonded warehouses at which the wheat would be off-loaded and siloed before transshipment over the Andes to La Paz. The auditors visited Arica periodically, on no fixed schedule in order to minimize the chance for theft or diversion. A special emergency arose when we received a cable from Washington that advised us that Senator Javitz of New York, while on a cruise from Santiago to New York, had observed the pillaging and improper storage of wheat at Arica when his ship docked nearby. We sent auditors down to investigate, coupled with a strong warning to the government, threatening to cut off access to PL 480 commodities. For several months thereafter we received no complaints. When another report came from Washington of a perceived impropriety in Arica, I immediately repeated the investigation and the warning.

The second recurring problem was the sale of wheat in neighboring markets like Brazil, Peru, and Paraguay where the price of wheat on the street was higher than in Bolivia. Just about every six months, the ambassador or I would receive a call from a Maryknoll priest stationed at Guajará-Mirim on the Mamore River, with one half of the city on the Bolivian side and the other in Brazil. The Father would report that PL 480 wheat, clearly marked for Bolivia, was on sale in the Brazilian city market. I would immediately advise Gene, who would fly an auditor to Guajará-Mirim on the next available plane. I would then go to see the minister of the Economy and tell him of the report and the news that an auditor was on his way. We would get no further reports of violations for the next several months. But, about every eight months a new call would be received and the process was repeated all over again.

In implementing our new program, David and I committed large amounts of time and effort to the community development program. We saw it as much more than an effort to help communities deal with some of their own pressing problems, but as the building block for self-government at the community level. The Peace Corps directors, first Arthur Purcell and then his successor Gino Baumann, shared that perception. The Peace Corps, with over a hundred volunteers working and living in rural communities, needed resources and tools to help the people help themselves. USAID had resources and tools but often lacked the ways and means for getting them to the communities. The community development program was the mechanism for USAID and Peace Corps to join forces to reach a mutually agreed upon objective.

One of my most difficult problems was convincing President Barrientos and the military that community development should be supported. They were advocates of the civic action program through which they had rebuilt popular support for the military among rural people. Civic action modus *operandi* was for the military to identify projects that rural people wanted, like a bridge, a farm-to-market road, a civic center, or a school and then the military would build it and give it to the community. The military might go to the community elders with a request to provide some labor, but most times little community participation was expected. The military essentially did the work for the community, delivered a finished product, and got all the credit. However, the communities frequently felt that the project was a gift and expected the military or the Ministry of Public Works to do whatever maintenance work might be necessary, since after all, it was not their own project.

Community development meant working with the community to help it identify what its needs are and provide assistance once the community commits its own resources for construction, orga-

nizes itself to carry it out, and agrees to provide on-going community support to maintain it. The critical difference was community organization and developing a sense of local ownership for the
project. The military didn't like the concept. They wanted the power to remain in their hands and viewed community development as
a threat to the civic action power base.

I spent hours in discussions with President Barrientos in our
late night meetings talking about the long-term implications for
the development of the country and building the capability of rural
people to help themselves. I would remind him of the shortage of
funds in the national budget and of the thousands of small projects
that were needed in rural areas to create the socioeconomic conditions needed for real long-term progress. One night, he reluctantly
agreed to let the community development program move forward,
but he stressed that he really preferred civic action.

In 1964 and 1965, on the Altiplano, we had found that Peace
Corps and USAID working together could bring solid results.
During the severe freeze of 1964, most of the potato crop had been
lost, except in one village where a Peace Corps volunteer had shown
a young villager a USAID-developed planting system that protected potato buds from the frost. The village elders were furious with
the Peace Corps volunteer and ran him out of the village for dese-
crating the age-old Aymara potato-planting practice. When the annual freeze came, it was more intense than normal and the village
lost its crop, except for that planted by the young man as taught by
the Peace Corps volunteer. Word spread rapidly across the Altiplano. Villagers came to see for themselves, and planting the following
year throughout the Altiplano applied the new planting system.
The 1965 crop flourished in spite of another hard freeze. The Peace
Corps volunteer had succeeded after years in which Bolivian technicians could not convince skeptical *campesinos*.

The second experience emerged out of the sheep-shearing project spearheaded by Utah State. Peace Corps volunteers in the villages were natural allies in helping *campesinos* learn how to shear
sheep, take care of the wool, and put the villagers in contact with
the cooperative marketing mechanism created by USAID. The wool
brought new cash resources to the countryside.

Every month, in my office, the director of the Peace Corps,

Gino Baumann, the Bolivian government program director, Major Ramirez, a group of Peace Corps volunteers, and USAID technical advisers met to monitor the implementation of the community development program. Gino and I took turns chairing the meeting, but we drew up the agenda together.

One of our first major problems was how to react to the community requests for projects. Bolivian government and U.S. technicians really wanted to set the priorities for the communities. David, Gino, and I, supported by most Peace Corps volunteers, believed that the program should respond to the priority defined by the villagers. We believed that the villagers had little reason to trust us—they had been repressed by governments for centuries, and why should they see us as any different? We had to gain their confidence. So, when several villages indicated that their top priority was a soccer field, David, Gino, and I approved building soccer fields. And then we went back to the community and asked, "What's next?"

The initial projects quickly sold the ministers of Agriculture and Education on the program. I systematically informed the ministers of Finance and Economy about the program's potential for promoting growth and integrating rural communities into the cash economy. Then, one night about eleven o'clock, the phone rang again. When I arrived at the president's house and we began sipping brandy, he said, "Irving, tell me about the community development program." After my explanations, he said he was committed to supporting it, and that he had told his trusted friend, Major Ramirez, that he understood the potential of the project to integrate the indigenous people into the political process.

The Not So Official Agenda

Ele's work with the wives' group continued to be a major contribution to the morale of the mission.

One of the Bolivians who always attended was Daisy Wende. She was not only the wife of former mission economist Ernesto Wende, but also the owner of one of the largest handicraft centers in the country. USAID had helped create *Artesanías Bolivianas* (Bolivian Handicrafts) in the early 1960s as part of a hemisphere-wide project by John Gallagher of Sears and Edward Marcus of Neiman-Marcus to promote marketing of Latin American handicrafts by providing technical assistance to artisans to increase production, develop quality controls, and improve delivery systems. Unfortunately, the production levels were not adequate to satisfy the demand in the mass markets of the more developed countries and the hemisphere-wide project imploded. USAID interest also died and it was decided to close *Artesanías Bolivianas*. Daisy made an offer to purchase it and the mission accepted.

Ele found out that Daisy was also a very talented dress designer and had plans for a number of special creations based on unique Altiplano patterns using Bolivian cloth. Daisy was invited to talk at one of the wives' meetings about her plans. The reception was enthusiastic and Daisy was invited to put on her first fashion show in our living room. Several wives agreed to be models. I was unable to attend the first fashion show by a Bolivian designer in the history of Bolivia, but rave reviews were heard all over the city. The major newspapers covered the event. The diplomatic community wanted a repeat. After the second fashion show, Daisy was invited to make presentations in Berlin, New York, and Miami as well as in neighboring countries. Daisy always said that it was Ele who gave her the courage to make her dream come true.

Ele also said no more black-tie dinners and proposed instead an annual barbecue in our garden. Since June is the winter season in La Paz, with the shortest days of the year, Ele chose to celebrate the barbecue at the end-of-winter, in early August.

Through friends at the German Embassy, she had located a slaughterhouse that prepared delicious smoked pork chops, and through a Bolivian friend she found a butcher who had some of the best, tastiest, and most tender beef in the country. She also took up an offer by the head of the U.S. Air Force mission to fly in hot dogs and hot dog buns from the commissary in Panama. She arranged to set up a barbecue pit in our yard to roast pork and beef. She had Eduarda prepare potato and other salads. She arranged for the brewery to deliver a keg, and set Zenovio up with an open bar. She decorated the garden and invited more than three hundred Bolivian, diplomatic, and country team members.

It was a great success. Vice President Adolfo Siles Salinas, almost all of the ministers, most of the diplomatic corps, Bolivian businessmen, and all of our American official colleagues and families attended. The top menu choice was the mighty hot dog from the Canal Zone. We had enough steaks and pork chops left to fill our freezer for some time. For weeks after the barbecue, wherever we went, Bolivians, diplomats and co-workers told us how much they had enjoyed themselves. The barbecue opened many doors for USAID, especially in the government and business community that had been closed before. Ele repeated the barbecue the next year, and we were transferred before we could hold our third in 1968.

One of the guests at the barbecue was Father Walter, who told me that the Canadian Fathers at Catavi thought the time had come to try to reopen a dialogue between the miners and USAID. The mine union was aware of the declining quality of the ore and the need to find alternative sources of employment for their members, a subject that I had broached in the not-so-successful meeting a year earlier. But the mine union leader did not want to talk to me, but rather with some other member of USAID. I consulted the ambassador, and we agreed to send the USAID Program Officer John Blumgart. We briefed him carefully before he went off on the following Friday for a meeting on Saturday.

John returned Sunday afternoon and called me to report. I asked him to delay his report until we could meet in the office Monday morning. But John persisted in spite of my continually saying, "John, wait until tomorrow morning." Finally John gave me the name of one of the union leaders who had talked with him. At which time, a third voice broke into the conversation to correct him! Well, we lived in Calacoto and our telephone exchange was an old fashioned model with about two hundred lines and was maintained twenty-four hours a day by an operator. Ele had long suspected that someone was listening in on her calls. So, we were always careful about anything we said on the phone. Now, I had clear proof that the operator, probably from one of the Bolivian intelligence services, was monitoring our calls. Monday morning I had to explain to John what had happened, and he agreed not to discuss substantive matters on the telephone.

As I pointed out earlier, everything that USAID or one of its senior staff did was the subject of conversation and often showed up in the local press. The ambassador and I frequently dealt with seemingly innocent occurrences that seemed to take on lives of their own. One such event took place after the opening of a branch of First National City Bank of New York in La Paz. USAID received orders from Washington that, in accordance with federal law, US-AID and embassy accounts had to be transferred from the Central Bank of Bolivia to the new branch. The USAID account of about US$16 million was the largest in the Central Bank, eclipsing the funds of the Bolivian government. The branch manager was John "Jack" Hennessy, later assistant secretary of the Treasury in the Nixon administration. The ambassador and I talked to Jack, and I met with the Central Bank president. Tensions ran very high when we finally set a date for the transfer.

The morning of the transfer, I received a call from the ministers of the Interior and Finance, formally protesting the transfer. They informed me that there had been a poker game in which U.S. Deputy Chief of Mission Bob Hurwich, USAID Controller Gene Barrett, and Bank Manager John Hennessy were among the players. They told me that their intelligence sources reported that part of Hennessy's winnings in that game was the transfer of the USAID account. I met with them at the Finance ministry and showed them the law and the instructions from Washington. They agreed that there was nothing improper and that the poker game had nothing to do with the decision. Nonetheless to avoid a recurrence, I asked the USAID controller to stop participating in the poker game.

Shortly after the barbecue, the embassy medical officer informed me that in September 1966, I would have completed sixteen months in the high altitude and that I had to take R&R. I said that I wasn't ready to take a break. He said that there was no waiver and that I should make plans to take altitude relief within six weeks.

So I went to see USAID Executive Officer Les Gottlieb to find out the options for our R&R. The government would provide Ele and me with tickets to one of several sea-level sites, including Miami, Panama, Rio, Buenos Aires, Lima and Santiago. We would receive per diem while traveling to and from our destination, but all expenses incurred while we were at our R&R site would be ordinary living expenses and not be reimbursed by the government.

That evening at home, I told Ele about our required R&R and the sites to which our airfare would be paid. She looked at me and said, "I've been to all of them. Going back would not be R&R for me." I gasped and in my usual initial reaction, "What do you mean? These are the sites that the government offers. Are you out of your mind?" I fumed and fussed, and she just sat and looked at me. After about ten minutes of my antics, she said, "Let me think about it. We will talk tomorrow night after we get home from our dinner party."

The following night when we arrived home and were getting ready for bed, she said very casually, "Well, I've done some thinking about the R&R. You know how much we loved Venice when we visited there in 1957? Why don't we take our R&R there? It's at sea level." I exploded, "We don't have the money right now to cover the cost. Think of the additional travel expenses and remember how expensive it was even then?" She just smiled and said, "Well, I talked to Les Gottlieb and the Pan Am agent today. The government will allow us to apply the cost of a trip to Miami to a longer flight, provided we use an American carrier. And Pan Am has offered us a great deal from La Paz to Rome and Venice for only a few hundred dollars more than the round-trip to Miami." She added that that we needed a change of pace, somewhere with different surroundings that would allow us to forget about the day-to-day pressures of the job. "Isn't that one of the objectives of an R&R?"

So I told Les that we were going to take R&R in Venice. He just looked at me as if he already knew more than I did.

The following evening we had dinner at the ambassador's, and Mrs. Henderson asked about our plans for R&R. I told her that we were going to Venice. She said, "A second honeymoon?" I guess I blushed. At home that night, Ele smilingly said to me, "Now we've decided on Venice, why don't we add Greece? You know how much you have always wanted to see the Parthenon? Pan Am offers a special deal if we add Athens to the ticket. You see, it's less than x dollars more." I am a creature of habit and I exploded once again. She just sat looking at me, with that certain stare that asked me why I am being such an ass. It didn't take long for me to realize that this was a good idea. She let out a short sigh and said goodnight. So I advised Les to add Athens to the ticket.

The third night we came home from a cocktail party and sat down to a light supper. Ele then said, "As long as we're going to Venice and Athens, why don't we go on Istanbul? Pan Am will allow us to go there for almost the same price as the flight from Venice to Athens—and that's a great deal. Now let's have none of your hysterics tonight. Just say yes!" I sipped my quinoa soup and surrendered. When I told Les the next morning, he said that he thought we would.

We advised Washington that I would be on R&R in Europe for most of October 1966 and that David and Em would take over as acting mission director and acting deputy mission director. Washington authorized the R&R and the substitutions, and added that I was to report to Washington for consultations before returning to post. So I was routed: La Paz–Buenos Aires–Venice–Athens–Istanbul–Washington, but the government would pay for La Paz–Miami–Washington–La Paz. Les so advised Pan Am. With all arranged I called Ele and told her our travel plans were now in place.

When I got home that night, I found Ele had other wrinkle. Pan Am had told her that the cost of a flight home to La Paz through Tokyo and California was exactly the same as the flight from Istanbul to Washington to La Paz. She was going to leave me in Istanbul and continue on to Beirut, Tehran, Delhi, Bangkok, Hong Kong, Tokyo, Hawaii and California. My ticket from Istanbul would give me a night in London and then a flight to New York and Washington. I said nothing. I had been outfoxed and let Ele glory in her coup. When I told Les the next morning, he said, "Yes, I know. I helped a bit."

When R&R came, we flew to Buenos Aires and stopped over in our favorite hotel, the Gran Hotel Dorá on Avenue Maipú. We had friends at the embassy who met us at the airport and took us to dinner. Pan Am advised us that it had no flight that day to Rome and that it had routed us on Alitalia. So, before going to bed I checked our Alitalia flight time for the following day. I was told that the plane had not yet left Rome and that it might be a few hours late. Thursday morning, the embassy advised us that the plane was still in Rome, and later that the flight would be delayed until Friday. We were really getting tense. Another friendly embassy couple took us home to dinner. The hostess made a couple of calls to Alitalia that night, and found that the plane was still in Rome.

Friday morning, the scene looked very bleak when the travel officer at the embassy called to tell us that she had arranged through

Pan Am to get us a reservation on Lufthansa that afternoon. We had to be in the airport in no more than one-and-a-half hours. With traffic and the distance, we had to leave immediately. A station wagon from the embassy would be at the Gran Dorá in fifteen minutes. We threw all our things in our suitcases, and I rushed down to pay the bill. We loaded up and went on the wildest ride of our lives. Ele was finishing packing as we lurched and weaved through traffic. I, the worrywart, thought that we wouldn't arrive on time. But we did, and were met at the Lufthansa counter by a most gracious clerk who said that they were waiting for us and had made arrangements with passport control to facilitate our boarding since we had diplomatic passports. At 2:00 p.m., we were ensconced by the window in two comfortable cabin seats, sipping a much-needed scotch.

The Lufthansa flight was wonderful. We arrived in Venice about nightfall, and it was raining. We had no hotel reservations, so Ele went to the tourist office and, with her luck, found us a room in a lovely hotel down the street from the Hotel Danieli on the Grand Canal that had just become available. We boarded the *vaporetto* (water bus) that took us to the landing just in front of the hotel and we were installed for five days.

We had a memorable time. Although it rained quite a bit, we visited every corner of the lagoon by *vaporetti*, visiting the Lido, Burano, Murano, and just about every other island. We leisurely enjoyed every church, museum, and art gallery and strolled the back streets. When we got lost, I used Spanish to find my way back; most of the Venetians thought I was speaking a strange dialect. The rain kept the crowds down and gave us much more time to explore the glories of St. Mark's and the Doge's Palace. We walked the Bridge of Sighs almost alone. We ate at little restaurants on the back streets and had our drink at Harry's bar.

It was still drizzling when we headed back to the airport for our flight to Athens. We were delighted to see bright sunshine as we approached the Athens airport. The embassy had made reservations for us at the Athens Hilton where we had an elegant room with a terrace overlooking the Parthenon. It was a magical sight when we came up from dinner with a full moon shining on that incredible ancient monument. The Alitalia debacle caused us to shorten our stay in Athens by one day, and Ele also canceled her stopover in

Beirut to make her scheduled meeting with friends in Tehran. Pan Am took wonderful care of us, and moved up my departure date from Istanbul to Washington.

So, we had just four days in Athens, and tried to take advantage of every minute. Day one we went on the pilgrimage to the Parthenon and endured the steep climb to wander around the foundations of Western civilization. The second day, we savored Athens and the antiquity museums. The third day we took a tour of Corinth and ancient Sparta. Our fourth day, we went to Piraeus and took the cruise out to Mykonos and neighboring islands. The four days flowed by so fast, and each vista of that rugged land delighted us. Each night after dinner we would sit on our balcony and drink in the beauty of the Parthenon by moonlight.

Istanbul was a short flight to another world. What an enchanting cosmopolitan city! Again, the embassy booked us at the Hilton and we had a comfortable room but very little view. We took a tour of the city and saw Topkapi Palace, St. Sophia, the old city, the bazaar, and the vistas of the Dardanelles. We rode the ferry to Asia, our first encounter with the world's largest continent. A friend who was the U.S. consul general treated us to a ride on the U.S. consulate's boat and we saw the waterfront from a unique angle. Since we had only allowed three days for our visit, it seemed to be over before it began.

We left for the airport early Sunday morning. We checked in at the Pan Am counter: Ele to Tehran and I to London and Washington. We did not see each other for almost six weeks.

Ele's flight was much more dramatic than mine. As the plane approached Tehran, the pilot announced that they could not land because of a typhus epidemic and that the Iranian authorities had advised Pan Am to continue on. The result was that Ele arrived in Delhi two days earlier than planned, at 3:00 a.m. in a darkened, almost abandoned airport. Ele and a lady from Atlanta, Georgia, found themselves at the Pan Am counter at about four in the morning with nowhere to go. Ele made a ruckus, Pan Am arranged for reservations for both ladies at a gracious old colonial hotel and sent them there in a Pan Am vehicle. The hotel, Ele described, was a vision from a Kipling story, with large, high-ceilinged corridors, rattan furniture, and large ceiling fans. She was escorted to her suite about 5:00 a.m., where a bearer had prepared a bath and left tea by the bedside. Mosquito netting covered the large Victorian style bed. She slept until noon, and when she began to stir, the bearer, who apparently had kept guard since her arrival, asked if he should bring her tea and biscuits. She called the Atlanta lady, and they had a light lunch and decided to rest for the remainder of the day. Ele called the embassy to make contact with Dr. Carl Nydel, who had been recently transferred to India from Bolivia as the regional medical officer. The Nydels were Ele's hosts for the rest of her visit to India. Ele explained her early arrival and Carl arranged for her to move the next morning to the air-conditioned Embassy-AID guesthouse that had none of the charm of the hotel, but its air-conditioning made living in the heat much easier.

Her stop-over included a visit to the Taj Mahal in its entire splendor. When she showed her slides to us in La Paz, she commented that the poverty surrounding it, with the emaciated children and the beggars, eclipsed the beauty of the building. Ele found India fascinating, especially the markets, the jewelry, the curries, and the saris. But the stark contrast between opulence and poverty made a greater impression on her and colored her perspective on the country.

Then she flew on to Bangkok where the wife of an agricultural adviser whom we had known in El Salvador met her at the plane and served as her guide. Ele stayed in a lovely garden hotel on the river. Her friend took her on tours of the city and countryside, and she did a lot of strolling on her own and found the jewelry and textile shops much to her liking. Over the years, whenever we got into conversation with friends about the trip, she would contrast the beauty and lushness of Thailand to the somber reddish-brown landscape around Delhi.

Next came Hong Kong, and she was on her own. The consulate had reserved a room for her at the Peninsula Hotel, and she was enthralled at its colonial elegance and service. The shopping was just beside the hotel and the ferry to Kowloon just across the street. She took the ferry across Hong Kong Bay and took the funicular up to the top of the hill that provides magnificent view of the harbor. She went on a special tour to Aberdeen because of her Scottish roots and rode the railway up to the Communist Chinese border. Ele resolved to revisit Hong Kong whenever the opportunity arose.

In Tokyo, Ele scheduled her time around visits to handicrafts centers, the Imperial Gardens, a Geisha ceremony, and a kabuki theater presentation. She took the fast train to Kyoto, saw Mount Fuji, and attended a class on flower arranging. She tried seaweed for breakfast, raw fish, sushi, and tempura. All too soon, she was back at the airport en route to Honolulu.

That was her first visit to the Islands. Pan Am got her a room at the Surf Rider Hotel, overlooking Diamond Head. She took a couple of tours and fell in love with the beauty and pace of life. Two days later she returned to California for a short visit with my mother in San Francisco, and then three weeks in Tulare with her mother, overseeing the marketing of the crops and reviewing the accounts from the South Dakota and California farms. She returned to La Paz for Thanksgiving.

I left Istanbul for London several hours after Ele had begun her round-the-world adventure. Pan Am had arranged for a businessman's hotel for me near Marble Arch. I arrived about dinnertime and asked if any theater tickets were available that night. The only performance that Sunday night was at the Palladium, where after a fish and chip dinner, I saw Pearl Bailey belt out, "Won't you come home, Bill Bailey." About midnight, I found myself lost near Marble Arch, and a London couple took pity on me and walked me back to my hotel. That was the end of my R&R.

When I arrived in Washington, the mood was somber. Vietnam had enveloped the Latin American Bureau. The AFP was no longer a priority on the Seventh Floor of the State Department, much less in the AID front office where the autonomy given the Alliance for Progress was never popular. Assistant Secretary Tom Mann, had become deputy secretary of state for Economic Affairs, and my five-minute "hello" with him was sandwiched in between two high-level policy meetings. Jim Fowler had taken over as deputy coordinator for the Alliance, but he expected to be reassigned to a post involving Vietnam. Ray Sternfeld and his deputy Dick Breen reviewed with me the reformed Bolivian program. They warned me that money was tight, with large transfers of funds from Latin America to Vietnam in the new budget guidelines. I had a short appointment with the new assistant secretary of state, Covey Oliver, whom I had come to know when he was ambassador to Colombia.

I had lunch with Jack Vaughn, now director of the Peace Corps, and his aide, Margaret "Lefty," who was later to become his wife; they understood better than anyone in the hierarchy what we were trying to do in Bolivia, but warned me that Vietnam was now top priority in Washington—over all other items on the domestic and foreign policy agenda—to prevent the falling dominos.

Back to Work

On my return to La Paz, the ambassador brought me up to date on the political scene, but did not tell me about the intelligence reports that Che Guevara was in the country. With David and Em, we analyzed developments and problems, project by project. Gene and Les gave me a detailed report on our finances, the flow of funds by project, and any red flags that required immediate attention. The program and capital development officers briefed me on progress and problems. The following day I met with each of the division chiefs and Gino Baumann of the Peace Corps. Within a couple of days, it was as if I had never been on R&R.

David and Em had maintained the same schedule of meetings with ministers and division chiefs. They had astutely resolved all the issues that had arisen in my absence, and there were none for me to fret about. Some changes had occurred: Clark Ballard went back to Utah State to become the vice president of the university, and economist Roberts replaced him as chief of the Utah State team. Dr. Holmes and the San Jose State team had worked out a schedule of teacher training programs for different levels of elementary and high school teachers. Dr. Holmes reported that several films on reading, grammar, and arithmetic designed to supplement classroom teaching had to be revised to overcome some technical and human glitches: for example, indigenous children wouldn't look at the screen whenever the instructor looked directly at the camera, for fear that the teacher would steal their souls. Chuck Shirley reported that heavy rains and flooding were inhibiting progress on road building. These were the operational problems that we faced week in and week out when implementing projects.

The closing months of 1966 were quite productive. We were getting much better data on farm production, marketing, and agriculture lending because of the new programs developed by Utah State. Utah State had also acquired breeding pairs of llamas and alpacas for research at its U.S. campus, and the research was already providing significant new information about the animals, their reproductive patterns, and measures to raise their fertility rates. Reports from school principals were positive about results in the classroom from the teacher training courses. School building in rural areas was on schedule. Repair of the Cochabamba–Santa Cruz road was progressing well. Romero Loza reported that he was pleased with the new procedures installed at the ministry of Finance and the Central Bank. Even so, there were many operational problems to be resolved.

When Ele returned a few weeks later, we joined the Lazars and other friends at one of the late night cafes in downtown La Paz where Andean and flamenco music was played while we sipped Andean liquors, *chicha*, or strong coffee. Ele sighted a fabulous painting of a devil dancer. She was captivated and offered to buy it. The artist was a young Peruvian, and he needed money. We bought it then and there. Someone nearby said, "The American bought the painting. Now (the artist, whose name I don't remember) can join Che." I thought nothing more about it until Ele reminded me some weeks later.

Ele shortly thereafter was elected president of the *Damas Diplomáticas*, and was invited in early January 1967 to play bridge at the home of one of the Bolivian members. During one of games, the ladies, talking in Spanish, commented that the number of planes flying over La Paz had increased. Another lady chimed in, "I think they are planes dropping weapons for Che. You know he is in the country somewhere."

Ele told me that night of the comment and I reported it to the ambassador first thing the following morning. He treated the comment lightly, saying, "We know exactly where he is." When I told Ele that the ambassador had not seemed impressed by the report, she was not convinced. She said, "Henderson did not say that Che is not in Bolivia."

A couple of weeks later, in late January or early February, I had an appointment to visit the rector of the University of Sucre to discuss possible collaboration in the teacher training program with San Jose State and the agricultural program of Utah State. The discussions were amicable and the university was prepared to cooperate but would be unable to cover any costs; it would cooperate if USAID covered all the costs, including professors' salaries and sprucing up the classrooms.

That evening, as I returned to my guest room at the Central Bank building, I was told that President Barrientos had arrived earlier that day and was in his suite on the top floor. After dinner, about 8:00 p.m., one of the president's aides knocked on my door and invited me to join the president for a brandy. As the president started to ask about my day, an aide came in and whispered something into his ear. Barrientos told me that a delegation of *campesinos* wanted to talk to him and asked me to go into a side room. For the next hour, I heard snatches of conversation in Quechua. When they left, Barrientos told me that the *campesinos* were upset by people on a nearby property who were "playing" at soldiers and talking to them about being proletarians when they had titles to their lands. The president gave orders for an army patrol to see what was going on and made a comment about smugglers operating in the region.

When I got back to La Paz the following day, the news broke that Che was in the country and that he was in Chuquisaca, the region where the *campesinos* lived. I have never been sure whether I lived a bit of history or whether the incident had been staged. I later learned that U.S. and Bolivian intelligence had information shortly after Ele and I had left on R&R that Che was somewhere in the Sucre-Chuquisaca area, but I am not sure that they had pinpointed the precise location. I know that shortly after my Sucre trip, President Barrientos and Ambassador Henderson flew to Texas to meet with President Johnson at his ranch, and that President Johnson agreed to provide US$5 million to the Bolivian Army to track down Che. Whatever the truth may be, that was a unique night in Sucre.

For what it is worth, I never believed that Che's target was Bolivia. He may have called his small force the "Bolivian Liberation Army;" however, from his choice of a base of operations and the tactics he used with the *campesinos*, I always believed that he was setting up a base in Bolivia to launch a take-over of his native land, Argentina. He knew of the political split between the Stalinists and Trotskyites in Bolivia and the odds for one or the other supporting him. I think he also knew that of all the high valley *campesinos* in Bolivia, none was more independent-minded than those in Chuquisaca since most of them had already received titles to the land they farmed. As adroit as he was in revolutionary tactics, I believe that he chose a locale where he could assemble and train his cadre at a base camp not too remote from the Argentine border and then, following the route of the Incas, penetrate Jujuy and Tucumán to take over his homeland.

21

Administering the Bolivian Program

Being away from La Paz on R&R had been no great concern for me. USAID was the hands of two excellent colleagues, David Lazar in charge and Em Melaven as his right hand man. David, Em, and I worked as a team as we designed the new USAID strategy. They moved ahead during my absence. I came back to La Paz full of energy.

An essential part of our long-term strategy was to change the image of USAID from the central contributor to the Bolivian national development program to just one of the international and bilateral donors committed to supporting it. The perception for a decade had been that the U.S. was not only the primary source of financial and technical support for the development program, but also the strategic planner and decision-maker. We made every effort to identify each USAID program and project as part of the plan of the Bolivian government while giving due credit to the U.S. for our contribution to the government's development plan.

We saw our job as helping to build the government's capability to do its own planning and design its own programs. We tried to emphasize to the government the need for changes in structures and policies and tried to avoid personalizing them. Our objective was to help them identify and overcome weaknesses in the public sector on terms that they understood and through measures they were capable of implementing. For a government with limited financial and technical resources, making such changes is not an easy or smooth process.

David, Em, and I could not do the day-to-day work with the ministries and in the field. We had to rely on our USAID colleagues to work with their counterparts to set the tone and define the image through day-to-day working relationships. We relied on them to alert us when we should meet with a minister and other key government personnel to resolve specific policy issues or deal with a bottleneck in project execution. When we met with ministers and government technicians, we tried to talk about their objectives and plans of action, and to link relevant USAID activities to them.

Building up the public perception of the development effort as an initiative of the Bolivian government did not mean that we were prepared to fund or support every proposal presented to us by the Bolivian authorities. We carefully reviewed each proposal. We recognized the financial crunch that the government faced and tried to help where our aid made sense. One principle that we never overlooked was that USAID funds would never be used for a project designed to do political favors or support a boondoggle. We were frequently confronted by some scheme or other to get USAID funds for someone's pet project. Usually, David, Em, or I would see a red flag and find some quiet behind-the-scenes techniques for killing a proposal—often through the minister of Finance or the minister of Agriculture.

Running a Mission Is Not Easy

The operating problems in 1966 and 1967 were tough. David, Em, and I were under pressure every day. The division chiefs were constantly receiving requests to provide resources. The availability of U.S. input for a given activity was frequently out of sync with operating timetables. Sometimes the quality of the equipment funded by USAID and provided by U.S. suppliers was defective. Often the counterpart technicians or funding agreed to by the Bolivian government came up short. In these situations, David played the bad cop; Em oversaw the internal operation of the Mission, and they allowed me to be the good cop.

Through all our problems, the one constant source of support was Minister of Finance José Romero Loza and his deputy, Jorge Jordán. The minister was focused on raising government revenues, modernizing fiscal management, and upgrading the technical quality and availability of government services to and for the people.

We talked out our disagreements and made many adjustments in our respective plans and operations, and we maintained an open and comprehensive dialogue.

The pressure on USAID to be the lender of last resort did not go away whenever the Agricultural, Mining, or Industrial Banks ran short of funds or when COMIBOL needed working capital. The minister and vice minister understood the rationale for our position not to be that lender, and we opened discussions on how the Central Bank should be reformed to define monetary policy and ensure liquidity in the economy—precisely the policies and practices that IMF had been urging on prior governments. We assigned Phil Fawcett, USAID's banking adviser, to work with Jorge Jordán to design the framework for a reorganized Central Bank, with rediscounting windows.

It took most of 1967 for them to develop an acceptable plan. As part of that plan, USAID agreed that repayments of those U.S. loans payable in local currency, especially from the sales of PL 480 wheat, become the initial source of funding for the rediscounting facility. We explored new income sources for the Central Bank to fund the facility, including the restoration of the national tax on real property that had been abolished after the Revolution of 1952.

The minister moved forward as quickly as politically feasible. He took great care to get the full support of President Barrientos before he acted. When Jorge Jordán was named president of the Central Bank, the plan was approved and we signed the agreement on the use of the designated repayments of U.S. local currency loans. On new tax revenues, especially the property tax, President Barrientos decided that he needed to build up political support for it before he sent it to congress.

At the same time, the other sectors of the USAID program demanded constant attention. One crisis arose over equipment purchased under an AID loan for a road maintenance project. The equipment delivered by the U.S. manufacturer was defective and heavy pressure was required to get it to replace that equipment.

Another crisis arose when a flood destroyed a key bridge in construction of the new highway from Cochabamba through the Chapare Valley to Santa Cruz. Unlike the hazardous mountain route that traditionally linked the two cities, the new highway was on a level plain. A big ceremony was planned to commemorate the completion of the bridge and USAID funding to complete the highway. Then came the news of torrential rains, extensive flooding, and the sweeping away of all but the two towers of the suspension bridge. Engineers working on the feasibility study for the remaining stretch of the road radioed in from treetops that they needed urgent help. David and I had to wrestle with whether this flood was a predictable disaster or was it a hundred-year event. We sent the chief engineer to take a look, and he reported that the damage was catastrophic and that local residents reported that the rivers had crested at the same levels several times in their lifetimes. The U.S. engineering firm constructing the bridge advised us that its insurance would cover most of the rebuilding. So, we recommended to Washington that rebuilding the bridge be authorized, but that new road construction be delayed pending further study of the flood threat. Engineers came down from Washington, and after field inspections, agreed with our recommendation.

Another road project caused us much concern after the inauguration of Barrientos. When I called on the new Foreign Minister Alberto Crespo, the father of our ex-USAID economist Jorge, he presented me with a copy of an agreement signed at the beginning of World War II in which, in return for exclusive U.S. access to Bolivian tin production during World War II, the United States agreed to finance the building of two trunk highways uniting the country. The first was the main east-west trunk highway linking La Paz, Cochabamba, and Santa Cruz, which the U.S. carried out. The second was a highway south-southeast linking Bolivia's two capital cities, La Paz and Sucre, through the mining region and down to a potential new source of petroleum in Camiri, southeast of Sucre. The foreign minister proposed that we open negotiations on the financing for the second road.

When I returned to my office, I consulted the ambassador, who had known of the agreement but thought that the Bolivian government had set it aside. We decided to make a preliminary engineering study of a possible route over some of the most formidable mountainous terrain in the country and its potential cost. That study reported that building a highway would be a major engineering feat, involving scores of tunnels and bridges as the terrain drops precipitously from the Altiplano to the tropical lowlands and that the cost was in the range of US$3 to US$5 billion, well beyond the scope of U.S. financing planned for Bolivia. We consulted the ambassador about how to say "no" to the Bolivian government and were weighing the options when President Barrientos shuffled his cabinet and named a new foreign minister. The new foreign minister never raised the matter again.

A recurring, time consuming task was reminding ministers of their commitments to match U.S. aid with their budget resources. One of the most difficult problems kept arising with the Ministry of Public Works on road maintenance. A large USAID loan covered the purchase of needed equipment and training for construction workers. The Bolivian government pledged an adequate budget for maintenance and personnel. Unfortunately, with the continuing budget deficit, the mission had to constantly remind the minister of Finance—and sometimes even President Barrientos—that the budget of the Ministry of Public Works had to include the agreed-upon funds. And, then, all too often remind the minister of Public Works that he should not use the maintenance budget to respond to political pressures for constructing some other project.

One of the most difficult issues was the negative attitude of Bolivian officials, including the military, toward the private sector. We found existing policies and regulations were rooted in colonial tradition and practices under which all private activity was strictly controlled by the Spanish Crown, with licenses and permits required to legally engage in production, services, and trade. It favored monopolies and public officials expected to share in the profits and receive under-the-table favors. The corruption associated with the licensing process pervaded the colonial and republican history of most Latin American countries.

We felt that the 1952 revolution gave the government a unique opportunity to transform traditional practices. The government had an opportunity to earn the trust of post-feudal *campesinos* by opening up the legal and economic systems to serve their needs. That included rapid distribution of titles to the land they had occupied, so they could operate as private farm entities and provide them access to credit and create private sector production and marketing businesses that they could own cooperatively or individually. New government policies and licensing practices were needed for this to happen.

David and I would introduce the importance of such changes with key ministers by advising them of reports we had received of delays in obtaining a government license from his ministry. The response was usually that they would look into the matter. After months of work, we convinced the minister of the Economy to liberalize government-wide regulations on the private sector; David and I were working with him on the text when he was dismissed in a cabinet shuffle. So, we had to start all over again.

David and I also worked with the Industrial Bank to foster a more favorable environment for the private sector. USAID had been the moving force in establishing the bank, loaned it funds for its initial working capital, and provided technical assistance needed in its internal review of loan requests and by bank clients on accounting, management, and production problems. We coordinated with the bank president strategies and specific approaches to streamlining bureaucratic practices and identifying incentives for small entrepreneurs.

Our work was complicated by the decision of the president to change his cabinet every six months or so; the only holdovers were his key allies: the minister of Finance, the minister of Agriculture, the minister of Public Works and the minister of the Interior. At one of my late night sessions with President Barrientos, I raised the difficulties we were having, and he calmly reminded me that he had told me to work with the minister of Finance.

The Community Development Incident

The Community Development Program (CD) had become a USAID priority. When Jack Vaughn became director of the Peace Corps, replacing Sargent Shriver, he advised Gino Baumann, the Peace Corps chief in Bolivia, and me that he supported the cooperation of Peace Corps and USAID in implementing the Community Development Program. Gino and I met regularly and made field trips together to oversee field operations.

After one of our monthly meetings on program developments, Gino stayed behind to talk to David and me about his concern that the principal USAID adviser was losing perspective and had chosen twelve Peace Corps volunteers as his "disciples" and that he was relying on the Peace Corps volunteers to communicate with his Bolivian colleagues and *campesinos* because his Spanish was so limited. The following day, I called him to my office and spelled out how important I considered the program to be. I urged him to stick to his technical role, watch his words and actions, and be more discreet in his dealings with both his Bolivian counterparts and the Peace Corps volunteers. I assured him that Gino, David, and I were in his corner, and would do everything possible to support the program.

I followed that office discussion with a visit to his home, where he was meeting with a group of Peace Corps "disciples." I told them of our support for their work and the need for them to recognize that CD was a Bolivian government program to which they were advisers. I also told them that President Barrientos was now personally interested and would be accompanying the Bolivian program director, Major Ramírez, on a visit to a community very soon.

The following week, President Barrientos did visit a community in which the people provided all the sweat equity to build a soccer field and the CD program provided the plans and equipment. The community was so pleased that the elders had decided on a second project: a two-room school building and a house for the teacher for which, they told the president, they were prepared to provide the land and all the labor. Barrientos was impressed. Unfortunately, this adviser commented in English to a newspaperman accompanying the president that he knew more about Bolivia than Barrientos and that the presence of the president was politicizing the CD program.

The following day, those comments were on the front page of several newspapers. The ministry of Foreign Affairs made known the government's displeasure. The same day, Gino advised David and me that the adviser's actions were causing ill feeling among those Peace Corps volunteers who were not his "disciples." In addition, his USAID deputy requested a transfer. Gino, David Lazar, and I reached the conclusion that we had to send the adviser home. When I told the ambassador our conclusion, he was distressed because, like me, he thought highly of his work, but agreed to support the decision. We called Washington and arranged for the adviser to be reassigned to Washington as soon as possible. He left by the end of the week.

But that was not the end of the affair. We continued the program at full speed with two other USAID officers, both Peace Corps graduates. However, the "twelve disciples" and the adviser contacted U.S. senators and accused me of taking arbitrary disciplinary action. Washington called me up to meet with the senators to explain the reasons for my action.

When I arrived in Washington, Jack Vaughn called me to his office where he offered to join me on the Hill if necessary. He offered to make Gino's reports available to any interested senator and made some calls in support of our decision. I spent four days meeting senators and everyone agreed with my decision. The one meeting that most concerned me was with Senator Bobby Kennedy. When I reached his office, I was greeted by his chief of staff, Frank Mankiewicz, whom I had met several times when he was Peace Corps chief in Peru. He immediately put me at ease and told me that the senator had received several letters from the "disciples," had talked with Jack Vaughn about the issue, and found no fault with the action. Frank then called around to the chiefs of staff of several other senators, explained what had happened and then told me that I need make no further appointments. I never heard from the senate again but for many years when I met some of the "disciples," I was often accused of not having treated the adviser fairly.

The Suit by *Ex-Servicio* Employees

There were other personnel issues throughout the year as David and I began to trim the staff. We eliminated several proposed new positions and those changes required lengthy discussions with the division chiefs. We also had two disciplinary cases in which we had to send technicians home. Each case required discussion with the affected employee, written warnings, and justifications for the disciplinary action.

The most time consuming and complex issue involved the Bolivian technical and administrative personnel who had been employed by the Agriculture, Public Health, and Education *servicios*. They had enjoyed relative job security and never missed a payroll even during political upheavals. When the *servicios* were terminated, they sued USAID for termination benefits under the Bolivian Labor Code provision that any substantial change in conditions of employment in the public or private sector was considered a termination and the affected employee was entitled to a termination benefit.

AID had included in the agreements to close the *servicios* that all the employees would continue to be employed by the Bolivian government with no loss of seniority or other perks and that there had been no change in the employment situation of ex-*servicio* staff. The AID legal office was assured by the ministry of Foreign Affairs that the government would oppose the suit on behalf of the U.S. government and USAID, and interpose the defense of sovereign immunity. When the Labor Court heard the cases, the ministry made no defense, arguing that the Supreme Court of Bolivia was the proper instance to present the sovereign immunity defense.

Two Supreme Court justices advised me that the USAID case was on the court's docket on a given date. David alerted the senior AID lawyer in Washington that the matter would be before the court on that certain date and asked him to remind the ministry of Foreign Affairs, who reassured him of the government's commitment. In fact, no one from the ministry appeared before the court, and the court reaffirmed the judgment of the Labor Court that USAID should pay US$4.5 million in termination benefits. The embassy and USAID were not informed of the decision until it appeared in an official Supreme Court publication some weeks later.

Then came one Friday night when I was clearing my desk, I made one last check of the in-box and found a letter signed by the ministry of the Interior with an order for my arrest that very night, for me to be taken to the central prison, and held there until the judgment was paid in full. The ambassador had already left, so I called the DCM. When I told him my problem, he said that he was hosting a dinner for the minister of the Interior and that in fact the minister had already arrived. The minister claimed that he knew nothing about the order and told me that he would countermand it on Monday. However, since the date of my arrest was that day, he instructed me to go directly home and stay there throughout the weekend. He would immediately dispatch a squad of national police to my home to prevent those already instructed to arrest me from taking me off to the notorious central prison.

So, while my secretary called Ele to advise her of the drama, I filled my briefcase with work for the weekend and went straight home. I arrived shortly before a ten-man police squad arrived at our front gate. The officer in charge advised us that the minister had personally selected him and his squad to protect us for the weekend and to stay until further notice. He and his well-armed men took up posts surrounding the house and at the front gate. The siege had begun.

At slightly before midnight, the second detachment arrived to arrest me. Two police squads were facing each other with a look of utter consternation on the face of the officer in charge of the second squad. From the safety of the library window, Ele and I observed the discussion between the two officers. The second one smiled and threw up his hands, and peace was restored. At this point, our cook Eduarda arrived with hot breads for all of the policemen.

Squad No. 2 departed shortly thereafter. Not Squad No. 1! It was a most contented police unit. They slept and stood guard in four-hour shifts. Eduarda, Elsa, and Zenovio found places for each of them to sleep or rest. Eduarda prepared meals for them and Elsa set up a makeshift dining room on the side terrace. Zenovio arranged for the men to take hot showers between shifts. Sunday was normally their day off, but none of them would leave us alone that Sunday.

Monday morning I got up early. The police squad was still there, half of them on the side terrace enjoying a quinoa cereal breakfast. The officer in charge warned me that I could not leave until he received instructions from the minister—indeed it was clear that he and his men were hoping that he had forgotten about them and that they would become permanent wards of my household. Alas for them, the embassy security officer arrived at about 10:00 a.m. with an official of the ministry of the Interior to advise the officer-in-charge that I was a free man.

Ele and I, joined by Eduarda, Elsa, and Zenovio, wished them well when a vehicle arrived to take them back to the police station. Shortly thereafter, in a much more orderly household, I said my thanks to Ele, Eduarda, Elsa, and Zenovio, and departed for the office.

There are two postscripts to that "terrible" weekend. First, Eduarda, Elsa, and Zenovio got two days free the following week to compensate them for their valiant labors in defense of the household, and we gave them a few extra perks. The second postscript is that, several years after Ambassador Henderson, DCM Bob Hurwich, David, and I had left Bolivia, the U.S. government paid the judgment in full, but no one seemed to remember how the judgment was issued, or the grueling ordeal of "my weekend of house arrest."

Official Visitors

That year, 1967, was filled with Washington visitors and important social events, but no congressional delegations came up to the altitude. I had hoped Dante Fascell and Brad Morse would bring the Latin American Sub-Committee of the House Foreign Affairs Committee, but Bolivia at that time was not a priority. Our only congressional visitor was Senator Montoya of New Mexico who came to look into a tax problem. Ambassador and Mrs. Henderson hosted him, and Ele and I had a dinner party for him. One of the senator's long-time friends was USAID Deputy Executive Officer José de Baca, whom the ambassador assigned to be the control officer.

Our most important visitor was Assistant Secretary of State Covey Oliver, with whom I had worked when he was ambassador to Colombia. The three-day visit was treated by the Bolivian government as a state visit. Ambassador Henderson and the Foreign Office met several times to work out the protocol, the formal meetings, and the state dinner parties. My office was not included in most of the formalities, but we were advised that the assistant secretary was to be accompanied by his deputy for the Alliance for Progress, James Fowler. So Ele and I were included in many of the events, but not in the formal dinner hosted by President Barrientos.

Ele and I were part of the official party at the airport to receive the assistant secretary and his party. As the plane descended, we formed a formal line in which, according to protocol, Ele and I were practically at the end of the runway. The foreign minister and the chief of protocol stood next to Ambassador and Mrs. Henderson at the head of the line. An honor guard faced the receiving line and the army band was primed to play the two national anthems. The ceremony went off perfectly.

Covey Oliver made a warm statement in fluent Spanish that delighted the Bolivians. He spoke of our common interests and ended with a reference to the great range of mountains surrounding the airport, saying, "If the mountain can't come to Muhammad, Muhammad must come to the mountain."

When the ceremony ended, we drove to the embassy where the ambassador went over the proposed schedule with the assistant secretary. He explained that there were no significant festivities for the first night, just a small dinner with the foreign minister at the embassy. The following day involved a series of meetings with key government officials and the state dinner at the presidential palace. The last day would include meetings at the embassy with the members of the country team, followed by a dinner at the embassy in honor of President Barrientos and General Ovando. Ele scheduled a special costume party for the USAID staff and their spouses to meet Jim informally. Covey Oliver said that it sounded like fun and it was added to his schedule after the embassy dinner with President Barrientos ended.

Jim Fowler was our houseguest and we set up USAID briefings for him on the second and third days of his visit. Covey Oliver added the USAID briefings to his schedule on the second day. So both visitors were briefed and met with senior USAID officers. My secretary made a cake for the occasion and served coffee and cake while the assistant secretary and Jim talked informally with the USAID officers.

David and I escorted Jim to a meeting with the minister of Finance Romero Loza, who spelled out our working relationship in upgrading the government's capacity to set fiscal policy and collect revenues. The minister emphasized that most of the revenues came from sales and import taxes and that the ministry's machinery was still so underdeveloped that it was incapable of administering sophisticated taxes, like an income tax. He pointed out that the government was exploring the imposition of some form of property tax.

After the meeting with Romero Loza, David and I explained to Jim how we were trying to link reinstituting the national land tax to the completing the issuance of titles to the *campesinos* for the land they had occupied since the 1952 revolution. I told Jim that on a recent trip with President Barrientos to his hometown of Tarata near Cochabamba, he had me meet rural labor leaders and community elders to get their reaction to reinstating the land tax. The president questioned the union leaders about their priority needs. They told him, in a mixture of Quechua and Spanish, that their members wanted the titles to their lands and resources to improve their crops. When asked by a Bolivian official about paying a land tax, they were negative until the official suggested that the tax receipt would be a confirmation of a *campesinos* title to the land. They became very pensive and some nodded their heads. President Barrientos suggested that they consider the proposal.

I continued that shortly thereafter the president had invited me to join him in Sucre for a similar meeting with local rural leaders. The reaction was about the same. That afternoon, the president proposed that the matter of a land tax be discussed at the national conference of rural leaders scheduled for Oruro in early 1968.

Then, David and I went over the progressive expansion of the national community development program, which we believed could empower communities to help themselves deal with immediate problems and provide the machinery to enable them to draw on services available from the government. We drew a picture of building bottom-up organizations at the same time as the ministries of Agriculture and Rural Development were being equipped to respond to community needs. Above all, we stressed that we were trying to involve the Bolivians themselves in the process, and to de-emphasize the role of USAID.

The costume party the second night was a delight. Ele took over. In her elegant, aqua-colored, flower-festooned, silk muu muu, she greeted about a hundred guests for the evening in honor of Jim Fowler. Eduarda prepared a buffet supper and Zenovio rolled up the carpets to make a dance floor. Ele had masks for the guests. By the time Covey Oliver and the Hendersons arrived about 9:30 p.m., the party was in full swing—and they quickly joined the dancing. It was a great party!

The following morning, David joined Ele, Jim, and me on the trip back to the airport. The assistant secretary said that Jim had briefed him on the meeting with the minister and the discussion with David and me. He urged us to get a package together as soon as possible since 1968 was a U.S. election year and Vietnam was dominating the agenda in Washington.

The Job Is Not All Work

David, Em, and I worked long hours, many of them with the minister and vice minister of Finance. I had several late night invitations from President Barrientos to ask me about the details that the minister and the president of Central Bank, Jorge Jordán, were putting together. He kept asking, "Where's the money coming from?" I kept trying to say that the money would come if we could formulate a sound program proposal. I stressed that the formulation had to be Bolivian; it could not have a "made in USAID" label on it. I kept the ambassador informed, which was often uncomfortable for me because normally the only relationship with a president is through the ambassador or with the ambassador present.

The pressure was getting to me, especially at the high altitude. But some extraordinary friends entered our life to help me reduce the tension. They were Lois and Ed Faisan. They became the out-of-the-office balance I needed.

Ed was not a career AID employee. He had been an advertising executive and was on a two-year contract to advise on marketing and private sector development. He had an instinct for identifying production prospects and the creativity to put together packages from production to the market place. His USAID colleagues were production engineers, Eli Hill and Dick Plummer, who could work with small entrepreneurs to resolve technical operating and production problems. He and his colleagues worked closely with René Balliván, the president of the Industrial Bank, and frequently did the technical analysis the bank needed in its loan approval process.

Ed and I spent hours discussing job creation in urban areas, the impact of rural-to-urban migration, and the new settlements of rural migrants taking shape near La Paz's airport at El Alto. Those new residents needed jobs as well as basic health and sanitation services, and Bolivia needed programs to deal with those needs if it was to avoid the horrendous urban slum problems then confronting Lima, Rio, Buenos Aires, and São Paolo. Soon, we built a friendship beyond the office; Ed, his wife Lois, Ele, and I made trips together to the Altiplano to look over prospects and enjoyed informal lunches and dinners.

Then one Saturday, in mid-1966, just before we went on R&R, I just ran out of steam. Although Ele made Sunday our day at home, I usually worked most of the day. That Saturday, Ele told Ed that she was worried about my health; and Ed agreed. They conspired to force me to take a day off each week. Ed, with his doctorate in psychology, was one of those unique people who understood how to put someone at ease. Lois, like Ele, was warm and intelligent, with wide-ranging interests. From that day forward, we spent most of our Sundays with Ed and Lois, even though they had three youngsters waiting at home. Sometimes we discussed books and plays, or just talked. Those Sundays turned out to be my lifesavers and allowed me to regenerate my energies for the following week's work. With David as my alter ego at the office and friends like the Faisans, my job in 1966 and 1967—with all the stresses and pressures—was as good as it could get.

In addition to our Sunday days of R&R, Lois and Ed were always looking for something special that we might do. We occasionally went to a fair on the Altiplano or attended a Bolivian play. One Sunday, they proposed that we rent a Bolivian National Railway carriage for a week-long round-trip to Potosí and Sucre. Bolivia had nationalized the railroad in the mid-1960s, taking it over from its English owners. The railways were built in the late 1800s and linked the Pacific Ocean port of Arica with La Paz, Potosí, and Cochabamba, with an electric tramline to Sucre. The equipment was brought over from Britain, much of it second-hand.

With the Faisans and a couple from the U.S. Army mission, we rented the private car that the president of the former British owners used. It came with three bedrooms and baths and a kitchen, with a Bolivian cook to prepare our meals. Lois and Ele went to the market and bought food for the trip. What a thrill—a railway car of our own for seven days and a ride over the Altiplano at 13,000–14,500 feet and its magnificent Andean peaks!

When we arrived at the Central Station, we were escorted to a magnificent old car at the end of the train. It was decorated in

Victorian red and gold, with damask wallpaper. The back of the car was a sitting room, with windows all around and an observation platform on the end. The bedrooms were quite spacious with full sized beds. The small bathrooms were quaint; the toilets worked, the washstands did not. The kitchen at the end of the car consisted of a wood stove and some ceramic cookware. The cook was a pleasant young man, who assured us that he had cooked for the former English president of the railways for several years. He took the food we brought on with a quizzical look and commented that he usually bought the food supplies at the stations along the route and presented his bill on the return to La Paz.

The train pulled out of the station about midday, and tootled across the Altiplano to Oruro, and in late afternoon reached Lake Poopó, a shallow, saline body of water populated by thousands of pink flamingos; the lake is their breeding ground, and their brilliant color made for a stark contrast with the browns of the surrounding desert. As the train crossed the lake, the flamingos were all around us. Most of them were roosting and just looked over at the train as it passed. A few took flight. Truly spectacular!

The next day, we chugged our way up another 1,500 feet to Potosí. It was an engineering miracle. When we reached the Potosí station, our car was detached and we made our way to a hotel for our first bath in almost three days. Our railway car served as our hotel. The following day, we took the tram over the mountains and steep gorges that separate Potosí from Sucre, the ceremonial capital of Bolivia. Sucre, where in colonial times the mining barons of Potosi, settled their families, is the land of eternal springtime, situated at about 9,000 feet in a lush valley.

We had a dazzling day in Sucre. Friends met us at the station and took us to their gracious homes, many dating from the late eighteenth and nineteenth centuries, with walls covered with colonial religious paintings from the famous Potosí School. The verdant greens of Sucre contrasted sharply with the stark rocky outcrops of Potosí. In mid-afternoon, we were en route back to Potosí for another hot shower and then bed on our private car. Early the next morning, we were hooked up again to the train and began the trip back to La Paz.

For my birthday in 1967, the Faison's invited fifteen couples to a black tie dinner. Lois decided that we needed to rise above our mundane world and do something special. She hired the Israeli Club of Bolivia to cater the dinner. As we arrived, elegant cocktails and *hors d'oeuvres* were served. The menu in elegant calligraphy was at each place setting. As each course was served, the waiters descended on each table with the precision of a military tattoo. Dessert was a flambé that only entered the dining room after complete darkness. A birthday dinner I will always remember!

Of all the social events of 1967, one of the most enjoyable was our participation in a truly historic event: the first Catholic-Protestant wedding in the history of Bolivia conducted jointly by ministers of the two faiths in a Catholic Church. We were living in the sunlight created by Pope John XXIII and his opening for the unity of Christendom.

The occasion was the marriage of Teresa Camacho Omiste, our USAID secretary, to Charles Hull III of the U.S. Marine Corps at the embassy. Charles asked the ambassador and me to be his witnesses. Teresa named President Barrientos and her uncle, General Ovando, to be hers.

The wedding was in the Chapel of the Church of the Carmen. The altar was shared by a Catholic priest and a Presbyterian minister. It was a beautiful, traditional marriage, with the bride in an elegant white gown and the groom in full-dress Marine uniform. The reception was an assemblage of some of the most important figures in the government, and Ele and I were treated like a part of the extended family of the bride and groom. Teresa and Chuck have had a happy marriage. Chuck got his MBA from the University of Maryland and became a successful stockbroker. Teresa, now a widow, is a renowned painter and sculptress and remains a close friend.

Ele maintained a heavy schedule of her own. She met each new family assigned to USAID and kept me informed of family problems that needed USAID attention. She also hosted or participated in embassy teas and was elected president of *Damas Diplomáticas* in late September 1966, even though she was not the wife of an ambassador. When I got home that night, Ele announced that she now outranked me. She was now a president.

The Irving School

Ele joined me on several trips to project dedications around the country. We took advantage of an offer from Gulf Oil Company to visit its installations in the Santa Cruz and Camiri area, where Che was eventually cornered and killed. We attended sheep-shearing contests at Altiplano fairs and were judges at one. We participated in ceremonies at Cochabamba, Sucre, and Oruro to dedicate schools and water projects funded by USAID. We visited the Okinawan re-settlement project outside Santa Cruz.

One of the most exciting for us was in August 1967 when the government of Bolivia honored me by giving my name to a two-room rural school in Tacachira that was built under the community development program. The materials for the school were supplied by the program and the labor by the community and located next to the soccer field that had also been built under the program. The community had agreed to pay for the teacher, and the Utah Part-ners supplied blackboards, chairs, and supplies.

The community was about an hour from La Paz by helicopter, but three hours by road and burro. A delegation consisting of Ele, Ed Faison, Chuck Brady, Major Ramírez, my secretary Peggy, and me left La Paz on the paved road to a site where we were met by elders of the village and mounted on trusty burros for the two and one-half hour trek over boulders and sage. We arrived at Tacachi-ra shortly before noon, and the village was bedecked with bright-ly colored paper flags and elegant hand-woven textiles. Ele and I hugged all and were led to a small platform in front of the school. Then we heard a helicopter; President Barrientos joined us, and the celebration became even more animated. We had a lunch prepared by the community, with *empanadas, chuño, chicha,* and Andean mu-sic. Barrientos dedicated the school and said some very flattering things about my contributions to Bolivia. When the program end-ed, Barrientos invited Ele and me to fly back to La Paz with him in the helicopter. We gracefully declined and stayed on with the community until it was time for us to make the burro ride back to the cars.

The following day, the *Novedades* newspaper, an independent daily with a Christian Democratic bent and not usually supportive of the United States, published an article by its leading political analyst, Paulovich, entitled "USAID on Burro." He praised us for staying with the community until the end of the ceremony and turning down the president's invitation to return with him for the twenty-minute helicopter ride. My secretary, Peggy, framed the article, which today hangs on my home office wall. Most of us returning from five hours on burro back had sore thighs and rear ends for the next few days.

A Marketing System

On St. John's Eve 1967, the longest and usually coldest night of the La Paz year, I was invited by the mayor of La Paz to join him at the annual city bonfire imploring the gods to return the sun. At the ceremony, the mayor raised his interest in building a new wholesale market complex to replace the one that had grown up over the last century. The following week, I was invited by the minister of the Economy to meet with the mayor, the minister of Agriculture, and the president of the Central Bank to discuss the new La Paz market proposal. I took Ed Faison with me.

The proposal was for a five-story ultramodern building with state-of-the-art facilities for receiving, grading, moving, refrigerating, and storing produce. The presentation was impressive, and the bottom line was the request for AID financing. Ed Faison had briefed me on an AID regional contract with Michigan State on agricultural marketing. So, I suggested that we bring a team from Michigan State to review the proposal. A pall fell over the room until the president of the Central Bank, Jorge Jordán, reminded the others that the use of AID money, whether dollars or local currency, would require a feasibility study and that the Michigan State analysis would be a necessary component of such a study. The result was a request for a Michigan State team as soon as possible.

The team completed its work in record time and presented a concise, insightful report. It found that, with some changes in systems and procedures, the existing facilities would serve the needs of the farmers and urban consumers for the foreseeable future. It also noted that the farmers, who had been little more than serfs before the 1952 Revolution, were now aware of the prices in any marketplace within seven hours of their farms. Why seven hours? Because that was the time it took for them to walk behind their llamas or burros to get the crop to the marketplace. They were well informed about the pricing systems and standards. It further found that the small farmers usually received the lowest prices and had little or no bargaining power. Michigan State said that what was needed were better storage facilities in rural areas to help farmers secure better prices and a better transport system to move produce to market, not the five-story building in La Paz.

The report made the mayor quite unhappy but caught the attention of leaders of the rural workers union. President Barrientos had introduced me to several of them to discuss community development and the possible reintroduction of the national land tax. When the president arranged for me to meet with the union's executive committee in the late summer of 1967, I was asked questions about not only community development and the possible land tax but also the marketing study.

Shortly after the meeting, Ele and I were advised that we were scheduled to take our home leave in the U.S. in late August, and would return to Bolivia for another two-year tour. I was not eager to leave, but the ambassador thought it would be a good time to go since I would be back before Thanksgiving and since David and Em were in place to deal with program operations and prepare the loan and grant proposals that Covey Oliver and Jim Fowler had encouraged us to present.

Home Leave

When we left in late August on home leave, I planned to be back in country no later than October 1 in order to complete the negotiations with the Bolivian government on the loan and grant proposals. David, Em, and I spent several days charting the work to be done in my absence, and the three of us tried to talk with the minister of Finance and the president of the Central Bank. That was frustrated by other government priorities, including the insurgency that centered on Che Guevara. When I left, David and Em were still awaiting the call from the minister.

Ele and I flew to Rio to spend a long weekend with Norche and

Steward "Stu" Van Dyke, the USAID director in Brazil. He had just returned from consultations in Washington, and I wanted to get a feel from him about the environment there. He alerted me to a wholesale change in the leadership of the Alliance and his concern about its perception of the Alliance program.

The following Monday, we flew to St. Thomas for a few days of rest before heading to Washington. I was worn out, and Ele did not want me to take the medical exams at State before I had relaxed a bit. Ele always knew when I needed rest because my hearing would go down and I would begin to shout, rather than moderate my voice. Those few days of sun and rest at the Virgin Islands Hilton rekindled my energies. I can also report that Ele enjoyed the duty-free shopping.

We arrived in Washington on a Monday. I was told to report immediately to Mel Spector. He had a clear message for me: the State Department is recalling you from AID and your tour in Bolivia will be over next July. Second, you have been selected by Tom Mann and Covey Oliver to be the bureau's candidate for the 1968–69 Senior Seminar on Foreign Policy. They have placed your name on the list of potential ambassadorial candidates. Third, he said, US-AID Bolivia was due for some immediate changes in its top leadership: Emerson Melaven was to be transferred after three years in the altitude, and David Lazar was on a list of senior AID officials to be assigned to Vietnam.

Mel then confirmed what I had sensed on my last visit to Washington: the Alliance had few supporters, and Vietnam was now the only priority for the U.S. government. He explained the changes in Alliance leadership. Jim Fowler had retired and been replaced by David Richardson. Ray Sternfeld had been appointed vice president of the Inter-American Development Bank and had been replaced by his deputy, Richard Breen. In addition, Donald Palmer, a career foreign service officer, had been named the Bureau's deputy assistant secretary of state for Economic Affairs. Mel confided that there were serious disagreements among the three.

He set up a lunch with my former colleague in Caracas, Bob Cox, who was then a senior White House official. Bob had co-authored Caracas briefing paper that Che Guevara had read out at Punta del Este.

Then, he gave me my schedule for the week. Ele and I had medical exams on Tuesday. I had briefings from the new assistant coordinator for the Alliance, the new AID program officer, and the Bureau's deputy assistant secretary for Economic Affairs. I was also to pay courtesy calls on Under Secretary of State Thomas Mann, AID Director Bill Gawd, and Assistant Secretary of State Covey Oliver. On Thursday, I had an appointment with CIAP President Sanz de Santamaría, and lunch with the president of the Inter-American Development Bank, Felipe Herrera, and Ray Sternfeld. Thursday afternoon, I was scheduled to meet with my old friend, Jim Boren, director of the Partners of the Americas. I would return to see Mel Friday afternoon before I left Washington.

As I was leaving Mel informed me that, at Jim Boren's request, our tickets in the U.S. had been re-routed to include visits with the Partners Groups in Arkansas and Utah, and that Governor Rockefeller had invited us to spend a night at Winrock Farms. So, we would be a week en route from Washington to Tulare, our base for home leave.

I had a lot of news to share with Ele that night. I arranged for Ele to join Jim Boren and me Thursday afternoon for a briefing on the Partners and our hosts. All I can remember is a blur of meetings and a lot of feigned interest. Vietnam was top of the agenda in every office I visited. At the White House, Bob Cox came close to urging me to move to the Asia Bureau of the State Department after the Senior Seminar, and bluntly called continued assignments in Latin America a dead end. Felipe Herrera and Ray Sternfeld were clearly upset at the loss of high-level interest, and I sensed that Sanz de Santamaría was frustrated with the CIAP's lack of support throughout Latin America.

Jim Boren was the exception. He was enthusiastic about progress in building partnerships in all fifty U.S. States and saw the Partners of the Americas as a potential force for building support for the AFP in almost every state's congressional delegation. He informed us that he was working with a group in North Carolina to form a partnership with Santa Cruz area and that Governor Rockefeller had convened a meeting of the Arkansas Partners during our visit. He confided that the most active partnership at the time was with Utah.

My last session with Mel Spector was short and sweet. He said that he had received our medical clearance for return to post, and that our return tickets to Bolivia should be in California when we arrived there. He said that David Lazar would be leaving La Paz in early 1968 for training before assignment to Vietnam and that David had accepted the news well.

Our trip to California included a visit to Arkansas, an inspection of the South Dakota farm and a meeting with the Utah Partner. The stop in Arkansas was a disappointment. The governor was called out of state and the organizing committee was not convened. We had lunch at Winrock Farms before moving on to South Dakota on a route that included three stops, long lay-overs, and arrival in Aberdeen, South Dakota at 11:00 p.m. in a blizzard, with the wind blowing so hard that we barely reached the terminal building before the attendants locked it up. That experience ended any thought of our moving our residence to South Dakota! We spent two days with Ele working with her tenant on marketing the crop, plans for next year's crop, and settling accounts.

We flew non-stop to Salt Lake City where the President of the Utah Partners, Gary Neeleman and his wife met us at the airport and presented us with a busy schedule that included a meeting with the executive committee of the Utah Partners and dinner at the Alta Club. Ele and I were excited by the plans outlined at the meeting and the interest of the Partners members. The following day, a Friday, we were invited by the vice president of Utah State University, Clark Ballard, formerly the Utah State team leader in Bolivia, to the university to discuss the plans of the team and the personnel it planned to assign to Bolivia in 1968. Saturday, we were guests in the university president's box at the traditional football classic between Brigham Young and Utah State. The stopover in Utah was one of those unexpected inspiring experiences that nurtures one's commitment to succeed.

Since I planned to be back in Bolivia in the first week in October, my time in California was slightly more than two weeks. I visited my mother for several days while Ele handled the ranch business in Tulare. During the ten days that we were together in Tulare, the local daily, the *Tulare Advance-Register*, on which Ele had worked for two years as the society editor, noticed that I had been listed in *Who's Who*. The editor called Ele's mother to ask about it. They sent a photographer and reporter to interview us, and our picture graced the front page of the newspaper. The article noted that the only Tulare County residents listed in *Who's Who* were Admiral Elmo Zumwalt; two-time Olympic decathlon champion, Bob Matthias; and the Tragens. We received a lot of dinner invitations.

I returned to La Paz in early October. It coincided with the Bolivian Army cornering, capturing, and killing Che. It was shortly after that word got out that Em and David were being transferred. The environment was uneasy. David and Em briefed me on the very slow progress over the last five weeks—slow, because Che had been at the top of the government's agenda. When I called the minister of Finance, he expressed his concern about their departure, and I urged him to help me expedite the work still pending. I advised him that we had a project agreement ready for signature, and he arranged a date on October 10 with the foreign minister for the signing.

I went alone to the Foreign Ministry that afternoon. I was ushered into the minister's office, and he greeted me with an *abrazo*. He was quite relaxed as I congratulated the government on the successful conclusion of the Che Guevara campaign. He motioned for me to sit down at his conference table on which the Project Agreement was duly laid out for signature. Then the phone rang and one of his aides picked it up and told the minister that it was urgent. The minister walked to the phone and I watched his expression change to almost shock. When he returned to the table, he took a sip of water. I asked him what happened. He looked at me and said that the U.S. government had asked for Che's fingerprints, but the soldiers in Vallegrande had no idea how to take fingerprints so they just cut off his hands. The minister stared at me and told me that he would send a note to my diplomatic colleagues about what had happened. We signed the project agreements very quickly and I left the foreign minister still seated at the table. I can't verify what occurred in Vallegrande, but I shall never forget the look on the foreign minister's face.

When I returned to the USAID Mission, I related the experience to David and Em. We just looked at each other until David said, "Just close that chapter and get down to the work we have ahead of us in the next twelve weeks." Then, the three of us spent long hours talking about the future of the USAID program. We laid out what we needed to do before David and Em departed. We agreed that David's successor should be someone who could work closely with the minister of Finance and the president of the Central Bank. That led us to nominate our banking adviser, Phil Faucett, to replace David as the deputy director. Washington would not approve our carrying the post of associate deputy director once Em left, since no other post in Latin America had a similar position. Mel Spector had warned me that that would probably be his office's decision.

Ele and I also suffered another grievous loss that November when Washington advised us that Ed Faison's contract was cancelled for reasons not related to his performance or security clearance. We had a dinner at our home with just the Faisons. They were uncertain about where to go. Ele suggested Hawaii—far away from the grapevine and somewhere they could fit right in. They did go to Hawaii, where Ed was hired as Professor of Advertising-Marketing at the University of Hawaii. Lois found an affinity for Oriental Art and earned an advanced degree in the subject. The children blossomed.

Much of December was spent attending farewells for David and his wife Nancy and for Em. They had become much more than office colleagues, they were close friends. They left a gaping hole in our advisory team—and all of us knew it. I cannot describe the emptiness I felt when they left, especially David's departure. He shared every decision with me, and his sound judgment and sense of justice helped keep me on an even keel. The minister of Finance and the president of the Central Bank President hosted a farewell reception in honor of David and Em. My two colleagues had earned the respect they received. Around Christmas, Ele and I gave them the crowning farewell with their diplomas as "S.O.B.s," Survivors of Bolivia.

Our world in La Paz had been severely jolted. The departure of three colleagues made my last months much more challenging. But there were two more jolts to come: a turndown in Washington, and the sudden departure of Ambassador Henderson because of his wife Dorothy's terminal cancer.

22

The End of My Bolivian Cycle

Two major activities on which we had concentrated in 1967 and 1968 were aimed at helping the government increase its income and raise living standards in rural areas through the community development program. By the time I left on home leave, the government and USAID were examining the restoration of the national rural land tax and a division of the proceeds between the national government and municipalities. Also under consideration was the creation of a facility at the Central Bank to help municipalities finance multiyear improvement projects. As the ideas took shape during 1967, the complexity and scope of the undertaking led both the minister of Finance and Ambassador Henderson and me to insist that we keep the proposal under wraps until we had worked out the details. In the Bolivian government, I knew of only three officials who were privy to our discussions: President Barrientos, Minister of Finance Romero Loza, and Central Bank President Jorge Jordán; on the U.S. side, the ambassador, David, Em, and I. We knew that the proposal could be sabotaged if it was leaked out before we could put the pieces together.

A Proposal Takes Shape

When I returned to La Paz in early October, David told me that nothing had moved forward since my departure with all attention focused on combatting Che Guevara. David and Em had been unable to meet with the minister of Finance or the president of the Central Bank. He also told me of uneasiness in the city, because of rumors about imminent changes in the cabinet and friction between President Barrientos and General Ovando over the army's campaign against Che. There was nothing that we were prepared to put on paper until we had clear signals from the minister. We had to make certain that an initiative as comprehensive and delicate as this had "made in Bolivia" written all over it.

My first interview with the ambassador on my return was quite tense. It was clear that he was under great pressure. He had taken President Barrientos to meet with President Johnson at his Texas ranch, and the president had promised US$5 million to help Bolivia locate and capture Che. The Bolivians were pressing for the money since almost all Bolivian government activities had been cut back or postponed in order to fund the operation against Che. When the ambassador queried the White House, he was told that AID was to provide the money, but AID balked at providing "budget support" since it had told the congress that no additional budget support would be given to Bolivia.

I called the minister of Finance and the president of the Central Bank to tell them of my return and asked for appointments. The minister of Finance saw me for a few minutes and arranged for the project signing at the Ministry of Foreign Affairs. When I called the ministers of Agriculture and of Education, their secretaries reported that they were tied up on "cabinet business."

It was not until early December that the minister of Finance finally called back to set up a working meeting. He and the president of the Central Bank regretted the delays that he attributed to the government's commitment on Che. He told us that the Bolivian government and the Central Bank were basically out of funds and that the five million pledged by President Johnson was urgently needed. I told him that those funds were not in my USAID portfolio, but that I would help in any way I could.

After that meeting, I proposed to Ambassador Henderson that I try to wrap the five million into the land tax proposal. He agreed, but said that he would continue to press Assistant Secretary of State Covey Oliver to get AID to release the funds with no strings attached.

When David, Em, and I met again with the minister and the Central Bank president, we asked them to begin writing the draft legislation and decrees to authorize the land tax, with provisions for tax collection by local governments, the decree to create the new window in the Central Bank, and other necessary approval documents. They and we were fully aware of the opposition of General Ovando and other cabinet members, but if we tied approval of those measures to the release of the five million and additional AID funds, the minister felt that cabinet approval could be obtained. Unfortunately, I did not get a late-night call from President Barrientos to discuss this approach.

We heard nothing more through the Christmas season. In January, after David and Em had departed post, Phil Fawcett, the new deputy USAID director, advised me that the president of the Central Bank asked him for assistance in preparing the blueprint for the new facility. The ambassador and I briefed him on the tax proposal and authorized him to work with the president of the Central Bank. Shortly thereafter, the minister of Finance advised me that he was setting up a team to prepare legislation for a new national land tax and reminded me that a key hurdle in our plan was gaining the support of the rural workers union and most were loyal to the exiled MNR and skeptical of the government's commitment to improve rural life and public services.

In late January, President Barrientos invited me to join him at a meeting with union leaders in Tarata, his hometown. The president once again asked the leaders how they felt about establishing a land tax to be collected at the community level and used in part for local improvement projects. He explained my presence by saying that USAID would consider helping out.

They were reticent to commit themselves. So, I asked how they would respond to restoring the land tax if, as part of its installation, all *campesinos* would be provided titles to the land they occupied and a percentage of the tax collected would remain at the community level to fund projects the community determined were its priorities. The conversation heated up and the union leaders began to ask questions of each other as well as to the president. They asked whether the community could elect the tax collector, whether the community could oversee the tax collector to ensure the money was not stolen, and how the land titles would be distributed. After considerable discussion, they asked the president for time to think over what commitments they would need from the government before they could give him an answer. They agreed to meet with the president and me on the eve of the national convention in Oruro, scheduled in about six weeks.

In the interim, the ambassador and I worked with the minister of Finance on a possible plan, as simple and transparent as possible, that could be discussed with the union leaders in Oruro. We proposed to create a straightforward land tax, easy for the people to understand, such as, a fixed amount per hectare per year for land planted with crops, a lesser amount for pasture land, and a higher amount for urbanized lots. A percentage would be earmarked for the community to pay for its priority projects and a percentage sent to the national treasury; Romero Loza wanted a fifty-fifty split; I suspected that the unions would want more. In addition, on payment of the tax, each *campesino* would receive a receipt that specified the boundaries to the taxed land and that receipt would be treated as a deed. To implement the system, each community would elect its own tax collector and set up a local committee to walk off the boundaries of the property if the *campesino* had no deed. There would be no complicated cadastral study—so as to save time and assure transparency to the *campesinos*. The Ministry of Finance would train the local tax collectors and prepare a standard accounting system for the money collected. We recognized that the process was imperfect and that installation would be difficult (an estimated two years). The revenue would be limited initially, but we all believed that the concept was critical for the long-term development of Bolivia—not merely fiscally but, more importantly, for promoting democratic development in rural communities across the country.

I got the call to meet the union leaders in Oruro the night before the convention. I did not accompany the president, nor was I included in his meeting with the national leadership. I met with the same leaders with whom I talked in Tarata and they told me that they were advising the president that they would not oppose a tax on land, provided the legislation contained the provisions discussed in Tarata. Those provisions they reminded me were: (1) each *campesino* would have title to the land he or she occupied before the tax could be levied; (2) the tax collector would be elected by the community and be responsible to the community for the monies collected; (3) 65 percent of the monies collected would be kept in the community for projects selected by the community and only 35 percent went to the national government; (4) the government would give priority in its budget to local projects proposed by the communities; and (5) each year when the *campesinos* paid their taxes, the government would stamp the "deed" as recognition of ownership.

It was a couple of days before the minister called me to his office. The president had authorized him to work with me on a proposal to present to the Bolivian congress and to Washington. He reiterated that the government was in a cash crisis and needed the five million dollars immediately. The ambassador called Covey Oliver to pressure AID for the immediate release of the money. AID refused, citing congressional considerations and its concern about the Bolivian budget deficit. The ambassador then proposed to President Barrientos that we use the proposed land tax to provide the *quid pro quo* for releasing the five million dollars, and the government agreed.

In late March, the minister appointed a task force of Bolivian lawyers to draft a complex bill to reinstall the land tax, with all of the features that the unions had indicated were critical for their support. Writing the law was a complicated process because it meant amending numerous statutes, including the organic laws on agrarian reform and tax collection. It was also only the first phase of the even more difficult process of implementing it.

No Support in Washington

An integral part of the package was an AID loan to the government of Bolivia to fund the Community Development Program. The ambassador, David, Em, and I had decided that, once President Barrientos had endorsed the program, the best way to ensure its continuity would be a loan that assured USAID funding for the next several years and annual counterpart contributions by Bolivia. That loan proposal was sent to Washington in early 1968; days after the meeting in Oruro, I was summoned to Washington to present the loan for approval. About the same time, I was also formally advised that I had been selected for the Senior Seminar on Foreign

Policy to begin in late August, and that Ele and I would be leaving before August.

I delayed my departure to early May in the hope that the land tax legislation proposal could be completed in April. But there were too many knotty questions to be ironed out, and the best I could bring with me to Washington was an assurance by the minister that, if the five million dollars were released, the government would have the legislation before the congress by June 30.

When I arrived in Washington, I found myself dealing with the new cast of characters in the front office of the Alliance. I could not turn to Bill Rogers or Ray Sternfeld for support. I expected little opposition to the community development loan, but the release of the five million dollars was still uncertain because all the t's were not crossed. When I laid out the land tax package to my colleagues in the AID program office, I was met with a mixed reception. The loan proposal was approved, but the land tax as the *quid pro quo* for the release of the five million was not received favorably.

Doubts were expressed about the Bolivian government's commitment and its capability to implement the land tax. Their skepticism unsettled me. I made several long presentations, but the spirit of innovation that had permeated the early Kennedy years of the Alliance had dissipated. The focus was on Vietnam and the Cold War, not on democratic development. When I described the proposal to Tom Mann, now under-secretary of state for Economic Affairs, he raised questions about the government's resolve. Covey Oliver said that he would rely on the judgment of his assistant secretary for Economic Affairs, Don Palmer. Colleagues like Jack Vaughn and Representative Dante Fascell gave their full support to the proposal and offered to help, but warned that the administration was a lame duck on the eve of an election and had no interest in disrupting the usual program review process. I explained the situation to Julio Sanjinés, the Bolivian ambassador, and he met with senior State Department and AID officials, but he received only polite responses.

In mid-May, I decided to make one last effort and met again with key State and AID officers. My last meeting was with the deputy coordinator of the AFP, David Richardson; when I left his office, I was depressed. He said that he would only agree to release the five million dollars if the government immediately enacted a

15 percent increase in import duties. I argued that that would be counterproductive and an incentive for smugglers and graft, not increased government revenues. He basically said, "Take it or leave it."

I went to the Bolivia Desk to call Ambassador Henderson for his help when I was told that his wife, Dorothy Henderson, had been diagnosed with cancer. When I phoned him, despite his grief, he agreed to ask Covey for another review of the proposal, but Richardson and Palmer demurred. My message to President Barrientos and Minister Romero Loza had to be: "The five million will be transferred on approval of an immediate 15 percent surcharge on import duties." I was devastated. To this day, I have wondered what else I could have done to get approval for the land tax as the *quid pro quo* for the five million dollars. Would the land tax have really led to greater grassroots democracy in the country? Would it have helped stabilize government revenues at the community and national level?

The night before I left for La Paz, I had dinner with Nancy and David Lazar. David was home on leave from Vietnam. My dinner partner was Holly Mankowitz, the wife of Bobby Kennedy's press secretary in the 1968 campaign, Frank Mankowitz. David commiserated with me and warned me that the Alliance was dead and all attention was on the "domino theory." After dinner, Holly drove me to my hotel and, after we said goodnight, I went up to my room and turned on the TV. There was Frank standing on a car in front of the Ambassador Hotel in Hollywood announcing that Bobby had been assassinated. What an unforgettable climax to one of the most tragic experiences of my government life!

It was no surprise that when I returned to La Paz, I was exhausted and needed a week in an oxygen tent before I could resume my duties. By then, Dorothy Henderson had been diagnosed with fourth-stage cancer, and emergency evacuation was ordered for treatment at Bethesda Medical Center. I well remember the sad journey we all took to the El Alto Airport to bid the Hendersons farewell.

Equally disheartening was my first meeting with Minister Romero Loza. He and I agreed that the worst fiscal medicine for the country would be 15 percent surtax on imports. He had already been advised by Ambassador Sanjinés of the outcome of my mission. The minister told me that President Barrientos felt that it would take all of his political skills to get the congress to approve the surtax and that, under the circumstances, he would have to delay submitting the land tax proposal.

The congress approved the surtax by June 30, and the five million dollars were released. The "Smugglers Union" held a great street demonstration in support of the surtax, including a serenade under my office window to thank USAID for their windfall! Government revenues did not increase appreciably as the result of the surtax, but the smugglers certainly made lots of extra money. What a pyrrhic outcome!

Leaving La Paz

Our departure from La Paz was bittersweet. Ele and I would have welcomed an extension of the assignment, but that was not to be. The rejection by Washington of the land tax, the departure of David Lazar and Emerson Melaven, which had removed two key players from the mission, and the sad departure of the ambassador had made the job much more difficult. But the continuing support of the Bolivian government, and the on-the-ground successes in implementing the program were some compensation.

The teacher-training program had drawn kudos from even the most anti-U.S. sectors of the Ministry of Education. They were equally pleased with the results of the redesign of the rural elementary school curriculum to teach Spanish as a second language. The Savings and Loan Bank had given a substantial boost to the housing sector and urban jobs. The credit union movement was attracting new members in rural and urban areas.

Above all, I was pleased with the broadening of the focus of the USAID program from building infrastructure to building the capabilities of people. The country certainly needed more physical and institutional infrastructure, but above all it needed to equip its people with the skills to improve their own lives and living standards and to plan for the type of government and society that best suited them.

Some of the most intelligent people I met were illiterate *camp-*

esinos. They had learned to survive in the most hostile social and physical climate possible. They had lived through Spanish and post-colonial regimes that denied them access to education and exploited their labor. They had learned to trust no one outside their immediate clan. They knew their problems, but had no idea how to resolve them. The challenge was to awaken their trust in those who really wanted to help them help themselves.

I watched two programs that were doing just that: the Utah State agriculture program in the highlands, and the national community development program. I saw the results and heard about many more from Peace Corps and USAID technicians.

On the Altiplano after the first experience with sheep shearing, sheep shearing contests became a standard event at local fairs. Then, shortly before we left Bolivia, my secretary Peggy Hook told me that a delegation of *campesinos* wanted to see me—she was a bit apprehensive because they were so gruff and dirty. In my office, one of the elders told me that they had heard on their new radios that there was to be a sheep auction in a place in Peru called Cerro de Pasco and they wanted to bid at the auction. They had 495,000 Bolivian pesos saved from their sheep shearing, and wanted me to authorize Tata (an Aymara term of endearment for a respected elder) Matthews of the Utah State team to use that money to buy new stock for them. The program had made an impact and Matthews had earned their trust and respect. A door had opened.

On a visit to a rural community outside of Cochabamba, the elders asked to meet with me. In a mixture of Quechua and Spanish, they said that they wanted an improved water supply for their crops, but the technicians wanted them to use it for drinking water. Prior to the community development program, the *campesinos* would not have spoken out, but would simply have accepted what the government technicians gave them. Now, they were learning that they had a voice in decision-making and were telling me of their priority for water use. They were given what they asked for— improving their livelihood mattered more to them at that time than safe drinking water.

We also missed some opportunities. I recalled the visit of a vice president of a major U.S. cereal company. Ele and I had him to dinner, and Ele served him quinoa soup, which he loved. Ele asked our cook Eduarda whether we had any more quinoa, and she said yes. So, Ele sent him some for breakfast the next day. A few weeks later, I received a cable from him asking how he could buy 25,000 tons of quinoa for a trial program to find out whether it would be acceptable in the U.S. as a new breakfast cereal. We discovered that the annual production of quinoa, which grows on marshland on the Altiplano, was merely 17,000 metric tons. While it is a high protein grain, foreign aid programs had invested very little money or effort in expanding quinoa cultivation, since it was just regarded as "peasant food" and "inferior" to wheat or corn. We had missed an opportunity to help Altiplano farmers develop a new cash crop.

The orders for our transfer to Washington arrived in mid-June, and we were to leave in late July. The government was advised the next day of my imminent departure. The embassy received a note from the Foreign Office saying that the government had awarded me the Order of Bolivar, one of Bolivia's most distinguished medals. The U.S. government authorized me to accept it. In mid-July, a few days before our departure, the Foreign Ministry held a ceremony at which Vice President Siles Salinas presided. Almost all of the cabinet and many of the public and private sector leaders with whom I had worked were in attendance. I was truly honored. That evening President Barrientos sent a car for me to have a brandy with him for the first time since I had left on home leave.

Ele supervised the packing. Phil Fawcett and I tried to clean up the last pending matters so that the transition to my successor would be as smooth as possible. We kept the farewell parties to a minimum in respect for the tragedy facing Douglas and Dorothy Henderson. The USAID staff gave us a warm farewell. I received my SOB, Survivor of Bolivia.

I received one other award from the Trotskyites that I also cherish. I had made an impression on them and they created a caricature of me called the "Condor Gringo," a bald, eye-glassed foreigner whose Spanish resembled mine and who was always getting involved in one Bolivian matter after another. I felt that I had made an impact if they were concerned enough about me to parody my speeches at inaugurations of schools, community development projects, and other public events.

Ele and I left Bolivia in late July. We left a part of our hearts there.

23

The Senior Seminar

Ele and I arrived in Washington in late July. Ele arranged for us to rent an apartment at the Towers where we had lived before our assignment to Bolivia. Old friends made us feel at home as soon the news of our return got around the corridors and we were feted to a series of welcome home dinners. This was the first time in three years that we were not on call around the clock and had time for ourselves. Ele was enthusiastic about getting back into her routine of monitoring the stock market and working with the American Association of Foreign Service Wives (AAFSW) on its project to amend Foreign Service rules that limited the rights of female officers and to broaden Department of State support of Foreign Service families.

A Time for Reflection

In the last week of August, I reported to the first session of the XI Senior Seminar that met on the top floor of the Foreign Service Institute (FSI), which was then located in Rosslyn. I joined my colleagues for coffee as we introduced ourselves. We were senior level officers from various U.S. government agencies, twenty-five in all. Fourteen were from the State Department, two from AID, two from the U.S. Information Agency, five from the Defense Department, one from the U.S. Department of Commerce, and one from the General Accounting Office. Most had never met before, and only a couple had worked together on prior assignments.

At 9:00 a.m., Ambassador Wesley Jones, the coordinator of the seminar, joined us and gave us the syllabus and work plan for the next nine months, together with a binder of information about the various speakers who would meet with us and about the visits we would make across the United States. The schedule included meetings with distinguished university scholars, the Joint Chiefs of Staff, top Department of State officers, key members of congress involved in foreign affairs, and government officials from other departments working on issues that impacted foreign policy formulation. The visits were to various regions of the United States that would expose us to the changes that were transforming our country. We were provided with an extensive reading list, including some that were critical of U.S. foreign policy.

There were some grumbles about the scope of program. Some wanted more attention to foreign policy issues, especially the Cold War and Vietnam. Some wanted a more structured approach to the work of the next nine months. Ambassador Jones listened carefully and simply reminded us that we were mature senior level officers capable of making our own judgments about our policies and the conditions in our country and that the program was intended to inform us as broadly as possible of various views on foreign policy and on conditions in the country so that each of us could make the best possible decisions in our future career assignments.

The seminar was a wondrous experience for me. For most of my adult life I had been immersed in Latin America, working on either foreign policy issues or development. For those nine months, I was engaged in thinking about broader issues and reacquainting myself with my own country and my country's capability to deal with not only the Cold War abroad but also the domestic revolution within. This was 1968, with the civil rights movement and the anti-Vietnam upheaval in full swing. In my Foreign Service cocoon, I knew little about this process, and the growing distrust of government. I had grown up in the Depression and World War II when government was our hallowed protector. Our debates were about how far we wanted government to act to improve our lot, not about limitations on its powers and opposition to wars undertaken to protect our perceived interest. The meetings around our conference table and our visits throughout the U.S. gave me cause to rethink many of the premises on which my career was built. Over the next several months, I would tell Ele of our seminar discussions and we would talk about their impact on our lives.

Our initial meetings featured presentations by senior State Department officials, including Secretary of State Rusk, followed by in-depth discussions around our conference table. Then, Dr. Herman Kahn, the director of the Hudson Institute, initiated a week of analyzing nuclear war, arms control, "mutual annihilation," and the "domino theory," followed the next week by a group of scholars, including Dr. Louis Kahn of the University of Pennsylvania, who focused on the urban, social, and economic transformation taking place in the United States. The Senior Seminar basically asked: "How can you represent your country if you do not understand the country as it is today?" Throughout those nine months we were engaged in rethinking some of the most important issues facing our nation and ourselves.

I still remember the question posed by Dr. Louis Kahn, "What is the role of the city in our culture? Is it a complex through which transportation and people move, or is it a place where people live and thrive? Why do we construct cities as we do? Is it for people or for economic convenience?" You can rephrase that question to apply to so many other aspects of our life as a nation or as an individual. It led me to reexamine my perspectives and objectives. I believe that that experience made me a more thoughtful and effective public servant.

The following weeks included discussions with the senior state, defense, and congressional leaders on U.S. foreign policy and the impact of domestic issues on it. Vietnam was the central point of our discussions. This was during the depths of the Cold War and Vietnam; the Tet Offensive had destabilized our position in Vietnam, the South Korean state was in crisis, and U.S. capability to face the multiple foreign dragons was in doubt. We had in-depth presentations on U.S. foreign policy and diplomatic relations in various theaters of the world. We probed our National Security and State Department invitees on the premises and relevance of their strategic and tactical positions in Europe, Southeast Asia, and the Middle East. No one mentioned either the Western Hemisphere or Africa. The Cold War and Vietnam had crowded everything else off the U.S. agenda, My colleagues and I spent hours around our conference table and in private discussions analyzing, hypothesizing, and speculating about the next moves on the world chess board and the *realpolitik* that was needed to protect and enhance the United States in such a hostile world. We concluded that the balance of power in Europe had stabilized and fear of further USSR expansion in Central and Western Europe had retreated, but that the potential conflict with China and the USSR portended over Vietnam and Southeast Asia, with serious doubts about the SEATO and our relations with India and Pakistan.

In this process, we had a week of meetings with the Joint Chiefs of Staff. A seminar member hosted the chief of his respective service. We met on consecutive days with the chief of Naval Operations, the chief of the Air Force, the commandant of the Marine Corps, the commanding general of the Army, and the head of the Joint Chiefs. Each made a presentation about the forces he commanded, their mission, and his perception of the threat facing the United States. Then, we were allowed to ask questions. One of my fellow seminarians, a Marine colonel and Vietnam veteran, asked scathing, probing questions about the Vietnam War—including our military strategy and the effectiveness of the tactics employed on the ground. On Thursday of that week, General Westmoreland sat at the table and was respectfully but relentlessly questioned about the effectiveness of the operations in Vietnam during his tour as supreme commander of armed forces. I heard my Pentagon colleagues challenge the gospel that I had not questioned in the daily reports on Vietnam we received in La Paz.

These experiences made me a skeptic of U.S. policy making. Throughout my career, I had accepted, without reservations, pronouncements from our policy makers. I often stifled my own concerns because I presumed that they, the best and the brightest, knew better than I and had access to information not available to me. It was at the Senior Seminar conference table that I realized how naïve I had been in not challenging decisions I thought were intrinsically opposed to the long-term interests of my country. It was during the Senior Seminar that I had time to rise above the daily routine of problem solving and look at the broader picture. It was in the Senior Seminar that I questioned how we could be the super power of the free world without focusing on all parts of the world, including Latin America and Africa. No books impressed me more than two on Vietnam: Frances Fitzgerald's *Fire in the Lake* which, drawing on history and knowledge of the region, destroyed the domino theory, and David Halberstam's *The Best and Brightest*, which laid out the mistakes in U.S. perceptions and policy making that led to the debacle in Vietnam. In retrospect, I believe that my frustration with the Washington decision not to support the land tax in Bolivia had prepared the ground for my "conversion."

Even more revealing for me were the visits we made across the country. I was exposed to the changing face of a country that was very different from that in which I had grown up. A social revolution was taking place. My career had taken me overseas from 1945 to 1968. My life revolved around my jobs in Latin American countries. On home leave, I was with my family for a few weeks in which the changes occurring in our society were not immediately perceptible. Reading about them in *Time* and *Newsweek* did not make them real to me. As Ambassador Jones bluntly asked us: how can you represent a country you don't know?

Our first field trip was to the New South with stops in North Carolina to visit the new Industrial Triangle, the traditional city of Charleston, South Carolina and dynamic Atlanta. We got a taste of the new vigor of the South, the rising black professional class, and the changes in the social and economic structures, and felt the tensions that the changes engendered when we walked into integrated meetings.

Our second trip took us to Boston and New York, with meetings with businessmen, bankers, academics, and political leaders. The feel was very different from that in the vibrant New South. While our briefings were absorbing and thought provoking, they lacked the vigor that I had felt in the New South. In our few days in New York, while we were studying its civic problems, from the mayor's office to Times Square, I was astounded to find that Atlanta had better municipal planning and development services than New York.

A third trip took us to Detroit, Cleveland, and Chicago. In Cleveland we saw a city in decay, reeling under years of urban neglect and poor leadership as industry had abandoned the area and Lake Erie had been degraded by pollution. In Detroit the era was promising with strong local leadership supported by the UAW and some businesses that were addressing immediate problems. In both cities, we observed urban decay and the racial divide between the black ghettos and the white suburbs.

In Chicago, we were introduced to the Daley regime, replete with Harvard MBAs leading urban renewal and economic development. In Chicago, each of us was assigned to ride in a police car for one night, and what an eye-opening revelation of racism was that for me! The night of my ride was just three months after the riots in Grant Park during the Democratic Convention, and my hosts were one white cop and one black cop. They were clearly not pleased to be working together. Most of my questions got non-committal responses. When I asked about Grant Park, the black cop said that the police had overreacted while the white cop said that you had to use force to keep the commies and malcontents under control. Nothing more was said until we got a call to deal with a robbery at the Greyhound Bus Station that they both called "the fruitcake capital of the universe." I was instructed to stay in the car while they investigated. The black officer came back to call for back-up, and I waited while they cuffed a Latino for petty theft and put him in the paddy wagon to be taken to jail. No more talk until we answered a call for a "domestic dispute" on the North side.

Our fourth field trip took us to the Midwest, Texas, and the West Coast. We visited the SAC (Strategic Air Command) and inspected nuclear rocket silos and were briefed by Boeing on aircraft planning and construction in Seattle. Outside of Omaha, we were also introduced to state-of-the-art large-scale corporate farm management. In Houston, we were given an in-depth briefing by NASA of its plans and operations, followed by a meeting with Jimmy Ling at his corporate headquarters. In his opulent Mandarin-style office, Mr. Ling, then the epitome of the new generation of industrial empire builders, outlined his plans for integrating and modernizing the U.S. steel industry. He feted us at a gourmet lunch at which his vice presidents munched on antacids as they dutifully agreed to everything their boss said.

That trip showed me that what I had heard at the conference table was indeed true: the industrial heart of the country had moved from the northeast and north central states to the New South, Texas, and the West. It convinced me that the family farm which had been the centerpiece of our agricultural policy and economy had practically disappeared as corporations bought up land and integrated production into their industrial food operations.

Our last trip took us to Puerto Rico, our only exposure to the Western hemisphere in the program. We flew to San Juan as guests of the governor of the commonwealth. We met with government officials and businessmen. The issue of independence from the U.S. was still vibrant, but it soon became clear that it was the bombast of a few. The U.S. provided political stability and an economic safety net. Operation Bootstrap had run out of steam and the new economic leadership lacked the vigor and vision of its creator, Teodoro Moscoso. Unemployment was high, and as U.S. citizens, Puerto Ricans could freely migrate to the United States mainland to find jobs. Federal funds supplemented island resources for infrastructure building and other programs. Many Puerto Ricans lived on social security and benefited from Medicare. The real issue that emerged from our briefings was whether the interests of the island were better served by statehood or by continuing the current commonwealth status.

Our visit to Puerto Rico also caused us a major crisis. The authorities booked us rooms at a fabulous hotel, and many of my colleagues arranged for their wives to join them there, flying on a commercial airline. Ele had a prior commitment that prevented her from joining the group. The commercial flight was hijacked to Havana and all of us, with the strained relations between Washington and Castro, were deeply concerned that the wives would be held hostage. For two days, we hung on all news from Havana and then learned that the aircraft and its passengers would be returned to Miami. All of my colleagues whose wives were involved arranged to fly to Miami to be with them. When we next assembled in Washington, my colleagues reported that their wives had been well treated and were less distressed by the experience than we had been.

Following the trip to Puerto Rico, the seminar program changed emphasis. Now, each of us was asked to submit a subject for individual study for the next two months, with a detailed plan of investigation, including any travel that we might deem necessary. Ambassador Jones met with us individually and asked us to justify the relevance of our proposed topic to the objectives of the seminar. Subjects ran from strategy in Southeast Asia, the role of Pakistan in SEATO, the effectiveness of the U.S. information program, to emerging African nationalism.

I chose *Tourism, a Sector for Development*. I proposed to look at the role of tourism in the development of the Pacific Trust Islands that the U.S. was nurturing toward independence. Ambassador Jones informed me that budget cuts limited overseas travel, and suggested that I look at the sector in a more generic way. So, I redesigned my proposal to look at the impact of tourism on developing countries.

I spent most of March and April on the project. Beside tons of reading, I went to New York to talk to industry executives and found that the major U.S. banks like Citibank and Chase financed most of the industry. I met with managers of successful tourism programs in several U.S. cities, including Honolulu. The trip to Honolulu allowed me to visit my mother in San Francisco in what turned out to be our last time together.

The paper covered tourism as an industry; its impact on the economy; the in-country conditions needed for the tourist industry to thrive; the multiplying effect on local industry, agriculture, and employment; and the source of international financing for various components of the industry from transport to accommodations.

The last month of the seminar was dedicated to the presentation of the papers. The seminar printed a limited number of copies for our use in the seminar, and I sent a copy of my paper to the bankers, travel agents, and other specialists who had counseled me. The Senior Seminar received requests for about a thousand more. The Dominican Republic's Ministry of Tourism obtained permission to translate it into Spanish. The Hawaiian Tourism Agency reprinted it. On later trips to Latin America, I found my paper in government tourist offices and on the bookshelves of large tourist companies. It was even cited by several governments in their requests for funding to international banks and AID for their national tourism program.

The Senior Seminar was a unique and rewarding experience. I found that it struck the right balance between foreign affairs and the socioeconomic and political changes taking place in our own country. We were reintroduced to the poverty and problems at home that needed attention as much the Cold War and the Alliance for Progress. I found that balance essential to reacquaint all of us with the country to whose service we were committed and to sharpen our thinking about a foreign policy consistent with our changing interests and values. As wealthy a nation as we then were, we needed to avoid throwing our resources at problems that we did not adequately understand. Hearing constructive dissent on domestic, military, and foreign policy made me appreciate even more the importance of full-scale analysis and discussion before making decisions. It was a tremendous mid-career experience, and one from which I still draw insight and inspiration.

The State Department discontinued the seminar in 2005 for budgetary reasons, a measure with which I disagreed. Senior State Department career officers need a year in which to stand back to look at the issues with which they deal daily in the context of the emerging economic and social conditions of our dynamic, ever-changing nation. I doubt that an experience at the War College or in academia would have been more rewarding.

Tragedies of Life

The Seminar gave Ele and me much more time together than previous assignments. I could almost always arrive home by 5:00 p.m. We had our weekends free to enjoy Washington together: the museums and art galleries, and exploring Georgetown and the Eastern Shore of Maryland. We played bridge with the Sherrys and other friends at the Towers, and went to the National Cathedral on Sundays. And, Ele had her special friend, Elizabeth LaCell, the Tulare City's Librarian, who kept her up to date on her mother and developments in Tulare. Ele had one void in her life that fall with the cutting of ties with her old office at the Department of Labor as old friends were no longer there; Clara Beyer and Gertrude Schermerhorn had retired, and Olive Clapper passed away.

Another sad note was the demise of Dorothy Henderson. We visited her at the hospital a couple of times, but toward the end the family felt that the cancer had so debilitated her that visitors were not convenient. I remember the memorial service for Dorothy and the deep affection of the family for that good lady. Most of our colleagues from the Bolivian mission joined the family at various times over the next few months to celebrate her life.

We remained in close touch with Bolivian Ambassador Julio Sanjinés and were frequent guests at embassy receptions and dinners. He conveyed messages from President Barrientos; one late in the year advised me that he expected to request the congress to approve the land tax in 1969. When a new ambassador was named to replace Douglas Henderson, Sanjinés invited Ele and me to a reception in his honor. Sanjinés suggested that he talk with me about Bolivia, the land tax, and community development. Unfortunately that did not work out. I recall clearly the afternoon in the spring of 1969 when the Bolivian ambassador notified me of the death of President Barrientos in a helicopter crash and his sad words that our plans had died with him.

At many of the receptions at the Bolivian embassy, we met Teresa and Chuck Hull, at whose wedding in La Paz I had been a witness. They had their first son, and her mother was staying with them at their home in suburban Maryland. We had a couple of family dinners together and were regaled with the latest news from La Paz, including the plans for General Ovando to run for the presidency to succeed Barrientos in 1969. Then, in mid-February we were invited to an April reception at the Bolivian embassy in honor of General Ovando who was returning from a tour of European capitals. On the day of the general's arrival in Washington, the Bolivian Embassy called to cancel the reception because of the death of President Barrientos.

Ele also began working on projects of the American Association of Foreign Service Wives (AAFSW) and planned to run for one of the officer posts. She postponed presenting her candidacy until she returned from her annual farm trip to South Dakota and California. But, those plans went awry midway into 1969.

After a lovely Christmas, we settled into a delightful, comfortable period in which life just seemed to flow along. Ele was going downtown three days a week to attend AAFSW meetings and check with her brokers. She got deeply involved in two AAFSW proposals to revise State Department rules and regulations on the rights of female foreign service officers and the participation of families in State Department orientation programs.

She also felt that the investment advice from her two brokers was not consistent with her reading of market conditions, and she decided one morning to drop into the Bache office on Connecticut Avenue where she met a young broker named Robert Wright;

she found him just right for her. He was to become our principal stock market advisor—and remains today. She thought she had her schedule in line for the next couple of years.

That changed on Memorial Day 1969, when on our return from the National Gallery of Art, we received a call from Tulare. At a luncheon of the Tulare Garden Club, Ele's mother had fallen and broken her right hip and wrist. Ele left for Tulare the following day and stayed with her mother for the rest of the year. Her mother was bedridden, and we had to hire a caregiver to take care of her during the day, but Ele was with her all night. Ele and I talked regularly by phone in the evening, and I could sense how frustrated she was with the lack of progress in her mother's recovery. I suspect that today's medical technology would have had her up and about in a few weeks, but in Tulare in 1969 the medical regime did not include physical therapy to speed up rehabilitation and recovery.

I missed Ele terribly. I still remember the emptiness I felt every night when I arrived home and ate dinner alone. There was no one to talk to at night about the highs and lows of each day. But I think that she had a much more difficult time than I. She set aside her plans to work with AAFSW and on investments.

Before Ele's mother's injury, I had been advised by Mel Spector that the State Department had selected me to become the next director of the Office of Argentine, Paraguayan, and Uruguayan Affairs. My new assignment would begin at the end of the Senior Seminar on June 1. I was to replace an old friend, William Krieg, whom we had known in Chile when he was chief of the political section of the embassy. Ele and I respected him, and I felt honored that I was chosen to replace him. The assignment turned out to be fortuitous since it kept me in Washington at a time when Ele needed my support.

24

Argentine, Paraguayan, and Uruguayan Affairs

In mid-June 1969, I assumed my new duties at the State Department as director of the Office of Argentine, Paraguayan, and Uruguayan Affairs. The purpose of the office was to promote and build support by those three countries for U.S. policy and tactical objectives. That required understanding what was going on in each country, working with each one to resolve problems arising between us, providing guidance and support for the U.S. embassies in the three countries, and developing a working relationship with each country's representatives in Washington.

The State Department budget does not allow for an overlap from one director to another. The new director is expected to learn on his/her own and often does not have the opportunity to be briefed by the predecessor on critical issues and relationships with counterparts in the embassies with which he/she is to work.

In my case, since I was at the Senior Seminar in Rosslyn, I met with my predecessor several times and received his guidance on the critical issues, especially long-term sore points, and on the office's relations with the ambassadors with whom I could be working.

I was also able to receive policy guidance from Deputy Assistant Secretary for American Republics Affairs (ARA) Jack Crimmins, a top-flight professional career officer, to whom I reported. Jack arranged my first meeting with Charles Meyer, the assistant secretary of state for ARA, and my formal induction into the routine of my new post.

My first action on the new job was to advise the three U.S. ambassadors whom I was to work (John Davis Lodge in Argentina, Ray Ylitalo in Paraguay, and Robert Sayre in Uruguay) that I had formally replaced Bill Krieg.

On that first day, I was advised that Deputy Office Director Bill Lowenthal was to be replaced the following Monday, and that two of my state desk officers were to be transferred to new posts within days. On my second day on the job, the periodic removal of files from the office to the storage repository in St. Louis took place. Ele was not there those nights when I went home to bemoan my fate.

On the third day, Jack Crimmins advised me that my old friend, Edward Marasciulo, had been selected to be the new deputy director; he arranged for Bill Lowenthal to overlap with him for a few days. The only remaining state officers who had served under Bill Krieg were Jack Whiting, the very competent Argentine desk officer, and Peter Askins, the talented senior AID program officer. The two new officers scheduled to join the office were David Cox on Uruguayan Affairs, and Charles Brayshaw, a young foreign service officer on his first assignment, for the Paraguay desk.

At our first office staff meeting, Bill Lowenthal helped us compile a list of all the "burning" issues facing us. We had a few immediate posers, but most of our agenda was made up of long-standing problems that had no easy solutions. When we finished the second week, Ed Marascuilo placed a statue of St. Jude on his desk, and told us that we needed the good offices of the saint of lost causes.

Then Ed and I called on the ambassadors with whom we would be working for the next couple of years. Our first was to the affable, veteran Argentine diplomat, Rafael Vásquez, who was the chargé d'affaires. The ambassador, Eduardo Roca, had resigned over policy differences with his government; the government was in the process of selecting his replacement. We had a long talk over the status of relations and measures that we might take to settle some of the pending issues. Next, we visited the Uruguayan ambassador, Hector Luisi, an urbane and talented lawyer who had been foreign minister of his country. We talked about the internal crisis in Uruguay and the threat of the *Tupamaro* insurgency. Our last visit was with the Paraguayan Ambassador, General Roque Ávila, the longtime associate of President Alfredo Stroessner; that meeting was short and quite formal.

Then, we got down to the day-to-day routine of the office. Each day began with reading the dispatches from the three countries, the intelligence reports, and the news digest of hemispheric and world events.

Ed Marasciulo and I divided up the work of the office. Ed concentrated on the AID agenda, went to AID staff meetings, and worked with Peter Atkins on project reviews and liaison with various AID offices. Argentina had terminated almost all its AID-funded projects. Uruguay had a few in health, education, agriculture, and public safety. The largest program was in Paraguay and was headed by one of AID's most effective directors, Peter Cody. Once a week, I joined them to go over developments and issues.

Once or twice a week I attended staff meetings convened by the assistant secretary and worked primarily with the State desk officers on political and economic issues. That required my understanding not only the immediate issues but also the overall political, economic, and social situation of each country, and the three were distinct—historically and contemporaneously. I set up special sessions on political and economic developments that the desk officer deemed warranted.

Ed and I encouraged each of the desk officers and the AID specialist to prepare background papers on issues or developments they thought required our collective consideration. If a policy issue arose, I was the channel for consulting Jack Crimmins. We set up a work schedule for either Ed or me to be in the office on alternate weekends, along with one of the State desk officers. We sensed that there could be a crisis at any time.

All three countries were our allies in the Cold War. They were signatories of the OAS Charter and the Inter-American Treaty of Reciprocal Assistance (commonly known as the Rio Treaty). However, bilateral relations were substantially different country by country. Argentina saw itself as a competitor with the U.S. for leadership in Latin America. Uruguay saw good relations with the United States as a guarantee of its independence from its powerful neighbors—Brazil to the north, and Argentina. Paraguay saw the U.S. as an important ally of its strongman who had committed to the U.S. in the Cold War. Relations between the U.S. and the three were not always cordial.

The immediate problems facing us with Argentina, the largest of the three countries, were related to its military dictatorship and its profound economic crisis. In the mid-1960s, the military had once again deposed the civilian government and chose General

Juan Onganía to be president. He assembled a technocratic cabinet headed by Economic Minister Adelbart Krieger Vasena to lead the economy out of stagnation. Krieger Vasena's reforms chipped away at failed economic policies and practices in place since World War II; he was trying to open up the economy and stabilize the monetary and fiscal situation. But his policies created large-scale unemployment as formerly protected infant industries failed and popular unrest grew violent. Krieger was fired and Onganía was under pressure by the armed forces as he sought to move forward the reform package. There was indeed a question about the durability of the Onganía regime.

In 1969, Paraguay was in the fifteenth year of the dictatorship of President Alfredo Stroessner and his Colorado Conservative Party. After a decade of civil war following the ill-fated Chaco war with Bolivia and years of economic crisis, Stroessner took power in 1954. Under Stroessner, there had been a gradual economic recovery as the country's predominately agricultural economy stabilized and improved. Political opposition was ruthlessly repressed, often in the guise of anti-communism. Reports of smuggling and government corruption were widespread, with stories of senior government power brokers lining their pockets.

In 1969, one of the oldest and most respected democracies in the hemisphere, Uruguay was on the verge of economic collapse. It was also confronting an insurgency born of deteriorating economic and social conditions: the *Tupamaros*, led by Raul Sendic. Uruguay had experimented with cradle-to-grave social security that bankrupted the small country and with a Swiss-style council of government that had brought government to a standstill. The crisis forced the two principal parties, *Colorados* and *Blancos*, to agree to return to the presidential system. In 1967, Jorge Pacheco of the *Colorado* party was elected president, with a legislature divided by proportional representation. The U.S. was committed to supporting the Pacheco government in reviving the economy and suppressing the *Tupamaros* for fear that another Castro or Allende Popular Front government would emerge on the Rio de la Plata.

The situation in three countries raised serious concerns, and shaping U.S. actions to deal with them required careful thought and study. Since Ele was in California taking care of her mother,

I spent my nights and weekends reading every book, academic study, and monograph I could find about them. I spent my lunches and weekends consulting government colleagues, academics, and specialists at think tanks who had experience working with and living in the three countries.

The Countries

I came to understand that this unique corner of South America had been the poor cousin of the Spanish Empire. No gold had been found in the area. Under the fifteenth century Bull of Tordesillas, most of the South Atlantic coast on the easternmost edge of the Spanish empire had been awarded to Portugal and its colony, Brazil. Under the fourteenth century Treaty of Windsor, Portugal was allied with Great Britain, and the Portuguese-British alliance made the South Atlantic dangerous waters for Spanish shipping. Hence, Spain deployed her political, economic, and military resources in the Caribbean and Pacific, and used the Pacific route to move the gold from Bolivia and Peru to Panama and hence to Spain. It did not develop the great harbors of the Rio de la Plata.

Argentina was one of the poorest and least populous colonies of Spain. It was administered under the Vice Royalty of Peru and primarily developed in the Tucumán area to supply food for the mines of Upper Peru, now Bolivia. Marauding Indian tribes controlled much of the pampas. It was 1776 before the Spanish decided to counter growing Portuguese and British influence in the Rio de la Plata by establishing the Vice Royalty of Buenos Aires, in the port city of little more than 4,000 inhabitants. After San Martín won independence in 1816, the country spent the next fifty years in civil wars as well as fighting the Indians in the pampas and Patagonia. National leaders fought over federation versus confederation, that is, whether to build a strong national government in Buenos Aires, or to have a confederation with power dispersed among the numerous provinces.

During that era, the British consolidated their interests in the South Atlantic by providing economic assistance to the young republic. Public and private British capital was invested extensively in developing ports, railways, and utilities. The great harbor of

Buenos Aires was dominated by British shipping, and all the British built railways converged on Buenos Aires, with few interconnections with other cities of the country. Scots brought organization and technology to cattle and sheep farming. However, the country's elite looked to Paris for education, culture, and fashion. The army looked to France and Germany for technical guidance, with the navy inclined to the British.

By 1870, the federation (nationalists) won the civil war and Buenos Aires became the permanent seat of government. The pampas and Patagonia were pacified. The economy then exploded. The population tripled, with a majority of its new residents coming from Italy. To Europeans seeking a new life, only the U.S. was more attractive for immigration than Argentina. At the beginning of the twentieth century, Argentina was one of the ten richest countries in the world, and Buenos Aires rivaled Rome and Paris as a great cosmopolitan city.

The national political system took shape, with the Conservative party the strongest force. The Conservatives stood for indirect election of presidents, powerful presidents in a centralized national government, and the union of the Catholic Church and state. The opposition Radical Socialists, modeled on the French party of the same name, fought for universal male suffrage, direct election of the president, and separation of church and state. When in the late 1910s, the Conservative government adopted universal male suffrage and direct election of the president, the Radical Socialists seemed unable to find a new political message and lost their appeal to the electorate. The Great Depression of the 1930s ravaged the economy as the export markets for meat and wheat dried up and brought on a political crisis. Election fraud throughout the 1930s wreaked havoc on political stability and popular support for elective government.

Throughout the first half of the twentieth century, Argentina saw itself as the natural contender with the U.S. for leadership in the hemisphere. It joined the Pan American Union when it was created in 1898 and saw it as a mechanism for promoting Latin American regional cooperation against the Colossus of the North. The two countries were competitors in the world's agricultural markets, and the U.S. banned all Argentine cattle and beef from entering its domestic markets because of endemic foot-and-mouth disease in Argentina. The two countries found occasional areas in which they cooperated, like the Pan American Sanitary Bureau's efforts to control yellow fever and other diseases.

In World War II, despite U.S. pressure, Argentina maintained neutrality. There were strong pro-Axis elements in the government, especially in the army and the Argentine "White House" (*La Casa Rosada*). In 1943, the armed forces led what appeared to be a pro-Allied military coup, but Juan Domingo Perón with his lady Evita challenged the pro-Allied leadership and emerged as the strong man of Argentina. His populist message propagated by Evita was the first in Argentine history to speak to the aspirations and needs of the common people, and made them the champions of the Argentine common man, *los descamisados* (the shirtless ones). A month before the end of World War II in Europe, Argentina declared war on the Axis even though Perón reportedly had pro-Axis sentiments and his relations with the Allies were severely strained. Peron became president in 1945 and was elected in a landslide in 1948.

By the end of World War II Argentine sales of wheat and beef to both sides during World War II had made it one of the richest countries in the world. Perón and Evita used that wealth to carry out their populist agenda. He went on a nationalist push to pay off the foreign debt, buy foreign-owned utilities and railways at extravagant prices, and promote new national industries to achieve economic self-sufficiency. He also gave the vote to women, developed social welfare programs for the *descamisados*, and subsidized pro-government labor unions to press for the rights of workers and higher income for the rural and urban workers. Peron's popularity remained high as government surpluses turned to deficits by the early 1950s. Perón achieved full employment, but he bankrupted the country in the process. In 1955, after Evita's death, he was deposed and exiled by the army. Civilian governments for nearly a decade grappled unsuccessfully with a deteriorating economy and rising social discontent until another army coup had brought President Onganía to power.

Paraguay had a very different history and was far less developed than Argentina. With little gold and fierce Guaraní tribes, the Crown entrusted the Jesuits with the territory and authorized them to set up Missions to convert the people to Christianity and develop a self-sustaining economy. Paraguay became a Jesuit-run theocracy until the late eighteenth century when the Jesuits fell out of favor and the Franciscans, backed by Portuguese and Spanish military, were sent to displace them. After independence from Spain, the first president, General Gaspar Rodríguez de Francia, decreed that the country be sealed off from all external influences and banned all schools and road building. However, his chief minister, José Francisco López, maintained an extensive private library in a remote rural area and educated himself. When he replaced Francia, he opened the country, created efficient public services and a national school system, invested in agriculture, and adopted policies to attract foreign investment. He led it to become one of the richest and most progressive nations of South America.

His son, Francisco Solano López, replaced him on his death in the 1850s. He was educated as a military officer at France's St. Cyr Military Academy and had ambitions of providing his landlocked country with a seaport on the Rio de la Plata. He inherited a booming economy and a full treasury. Paraguay reportedly had nearly one million inhabitants, while his Rio de la Plata neighbors were no larger: Argentina had perhaps a million people and Uruguay, 300,000. Argentina was engaged in its final Indian Wars, and Uruguay was emerging from a series of civil wars between conservatives and liberals. Solano López exercised absolute power in a prosperous Paraguay and believed that with the military prowess he had learned at St. Cyr, he could defeat his neighbors. Borders in the region were ill-defined, and Paraguay was periodically engaged in border skirmishes with both Brazil and Argentina. So, in 1864, Paraguay went to war with Brazil, a country of ten million inhabitants, over a disputed border and with Argentina and Uruguay to obtain a deep water port on the Rio de la Plata. Thus began the War of the Triple Alliance. For five years, the bloody war rolled on until Brazil cornered and killed Solano López. For Paraguay it was a war of national genocide, with only 2,500 males between the ages of eighteen and fifty-two left alive.

Paraguay lost not only most of its male population, with women outnumbering men by at least four to one, but also 54,000 square miles of its most productive farmlands to Argentina and the disputed territory to Brazil. Brazil occupied and governed Paraguay for ten years and allowed it to remain independent because Brazil wanted a buffer zone between itself and Argentina. Argentina, Uruguay, and Brazil imposed huge indemnities that impoverished Paraguay for decades and that were not fully paid off until World War II, seventy years after the War of the Triple Alliance had ended. Paraguay was also allowed perpetual rights to use the river systems through Argentina down to the Rio de la Plata and special privileges at Argentina ports. Brazil agreed to build a highway to a Brazilian Atlantic port and provide duty-free status for products landed at that port bound for Paraguay.

The only consolation for Paraguay was an arbitration award in 1879 by U.S. President Rutherford B. Hayes. The four countries agreed to submit to the U.S. president their dispute over control of the Rio Verde tributary of the Pilcomayo River. The arbitration favored Paraguay, and Hayes became a hero in that country. A vast Chaco Province in Paraguay is named after him, as well as the province's football team, the *Yanquis*; Paraguayans are the only Latin Americans who chant, "*Arriba los Yanquis!*" (Go Yankees!), in a public stadium.

From the War of the Triple Alliance to the Chaco War with Bolivia, Paraguay was in a state of unending civil war, with one general after another contesting for power. Its population gradually recovered, some say with a blind eye to polygamous marital arrangements. By the time of the Chaco War, Paraguay was estimated to have about one million people again. In that war, it lost another 30,000 fighters while its Bolivians opponents lost about 65,000. Civil war broke out again in the 1940s and ended only after Stroessner took power. The fifteen years under Stroessner was one of the longest periods of peaceful development since the time of José Francisco López.

Uruguay had a quite different history. Uruguay was settled by gauchos from Central Argentina who came in their covered wagons (*caretas*) with a fierce sense of independence and self-reliance. The hero of the independence movement, José Artigas, was a strong democrat and advocate of elected government. By the mid-1850s, the liberal party, the *Colorados*, had come to power and for more than century won election after election over the conservatives, the *Blancos*.

The *Colorados* in the first years of the twentieth century championed broad citizen participation in government and, by the 1940s, installed cradle-to-grave social welfare programs. It was hailed as one of the best functioning democracies in the region. The social program established liberal retirement benefits, with relatively young retirement ages to qualify for benefits. The system was financed by taxes on the profits made from international trade in wheat and cattle. However, the government failed to provide incentives for reinvestment in sustaining production, and they were bled dry, leading to a severe economic crisis in the late 1950s and 1960s. The Uruguayan peso that had stood at two pesos to the U.S. dollar for decades dropped precipitously to one thousand to a dollar. The country was on the verge of bankruptcy.

The economic crisis was compounded by a political vacuum of power when its experiment with the Swiss-style Council of Government system resulted in indecision and lack of government action on almost all issues. Facing a national implosion, a multiparty decision was made in 1966 to return to the presidential system. With the economy in a shambles and popular discontent almost universal, a new political force, the Broad Front (*Frente Amplio*) brought together the parties to the left of the *Colorados* and threatened "the tired old men" who led the besieged *Colorados*. At the same time, impatient allies of the *Frente* formed an insurgency, the *Tupamaros*, led by Raul Sendic. In 1967, Jorge Pacheco, the standard bearer of the *Colorados*, was elected president.

Uruguay obtained economic aid from the U.S. to stabilize the economy, but the depleted financial and institutional resources of the Uruguayan government made progress extremely difficult. Both governments were concerned that the *Frente Amplio* could give rise to a pro-Soviet regime, which led the U.S. government to provide counterinsurgency assistance similar to what AID had provided to Brazil, Vietnam, and other countries. Democratic Uruguay was in danger, and that became my number one concern.

Relations with the Embassies

After the courtesy calls on the three ambassadors, I suggested that we set up regular meetings to deal with issues on our respective agendas. The Argentine and Uruguayan ambassadors were enthusiastic and agreed to informal working sessions with Ed and me once every two weeks. The Paraguayan ambassador felt that we did not need to meet regularly, so we left it that we would meet whenever either one of us felt it necessary.

The Argentine chargé, Rafael Vasquez, suggested that each of us prepare a list of outstanding issues. I agreed and suggested that Jack Whiting, the desk officer, join us and that Vasquez bring whichever of his senior officers he thought best informed on the issues we would be discussing. I invited Vasquez to meet at State for the first meeting and suggested that we have lunch in the Executive Dining Room after the meeting. Vasquez returned the invitation and we began a year and a half of open discussion.

The Argentine embassy staff was substantial, with specialists in economic, political, and military affairs. Vasquez introduced Jack, Ed, and me to the members of the embassy as well as to senior officers of the Argentine military missions who usually worked only with colleagues at the Defense Department. We were invited to their homes and reciprocated with lunches at State. When they compiled their agenda, Jack and I had not been aware of some of the priority issues raised. High on the list were the limitations on access of beef, pear, and apple to the U.S market and a decade-old negotiation for the Argentine acquisition of naval vessels. On some items, Jack had information in our active files; on others, we had to contact the State Department File Repository in St. Louis for background papers.

This process placed all our concerns on the table. Maybe we couldn't resolve every one or even make a dent on many, but we had them before us and we could understand the matters that were eating away at our relationship. As we discussed each issue, I would invite other U.S. government colleagues who were more knowledgeable about them to join the discussions. I felt that my job was to create a cooperative environment in which we could understand and respect each other. My experience had been that once an amicable working relationship is created, talking about business becomes easier and more conducive to finding common ground.

One lunch in the fall of 1969 that I still vividly recall was with former Argentine Ambassador Eduardo Roca. He had resigned in late 1968 over policy disagreements with the Onganía government. Eduardo Roca was the grandson of two-time Conservative Party President Julio Argentino Roca at the turn of the twentieth century. His grandfather built a mansion that he planned to offer as the official residence of Argentine presidents. When his offer was declined, he sold it to the U.S. government for our ambassadorial residence, as it remains today. Ambassador Roca gave me a history lesson on the failure of successive Argentine leaders and political parties to develop effective political institutions and blamed the resulting political vacuum for the discontent of the Argentine people and the rise of Perón. Roca was deeply concerned about the political situation and warned me that deteriorating economic and social conditions in his country threatened the stability of the government.

Relations with the Uruguayan ambassador were quite different. He ran a small embassy with two or three aides of considerable ability, but it was essentially a one-man operation. Ambassador Luisi, a successful lawyer and foreign minister before his assignment to Washington, had played an active role in the re-establishment of the presidential system and in confronting the insurgency. He saw his job as critical to the survival of the democratic institutions of his country. He knew all of the significant political personalities in country, including President Pacheco, to whom he had direct access. Each discussion with him was a lesson in the decision-making process of the Uruguayan elite and his descriptions of the key policy makers gave me an insight into what decisions I should expect that government to make.

We met every other week for the next year and a half. We became good friends and we shared a common concern—not merely to counter the threat of the *Tupamaros*, but to rebuild democratic institutions. We were equally concerned about reports from Montevideo of police and military "death squads" that were rounding up suspects and disposing of them and believed such practices were counterproductive. We gave those reports serious attention and investigated them in both Washington and Montevideo, My inquiries to Byron Engel, chief of the AID Office of Public Safety, assured me that AID had nothing to with death squads or any activities outside of the traditional technical training of the local police.

The Paraguayan ambassador met with us only occasionally. He

usually had his deputy chief of mission raise matters with us, often related to some aspect of the AID program. So it was with some surprise that I received a request from a Washington lobbyist, a one-time national republican committeeman, for an appointment to discuss a proposal from President Stroessner.

The lobbyist presented a detailed plan to convert Paraguay into an "Anti-Soviet Aircraft Carrier" in the heart of South America. The proposal called for a U.S. and Paraguay military cooperation treaty to build a mammoth air force operating center in Paraguay from which the Western Allies could counter pro-Soviet military and subversive activities in South America in return for training and supplying planes and equipment for an elite Paraguayan force that would be available to assist the U.S. in the event of an emergency. He advised me that he was in contact with officials at the White House and the Defense Department as well as at State. He wanted my office to be informed because he expected early positive action at the highest levels of the U.S. government.

I immediately presented the proposal to Assistant Secretary Meyer and Jack Crimmins, and voiced my objection to it. They agreed, and Jack contacted his counterparts at the White House and the Defense Department, and found that they had no interest in the proposal. We deep-sixed the presentation, and they left me to tell the lobbyist that his proposal was going nowhere.

Visit to the Countries

I had been on the job for about six weeks when Assistant Secretary Charles Meyer advised me that it was time to meet the leaders of the three countries in person. I was apprehensive about leaving the country because Ele's situation was worrisome—her mother was making very slow progress in recovering from her broken hip, her wrist was not healing well, and her doctor kept her confined to bed. Ele had been in Tulare all summer and the heat and worry had taken its toll on her.

In 1969, Ele and I communicated primarily by letter. We wrote several times a week and tried to talk every Sunday. Her letters reflected a sense of despair. Her grandmother had died following a broken hip, and now her mother. She seemed to lose interest in everything outside the immediate problem in Tulare. I was afraid that if I took the trip to South America, she would feel abandoned.

I wrote her to say that the assistant secretary was pressing me for a date to visit the countries. The following Sunday, she said that I should make the trip and that, on my return, she would join me in Washington for a week or two. So, my trip was on.

In their briefings, the assistant secretary and Jack Crimmins spelled out their concerns about the situation in Argentina and Uruguay, and specified matters that they wanted me to explore; while the assistant secretary was not a career foreign service officer, he had an excellent grasp of the short and long-term issues. He also told me to tell the ambassadors that he hoped to visit their countries in the near future.

My itinerary took me first to Buenos Aires, then to Asunción and Montevideo. On my return trip, I was to consult with South Com, the U.S. military command center for Latin America situated in Panama. There was no non-stop flight from Washington to Buenos Aires; it was a sixteen-hour flight, including a four-hour layover in Miami.

I arrived in Buenos Aires about midday and was taken to the ambassador's residence where I was to stay for the next four days. Ambassador John Davis Lodge, his wife Francesca, and Deputy Chief of Mission Mike Barall were waiting for me. They presented me with a detailed program, and informed me that dinner that evening was with the owner of the newspaper *El Clarín*. I gratefully grabbed a bath and a siesta.

This was the house that Eduardo Roca's grandfather had built to be the Argentine White House. It was truly a palace, built of marble, with a central staircase that rivaled noble homes in Europe. Its rooms were gracious and large, designed to host hundreds of people at receptions and balls. My bedroom for my four days was the suite that President Franklin Delano Roosevelt had used during his historic "Good Neighbor" visit in 1936, and I slept in the Roosevelt bed. The bathroom was big enough to hold a Ping-Pong table. I felt like a little kid who had won the jackpot!

Dinner at 8:00 p.m. was black tie. The owner of *El Clarín* was one of the most powerful women in the country. I joined Ambassador Lodge and Francesca in greeting the dinner guests. We had a lively dinner that lasted until after ten o'clock, enlivened by the ambassador's leading us in singing Argentine and U.S. songs after dessert. We talked little business, but a lot of getting to know one another in preparation for serious discussions later in my stay.

The next morning, the ambassador took me to the chancery in central Buenos Aires. We had little substantive discussion until we entered a secure conference room outside the ambassador's office. Since the chancery was on several floors of a commercial building, there was concern that eavesdropping devices might be located on nearby floors or adjoining buildings. I met the country team and was given an in-depth briefing by State Department, CIA, and military members of the mission. The ambassador said that he would accompany me later that morning to a protocol visit to President Onganía and from that time forward, Deputy Chief of Mission Milton "Mike" Barall would be my constant companion.

We then went over three days of visits. A working session and luncheon that day with the foreign minister, who was to accompany the president during my courtesy call. Later that afternoon, I was to call on the minister of the Economy. The following morning, I was to meet with the chief of the Armed Forces, and later that day, with the minister of Planning. Lunch was to be at Mike Barall's residence with several academics and newspaper editorial writers. That evening there was a small dinner party to meet key embassy officers and their wives. My last full day was devoted to meeting political leaders, including supporters of ousted President Perón, former President Aramburu, and exiled President Frondizi. At midday, the ambassador hosted a lunch at the embassy for Argentine labor leaders, many of whom I had met when I served as regional labor adviser, and some of whom I knew were clandestine Peronists.

My impression from the four days in Buenos Aires was that serious internal trouble was ahead. Perón was the elephant in the room that no one talked about. The Argentine economy was improving, but Onganía was about to tackle the special privileges of the military industrial complex (*Abastecimientos Militares*) and it was clear to me that the military was not about to let its sacred cow be touched. President Onganía had mentioned the economic measures that he had already approved, and said that his minister of the Economy was preparing new actions to open Argentina up to foreign investment and access to the world money markets. The minister, Luis May, was not specific in our discussions but made clear that he was about to tackle sacred cows of the armed forces. The minister had been trained at Columbia University on an AID fellowship before the Peronists forced the University of Buenos Aires to cancel its university-to-university agreement.

Every official I talked to warned me of the restiveness of the High Command with the direction of economic policies and the power it wielded in the country. Nowhere did I sense that more than when I walked into the armed forces conference room. There was a map on the front wall that showed the world from the Argentine perspective: Argentina in the center with the rest of the world on a much smaller scale and, within Argentina, the layout of military bases.

Discussion of the political climate revolved around the Peronist Party even though it had been proscribed in 1955 when Perón was ousted and exiled. However, no other party had filled the vacuum. The military, after a period of national reconciliation, permitted two elections, the first won by conservative Aramburu and the second, by a more liberal Radical Socialist Frondizi. When Frondizi began talking of reconciliation with the Peronists, he was overthrown in a coup. Everyone I talked to stressed the determination of the military not to allow the Peronists to return to power. There was no doubt of their anti-communism, and little doubt of their discomfort with liberal democratic institutions. I felt an aura of pessimism in everyone with whom I talked. The academics speculated about the root causes of the failure of successive regimes to build effective democratic institutions, but no one seemed to have answers.

When I left Buenos Aires, I was genuinely concerned about what was to happen in the country. The military was all powerful and not inclined to give Onganía much leeway. In the Cold War setting, the U.S. would not risk pressure on the military for fear that it would provide an opening for the USSR. Having talked to senior military, I was convinced that if Onganía were ousted, the succeeding government would be less disposed to reform and more repressive. My embassy colleagues had a similar perception.

The trip to Asunción on *Linea Aérea Paraguaya* (LAP, the Paraguayan national airline) was pleasant. As we approached Asunción, the public address system played a musical tribute to President Stroessner. That set the stage for my four-day visit.

U.S. Ambassador Ylitalo invited me to be his guest, and I was whisked from the airport to the embassy compound and the ambassador's residence. It was a Saturday and the ambassador invited all the members of the country team to a cocktail and briefing in the late afternoon. There were several old friends to greet me, including USAID Director Peter Cody, whom I had first met in Mexico.

The briefing was all about Stroessner and his control over every aspect of Paraguayan life. The order and security that he had installed fifteen years previously had been welcomed by people after living through decades of civil warfare and the Chaco War. However, Stroessner exercised an iron hand and tolerated no dissent. He and his henchmen had installed a graft-ridden regime that took advantage of every opportunity to line the pockets of key officials—and everyone in the administration seemed to take his or her piece of the action. Peter Cody and the Peace Corps director were the positive face of the U.S.; they were engaged in institution building and grass roots development designed to set the stage for a change when the Stroessner era ended. By the time we sat down to a family-style dinner, I knew what to expect from the meetings scheduled for Sunday, Monday, and Tuesday morning.

Ambassador Ylitalo had been transferred to Asunción from Tijuana, Mexico, where he had been consul general. He was the first South Dakotan ever to serve as an ambassador. He was intelligent and dedicated. He found learning Spanish extremely difficult, but he was fluent in Finnish and other Scandinavian languages. On the other hand, his children were totally comfortable not only in Spanish but also in Guaraní, the second official language of Paraguay. I remember his daughter entertaining us after dinner with Guaraní songs as she played a Guaraní harp—some of the most enchanting music I have ever heard.

On Sunday, the ambassador took me to the opening game of the Paraguayan League soccer season. The Presidente Hayes *Yanquis* team invited the ambassador to kick the ball to open the season—to the cheers of the *Yanqui* rooting section, *"Vivan los Yanquis"* (Go Yankees). On Sunday evening, the ambassador and Mrs. Ylitalo took me to dinner with the foreign minister and his key advisers at the Foreign Ministry.

Early Monday morning, President Stroessner invited the ambassador and me to a short meeting in his office. He welcomed me and assured me that his ministers were prepared to cooperate with the U.S. in every way possible, especially in combating communism in South America. Leaving his office, the Economic Counselor and Peter Cody accompanied me to a long meeting with the minister of Finance, General Barrientos, who had assumed his post when his friend and colleague, General Stroessner, became president. I was told that he knew where every body was buried and the destiny of every penny that entered and left Paraguay. We spent several hours discussing every aspect of the country's fiscal and monetary situation, as well as the AID program, pending Paraguayan loan applications in the Inter-American Bank and the World Bank, and the agenda for pending discussions with the International Monetary Fund. The minister asked for U.S. support of Paraguayan loan requests. I might add that the Paraguayan ambassador in Washington had never raised any of these issues with us. I also met with the ministers of Planning, Agriculture, Education, and Public Health before dinner at Peter Cody's home.

Tuesday morning, before I left for Montevideo, the embassy set up a couple of interviews with opposition leaders. We knew that every step I took was shadowed by the Paraguayans, so the meetings were carefully arranged to limit the chances of compromising the people with whom I was to meet. One of them was an old friend from I House Berkeley, and another was a student leader whom I had met at AIFLD in Washington. They confirmed the continuing use of torture by the secret police and were clearly on edge for even meeting with me.

Just as I was about to leave for the airport, a gentleman asked to see me at the ambassador's office. He gave me a package with a picture of my meeting with President Stroessner—and an invoice for US$7.

I took the daily flight of the Uruguayan National Airline from Asunción to Montevideo. On arrival, an embassy officer moved me quickly through the airport since the *Tupamaros* posed an immediate threat to my security. I was taken to the residence where Ambassador Robert Sayre invited me to be his houseguest. I was taken up to the Eisenhower Bedroom. Yes, once again I touched fame! In 1959, on his historic visit to South America, this had been the suite in which Eisenhower had stayed.

I went to the chancery after lunch and met with Ambassador Sayre, one of the most competent and incisive officers with whom I worked. He gave me a detailed analysis of a country on the verge of collapse, and came right to the point about the challenges facing President Pacheco and his *Colorado* cabinet of senior citizens. Pacheco had brought together very able advisors who averaged seventy years of age, but they were groping with political and economic issues with which they had little experience. Economic Officer Bill Kneeper and Political Officer Jim Tull filled in the details, and the CIA chief spelled out the opportunity the morass offered the insurgents. Unlike Argentina and Paraguay, the military was not eager to step in; they wanted to ensure the constitutional system with civilian political leadership. In those four days in Uruguay I met with key civilian and military leaders. No pomp or ceremony, just immersion in the crisis!

My courtesy call was not on President Pacheco, who was ill, but on Vice President Alberto Abdala, who was not considered to be particularly friendly to U.S. interests and not a member of the president's *Colorado* Party. Our meeting was quite formal until he asked me if I had ever been to Yankton, South Dakota. I replied that I had, and that my wife had inherited a farm in nearby Aberdeen. We started talking about South Dakota, and the visit went well beyond the fifteen minutes that he had scheduled. It turned out that his brother had migrated to Yankton and that he had boarded the wrong ship in Beirut and ended up in Montevideo instead of New York. We sipped coffee and talked about the United States and U.S.-Uruguayan relations until his secretary came in almost an hour later to remind him that he had other appointments. We stayed in touch for several years.

That evening, Ambassador Sayre invited President Pacheco's key economic advisers to dinner at the residence. Most of them were in their sixties and seventies, and all had been long-time political activists, several had been presidents of the Central Bank or cabinet ministers. All were committed to the resurgence of a democratic Uruguay. They were the brothers and heirs of the Middle Way democracy with social justice. Now they were faced with the consequences of not recognizing the cost of the "cradle-to-grave" social security and not including measures to stimulate economic growth in order to finance it.

These were people I truly wished to help. They were committed to freedom and human rights. They had worked for many years to help their country establish institutions capable of protecting the interests of their fellow citizens. None of them was a rich man; none had been accused of corruption, only of making poor economic decisions. As I listened to them talk about the problems and their frustrations, it was clear that, while they were all prepared to support drastic measures needed to right the economy, there was little agreement on specific actions to be taken. Their diagnosis was correct: they had to stop the spate of bank failures and businesses closings, and they had to face the reality that revenues were less than social obligations and that the reserves were almost gone. But they were reluctant to dismantle or reform the social security system that they themselves had helped design and install.

With almost 25 percent of the Uruguayan populace dependent on social security payments for their income, this was the key issue they had to face. Since the Uruguayan peso had dropped in less than a decade from two pesos to the U.S. dollar to 1,000 to the dollar, a pension of one hundred pesos that had been worth fifty dollars ten years previously was now worth about ten cents a month. Health services had to be closed because the budget could not cover the costs of operation, and the sick were being turned away from clinics and hospitals. After years in which all the profits had been taxed away to support social programs, agriculture had become unprofitable and generated only minimal foreign exchange earnings. Unemployment in this highly urbanized society, with one third of the population living in Montevideo, was escalating.

They urged the ambassador and me to provide some short-term financial relief to save their democracy. The anti-communist card was played several times during the evening, saying that greater austerity would give the *Tupamaros* an opening. They urged us to consider a bridge loan from the U.S., but the ambassador and I reminded them that the U.S. needed a plan from the Uruguayan government as the basis for our considering any assistance. We also reminded them that the IMF had indicated several specific financial and budgetary measures that had to be taken in order to trigger IMF support, and that the U.S. government supported the IMF proposals.

After my eight days in Argentina and Paraguay, my commitment to Uruguay was firmer than ever, but the Uruguayans had to take the lead on the road back to solvency. It was tough for the ambassador and me not to be more forthcoming. But without measures by the government to deal with the causes of the economic and social disaster, throwing money into Uruguay would only postpone the day of reckoning. With all the potential negatives, we saw no alternative but to urge them to present a viable financial plan to allow us to help them.

The rest of my stay in Montevideo was dedicated to assessing the immediate threat posed by the *Tupamaros*. I was introduced to student leaders and newsmen who claimed to know the leaders of the *Tupamaros*. They all believed that they were an indigenous group with leftist leanings. Few thought they were controlled by outside forces such as Castro, the USSR, or the Brazilian militants. They were clearly a threat to Uruguayan democracy but my question was: what could the U.S. do other than support the country's elected leaders until the government presented us with a socioeconomic plan to deal with the crisis? The ambassador agreed.

I met with senior Uruguayan military and police officials who, unlike those in Argentina or Paraguay, expressed little interest in running the government. After over a hundred years of civilian government, they stressed that their role was to support the Constitution. They also said that they were not trained to deal with economic and social issues. They bemoaned that they lacked more than elementary counter-intelligence capability. One general commented that in prior years, they had spent more time preparing for civic parades than handling civil disobedience. They did express their appreciation for U.S. support to deal with the *Tupamaros*, especially building up their intelligence and counter-subversion forces.

Only one afternoon was dedicated to the USAID program. It was small, with agriculture as its primary focus. I talked with the minister of Agriculture and an AID technician about the inputs needed to revitalize wheat and cattle production, as well as to introduce some additional cash crops such as citrus and alfalfa. I regretted that my scheduled meeting with the USAID police mission was cancelled at the last minute because of an emergency, since over the past two days I heard veiled comments about police brutality and insinuations that the USAID police mission had been involved. I wanted to discuss this with the team leader, even though the ambassador told me that he had instructed them against any teaching or involvement in the use of torture or other prohibited practices in questioning suspects. I made a note to talk again to Byron Engel, director of the worldwide Police Advisory program on my return to Washington.

I flew from Uruguay to Panama for two days of consultations with South Com. Ambassador Charles Adair invited me to stay at the embassy residence. That was fortuitous, because it provided an opportunity for the ambassador and me to get to know each other. I was aware that Ambassador Adair was slated to move to Uruguay and Ambassador Sayre to come to Panama. I shared with him my perception about the situation in Uruguay. His questions were penetrating and to the point. He earned my respect and made me feel very comfortable working with him.

Ambassador Adair accompanied me to my meetings with the general in charge of South Com and his officers working on Argentina, Paraguay, and Uruguay. With Ambassador Adair preparing for a transfer to Uruguay, the briefing was comprehensive, followed by an in-depth analysis of concerns about the military situation in the area and the threats of subversion. The Cold War was in full play and the possibility of Soviet exploitation of the political and economic situation in each country was aired in great detail. I expressed my concern over the internal situation I found in each country as well as the rumors of U.S. involvement in the treatment of prisoners in Uruguay.

My former deputy in Bolivia and close personal friend, David Lazar, had been transferred from Vietnam to Panama as AID mission director. He and his wife Nancy invited me to dinner on the last night of my stay. I remember that night very well, July 16, 1969, the date on which man first walked on the moon. We had a warm family dinner and talked about personal things. As the evening progressed, Nancy and David invited the maid, the cook, and the gardener to watch the historic moon landing on television. We were awestruck by Neil Armstrong and his "One giant step for mankind." David asked the maid and cook for their reactions and they seemed very excited. Not the gardener! He said to us, "You gringos can put anything on television. Now, you want me to believe that you gringos reached the moon?" He shook his head and left the room.

My report to the assistant secretary and Jack Crimmins was not a happy one. While I stressed the quality, objectivity, and outreach of our missions in the three countries, I advised that we should expect a bumpy road ahead in the Rio de la Plata: instability in Argentina, an unsavory government in Paraguay, and crisis in Uruguay. The whirlwind trip had made quite real the perceptions and insights I had accumulated from my readings and my initial dealings with my counterparts in the three embassies in Washington.

I also called Byron Engel, director of the worldwide Police Advisory program, for an appointment and was told that he was unavailable. I was referred to the chief of Latin American operations who listened politely to my concerns about the situation in Uruguay and assured me that the police program flatly opposed the use of torture and brutal methods in questioning suspects. However, I was further told that I had to understand the real world as it is and that, in the Cold War, the U.S. had to use "enhanced" techniques to thwart our enemies—but those techniques did not involve torture or brutal methods even if our enemies used them. I was also politely told that the police program knew what it was doing. As events in Uruguay evolved over the next two years, culminating in the murder of USAID Chief Police Adviser Dan Mitrione, I was disgusted by my naiveté at accepting what a fellow officer had told me. Maybe I could have made a difference.

The Storm

The next year was one of the saddest and most frustrating of my life. St. Jude, the saint of lost causes, pervaded my life.

On my return from the Rio de la Plata, my office colleagues and I began a process of assessing the importance of our relations with

Argentina, Paraguay, and Uruguay with the central themes of our foreign policy. For all practical purposes, the Alliance for Progress was no longer a priority. Since the Cuban missile crisis and the *de facto* U.S.-USSR understanding that Castro would not be "unleashed," and our increasing commitment in Vietnam, U.S. interest in Western Hemisphere affairs had declined dramatically. Mexico and the Panama Canal had a life of their own. Only the threat of communist subversion in a given country seemed to awaken any interest above the assistant secretary for Inter-American Affairs.

The American nations had agreed to a nuclear-free area. The OAS member states were military allies under the Rio Treaty. We had joined the Latin Americans in creating the Inter-American Development Bank to help finance country development. I perceived that policy makers believed that was all we needed to do for the moment in the Americas, barring some unforeseen emergency.

In this context, the Rio de la Plata countries were not candidates for much high-level policy attention. My colleagues and I estimated that our ability to awaken high-level attention to resolve political issues or allocate special resources to respond to economic needs was limited. We were already providing counter-subversion assistance to Uruguay. We had open lines of communication for dialogue with the leadership and opposition elements in Argentina and Paraguay. AID and the Peace Corps were assets in helping the countries solve problems. Che Guevara was not alive to lead the *descamisados* to establish a new Castro domain in Argentina. Corruption in Paraguay was not yet tied into the international drug cartels. The Brazilian military, though fiercely nationalist, were not prepared to let the *Tupamaros* on their southern border pose a threat to the internal order they were imposing on their homeland. Our trade and investment were not as large there as with other regions of the Western Hemisphere. There was little demand for bilateral military cooperation and interdependence.

Hence, we concluded that the primary U.S. interest was to be alert to developments and be in position to react if anything untoward happened that affected negatively our priority national interests. This meant that the Rio de la Plata was not likely to attract much high-level interest over the next couple of years and ours would a holding action. In this context, we focused our work plan. When I consulted the assistant secretary, he agreed.

The assistant secretary also advised me that he planned to make an official visit to each country in the Latin America to meet each head of state personally. In March 1970, when he made his official visit to the Rio de la Plata, he invited me to accompany him. He was accorded the treatment usually given to the secretary of state—he was met by the foreign ministers and chiefs of protocol and was given lavish banquets. In Paraguay, he was met at the airport by an honor guard that he reviewed under the watchful eye of President Stroessner seated in his car a few yards away. We met with the heads of state in all three countries, attended country team and ministerial meetings, and stayed in the ambassadors' residences. Secretary Meyer was in the Roosevelt and Eisenhower suites. Fog closed the airports in Buenos Aires and Montevideo, so we had to cross the estuary by boat and missed the official dinner with Uruguayan President Pacheco. In all three capitals, the scope, flavor, and depth of the discussions and analyses differed little from those I had experienced a few months earlier, with little sign of alleviation or improvement. The tone of the assistant secretary's remarks closely followed my office's perception of the priority afforded the region at that time.

Over the next few months, my office colleagues and I maintained our routine. We met with our counterparts at the three embassies and with our counterparts at State, Defense, CIA, AID, and USIA. We monitored CIAP and IDB meetings on the three countries. We read the daily intelligence and press reports on the countries. We were waiting for something to happen.

But first something happened to Ele and me. I flew out to California for Christmas, saw my mother in San Francisco, and we celebrated Christmas together in Tulare. Ele's mother's wrist had improved so that she was now able to take physical therapy to walk again. Ele agreed that she would find a rehab facility in which she could place her mother for a couple of months until she was able to walk well enough to go home. In January 1970, Ele found what she thought was just the right facility. She arranged for her mother to be admitted, and then flew back to Washington.

I well remember February 22, 1970. Ele and I had spent the day with our friends, the Guthries. It was one of those lovely early spring days in which the gray of winter had been replaced by sunshine. We had a late lunch at the Guthries and arrived home to hear that an urgent message was waiting for us from the nursing home. We hurried upstairs and Ele made the call. Her mother had died along with most of the other patients at the facility by a deadly wave of influenza. We were not prepared for the news, but had to react immediately. We arranged with United to fly the following day. We made funeral arrangements. We called friends in Tulare to tell them the news. The good feeling we felt on leaving the Guthries had turned to sadness.

The funeral was a sad occasion and Ele decided to stay in Tulare to handle the settlement of the estate. While it was a modest one, the paperwork was still demanding. Ele hired a Harvard-trained estate lawyer to prepare and file the federal and state papers. The work dragged on for weeks. The lawyer missed deadlines for requesting exemptions and Ele called on me to help out. I spent evenings and weekends researching the relevant laws. In fact, I prepared almost all the documents and explanations that the local lawyer ultimately submitted. Ele talked to state and federal officials.

The spring of 1970 was one in which Ele and I, at opposite ends of the country, found empty and frustrating. It was late June before she locked up her mother's and grandmother's side-by-side houses, turned them over to a security officer to look after during her absence, and returned to Washington.

On her arrival, it was clear Ele was not well. Her preoccupation with her mother's passing had led her to postpone the treatment that her doctor in Tulare had been urging. She felt that rest and quiet would do the trick. Meanwhile, reports from San Francisco were that my seventy-six year old mother's health was also deteriorating. My brother-in-law did not seem too concerned, but I sensed during our weekly telephone calls that something was awry. I talked to Ele about my going to San Francisco, but she asked me not to leave her until she felt better.

In spite of this difficult personal environment, I kept up my bi-weekly meetings with the Argentine and Uruguayan ambassadors.

In January 1970, a new Argentine ambassador, Pedro Real, arrived. He was from the Conservative Party and was a strong advocate of improving relations with the U.S. However, we seldom met without his political counselor, Mario Campora—an ardent Peronist. Ambassador Real, Mario, and I had long discussions about legal principles and U.S.-Argentine relations. Mario was the nephew of Héctor Campora, the Argentine journalist who was to become president of Argentina later in the 1970s when the military restored civilian government. My dialogue with the ambassador and Mario continued for many years after my tour as office director ended.

Over several months we made little progress in solving issues on our agenda. We made a special effort to find an accommodation on the U.S. tariff on apples and pears, but the U.S. Department of Agriculture made it clear that business interests in Washington and California held the cards and were not prepared to consider any competition. The ambassador rarely raised requests for military equipment; he let his military attachés discuss those matters with their counterparts in the Defense Department.

After Ele's return, Ambassador Real made Ele and me frequent guests at dinners and receptions at the embassy. The Argentines seldom invited senior U.S. administration officials or members of congress to their dinners and receptions, preferring Defense Department officials, businessmen, and lobbyists. One of the receptions they hosted was for Neil Armstrong and Buzz Aldrin after the moonwalk. I accompanied the guests of honor from the White House to the embassy. Ele and I witnessed Armstrong's gesture of giving his watch to an Argentine officer who admired it.

Mario Campora also took me to a number of *parrilladas* (barbecues) hosted by various embassy members. They were masters of roasting steaks. At one of them, in June 1979, at the home of the Argentine Air Force attaché, I was drinking a beer with the chief of the Argentine Military mission, General Roberto Levingstone, when an aide rushed over to advise him that Onganía had been deposed and that the Military Junta had chosen him, General Levingstone, to be the new president. I watched while the general and his wife said their goodbyes and left to pack for the flight home. Frankly, I was distressed because I had found Levingstone to be a hardline nationalist and politically close-minded. As we drove home, Mario was very tight-lipped but clearly unhappy at the turn of events. Ambassador Real cancelled our bi-weekly meetings for the next couple of months.

The situation with Uruguay was equally disturbing. I spent a lot of time with Ambassador Luisi and his wife Blanca. Ele and I along with Ed Marasciulo and his wife Eileen were frequent dinner guests, both at small family dinners and larger receptions, usually in honor of key members of the Nixon cabinet, like Secretary of State Rogers, Attorney General John Mitchell and his wife, Martha, and the Secretary of Commerce and Mrs. Stans. The ambassador was building a coalition of friends in the administration as the news from Montevideo became increasingly ominous.

The Uruguayan economy was not picking up as the government had hoped. Violence in the usually peaceful country was on the rise. Raids by the *Tupamaros* were increasing in number and intensity. The reaction by the government was increasingly severe. That summer, Ed and I took turns at night and over weekends on "security watch." The Department of State had not yet set up a "Crisis Center" and each office basically took its own measures. Ambassador Adair reported the measures he was taking to protect the embassy and the staff. The tension was extremely high. Ambassador Luisi was concerned about a coup and we used State Department channels to help him communicate with President Pacheco.

Then on July 31, we received the cable from Montevideo that Dan Mitrione, a USAID public safety adviser, had been kidnapped by the *Tupamaros*. Ed and I spent the next ten days almost around the clock in the office. Ele and I had planned a dinner for the Luisis at our apartment and Eileen had come over early to help. We never had that dinner. We got home two nights later. Jack Crimmins became part of my office and helped us develop our communications hotline with Ambassador Adair. Ambassador Luisi also made our office his, and we provided the secure communications with the president of Uruguay's office. I remember a Saturday night when Under Secretary of State William Macumber, Jack Crimmins, and I worked as a unit in getting instructions to the ambassador. I was under pressure to fly to Montevideo, but argued that the ambassador was top-flight and knew exactly what needed to be done. He had the necessary contacts with the Uruguayan government, and certainly shouldn't have to worry about taking care of any additional Washington hands.

For ten days, we were in crisis. The *Tupamaros* wanted freedom for one hundred fifty of their jailed comrades in return for the freedom of Mitrione. President Pacheco and we said no. I agreed with the U.S. policy because I believed—and still believe—that if we agreed to pay ransom for one American, terrorists around the world would place a price on every other U.S. national abroad, and kidnapping could be a standard operating tactic of all our adversaries. The pressure on us to make a deal was heavy, and I well understand the humanitarian reasons for it.

Some days the news seemed good. The Uruguayan counter-insurgency group located and captured Raúl Sendic, the *Tupamaro* chief, who told his captors that there was no intention to kill Mitrione and that the wounds he suffered at his kidnapping had been treated and he was recovering. After the capture of Sendic, apparently the cell holding Mitrione lost contact with headquarters and panicked. Mitrione was killed on August 10, 1970. Our job at the embassy was to transport his family and his remains back to his home in Richmond, Indiana.

About the same time, a USAID agricultural adviser, Claude Fly, was also kidnapped. But Ambassador Adair was able to coordinate with the Uruguayan authorities for his release and travel back to the United States.

Those were harrowing experiences. In the context of Vietnam, it may have been a minor issue. But to those of us—Uruguayan and American—involved in the ordeal, it was terrible. I will never know whether Mitrione was targeted because of his involvement in teaching torture techniques to the Uruguayan "death squads" or, as Raul Sendic claimed, he was just a convenient target to kidnap. I will never know if there were measures we should have taken to better protect our colleagues in the field. I do know that there was no one better than Ambassador Adair on the spot to handle day-to-day problems.

When it was over, I took a day or two off to be with Ele. She was a rock.

A Diversion to Santiago

I went back to work on the Monday following the killing of Mitrione, and was called to the office of the Assistant Secretary of State Charles Meyer. He advised me that the Committee for the Alliance of Progress (CIAP) had convened an expert meeting on popular participation to meet in Santiago, Chile the following week, and that he and Herman Klein, the coordinator for the Alliance for Progress, had selected me to be the U.S. delegate. He told me that he thought that it was a good time for me to get out of the office and added that Jack Crimmins and Ed Marasciulo could hold down the office for a week. I called Ele and asked if she had any objection. No objection she said—provided the time away from Washington was only a week. So, I agreed.

Herman Klein provided me with the background documents and policy instructions. I arranged to leave on Saturday and return the following Saturday. When I got home that night, Ele was clearly suffering considerable discomfort. She only looked at me and said that the Mitrione crisis had to be handled. She agreed to see a doctor at George Washington University Hospital while I was away. Ed offered that the Marascuilos would help out if needed.

When I arrived in Santiago, I was met by USAID Director Dean Hinton, and taken to his home. He told me that he had to go to the U.S. to settle some matters related to his divorce and wanted me to housesit for him. He also told me that two old friends, William Thayer, currently rector of the Universidad Austral, and Father Roger Vekemanns had played a major role in convening the experts meeting. They were scheduled to meet with me the following day. He advised me that the ambassador would also meet with me the following day and that the embassy would hold a reception in honor of the delegates.

The ambassador informed me that the presidents of Chile and Venezuela had jointly called on CIAP to sponsor the meeting and that it had a strong Christian Democratic tinge to it. The two presidents feared that the Alliance was becoming a top–down operation and felt that more attention and resources should be dedicated not only to social development projects but also to activities at the grassroots to involve the people in the development process. It sounded like the community development program in Bolivia. He offered me an office and his assistance in getting ready for the meeting.

At the inaugural session, I was pleased to see that the Venezuelan delegate was Adela Calvani, the wife of my friend Arístedes

Calvani, then Venezuela's foreign minister. Not all the countries were represented, but several were from governments with military dictatorships. After the first session, Adela invited me to meet with the Chilean, Colombian, and Mexican delegates to discuss cooperation in drafting the document and avoiding confrontation with "unfriendly" delegations.

The drafting sessions were long and often contentious, but the language adopted reflected the Christian Democratic philosophy. The document was called "Popular Participation in the Development Process"—not "community development" as U.S. specialists had traditionally defined the process. Most of the recommendations were consistent with the techniques and processes used in projects supported by AID. The text proposed much greater community involvement in project design and implementation than was the practice in Latin America, where government planners and administrators pretty well told the people what was going to happen to them. Implementing the recommendations meant a much greater emphasis on education and information sharing than any government in Latin America had ever done. It basically set goals and norms for societies that were much more mature than those in the region. It is still good reading and its goals are still laudable.

The experts meeting ended on a strong vote of unity, thanks in great part to the role played by Chilean President Eduardo Frei and Adela Calvani in seeking consensus and understanding with technicians from "unfriendly" governments. The president not only opened the meeting and met the delegates after his address, but also invited us to tea at the *Moneda*, Chile's presidential palace, where he discussed the issues under consideration. Sra. Calvani had special dinners to involve Brazilian, Argentine, and other delegations to share in the drafting work.

My week in Santiago came at the height of the campaign for the presidency of Chile between ex-president Jorge Alessandri, Salvador Allende, and Radomiro Tomic. The polls indicated that Allesandri and Allende were almost in a dead heat, while Tomic, the Christian Democrat, was trailing. Since the early 1940s when the Popular Front elected Aguirre Serra, the Chilean electorate had been practically split, with a third on the right, a third in the center and a third on the left. In 1958, Alessandri of the right had won by a whisker over Allende. In 1962, the right withdrew and threw its support to Frei, the centrist Christian Democrat, to prevent an Allende victory. Since the 1964 election, a faction of the Christian Democrats split with Frei and joined Allende. In this election, Tomic had refused to withdraw and throw his support to Allesandri to stop Allende. I suspect that Frei would have been re-elected if the Chilean Constitution had allowed him a second term.

Each night I listened to political presentations on TV after the expert meetings. The Chileans were night owls and stayed up after dinner to listen to the candidates. I watched a tired old man, Jorge Alessandri, trying to exhort his followers and to win over centrist voters. I watched Tomic talk over the heads of the electorate about social and economic development issues in terms that only technocrats could understand. I watched Allende hold masterful press conferences in which he surrounded himself with his key socialist, communist, Radical, and ex-Christian Democratic allies, and let them answer questions posed by newsmen and members of the audience on which he said "They were better informed then I."

Chilean and embassy friends told me that Alessandri was the sure winner. Before I left Chile, I saw my old friend Bob Hurwich, who had been sent from Washington to monitor the election. He said that polls indicated a slight edge for Alessandri. I said that I didn't believe the polls and that I thought Allende was building strength by the way he was projecting himself as a reasonable leader who listened to his advisers, including centrists. The election was close, and Allende won over Alessandri by a few thousand votes.

Ele's Health

When I returned to Washington, I found that Ele had spent the entire time in bed and had hardly eaten anything. I took leave to take care of her and arranged for a medical appointment as soon as possible. I found it very difficult to find out what was bothering her. Unusually for her, she was almost constantly in tears, and I found it almost impossible to comfort her. Finally, we got an appointment with a doctor and found out that she had severe pain in the uterus and excessive bleeding. She was convinced that she had cancer and that she was fated to die.

The doctor's diagnosis was that she did not have cancer but needed surgery to stop the excessive bleeding. He would need to treat her for two weeks to stabilize her health before surgery and set the date for the second week of September. I went back to work but accompanied her twice a week to the doctor's office for the preparatory treatments.

Then, in early September my mother called from San Francisco to tell me that her health was failing. Since my sister had passed, she wanted me to come to San Francisco to take care of her affairs. I had a dilemma, but I decided that I could not leave Ele. I dearly loved my mother and was devastated by the news. I knew that my brother-in-law and my niece and nephew were available to comfort her—but there was no one but me for Ele. And Ele had to come first. With a heavy heart, I contacted the son of a friend in San Francisco to prepare my mother's will. I hoped that I could get Ele home and convalescing and then fly to San Francisco. I talked to my mother every day and she seemed to be getting weaker. On the day Ele was taken to surgery, she passed away.

It was several months before Ele really recovered, and I can never truly thank Eileen and Ed Marasciulo for their loving assistance. Ed joined me every day in visiting her in the hospital and arranged to bring her home. Eileen spent afternoons with Ele while she recuperated. The Guthries, the Sherrys, and other friends pitched in and made it possible for me to work. Assistant Secretary Meyer and Jack Crimmins made it as easy as possible for me to do my job.

For Ele and me it was a time for refocusing our lives. We came together in the recuperation period and recommitted to each other more profoundly than when we first married. Our parents had passed. My sister had passed. Ele was my family, and I was hers. Career or other considerations mattered little. Our primary responsibility was to each other, and our love bound us tightly together from that week in September 1970 to the end of time.

25

The Inter-American Foundation

In late September 1970, following my return from Chile and a few days after Ele's surgery and my mother's passing, Assistant Secretary Charles Meyer called me to his office to meet with George Cabot Lodge, with whom I had worked when he was assistant secretary of Labor. The secretary told me that George, with White House approval, had requested my detail for four months to work with the board of directors of the newly established Inter-American Social Development Institute (ISDI).

George told us that President Nixon appointed a six-person board of directors and named him the vice chair and assigned NSC Latin America Policy Advisor Arnold Nachmanoff to act for the board until its first meeting in November. At that meeting, an options paper was required for the board to determine ISDI policies and operating procedures. When they consulted Congressmen Fascell and Morse, the sponsors of the legislation, the congressmen suggested that I would be a good choice to advise the board since I had worked with them on the legislation. The assistant secretary said that he had agreed to the detail and that it would begin the following Monday. I was taken completely by surprise.

Preparing the Options Paper

The next Monday, I met with Arnold Nachmanoff, who advised me that the White House established a temporary ISDI headquarters in a nearby building. They had already requisitioned the furnishings and equipment for the office, and had confirmed plans with the board chair, Augustin Hart (vice president of Quaker Oats Company), to convene the first meeting of the board in November.

He also told me that I was to head a study group to prepare the options paper for the board, that the study group would include another State Department officer and two private consultants selected by the White House (James Ragan and Godfrey Harris), that I was to make a progress report at the November meeting and that the options paper was to be considered by the board at its second meeting scheduled for the third week of January. He also said that the White House would review the options paper carefully before it was presented to the board. His comments and tone conveyed a message that the White House and AID were not enthusiastic about ISDI.

My State colleague, who was awaiting an overseas assignment, worked with me for a week or so before leaving for his new assignment. We laid out a schedule for consulting experts on Latin American development across the country, and prepared a questionnaire for the interviews. Jim Ragan and Godfrey Harris joined me in reviewing the questionnaire and set a December deadline for the first draft of the presentation. I then consulted the specialists in person or by telephone. I made a couple of overnight trips to New York, Boston, Austin, and Miami—always hurrying back to take care of my convalescing Ele. By late October, I put together an outline for the report. I met with the board in early November, and was authorized to proceed with the paper.

By early December, I produced the first draft, which was crafted in typical State Department format and language. Godfrey and Jim took one look at my brainchild, and said that it would not fly for a high-powered board headed by corporate executives. They edited my "bureaucratic presentation" into a concise document. They had few words on each page, carefully chosen to say precisely what the board needed to consider, with rationale and comments in short phrases in left hand columns and options on the right. They conveyed ideas with a minimum of words.

Even as the work piled up, I tried never to be far away from Ele. I did the cooking every night, and often served breakfast and dinner to her in bed. In retrospect, the assignment to ISDI was providential because it made my days much more flexible and allowed me to spend more time with Ele and provide her the help she needed. If I had to be away overnight, Eileen Marasciulo or some other friend would look in to make sure that Ele was all right. When I had to fly to Los Angeles for a meeting at the Western White House so that Nachmanoff and his NSC bosses could review the draft in detail, I was on the phone with Ele twice a day.

We finished the document in early January 1971, and submitted it to Nachmanoff at San Clemente a couple of days before the ISDI Board was to meet. NSC made some changes before authorizing me to have it delivered by special messenger to each member of the board.

Before the board meeting on January 21, I was interviewed for the post of Executive Director of ISDI and told that I was one of the two or three finalists that the board was considering. I frankly had very mixed feelings. The honor and the challenge were great, but I really wanted out of Washington. I was always happier working in an embassy or USAID mission than in the bureaucratic maze of Washington.

In January, after I returned from San Clemente, Mel Spector, still the administrative director for the State Department American Republics Area (ARA), advised me that Jack Crimmins was recommending my appointment in June 1971 to be Deputy Chief of Mission (DCM) in Argentina, and that Bill Stedman, then at the Senior Seminar, was to replace me as director of the Office of Argentine, Paraguayan, and Uruguayan Affairs. I was also advised that I had scored high in the evaluation ranking of FSO-1 officers.

When I told Ele that evening that we would be assigned to Buenos Aires in mid-1971, she became quite upset. She was apprehensive about going overseas until she settled her mother's estate in Tulare, stressing that she needed me nearby. Communicating and consulting with each other from overseas was not an easy job in 1971 since we didn't have fax or computers, and international phone connections were still costly and often not reliable. She really wanted us to stay in the States at least one more year. When I raised that with Mel, he understood but pressed me to accept Buenos Aires—which I reluctantly did.

After a quiet Christmas, as Ele grew stronger, she began planning to return to Tulare to get her affairs in order before going to Buenos Aires. She felt very alone with her mother gone and was concerned about what might happen if I were to suffer the fate of

Dan Mitrione. On New Year's Eve when Chet Guthrie asked Ele why she didn't sell the two pre-World War II vintage houses, she replied that they represented her roots and gave stability to her life in the event that something unexpected happened and she was left alone. My message from Ele was clear.

At the ISDI board meeting of January 21, 1971, the board approved the policies and procedures to govern ISDI and appointed Bill Dyal, formerly of the Peace Corps, to be the first ISDI director. Bill asked me to be his deputy in setting up and organizing the Institute. However, with my detail over, I went back to my office director's chair. I was working at State when Nachmanoff called me to his office. When I walked in, there were three other people present: a senior State Department officer, a representative from the State Department Office of Personnel, and a senior White House official. Nachmanoff made it clear that the White House wanted me to take Bill's offer to be his deputy. The administration wanted me as "a stabilizing force at ISDI." It was made clear that my options were limited. The decision was being made for Ele and me.

On returning to State, when I advised Assistant Secretary Meyer, who had been appointed a member of the ISDI Board, about what had just happened, he seemed not surprised. Mel Spector and Jack Crimmins were not pleased because they thought that going to ISDI was a bad career decision.

In February 1971, the State Department approved a two-year detail to ISDI. Ed Marasciulo was named acting director for Argentine, Paraguayan, and Uruguayan Affairs until Bill Stedman completed the Senior Seminar course in June. Ele returned to California in late February just as I made the transition from State to ISDI.

ISDI

ISDI was a creation of congress, not the executive branch. Its primary sponsor was the Subcommittee on Inter-American Affairs of the House Foreign Affairs Committee, specifically the subcommittee chair, Dante Fascell of Florida, and the ranking Republican member, Bradford Morse of Massachusetts. The congressional mandate was to support social development in Latin America and the Caribbean. The creation of ISDI reflected the subcommittee's disappointment that the Alliance for Progress was skewed to financial transfers and economic assistance. ISDI was intended to complement the Alliance and focus exclusively on enabling people to participate in and share the benefits of development. The legislation authorized an initial $50 million to establish ISDI and initiate operations. The ISDI study group prepared the options for the board to determine how ISDI was to meet the objectives.

ISDI was set up as an independent federal agency that reported directly to the White House, not to State or AID. A board of directors selected by the president was its governing body. The first board included: Augustin Hart, Vice President of Quaker Oats as president; George Cabot Lodge of Harvard Business School as vice president; Charles Robinson, president of Utah Mining; Governor Luis Ferré of Puerto Rico the administrator of AID, then John Hannah, and the assistant secretary of state for Inter-American Affairs, then Charles Meyer. All were distinguished Republicans and had strong opinions on the role ISDI should play.

The board determined that ISDI's objective was not to create its own program, but to support Latin America and Caribbean initiatives whose goals were aimed at (1) greater and more equitable distribution of income, goods, and services; (2) creating greater opportunities for people to participate in the critical decisions and processes that affected their lives; and (3) amelioration of societal conflicts arising out of the development process and forging linkages among conflicting groups. In working toward that objective, ISDI was to act independently of both AID and State, but the director was instructed to work with State and AID to open direct lines of communication with ambassadors and AID directors in those countries in which ISDI decided to fund projects.

The board decided that ISDI's mission was to respond to the needs of the people of the region, as the people themselves defined them, and to help them achieve their goals. It rejected the idea that ISDI would manage or operate projects on its own. It could stimulate interest in social projects, and was directed to bring together information on how to promote social development in Latin America and the Caribbean. Bill Dyal later summarized ISDI's role as an enabler.

In its discussion of the objectives and role, the board determined that ISDI itself should identify promising projects developed by local Latin American and Caribbean groups, and not rely on private voluntary organizations (PVOs) such as cooperative, labor, and educational groups, to present projects for ISDI consideration. The board based this decision on the legislative history and the fact that the language of the act made no mention of supporting U.S. PVOs working in the region.

The board was offered five categories of projects for possible funding: civic improvement, physical wellbeing, capital generation, job creation, and social fulfillment. The study group provided outlines of projects in each of the five categories based on projects financed by the U.S. government, OAS, the UN, and other international agencies and major foundations. It then analyzed projects in each category to show their potential impact on innovation, government involvement, ISDI visibility, risks of failure, relevance to U.S. foreign policy interests, and domestic interests in the host country. The board authorized ISDI staff to consider possible projects in all five categories and weigh the opportunities and risks of each proposed project.

To initiate operations, the board authorized a staff of fifty to seventy people, to be built up over the first three years and set a limit of $7 million for planning, programming, and evaluation, with the balance for funding approved projects. It anticipated that in the buildup process only a limited number of projects would be ready for approval in the first year of operations.

Bill Dyal took leadership from day one, and set the tone and orientation of ISDI. He was a charismatic personality who wanted a very different type of government agency—one that was open, as non-bureaucratic as possible, and responsive to the needs of the Latin American and Caribbean people as they defined them. In March, he located office space in Rosslyn, Virginia and oversaw the planning and layout of the office space to give it a feeling of openness and sharing. I fully shared his plan and design.

Setting up a new organization was quite different from any job I had been involved in before. I had experience with the Pan American Sanitary Bureau and the Mexico-U.S. Commission on Foot-and-Mouth Disease in beginning new operations within an existing structure. However, my new job required defining the structure and the rules and procedures that the new entity was to live by. My initial assignment was to draft the organization chart, the operating rules and regulations, and job classification standards that were consistent with U.S. civil service norms but flexible enough to meet the board's guidelines.

After drafting the initial organization and program framework, I prepared employment and personnel regulations consistent with U.S. government requirements. I drafted the first operational plan and projection of field visits and the initial outlines of project documents, including the framework for field investigation and interviews with prospective applicants. Much of what was done, we knew, would be modified or adjusted as we moved into operations, but we had to start somewhere.

The next assignment involved setting up an evaluation system. One of the key functions of ISDI was to build up understanding of the social development process, in other words, make ISDI's efforts a learning process. That meant from day one, we had to build evaluation into each project ISDI considered and to involve the Latin American and Caribbean recipients in it as much as ISDI itself. We studied evaluation systems set up by AID, the UN Development Program, foundations and bilateral assistance agencies. We analyzed social development programs sponsored by other entities to try to identify what worked and what did not—and why. We found that assessing results was not feasible unless the goals and specific actions to be taken in achieving the goals had been spelled out in original project plan.

Bill also asked me to work with Charles Meyer and John Hannah on procedures for consulting with ambassadors and AID directors in the field to avoid misunderstandings about ISDI intentions and to explain our project selection process, and relationships with grassroots organization. It was important that they be informed about what ISDI was doing in country and to obtain their advice about the *bona fides* of grassroots organizations being contacted. We worked out a procedure for building those relationships.

The selection of the staff was critical. With the board's limit on the size of the staff, that meant selecting the right people from day one. Bill took charge of recruitment. While he saw the need for a handful of long-term staff members, especially those engaged in building the learning process, and overseeing program operations, he looked for people who were not afraid to experiment with new approaches to dealing with basic social problems and willing to contribute to the learning process. He did not want them to look on ISDI as a lifetime career, but as a place to acquire expertise and then use that expertise in future career assignments.

Some of the first appointments were key people who participated in the creation of ISDI. Ricky Bennett, who had worked on the legislation that created it, was enticed away from the Inter-American Sub-Committee of the House Foreign Affairs Committee; she created the library and learning process. Having worked with Congressman Fascell, she had access to project materials throughout the government. Another key member was Paul Bell, a colleague of Bill's from the Peace Corps, who had in-depth knowledge of the grassroots programs in the region; he headed up the operations staff. A third was Bob Machek, from the Office of Management and Budget (OMB) who had worked with the study group and had an overview of the White House attitudes on ISDI; he became part of Paul's core staff. The fourth was Linda Lee from Congressman Brad Morse's office; she had helped draft the legislation and became the first legal counsel.

Those staff members who were to work with grassroots and civic organizations overseas were called representatives. The qualifications called for generalists fluent in Spanish and Portuguese, rather than subject matter specialists in social development. We felt that the staff needed to have a broad view of the subject matter and be prepared to draw on expertise when needed in considering individual projects. Many of those hired as ISDI representatives were ex-Peace Corps veterans who had lived in villages or overseen community projects during their overseas tours.

As we initiated operations, we were pressured by PVOs with social programs in Latin America and the Caribbean for an inside track to funding for projects and activities they supported in the region. They sought to have us hire many of their field staff and bring their on-going projects with them. Having served as chief of social development in the early years of the Alliance for Progress, I knew many of them, and it is not easy to tell people you respect in other organizations that you don't think they fit the recruitment criteria of your new institution; I'm afraid that I alienated a few.

When I advised the PVOs of the board decision not to directly fund their projects in Latin America and the Caribbean, several PVO's asked the board to reverse its decision. The board consulted Congressmen Fascell and Morse and was told its policy decision was consistent with the intent of the legislation. The board stood firm and advised the PVOs that ISDI would not give special preference or treatment to projects proposed by or tied to a U.S. PVO.

Moving into operations was a tumultuous period. Paul Bell installed the program review system. Some Peace Corps veterans thought that we should just finance activities without a project review process. In that first year, we had long, sometimes heated discussions over the approach and relationship of representatives with project proponents. It was clear that representatives should listen to the organizations and individuals and encourage them to present viable plans for dealing with problems. But what about those groups who had identified problems and yet were unable to provide meaningful action plans? Some advocated that ISDI's exclusive role should be limited to reviewing proposals as presented since the proponents were the people who knew their own problems and were ready to deal with them. Others believed, as I did, that, when people identified a problem, the representative should help them by telling them how others had dealt with similar problems and work with them in thinking through what might be done.

My experience in several Latin American countries had led me to conclude that some of the sharpest people I had met were illiterate peasants who had learned to survive but needed help understanding why they had their problems and what processes and tools were available to overcome them. Those well-meaning people usually did not have access to information that could help them identify possible solutions. I strongly felt and still believe that the representatives needed to encourage a constructive two-way dialogue—a dialogue in which ISDI listens to the people and their perceptions of their needs, and then helps them with information about possible actions that might deal with those needs. The purpose of the library and information center, I felt, should be to provide the representatives with information about processes that had succeeded or failed and the reasons for the results—and for the representatives to share that information with the grassroots groups with which ISDI interacts.

ISDI Operations

The board met once a quarter. Preparing a progress report to them was a top priority. Bill usually prepared the report himself, with input from each of us. But the style and tone was his. He prepared for meetings by considering what issues might arise and weighing appropriate responses. I admired, and suspect envied, the ease with which he was able to present the issues and respond to board questions. He had the knack for making the right response to just about every question or comment. He had style and substance that made him certainly the right choice for the top job in an organization in its initial phase of operations. I learned a great deal from him that I found extremely helpful in later assignments.

The board meeting usually lasted a full day, occasionally two, at ISDI headquarters. At the end of almost every meeting, board members raced for planes to be back at their home offices the following day. I recall only one board meeting not at headquarters—that was in Puerto Rico, in the offices of the governor. It was the only one in which socializing overshadowed the business, and provided an opportunity for the board and staff to become better acquainted.

The first chair was Augustin Hart, a seasoned corporate executive. He presided over the board adroitly and expeditiously. The board focused on the program and raised probing questions about actions that did not meet their expectations. It went over the financial statement and demanded detailed explanations and justifications for expenditures. From its first meeting, the board dealt objectively with the issues and treated the staff as professionals.

By the third meeting, the board put pressure on us to begin project funding. Spending money on organization and recruitment needed to be matched by field operations. Congressmen Fascell and Morse were concerned that their brainchild might fizzle. AID was arguing that the money should be allocated to it rather than to the new entity and contacted board members with proposals to integrate project identification and selection into AID's established machinery.

Bill responded by speeding up our original timetable. To get the staff up and running, Bill convened weekend retreats to build cohesion, defuse conflicts, talk out objectives, operating problems, and personal concerns. The informality of the retreat and the free flow of ideas outside of the office had its merits. For me, however, with my hearing deficiency, the retreat was a time of great stress since I could hear only a portion of the discussion and often lost track of the interplay among the staff members. Sometimes after a retreat it would take me several days of questioning other participants to understand fully the implications of the discussions.

I was not directly involved in project operations but was on the project approval panel. Project operations were Paul Bell's bailiwick and he was a jewel. He was the leader of the representatives, most of whom he had known in the Peace Corps. The representatives were fifteen to twenty years younger than I, and for the first time in my career I felt like an old timer. Their learning experience in the villages of Latin America had been different from mine and they had less concern about the bureaucratic issues that I had faced in my assignments and were not inclined to consider the lessons I had learned in overseeing similar project operations. They wanted to learn for themselves and frequently the implied message was, "We know better and are not going to repeat the mistakes that your generation made."

The first projects presented for consideration were in the fall of 1971. Initially they were sketchy, with critical elements not included. Additional information was needed to clarify the goals, the precise activities to be funded, and the benchmarks to be tested in the evaluation process. Some representatives revised their presentations; others went back to countries to obtain missing pieces. We knew that we were experimenting and trying to find our own style and *modus operandi*. We were trying to apply the lessons learned by the Peace Corps, AID, and others to get superior results with the limited resources at our disposal. By the last quarter of 1971, less than a year after opening its doors, the first projects were approved. ISDI was a functioning institution.

The Inter-American Foundation (IAF)

At the end of 1971, Bill proposed to the board that ISDI change its name to the Inter-American Foundation. The name ISDI had created confusion about our purpose and goals with Latin American and Caribbean institutions since the word "institute" to them denoted a university activity of some type. When Bill presented his recommendation for a change of name to Congressman Fascell and the board, they unanimously approved the change and in 1972 the necessary legal steps were taken to rename ISDI, the Inter-American Foundation (IAF), and that is the name it carries today. The board changed Bill's title to IAF president, and mine to vice president.

The name change was followed by a major redesign of our office space. Bill brought in the Miller Company, who replaced offices with the open space concept. Only Bill's office and the board meeting room remained enclosed. All the rest of us were reconfigured into cubicles with working space and no doors. Several small conference rooms were set up in which staff members could meet privately for discussions. The watch phrase was, "Sharing in a common cause."

My first reaction was negative, but once the configuration was in place, I became quite comfortable. I didn't feel any loss of privacy. I found that everyone respected everyone else's space and that my ability to work was in no way inhibited. In fact, it did promote closer working relations and easier cooperation.

Even with the office design, as we moved into operation, I began to feel like the fifth wheel in the management and operation of IAF. I participated in the project selection process, but not in project identification. When a contact at one of the PVOs would give me a lead on a promising group or activity in Latin America or the Caribbean, I would pass the information on to Paul and the appropriate representative for the country and recommend that the representative take a look on his next field visit, but I seldom even got a call back. When I would ask about the possibility, sometimes, the representative would tell me that he didn't have time to visit the group or activity, making me feel that I was not considered a reliable source or that recommendations by a PVO were suspect. So I stopped following up on proposals.

My routine became office-bound. My interest in working with the IAF had been to broaden my field experience with people-oriented projects, not to hold down a Washington desk assignment. I had already had that experience in Institutional Development in the early years of the Alliance for Progress. During my two years at the IAF, my only visits to Latin America were special assignments that Bill gave me to deal with specific issues: one to Barbados, one to Central America, and one to Uruguay. I talked regularly with the representatives about projects, but increasingly I found myself sounding like an old-timer who was reminiscing about the good old days.

On several occasions, at the project approval meetings, I raised questions when I saw an IAF proposal repeating mistakes that had been made in earlier AID projects with which I had been associated. Those questions were usually passed over or treated despairingly. Sometimes their responses were that their experience in Peace Corps was different than my experience in AID. My younger colleagues had the fire and enthusiasm that comes with discovering the world and trying to help people find simple answers to complex problems. Those experiences contributed to my feeling that I was not really part of their team.

The generational gap led me to spend less time with the IAF representatives and more time with Ricky Bennett in the information center analyzing past AID, UNDP, and Peace Corps projects. We felt that a major role for the IAF was to be a repository of information on what makes for successful social development projects. No other agency—neither USAID, UNDP, other international agencies, nor national institutions—had focused systematically on building such an information base.

Ricki's goal was to identify the factors that the IAF needed to analyze when putting together a project and to design projects that optimized the chances for success. In addition, I joined her in looking for the reasons a project was deemed successful or unsuccessful. We spent hours categorizing problems that those projects addressed as well as the approaches and inputs used in the projects to deal with them. We looked at the involvement and participation of communities and people being helped in planning their own projects and their role in overseeing implementation and operations.

We sought to identify who designed the projects, what the operating structure and dynamics were, who benefited from it, and what role the beneficiary played in its planning and operations. Patterns of success and failure began to appear. While our sample was small, we tried to organize the information systematically and began to play with models of what worked and other models of those that did not produce positive results.

Just as we moved into designing the system, Ricky fell ill with a recurrence of a cancer that had been in remission for several years. She was out of the office for much of 1972 until her untimely death.

While I cannot remember all the elements we identified for the design and operation of a successful social development project, I recall that they fell into the following categories: first—the need for and viability of the project; second—the clear definition of objectives and the actions to be taken to achieve them; third—the quality and creditability of the leadership and its openness to the community it supports; fourth—understanding by the community of the goals for the project and the steps to be taken to achieve the goals, so the people would feel that they owned the project; fifth, periodic open reviews of progress and problems in which the community participates; and sixth—a good feedback system in which keeps the community informed of actions being taken to resolve problems.

When I was invited to participate in a panel on social development at the University of Pittsburgh, I decided to present our initial findings and tried to shape them into a model. I spelled it out in my presentation, and was taken aback when one of the panel members called it "obscene." He claimed that the Alliance for Progress had failed and asked how I dare presume to set forth a model on social development. I was too flabbergasted to answer, and forever regret that I did not respond. No matter whether the Alliance had failed or not, we had a great deal of experience and we needed to learn from it. I continue to believe that one of our greatest challenges is to find processes for involving people in the development process—in every country of our world. No one model will work in each and every environment, but elements can be identified from our extensive experience to help improve the planning of social projects and the phasing of timely and consistent flows of technical and monetary support.

My last major assignment at IAF was to investigate the interest of foundations and private donors in funding the emerging program. In its first meeting of 1972, the board asked Bill to investigate the prospects for additional funding from non-government sources. Bill assigned me that job. For the next six months, I combed through foundation source books and read the annual reports of major foundations, banks, and corporations to ascertain if they had interest in Latin America or social development. I contacted each one that looked promising and made arrangements for visits. I was given appointments by more than a dozen senior officials. Most of them gave me considerable time for my presentation about IAF, but ultimately, the message was that they were not prepared to consider funding a U.S. government entity, especially one with no track record. Come back in five years; if the IAF has achieved good results, we might reconsider.

Many were interested in what the IAF was set up to do. Many wanted to be kept informed. Some even promised to consider financing a specific project developed by the IAF if it met the organization's interest and criteria after its own staff had made an independent review—but they would fund the project independently of the IAF. Several offered to meet with the IAF periodically once we had a portfolio of projects to discuss. Not one was disposed to enter into a working arrangement at that time.

Neither the board nor Congressman Fascell seemed surprised. None of them had expected an enthusiastic response to a request to fund a U.S. government creation—even one they admired. I quoted to the board members the words of Martha Muse, then president of the Tinker Foundation, "Private foundations are built on their independence and are wary of government participation. Government grants come with lots of strings attached. We may understand your interest, but we are not very likely to work with you until you have a track record and we can recognize that working with you is to our mutual advantage."

The last few months of my two-year detail were spent on routine activities. I went to board meetings and project review committee sessions. I read project progress reports, many with red flags that inevitably occur as you proceed from planning to action, but it was too early to predict what the results of the IAF program might be. I was in that very uneasy situation of not knowing how to make a further contribution. I was not too happy and I am sure that Bill, Paul, and the others were not too pleased with having me around.

My discontent was accentuated by Ele's prolonged stay in Tulare. After Ele recovered from her surgery, she returned to Tulare to complete closing her mother's estate and getting her mother's and grandmother's houses ready for rental. She was pretty much on her own. Unlike in 1971 when she was settling her mother's estate, I could give her very little help. In 1971 I helped out by preparing legal research and drafting proposed estate submissions to state and federal authorities. This time I couldn't advise her about building codes or how to deal with difficult city inspectors. She had to make her own assessments of contractors and technicians. She had no close family to call upon and did not feel comfortable discussing her problems with old friends. So, for 1972, we had little to share, just commiserate about her problems in Tulare and mine in D.C.

Once the houses were ready, Ele looked for a management company to rent and look after them; Tulare was not a good housing rental market, especially for middle or upper income houses. She determined her best choice was the Security Pacific Bank's Trust Department that already oversaw the Pixley ranch. She obtained written commitments of due diligence and negotiated a one-year renewable contract, which would minimize the need for her to go back to Tulare every year. She wrote me that she wanted to concentrate her time on work of the American Association of Foreign Service Wives (AAFSW), and on our investments. By the early fall, she left to visit the South Dakota farm en route back to Washington.

Ele returned to Washington in time for Thanksgiving with the Guthries and one of Chet's special hickory-smoked turkey masterpieces. That afternoon, she seemed to relax for the first time in months. She was with friends, and we talked about politics and the implications of Nixon's second term, and our impending withdrawal from Vietnam. Watergate was not yet a full-grown scandal, but the landslide defeat of George McGovern had apparently given Nixon a free hand to deal with the national and international agenda. Ele told me that it was a relief to talk about issues that didn't involve the houses, farms, or going to town for supplies.

One of the topics we discussed that Thanksgiving was the upcoming end of my assignment with the IAF. Chet had formed a consulting company that was contracted by various government agencies to provide services or manage projects. His office was also in Rosslyn, just a couple of blocks from the IAF. Many an evening he would call to offer me a ride home. He was well aware of my frustration and had counseled me to put the experience in perspective now that the IAF was operational. He reassured me that it was time for a new assignment.

With Ele home, I relaxed, having her light up the holidays. We enjoyed being together, going to the Smithsonian, partying with friends, and postponed investment and personal decisions until we got a clearer idea about our next assignment.

The IAF Chapter Closes

In the fall of 1972, pending the outcome of the election, discussion of future senior assignments in the State Department was on hold. Charles Meyer informed Bill Dyal and me that he would be returning to Chicago after the election. His senior deputy now was my good friend, Bob Hurwich, who had been the deputy chief of mission in Bolivia during the first couple of years of our assignment there. Charles, Bob, and I had lunch in late November and discussed a future assignment. They said that they did not foresee many Latin American ambassadorial assignments coming up, and that those that might open up would probably be filled not by career officers but by political appointees. They reviewed with me several possible deputy chief of mission posts that might come up in 1973. Charles said that Bob would be my contact point for the next few months and assured me that on the termination of my detail, I would have an assignment in the inter-American area.

Mel Spector and other friends in the State personnel office assured me that State personnel was expecting me back in the first quarter of 1973 and that I was being considered for several assignments, including a few outside the Western Hemisphere and urged me to be flexible when offered an assignment. In February, Bob Hurwich advised me that I would soon be offered a choice of two posts in early March when my detail ended. I kept Ele fully informed, and having her there to share my concerns was incredibly comforting.

I am pleased to have played a small part in the initial phase of the IAF's life and consider the experience an invaluable part of my professional life. I have kept an eye on development of the IAF over the last forty-five years and welcome the recognition it has received for its contribution to social development in Latin America and the Caribbean. I remain committed to its mission.

I am also proud that in 1983, I was once again a candidate for its presidency—only to come in second to Deborah Szekely, a most dynamic and innovative civic leader who led IAF through new frontiers during her decade as its president. During Debbie's tenure as IAF president, she made a special effort to bring together the principal social development specialists in Washington, D.C. to share their experiences and help one another move forward their work in the region. I was one of those whom she drew on. She organized and hosted monthly breakfasts at the Mayflower Hotel at which we discussed not only specific grassroots projects in various countries but also systematic approaches to building local leadership; micro-finance; promoting entrepreneurship and income producing activities at the grassroots; and opening lines of communication between government agencies and grassroots organizations.

Debbie's work coincided with my efforts to develop the Social Development Department at the Organization of American States (OAS). I drew on the Foundation's experience and Debbie's initiatives to help me define the areas of work on which to concentrate the OAS program. Working with her during her IAF years led to a respect and friendship that abides to this day.

26

Back to Central America

1973 began with considerable uncertainty. My two-year detail at the Inter-American Foundation was coming to a close. The re-election of President Nixon brought changes at the State Department: Secretary Meyer left on December 31, and Henry Kissinger became the new secretary of state and was fielding a new team. Most ambassadorial vacancies would be "in play politically" and few deputy chief of mission or office director slots would become available until the summer.

In February 1973, Bob Hurwich, then acting assistant secretary of state for Inter-American Affairs, asked me to consider one of two assignments: either director of the U.S. Mission to the Central American Common Market (ROCAP), or deputy to Herman Kleine, the assistant coordinator for the Alliance for Progress. Bob knew I wanted an overseas appointment, but he and Herman wanted me to join the front office of the combined State-AID Bureau. Being Herman's deputy would involve me in the bureau's policy decision-making, supervision of field operations, and relations with congress. On the other hand, ROCAP was a joint State-AID operation, funded primarily by AID, which combined the multicountry political and development components of U.S. interests in Central America.

When that interview ended, I went down the hall to Herman Kleine's office for a long talk, and then discussed matters with my good friend, David Lazar, the newly appointed director of Central American Affairs. Both men briefed me on the job they would expect me to do, and gave me no illusions about the problems involved in either one. Then I consulted Ele, and we chose to return to Central America.

The nearly five years that Ele and I had spent in El Salvador had been rewarding and happy ones. We had been in all five countries of Central America and were fairly well informed about the issues and prospects. We knew that ROCAP would be a tough assignment, not only because of the political crisis in the region but also because of the tension between ROCAP and the embassies in each of the countries over jurisdiction and relationships.

ROCAP

The Regional Office for Central America and Panama (ROCAP) had been established by Kennedy in the early days of his administration to support Central American efforts to create a common market and build a regional development program. The political systems in all the countries except Costa Rica were military dictatorships. The outlook country by country for democratic openings was not promising. The economies of the six countries making up the Central American Isthmus were too small and resource-poor to promise substantial improvement in GNP or living standards. The UN Economic Commission for Latin America (ECLA) and a new generation of Central American economists and political leaders had pressed for regional economic integration in the 1950s, and the Kennedy administration found the efforts promising enough to embrace the regional approach and created ROCAP.

Central America occupies a strategic location on the Caribbean between Mexico and the Panama Canal, and was a potential target of opportunity for the USSR and its ally Fidel Castro. Even after the settlement of the Cuban Missile Crisis and the USSR's commitment to restrain Cuban interference in other American Republics, the weakness and instability in the region were deemed serious U.S. security concerns. ROCAP was created as much for U.S. policy reasons as it was to support regional political stability and development.

ROCAP was a separate mission, not part of an existing U.S. Embassy. It was financed primarily by AID, but had a complement of State economic and political officers to cover regional developments as well as a team of AID development specialists.

The director of ROCAP was accredited as the U.S. representative to the Central American regional political authority. He reported to the assistant secretary of state for Inter-American Affairs on political and economic policy matters and on economic and technical aid programs to the deputy coordinator for the Alliance for Progress. He recommended political and economic policy for the region, especially on the efforts by the six countries to integrate politically and economically, and directed U.S. economic and technical assistance to the Central American regional bodies. The director was treated as comparable in rank to an ambassador, but without the title.

The first ROCAP director was Henry DuFlan, who had been deputy secretary of defense in the Eisenhower administration. He was a successful businessman who was a classmate and friend of President Kennedy. Henry was offered the title of ambassador, but wasn't concerned about such formalities. As he later told me, "I just wanted to tackle the challenge and help develop a new approach to Central America. I wasn't interested in the title of the job." Henry also said that in 1961, President Kennedy had told him that he was considering phasing out separate economic and technical assistance programs to the six countries and consolidating them in ROCAP. Henry added that he advised the president against taking such action at that time because of the great differences in political, economic, and social conditions in each of the six countries and to focus ROCAP on the regional economic integration.

Including Panama in the mission with the other countries was a geographical consideration, but made little sense historically, politically, or economically. The Vice Royalty of Nueva Granada, headquartered in Bogotá, had governed Panama in the colonial era while the Vice Royalty of Mexico oversaw the other five countries. Panama's economy was geared to the transshipment of Andean gold and silver to Spain, while the other five were essentially agricultural. Four of the countries had lived under feudal land systems, with ownership concentrated in a handful of favored families. Costa Rica had been settled by Spanish farmers who worked their own lands. None of the six had significant gold, silver, or other mining operations.

By the mid-1960s, the differences in political and social development and economic interests led Panama to withdraw from the integration movement and from ROCAP. As a result, the name of the mission was changed to the Regional Office for Central American Programs.

When ROCAP was created, it did not include Belize, the other state in Central America, since it was then called British Honduras and was still part of the British Empire. If Belize had been included, Guatemala would have withdrawn from ROCAP because of a century-long dispute with the United Kingdom. Guatemala claimed that the U.K. occupied the territory unlawfully, while Britain countered that Guatemala had ceded it in return for a commitment to build a railway from the Caribbean coast to the interior of Guatemala.

Starting the Assignment

I was sworn in as ROCAP director by Herman Kleine, acting coordinator for the Alliance for Progress, in a ceremony on the eighth floor of the State Department. Bob Hurwich, and most of the senior staff of the joint State-AID Bureau for Latin America and the Caribbean joined us, along with all of the ambassadors from the Central American countries and Panama. Ele stood beside me.

Then the formal briefings began. Since Charles Meyer had departed, and Jack Kubisch, his presumptive successor as assistant secretary of state and coordinator of the Alliance, was awaiting confirmation by the Senate, my primary briefers were Bob Hurwich, Herman Kleine, and Dave Lazar. The picture they painted was bleak at best.

The Central America integration movement and the development of the Central American Common Market (CACM) were in crisis. The 1968 Soccer War between El Salvador and Honduras had brought them to a standstill. My briefings focused on what might be done to settle the dispute and to re-energize regional cooperation. It was clear that neither the White House nor the seventh floor of the State Department had much interest in the region, except to ensure that Cuba or the USSR did not take advantage of the situation. The primary focus of the United States was on Vietnam and the *realpolitik* of the Cold War.

Bob Hurwich and Dave Lazar briefed me on the political situation in the five countries and the serious tensions among them. Weaknesses in their internal economies and the accelerating rural to urban migration were placing ever-greater strains on government resources. Actions to deal with the crisis required intergovernmental cooperation and regional programming. Thus, it was in the strategic interest of the U.S. government to promote closer economic and political cooperation in the region, looking to eventual economic and political integration.

My briefings by Herman Kleine and his aides were focused very differently. They told me that the Alliance had little support in either the Nixon administration or Congress, that funding for Latin America had been severely cut back to support programs in Vietnam and South Asia, and that ROCAP was one of their targets for cost cutting and possible elimination. Herman gave me a copy of a report prepared in 1972 by a commission headed by Larry Harrison, then director of programming for the Alliance for Progress, that questioned the relevance of ROCAP in the aftermath of the Soccer War. Herman also informed me that he personally was inclined to cut back or eliminate ROCAP but was postponing a decision in the face of the political concerns of his State Department colleagues, especially after the decision was made to send me to ROCAP. He confided that I had been chosen to help the Central Americans find a formula for revitalizing regional integration and finding their way past the Soccer War.

The assignment to ROCAP coincided with one of the most important political events of the second half of the twentieth century: Watergate. Watergate promised that even less attention would be given to a lesser trouble spot like Central America; Vietnam and Watergate would absorb all the high-level energies of the administration. All of my other briefings in the executive branch and congress reflected this preoccupation with Vietnam and Watergate.

Ele and I were equally absorbed by Vietnam and Watergate. Being in Washington, Watergate seemed more immediate and threatening. We were transfixed by the hearings conducted by Senator Sam Ervin and the revelations in the *Washington Post, Time,* and *Newsweek.* We were glued every evening to the news and commentaries on TV. Ele kept detailed records of developments, filled boxes with clippings, and made extensive notes on congressional proceedings. When names of Watergate participants whom we had met appeared in the press, we were often shocked by the revelations—like the testimony of John Dean, who had been a lifeguard at our swimming pool one summer and married the daughter of our neighbor, Senator Long of Missouri. Even getting ready to move to Central America, our principal topic of conversation was Watergate and its meaning for constitutional governance in the United States as well as its effect on our political image abroad. There were times that I wondered if my assignment made sense. What could we do in Central America? Did the administration have credibility there or anywhere else on the planet?

As the time drew near for our departure for Guatemala City, Ele and I had long discussions about the implications of Watergate for my job. Ele firmly reminded me that I was a career foreign service officer and that I was to serve our country, not merely the current incumbent of the White House or the seventh floor of the State Department. My duty was to do the job that I was assigned—no matter the political mess or my personal feelings. When I proposed declining the ROCAP post, Ele and David Lazar read me the riot act—and that was that!

The last three weeks in Washington, Ele supervised packing up our personal effects for shipment to Guatemala and most of our furniture for storage in the Washington, D.C. area. We were assigned the furnished government residence of the ROCAP director. The storage company had a high volume of work and had to move our furniture several days before our departure. So we virtually camped out in the apartment, sleeping on mattresses on the floor, watching the TV reports on Watergate, and eating off dishes loaned us by friends. I vividly remember crawling in and out of bed with the voice of Sam Ervin filling the bedroom.

Taking Over at ROCAP

I went directly to Guatemala while Ele took a flight to South Dakota and California to check on the farms and houses. On my arrival, I was met by colleagues: Don Finberg, the about-to-be-reassigned deputy director of ROCAP; Rudy Jonke, the ROCAP executive officer, and Les Gottlieb, the executive officer for Guatemala, who had been with me in La Paz. They whisked me to my residence where the senior staff was waiting: Bob Parker who had just been named to replace Don Finberg; Bob Allen, the political officer; Charles Buchanan, the operations officer; Bob Eyre, the program officer; John Kahle, the regional legal officer; Don Fiester, the chief Agriculture officer; Bob Davis, the chief engineer; Warren Wolff, the loan officer; Chuck Flinner, the controller; and John Kilgore, the regional housing adviser.

They briefed me on the ROCAP program and its staff, and advised me that the following morning I was to meet with the U.S. ambassador to Guatemala, William Bowdler, with whom I had worked on earlier assignments. They also told me that the embassies in Costa Rica, Nicaragua, El Salvador, and Honduras were informed of my arrival at post.

The meeting with Ambassador Bowdler was substantive. We were joined by AID Mission Director Ed Coy, another good friend who had succeeded me as AID mission director in Bolivia. As was his style, Bowdler told it as he saw it: the situation in the region appeared to be even worse than I had suspected from the briefings in Washington. The shadow of the still unresolved Soccer War between El Salvador and Honduras continued to block political discussion among the countries. The Organization of Central American States (ODECA), headquartered in San Salvador, was barely functioning, with most of the five governments in arrears on their annual payments. The Central American Secretariat for Economic Integration (SIECA) was bogged down and unable to move forward proposals for expanding intra-regional trade.

The following Monday, I met most of the twenty-three U.S. and thirty Central Americans on the staff of ROCAP at the offices downtown across the street from the National Palace. To get to the building we had to drive through the narrow city streets that posed a security threat; Guatemala was considered one of the most dangerous assignments for U.S. officials in the Western Hemisphere. The ambassador rode in an armored car with bodyguards, followed by a car with armed officers. Mine was a special car reinforced for security, with a follow car and two armed guards. We sped through traffic and stop lights, with some harrowing experiences. For the first time in my career, there was an armed guard on twenty-four hour duty at our residence, and our instructions were never to leave home or office without the guards. From day one in Guatemala, personal safety was an integral part of every experience and activity.

My first month on the job was series of briefings. I met with the regional authorities: Dr. Roberto Mayorga Cortés, executive secretary of the Executive Secretariat for Central American Economic Integration (SIECA); Dr. Enrique Ortiz Colindres, president of the Central American Bank for Integration (CABEI); and Dr. Mario Martínez, executive secretary of the Central American Institute of Science and Technology (ICAITI). I had initial telephone conversations with U.S. ambassadors in Costa Rica and Nicaragua, as well as the chargés in El Salvador and Honduras, and arranged for trips to meet with them and be introduced to presidents, foreign ministers, and national officials in charge of Central American integration policy. Don Finberg and Bob Parker scheduled in-depth briefings by each of the senior staff who had been waiting for me at my residence the day of my arrival. Most were frustrated by the delays in program execution. One specific example was in the housing industry. The ROCAP housing adviser, John Kilgore, had lined up millions of dollars from the U.S. private sector, under the AID Housing Guarantee Program, to finance the manufacture of building materials in the region to be used for the construction of thousands of middle-income houses. The critical element for the program to move forward was the creation of a Central American rediscounting facility in the Central Monetary Commission (CMCA). In 1967–8, the countries had agreed to create the CMCA as the central bank for the five countries, a regional adaptation built on the model of the International Monetary Fund (IMF). The CMCA was to include a housing window through which the five central banks could rediscount mortgages already discounted by each country's central banks from national saving-and-loans associations and licensed commercial banks. Then came the Soccer War and for five years there had been no movement. So, John advised me that he had agreed to a transfer to Panama to work with its Central Bank on a national housing finance program.

My colleagues laid out project after project in agriculture and industrial development that, like the housing program, were ready to go if the impasse in Central American integration could be broken.

After the departure of Don Finberg, Bob Parker took over as deputy director and became my close colleague and adviser for the next two years. Bob was a veteran of AID programs, and his work in Vietnam had uncovered significant cases of misuse and mismanagement of AID funds. He was a meticulous officer who made certain that, before a decision on any issue was made, we had comprehensive data on the situation in the region, the conditions in each of the five Central American countries, and the competence of the Central American regional and national bodies involved. He was well respected by our senior staff, which was especially important since our mission, while relatively small, was made up of highly qualified veteran professionals.

Status of Central American Integration

After those four weeks of briefings and initial visits to the countries and integration bodies of Central America, I had chapter and verse on the stagnation of regional integration since the Soccer War. U.S. concern over Vietnam had left the five countries to work through the crisis pretty much by themselves. Bitter feelings by the military on both sides prevented any progress. It was like the aftermath of a fight between brothers, with neither one ready to concede that he was at fault. Several had tried to broker an agreement, including Ambassador Bowdler and the Costa Rican Foreign Minister Gonzalo Facio. Others like Nicaraguan strongman Tachito Somoza and the Guatemalan military seemed quite satisfied with the status quo, in spite of occasional lip service.

Integration and the Common Market were innovations that challenged the established order. The five sovereign states of Central America had failed in an earlier attempt to forge a regional political union after becoming independent of Spain in 1822 and Mexico in 1825. They sought to establish the Confederation of Central American States under Honduran General Morazón, and it lasted until 1838. A similar initiative the 1890s was aborted on inception. Lack of an interregional communications and transportation network had isolated the countries from each other, and led to the emergence of local power blocs that resisted sharing power with their neighbors. Each of the five countries had more commercial and political connections with Europe, the United States, and Mexico than they had with each other. The first paved land connection among all five countries was the Pan American Highway built with U.S. assistance in the 1930s. It was only after World War II that the countries established direct communication links.

After World War II, they began to consider ways and means of increasing their voice in world and hemispheric affairs. Some political leaders revived the dream of the Central American Confederation, and young economists and businessmen, trained in the United States and Western Europe and influenced by ECLA, called for a Central American Common Market.

The first step was the creation in 1950 of the Organization of Central American States (ODECA), headquartered in San Salvador with a small secretariat. It was a loose political framework that provided a regional forum in which foreign ministers could discuss issues and try to hash out common positions. As a former secretary general of the Organization of American States (OAS), Alberto Lleras Camargo, so wisely observed in the mid-1950s, "An international organization is only as useful and effective as its member states allow it to be. It is the sovereign members who govern it."

In the 1950s, the Council of Ministers of the Economy was formed and in 1960 it reached agreement on the framework for a free trade area, which they called the Central American Common Market (CACM). In 1963, the Council agreed to a treaty of economic integration and the establishment of the Secretariat for Economic Integration (SIECA) to implement the CACM and the integration process. In 1961, the Council also created the Central American Bank for Economic Integration (CABEI), and in 1964, the Central American Tourism Authority (ATCA).

Paralleling the trade efforts, the economic ministers in 1960 moved to create a Central American financial system. In 1961, the Central American Clearing House was set up in the National Bank of Honduras. The presidents of the five Central Banks spearheaded the creation of the Central American Monetary Authority (CMCA) and the Central American Monetary Union, looking to create a central bank for the region. Plans had advanced for a common currency for the region, called the Central American peso. Then came the Soccer War! Honduras withdrew from negotiations. An agreement in 1969 to move forward the Monetary Authority failed because of Honduran refusal to ratify.

Throughout this process, ROCAP supported the organization and program of SIECA. ROCAP's economists helped compile and analyze economic data, build a regional database, and develop a comprehensive economic development information center. It provided financial and technical aid for regional development seminars and projects. It supported integration agencies set up to further inter-country cooperation, including SIECA headquartered in Guatemala, ODECA in El Salvador, CABEI in Honduras, the regional tourist ATCA in Managua, and CACM in Costa Rica. At least one integration agency was headquartered in each Central American capital city.

Until the Soccer War in July 1969, the integration movement had made substantial progress in building a common market by adopting, *inter alia*, common customs nomenclature, standards and procedures, industrial trademark protection, a regional highway network, a plan for a regional energy grid, and a telecommunications policy. As I pointed out earlier, the five countries had reached technical agreement on the creation of the regional central bank and a common currency.

Those accomplishments were especially impressive since the integration movement was led by political reformers, economists, and technocrats with limited political bases in three of the countries. Indeed, they faced the opposition of the traditional power brokers and the military in Guatemala, Honduras, and Nicaragua. Costa Rica with its democratic political system reluctantly participated with its more authoritarian partners, and probably only El Salvador was enthusiastically committed. But for nearly a decade, they had staked out new paths to progress for Central America.

The progress ceased when women from El Salvador and Honduras were assaulted during soccer matches in Tegucigalpa and San Salvador, and the two countries went into a short, bloody war that ended with a truce that lasted over a decade until the Peace Treaty was signed at the OAS in 1980. The fallout not only shut down the integration movement but also led to the expulsion of tens of thousands of Salvadorans, many of whom had been small shopkeepers and businessmen in the interior of Honduras. They were "dumped" into the San Miguel region and became a source of tension with the local populace, and perhaps one of the causes of the later Salvadoran Civil War.

The Soccer War scuttled further discussion of forming the customs union and the regional capital market. The foreign ministers met to try to revive negotiations, but Honduras opted out. The economy ministers proposed an interim mechanism to continue governing the Common Market until Honduras rejoined as a full member, but that stalled in 1971 when Honduras opted out of the CACM and set high protective tariffs on products from the other four countries.

By July 1973, the resurgent military backed by traditional oligarchs in El Salvador, Guatemala, Honduras, and Nicaragua were sidelining progressive young professionals and forcing them to emigrate to jobs outside Central America. The integration movement may not have been dead, but it was barely limping along.

Only CABEI continued to function normally, and it was financing the construction of regional infrastructure projects, primarily for roads and power. It also managed a regional fund to guarantee certain investment capital and handled a limited number of business and housing projects. CABEI could finance itself from its fees and interest on its loans.

ODECA and SIECA, dependent on annual quotas paid by the five member states, were hampered in their operations since only Guatemala and El Salvador were current in their payments; Costa Rica and Nicaragua, facing fiscal shortfalls at home, were late, but promised early compliance. Honduras declared itself free of any obligation, including pre-1971 arrearages.

The United States and other international donor agencies continued to fund specific regional projects, but did not provide institutional or budget support. Access to those donor funds depended on the quality and capability of the ODECA and SIECA staffs. ODECA had only a skeleton group at its headquarters in San Salvador. SIECA had lost several key specialists but was able to conduct studies, manage meetings of Economic and other technical ministries, and prepare specific projects for the countries to consider. SIECA, not ODECA, was the functioning center of what was left of Central American integration in 1973.

The political and social situation in the five countries was not good. In the largest Central American country, Guatemala, repressive measures controlled and silenced the political opposition, especially the land-hungry indigenous people—roughly 55 percent of its eleven million people. In the latter half of the 1960s, a virtual civil war existed in which the U.S. military openly trained and supported the Guatemalan army and air force to repress dissent, with the U.S. acting out of its Cold War concern that Fidel Castro could gain a foothold. In 1968, U.S. Ambassador John Gordon Mein had been assassinated by rebels on the streets of Guatemala City, and the Guatemalan military responded with further bloody strikes of retaliation throughout the country and political assassination. Guatemala was *de facto* a military dictatorship, with only nominal respect for human rights and judicial processes.

At the other end of spectrum was Costa Rica, a fully functioning democratic state with a record of respect for human rights and a succession of elected governments, in which opposing political parties often replaced each other in peaceful constitutional transfers of power. In 1947, José Figueres and his PLN Party (*Partido de Liberación Nacional*) successfully overthrew a military-oriented government, abolished the armed forces, and installed the contemporary political system. There was an effective system of checks and balances, with an independent judiciary and a fully functioning Congress.

Costa Rica was historically unique in Central America. Settled by Spanish farmers who killed off the indigenous population and took over their land, there were few large land grants. Costa Rica did not have the extremes of wealth and poverty that existed in its four northern neighbors. Throughout its colonial and republican history, unlike its neighbors, Costa Rica had invested in education for its fairly homogenous population. In its four neighbors, education was for the elites, mainly the Creole upper class, with the indigenous native population largely excluded.

El Salvador, Guatemala, Honduras, and Nicaragua had little experience with representative democracy. They had been governed since independence by a succession of military leaders, usually selected and sustained by large landowners. Power was transferred more often through revolutions than elections, creating few political institutions and little experience in constitutional governance. The nominal political parties that existed were the Conservatives, who advocated unity of church and state, and Liberal, who favored separation of church and state.

Guatemala and Honduras were the personification of Banana Republics—countries whose governments responded whenever the price was right. And it was the United Fruit Company and its banana production that became the corporate image of the manipulating foreign entity. It exploited the Caribbean coast of Central America to produce bananas for the U.S. and European markets. From the late nineteenth century, the company made sure that governments adopted and maintained policies that protected the interests of its banana business, its railways, and its maritime shipping company—the Great White Fleet, popularly known to Central Americans as the line on which, "Every banana's a guest, every passenger a pest."

El Salvador, the only Central American country with no Caribbean coastline, had no commercial banana production. The only significant United Fruit Company investment was in the International Railway of Central America (IRCA), which runs from the Guatemalan port of Puerto Barrios on the Caribbean to the Salvadoran port of La Unión on the Pacific Ocean's Gulf of Fonseca. El Salvador is the smallest of the five republics in territory, but it is the most densely populated. Its indigenous people, the *pipiles*, had a reputation from pre-colonial times for their fierceness. Throughout its colonial and republican history, there were bloody insurrections suppressed by one military strongman after another.

In the 1950s, El Salvador began a transition toward more democratic political processes. However, the Soccer War had once again thrust the military into the center of power. In 1972, the mayor of San Salvador, José Napoleón Duarte, a Christian Democrat civilian who advocated that the "military return to the barracks and stay out of politics," had amassed a substantial lead over his military opponent, with a reported 65 percent of the vote tabulated. At 11:00 p.m. on election night, the military moved into the vote counting center, seized the ballot boxes, and shut off television coverage. Four days later, they announced that the military candidate had been elected, with a vote that defied any reasonable projection based on the tabulations on election night. The election fraud went unchallenged, even by the U.S. and Western democracies, and cast a pall on popular expectations for reform through a peaceful political process.

In Nicaragua, one family had dominated the political scene for over thirty years: the Somozas. General Anastasio Somoza García, known as "Tacho," had seized power in the late 1920s after the U.S. Marines occupied the country to secure payment for defaulted Nicaraguan debts. Somoza was from the Liberal Party, which, since independence in the 1820s, had alternated power with the Conservatives more often through military coups than constitutional transfers of power. Tacho ran the country with an iron hand until his assassination in 1957. Power then passed to his older son, Luis Somoza Debayle, who initiated moves to open up the political and economic system. Those moves were abrogated when his younger brother, Anastasio "Tachito," who attended West Point, succeeded him.

In 1972, Nicaragua was wracked by a monster earthquake that devastated the capital city, Managua. Tachito took advantage of the earthquake to consolidate economic and political power. Rumor had it that, while his father's cut of business operations was 8 percent, Tachito raised his to twenty and moved into business sectors like banking and insurance that his father, Tacho, had left to others. The result was broad based opposition to Tachito.

Honduras, throughout its history, had passed power from one military figure to another, from Conservative to Liberal, from one family to another. It was a country known for its Wild West traditions and the law of the *pistola*. In the 1960s, during the early Alliance for Progress days, the military allowed the election of a liberal civilian president. The United Fruit Company, concerned about growing Castro-communist influence among its workers, gave access to the AFL-CIO to help its workers counter the red penetration. The opening to democracy closed abruptly with the Soccer War, and the military openly seized the reins of government and rebuffed efforts to revive the regional integration process.

The political situation in the five countries was unfavorable for an accommodation. Each military president saw himself as the natural leader and had no stomach for sharing power with the other four presidents. Costa Rica was deeply concerned by the authoritarianism in its four northern neighbors and was not prepared to support any military officer to lead regional efforts.

The situation with the economies of the region was not much brighter. When the integration process began in the early 1950s, there was little intraregional trade. The five countries sold commodities—principally coffee, bananas, meat, and raw materials—to the U.S. and European markets, and bought consumer goods from them. There was no regional financial market; they looked primarily to the U.S. for capital. Banking was a traditional commercial operation oriented to the needs of exporters and landowners. Manufacturing was rare, except for some textiles on the north coast of Honduras developed by Lebanese newcomers, and food processing plants owned primarily by foreign companies. The region had few mineral and petroleum resources. The per capita income was among the lowest in the Western Hemisphere. Public education, outside of Costa Rica, barely covered basic elementary schooling for most of the urban children.

After World War II, the five countries began to explore together ways to strengthen and modernize their economies. With few natural resources other than agriculture products, the opportunities for increasing non-agricultural employment and economic diversification would have to come from developing a market large enough to support efficient regional manufacturing and service industries. The assistance they received from the U.S. through the Institute of Inter-American Affairs (IIAA), had been technical assistance in agricultural development, education, and public health. From ECLA they received assistance in economic planning, including the creation of national planning commissions and promotion of economic integration, regional trade, and more diversified economic development—sometimes at odds with the U.S bilateral trade interests.

As late as 1958, exports from the five countries totaled only US$428 million, a scant 20 percent attributable to intra-regional trade. By 1963, as the integration framework became functional, the intra-regional percentage rose to over 50 percent of the US$518 million in total exports. By 1968, the total trade of the five countries had doubled and the intra-regional trade then reached over 65 percent, with products manufactured in the region accounting for most of the intra-regional trade. The byproducts of the increased manufacturing were the rapid growth in value-added, a rise in non-agricultural jobs, and much-expanded public and private infrastructure.

The region also had traditionally suffered from trade deficits, and the countries set up a mechanism for regional action to negotiate agreements; that process had ceased when Honduras blocked joint action in 1969.Throughout the late 1950s to the Soccer War, there had been steady substantial growth in GNP and GDP.

Unfortunately, the benefits did not fall equally among the five countries. El Salvador and Guatemala had more capital and entrepreneurship to take advantage of the expanding regional market. Costa Rica was slow to recognize the advantages, but became a much more active participant as the market grew. Honduras and Nicaragua were clearly the least benefited. Whatever the reason, Honduras felt the most aggrieved, and was demanding special advantages when the Soccer War broke out.

After the Soccer War, El Salvador could no longer move its products overland through Honduras to Nicaragua and Costa Rica, having to rely on a ferry from La Unión, El Salvador to Corinth, Nicaragua, that was owned by Tachito Somoza—and the ferry rides were not cheap. Guatemala took advantage of the stalemate and neither Nicaragua nor Costa Rica had developed enough new plant capacity or products to increase intra-country trade.

Regional Development Program

The *raison d'être* of ROCAP was to support Central American integration. The ROCAP Program had a political and economic focus. It carried out the reporting and analysis functions of a typical embassy but also provided economic and technical assistance to the various bodies created by the Central American regional authorities as an AID Mission.

After reviewing the economic and technical program mix, I asked why there was so little attention to the social dimension of development, I was reminded that that reflected the priorities of the countries and that the regional leaders did not find conditions ripe for dealing with social issues *per se*. When the Soccer War broke out, negotiations on a blueprint for free movement of labor among the five countries were shelved. SIECA's plans for manpower studies were put on hold. It had not broached the design of a region-wide elementary school system (with standard curriculum and textbooks on reading, writing, arithmetic, and social studies), because of the failure of the 1950s textbook program over nationalist and ideological differences among the five countries. Initial discussions for a regional health program floundered on concerns by national health leaders that a regional effort would divert their limited budget funds from national to regional priorities.

ROCAP's top priority was to strengthen SIECA's economic and technical staff and support its establishment of a regional statistical and information system and network. ROCAP Economist Clark Joel was the technical adviser to SIECA on the regional databases and collection systems, and I was advised that ROCAP had the most comprehensive and respected data on economic and social development in the region. Clark also provided technical advice to SIECA on seminars, workshops, and studies on economic conditions in Central America and on the prospects for regional products in world markets. It also financed scholarships for SIECA, private sector managers, and officials of member governments to overseas seminars and plant visits in the United States.

ROCAP's second priority was support for CABEI. Warren Wolfe, a veteran Capital Development officer, was ROCAP's liaison with CABEI and monitored U.S. loans to the bank. He started his briefing with an organizational chart of the bank and an introduction to its key officers. He advised me that its banking and oversight competence was in the area of infrastructure loans, and that it was building its technical and staff capability in other lending categories. In addition to CABEI, he oversaw regional loans from ROCAP to other Central American public and private entities. He detailed the procedures his office followed in investigating each request for a loan, in preparing recommendations for ROCAP's response and, if considered promising, drafting and submitting the documentation for AID Washington consideration. He then outlined how his office, once a loan was approved, worked with the operations director and technical specialists to ensure that the funds were expended in accordance with the terms and conditions established in the loan agreement, and to provide for periodic inspections and evaluation of the borrower's performance.

The third priority area was the oversight by the engineering division, headed by Bob Davis, of regional infrastructure projects, by both ROCAP and the five country USAIDs. It inspected the construction of AID-financed roads, schools, housing, water and sewerage systems, and the regional power grid. It also advised CABEI in its review of engineering aspects of projects under consideration for funding.

Bob Davis and his staff, on a map of Central America, identified the various projects designed to modernize the region's transportation and power grid and laid out the problems they faced in moving projects forward. He pointed out that, when projects for the long-term benefit of the region seemed to conflict with some immediate national interest, they were being sabotaged in the multi-country approval process. They cited as a prime example the loan to build the highway intended to link the main ports of Guatemala and Honduras—Puerto Barrios, and Puerto Cabello respectively. When constructed, the Guatemalan section of the highway reached the Honduran border some ten kilometers away from the connecting Honduran segment because the Guatemalans feared the better-endowed harbor in Honduras would divert shipping to Puerto Cabello. As far as I know, that is the way it still is today. This jingoism had intensified since the Soccer War and was holding up final approvals for projects, seeking to revise project plans for narrow national interests, or induce CABEI to promise to finance a pet project in return for approval.

The fourth area of the ROCAP program focused on agriculture and rural development program. Don Fiester and his colleague Phil Church gave me a status report on a loan paper being prepared by SIECA to improve agricultural production and farmer income in the CACM member countries. Based on years of research and experimentation, much by Don and Phil themselves, it was aimed at incorporating subsistence farmers into the cash economy through multiple cropping and planting new dry season crops with technical, financial, and marketing assistance. Their research showed that much of the land in the region was cultivated only during the rainy season and that during the dry season it lay fallow, providing little food for the cities or income for their families. It also identified that only one third of the farmers in the region owned the land they cultivated; that another third leased land or raised crops designated by the landlord; and that the remaining third were squatters who moved onto unused land, burned the foliage and trees, and grew subsistence crops until the land wore out or they were driven off. Additional research was needed to better understand the complex patterns of land use and land tenure in the region, and the loan provided funds for that purpose.

Don then detailed how the loan would involve the two most important research centers in Central America—the Inter-American Institute for Cooperation on Agriculture (IICA) in Torrialba, Costa Rica, and the Pan American School of Agriculture in Zamorano, Honduras. IICA was founded by the OAS as the hemisphere-wide research center for agricultural development and had pioneered agricultural cooperation in the Western Hemisphere. It had a broad agricultural research program and good facilities—even though its work was being overshadowed by international centers on coffee, potatoes, rice, and other commodities (which received substantially greater financing from the UN and private foundations). Zamorano was set up by the United Fruit Company to train agronomists, initially for the company operations and later expanded to agronomists and agricultural technicians from not only Central America but also countries around the world with similar climates and soils.

The loan was to include funds for IICA to coordinate applied agricultural research and extension in the five countries and provide expert assistance to the five countries on implementing the loan. Loan funds for Zamorano would cover specialized training for extension agents and farmers in advanced production techniques. Zamorano had ties to California State Polytechnic University (Cal Poly) in San Luis Obispo, providing it access to the latest scientific advancement in agriculture and state of the art training systems.

During the discussions on the proposed loan, we considered efforts in the late 1960s and early 1970s to work out a regional agreement on the free movement of labor. Don traced the generations old yearly migration of farm labor from Guatemala to Nicaragua for picking the major cash export crops: coffee, cotton, and sugar. The

CACM authorities were proposing a regional legal framework for that movement and some protection for farmers and migrants. The Gordian knot in the negotiations had been the rights of migratory farm labor. Many migrants were small farmers or squatters who left their acreage to pick crops during the harvesting season, usually in the last six months of the year. They crossed borders without any controls or protections. The negotiations had dealt with a system to ID them, the framework for a minimum wage, and some form of social security.

When negotiations broke off, SIECA was preparing basic studies of the impact of the annual migration on workers, conditions of migrant laborers, and their impact on regional economic development. The initial data indicated that the long absences of the male workers resulted in mothers becoming the stabilizing force of the migrant laborer family and that male migrant laborers frequently changed spouses, with a high incidence of children born out of wedlock. It also raised questions about the capability of any of the countries to provide education, social welfare, and health services for this annual cross-border migration and that this migratory labor pattern went to the core of the endemic unemployment problem faced by four countries.

The fifth program area of ROCAP was technical support for the industrial sector and diversifying foreign exchange earnings. This line of action had four major components. The first was financial support for the Harvard Business School initiative to establish the Central American Institute of Business Administration (INCAE). Led by George Cabot Lodge, the Harvard team set up the institute on the hills overlooking Managua, on land provided by the Nicaraguan government. Harvard prepared the curriculum and teaching materials in Spanish and supplied the initial faculty. Harvard trained Central Americans for faculty assignments and had maintained its presence and interest by using its own resources after those from ROCAP terminated. By 1973, a Nicaraguan, Dr. Enrique Cruz, had become its first Central American director. Dr. Cruz was the brother-in-law of our I House friend Luis Carrión. INCAE attracted the best and brightest young businessmen in the Isthmus, and its MBA was a prestigious degree. Its graduates were modernizing traditional business models in all five countries. INCAE left Nicaragua after the Sandinistas took power and operates today from its campus in Costa Rica.

The second component was direct technical assistance to business leaders. ROCAP financed bringing retired U.S. corporate leaders to Central America to advise companies throughout the region on measures to increase their efficiency, install cost control systems, and improve product quality in order to better compete in the internal and export markets. Although high tariffs protected regional manufactures from external competition, SIECA aimed to stimulate exports as well as domestic consumption—and that required constant upgrading of quality and design to compete in the world market. Infant industries and fledging entrepreneurs needed substantial on-the-job aid.

The third component was financial and technical support to ICAITI, the Central American technological center set up to advise and assist public and private industrial, agro-industrial, and service companies to improve the efficacy and effectiveness of their operations. ICAITI had the best facilities in the region for research on and testing of materials. It received requests from private industries in all five countries for technical assistance, and had a working relationship with the U.S. Senior Executive Corps to provide retired U.S. executives on short-time assignments to help local companies resolve specific management, technical, and operating problems. ROCAP financed certain projects undertaken by ICAITI and had on that staff a full-time industrial engineering adviser paid by ROCAP, Eli Hill, my former colleague from Bolivia. Its work had substantially improved production in the region and helped make several products competitive in world trade.

The fourth was support of regional tourism. Tourism had great potential for generating foreign exchange earnings, and ROCAP helped finance the program of the CACM's regional tourist agency ATCA, headquartered in Managua It funded technical assistance to identify and design tourist packages that could attract large-scale private investment in tourist facilities and long-term jobs for tens of thousands of white and blue-collar employees. I was pleased that the Spanish version of my Senior Seminar paper, "Tourism as a Tool for Development," was being used by both SIECA and ATCA.

In 1968, several proposals were ready to be launched, including the Mayan Circuit of Tikal, Copán, the Guatemalan Highlands, Yucatán and Chiapas; the ecological reserves being set up in Costa Rica; the Guatemalan lake region with the indigenous culture of Chichicastenango and the beauty and ruins of Antigua; the unique lakes of Nicaragua; and the beaches of the north coast of Honduras. Plans were being drawn up to attract private investment in hotels, transport, and facilities coupled with CABEI financing of roads and other infrastructure. However, the Soccer War intervened and the countries were unable to find common ground on implementing the plan. The agency was essentially moribund.

Ele's Arrival

Ele arrived six weeks after me and settled in quickly. Ambassador and Mrs. Bowdler had us to dinner the night following her arrival. The Parkers had a buffet dinner for all the ROCAP staff and their wives. The Coys invited us to a buffet for all his Guatemala USAID senior officers and their wives. Then Ele and I hosted a reception for Secretary General of SIECA Dr. Roberto Mayorga, his deputy, Dr. Rodolfo Quiroz, and other SIECA department heads and their wives. We hosted a second reception for key Guatemalan officials associated with the integration movement, including Minister of Planning Gert Rosenthal. Within three weeks, Ele had met most of the key people and their wives with whom we would be working.

She took charge of our two-story art deco style house, surrounded by a large garden and spiked metal fence. There was a large steel gate at the entrance a few feet in front of the house, beside which was a guardhouse where Guatemalan policemen protected us twenty-four hours a day.

The interior reflected the taste of the 1920s: spacious light and airy rooms. It had a formal living room, a dining room, a music room, a half bath, kitchen and pantry on the first floor, with a terrace around the back that opened onto the garden. On the second floor, there were two bedrooms, one a master suite with walk-in closet and bath, and a guest room with its separate bath. In a separate building off the kitchen were two maids' rooms and a bath. There were fireplaces in the living room and the master bedroom. It was a wonderfully comfortable modest house to live in—not the most modern or luxurious, but so easy to enjoy.

The house needed painting and a few touches, and the owner who lived next door agreed to paint. Ele chose soft greens and yellows for the walls. She also convinced the landlady to glass in the terrace. The terrace is where Ele and I spent many happy hours. Whenever I brought work home on the weekends, I set up a work area overlooking the garden where I could take a break to watch the humming birds (*tzum-tzums* to the indigenous people of Guatemala) and enjoy the orchids growing wild in the trees. Ele loved to read and listen to records, often Guatemalan marimbas, in the quiet of that terrace.

She had two immediate problems. Our cook, a fabulous chef who had spent ten years at the French embassy, decided to open her own catering service; she had saved enough money to buy a small house and equip a large kitchen. She gave Ele time to find a replacement. In addition, the maid took another job and had to be replaced. Through embassy and ROCAP contacts, Ele was able to line up a number of candidates and, within a week, found new staff. The cook was an elderly lady named María from Alto Vera Paz, whose bearing and poise belied her inability to read or write. María was a joy to be around, always smiling and always prepared to help. Ele said that, if she told her a recipe once, María never forgot any detail of it. She prepared Guatemalan and European cuisine, baked Danish pastries and cakes, and prepared vegetables and pasta al dente that never disappointed.

The maid Ele chose was Rosa, the niece of a maid who worked for a friend. Rosa was the happiest person I can remember. She had a smile on her face and a helping hand at any hour of the day or night. Her problem was that she was a klutz who could break anything in sight, even when she took special care. I well remember her downcast eyes as we arrived home one evening to her announcement that she had knocked over a vase while trying to put flowers in it, "Ay, *señora*, I don't know what happened." Ele would give her a light lecture—much softer than one I would get for a similar misdeed—and then Rosa absorbed her scolding, peered into the Ele's eyes and they both would be smiling.

Most of our social life revolved around the job. We seldom went off on our own since we had our ever-present police guards. We didn't bring our own car to Guatemala because of concern for personal safety. So, everywhere we went for three years, we were a party of six: my driver, the police in the follow car, Ele, and me. If we went for a picnic, María would make a basket for six people. If we were invited to an event or a dinner party, there would be four people waiting for us. If I went to the airport, I was surrounded by my police protectors. I sometimes believed that I was a more identifiable target than if I had been alone.

One night shortly after Ele arrived, we decided to see a movie in a theater not far from our house. As required, I advised the police escort of our plans. When we got to the theater, we were ushered into a row in the back of the theater—it had been cleared of all other patrons. An armed policeman sat at one end of the row, another policeman similarly armed at the other end. We were seated in the middle of the row all by ourselves—we never felt more conspicuous targets in our whole lives. We never went to another movie during the rest of our tour in Guatemala.

Doing the Job

One of my first efforts was to build working relationships with my Central American counterparts. That meant not only the officials of regional organizations, but also the key officials in the five governments who dealt with Central American integration, like ministers of Foreign Affairs, Economy, Development, Planning, Finance, and Central Bank presidents. My job required an up-to-date understanding of where they stood on regional issues and to reflect them to Washington.

This was definitely not the role I played as a mission director in Bolivia, where I had looked to the ambassador for political guidance. In this post, I reported to the assistant secretary of state in Washington for political guidance and to the coordinator of the Alliance for Progress on matters involving U.S. support for regional development programs. This placed me in a very delicate relationship with all five ambassadors, and I had to avoid sending signals to Washington to which the ambassadors might not agree. Hence, there was a need to maintain close working relations with each of the ambassadors and touch base regularly to ensure that ROCAP and the five embassies were on the same wavelength. In addition,

ROCAP had to rely on intelligence from the embassies since our office did not have a secure area. Every morning, Bob Allen, Bob Parker, and I received the daily intelligence summary and copies of the dispatches to and from the five embassies, but we did not have access to the sensitive, highly classified materials.

That was no easy balance to maintain. Most ambassadors focused on their bilateral interests and frequently looked on regional political and development interests as undermining their authority at the national level. Some ambassadors, like Bill Bowdler and later Tom Meloy in Guatemala and Pete Vaky in Costa Rica, understood the interplay between regional and national interests and the need for close cooperation between ROCAP and his embassy.

I visited each country regularly. My first action on each visit was to call on the ambassador and have a detailed talk about the local political scene and regional issues. Then I would call on the key ministers dealing with regional affairs, often before I met with officials of the regional organization headquartered in the country. I also set up appointments with Central American colleagues with whom I worked during the El Salvador assignment and friends from International House Berkeley. I often got a very different picture of the situation in country from the regional personnel and personal friends than from the embassy or the national authorities.

After my first visit to the five countries, I was struck by the lack of information and interest among the key embassy staff members about the policies and situation in neighboring countries. The development of a Central American regional authority was not on their agenda. Only occasionally would I find a deputy chief of mission or a political or economic officer who had any background on regional issues, and few of them knew their counterparts in neighboring countries.

Regional policy could not be made in vacuum. Inputs and assessments were needed from the five embassies. I began wrestling with the problem of what ROCAP could do to keep senior staff in each embassy informed about regional developments and encourage their input. ROCAP needed to know what national officials thought about regional issues. We needed a systematic two-way information flow.

The effects of the Soccer War were apparent in my conversations with officials of all five governments. They made clear that their political interests were centered on national issues and that the enthusiasm for regional cooperation had significantly waned. Only in El Salvador and Guatemala did I find senior civilian, political, and business leaders urging the resurgence of regional programs as the modus operandi for stimulating economic growth and promoting more democratic, non-military governments. In Honduras and Nicaragua, the military running the countries talked with me only about national power and national interests. The only information they wanted was on what regional programs they could get for their countries from the U.S., CIAP, and the international banks if they "cooperated."

When I met with General Osvaldo López Arellano, then president of Honduras, at his military headquarters in late 1973, he said in effect, "Let's be practical. There are four generals running the countries. Only one of us really can lead Central America, and the other three won't let that happen. So, all we expect from the regional mechanisms are financial resources that help us carry out our national programs without having to burden our people with too many more taxes."

At my meeting with General Arturo Armando Molina, president of El Salvador, he gave lip service to regional integration; but I felt that he was saying what he thought I wanted to hear, not what he was interested in or prepared to do. In Guatemala, my visit to General Carlos Manuel Arana Osorio was purely protocol and he left no room for discussion.

In Nicaragua, Ambassador Turner B. Shelton took me to the office of President Anastasio Somoza Debayle (Tachito) for not only a meeting but also an elegant lunch of lobster and crepes. The president told me of his plans to rebuild Managua after the devastating earthquake of 1972, expand public education, and nurture popular participation in all phases of Nicaraguan life. He pledged his support for finding a solution to the Soccer War. He said all the things that I wanted to hear, but his track record belied his words. As Ele said to me that evening after my return flight to Guatemala, "He researched you down to your underwear. He used all the catch phrases you used over the years. You have to determine if his actions indeed match his words."

In Costa Rica, the civilian leadership with its democratic principles was at first reluctant to join the integration movement. It had established close working relations with the U.S., the UN, the IDB, and the World Bank. President José Figueres and his successor Francisco Oduber had reservations about dealing with the military dictators next door, and warmed up to the Central American Common Market only when they saw potential benefits for their country's development. Talking with them was much less formal than with leaders in other countries. I had met President Figueres several years earlier at the home of AFL-CIO Chief of Latin American Affairs Serafino Romualdi. The president invited Ambassador Viron "Pete" Vaky and me to his residence for a "quiet talk." He was clearly skeptical about the advantages to Costa Rica of economic regional integration. A day later, I had lunch at DCM Lyle Lane's residence with ex-President Francisco Oduber (he succeeded Figueres as president again in 1974) and Foreign Minister Facio. We had a far-ranging discussion of the situation, marked by their deep concern about the deteriorating economic and political outlook in the region.

Given the deep divisions among the countries, I felt that bringing the embassy officers into a dialogue not only with ROCAP but also among themselves was a priority. So, I asked Bob Allen and Bob Parker to help me put together a proposal to submit to Washington to have ROCAP sponsor periodic meetings of the DCMs, and political and economic officers to discuss the situation in the region and work with ROCAP to design and develop appropriate lines of action.

Meeting of Central American USAID Directors

In late 1973, a meeting of mission directors from the AID Missions in Central America was convened in Honduras. My good friend Ed Marasciulo was the AID director in Honduras and proposed for safety reasons that we meet outside of Tegucigalpa, at a Caribbean resort, St. Anthony's Key. The resort was built around a lagoon, with individual bungalows and a main building complex with meeting and dining rooms. The owners allowed us to bring our wives at no extra cost. So, all of us brought our wives.

Ele and I flew on a DC-3 to the conference. The rainy season wasn't over—and my most salient remembrance of our weekend at St. Anthony Key is the deluge that didn't stop from our arrival until our departure and the rough water in the lagoon as we were ferried back and forth to meetings and dinner.

The roofs of several bungalows sprung leaks. I shall never forget the scene in the neighboring bungalow of Fran and Bob Culbertson, the AID mission director in Nicaragua, sitting on their bed with open umbrellas in hand to try to keep the rain from drenching them. There was no sunbathing or vacationing during that meeting!

Our meetings spelled out the troubles of all five countries. The directors felt that regional integration was, at least for now, a minimal factor in Central America and that each mission would have to program for its country without expectations of regional incentives to spur national growth. Bob Culbertson and Ed Marasciulo both blamed the stagnation on the lack of progress on regional integration and reported that they   were pressing for action to break out of the impasse. Ed Marasciulo reminded us that Honduras as the least developed country in the region wanted special treatment as the *quid pro quo* for breaking the impasse. Ed Coy pointed out that the Guatemalan military resisted pressures from the other governments to offer additional special incentives for Honduras and Nicaragua as "pay-offs" for reviving the CACM.

Ed Johnson, the Salvadoran director, reported that the country was suffering greatly as the manufacturing boom went bust after the Soccer War because it lost land transport access to its formerly vibrant markets in Honduras, Nicaragua, and Costa Rica. Political unrest was growing after the military's blatant theft of the 1972 election with hardline generals in control, and the generals blamed a small group of Honduran entrepreneurs, mainly Lebanese shirt and garment manufacturers in San Pedro Sula, for boiling the pot and unduly influencing the Honduran military leadership. He also warned that, while there was no evidence of an armed uprising against the government, a wave of violence, possibly tied to a faction of the military, was targeting progressive young business and political leaders who, like the exiled winner of the 1972 presidential election Duarte, had fought for economic and political reform.

The USAID director in Costa Rica attributed the five-year downturn in that country's economy since the Soccer War on the statist economic policy that gave little support to the private sector. The country's trade deficit accentuated because of rising imports for the rapidly urbanizing middle class. On the other hand, agricultural and non-farm production was not increasing because of the lack of incentives and skimpy information about potential markets. The budget deficit was troubling and the government was focused on austerity measures to keep it under control.

In addition, Costa Rica had no civil service laws. With each change in administration, even when the governing party won re-election, there was a tendency to replace staff from top to bottom. The mission was besieged with requests for training new specialists and technicians to replace those who were let go. As a result, progress on programs and projects was behind schedule and project costs were mounting. The other four mission directors bemoaned similar experiences, noting that almost all appointments were political and often only those with ties to the military were retained. We discussed whether SIECA could spearhead regional action for assuring continuity in key technical posts in the national governments.

I reported that the regional organizations were barely limping along. The days when Harvard and the Brookings Institution collaborated with SIECA in analyzing and projecting regional development had basically ended with the Soccer War. Many of the key economists and technicians who staffed SIECA had left for more permanent posts in the IDB, World Bank, IMF, and private banks. Regional trade and investment in import substitution businesses continued to grow, but now at a feeble pace. CABEI was still making loans, but its capability was limited to certain infrastructure projects, especially roads and dams. The region now needed additional banking facilities, like the dormant Central American Monetary Authority central bank, to provide greater liquidity; and the generals just weren't interested.

Our colleagues from Washington, led by Herman Kleine and David Lazar, made it clear that money was tight, that our funding levels would be further reduced, and that USAID and ROCAP should rethink and consolidate priorities and programs. Then they advised us of rumors of pending changes in Alliance leadership, with the appointment of the current assistant secretary of state for Inter-American Affairs, Jack Kubisch, to be ambassador to Greece and of Bill Rogers, the former deputy coordinator of the Alliance, to replace him. We speculated on what such a change would mean in light of Bill's recent book, *How The Alliance Lost Its Way*. Our Washington colleagues surmised that nothing short of armed intervention by the Soviets or Cubans would revive high-level U.S. interest in the region.

Over the next two days we discussed this grim panorama. In the discussions, only Ed Marasciulo joined me in supporting regional integration. Nonetheless when we finished, all agreed that regional cooperation was critical to development of their countries. All recognized that none of the countries had the resources or capabilities to make meaningful progress on its own. We also agreed that the political environment in each country, and the region, required us to involve State Department officers in our future meetings because of the political cast to development issues.

I then presented my proposal to have ROCAP establish periodic meetings of embassy officers from the five countries. All the directors felt that such an initiative would be useful to help embassy officers better understand the objectives and scope of national programs as well as the issues of regional integration. Our Washington colleagues promised their support.

The rains stopped on the last day of the meeting. The DC-3 flew most of the participants to the airport in San Pedro Sula. Ele and I joined the Marasciulos on a visit to the new Dole pineapple plantation on the north coast of Honduras. Dole had bought out the Standard Fruit Company and was replacing bananas with pineapples when it found the soil and climate just right. It was closing down its high labor-cost operations in Hawaii and moving them to Honduras.

We spent a day being briefed on the operations and the company's investment plan. We stayed at the Dole Guest House and had long discussions about production and marketing plans, relations with the Honduran government, and labor-management conditions. The manager was clearly uncomfortable talking about the balance he had to maintain with the generals and colonels and the difficulties he had in obtaining permits to bring in machinery as well as facilitate exports. The unions were active, and he told me that the pro-U.S. labor leaders were being outflanked by radicals who sounded like Fidel Castro.

Treading Water

Preparing a program strategy and a budget request for the next fiscal year was a challenge. While the environment for regional integration looked like a far-fetched dream, the cold economic and political reality remained that the five countries individually could not achieve the economies of scale needed for self-sustaining economic growth, attracting needed investment, generating new jobs, and accessing world markets, much less for financing education, health, and social services for the rapidly increasing population. If the region was to continue the transition from mercantilism and feudalism to a modern capital formation and productive economy, it had to renew its efforts to build a regional system.

No outside entity—not the United Nations, the United States, nor the OAS—could do it for them. External agencies could provide technical and financial help, but the effectiveness of that help depended on the capability of the regional institutions themselves. So, ROCAP had to make helping the Central Americans to find their own way as the focal point of our efforts.

The question I faced was tactical. What was needed to sustain the wobbling regional institutions while looking for a solution to the Soccer War? My initial visits to the five countries had indicated that little political will existed in any one of them.

Perhaps the U.S. could pressure the generals, especially in Honduras, to work out an accommodation, but that seemed unlikely without some formula that had promise of succeeding. I felt that, if ROCAP could find that formula, it might generate sufficient interest in Washington to induce Honduras and El Salvador back to the negotiating table. I was authorized to talk to leaders in both countries to see if there was such a formula. In the meantime, we focused ROCAP support for SIECA and CABEI on strengthening their planning and operational capability and providing high-level training for Central American economists and technicians. We requested Senior Economist Clark Joel to recommend measures to support SIECA and the Loan Officer Warren Wolfe for those related to the Central American Bank (CABEI).

ROCAP also curtailed support for several projects that were not central to this tactical approach. We eliminated assistance to: (1) the regional tourism agency (ATCA) and (2) the moribund political arm of the integration process (ODECA).

As part of this approach, funds were requested for a three-day meeting per year for the five embassy DCMs to meet together with the senior ROCAP staff in order to inform each other on developments in their respective countries and in the region and to devise ways of improving inter-country communications and cooperation. We also proposed that economic and political officers from the five embassies meet periodically with ROCAP. When I also detailed this proposal to the ambassador to Guatemala, Bill Bowdler, who was being transferred to Washington as the senior deputy assistant secretary of state for Inter-American Affairs, he embraced it.

Shortly after Bill took office in Washington, I was called to Washington for consultations with Bill Rogers, Herman Kleine, and him. They informed me that the Latin American regional integration of AID and State was being undone and that ROCAP was to become an AID operation. Even so, Bill Rogers offered me a direct line to consult with him, and Bill Bowdler helped me present the proposal for meetings of embassy officers with ROCAP. Herman Kleine was not enthusiastic, but agreed to give it a try.

In the discussions with the AID senior staff, I sensed a deep skepticism about not only my proposal but more profoundly, about the Central American regional movement. I certainly shared doubts about whether the impasse in the region could be resolved.

On my last day, I met with Herman Kleine, who told me once again that the continued existence of ROCAP was in doubt once AID assumed direction of economic and technical assistance in Latin America. He was to become regional administrator of AID for Latin America and the Caribbean, and offered me once again the post of his deputy.

He took me to meet the new administrator of AID, Daniel Parker, who listened carefully to my outline of conditions in Central America. He was acquainted with the region from his years as the CEO of the Parker Pen Company; my perceptions coincided with his. He also responded favorably to my program proposals. I left his office feeling a lot better about the future of ROCAP. I declined Herman's offer.

On my return to Guatemala City, Bob Parker and I worked closely with Program Officer Bob Eyre to prepare adjustments in the program and to set the framework for the Fiscal Year 1975 program presentation that was about to be submitted to Washington.

Then we settled into a routine. Bob Parker, Warren Wolfe, and I made a monthly trip to Tegucigalpa to attend the CABEI board meetings at which proposed loans were considered, many of them from funds provided by AID. I met weekly with SIECA Secretary General Roberto Mayorga to review progress and problems. I continued to go to San Salvador periodically to meet with the caretakers of ODECA and to get the latest gossip about tensions and prospects for an agreement to end the Soccer War.

Bob Parker and I went individually on field trips with Bob Davis and Don Fiester to see first-hand the operational problems they faced. I can still taste that dust and feel the stifling heat driving over the CABEI-financed Nicaraguan highway from Managua to Bluefields on the Caribbean. Bob Davis took Ele and me on an inspection of the CABEI-financed road from Guatemala to Tegucigalpa, through Esquipulas, the home of the relic holy to millions of Central Americans known as the Black Christ. The highway had opened up a potentially rich new agricultural area where tree crops could be grown profitably with easy access to good seaports for shipment to potential export markets. My driver and follow car were especially concerned because the Guatemalan military had recently chased armed insurgents out of entrenched positions near the highway.

On that trip we visited a couple of agro-industrial plants that received technical advice from ICAITI. Using funds provided by ROCAP, ICAITI provided technical assistance to plant owners on production problems, the installation and adaptation of machinery, and layout for efficient plant operations. ICAITI had arranged with the Executive Service Corps to provide short-term operational guidance by retired U.S. businessmen. I especially welcomed the opportunity to visit infrastructure, industrial plants, and food processing facilities in the five countries because I could compare the current conditions with those I had seen in two or three countries during my El Salvador assignment. In the 1950s, there had been little road infrastructure, few operating plants, and even fewer progressive businessmen. A great deal had improved, but the countries were still in the early stages of development and lacked much of the infrastructure, the industrial base, and the work force to make a giant leap forward.

Don Fiester took me on visits to IICA and the Pan American School of Agriculture at Zamorano. The director of IICA, Dr. Araujo, a distinguished Brazilian agronomist, did not see IICA as a Central American center, but as the hemisphere-wide planning and oversight arm of CIAP on rural development projects. He expected additional CIAP appropriations to build up his staff in San José and expand research facilities in Torrialba. Unfortunately, over the next two and half years, CIAP resources dried up and Dr. Araujo's expectations evaporated.

At Zamorano, Don and I toured the facilities and met with the students from all over the hemisphere. We were briefed by the director and his Cal Poly advisers on their programs, plans, and budget. They were in good shape and received strong support from the Honduran Ministry of Agriculture. It was a first class facility, far better than most I had visited in Latin America and the Caribbean. And there was no doubt of its interest in cooperating with Don in training national research and extension agents from the five Central American countries and for assisting small farmers on multiple cropping and new crops for the dry season.

Life in Guatemala

Ele thrived in the altitude. Her low blood pressure seemed to give her more energy and get-go in the altitude of almost 5,000 feet than at sea level. Its indigenous culture captivated both of us, as did spring-like climate year round. We almost bought a retirement home in Antigua—if only the political and social environment had been less conflictive!

Ele ran the household, with María and Rosa for most of our nearly three years at post, and it was a happy place. When María fell ill, we hired a temporary replacement, a lady who had worked for fifteen years as the cook for one of the elite families of the country. She was an excellent cook, and we paid her a higher wage than she had received from her former employer. Ele instructed her: "Keep honest accounts of any money I give you, and ask me before you take any food out of the house. You will eat what we eat, as well as any additional tortillas, corn, or beans you need to round out your diet. Just tell me about it." Nonetheless, the new cook was fired a month later when Ele caught her skimming off money and smuggling nightly packages of food out to her family. When Ele confronted her, she responded that was the practice in her former place of employment and she couldn't adjust to the strange system in our household—even with her higher monthly salary. With Rosa's help, Ele did the cooking until María returned.

Running the house was only one aspect of Ele's life in Guatemala. She was active in the diplomatic and embassy wives' organizations. As I noted earlier, shortly after our arrival at post, the Bowdlers were transferred to Washington and there was a hiatus of several months until Ambassador Francis "Frank" Meloy, Jr. arrived. He was a bachelor and brought no female relative to serve as his hostess. That role fell to the DCM's young wife, a charming lady with small children. She and Ele became fast friends and Ele helped out when family matters required the young wife' attention. Ele often found herself taking the role of the senior U.S. diplomatic lady at post. She enjoyed working with the ladies and followed the same guidelines that she had applied in Bolivia. The ladies chose their own priorities and activities, organized their own meetings, and elected their officers. They did not want typical charity work or to roll bandages at the hospitals.

For finding good works to do, the ladies were fortunate to have the advice of a remarkable American expatriate, Sam Green. Sam made a fortune in New York real estate before coming to Guatemala on a visit; he fell in love with the country and its people. He built a comfortable home on a hilltop overlooking Lake Atitlán, with a breathtaking view; if I remember correctly, it was 170 steep steps from his terrace down to the lake. He also built a dirt road to his front door from the highway. And, indigenous people approached his front door for help. They came with requests for help in building water supplies, bridges, latrines, and cooking stoves. In keeping with the tradition of this feudal society, the village elders had come to the great lord to ask for his charity. Sam said, "No charity." Instead, he offered to match every penny they raised in the community and every hour of labor the people pledged. No charity, but friendship and cooperation!

When more requests came from other villages, he responded in the same way, and soon found himself engaged in projects all around the lake. He provided technical engineering advice to the community workers and advised them on managing their resources and building more economically viable communities—as he said, "grass-roots democracy." As the projects grew, he asked for the help of Guatemalan and American friends. Thus was born the *Fundación del Centavo*, the Penny Foundation, one of the most effective organizations of its kind in Latin America and now run by civic-minded Guatemalans.

Ele introduced Sam to the embassy wives. Several had worked with the foundation on various rural community projects. Ele proposed that the embassy wives use the Sam Green model for their local projects, and they were enthusiastic. They found a community called Chimautla, well-known for its beautiful gray pottery, *ollas* (cooking pots), and sculptures of birds and angels, which provided the community with most of its cash income. Twice a month, the ladies went out to the village and worked with the women on a variety of civic development projects and were gratified to see those women build their self-confidence and carry out projects to improve their community, especially the education of their children. Unfortunately many of those improvements were devastated by the terrible earthquake of 1976.

The embassy ladies also worked with a group of nuns in Guatemala City to help them develop programs for abandoned and runaway girls who subsisted in the center of the city and who were an increasing cause of crime. Ele said that the nuns were usually from rural families who had little formal education themselves. They taught the girls what they could, mainly embroidery and some truly exquisite pieces were produced. They asked the "foreign ladies" to show them how to develop other projects that would teach the girls skills so that they could make their own living.

The ladies also supported a project run by priests and private charities to rescue some of the thousands of street boys who lived on the streets of Guatemala City. The numbers were overwhelming. Birth rates had risen as infant mortality declined, and older boys in rural areas increasingly left home to find jobs in the city to help their impoverished families in the countryside. They had no skills, and most were illiterate. Only a handful could find jobs as food handlers or hauling carts. Most ended up in gangs that extorted money from shop owners or robbed pedestrians. What was needed was a government program, but our contacts in religious organizations and welfare centers told us that the government officials bemoaned that their limited resources were being channeled to make up for centuries of neglect in public education.

The ladies also called on the chief education adviser for the US-AID program in Guatemala, Peter Wright, to advise them on ways they could provide additional resources for the cash-strapped school system. Several joined Peter and his wife and Ele and me on visits to elementary schools and centers across the Guatemalan highlands. The schools we visited had equipment and teaching tools inferior to those in similar rural schools in Bolivia. Even in Guatemala's second largest city, Quetzaltenango, the facilities were well below what I had expected. Peter Wright made it abundantly clear that the resources of both the Guatemalan government and the USAID Mission were woefully inadequate, and certainly did not have the capability of dealing with the problem of street kids. The U.S. ladies made a valiant effort to provide money and supplies for some schools.

In addition to her work with the *Damas Diplomàticas* and embassy/AID wives, Ele entertained a steady flow of official visitors and friends who made their way to Guatemala. Every visitor meant a trip to Lake Amatitlán, Antigua, Atitlán, and the market at Chichicastenango (called Chichi by all us natives). Ele often took lady visitors to the central market of Guatemala City with its dozens of booths full of handicrafts, pottery, and textiles that the incredibly talented artisans produced.

In the markets, buying meant bargaining and never divulging the apple-of-your-eye on the first round. To the market ladies, a good bargaining session was as important as the ultimate sale. Ele enjoyed the give-and-take, with all the long faces, shrugs, and dramatic dialogue. And what pleased her was that she was always welcomed back when she brought another visitor. I might add that, whenever Ele went alone, she came home paying a lot less than when she had visitors in tow.

We had few visitors from U.S. universities or think tanks. I recall only two academic visitors in my two and a half years at ROCAP: George Cabot Lodge of Harvard Business School, who stopped over en route to direct a seminar at ICARE, and Dr. Charles Denton, chairman of the political science department at Fresno State University, who wanted to explore a possible university contract to support SIECA and ODECA. Ele welcomed them to lunch, cocktails, or dinner as their and our schedules permitted.

We had many official visitors from various U.S. government agencies and members of Congress and staff of Senate and House Committees dealing with Latin America. Cuban influence in Central America was a major concern. For each visiting delegation, we arranged formal briefings at the office followed by informal meetings at our home, often at lunch and dinner. When Congressman Dante Fascell and his wife Marie, or Claude Pepper and his wife Mildred came to the country, Ele often spent her days with the wives, especially since our ambassador was a bachelor.

The Fascells came on a personal visit before Christmas in 1973. They wanted a little time to relax with their longtime friend, Henry "Hank" DuFlan, the first director of ROCAP. On retiring from ROCAP, the DuFlans bought a colonial house in Antigua and refurbished it with colonial furnishings and Guatemalan handicrafts. Hank invited Ele and me to join them on the weekend and participating in the discussion was a wonderful experience.

The DuFlans became our close friends. I consulted him often about developments in the region and avoided many missteps by listening to his wise counsel. In addition, both of them were experts in the folk arts of the indigenous people and had accumulated a world-class collection of Guatemalan *huipiles* (the colorful blouses worn by the women). Each community had its own design. The DuFlans had examples from almost every village in Guatemala, including some exceptional nineteenth century beauties. By the 1960s, many of the *huipiles* were being made in factories, and village weaving was rapidly disappearing. The DuFlans taught us how to distinguish between the traditional and machine-made garments and helped Ele identify and purchase many of the *huipiles* in the collection now at the Museo de las Américas in Denver.

The visit by Claude and Mildred Pepper was extra-special. Claude came to Guatemala as a speaker for a regional savings-and-loan conference. They stayed at the hotel in which U.S. and Canadian conference leaders were housed, just a few blocks from our house. John Kilgore had been instrumental in having the meeting convened in Guatemala and was the technical adviser on the agenda and conference arrangements.

One of the high points of the conference was a visit to a housing project in Antigua financed under the AID Housing Loan Guarantee Program. The president of the U.S. Savings and Loan Association and John Kilgore made it a special occasion, with a marimba band and speeches by the homeowners. After the program, Ele and I took the Peppers to see the ruins of the cathedral and houses in the area—and found a monument commemorating the terrible eruption of the Volcano Agua that poured millions of gallons of superhot water onto Antigua. The congressman asked me to translate its inscription and, when I read him the date, he in his southern drawl exclaimed that the date was also that his birthday, September 8. He quickly added that it happened a century or so before he was born. We celebrated that birthday for several years before he passed away.

Ele and I also attended many official dinners, both for regional Central American and Guatemalan events. We were treated by the Central Americans as a chief of mission and often paired with senior officials from other Central American countries at presidential and Foreign Ministry events. Ele had an array of dinner dresses and ball gowns, and we seldom traveled to the other Central American countries without packing my tux and one of her long dinner dresses. At the inauguration of General Lagerud as president of Guatemala, Ele wore a forest green ball gown that drew praise from the president-elect's wife, Helen, and led her to invite Ele to several informal lunches before we were reassigned to Panama in 1975.

We did a lot of entertaining at lunches, and Ele worked with María, our cook, on the menus and on decorating the table. Ele tried to keep our entertaining as informal as possible. Several times during the first year in Guatemala, we had working lunches with

SIECA, CABEI, and other regional and national officials in the garden, where we set up a long table in a flat area near the corner fence. The last such lunch honored the Guatemalan minister of Planning, Gert Rosenthal, and had an agenda of measures to strengthen the SIECA staff. We also talked about potential new regional initiatives that Gert felt his government might consider sponsoring. After the lunch, Ambassador Meloy called me to his office to advise me that a suspicious car had been spotted circling my home, and that an outdoor lunch could well entice certain elements to attack the house. Ele took a second look at the exposed garden and we never had an outdoor lunch again.

Ele always helped me through difficult situations and found a way to calm the waters. One evening we came home from a party with our ROCAP colleagues, and I thought that I had been very clever with several witty remarks. When we got home, Ele, as she inevitably would do, looked at me and asked, "Do you realize that you offended several people by your snide remarks? Didn't you realize that you opened up delicate matters for several of our colleagues? I think that you should call them tomorrow and apologize."

A New Headquartes Building for ROCAP

In late 1973, the U.S. regional security officer for Central America told me that he had serious concerns about the safety of our offices in downtown Guatemala City and our daily drive through the narrow streets of an increasingly crime-ridden central area. He advised me to move our office closer to the new U.S. Embassy building in Zone 10.

This made sense. ROCAP staff told me of overnights in the office by my predecessors during failed military coups and anti-government demonstrations. The controller, Chuck Flinner, pointed out the high cost of maintaining a separate guarded parking area near the office building and reported break-ins near the ROCAP garage. The administrative chief, Rudy Jonke, presented data that showed substantial savings if we combined our vehicle program with that of the embassy and USAID. So, we set out to find a new headquarters building close to the embassy.

Not long thereafter, Bob Parker met a builder who was putting up a four-story edifice around the corner from the embassy. He said that he would be pleased to rent the building and adjust his construction plans to meet our operational and security needs. We negotiated a favorable long-term lease, and prepared to move in as soon as the building was completed. By mid-1974, we made the move.

Ele and the wives decided that we should have a formal moving-in ceremony. They decorated the building for the occasion. The landlord agreed to paint the walls in colors suggested by them. The ladies and the administrative officer selected plants for the interior of the building that made it an elegant government office.

We invited the Archbishop of Guatemala City to the inauguration, and he agreed to do the blessing. The guest list included the acting director of ODECA, the secretary general of SIECA, the president of CABEI, the director of ICAITI, the foreign ministers, the planning ministers, and the ambassadors of the CACM countries. Ele and the ladies prepared a reception, with food and drink befitting the occasion. Our cook María made an assortment of sweet buns that disappeared almost before they reached the serving tables. Ambassador Meloy and the SIECA secretary general joined me in cutting the ribbon to open the building.

The move was a good one. The consolidation not only reduced our administrative expenses but also allowed me much closer ties to both Ambassador Meloy and my colleague Ed Coy, the US-AID-Guatemala director. The working conditions were ideal for the ROCAP staff. The offices were bright and the facilities much more modern than those downtown.

Ele made that office the most attractive that I ever enjoyed. Not only was it just the right size with excellent lighting, but it was graced by one of the most appreciated gifts that Ele ever gave me: a Honduran mahogany wood sculpted panel, about four by three feet, of Mayans planting corn—a motif of hope and promise for the Mayan people. That panel was in every office I occupied from that day forward and is now at the Museo de las Américas in Denver since I have no room to display it properly in my retirement apartment.

Friends Came A-Visiting

Our good friends the Guthries were with us for Easter 1974. Dorothy, the artist, loved to paint flowers and how she enjoyed our garden! In the almost unending springtime in Guatemala, after a dreary winter in Washington, D.C., Dorothy reveled in sketching the orchids, roses, off-pink patience, and hummingbirds that made our garden their home. Chet came to the office with me and gave all of us the value of his extensive experience in foreign assistance programming. And the Wrights invited us to be their houseguests in Antigua for the Good Friday to Easter spectacle, with the streets covered with elegant carpets made of flowers and chalk. The Wrights, the Guthries, the DuFlans, and the Tragens walked from church to church to the *Alcaldía* (city hall) to keep eager eyes on the craftsmen who prepared the carpets and arranged the flowers. We watched the processions on Friday, Saturday, and Sunday. This was Ele's and my first Easter in Antigua, and it was unforgettable. Even our visits to Chichi placed second to the allure of Easter in Antigua.

After the Guthries left, we took a short vacation to Yucatán and Guadalajara. We had never been to the Peninsula and were intrigued by the Mayans. We had been to Tikal and Copán, and now we wanted to see Chichén-Itzá and Uxmal. We arrived in Mérida and hired a tour company to take us around for three days. And what spectacular ruins! The hot semi-arid plains of Quintana Roo and Yucatán can be very warm in April, and that year was no exception. In the heat, climbing the pyramids was a chore—and getting back down an adventure. I confess that Ele mocked me as I climbed up—and laughed as I sat down to descend the steep steps on my rear end.

From Yucatán, we flew to Guadalajara to spend a few days with Sally Phipps Korkawski, the daughter of our long-time friend Helene Phipps Tubbs. Sally had a lovely apartment in the city and a time-share condo in Puerto Vallarta. Being with Sally was like being with family. We visited the wonderful museums, music centers, and book fairs in the city and spent a couple of days resting in Puerta Vallarta before Ele went onto California and I returned to ROCAP.

Sally visited us in Guatemala later that year, and Ele treated her to the handicrafts of Guatemala and the beauties of the lakes and Chichi. That Sunday at Chichi, Sally, Ele, and I climbed up the hills around the city to watch the *shamans* lead the people in prayers to the age-old deities to ensure that their messages got to the Supreme Being, just in case those from their personal altars inside the Catholic church in town had not.

For Easter 1975, we were graced by the visit of our good neighbors at the Towers in Washington, the Sherrys. We booked rooms at the Hotel Antigua since the DuFlans and the Wrights had houses full of family. We went up to Chichi on Wednesday and spent the night at the marvelous Mayan Inn and walked around the special holiday booths, full of textiles and ceramics, and the food stalls until we nearly dropped. Faye with her artist's eye was captivated by the color and designs of the textiles. Then, we spent three days in Antigua and repeated the experience of the year before. Believe it or not, it was even more wondrous than the year earlier. We spent every available minute visiting the churches, watching the street artists at work, and trying to decide which street carpet we liked the best.

We had only two bedrooms in our home, one of which we used as a guest room. Sometimes we had conflicting calls on its use. I remember when my nephew Gary told us on a Wednesday that he was coming to Guatemala on Friday, we already had an official visitor from Washington as our houseguest, and he planned to leave his bags at our house while he took a field trip to inspect some ROCAP loan projects in the interior of the country. We found a comfortable pension for Gary and took him to Antigua, Lake Atitlán, and Lake Amtitlán, but couldn't get back to Chichi. We had a great four-day visit, but truly regretted that we had been unable to have him stay with us.

On another occasion, our good friend Billie Heller from Beverly Hills accompanied Helen O'Connell, the popular singer and former host of the *Today Show*, to Guatemala for a couple of days before going to San Salvador for the annual Miss Universe Pageant. We accompanied them to a reception at the embassy and became their official guides to see Atitlán and Antigua. We ended up spending five days together since I had a commitment at ODECA and with the Salvadoran Foreign Minister the day before the Miss Universe finale.

Both were captivated by the beauty of the Guatemalan high-lands and the capabilities of the indigenous weavers and artisans. We talked about culture, politics, the woman's movement, and the Equal Rights Amendment, as well as the emerging post-Vietnam world. Helen and Billie flew to San Salvador on Thursday for the pageant. Ele and I drove over Thursday night and stayed with the chargé at the U.S. Embassy, who accompanied me to the meetings on Fridays.

After the meetings, I took the chargè to meet Helen and Billie at the Salvador Hilton. Helen was at rehearsals, but Billie was in bed with a terrible case of diarrhea. The embassy doctor was called while Ele and I tried to help Billie. When Ele went to ask for clean towels and fresh bedding, she discovered that the maid was mixing water from glasses half full into pitchers and delivering the pitchers to guests asking for water. Ele called the hotel manager and told him what was happening. He confessed that, because of Miss Universe, the hotel was full for the first time in months and that he had hired several part-time workers to take care of the rooms. When she threatened to call the minister of Public Health, the manager agreed to take immediate measures. We were later informed that all of the finalists on Billie's floor had the same symptoms and that several had withdrawn because they were so weak. It took Billie several weeks to recover from the effects of dehydration.

Ele and I joined the U.S. chargé and his wife in the diplomat-ic box at San Salvador's then brand new indoor sports arena and watched a truncated show. Beside the several contestants too ill to appear; one fainted during the performance, and several others were too weak to perform their dance routines. All I recollect of that Miss Universe event is the medical crisis.

A special houseguest was one of Ele's young cousins, David Leonard. He was graduating high school, and his parents let him come down to spend his summer with us. He explored Guatemala City, riding the buses, interacting with the street boys, and seeing the sites. He flew over to Tikal and slept in a hammock at a local hotel. We included him on a trip with a visiting congressional del-egation that took him to Antigua, Amatitlán, and Chichi. He also joined Ele and me on a trip by car to the other four Central American countries where I had work assignments related to the agricultural loan package, ROCAP and CABEI infrastructure projects, and a SIECA meeting on monetary policy in Costa Rica. That trip became a voyage of discovery for David—a new view of a world quite different from the San Joaquin Valley of California. He wanted to pay his own way, so we let him stay in the typical hotels in which our driver usually stayed. He was eager to try out his Spanish and talked to people on the street and went off to see the sights while Ele and I were working. We also included him in embassy and foreign ministry receptions and parties with colleagues and friends in San Salvador, Managua, Tegucigalpa, and San José.

When it was time to go home, David decided to trade in his air ticket in favor of the train to the Mexican border and then by bus and train to Mexico City and a few days on his own in the Aztec capital before flying home. Ele and I advised against making the trip since the Guatemalan track to the Mexican border did not connect with the Mexican passenger train, only a freight line that required hanging out on cars for some sixty kilometers inside Mexico, followed by buses on the road north to Mexico City. But he convinced his parents. When he began his trip home, María made him a lunch befitting a growing teenager. Rosa hugged him for good luck. Ele and I advised him to change his plans even as we drove to the railroad station. David did what David had decided to do. So, we wished him well as he boarded the train.

His trip home was truly adventurous! When we saw David several months later, he gave us a vivid account of his bus rides with chickens and pigs, tortillas, rice, and beans, the warmth of the Mexican people, and the shower he took when he arrived at the City of Mexico. His only real fright came when he got off the train at the Guatemala-Mexico border and was confronted by Mexican soldiers pointing their rifles at those wending their way up the track to cross the border.

Meeting of Central American Ambassadors

Early in 1974, Deputy Assistant Secretary of State for Inter-American Affairs Bill Bowdler convened a meeting in Guatemala City of the U.S. ambassadors in Central America. Bill had been ambassador in El Salvador and Guatemala and was the most knowledge-able officer on Central America in the Washington hierarchy.

Three of the five ambassadors had only recently arrived at post: Frank Meloy in Guatemala, Jim Campbell in El Salvador, and Phil Sanchez in Honduras. Turner Sheldon was in his second year in Nicaragua as was Pete Vaky in Costa Rica. Only Vaky and Meloy were career foreign service officers.

Bowdler opened the two-day meeting and placed me on his right at the head of the table. He called on us to work together to find a solution to the Soccer War impasse and revive the integration movement.

He advised us that Latin America was not a priority for U.S. strategic policy makers in the post-Vietnam world, but that Rogers and he wanted a stable Central America. He advised us that Kissinger and Rogers were moving ahead with the negotiations for a new Panama Canal Treaty, since the U.S. with its airpower and a two-ocean navy no longer saw the Panama Canal as a critical factor in U.S. national defense.

Early on in the meeting, I was asked to make a presentation on ROCAP. My focus was primarily political, not economic or developmental. I pointed out that progress in regional integration demanded an early end to the Soccer War and that until Honduras returned to active participation in ODECA and SIECA, there could no meaningful forward movement on the stalled initiatives on freer trade, regional monetary policy, a telecommunication network, and a regional power grid. I warned that, without the regional framework, each of the five countries would not have the resources to reach their national development goals. I did not explicitly say that Honduras and Nicaragua, often supported by our embassies, put obstacles on the road to finding a solution. I then laid out my proposal for ROCAP to sponsor, together with the ambassadors, a flow of information among the embassies and ROCAP on conditions in the neighboring countries and to convene periodic meetings of embassy officers with ROCAP to facilitate our working together to assist the five countries in overcoming the impasse.

Specifically, I proposed that early in 1974, the five deputy chiefs of mission meet in Guatemala for a day, preferably over the weekend, and talk together about the issues that the U.S. was facing in dealing with the host governments and in analyzing national attitudes and obstacles to regional cooperation. That would be followed by two additional meeting of ROCAP and embassies officers: (1) a three-day meeting of the embassy economic officers with ROCAP and SIECA economists to acquaint them with the resources available in the region; and (2) a weekend meeting of political officers and ROCAP to work on a coordinated effort to consider political issues in the region.

The first issue that arose was the cost of the meetings. None of the embassy budgets had funds for inter-country travel, nor did their work plans contemplate dedicating much time to regional affairs. Two of the ambassadors took the position that their mandate and focus was on U.S. bilateral relations and that the regional issues added a burden on their already overworked small staffs. I offered to ask AID to fund the three meetings. Bowdler, Meloy, and Vaky welcomed the offer, and Bowdler agreed to talk to Herman Kleine to get approval for the funding.

As the meeting progressed, the critical importance of regional cooperation, if not integration, kept creeping into the discussion of bilateral political, economic, and trade issues. I listened to the ambassadors describe priority problems that usually hinged on technical capability, inadequate tax bases, ineptness of national leadership, and corruption—some of which could be alleviated by moving forward on pending monetary agreements and expanded intraregional trade. Three of the ambassadors reflected that they had never read the CACM agreement nor knew of the monetary agreement treaty. During that discussion, I expressed my doubts that the CACM then or in the near future could provide leverage to deal with corruption and deficiencies in national leadership.

At the meeting, Bill Bowdler said that the top priority on my agenda would be to work with the ambassadors to find a formula for ending the Soccer War. That led to my visiting the foreign ministers and planning ministers of both El Salvador and Honduras. They were civilians who told me that they wanted to put the conflict behind them. There were sticking points over land and expulsion issues, but above all, there were the generals and their susceptibilities. The solution had to save face for them. The Hondurans suggested that the disputed land issue might be resolved by making it a Central American regional reserve, with the flag of Central America flying over it. Salvadorans suggested that a fund be set up to indemnify their countrymen expelled from Honduras. Both required careful discussion under the leadership of a third country, preferably the U.S. Both would require some funding, with a ballpark estimate of $50–100 million. I also met with ODECA and SIECA regional officials who pointed to the U.S. as the preferred mediator. When I reported my findings to Washington, I was told that Vietnam and Watergate were the only topics on which high-level attention was focused and that the ambassadors in Honduras and Nicaragua did not look kindly on ROCAP's involvement. I discovered that Tachito, with his connections in the U.S. Congress and Defense Department, had already pooh-poohed the idea. The only informal response I received was a polite "interesting, but not doable."

I hoped that the meetings with the DCMs, economic officers, and political officers from the five embassies might come up with some new approaches. We had frank discussions, but the best we could do at the first meeting was set up a systematic flow of information to and from ROCAP and the five embassies. On the economic side, we agreed to create a new series of regional statistical and economic information that was needed by the five embassies.

Just as we started to develop closer political and economic relations in the region, Washington made a profound bureaucratic decision. The Alliance for Progress was declared to end in mid-1974 and the combined State-AID inter-American structure was disbanded. State would have its structure and offices for the countries, and AID would have its own. ROCAP would be financed by AID and its mission would no longer include a political dimension. ROCAP's role was exclusively to provide development assistance to the Central American Common Market, with political and policy matters handled by the State Department. I could not then, nor can I now, rationalize those decisions about ROCAP and the U.S. interests in Central America.

A Seething Volcano

From the day I began my tour as director of ROCAP, the rising level of violence in the region—except for Costa Rica—deeply concerned me. The unrest and the breakdown in dialogue among the countries and with political factions inside countries was a constant theme in my official discussions and personal conversations. Almost everyone warned me about the increase in street violence and criminality in Guatemala City, San Salvador, Tegucigalpa, and San Pedro Sula. In Managua, my friends told me about the guerrillas in the hills and said that the 1972 earthquake had made people less fatalistic about the inevitability of the Somoza dynasty and that civic groups were preparing to confront Tachito with armed force if necessary. The conditions had changed radically since I completed my assignment to El Salvador in 1957.

The continuing reports of army suppression of indigenous communities in Guatemala were ominous. Shortly after my arrival, I contacted the rector of Landívar University, the institution that had been selected to continue the rural leadership program initiated by Father Twomey of Loyola of the South. When he heard the purpose of my visit, he was very uncomfortable and cut our interview short by telling me that Landívar was no longer involved in the program. Several weeks later, I learned that the Guatemalan military considered the leaders we trained were subversive because they tried to organize cooperatives. The military then "liquidated" them and arrested the Landívar professor who had taken over from Father Twomey. It was the first of many reports about "police action" against leaders in several communities that Loyola and Landívar had been helping. Guatemalan military officers told me that they didn't want any "leadership" in rural communities except themselves.

In Guatemala and El Salvador political assassinations, popularly blamed on the military, were further polarizing national life. As I sadly learned when I traveled in the interior of Guatemala, there were areas of the country that the police escort proscribed my visiting as "unsafe" because of guerilla activity and the danger of an ambush.

My old friends in El Salvador warned me that the situation in the country was tense. One feared that an armed rebellion against the military was building after it seized the ballot boxes in 1972 and exiled the apparent winner. Reform leaders who had emerged on the right and in the center of the political spectrum had been assassinated, whether by the far right or the far left, no one seemed sure. I was told of serious unrest in the southeastern region of the country around San Miguel where tens of thousands of people had been expelled by Honduras, with little prospect for productive employment. Large numbers of Salvadoran farm workers found their income sharply reduced because they could no longer follow the crops as they had traditionally done—their movement across borders was blocked by the military in Honduras and Guatemala. When I raised those concerns with U.S. embassy officers, I was assured that there was no evidence of "unrest" and that there was little chance of the same type of violence in El Salvador that existed in the Guatemalan countryside or in the emerging Sandinista insurrection against Tachito.

In Honduras, on each visit, I was warned of the growing urban violence. Honduran middle class friends expressed concern about extortion by criminal elements, which they thought the military tolerated. Squatter towns were mushrooming around Tegucigalpa and the North Coast cities, many made up of migrating families from rural areas disrupted by the Soccer War. Older labor leaders whom I had known in the 1950s reported the presence of Cuban-trained organizers on the North Coast who were undermining the union leaders trained by AIFLD. After my one road inspection trip from Guatemala City to Tegucigalpa, my Guatemalan police escort ruled out any further land trips to Honduras because of rising activity by "bandits."

Nicaragua was another deep concern. Old friends in the government avoided talking to me except at private dinner parties when they were sure government informants were not around. U.S.-trained economists and technicians at the Central Bank were seething over Tachito's "removal" of over US$100,000,000 in earthquake relief funds from the Central Bank to his own private bank. My I House friends of both the Liberal and Conservative parties told me of armed guerilla groups fighting in the hills, and that many of their sons like those of Luis Carrión were already committed to the Sandinistas. I was warned not to make another road inspection on the highway across the country to Bluefields on the Atlantic because the government had lost control of parts of the road. My colleague Jim Cheek, the political officer at the U.S. Embassy warned that the Somoza regime was coming apart. Others told me that it was time for the U.S. to drop its decades-old support of Somoza and relegate to history a comment attributed to President Franklin Delano Roosevelt in the 1940s—when asked how he could stand for the Four Freedoms and still support Latin American dictators like Trujillo and Somoza, FDR reportedly quipped, "They're bastards, but they are our bastards."

Costa Rica raised other concerns. While the level of violence and crime seemed manageable, colleagues and friends warned me that there was considerable discontent because of the stagnant economy, rising unemployment, and accelerating rural-to-urban migration. The demand for public services, from infrastructure to education and health, was escalating at a rate that the public sector could not satisfy. Controls on the private sector stifled new investment. A growing minority advocated importing the Cuban Marxist model of state control and state financing of needed industrial and agricultural enterprises—and a rejection of regional cooperation. A functioning democracy with more teachers than policemen, it had just completed a model presidential election; no one contested the honesty of the count. The candidate of President José Figueres' FLN Party, Francisco Oduber, won a narrow victory. He stood for the same government-directed economic policies and there was real concern that those policies were not appropriate to deal with the deteriorating situation.

These concerns by the middle of 1974 led me to send a classified message to Bill Rogers that began, "Central America is a seething volcano of the western edge of the Caribbean, our Mare Nostrum." In probably more ambling prose than necessary, I laid out my concerns and asked for U.S. leadership in the region to prevent further deterioration, specifically by bringing the five countries together to end the Soccer War impasse and revitalizing the Central American integration process. I received comments and questions from Bill Rogers, Bill Bowdler, and others in response to the letter. But Washington's interest was on Watergate, the opening to China, and the exit from Vietnam. The ambassador in Honduras told me my concerns were unfounded; the ambassador to Nicaragua said my concerns were "distorted;" our ambassador in El Salvador said that the military was in firm control and that there was no prospect of an armed insurrection there. The ambassadors in Guatemala and Costa Rica were annoyed with me for sending the letter without clearing it first with them, but they did not disagree with my thrust and concerns. Since it was a classified message, I do not have a copy of it, and I can't revisit the persuasiveness of my arguments. But as the violence built up in the region, I have often wondered whether a strong U.S. response in 1974 could have avoided many of the questionable and expensive interventions that we had to make since the mid-1970s.

ROCAP Redesigned and One Last Effort

The Alliance came to an official end in the middle of 1974 about the time that Nixon resigned over Watergate. The integrated Inter-American Bureau was dissolved and State and AID set up separate regional offices. This meant working exclusively with SIECA, CABEI, ICAITI, and the other technical units even though their ability to function effectively depended on a political solution to the political impasse.

To make clear the new alignment of responsibilities, the director of the Latin American Bureau of AID, Herman Kleine brought a team of senior advisers to ROCAP for a meeting of USAID mission chiefs in early November 1974. The AID directors in the five countries were Ed Coy, USAID/Guatemala director; Ed Anderson, USAID director El Salvador; Bob Culbertson, USAID director Nicaragua; Frank Kimball, the new USAID director in Honduras, and Arnie Arneson, the USAID representative in Costa Rica where the AID program was being phased out. Herman's team included Dave Lazar, the director for Central American Programs in AID; Larry Harrison, director of Latin American Program Development; Marshall Brown, director of the Latin American Loan Office; and Kenneth McDermott from the central office of AID.

Washington laid out the new relationships between State and AID and the role of ROCAP and the five missions. We were advised that the situation in Washington was still fluid, as Bill Rogers pushed through the separation of State and AID functions. We were also advised that Costa Rica was no longer considered an underdeveloped country under AID's criteria and no longer eligible for loan and grant assistance; however, it would be offered training grants and services through regional programs of ROCAP, AIFLD, and U.S. cooperative organizations.

Then, Herman conducted a series of separate programming sessions, with each USAID Mission and ROCAP. The Washington team reviewed the ROCAP proposed program for the next fiscal year before we met for lunch with SIECA Secretary General Mayorga. He spelled out the continuing impasse in the CACM. After lunch, we had a lively debate, at which it was decided to maintain ROCAP as a mission, with its primary role as supporting SIECA efforts in regional agricultural development and on monetary policy, including reviving efforts to create a region-wide mortgage rediscount facility. It was also decided that IDB would be encouraged to replace ROCAP as the primary financer of CABEI road, energy, and telecommunications networks projects.

Fortunately, outside the meetings, I spent time with David Lazar, who told me that he had opposed the separation of State and Aid and had had little success in getting Bill Rogers to focus on Central America. He agreed with my grave assessment of conditions in the region and considered regional integration the only viable route for Central American political stability and economic growth, but saw little hope for Washington action to revive the integration movement. He then confided to me that his friend and colleague from the National War College, General Brent Scowcroft, had asked him to join the National Security Council at the White House as his Latin American adviser. He said that he was available, but warned the general that State might balk at having an AID officer assigned to that post. We agreed that it was a great opportunity and I urged him not to turn it down.

During the meeting, Herman Kleine once again offered me the post of his deputy. I was frankly not interested in another Washington assignment and was not sure where AID was headed. Deputy Assistant Secretary Bowdler had already told me that he wanted me to return to a State Department assignment and shortly thereafter called me from Washington to ask me to go to Venezuela as the DCM. I would have accepted the offer for any post other than Venezuela because I knew that Ele would not agree to go back to the country where she had been the target of terrorist attention. I declined both.

After the Kleine visit, my work changed. Now, in dealing with officials in the five countries on integration questions, ROCAP worked through the five U.S. Embassies. When I visited countries, my meetings were arranged by local embassy or USAID officers who accompanied me on most visits. Only with CACM officials or regional organization located in the country did I make my own appointments. I continued to make the monthly flight to Tegucigalpa to attend CABEI meetings. I attended the graduation at INCAE in Managua. I went to San José for discussions with IICA Director Araujo on IICA cooperation with the proposed ROCAP agricultural sector program. I did not go over to El Salvador since the embassy there now handled contacts with ODECA.

In the winter of 1974–75, Bob Parker and our senior top staff systematically evaluated progress on ROCAP loan and grant projects. He also organized the review of the proposed loan for the regional agricultural program; I was a member of that loan review committee. We challenged Don Fiester and Phil Church to justify the proposed objectives and planned operations, especially the rationale for supporting small farmers in the five countries. We also called in SIECA technicians and raised the same questions with them. We found that, while they used the same terminology, their conception of the program, objectives, and timetables were substantially different from ours. So we had long policy and program talks with SIECA before revamping the loan paper and submitting it to Washington. The loan proposal provided for periodic evaluation sessions throughout the implementation of the project to ensure that both parties remained on the same wavelength.

Preparation of that loan document illustrated how far we still needed to go in Central America to have a seasoned partner in analyzing problems and prescribing potential solutions. This was not a matter of who was right or who was wrong. It was a question of recognizing that countries at different stages of development have different perceptions of problems and possible courses of action to meet them. We could agree on the problem, but we needed careful discussions before we came together to chart possible solutions. Above all, it had to be the Central Americans' project in which we were assisting them to plow new ground.

Early in 1975, I was called over to the office of SIECA Secretary General Mayorga for a meeting with Gert Rosenthal, the Guatemalan minister of planning. Mayorga wanted to put together a new package of incentives to induce the generals in Tegucigalpa to rejoin the CACM. The economic and trade situation in the region had deteriorated badly according to the latest data that SIECA and ROCAP had compiled. Mayorga went over the package of fiscal incentives that Gert had put together in 1973 and that the generals in Honduras had rejected. He then outlined the objections of the Hondurans and proposed that it was time for a new initiative that responded to those objections. Gert agreed.

Mayorga asked for ROCAP's help in putting together a new proposal for the ministers of Economy to consider at their meeting in June 1975. None of us believed the problem was technical, but political. SIECA had to put together a political package with sufficient incentives to entice the Hondurans back into the CACM. I agreed to help and asked Clark Joel and his economic staff to provide the technical support that might be needed.

I called David Lazar, to brief him on the meeting and ask his advice about any input the U.S. might want in the package. I also alerted him to the need for putting some pressure on Honduras and Nicaragua at the right time. David was noncommittal; the most he would promise was to explore the prospects. I understood his position. The Cold War was virulent. The exit from Vietnam had not been pretty. Fears of growing Soviet influence had led to the overthrow of Allende in Chile and the U.S. ambassador in Tegucigalpa was working closely with the Honduran military to counter Castro's growing influence in that country. Those concerns were compounded by Nixon's resignation and his replacement by President Ford.

Without a "no" from Washington, ROCAP worked closely with Mayorga and Gert Rosenthal in preparing the paper and planning for the June meeting. Mayorga also received assistance from Enrique Iglesias, then executive secretary of ECLA (the UN Economic Commission for Latin America and later president of the IBD).

At the meeting, the ministers approved the SIECA proposals and negotiated the Second Protocol to the General Treaty of 1960. In September 1975, at the Central American Summit, the five presidents approved the Second Protocol and called for legislative action in early 1976 to implement the new integration measures. The Second Protocol was ratified by four of the five countries in early 1976. Why Honduras demurred and never ratified I do not know.

In 1976, the primary focus of attention in the region shifted to the Sandinista insurgency in Nicaragua.

Departure from ROCAP

In May 1975, the Parkers' tour with ROCAP came to an end. Ele and the embassy wives organized a series of farewells for the couple, who had been friends and partners in running this complex mission. Bob had been meticulous in overseeing ROCAP operations and made sure that all our records and accounts were in apple-pie order. He never excused sloppy reporting or record keeping, incomplete documents, or feeble explanations. I was extremely lucky to have had two such excellent deputies as David Lazar in Bolivia and Bob Parker in ROCAP.

Bob had been active in almost all mission activities. He and Bob Davis had organized the ROCAP softball team, with a few ringers from the Marine detachment at the embassy. The Parkers were great hosts and always seemed to be ready to lend a hand when visitors came to town. When an AID programming team came down in early 1974 from Washington, the Parkers hosted a cocktail reception for nearly seventy people so that Ele and I could host a small lunch for top Washington officials with the SIECA secretary general and the president of CABEI.

Shortly after the Parkers left, Ele and I received home leave orders. By that time, David Lazar had moved from AID to the National Security Council as Latin American advisor.

The following day, Bill Bowdler called to ask me to take on a dual job in Panama—as economic counselor of the embassy and USAID director. He said that negotiations on the Panama Canal Treaty were reaching a stage where I could be useful to the team negotiating the treaty. On the call was Herman Kleine, who recommended that I accept the assignment even though he preferred my becoming his deputy. I talked to Ele, and although the tropical climate and the humidity were not our cup of tea, we accepted. The necessary paperwork was not ready when we left on home leave in September. Our orders read, "Home leave and return to Guatemala." I left the mission in charge of the new deputy director, Barry Sidwell, and we flew to Los Angeles. Billie Heller met us there and took us on our second trip to Las Vegas as guests of Liberace. We saw the shows and rested for a few days before we made our way to Tulare.

Ele's mother's house was vacant; it was up for rent but had no occupants. So we moved in there for the month of October. It was very strange not to have Ele's mother there and not to be planning a trip to San Francisco to visit my mother. We saw friends and dined out every night. Ele took care of farm business and made certain all our business affairs were in good shape. It was that October when we realized that Ele and I were really the only family we had.

We flew back to Washington in mid-November to a glorious Indian summer weekend. Ele and I had our physicals as the final step for the transfer to Panama. I spent four days being briefed on the new assignment, meeting with the Panama Desk of State and AID, Herman Kleine, a substantive session with Ambassador Ellsworth Bunker, the chief of the team negotiating the new Panama Canal Treaty, and Harry Shlaughterman, who had replaced Bill Rogers as assistant secretary of state for Inter-American Affairs.

Our week in Washington was a succession of lunches and dinners with friends. We were guests of Congressman Dante Fascell and Claude Pepper at lunch on Capitol Hill. We had dinners with Frances Howard, the Guthries, and the Sherrys. We sneaked off for a few hours at the Smithsonian and the Mellon Gallery. We flew back to Guatemala for a week of packing and saying our goodbyes. SIECA Secretary General Mayorga honored us at a dinner at which the mood was definitely upbeat since only a few days earlier, at the November 1975 Summit, the five presidents had endorsed the Second Protocol and the revitalization of the CACM.

Ambassador Frank Meloy hosted an elegant dinner in our honor and especially thanked Ele for her work with the embassy wives and for stepping in to assist him when needed. I suspect that he regretted Ele's departure much more than he did mine. Little did we realize that would be the last time we would see Frank alive. Shortly thereafter, he was named U.S. ambassador to Lebanon and was assassinated in his official car as he moved through Beirut on a peace mission to help settle the civil war then raging in the country.

The farewell party that most touched Ele and me was that at which our colleagues in ROCAP honored us. Our colleagues gave us a remembrance that Ele and I cherished: a poster of the city of Antigua signed by all the Central Americans and U.S staff. It has hung in my home office ever since, and every time I look at it, I remember ROCAP and think about what might have been.

A footnote to our ROCAP assignment came six weeks after we reached Panama. Guatemala suffered a terrible earthquake. It was the third time a serious earthquake had occurred shortly after we had left a post for a new assignment. General Torrijos, the strongman of Panama, heard of those coincidences, and the first time he invited me to breakfast, he quipped, "Please tell me before you are reassigned, so I can get out of the country before the "*terremoto*" (earthquake)!" In Spanish political slang, a *terremoto* could also mean a massive political upheaval.

27

Panama

The flight to Panama from Guatemala took only a few hours but it took Ele and me from one world to another. The economies and social order of Guatemala and Central America were agrarian based. Panama, on the other hand was a trading center—a mixture of cultures and traditions unique in Latin America. The differences are even more striking when one lives and works there after our tour in ROCAP.

On the plane down, I was quite upbeat about the prospects for the CACM and an end to the Soccer War. In their summit just days before we left Guatemala, the five Central American presidents, including the Honduran, had approved the Second Protocol as the basis for revitalizing the integration movement and called on their congresses to draft necessary enabling legislation by February 1976. A participant told me that the presidents had agreed to work together to find a formula to end the Soccer War. I felt that ROCAP had played a positive role in preparing the Second Protocol and that I could close that chapter of my life on a positive note.

However, soon after Ele and I moved to Panama, the Sandinista threat to Tachito took center stage, following the devastating earthquake in Guatemala. Costa Rica prepared for another election. The Honduran legislature did not ratify the Second Protocol, and the impasse following the Soccer War was allowed to drift on for another five years. My expectations faded quickly.

The briefings in Washington made clear that my primary assignment was to provide Ambassador Bunker's team with economic information on the Panamanian economy useful in the negotiations of the new Canal treaty. A strong and effective USAID program was the U.S. expression of its desire to cooperate with Panama—an ingredient in building a favorable environment for the negotiations.

Our New Home

We were met at Tocumen Airport by the executive officer of the embassy, John Hedberg, and the executive officer of the AID Mission to Panama, Rudy Fascell (whose brother was Congressman Dante Fascell), and their wives.

They whisked us through Customs in record time and took us to our house in the Golf Area of Panama. It was a gracious, tropical one-story rambler with a covered verandah that opened onto a garden with a swimming pool; it had been designed by the renowned architect Edward Durrell Stone while he supervised the construction of the El Panamá Hotel. The garden was surrounded by a barbed wire fence that looked onto Panama's private golf club. At each end of the garden were mango trees, a banana tree on the left side, and several fruit palms along the fence with the golf club. Off the kitchen was a separate building with two rooms and bath for our housekeeping staff: one cook-maid and a houseboy-gardener. It looked exotic, but as we found out, it was located in a low-lying area that did not catch the breezes and was not very practical for the kind of living and entertaining that we were expected to do for the next couple of years. But on that delightful December day, it was a beautiful new home for us.

Our Golf area neighbors were well-known Panamanian businessmen, politicians, and influential citizens. To our left lived the foreign minister of Panama, Aquilino Boyd, and to our right, the Tennessee-born widow of the owner of the famous horse race track where General Remón, then president of Panama, had been assassinated in 1956. The widow was the spitting image of my mother-in-law, and her Tennessee charm was undeniable. Across from her house lived then Colonel Manuel Antonio Noriega, the infamous G-2 of the Panamanian National Guard and ally of Panamanian strongman Omar Torrijos. The widow told us the Noriega house was a gift in gratitude to Noriega by her late husband for dedicated service. She also told us that Noriega and his brother were protégés of her late husband, who had found them living in the notorious slum close to the Amador entrance to the Canal Zone and subsidized their education and military training. Those neighbors were so well connected that twice in our two years in the residence we were awakened in the wee hours of the morning when bombs went off in unsuccessful attempts to dispose of one or another of them.

When our personal effects arrived from Guatemala a few days later, Ele set about decorating the house. She wanted to give it a tropical flavor, with as much wrought iron and glass as possible and very few traditional sofas and chairs. She wanted it comfortable for entertaining since one of our responsibilities during the negotiations for the new Panama Canal Treaty would be to build bridges to key ministers and provide a setting for discussions between them and U.S. executive branch and congressional visitors.

One of the problems that worried Ele from the day we arrived was the lack of security in the house. Since the only bathrooms were in our living quarters, we couldn't lock them when we had visitors, and the large open patio off the bedrooms invited thieves or other mischief-makers. She arranged for the regional security officer to examine the house just days after our arrival, because she felt that we should consider moving if the house were not better secured.

The regional security officer turned out to be Jim Ellis, who had been our neighbor and friend in Caracas. He told Ele that he had advised against renting the house for many of the same concerns she raised. He recommended that we ask the landlady to put a guest bathroom in the study next to the kitchen, so that during receptions, we could lock off our living quarters. He also recommended that the patio off the bedrooms be closed off and that certain other measures be taken. Ele and I decided to hold off decorating the house until it was made more secure. Jim told Rudy Fascell what needed to be done. Rudy met with the landlady and she agreed to make the necessary changes if Rudy would agree to a long-term lease that would allow her to amortize the expenses over a five-year period.

After we left Panama two years later, an AID auditor picked this security action as an example of excessive spending by a senior AID officer under the Nixon-Ford administration—and then leaked his finding to the famous Washington muckraker Jack Anderson, who published it in his column. We were notorious for several months as Mr. Anderson repeated his charges. The AID inspector general made a thorough investigation of the accusations. He determined that all of the changes to the house had been consistent with the rec-ommendations of the security officer, that the rent charged for the house had been in line with prevailing Panamanian standards, and that the cost of the changes undertaken had been in fact covered by the normal rental payments. Nothing ever appeared in the news-papers about the inspector general's findings. For months after his report, we were still being pointed out as "those people named by Jack Anderson." Ele and I were horrified by the experience, espe-cially after we had taken special care to prevent extra expense to the government. In fact, had we followed Ele's initial instinct and moved to a more secure house or apartment, AID would have had to pay a higher amount to terminate the existing lease and move us to a new residence.

Panama: The Unique Country

Getting started in the new job was easy. On my first full day in Pan-ama, I met with Ambassador Bill Jordan, a former newsman, and DCM Ray Gonzalez. They made clear what they expected of me both as the economic counselor and the AID director and briefed me on the latest developments in the treaty negotiations.

Next I met with George Rublee, the deputy director of the AID Mission, AID Program Officer Bernie Chapnik, Controller Bill Nay-lor, and Executive Officer Rudy Fascell. By the end of the week, I had met all of the embassy officers and the AID staff. In the second week, the ambassador took me for briefings by General Harold R. Parfitt, the governor of the Canal Zone, and the senior officials of the Panama Canal Authority.

U.S. relations with the Republic of Panama were unique. It had been the U.S. fleet that facilitated Panama's independence by pre-venting the Colombian fleet from suppressing the independence movement. It was the U.S. government that had constructed and maintained the Panama Canal, the lifeblood of Panama. Those his-toric events had created a special relationship. No one has told this history better than David McCullough in *The Path Between the Seas.* Panama existed because of U.S. intervention, but now it wanted control over the Canal, the *raison d'être* for that intervention.

Panama was one of the earliest acquisitions of the Spanish Crown in the New World. Barely five years after Balboa first crossed the Isthmus in 1510, the Spaniards founded the City of Panama. As early as 1520, the Spanish Crown recognized its strategic importance and began investigating the possibilities of building a canal from ocean to ocean, but that proved technologically beyond reach. As the great deposits of gold and silver were discovered in Peru, Panama became the indispensable transit point for moving those riches to Spain. Its inhospitable climate and the prevalence of yellow fever stunted the country's growth and kept Panama City a small town ruled by the Viceroyalty of Nueva Granada based in Bogotá.

Officials reluctantly left the comforts of Bogotá to supervise the movement and accounting for gold and silver moved by caravans of surefooted mules from the natural harbor of Panama City on the Pacific Ocean to Portobelo on the Atlantic. There, armadas of cargo and warships ferried it back to Europe to finance the glory of Spain for almost three centuries. Thousands of seamen died of yellow fever each year in Portobelo while they waited for the wagon trains, always on the alert for the English and French buccaneers who periodically raided the Caribbean port to steal the wealth awaiting shipment.

After independence from Spain, it became a sleepy province of Colombia as the shipments of gold and silver came to a halt. The visions of constructing a canal lay dormant until gold was discovered in California and the Manifest Destiny of the United States carried us coast to coast. U.S. financial interests headed by William H. Aspenwood and his Pacific Mail Steamship Company obtained a charter from Colombia to build a railroad across the Isthmus. The railroad completed in 1855 made substantial profits until 1869, when the transcontinental railroad opened a faster land route from the East Coast to the West Coast of the United States.

In the 1870s, fresh from his great success in building the Suez Canal, Ferdinand De Lesseps obtained a charter from Colombia to build a canal. In spite of his efforts, including building a hospital in Ancón, yellow fever, more than the engineering obstacles, devastated his ambitions. When his financing dried up, he had to give up his quest.

Throughout the latter half of the nineteenth century, the power-ful families of Panama fought for independence. In 1903, they found a powerful ally in President Theodore "Teddy" Roosevelt. Panama-nian and U.S. interests coincided: the U.S. wanted the concession to build a canal for strategic purposes, and the Panamanians wanted their independence from Colombia and were prepared to grant the concession. So, when Panama declared independence and installed Manuel Amador Guerrero as president, Teddy Roosevelt ordered a U.S. flotilla conveniently situated in strategic Caribbean waters to block Colombian naval vessels from Cartagena from intervening. Thus the Republic of Panama was born in November 1903.

Days after its creation, even before the formulation of the first Panamanian Constitution or election of its first president or con-gress, the Hay-Bunau-Varilla Treaty was signed in Washington, D.C. It recognized the independence of Panama and awarded to the United States a ninety-nine year concession to build a canal, with sovereign authority for the life of the concession over a ten-mile strip of land on both sides of the proposed canal. Yellow fever was conquered due to three incredible Americans: physician sci-entists Dr. Walter Reed, Dr. William Gorgas, and Engineer George Goethals. Drs. Reed and Gorgas led the attack on the *aedes aegpti*, the mosquito vector of yellow fever. Engineer Goethals not only built the Canal but also drained the swamps in which the mosqui-tos thrived and bred.

In the years since independence and the opening of the Panama Canal, Panama had evolved very differently from the other coun-tries of Latin America. Its economy relied on the revenues and ser-vices that flowed from the Canal and its operations. It was the nar-row Isthmus and the commerce it brought that was the economic engine for the country, which had little more than 1,700,000 inhabi-tants. Its provinces of Bocas del Toro and Chiriquí had large United Fruit operations, but those operations contributed little to national revenues. Running through the center of the country were the steep mountains of the Cordillera where there had never been much min-ing development and only occasional traces of gold or silver. Most of the land was more suited to cattle raising than agriculture.

The central element in Panama-U.S. relations was the Canal. In the first half of the twentieth century, the Canal had become the commercial lifeline between our two coasts and the vital waterway for moving our navy from the Atlantic to the Pacific. Then, in the Cold War, the U.S. developed a two-ocean navy, with aircraft carriers too large to transit the Canal. The use of rail and highway networks within the United States reduced our reliance on commercial shipping through the Canal.

From the outset, Panama questioned the validity of the Hay-Bunau-Varrilla Treaty, and was equally unhappy about its share of Canal operating revenues. Resentment was exacerbated by the Silver and Gold Roll wage system adopted by the administrators of the Canal for workers doing essentially the same job: Gold Roll and higher wages for U.S. citizens and Silver Roll for Panamanians doing the same job. Many on the Silver Roll were children of black Jamaican, Barbadian, and Trinidadian workers hired to build the Canal; their skills and knowledge of English gave them an edge over their mestizo countrymen. With time, the two had found common cause and forced the end of the Gold Roll.

Tensions built up after World War II, with occasional violent confrontations. Politics in Panama centered on relations with the U.S. and the return of the Canal Zone. Strong nationalist candidates became more vocal in their opposition to the status quo. The U.S. usually controlled the political arena by its influence over the National Guard, a nation-wide police force. Panama did not have a military force to defend its borders; that task was assumed by the U.S. armed forces based in the Canal Zone and at other strategic points throughout Panama. I remember U.S. officials saying to Panamanians during my assignment there in the mid-1950s that they should be pleased not to bear the budgetary burden of a standing army, air force, or navy, "Aren't you satisfied with the protection we give you without any cost to you!"

That argument grew increasingly threadbare in the 1950s as the nationalist party of Arnulfo Arias Madrid gained strength. When Arias was elected president of Panama on the wave of anti-U.S. sentiment, he called for the immediate annulment of U.S. treaty rights to the Canal Zone and Panamanian assumption of sovereignty over the Zone. The Arias government was overthrown by a coup led by the National Guard, with the support of the United States. That coup in 1968 brought to power a new generation of National Guard officers led by General Omar Torrijos Herrera. While Torrijos never assumed the presidency, he became its strongman and directed the government from his office inside National Guard headquarters.

General Torrijos was not from the traditional white upper class, the *rabiblancos* that had led the revolt against Colombia. The indigenous and mestizo were largely neglected and education and other facilities for them outside of Panama City were minimal. The other racial group was the black minority, largely descendants of Caribbean workers brought in to build the Canal; many of them were Canal or Canal Zone employees and were uneasy about any change in the treaty relationship.

Torrijos came from a middle class mestizo family from the Province of Herrera. Like many ambitious and enterprising mestizo youth, he made the National Guard his career. He rose through the ranks and built alliances with his fellow officers. While the leadership of the Guard had been *rabiblanco*, the middle and junior levels had become increasingly mestizo. Torrijos became their leader and posed an ever-increasing threat to the traditional leadership. He was considered so serious a threat that he was sent as an attaché to El Salvador in the mid-1960s. When the U.S. made a deal with the Guard's traditional leadership to overthrow the nationalist Arias, the mestizos took control and brought Torrijos back to Panama. In less than a year he emerged as its unchallenged leader and strongman of the government.

Torrijos prided himself on his relationship with the common people and his championing of their needs and aspirations, especially those in the interior of the country where he had been born and reared. Many times he told me about his assignments in different areas of the country and how he came to live and work with the "little people," mestizo and black. An experience he especially talked about was keeping law and order in the black neighborhoods of Colón from his radio patrol police car and the friendships he developed with the black community who joined him and the political party he formed, the PRD (*Partido Revolucionario Democrático*). He was a populist who talked in simple, pragmatic terms—not in the jargon or dialectic of socialists or communists. He was street-smart and an avid nationalist.

He had the typical Panamanian love-hate relationship with the

United States. He told me one evening that he admired our military and financial power, but hated having the presence of that power and wealth thrust into the face of every Panamanian every day from the Canal Zone. That, he said, made him feel like a second-class citizen in his own country. He wanted a new relationship "of respect" with the U.S., based on the return of the Canal Zone to Panama. Once during a meeting with Nicolás Barletta, the minister of Planning, he talked of his desire to strengthen the economy of rural Panama with schools so that they would be as good as those in the capital. "But," he added, "the Canal is our biggest asset and that means most of our investments will have to be in Panama City and Colón, our great commercial and trading centers."

In the nearly two years I was assigned to Panama, there were many occasions on which I disagreed with Torrijos and his government, especially when the evidence revealed government officials selling favors to help the Colombian drug cartels move narcotics northward. When once or twice I had the opportunity to tell him that I thought there were serious domestic problems he should be dealing with, he just looked at me and shrugged his shoulders. I had my opinion and he had his. He listened, but did what he thought was best for Panama.

Above all, he wanted a new treaty and he understood the political environment in Washington in the aftermath of the Vietnam War. He knew the critical role that the Canal played in moving supplies to Southeast Asia and commented several times that he hadn't expected an effective dialogue until the Vietnam War ended. Nonetheless, at every inter-American meeting, Torrijos confronted us and rallied Latin American and Caribbean countries to his side with his accusations of U.S. "foot-dragging" on negotiations. Few countries had confidence in Panama's ability to run the Canal, and many questioned the viability of the U.S. ceding control and management of the Canal, but all Latin American and Caribbean nations wanted the U.S. to initiate discussions to redefine our status in the Canal Zone. Torrijos told me he believed that the U.S. needed a new relationship with Panama to protect our interests and keep the Canal functioning.

With our withdrawal from Vietnam, the importance of the Canal to U.S. vital interests had changed radically, especially after the opening to Red China and the creation of separate fleets for Atlantic and Pacific operations. Widely circulating in Panama was an estimate by a U.S. military expert that over 100,000 U.S. troops would have to be deployed to the Canal Zone to protect it from an unfriendly attack through or by Panama. That was coupled with a serious doubt that the vital installations could be kept operating in the face of persistent guerilla operations and concern that the cost to the U.S. financially and diplomatically would be enormous—an expense that the country could not easily absorb in light of the worldwide recession and inflation at home.

President Nixon determined that it was time to deal with the Canal issue and establish a new *modus operandi* for living with Panama and protecting our interests in the Canal. The administration called on Ellsworth Bunker—businessman, diplomat, and seasoned negotiator—to complete this delicate search for a new relationship with Panama and to protect the integrity of the Panama Canal.

The Assignment

My immediate boss was Ambassador Jordan. He set the policy, and I was part of his country team. I was not directly involved in the Canal negotiations and depended on the ambassador to keep me informed on the status of negotiations and specific information required by the negotiators. I had two quite different jobs. First, as economic counselor, I directed the work of a traditional economic unit in the embassy—analyzing and reporting on economic and commercial developments and trade relations and working with businessmen and investors, plus the additional task of providing the treaty negotiators relevant financial, trade, or other economic information. Second, I directed the USAID mission and its package of development programs designed to strengthen cooperation between our two countries and hopefully improve the environment in which the negotiations were taking place.

In our initial meeting, the ambassador noted that my relationship with top-level Panamanian officials would be different than other embassy officers since, as director of the USAID Mission, I would inevitably be in contact with both Torrijos and Noriega. He underlined the need for me to maintain a strictly official relationship with them. In the next two years working with the ambassador, he never had to raise that issue again. As a member of his country team, I kept him fully informed of my work in both jobs, and of my numerous contacts with General Torrijos and Colonel Noriega.

I had two different offices—one at the embassy on the Bay of Panama, around the cove from the historic old center of Panama City. The other was in a building a mile or so away on a hill overlooking the Bay of Panama—and what a view it was! I spent more time in my USAID office, but my work was almost equally divided between embassy and USAID. My driver, Mr. Nichols (I never knew his first name), was the well-educated son of a Barbadian who helped construct the Canal and was part of the second generation Caribbean community that occupied technical jobs on the Canal to which indigenous population aspired but often lacked the English to qualify. From the many hours we spent together driving between the two offices, I learned how concerned the black community was about any change in the status of the Canal Zone.

My first few weeks were mainly spent at the embassy getting up to speed on the reporting functions of the economic unit, while George Rublee ably ran USAID. Then, I concentrated on the AID program, which focused on infrastructure, education, and public health projects in and around Panama City. Agriculture and rural development was not the top priority as it was in Bolivia or ROCAP. In those initial briefings, I was impressed by the superiority of the economic data at the USAID Mission over that of the embassy. The USAID economic section was staffed with professional economists, who worked closely with the Panamanian Planning Ministry, the Central Bank, and the Ministry of Finance; they accumulated in-depth data on the various sectors of the economy, GNP, GDP, government revenues, and public debt. The embassy economic unit was staffed by one U.S. foreign service officer and one local economist, and most of its data and reports were related to trade and U.S. investments in Panama, with only spotty information on the Panamanian economy or the structure of the public sector finances. I found that the embassy economic office had occasionally drawn on the USAID economic section for help in providing data for reports, but the two units did not meet regularly or share their information systematically. So, I brought these two units together and developed a systematic reporting and analytical program.

Central to my doing both jobs was understanding the structure and dynamics of the Panamanian economy. Fortunately, I found my guide in the then minister of Planning, Nicolás "Nicky" Barletta Vallarino. With a Ph.D. in development economics from the University of North Carolina, he knew the subject matter, understood the economy and sociopolitical environment, and saw the potential of his country. He was a key member of Torrijos' team and had convinced him that Panama's future was to convert it into a Latin American financial center that complemented the commercial and trade flow through the Canal. In our first meeting, Nicky showed me the detailed ministry studies that demonstrated the critical importance of the Canal to his country's development, with its limited domestic market, poor quality of the soils, and absence of mineral/hydrocarbon prospects. He then laid out his plan to build an international banking and investment center and a series of free ports to attract light manufacturing that served the transportation and financial sectors. He saw the package creating good-paying private sector jobs in and around Panama City and Colón. Nicky and I met every two weeks for a working session and lunch until his appointment in 1977 as vice president of the World Bank for Latin American operations.

As part of the long term development strategy, Nicky was planning integrated socioeconomic programs in the provinces to increase agricultural and livestock production, expand local employment opportunities, and delay large-scale migration of rural poor to the already bursting slums in Panama City and around the Canal Zone; in those projects, he placed great importance on education and programs to raise and diversify skill levels. His plans also included alleviating the serious energy problem facing his country by preparing a master plan for traditional and non-traditional sources that could attract public and private sector funding; Panama had few sites for hydro-electric facilities and no evidence of oil or gas resources.

In our discussions, Nicky set limits on the relationship with USAID. He told me that, while his government wanted to work closely with USAID, it also wanted to establish its independence in the pursuit of its own objectives and would look to the international banks, the IDB, and the World Bank, as its primary source of development funding. He suggested that the most helpful role for USAID would be to work with Panama in developing sector programs and projects, primarily in the soft sectors, like education and rural development, which the IDB and World Bank at that time were reluctant to consider.

Fortunately, the USAID program and economic staff shared many of Nicky's perceptions and that made the USAID component of my job much easier. When I completed my in-depth review of the USAID program, it became clear that my predecessor Alex Firfer had already honed the USAID program to reflect the role that Nicky had proposed.

The mission was relatively small, with about thirty U.S. advisers and support staff. Its operating divisions included rural development, education, population, and urban development. My first in-depth briefing was on rural development. The division was headed by a very able agricultural economist, Eric Shearer, who like Don Fiester in ROCAP, thought outside the box. For nearly thirty years, the U.S. had worked with Panama on agricultural development through the research station and extension service. In recent years, its priorities shifted to financing farm-to-market roads and supporting farm credit programs. Eric was now refocusing on sector planning for specific geographic areas in much the same terms as Nicky had discussed with me.

Eric described its limited agricultural potentials, with leached soils that could not sustain large field crops outside of bananas. He reviewed the agriculture potential of each zone of the country. In much of the central zone, small subsistence agriculture predominated, and the Azuero peninsula and Chiriquí prospects for profitable livestock operations were promising. United Fruit had installations in Chiriquí for both cattle and banana production. In Bocas del Toro province, banana was the primary crop, almost all exported by United Fruit or Dole. The Darién area southeast of the Canal Zone was an inhospitable area where several thousand indigenous people lived in small tribal communities and subsisted on traditional corn, manioc, and bean crops.

Eric advised me that efforts to introduce new crops had not been successful, citing the experience of U.S. billionaire Daniel Ludwig, who had lost millions trying to build a large-scale orange juice industry on the lower ridges of the mountains of Chiriquí. The soil was inadequate to support the thousands of orange trees needed for a profitable operation. Nasty labor disputes with political overtones, coupled with unfavorable marketing projections, caused Ludwig to pull out. The government was organizing cooperatives to carry on the experiment and was seeking funds for the project. Nicky did not encourage USAID support for those cooperatives.

Eric proposed that we consider a project in livestock production, especially in the lesser-developed provinces of Coclé, Azuero, and Herrera. He saw the possibility of a profitable integrated high quality meat industry that would not only satisfy Panama's demand but also offered potential for export. He pointed out that there was a shortage of protein in the diet of the average Panamanian living in the interior of the country and that the internal market system did not reach many outlying communities.

The nutrition theme was continued when I started my briefings with Dr. Felix Hurtado, the chief of the population section, the successor to the Public Health *servicio*. That *servicio* had been one of the largest USAID activities for two decades; it nurtured the creation of the health ministry and its countrywide programs of maternal and childcare, disease control, and rural health services. It was phased out in the early 1960s and both governments determined that the new focus for assistance in public health should be population planning. Dr. Hurtado felt that, while the budget for the ministry was relatively high and included good training programs, health services in Panama, especially in the interior, had not yet reached acceptable international standards.

The shift to population planning was designed to provide public health services to control communicable diseases and prevent an unmanageable population explosion Panama is a secular country, with a highly diverse population. While the majority was Roman Catholic, the influence of the Church was limited and the government felt little pressure when it introduced a national family planning program. With the Canal Zone next door and a large contingent of U.S. military stationed there, Panama had a large-scale sex business and sexually transmitted disease rates were high. The population program had been operating for several years, and both the U.S. and Panama considered it a success and had agreed to phase out U.S. aid over the next couple of years.

My discussions with Dr. Hurtado went far beyond the population program. He knew Panama well and described the great variations in medical and social conditions across the country. He described the poor economic conditions in much of the interior, especially in the enclaves of indigenous people in Coclé and Herrera provinces. He urged me to look at integrated development programs for those enclaves rather than sectoral programs in education, agriculture, and health.

Next I met with Dr. Richard Greene, the education adviser. He headed a small staff: a curriculum specialist, a teacher trainer, and a textbook adviser. Their offices were in the ministry across the hall from the minister. Education had been one of the first *servicios* created during World War II and initially concentrated on vocational training and literacy to satisfy the needs of the U.S. military bases in Panama and the Canal Zone. After World War II, the *servicio* shifted its emphasis to curriculum development in elementary education and teacher training, and a significant number of Panamanian teachers received specialized training. After the *servicio* was phased out in the early 1960s, the program focus remained unchanged. A new program proposal for USAID assistance to strengthen the institutional structure of the ministry ran into political opposition of the Teachers' Union, led by a sister of General Torrijos and was scrapped. The political environment for the program was uneasy, and periodically the union staged demonstrations against the USAID education program and advocated the exclusion of U.S. advisors and assistance until the United States "returned the Canal to Panama."

Dr. Greene reported that, in spite of the political environment in the ministry, most of the ministry staff and the teachers in the primary and secondary schools supported the current program. He showed me the schedule of teacher training courses that the ministry had approved for the next year and the U.S. institutions that would provide the training. He also identified several fellowships for Panamanian teachers who were being trained to replace current USAID advisers and anticipated that in the near future the program could be carried out without USAID support.

The last item raised by Dr. Greene was the textbook program, the vestige of the one started nearly twenty years earlier as a regional Central American program. In the other five Central American countries, national differences had stymied the effort, but in Panama it had some success and led to the ministry's textbook writing program that USAID continued to support.

My introduction to the USAID program was completed by meetings with Candeloro "Bud" Donato, chief of the Urban Development Division. Bud was an engineer and his staff consisted of four engineers and a housing adviser. This division had been created to help deal with the dreadful slums in the urban areas adjoining the Canal Zone. Along the miles-long barbed wire fence that separated the Canal Zone from the cities of Panama and Colón, the Canal Zone side was U.S. suburbia, while on the adjoining Colón and Panama City side were sprawling eyesores—a contrast of great political significance. Bud's division was charged with advising and helping the Panamanian Ministry of Public Works and Housing to design and carry out projects to alleviate this situation.

In the 1880s, Panama City and Colón, with the construction of the Canal, mushroomed from small tropical towns into rundown urban conglomerations to accommodate the labor needed to build the Canal. De Lesseps built small houses for his laborers at the edges of the cities with few comforts that were meant to last only during the time of construction. Almost a century later, they were still there—eyesores and centers of crime in the strategic area abutting the Canal Zone. In addition, on the Panama City side of the fence, non-descript concrete multifamily units were built to house workers needed for blue-collar labor at the Canal, and they too had become eyesores and crime-ridden. A more opulent middle class city had been taking shape, away from the Canal Zone and the older neighborhoods, and both governments believed those focal points of poverty and crime needed to be replaced. The urban development division was the U.S. response.

Bud spelled out a unique AID program that included advice on urban planning and the provision of basic services such as sewers, utilities, streets, and lot development. In addition, it was drawing on AID housing guarantees to build new low-cost housing to help slum dwellers become homeowners. Bud described a Panama City project, with the enthusiastic support of the Ministries of Planning and Public Works, to turn the largest and most dangerous slum of the city called San Miguelito into a settled urban community. They planned to start with staking out and paving streets and laying the water and sewer systems, culminating in the conversion of squatter occupancy into ownership of adequate and sanitary housing.

Working closely with Bud was John Kilgore, AID's regional consultant on Housing Guarantees. John had moved from ROCAP when plans for the Central American regional monetary authority were placed on hold. John administered the AID housing guarantee program for Latin America that provided AID loan guarantees for eligible house projects. He found that, based in Panama where scores of international banks had headquartered their Latin American operations, he could negotiate financing for housing projects in various countries. One of John's current projects involved working with the Panamanian Central Bank and Nicky Barletta to create a tertiary facility for discounting housing loans not only from Panama but eventually the five Central American countries.

By the end of the first month, I was ready for work.

General Omar Torrijos Herrera

I first met General Omar Torrijos Herrera near the end of my first month in Panama. The ministers of Planning and Public Works invited me to the inauguration of a housing development just a few kilometers northwest of the Canal Zone. Tenants from one of the De Lesseps eyesore districts had formed a housing cooperative with the assistance of the U.S. Cooperative Housing Association. USAID technicians had helped the community of more than a hundred Panamanian families find an architect to design a modular house on a substantial lot. The modular house had a bathroom, a basic kitchen, one or two rooms and space to add additional rooms as the homeowner could afford them. The government of Panama provided the new owners with water and sewerage. USAID had also facilitated financing the development through a Housing Guarantee. This was a joint Panama-U.S grassroots project. The inaugural ceremony was at the entrance to the new community. It was a bright, sun-filled Saturday in early January 1976, and anyone who knows

Panama knows that the first four months of the year it is blessed with one of the best climates on our planet. The environment was friendly and informal, festooned with U.S. and Panamanian flags. I arrived in Nicky Barletta's car, but arranged for Mr. Nichols to bring Bud Donato, John Kilgore, and a representative of the U.S. cooperative movement.

Nicky and I were invited to an area at the front of the community and waited for General Torrijos to arrive by helicopter. He was accompanied by his relative and close friend, *Guardia* Colonel Roberto Díaz Herrera, and two female *Guardia* officers. He was very informal and joked with the Panamanian homeowners, giving a hug to men and women alike. A few minutes later, he was led over to the area where Nicky and I were waiting. He welcomed me to Panama and then made a short speech in colloquial language that said very little about the U.S.-Panama cooperation that had made the project happen and then cut the ribbon. He invited me to join him as he walked around the community. He greeted family after family like long-lost relatives. Several times, one of family members mentioned a problem that they were facing. For some, he took money from the box that one of his aides carried, and other times, he would ask the aide to prepare a note for some government official or businessman asking him to solve the problem. Never once did he introduce me to one of "his" people, but he kept me by his side.

When we finished, he spotted a pond nearby and jumped in fully clothed. And many of the official party jumped in after him. They splashed around for a few minutes. Then Torrijos climbed out, went over to a small room accompanied by one of the female Guard officers. I simply watched the spectacle. I had not been prepared for the splash but merely smiled and enjoyed it. When he had dried off and put on a fresh uniform, he emerged from the room totally relaxed and came over to me and said, "I think we will get along. You did not jump into the pond to please me. You think for yourself."

At that point, Nicky came over to announce that he had another appointment and that I should stay with the general. He told me that the general had a free seat on the helicopter and invited me to join him on the way back. I don't know why I declined, but I did, just as I had in Bolivia when President Barrientos offered Ele and me the ride home from the school dedication. Torrijos smiled and walked away with his two female Guard officers. I rode home with Mr. Nichols and my USAID colleagues when the festivities ended.

A few days later, I was invited to a strategy meeting at the general's residence at Farallón on the Rio Hato Airbase, about 100 kilometers northeast of Panama City; Rio Hato had formerly been a U.S. air force base. Torrijos called this "my home away from home, my base of operations." It was the first of about six sessions that I spent there at his invitation over the next eighteen months. I went up with Nicky Barletta that day.

The topic was USAID support for the new Panamanian development plan. We arrived in time for a breakfast of cold fried eggs, bacon, melon, and coffee. Torrijos and two or three of his associates, including Colonel Roberto Díaz Herrera, sat around the table talking. The general told me that he valued U.S. aid, but wanted to wean Panama from dependence on the United States. He made it abundantly clear that he admired and respected Nicky Barletta and encouraged me to work closely with him. He had his usual female Guard associates around and periodically would go upstairs with one of them for up to half an hour, leaving Nicky, Colonel Díaz Herrera, the others, and me to talk.

Just before Nicky and I left about noon, Torrijos said that he wanted me to meet the minister of Agriculture, Colonel Rubén Darío Paredes, as soon as possible. I don't remember his exact words, but Torrijos told me that Paredes was more than a brother National Guard officer, but one of those whom he trusted and who would probably succeed him as chief of the Guard if anything were to happen to him. Even Nicky seemed surprised by the frankness.

My next meeting with the general was in early March 1976 when he invited me to fly with him to Santiago, Herrera Province. Colonel Rubén Darío Paredes was the only other passenger on the plane. Paredes was grappling with his assignment as minister of Agriculture. He was a disciplined officer who was trying to get on top of a very difficult assignment. We talked about the agricultural problems of the country. Paredes clearly was more comfortable talking about livestock than field crops. When we reached Santiago, we went to the family home where I met Torrijos' sisters. I well remember their strong opinions on Panamanian and world politics. One of his sisters was the leader of the Teachers' Union and had much more of a Marxist tinge to her views than I had observed in my discussions with the general. Neither the general nor Colonel Paredes said much during dinner; the ladies dominated the conversation. After dinner, Torrijos flew to another home he had in Coclé Province while Paredes and I flew back to Panama City.

In early May, Torrijos invited me to fly with him to a spot in the high Cordillera of northwest Panama, close to the continental divide, about half way between Chiriquí on the Pacific and Bocas del Toro on the Atlantic. I was told that, according to some geological surveys, the site contained the largest undeveloped copper deposits between Peru and Arizona. We were accompanied by one of his advisers who was seeking financing to develop the site. He told me that he had brought my predecessor there and had shared with him his excitement at the prospects of copper mining to diversify Panama's economy. The adviser told me that investors were cool to the project because of the isolation of the site and the lack of infrastructure, including roads, port, and other facilities to move the ore to market. In my mind's eye, I could see the importance of this potential to the economy if it was a high quality cooper deposit, but I saw a minimum investment of several billion dollars just to set the infrastructure in place. The question put to me was whether USAID would consider doing the feasibility study for the development of the site and provide seed capital for constructing the port and road network. I said that I would need much more information about the geological studies and the terrain before I could give a response. We had a quiet flight back to Panama and the proposal was never raised with me again.

Interacting with General Torrijos was a unique experience. I remember his special gift of mingling with his compatriots. I also remember that ever-present cash box and the steady flow of cash to those who asked for his help. I will never forget those extremely attractive National Guard women who responded to his every need—and how often he appeared to need their services. Above all, I remember the Saturday morning breakfasts at Farrallón and can occasionally sense the taste of those cold fried eggs and bacon. I remember the shrewd man who made tough decisions, including that of agreeing to a new Canal treaty that met his central objective of regaining control over the Canal Zone but did not include a platter of economic goodies from the U.S. He told me one morning in Farrallón that he believed Panama could develop its own economic future if it controlled the Canal, and that was his bottom line.

I never believed that Torrijos improvised. I always felt that he knew exactly what he was doing and why. He was a master at tweaking Uncle Sam's whiskers and playing the cards that made us stop and listen. He also had a special feel for timing. He went to visit Fidel Castro in Cuba at a time when Washington was unhappy with Castro's adventures in South America and Africa. I don't think he ever was pro-Castro, but Castro was convenient for his purposes. He convened the 150th Commemoration of the 1826 Latin American Congress to remind the U.S. that Panama had the united support of Latin America in negotiating the Canal Treaty, including those countries with constitutionally elected governments and those with the military dictatorships. He played with the Third World Movement to show his independence of the United States. He was just street smart. He should never have been underestimated.

Colonel Manuel Antonio Noriega

In all my conversations with Torrijos, one name he never mentioned was Colonel Manuel Antonio Noriega. He never included Noriega on a trip I took with him. He must have known that I knew about Noriega, who was my neighbor across the street. He must have known that I had been briefed about his role as G-2 and his reputation as the bagman for Torrijos. Certainly he knew that I had been told of Noriega's role in warning him of a coup attempt (reportedly with U.S. concurrence) to replace him as Commander of the *Guardia* when he was away on a trip to Mexico. I came to know Colonel Noriega through my neighbor, the widow of the owner of the local racetrack. She had told us that Noriega was her husband's protégé. It was the widow who brought us together.

Ele and I had been in Panama only a few weeks when our Tennessee lady neighbor invited us for cocktails. We thought that very friendly and had a delightful initial discussion with her about her meeting her husband, her life in Panama, and her husband's death.

About half an hour after we arrived, another guest dropped in. It was Colonel Noriega himself. After a warm *abrazo* with our hostess, he said to Ele and me, in Spanish (I never spoke English with him) that he thought it was an appropriate time and place for us to get to know each other.

After a brief conversation together with the ladies, he asked if he could have a private word with me. We took our drinks into a small room that appeared to be the family office. The colonel wasted little time in telling me that he wanted me to meet some of his associates who were interested in urban development. He thought that they could be useful partners with USAID in developing some of the urbanization plans for Panama City, especially the water and sewer installations for the San Miguelito area. He implied that an arrangement could be worked out that would be beneficial for all parties and ensure expeditious approval of USAID plans and timely execution under budget.

I thanked him for his interest, but reminded him that the U.S. government had established bidding procedures that we were required by law to follow. If his associates wished to submit bids at the appropriate time, the proper authorities would consider them like any other bid. He then presented several other variations on the same theme, but I stuck to my text. Finally, he just looked at me and said goodnight. As soon as I got home, I took a shower. I reported the conversation to Ambassador Jordan the next morning—and warned my USAID colleagues.

Over the next eighteen months, we were invited three more times to our neighbor's home for cocktails. Three more times, Colonel Noriega arrived unannounced and proposed various schemes about ways to expedite the implementation of USAID urban and housing projects. Three more times, I stuck to the U.S. government regulations. Three times more, I went home to take a shower, reported to the ambassador and warned my USAID colleagues.

One of the cocktail invitations came a few days after Torrijos returned from his official visit to Cuba and Fidel. Noriega had been a member of the delegation. That evening, he told Ele and me that Fidel had not impressed Torrijos and that Torrijos had found the conditions in Cuba to be very difficult for the Cuban people. He spent half an hour making the point that Torrijos and Fidel did not get along well together. When I recounted the experience to the ambassador, he told me that Torrijos had already talked with him and given him much the same message. It was clearly Torrijos' making sure through every available channel the U.S. got his message. Torrijos never lost sight of his goal: the new Canal treaty.

Doing the Job

My assignment as economic counselor was made infinitely easier in early 1976 when Dan Daniels was appointed as the embassy economic officer and Carl Gleason arrived as the senior USAID economist. The two were a natural fit and made it possible for me to coordinate the activities of the two entities and provide the in-depth analyses that Ambassador Bunker and his team needed for the Canal negotiations. Carl was a professional economist with background and experience in national accounts and development economics. Dan was a trained economic reporter, with a solid economic and political background. They complemented each other and, even better, they respected and liked each other.

The economy of Panama was in a mess. Torrijos had undertaken expensive rural development and education projects for which he borrowed money. His initial policies had discouraged investment and created distrust with both the local business community and international investors. Public sector income barely covered current expenses and sources of credit were rapidly drying up.

Carl and Dan provided detailed analyses of the financial position of the Panamanian public sector that laid out how serious the financial pinch was. Panama was a dollar economy, with its balboa (Panama's currency) at par with the dollar. The dollar circulated freely in Panama and was in greater supply than the balboa. The statistics showed that the government was running out of money and the tie-in to the dollar made it practically impossible to turn on the printing presses. Moreover, since the Canal operated on the dollar standard, the government's ability to act was further limited. The analyses made it clear that Panama needed an agreement to shore up its internal economy and avoid defaults on its foreign loan obligations. Ambassador Bunker told me later in Washington that this information gave the U.S. negotiators an extra tool in the bargaining process.

Panama, like most countries, developed and developing, had its fair share of graft. The cash box that Torrijos carried around was patent evidence of unusual government payouts, and I have no doubt that drug money and other pay-offs earned favors with government insiders. There are no instant or permanent cures, as history demonstrates repeatedly in every country around the world. But bringing corruption under control probably starts with discipline in public finance and establishing rules and regulations to govern both the expenditure of funds and the conduct of public servants. Requiring governments to deal with their fiscal realities is a critical step in bringing integrity to the public sector. I wrestled with what impact the USAID program could have on that problem; unfortunately it was not substantial enough to put pressure on the government to undertake reforms.

Most of my time was dedicated to planning and implementing the USAID program. That job was made infinitely more complicated after Deputy Director George Rublee completed his tour and was replaced by a first-term appointee with no previous AID experience—a political appointee and, according to Herman Kleine, sent to Panama to learn from my associates and me. We gave him comprehensive briefings by each of the divisions and assigned him to field trips to observe projects in operation. I included him in my bi-weekly meetings with the Planning minister, until Nicky objected to my deputy's loose talk with third parties after the meetings. All of us in the USAID Mission made every effort to bring him up to operating standards, and I regret that we were unable to meet the challenge, as his performance over the next eighteen months demonstrated.

In 1976, the Planning Ministry proposed that we concentrate our resources on regional sector programs. Nicky laid out a comprehensive proposal for a multi-sectoral program in one of Panama's least developed areas, the Azuero Peninsula. His plan was to test and refine the program in Azuero and later adapt it to other underdeveloped provinces like Veraguas and Coclé with future funding by the IDB and the World Bank.

While USAID was enthusiastic about Nicky's approach, the first question we discussed was whether Azuero was the right choice. Some preferred Veraguas Province, with its enclaves of semi-autonomous indigenous people who were undoubtedly the poorest and most disadvantaged in the Republic. Others suggested that Herrera, the home province of Torrijos, would generate better political support. After careful analyses and on-the-ground visits, we agreed on Nicky's choice.

A joint team drafted the loan paper for AID funding. In over twenty years of experience, this document was the first that was truly a joint operation. Bernie Chapnick, Carl Gleason, Eric Shearer, and Dr. Hurtado worked closely with Nicky's team in the analysis and drafting process and negotiated almost line by line to ensure that the language reflected our mutual understanding. Both sides understood the problems to be addressed, and the time frame for achieving short and long-term objectives. Both parties signed off on the objectives, the plan of operations, the short and long term course of action, the guideposts that we would use to appraise progress or problems, the contributions of each, the repayment schedule by Panama, and all the other components of a loan application—and we agreed on the obstacles to be overcome.

In the drafting process, Nicky and I, with all our key collaborators, spent several days in Azuero, talking to local officials, large and small livestock producers, representatives of the major utility suppliers, businessmen, and bankers. We explored with them the demands on their facilities and their readiness to cooperate. We talked to ministers about what their ministries would be expected to contribute and how much those inputs would cost. With Torrijos' full backing, Nicky talked to legislators about the action that might be required of them to authorize special powers for the authorities in charge of the regional development process. Drafting this proposal was not as much a negotiation as a coming together on priorities and action. One sour note occurred when we tried to involve my deputy in the work. Because he misunderstood what we were doing and tried to push his weight around, we had to bench him.

In my covering letter of transmittal, with a written endorsement by the ambassador, I pointed out the proposal had been jointly drafted and emphasized the urgency for Washington approval— both from the unique opportunity it provided USAID to work on a regional multi-sectoral development project and as a political statement of U.S. goodwill in the Canal negotiations.

In Washington, however, it ran into the new bureaucratic requirement that delayed consideration of field requests. A group of businessmen, some of whom had been AID technicians, had set up consulting firms and lobbied successfully in Congress and the Executive Branch to require "expert" review of loan requests before AID approval. These were the "Beltway Bandits," who charged for not only for their expertise but their overhead. So, the "experts" had to review the document in Washington and in the field before the AID loan committee could consider it. The Latin American Bureau advised that it would take several months and half a million dollars to review the proposal in-depth before the loan committee could initiate its review.

I don't recall how much time was consumed by this "expert review" process. I only remember that the "experts" had little competence to assess the proposal and that it took so long that, when finally approved by AID, many of the critical conditions for a successful undertaking were no longer in place—starting with the appointment of Nicky Barletta to be a vice president of the World Bank, a position that required far more expertise than the Beltway Bandits possessed. The delays defused the interest and excitement on both sides. I was transferred before the project got underway. A year later, in Washington, Nicky and I lamented about what might have happened.

Nicky and I also worked on a second regional development project that Washington ultimately did not approve. It was designed to deal with two problems at the same time: the deterioration of the watershed for the Canal, and the poverty of the people in Coclé Province adjoining the Canal Zone. Slash-and-burn subsistence farming and cutting trees for firewood posed a substantial threat to the tropical forests on the northwestern side of the Canal. The amounts of water needed for the operation of the locks of the Canal, as well as the navigation through Lake Gatún, were enormous. Any substantial reduction could cripple Canal operations.

So, we designed a project to protect the watershed by getting the subsistence farmers who inhabited the area directly involved in protecting it and at the same time increasing their income and raising their living standards. With Eric Shearer's guidance, we explored tree crops that might bring in substantial income to the farmers and stabilize their living habits. The proposal called for the government of Panama, with technical support from USAID and the Turrialba research center in San José, Costa Rica, to introduce Coclé farmers to income-producing tree crops, help them settle in communities where schools and health facilities would be available, and assist them to conserve and enrich the soil and tend the crops in place of their traditional "slash and burn" practices, thus protecting the tropical forest and water supply for the Canal. In addition, the Panamanian government would provide training for the farmers in forest protection and pay them a small monthly wage to serve as fire wardens and fire fighters.

Nicky departed before the project was fully defined, but his successor, Gustavo Gonzalez, was equally committed. Ambassador Jordan and the governor of the Canal Zone were especially pleased because of their concern about the accelerating denuding of the watershed. In light of the administrative delays to the Azuero proposal, the ambassador and I decided to send the proposal to Washington with less comprehensive detail than the Azuero document since we expected the Beltway Bandits to come down, at which time their questions could be answered and the details completed. AID Washington turned down the proposal, but I understand that the government of Panama later implemented a similar plan on its own.

Working with Panamanian Officials

In administering the USAID program, I developed close working relationships with three ministers: Agriculture, Rubén Darío Paredes; Education, Arístides Royo; and Public Works and Housing, Tomás Altamarino Duque.

Paredes invited me to accompany him on several field trips. He didn't have much specialized knowledge about agriculture, but his questions indicated that he was trying to learn as much as he could about the functions and services of his ministry. Like Torrijos, he was people-oriented and seemed to be genuinely touched by the plight of the small subsistence farmers whom we met. He also was a good judge of people and only seemed to trust those he felt were objectively answering his questions. He always dressed in military fatigues on our trips and insisted on maintaining proper decorum in dealing with his subordinates and co-workers.

Many of our trips were for a day, sometimes by car and occasionally by plane. The USAID Rural Development Chief Eric Shearer usually accompanied us. Eric often knew more about the soils and conditions at each site than the ministry's field representatives. Eric was discreet and never contradicted a field official in front of the minister. He would find an appropriate way to add a dimension to the presentation so that the field official did not lose face and could say, "Thank you. I had forgotten to mention that."

One of our most fascinating trips was to the Darién, most of the time over unpaved roads. We overnighted in the indigenous zone known as Emberá. We slept in hammocks that night with mosquito netting and ate a supper of rice and beans with the local farmers and community leaders. I got a personal view of the primitive level of life on which those people survived and got a detailed briefing on the poor quality of soils that meant large-scale efforts could only produce marginal improvements in production. Even the potential for tree crops and cattle raising seemed minimal.

On that trip, I asked Paredes why the government of Panama had resisted efforts to build the Pan American Highway down to the Colombian border. He said very simply, "If we complete the road—and I think that it is now technically possible—Panama will be swamped with poor Colombian farmers who live on the other side of the border. It will also give Colombian drug traffickers an overland route to move their stuff northward. It is better to keep the road unbuilt until both Colombia and Panama are better able to control the border." I never raised the question again.

On the way back, we visited the water project and dam that was being constructed with Yugoslavian money. Eric had told me that the feasibility study did not justify either U.S. or IDB support for the construction, and that the water resources were insufficient to sustain the expanded sugar cane production planned for the region. As the minister and I went over the site and reviewed the project, we discussed the issues that had undermined U.S. and IDB interest in making a loan.

Six months after our visit, President Tito and General Torrijos formally dedicated the project and opened the sluices of the dam.

I was not present but I watched the ceremonies on TV. After the speeches and the formal pushing of the buttons to open the sluices, General Torrijos, true to form, jumped into the water fully dressed. I will never forget the amazement on President Tito's face! I was told that Tito was formal and proper in his relationships, and was fully unprepared for Torrijos being Torrijos.

A few weeks later, the minister of Health joined Colonel Paredes and me in a visit to an indigenous village in the mountains of Veraguas to introduce tilapia to people who had a major protein deficiency. The Ministries of Health and Agriculture had joined forces to help indigenous communities deal with perennial problems of malnutrition, with coordinated programs for rural health posts and improved crops. The ministries requested USAID assistance and USAID arranged to introduce tilapia from the Philippines as a way of adding protein to the diet. USAID financed the acquisition and delivery of the fish, and worked with Panamanian agricultural agents to stock the lakes and ponds of the central Cordillera, as well as teach the villagers how to protect the food supply and how to fish properly. Now the task was to introduce the people to eating fish, as fish had never been part of their diet. A fish fry with corn, yucca, and beans was held, and we joined the villagers in the feast. Fish became part of their diet.

On another trip, Paredes invited me to join him on a visit to Bocas del Toro to observe the new technology that the United Fruit Company had introduced. We spent the day at the plantation headquarters being briefed on the new methods of banana storage and transport and on the preparation of a new banana by-product, banana chips. The company hoped that these banana chips would find ready acceptance in the U.S. and European markets and compete with the potato chip. They tasted good, but have never quite captured the marketplace.

Paredes also took me to Boquete in the mountains of Chiriquí, truly a Swiss-like oasis several thousand feet above the cattle and banana lands that made Chiriquí the most productive agricultural area of the country. We visited horse farms, temperate climate orchards whose production, though small, was being exported, and a coffee plantation that was being modernized to supply high quality mountain beans for the world market. We talked to agricultural businessmen about contacting the Executive Service Corps for advisers on improving their production and accounting practices. Later we flew down to David, the provincial capital, where we reviewed the efforts of the cooperatives trying to revive the orange groves that Mr. Ludwick had given up on.

The professional relationship developed into a personal friendship. The Paredes invited Ele and me a couple of times to small family dinners with their two young sons. They lived in a comfortable middle class house, and their pride and joy were their sons. They told us of their ambitions for their education as professionals who would contribute to the development of Panama. Both boys were learning English and Ele engaged them, to the delight of their parents, in a discussion of their schoolwork. I remember that evening very vividly because of the events that led to the end of Rubén Darío Paredes' political life.

After General Torrijos' death in a plane crash in 1981, Colonel Paredes became General Paredes, Commander of the National Guard, just as Torrijos had planned. In 1983, in order to run for the presidency to succeed then President Arístides Royo, he resigned as commander and was succeeded by Antonio Manuel Noriega. Immediately upon assuming command, Noriega called Paredes to tell him to abort his candidacy because his two teenage sons had become involved in drug trafficking. It had been Noriega himself who had lured them into the clutches of the Medellín drug cartel and set the trap for eliminating Paredes as his rival for running the country. Paredes withdrew from the presidential race and Noriega became the kingmaker. The older son went to Colombia to try to clear his name and was killed. Paredes brought his younger son to the U.S. and had him turn himself in to the Drug Enforcement Agency. He served a prison sentence and resettled in Florida where he and his family are building the professional life his parents had hoped for him. In the late 1980s and early 90s, when I was executive secretary of the Inter-American Drug Commission, I saw the Paredes family occasionally on trips to Panama. They shared with me their pain about their sons and their commitment to post-Noriega Panama.

The second minister with whom I developed a special relationship was Minister of Education Dr. Arístides "Risti" Royo, whom

Torrijos chose to be the president of Panama in 1978, the year after we were reassigned.

I first met him only weeks after my arrival in Panama. Dr. Greene set up a meeting in the minister's office to review the plans for teacher training seminars and curriculum planning. He impressed me with his understanding of the work to be carried out and his choice of the Panamanian ministry counterparts with whom USAID was to work. The minister made it very clear that he was in charge and that he would tell USAID what was to be done, when, and how. The meeting started out very formally but became more cordial as it evolved. We ended on a warm personal note and agreed to meet as often as was necessary to keep the program moving forward. While we did not develop a personal family relationship with Royo, he was my guest for luncheon meetings with senators and congressmen who came on fact-finding missions as the Canal treaty negotiations moved forward.

Shortly after that first meeting, Nicky Barletta had Minister Royo and me together at a planning session in his office. The environment was less formal. We had no trouble reaching agreement on the proposal presented by Nicky. I found during the months that we worked together, we could find agreement more quickly outside of the Ministry of Education where we often had bristling sessions under the eye of the Marxist-leaning Teachers Union. The more I worked with him, the more I came to appreciate his ability to maneuver through situations and get the solutions that he wanted. He was very pragmatic, not ideologically oriented. We took no field trips together. We did not appear jointly at school dedications or seminar openings as had been usual in other countries. The political climate required USAID to be low key—except when the minister needed to portray USAID as the villain in some problem generated in the internal politics of the ministry.

There was one hot, humid day in 1977 when he called me urgently to his office. Dr. Greene did not know why. The traffic was horrendous as Mr. Nichols drove down to the Old City of Panama where the ministry was headquartered. The ministry building was surrounded by a picket line of teachers and reporters through whom I had to fight to get to the minister's office. In view of the crowd, he kept me waiting fully ten minutes—and I was getting very uneasy. When I was finally ushered into his office, I was given a lecture about how USAID had caused the problem that prompted the staff to walk off their jobs. Newspaper cameramen came in to take pictures of the minister in control, and I did not lose my cool nor look away from the minister. He glowered and I departed. I fought my way out of the building and drove to the embassy to report to the ambassador. To this day, I don't know what USAID did to merit the tongue-lashing, even after looking at the photos and reading the accounts in the pro-government newspapers the following day.

The third was Tomás Altamarino Duque, the minister of Public Works and Housing. He was a seasoned business executive with a business-like approach to getting things done, and negotiating with him was straightforward. He meticulously defended the interests of his government, but he also understood and respected U.S. government rules and regulations. He never raised convoluted or extraneous matters to confuse or drag out a problem. Out of this positive working relationship, we became friends, and Ele and I enjoyed informal evenings in his home in the family recreation room.

USAID shared with the minister a common interest in transforming the slum areas of the city and promoting private home ownership. He listened to suggestions from Bud Donato and John Kilgore about the engineering and financial dimensions of the urban renewal projects, including the urbanization of the San Miguelito slum, and for resettling residents being displaced by his plan to raze hundred-year old deteriorating wooden structures built by De Lesseps on prime land near the center of the city. I suspect that USAID support helped the minister deflect pressure from politicians who wanted to make special real estate deals.

When the plan to tear down and redevelop the De Lesseps structures was finally approved, the pressures increased. Yes, I did receive an invitation from the lady next door for a cocktail—and yes, Colonel Noriega had a scheme to discuss. No, I did not succumb to his proposition, which, of course, I had expected. Yes, I reported the Noriega incursion to the ambassador.

When the project was approved following U.S. government bidding procedures, I participated in the ceremony to inaugurate the redevelopment program, and the minister presented me with an iron grill from one of the houses. That grill became part of Ele's handicraft collection that we donated to the Museo de las Américas in Denver, Colorado.

Ele, The Indispensable

No other assignment better demonstrated the pivotal role Ele played in my doing my job. She was occupied every day with planning or carrying out some official function, many of which were tied to building support for the new Canal treaty. In no previous post was she required to entertain so often and for so many. She had very little time for personal interests and no other post taxed her health as did the tropics of Panama.

Ambassador Jordan tasked us with building ties with key ministry officials to improve or consolidate their willingness to cooperate with the U.S. in redefining our role in Panama. As I had found out in my contacts throughout the Panamanian government, there was a substantial reservoir of goodwill but almost as much distrust. Ele and I opened our home to as many senior and middle government officials and their families as we could.

In 1976 and 1977, during the pleasant, lower humidity months from January to May, Ele planned late afternoon picnics in our backyard every couple of weeks for career ministry officials and their wives; we averaged thirty to forty invitees and ten USAID and embassy colleagues. Ele set up a serving table in the garden with hot dogs, hamburgers, chips, salads, fruits and other goodies, with smaller tables for four to six around the garden for people to sit as they ate. We served scotch and beer, as well as soft drinks. Outdoor entertainment at our house had to end by about seven o'clock, because the fruit bats came out in force after dark and constantly zoomed around us. Their radar was impeccable and they never hit us, but we were always concerned by their presence.

Ele had to plan our social life in a house that was not meant for entertaining. It was elegantly designed, but had no dining room. It was intended for a family, not as an official establishment. As I said earlier, the only bathrooms were in the family quarters and the architect had not provided for many non-family guests. And, while the picnics worked well in the dry season, Ele could not handle a large number of guests in the other seven months when it was humid and rained nearly every day. So, in the rainy season, Ele planned smaller buffet dinners with small tables arranged in the living room.

As I remember we had some official entertainment at our home every week for nearly two years. Ele always managed to arrange an attractive table and a tempting menu. She did all the shopping, going to the market in Panama City for fruits and vegetables and to the U.S. Commissary in the Canal Zone (to which we as U.S. government employees had access). She quickly learned Panamanian tastes and honed the menus to those tastes. Ele managed it all, including the financing. USAID provide us with an entertainment allowance of about $2,400 a year, a portion of which we shared with other senior USAID officers and about $1,200 a year from the embassy. We paid a substantial amount of the entertaining from our own pocket, and Ele carefully kept accounts and minimized damage to our bankbook.

We also had almost nightly work-related social obligations. There were dinners and cocktails with Panamanian officials, colleagues at the U.S. Embassy and USAID, government or military in the Canal Zone, or other embassies. In addition, Ele and I had friends from I House Berkeley and met new Panamanian friends that led to casual dinners and cocktails in many of the homes of *rabiblancos* and the new generation of businessmen who looked beyond Torrijos to a civilian Panama owning and operating the Canal—with close working relations with the United States. Each dinner with Panamanians helped us understand their country and their view of ours. What we heard was not a reversion to the past, but the building of a political and economic system that was more open and progressive. Ele and I were impressed that the mindset was so different from what we had experienced in other Central American countries.

As she had in previous posts, Ele actively participated in the American wives' association and the *Damas Diplomáticas*. The embassy wives met monthly and were engaged in a number of community projects that dealt with medical and social problems that beset the poor. With the diplomatic wives, she participated in planning the annual bazaars and attended the luncheons and teas. One other group she joined was the association of women writers based in the Canal Zone, where she met some talented ladies who shared her interest in writing and gave her another perspective on the interaction of the Canal Zone residents with the people of Panama.

Through her association with *Damas Diplomáticas*, Ele made many friends with the wives of several other diplomatic missions in Panama. Her friendship with the wife of the British ambassador led to one of the most exceptional invitations of our career. Her Majesty Elizabeth II had been touring Australia, New Zealand, and the South Pacific on her yacht *Britannia*. From Fiji, the queen flew back to Britain while the yacht steamed across the Pacific en route home to England. When the *Britannia* reached Panama, the British ambassador and his wife invited a small group, including Ele and me, to dine on the yacht. We were thrilled. The ambassador gave us a tour of the ship and a briefing on its various adventures and we had cocktails and dinner at the royal table. Ele could also report that when she went to the ladies room, she sat on the royal throne!

In Panama we also met friends from earlier postings—the Ellises, the Olsons, and Peggy Hook. They helped us get acquainted with life at post and alerted us to potential problems that we needed to avoid. Our friends from I House Berkeley gave us unvarnished insights into daily life. We often saw Dr. Julio Wong, a senior surgeon in the Army Canal Zone, and his wife Marge. Julio, after his undergraduate years in Berkeley, graduated from Johns Hopkins Medical School and did his surgical residency at Washington University School of Medicine in St. Louis. Julio brought us a different perspective on Panama since his family came from China during the construction of the Canal, made its fortune in trade (Julio used to jest that "not all of it was legit"), and settled into Panama's sophisticated multicultural society. When we got together, we talked local politics, sometimes relaxing at our pool and sometimes at dinner at the best Chinese restaurants in the city.

Two other I House Berkeley colleagues were Dr. Bernardo Lombardo, the ailing rector of the University of Panama, and Octavio Sousa, an official of the Panamanian Institute of Social Security. Bernardo was in dialysis when we arrived in Panama and we met only at his home. He opposed the military assumption of power in his country and the U.S. operation of the Canal Zone. He advocated a change in the internal balance of power and a new relationship with the U.S. In my first visit, he joked that the embassy and Torrijos would not be pleased to hear of my visit, and added that Noriega kept a sharp eye on who visited his house. Bernardo died shortly after our arrival.

Octavio Sousa gave us a quite different insight into Panama. He felt that Panama needed the strong leadership that Torrijos provided as well as a new relationship with the United States. As far as we could ascertain, Octavio was much more akin to the average Panamanian who was looking for a better future and working hard to make ends meet.

Visitors

The Canal was the hot political topic in Washington, and we had a succession of influential senators and congressmen to see the situation for themselves, especially as the treaty negotiations heated up. Some were serious, while others seemed more interested in advising the folks back home that they were protecting "our" Canal. Almost every week, the ambassador, the governor of the Canal, and the commanding general of the Southern Command, Lt. General McAuliffe, were briefing a dignitary or a delegation. They invited me to participate in many of those briefings, and to attend receptions and dinners for the visiting dignitaries. Ele usually accompanied me and was a very persuasive advocate.

The ambassador often asked us to arrange for a special lunch for a senator or congressman to meet privately with key ministers, like Nicky Barletta or Risti Royo. Ele would arrange the lunch, often in our garden where the key participants could talk comfortably. We had six such lunches at our home. I recall three quite well: one, with Senator Javits of New York and Nicky Barletta; the second with Senator Paul Simon of Illinois and Minister of Education Royo; and the third with Congressman Rhodes of Arizona and the minister of Education and Minister of Public Works Altamarino. I served as interpreter when needed, but mainly Ele and I let the principals thrash out their concerns and answer questions. The third lunch was one of the most interesting because the congressman had arrived very skeptical about a new treaty and left almost convinced of the need for a new treaty.

One or two congressional staffers came to inspect the USAID Mission and check our programming and finances. They kept US-AID Executive Officer Fascell, Controller Bill Naylor, and Program Officer Bernie Chapnick very busy during their visits. As a rule, Ele and I would invite the staffers to dinner, together with the USAID officers with whom they would be working, to help build personal ties with the visitors. One senior staff member of a House Committee arrived with a very adversarial view. As I had in all such visits, I invited him to dinner at my home with my USAID colleagues. He was hesitant but finally agreed. Ele put on very simple buffet dinner, and in the informal setting he talked with my USAID colleagues and their wives. They worked out a plan to expedite the investigation that he was about to undertake. As he left our house, he handed Ele ten dollars to cover the cost of his dinner. He said very haughtily that he was not going to be "purchased" by a dinner, and ten dollars was what he had expected to spend for dinner that night. Ele and I refused to take his money but avoided a scene. We had never had such an experience before and we were frankly miffed. Dinners that did not involve Panamanian counterparts were not considered eligible for reimbursement under U.S. government regulations and we never expected remuneration for doing something that we felt was part of the job. Ele and I felt that it was indeed unfortunate that friction between the two branches of government had become so petty. By the way, the report that the staffer prepared identified some very minor problems that needed correcting—just enough to allow him to justify his trip and affirm his "independence." USAID thanked the committee for its insights and made the adjustments.

We had only one houseguest during our tour in Panama and that was Elizabeth LaCell, the retired city librarian of Tulare, California, one of Ele's oldest friends. Elizabeth played a special role in Ele's life. Elizabeth had never traveled much and never been outside the United States. So, this was to be the great adventure for her lifetime: her first passport, and her first trip overseas!

Elizabeth stayed with us for only two weeks. Friends, official and personal, allowed us to bring her with us on all our invitations. One of the high points of her visit was when I included her on an official visit to the free port and industrial zone near Colón for the inauguration of a new assembly plant. On the way back, we took a short diversion to Portobelo to show Elizabeth where the caravels had loaded up gold and silver to take back to Spain and where Sir Francis Drake had made one of his most successful seizures of Spanish wealth. We walked the hills where the Spanish fortifications had been installed and marveled at Drake's astuteness and daring in the face of such forbidding terrain. For Elizabeth, many of the history books she shared with generations of Tulare students came alive.

Special Occasions

A special dimension to being the USAID director was making official visits to various provinces to inaugurate projects or review USAID supported programs. I took Ele with me on those visits. Sometimes, she would be the honored guest to cut a ribbon at the opening. Her smile was infectious and the results inevitably made my job easier.

We journeyed together to Chiriquí, Bocas del Toro, Colón, Veraguas, Herrera, Santos, and the Kuna home islands. All our visits were quite informal and frequently involved our being introduced to pet projects that the local officials could not induce Nicky Barletta or his successor Gustavo Gonzalez to include in the Ministry of Planning's priority list of projects. Often Ele and I would express our interest in the project, but said, "So sorry, its status is a matter between you and the minister of Planning." Once or twice there would be a proposal interesting enough for me to raise with Nicky or Gustavo. My job was to be supportive of the priorities that the government of Panama had set—not a time to introduce proposals that might ensnarl the negotiations.

By far the most interesting visit that Ele and I made was to the main island of the Kuna Indians. The Kunas are a self-governing commonwealth within Panama and make their own decisions on most domestic matters. A delegation invited Ele and me to be their guests for a ceremony to open a project for which USAID provided technical and monetary support. I cleared the invitation with the ambassador and arranged for a party of USAID officers to accompany me.

We flew to the Atlantic coast of Panama, and were assigned canoes to take us to the island. On arrival, there was a formal ceremony of greeting with the chief of the tribe and then the dedication of the project, followed by dinner at the government-run hotel. The hotel was not large, probably about ten rooms—very tropical with a thatched roof. The dinner was a delicious assortment of seafood and shellfish, with several toasts of friendship. Then we were shown to our rooms, immaculate and comfortable with private bathrooms where we were locked in for the night. The Kuna chief explained to me that this was their law to protect Kuna women from the visiting males. The electricity was off by 10:00 p.m. We had a quiet night and, after an abundant breakfast and farewell ceremony, went back to the airport by canoe for our return to Panama. Ele and I cherished that visit.

Another very special trip was when we were invited on the commemorative train ride across the Isthmus on the Panama Railway. We joined Governor Parfitt and Ambassador Jordan, as well as Panamanian and U.S. officials, for a box lunch on reconditioned passenger cars that took us over the famous route that opened in 1853. Riding along the northern edge of the Canal showed us the terrain and the tropical vegetation right outside our window and let us relive the concerns and expectations of those who had ridden the railway so many years ago.

We also celebrated the U.S. bicentennial in Panama. The ambassador had an official reception at which we worked, as did all our embassy and USAID colleagues, greeting Panamanian and diplomatic guests. Then we were invited by Governor Parfitt and General McAuliffe to sit in the official box to observe the parade and festivities in the Canal Zone. After the parade, at the governor's reception, we watched on a giant television the parade of ships in New York Harbor.

The governor also honored me by selecting me to deliver the annual address on Law Day that bicentennial year in the principal courtroom of Canal Zone. General McAuliffe also invited me to deliver an address on U.S. constitutional law at the School of the Americas, the officer training school for Latin American military officers, then located in the Zone.

One special experience occurred during the state visit of Marshall Tito of Yugoslavia and his wife Jovanka to dedicate the dam and irrigation project for the upper Darién sugar project. Ele and I were not included in any of the official proceedings, but we ran into them at the Holiday Inn, an elegant circular building on a hill over-looking the ocean and the Old City of Panama. It was the evening of the state dinner that coincided with a USAID hosted reception commemorating twenty-five years of cooperation between the U.S. and Panamanian cooperative movements.

Without our knowing it, the time to begin the USAID reception coincided with the departure of the Titos and Torrijos from the Holiday Inn for the state banquet. Ele and I arrived in our official car just as the Titos and Torrijos reached the front door of the Holiday Inn. Our driver, Mr. Nichols, got out of our car to let Ele out—but Marshall Tito thought it was to let him enter! The Marshall ended up almost in Ele's lap and my head almost invaded Jovanka's breastplates before Torrijos, furious at the hitch, screamed that this was not the official car for the Titos. Torrijos glared at Mr. Nichols and me as an aide directed the Titos to a car ahead of ours. That was as close as the Tragens ever came to the Titos.

A European Vacation

By the middle of 1976, the ambassador advised the Country Team that the terms and conditions for the new treaty had been agreed upon and the remaining details were more administrative than substantive. The pressure was off. So Ele and I decided it was time for a vacation. Ambassador Jordan allowed us three weeks in late September. That would give Ele and me some time together before she made her annual farm trip in late October. We decided to go to Munich for Oktoberfest and to accept an invitation from our friends, Elizabeth and Nathaniel Davis, to visit them at their new post—he had been appointed U.S. ambassador in Switzerland after finishing his term as director general of the U.S. Foreign Service.

Ele made arrangements with Pan American to fly to Frankfurt and return via Geneva and bought Eurail passes. She studied the places of interest in southern Germany and she selected Augsburg as the hub for the first ten days and Geneva after our visit with the Davises in Bern. Augsburg was chosen because it was only an hour's ride outside Munich with the hotel rates half those in Munich and by train only an hour from the Rhineland where we could revisit special places that we had enjoyed on earlier visits.

The tour books reported that the weather in September–October could be quite cold in Bavaria and Switzerland, so we packed for coolish weather. Knowing that she would be traveling to South Dakota after our vacation, Ele decided to wear her full-length Persian lamb coat.

The first week in Augsburg was a dream. The weather was warm and sunny. We loved the city and visited every attraction, especially the old guild centers and museums. The restaurants were excellent and the prices within our budget. Our Eurail passes allowed us to make two day-long visits to Munich and enjoy the old town center with its wonderful cathedral clock, Ludwig's magnificent palace, and the wine cellars. Two other days, we took the train back up to the Rhineland, revisiting Heidelberg, Wiesbaden, Bamberg, and Wurzburg.

The hotel in Augsburg was overbooked and required us to leave earlier than we planned. The day we left was the first cold day of our visit, and Ele wore her Persian lamb as we headed south to Buchloe, a stop on the mainline between Munich and Bern. The guidebook said that it had a small railway hotel located across the street from the station.

It had started to drizzle when we arrived in Buchloe, so I asked Ele to cross over to the hotel to check on rooms while I guarded our three bulky bags (which did not have wheels in those days); carrying them on and off the train had worn me out. Ele did not notice the curb outside the station and fell in the street. She hobbled back in disarray. The heavy coat did not help, and her chagrin on falling was even worse. So I went across the street. No one spoke English, but we managed to obtain a lovely big front room on the second floor.

Once we got settled, I asked Ele if she wanted to rest. She said no. Her ankle was bothering her, but she wanted to see Ludwig's Neuschwanstein Schloss—less than an hour by train. On the train, Ele's right ankle started to swell. When we arrived, we saw the Schloss loom up before us, and I asked Ele if she was okay. She replied that she was eager to see the inside of this fairytale castle. So we joined a tour for English speakers, walked up hundreds of stairs and ambled through the great flag-festooned halls. Ele's ankle became more and more swollen, and finally she said she couldn't walk any further. With help from another tourist, we half carried her back to the train station.

Ele was in agony all the way back to Buchloe. She steadied herself on me as we made our way back to our hotel room. When I got her settled on the bed, I asked our landlord for ice to treat her ankle. I knew that the word for ice in German is *"eis;"* so I asked the landlord for "ez" as if it were Spanish or Portuguese. He called his wife and they began to understand that Ele had a health problem and needed help. The wife's mother, a true German grandma, came in, took one look at Ele and said, "ice." Grandma took over: she iced Ele's ankle, brought her chicken broth, and sent for the family doctor. The doctor, who spoke some English, checked Ele's ankles and leg, and said that she had a sprain and would be fine, but that she had to keep off the foot for at least two days. He also sent me to the pharmacy for a salve to rub on her ankle every few hours to help reduce the swelling.

Then, it started to rain, and it rained the following two days. Grandma took care of Ele and brought her meals, excellent home-cooked German feasts. I went to Munich on the next day until the rain forced me to beat an early retreat; the other it rained so hard we both rested. The last night, Ele was on her feet again and we had dinner downstairs with the owner and his family. On Saturday, we took the train to Bern. Grandma helped me carry the bags over to the station and made sure that Ele had no problem getting on the train. We exchanged Christmas cards for several years before Grandma died.

On arriving in Bern, we took a cab to the embassy, a veritable jewel. We had a wonderful family reunion. Elizabeth had the embassy doctor check Ele's ankle, and he pronounced it well-taken care of, but recommend *"eis"* on it at night. Nat took us to Interlaken for a truly memorable day and the last day, Elizabeth, Ele, and I did some sightseeing and revisited the bears of Bern.

The following day we took the train to Geneva, where we spent three relaxed sunlit days, with boat trips on the lake to the Prisoner of Chillon, visits with old friends at the Palais des Nations and at the World Health Organization, and a walking tour of the heart of Calvinism. What I remember best were our daily lunches at the department stores. Ele loved to go shopping and she had read of the great department stores in Geneva. Well, she walked me through every one! On the third day, in the dining room of one of the stores, as we finished lunch, she sipped her tea and remarked, "I think I know what turns the Swiss on." I asked, "What?" Smiling brightly, she said, "After visiting the department stores and looking at all the lingerie and food displays, I know that the Swiss love to eat in bed."

Leaving Panama

Our home was the center of our life in Panama. But, we were always concerned about safety. We always had a feeling that someone was watching. It may have been our concern over the presence of Colonel Noriega across the street or our Tennessee widow on one side or the foreign minister on the other side. It may also have been the absence of a back fence; the back of the yard had a link fence with meager vines growing on it as it opened up onto the golf course, giving golfers a clear view of the living rooms, the bedrooms, and the garden.

That feeling of unease magnified when the government of Panama acquired the golf course for a public park, and we had people picnicking on the greens across the fence. Ele had to give up her afternoon swim because, whenever she was alone, men would come up to the fence and expose themselves.

On the occasions I had to be away, Ele felt especially vulnerable. Indeed, on two occasions in 1977, people broke in over the back fence and stole items, included two chaise lounges in the covered patio. A third occasion occurred when I had been called to Washington on consultation. She heard someone trying to enter the locked patio outside our bedroom and rang for help from the maid and houseboy—no one answered. She went to their rooms get help and found them in bed together. She blew up. She called Rudy Fascell for help and had them fired on the spot. She felt that the people we had hired to take of her had abandoned her in a time of need.

On my return the following day, Rudy briefed me on the events of that night and told me that he provided guards for the house.

When I advised Ele that we were being transferred to Washington, she broke down and, in tears, told me of her fears and her desire to get out of the house. She also told me for the first time that for several months she had been suffering from severe pains in her neck and shoulders but had not mentioned them because she didn't want to distract me from the job. The only other time that she had broken down was in Venezuela when our upstairs neighbor had been kidnapped by being mistaken for Ele.

Rudy helped me as best he could to keep her protected until we left. For our last few weeks in the residence, Ele tended to the house and prepared our meals. She went through the motions and smiled graciously through our farewells, but she ached inside.

The timing for our reassignment came shortly after agreement was reached on the new canal treaty in September 1977. A few days later, I received a call from the then Assistant Secretary of State for Inter-American Affairs Viron "Pete" Vaky, asking me if I was interested in returning to Washington as the deputy U.S. representative to the Organization of American States (OAS). I told him that I would discuss it with Ele. We talked at lunch and she was enthusiastic, and so I advised Pete that afternoon and he in turn alerted Ambassador Jordan. The appointment depended on the concurrence of the ambassador-designate, former Wyoming Senator Gale McGee, once he was confirmed. I was called to Washington in mid-November. My conversations with Senator McGee went very well and he signed off on my appointment.

When I advised the USAID staff of my departure, the reaction was not good. The delay by AID/Washington in approving the Azuero integrated regional development project had created complex problems getting it off the ground. USAID's closest collaborator in the Panamanian government, Nicky Barletta, had departed and his able replacement Gustavo Gonzalez did not have Nicky's political clout or the ear of Torrijos. Bringing together several ministries to cooperate and then assigning the right people to work in the field were difficult tasks in the best of circumstances, and now Gonzalez found himself enmeshed in a variety of political and bureaucratic disagreements that frustrated efforts to get the program moving.

I know of no better example of the importance of timing to initiate a project than the Azuero. When we completed the negotiation and drafting of the loan request, Nicky had not only Torrijos' approval for each step in the implementation process but also that of each affected ministry for its commitment of money and technical support for each major project component. A year later, Nicky wasn't there and the ministers and Torrijos had moved on. What had looked so promising one year ago now presented USAID and its counterparts with serious concerns.

In addition, the performance of the deputy USAID director had presented one problem after another, even though I dedicated a great deal of time to training him. There was deep resentment among the senior staff that someone without any preparation had been appointed to be their supervisor. Every time the deputy had been left in charge, he made decisions that had to be corrected on my return. He was not a quick learner and frequently misinterpreted the information being provided him, to the dismay of his USAID colleagues.

Unfortunately, dressing him down for bad judgment didn't do much good because shortly after I left post, someone got to him while he was acting USAID director and he attempted to award a substantial construction contract for the San Miguelito project to a single bidder, contrary to AID/U.S. government bidding procedures. The loan officer, the administrative officer, and the controller blew the whistle, and the ambassador requested his removal. Having a senior officer who does not earn respect can destroy an organization.

Morale among the local USAID employees was bad because they sensed that the USAID Mission would be closed once the new treaty was negotiated and the current projects were completed or phased out. Many had been with the USAID since the 1940s, and they saw their futures much in doubt. None of us in senior USAID posts could give them much reassurance.

Several U.S. colleagues, like Bernie Chapnick, made no secret of their intention to leave AID because of the policy direction they saw the agency taking. Senior technicians saw their jobs being phased out and given to contract personnel who earned more money as Beltway Bandits than they received as USAID technicians. Downsizing permanent staff was the tone of communications from Washington, and the U.S. and Panamanian technical and administrative staff felt very vulnerable.

Even in that environment, the USAID staff gave us a warm and affectionate farewell. They presented us an elegant reproduction of one of Panama's most elegant gold *dijes* that I shall prize for the rest of my life. That party and the *abrazos* from all of my Panamanian colleagues are a cherished memory. I have been fortunate to have seen many of them on later trips to the country.

The ambassador gave us a farewell reception at the embassy to which he invited my colleagues in the Panamanian government as well as embassy and USAID staff. The governor of the Canal Zone had an afternoon reception to which he invited members of the Canal Zone government and the Southern Command with whom I had worked.

The Panamanian farewells were much less formal. President Lakas, whom we had met at dinner parties, invited Ele and me to tea at the official presidential residence in the Old City of Panama. Colonel Paredes invited Ele and me to cocktails at the headquarters of the *Guardia Nacional*, and General Torrijos dropped by. It was the only time that Ele met him. He very tersely told us that I had done a good job and that he considered me a friend of Panama.

As I was wrapping up my work at the office, Ele was supervising the packing of our effects. She was one very unhappy lady. The crew that USAID sent over was inept and careless. She blew her top when one of the packers could not fit one of the Honduran ceramic roosters into the packing crate, and snapped the tail off. Ele ordered the packers out of the house and called Rudy Fascell for replacements. When the new team arrived, it was made up of professional packers. Even so, Ele did not leave the house again until the last crate was sealed.

The USAID and embassy staff came to the airport to see us off, and the Panama chapter of our lives closed.

PART IV

MULTILATERAL DIPLOMACY: THE ORGANIZATION OF AMERICAN STATES (OAS), 1977–1994

28

U.S. Mission to the Organization of American States

My concern on the flight back to Washington was Ele's health. We had arranged for an apartment in our building where we had lived on prior Washington assignments, the Towers on Cathedral Avenue. When we arrived at the apartment, Ele sat me down and told me how difficult the last couple of years had been on her. Her protracted recovery from surgery, the strain of the death of our mothers, and the combination of heat, humidity, and official duties in Panama had taken their toll. Now, she needed medical care and time to recoup. She told me that she would do only the necessary until she felt better.

The following week when we took our medical examinations at the State Department, she reported her problems and wondered if she had cancer. She was sent to Georgetown University Hospital for a battery of tests. The test results showed there were no signs of cancer, but did not pinpoint the cause of her problems. Her health did not improve, and I noticed that she lacked her usual spark as she joined me in the required introductions to U.S. Ambassador to the OAS Gale McGee, Secretary General of the OAS Alejandro Orfila, and the key ambassadors of the other OAS member states.

Finally, I asked her if she would meet my personal physician, Dr. John Latimer, who had diagnosed and taught me how to live with a chronic liver problem that lingered from a jaundice attack I suffered in Chile. Ele felt at first that she should let State Medical take charge, but after several weeks of no progress and enduring pain, we went to see Dr. Latimer. He examined her thoroughly and then asked her a series of questions that related to our lifestyle in Central America and Panama. He asked us if we had had air conditioning in our bedroom. We said, "In Guatemala, no. In Panama, twenty-four hours a day, all year round. In fact, the bedroom windows were simply for light and did not open." Then, Dr. Latimer asked Ele to lie down on the floor on her back. He gave a series of exercises involving raising her legs up several inches from the floor and then her neck and head. After about five minutes, he asked her to stand. And for the first time in months she said that she felt little or no pain. Dr. Latimer opined that the air conditioning constantly passing over her head and neck night after night had inflamed the muscles and tendons of her upper body. He also warned her that it was a problem whose effects she could control through exercises but never eliminate. He gave her a schedule of daily exercises to alleviate the aches. He took great care to help her deal with her other emotional concerns. Ele asked Dr. Latimer to advise State Medical of his diagnosis. He became her Washington doctor until he retired.

Assuming the New Post

When I reported to work on the Monday morning after our return from Panama, there were no formalities. I reported to personnel where I signed papers, reported to the executive officer for the Inter-American Bureau, still my good friend Mel Spector, and was escorted over to my new office on the sixth floor, adjacent to that of the ambassador Gale McGee. I was duly impressed when Mel told me that my office had been used for many years as the hideaway for Eleanor Dulles, the eminent European specialist and sister of the former secretary of state, John Foster Dulles.

The ambassador gathered the staff in his office to meet me. The mission was relatively small: the political officer, Mark Dion; the special assistant, Liz Hannifin (who had been on the ambassador's staff for eighteen years in the Senate); Frank Starrs, the economic officer; Donald Stewart, the liaison with the OAS Secretariat and other member states; Margarita Riva, a recently hired young officer, who dealt with the OAS Education, Science, and Culture Council (CIECC); and Faye Armstrong, the regional legal specialist from the State Department Legal Adviser's Office. The mission also had three secretaries: mine was Mrs. Helen May.

Mark Dion and Frank Starrs then briefed me for a week on the range of issues at the OAS. They gave me an overview of the weakened OAS in the post-Alliance for Progress world, the problems of working with Latin American delegations (the majority of which represented military regimes), the impact on decision-making by the accession to the OAS of eleven newly sovereign Caribbean states and Suriname, and the continuing unrest in Central America (especially El Salvador, Guatemala, and the Sandinista-led revolt in Nicaragua). Mark Dion acquainted me with the policies and rules of procedures of the OAS councils and the functions of the OAS Secretariat. I also met privately with each of my colleagues for briefings on the hot issues on the OAS agenda, the position of the Latin American and Caribbean delegations, and information on the chiefs of delegations with whom I would be working.

My colleagues were not optimistic about the interest of the State Department and the White House in working with or through the OAS on priority regional issues. That, they noted, was reflected in the diminished size of the mission compared to the Alliance years when the chief of mission, a politically prominent presidential appointee, had one or two career ambassadors to support him on political and development/economic affairs, and each career ambassador had a staff of career officers to support him. They alerted me that the deputy chief of mission would do most of the day-to-day negotiating with the other missions at the OAS, and the importance the Latin Americans attributed to the rank of the officer with whom they were dealing. They pointed out that, for a decade prior to the appointment of Robert White (my predecessor) the deputy had been a senior career officer who had served as an ambassador before his appointment as deputy and carried the rank and title with him. To the ambassadors of the other thirty-three active member states he was a co-equal. However, my predecessor, a very able and respected career officer, had not been an ambassador and his lack of rank complicated his negotiations on delicate day-to-day issues since the Latin American and Caribbean ambassadors did not view him of sufficient rank to speak for the U.S. I was warned that I would face similar problems.

When President Nixon ended the Alliance, the size and importance of the mission had been cut back sharply, along with U.S. financing for the OAS. They added that many career officers now believed that an assignment to the mission was a dead end. Aware of that perception, Ambassador McGee told me that one of his priorities was to build up support for the OAS at the White House and among his former colleagues in the Senate.

At a staff meeting with Assistant Secretary Vaky, Ambassador McGee raised the question of the rank of the deputy and was instructed to work with Mel Spector in presenting a request to the appropriate State Department office to establish rank and title of ambassador to the office of deputy chief of mission to the OAS. Secretary Vaky pointed out that he might be called on to use the mission for delicate negotiations on the deteriorating situation in Central America, and wanted the deputy chief to be in a position to handle detailed, quiet negotiations with key Latin American ambassadors since Ambassador McGee had little knowledge of Spanish or Portuguese. Two years were spent writing justifications and receiving rejections. In the Reagan years, my successors were given the rank and title of ambassador.

The assistant secretary included me in his regular staff meetings with his deputies and policy planning advisor. He shared his vision for a new hemisphere-wide strategy to replace the Alliance, an "overarching policy" in which the OAS would play a significant role. He tasked me with drafting policy papers about the U.S. relationship with the OAS. He shared my concerns that the Alliance had not had adequate time to build a solid institutional base to achieve the fundamental changes that the Charter of Punta del Este had defined. This "over-arching" strategy included hemisphere-wide cooperation to improve the capacity of governments in Latin America and the Caribbean to deal with the complex political, economic, and social changes sweeping the region.

My initial contact with the OAS was delayed until early 1978 because the OAS Permanent Council was in recess. Most of the representatives and senior OAS officials were on vacation in their home countries. It was mid-January before Ambassador McGee introduced me to Secretary General Alejandro Orfila and Assistant Secretary General Jorge Zelaya Coronado. That was my first official visit to the stately headquarters building of the Organization of American States, at Constitution Avenue and 17th Street, down the Ellipse from the White House, built with Andrew Carnegie's generous donation and inaugurated by President Taft in 1910.

The secretary general had a large suite of elegant offices on the second floor of the main building. Orfila had been Argentine ambassador to the U.S. before his election as secretary general in 1975. Zelaya Coronado had a suite of offices on the right-hand corridor on the first floor. He had been a Guatemalan diplomat for most of his career. Since the OAS was founded in its current form in the late 1940s, the secretary general had been from a South American country and the assistant secretary general from the United States. In 1960, during the Alliance years, the U.S. opted not to present a candidate and instead, supported the election of a Central American.

The conversation with Orfila, while essentially protocol, touched on a troublesome item on the agenda of the Permanent Council when it reconvened in late January, and on his concern about declining U.S. support. Orfila expressed hope that President Carter would re-examine U.S. policy, especially since only a few months earlier, the president had chosen the OAS as the site for signing the Panama Canal Treaty with Panama's Torrijos.

The meeting with the assistant secretary general took on a different tone. His primary role was that of secretary to the Permanent Council and officer in charge of the conference staff. Zelaya discussed with me the operations of the Permanent Council and its committees, and called in the director of the conference staff, Cuban diplomat in exile Guillermo Belt, who explained the rules that governed debate in the Permanent Council. He described the role of the General Committee and the committees that dealt with the Economic and Social Council and its Secretariat and the Education, Science and Culture Council and its Secretariat. I was also introduced to the rabbit warrens that served as offices for the OAS conference staff and many of the senior advisers to the secretary general. In 1905, when the building was designed, no one had anticipated the requirements for the staff of an inter-American organization in the 1970s.

I was stimulated by the possibilities for the job. I made plans for establishing working relationships with the delegates from the other thirty-three active member countries. I planned meetings with the senior officers of the Secretariat to better understand their functions. As I told Ele, it would be a different assignment from any that I had had before and one that would require all my diplomatic and technical skills and legal and management experience. To this day, every time I enter the main OAS Building, one of the most beautiful edifices in Washington, D.C., that old excitement stirs me and I remember that once I knew everyone working in the building and I had a job to do there. It still symbolizes for me the possibilities for inter-American cooperation, even in the current jaded world.

Getting into the Job

The first few weeks on the job, I spent on reading about the OAS, called on the principal representatives from the other member states and met State Department colleagues knowledgeable about it.

Inter-American cooperation was initiated in 1889–1890 when then U.S. Secretary of State James J. Blaine invited representatives of the other independent Western Hemisphere countries to meet in Washington to discuss commercial and legal issues of common concern. Blaine saw Latin America as a key U.S. sphere of influence. Building on the 1823 Monroe Doctrine that promised, "U.S. retaliation against any act by the European powers to recolonize the Western Hemisphere or to intervene in the affairs of the independent Latin American and Caribbean States," Blaine sought to build a special relationship with the American Republics through trade and U.S. investment.

In the late nineteenth century, the U.S. was a growing manufacturing and capital formation power with almost 80 million people. Latin America and Haiti, with 50 to 60 million inhabitants, were producers of raw materials, dependent on the European metropoles for investments and trade. They had classical mercantile economies, with feudal agricultural systems. Several had lived through incessant civil wars and military dictatorships since independence, and only a handful had functioning elected representative governments. On the other hand, the U.S. had emerged with its political institutions intact after the Civil War, glowed in the era of Manifest Destiny, and had enjoyed both territorial and economic expansion.

Sixteen Latin American countries and Haiti responded to Blaine's invitation. They accepted the agenda on trade and juridical issues, but also wanted to open discussion on ways and means of restraining the unilateral use by the U.S. of its growing power.

They were clearly concerned about United States' intervention in Mexico and Central America and the threat of gunboat diplomacy to exact payment of external debt. The Latin Americans wanted inter-American ground rules restraining unilateral military action by the U.S., not merely by European powers.

At the 1889/1890 Conference of Washington, an agreement was signed to cooperate on peacefully resolving commercial and juridical disputes and to create the International Union of the American Republics that set up periodic meetings of governments to deal with trade, juridical, and other issues of common concern, with the U.S. State Department serving as its secretariat. Several meeting were convened on specific issues.

In 1901 in Buenos Aires, the countries agreed to hold a Conference of Foreign Ministers every four years, established the Pan American Union (PAU), broadened the agenda and gave the organization a secretariat, independent of the U.S. Department of State. It was not empowered to constrain U.S. use of gunboat diplomacy in spite of several impassioned speeches. One Latin American diplomat called the PAU "nothing more than an elegant debating society."

It had no power to take collective action when U.S. naval vessels and marines moved into Venezuela, Haiti, or Nicaragua to collect customs receipts to ensure repayment of debts owed to U.S. and other bondholders. The PAU took no action when the U.S. intervened militarily in Mexico during the 1910–1920 Revolution. In the words of Theodore Roosevelt, "We respect the sovereignty of the American Republics consistent with the Monroe Doctrine. But when sovereign states do not live up to their international agreements, they have to suffer the consequences—and the gunboats are there to punish those who misbehave."

In 1920, U.S. educator and Latin American specialist Dr. Leo Rowe was appointed PAU director-general. For the next twenty-five years until his death in 1946, he built the PAU into a respected center for inter-American dialogue in addition to the regular quadrennial conferences on political, economic, and legal issues. He convened technical conferences and formed inter-country commissions on matters of common interest, such as women's rights. His vision of inter-American cooperation influenced the policies of

Franklin Delano Roosevelt, who ended the era of gunboat diplomacy and championed the Good Neighbor Policy.

During World War II, most of Latin America joined the Allied cause, supplied raw materials, and provided bases for the war effort. With the advent of the Cold War, President Truman and Secretary of State George Marshall sought a firm commitment by Latin America to combat USSR-Communist infiltration. The U.S. was concerned by the appeal to Latin American reformers of the Soviet development model of state control over the means of production as the formula for replacing their mercantile and feudal structures that were devastated by the Great Depression of the 1930s and the effects of World War II. The Cold War and the winds of change in Latin America set the stage for a new inter-American negotiation on a relationship that went far beyond the context of the Pan American Union.

In Bogotá in 1948 against the background of one of Colombia's perennial civil wars, the U.S. proposed a military alliance to commit the member states of the PAU to support the Western Alliance in the Cold War and for collective security arrangements in the event of an attack by the Soviet Bloc against any member state, or a communist-led subversion. In return, the Latin American states called for U.S. commitments to support regional political, economic, and social development and to contain unilateral U.S. action against any one of the countries. While street fighting took place around the building in which the delegates were meeting, George Marshall negotiated the Charter of the Organization of American States (OAS), and the framework for a Mutual Defense Pact, formalized later in Rio de Janeiro and popularly known as the Rio Treaty.

The key commitments spelled out in the charter are found in Chapter IV on the Fundamental Rights of States and in Chapter VI on Collective Security. Articles 19 and 20 of Chapter IV establish the principle of non-intervention of one member state in the internal or external affairs of another member state, including prohibiting the use of coercive measures of an economic or political character. Article 28 stipulates that, "every act of aggression by a State against the territorial integrity or inviolability of its territory or against the sovereignty or political independence of an American State shall be considered an act of aggression against the other American States."

Article 29 further empowers the member states to make special treaties to enforce the principle of collective security.

Chapter VII of the charter, titled "Integral Development," is one of the most comprehensive commitments to cooperation for development in any international accord. It stipulates that, "to ensure international social justice in their relations and integral development for their people as conditions essential to peace and security," the member states are to work together on economic, social, educational, cultural, scientific, and technological development. It calls for long-term intergovernmental cooperation through the OAS to achieve the long list of goals. The chapter reflects the hopes of the hemisphere after World War II to avoid not only another such war but an economic crisis like the Great Depression of the 1930s.

Following the adoption of the Charter, the member states negotiated and signed the Inter-American Treaty of Reciprocal Assistance—the Rio Treaty. It gave treaty status to the Inter-American Defense Board, which was created in 1942 to facilitate wartime cooperation among the military forces of the member states.

What the charter did not create was a strong secretary general with authority and powers like those given to the United Nations secretary general. The OAS secretary general was made an administrator of the programs and actions authorized by the member states. This reflected Latin American concern that the U.S., with its money and power, might take control of the OAS and impose its will on them—especially since its headquarters would be in Washington, D.C. So they created the Permanent Council to meet year round at OAS headquarters and oversee the implementation of policies determined by the annual General Assembly of Ministers of Foreign Affairs. As Dr. Alberto Lleras Camargo, the first secretary general of the OAS and former president of Colombia reflected, "The OAS is neither good nor bad, in and of itself. It is what the member governments want it to be, and nothing else."

In the case of the OAS, the disparity of power between the U.S. and the other member states created *ab initio* a tension over its financing. In 1948, the U.S. generated about 90 percent of the GDP of the hemisphere, and had about 50 percent of the population. It had the strongest military force in the world; none of the other member states could compete. However, if the U.S. were to cover 90 percent of the budget, the OAS would essentially become a dependency of the U.S. and that was politically unacceptable. The compromise reached provided that the U.S. would pay two-thirds of the annual budget, with the balance distributed among the other twenty member states based on per capita income.

During the 1950s, the OAS General Assembly met annually and supported the U.S. in the Cold War in spite of the tensions created by the CIA's role in the overthrow of the elected Arbenz government in Guatemala and the anti-U.S. accusations from Peronist Argentina. Joint military exercises were carried out periodically and the U.S. was acknowledged as the leader of the hemisphere.

But the winds of change were blowing throughout Latin America in the 1950s. The traditional economic system continued to unwind. The growing middle class pressed for fundamental political, economic, and political change. The growth of the population led to ever-greater rural to urban migration and young people, now the majority in most countries, were demanding better job opportunities. Most governments lacked the institutional capability and trained leadership to substantively react to the mounting pressures and unrest.

Instant communications made the region aware of the Marshall Plan and the European rehabilitation. In 1958, Brazilian President Kubitschek, drawing on Chapter VII of the Charter, called for a hemisphere-wide development plan, "Operation Pan America." President Eisenhower asked his brother Milton, president of the Johns Hopkins University, to advise him on measures that the U.S. could take to deal with the problems that threatened the stability of the hemisphere. Milton Eisenhower identified U.S. cooperation with Latin America to support economic and social development as the medicine for stabilizing the region.

Then came Fidel Castro! With the advent of the Cuban Revolution, the U.S. turned to the OAS and called for inter-American action under Chapter IV for collective security, and Latin America called for action under Chapter VII on Integral Development. The OAS suspended Cuban membership in 1962, while the U.S. took action to support the development of the other Latin American member states.

Under Chapter Vii, the Eisenhower administration embraced

the creation of the Inter-American Development Bank (IDB), and the U.S. provided most of the initial capital. After the Bay of Pigs fiasco, President Kennedy proposed the Alliance for Progress (AFP), quite similar to the proposal made by Brazilian President Kubitschek three years earlier. The Alliance for Progress was created in Punta del Este, Uruguay in 1961 with an initial life of ten years, and the U.S. committed $20 billion over its lifetime. The OAS was chosen as the institutional home for the AFP and its economic and social development secretariat grew exponentially.

When, after the Cuban missile crisis, the U.S. and the USSR reached an understanding on limiting Cuban subversive activities in the region and the Vietnam War took center stage, U.S. interest in the Alliance waned. With Cuba constrained, U.S. policy makers did not envision a strategic role for Latin America in winning the Cold War. In addition, the progress in achieving AFP objectives was disappointing. The weakness of national institutions and the lack of competent management undermined U.S. interest and led to policy decisions to cut back its financial and technical support. In 1974, on the tenth anniversary of the creation of the Alliance, President Nixon declared it at an end. From that date, U.S. political and financial support for the OAS and its program steadily declined.

I was taking up my post at a time when most Latin American governments interpreted U.S. actions as disengagement from hemispheric affairs except for certain agenda items of specific U.S. interest. The Carter administration advocated support for human rights and fighting poverty, not integral development spelled out in Article VII of the OAS Charter.

The OAS Member States

Each of the thirty-three active member states was represented by an ambassador to the OAS. The larger countries had embassies separate from that to the U.S. government. Smaller countries, such as El Salvador, Haiti, Honduras, Nicaragua, and new member states from the Caribbean, accredited their envoys to the U.S. to be their representatives to the OAS. Cuba remained a member even though it had been suspended in 1962 for its aggression against other member states and its self-proclaimed Marxist-Leninist government was deemed "incompatible with the principles and objectives of the inter-American system."

I made an initial courtesy call on each one. Most visits lasted about an hour, over coffee. Some visits turned substantive. One of my first calls was on the ambassador of Nicaragua, Guillermo Sevilla Sacasa, who was also the dean of Diplomatic Corps. He was one of the savviest men in Washington, having served since 1943. He was the brother-in-law of the assassinated dictator Anastasio "Tacho" Somoza and uncle of the current president "Tachito" Somoza. He told me in careful chosen language that he was well aware of the seriousness of the Sandinista movement and of his nephew's growing unpopularity. He said that several of his Latin American colleagues had told him about my work in their countries and of my friendship with Assistant Secretary Vaky. He asked me to assure the assistant secretary that he was always available to help the U.S. work out a "peaceful solution" to the current crisis.

Another early meeting was with Mexican Ambassador Rafael de la Colina, called by all of his colleagues in the Permanent Council "El Maestro." He was then in his late eighties and had served as Mexican Representative to the OAS for decades and was reputed to know the background and rationale for almost every OAS decision. In an interview that lasted well over an hour, he stated that his government would oppose any initiative in the OAS that might be seen as intervening in the internal affairs of any member state. He made very clear his government's concern that any such precedent might be used by the U.S. to intervene in domestic Mexican political affairs. As the old adage goes, "Mexico is far from Heaven and so close to the United States."

On consecutive days, I met with the representatives of Colombia, José Gori; Costa Rica, José Rafael Echeverría; Panama, Nander Pitty Velasquez; and Venezuela, José María Machín. They were the so-called anti-dictator bloc among the Latin American delegations and were critical allies for any initiatives by the U.S. on protecting human rights. All four assured me that they were prepared to support the United States. They also urged me to talk with Argentina, Brazil, Chile, and Peru since they sensed that those ambassadors would be interested in working with the U.S. if the issues were shaped appropriately.

After those meetings, I reported back to Ambassador McGee, Assistant Secretary Vaky, and Policy Planning Chief Luigi Einaudi. They authorized me to call on the Argentine, Brazilian, Chilean, and Peruvian delegations and open lines of communication with them. So, the following week, I visited the Argentine representative, José César Caraceles, a veteran diplomat with whom I had worked during my tour as director of Argentine, Paraguayan, and Uruguayan Affairs. Our meeting was formal but friendly. I cited the deep concern of my government with the repressive measures being taken by the military regime in his country and my expectation that our two countries would be on opposite sides on many issues at the next General Assembly. Nonetheless, we agreed that there were some issues on the OAS agenda on which we could cooperate.

The meeting with the Brazilian ambassador, Alarico Silveira, was also formal but more open. Once again, the authoritarian measures being taken by the military government in Brasilia meant that there were sharp disagreements between our two governments, but he and his deputy, Ney Mellos Mattos, both influential members of the Brazilian career foreign service, *Itamaraty*, assured me that Brazil wanted to work with the U.S. in the OAS.

The third meeting that week was with the Chilean Representative, María Eugenia Oyarzún, a prominent Conservative Party member with direct access to Pinochet, to whom she had thrown her support right after the coup. Our meeting was more personal. She knew of my long association with Chile and my work with former Christian Democratic Labor Minister Guillermo Thayer. She pressed me to be more understanding of the reasons why Pinochet had to use strong measures to root out the Chilean Communist Party and Soviet influence. We agreed to disagree but to keep in contact on issues that would arise in the OAS.

The following afternoon I went to the Peruvian Mission to talk with Ambassador Luis Marchand Stens. A senior member of the Peruvian career diplomatic service, he was knowledgeable and urbane, clearly not comfortable representing a military government. We had a wide-ranging discussion that laid the basis for a constructive working relationship in the OAS and a personal friendship in later years when he was minister of Foreign Relations.

I next visited the three principal Caribbean Representatives: Oliver Jackman of Barbados, Alfred Rattray of Jamaica, and Victor McIntyre of Trinidad and Tobago. All three had been leaders in the independence movements in their countries and were staunch supporters of open democratic political systems. They wasted little time on niceties. They came right out and addressed the issues and wondered why it took so much time and effort to get their Latin American colleagues to get to the point. They bridled at the arcane rules used at the OAS. They complained of U.S. positions in the OAS on trade and development but, on civil rights and political matters, they were aligned with us. I remember Oliver Jackman pointedly asking me if I had some special reason for my visit, and his smiling when I said that I just wanted to get to know the people with whom I would be working.

Over the next several weeks, I called on all the other delegations. Most of the discussions were pleasantries. Some, like the Bolivian, Guatemalan, Honduran, Paraguayan, Salvadoran, and Uruguayan, were with people with whom I had worked earlier.

When I completed my rounds, I found a deep division on democratic institutions and human rights and a common concern in all the Latin American and Caribbean countries about the role the U.S. saw itself playing in the OAS and its disposition for dealing with development and trade issues in the inter-American body. Most ambassadors raised specific questions about the U.S. agenda for the IA/ECOSOC and CIECC, whose programs were esteemed in their countries and generated a steady flow of requests for further aid from senior officials in their respective home countries.

The other topic raised in each interview related to the U.S. pressure to reduce its quota payments to the organization and the political implications of requesting the change in the formula agreed upon in Bogota in 1948. I was asked by almost all the ambassadors about the real objective of the U.S. in seeking to reduce its quota from two-thirds to "less than 50 percent." They did not buy the U.S. argument that no one member state should pay more than 50 percent of the budget of any international organization. The U.S. pointed out that in the United Nations, its quota had been cut from one-third to one-quarter in the early 1960s with the admission of West Germany and Japan. They answered that the situation at the

OAS was far different from that in the U.N. At the OAS, a reduction in the U.S. quota would require increasing contributions from the existing member states. As the Brazilian and Peruvian representatives made very clear in my initial visits, their governments were not prepared to increase their percentages of the OAS budget at all, and were opposed to the U.S. proposal since it required increasing the quota payments by the existing member states.

I reported the gist of my discussions to Pete Vaky and Luigi Einaudi. They appreciated the concern expressed and urged Ambassador McGee and me to be as open and constructive as possible, but offered no assurances that priority issues, including those related to development, would be handled multilaterally instead of bilaterally. They instructed us to keep the lines of communication open to all OAS member states, but to channel our efforts to support the non-military governments.

On the quota question, they authorized me to talk with NSC liaison officer to the bureau, Robert Pastor, about the issue, while Vaky and Einaudi took the matter up with the Seventh Floor. The response from the NSC and Seventh Floor was negative. We were authorized to soft pedal the subject, but our position was unchanged: Ambassador McGee and I need not press for a reduction in the U.S. quota; however, if the matter was raised by any OAS member state, the U.S. representative was to respond that our position was unchanged.

Working in the OAS

The Permanent Council resumed its work on the fourth Wednesday of January 1978. It met in the Council chamber on the first floor of the OAS building. It was convened to meet twice a month on Wednesdays, except during its summer and winter recesses and during the annual General Assembly, usually scheduled for June. Much of the council's work was to prepare the agenda and working papers for the General Assembly.

The Council was chaired by a representative of a member state and the occupant rotated quarterly in alphabetical order. The secretary of the council, the OAS assistant secretary general, advised him on agenda items, rules of procedure, and OAS precedents. The

OAS secretary general had the right to participate in the deliberations, but no vote.

The chair, the secretary general, the assistant secretary general and their advisers were seated on a dais overlooking a long semicircular table for the country delegations, arranged in alphabetic order by name of the country in Spanish. Hence the U.S. was *Estados Unidos de América,* seated between El Salvador and Grenada.

The agenda for bimonthly meetings was prepared by the assistant secretary general and the conference staff in strict accordance with rules on how items could be brought to the floor of the Permanent Council. Many items were brought to the council by (1) one of its standing committees, e.g. the Political and Juridical Committee or the Finance Committee, (2) a motion from member states, or (3) a proposal from IA/ECOSOC, CIECC, the Commission on Human Rights, or the Inter-American Commission of Women. The secretary general could also introduce an agenda item, but he usually consulted widely with the key delegations before doing so because of the reluctance by most Latin delegations to allowing the secretary general latitude to act without their prior consent. As I pointed out, the charter had created a weak general secretary and powerful Permanent Council, and the Latin delegations, especially of the larger countries, intended to keep that way.

Meetings were conducted in the four official languages of the OAS: English, French, Portuguese, and Spanish. The interpreters were key players in the discussions, and they prepared for each meeting by studying the agenda items and background papers in all four languages. Usually they were right on target, but occasionally they missed the point and provoked misunderstandings and vehement debates among the delegates. For that reason, while Ambassador McGee listened in English, I had on the Spanish or Portuguese channel. So, when the ambassador would turn to me and say, "What did that mean?" or, "The U.S. can't accept that statement," we could compare our understanding of what was said and call on the speaker to verify what he said or meant. On those occasions when the interpreters had in fact got the speaker's point right and the speaker's intention was considered a slur on the policy of a member state or the attitude or position of another delegation, the debate could become acerbic, even bloody, but most problems came from a faulty interpretation.

For each agenda item, the secretariat prepared a working paper. Delays in delivery of agendas and papers could become a *cause célèbre*. The secretariat was mandated to deliver them on the Thursday or Friday before the next Council session. Delays in delivery could generate heated discussions, even motions of reprimand. Sometimes, the problem had been with a delegation that wanted to keep the agenda item from being discussed, and it played the offended party while the secretariat squirmed. I noticed that the secretariat always knew how to get appropriate payback for having been made to squirm.

The U.S. delegation prepared position papers on each agenda item and required policy clearance on what we could say and how we should vote. Sometimes the issues had to be vetted by the secretary of state's office or the National Security Council or even the president. A briefing book was prepared with the background of the agenda items and the U.S. position. If we didn't receive our instructions in time, we would request a postponement because "there was insufficient time to obtain instructions from my government."

The rules of procedure were complicated and time consuming. Most of my colleagues in the State Department and AID thought them arcane. They wanted to get down to business on the issues. However, I had learned in my assignments in so many Latin American countries that to get something done, we gringos had to understand the rules of the game in each country. No two were alike. Political, social, and psychological factors were often more important than the dollars and cents. Each country had worked out its own formula for getting things done—often quite different from ours. The OAS was no different. We had to learn how to play in the arena before we could expect to have a real impact.

The Latin American and Caribbean delegations understood us better than we understood them. They had set up many of the rules to protect themselves from action by the United States. And I for one found it a challenge not only to use the forum for the promotion of inter-American understanding but also for advancing the U.S. agenda, especially promoting political democracy and protecting human rights.

Multilateral diplomacy required the U.S. Mission to build personal as well as official relationships with the key actors on the floor of the Permanent Council if we were to get the body to deal with key issues on our agenda. Prior consultation with the other member states was required to move an initiative forward, and I found that, if the U.S. had not carefully briefed other countries of the importance we attributed to a proposed resolution or other action, it would fade into the woodwork, just as happened often in our bilateral dealings.

One of my immediate objectives, and fortunately my colleagues in the U.S. Mission were similarly inclined, was to understand the power balance in the Permanent Council, the ground rules, and ways of getting things done. It was not a static game. The personalities changed. None of the senior U.S. staff was on assignment for more than three years; most of my Latin American and Caribbean colleagues were also subject to rotation. Each had his or her career interests beyond a tour at the OAS, and no one was prepared to rock the boat very much unless the conditions were advantageous to her/his country and to her/him.

One of the practices that the U.S. Mission followed was to have members of our delegation arrive on the floor early and chat with delegates as they arrived. By the time Ambassador McGee and I arrived, our colleagues already had a feel for the mood of the meeting and this allowed us to consider the need for a change in position. Whenever Ambassador McGee or I believed the matter of significant importance, we would ask to table the item until the next meeting "since our government was still studying the issue." On some matters after evaluating the reports on issues likely to arise, we would consult with other delegations about alternative wording of a proposed resolution before the agenda item was presented.

This flow of work in the OAS was the essence of multilateral diplomacy. It gave the member states a place where they could meet regularly and discuss their concerns, needs, and aspirations, ameliorate tensions, and promote collective action to erase a cause of intergovernmental confrontation. The fact that the U.S. was the economic and political superpower and the other members relatively weak made the OAS unlike any other body in the world, and offered the U.S. a unique opportunity to build a relative consensus and a sense of goodwill that enabled member states to look to the

OAS as the place in which they could talk out their problems without fear of reprisal.

During Council meetings, there were constant consultations and negotiations among the delegations. Almost all of the Latin American representatives looked to the delegation of Mexico for advice and counsel. They would consult Maestro Rafael de la Colina, and seldom proceeded with a proposal that he could not support. On legal issues, the wording of proposals would be consulted informally with Galo Leoro, the representative from Ecuador and long-time chair of the Juridical and Political Committee. The Brazilians were consulted on economic and budgetary questions, but essentially kept their own counsel. The Brazilian ambassador seldom left his chair to talk to other delegations, but his very competent advisers frequently consulted with other South American delegations and us. The Latin American non-military countries looked primarily to the Venezuelan delegation for leadership. The Chilean and Peruvian representatives, while representing military governments, regularly talked with representatives from the democratic bloc, especially Venezuela, Colombia, and Costa Rica. The Caribbean countries tended to keep to themselves. Occupying the chair next to the U.S. was Grenada, and almost never did he consult with his Caribbean colleagues on the floor of the OAS. If the Caribbean states coordinated positions, they did it before they arrived. Throughout the meetings, the U.S. would be consulted informally about our attitude toward a proposed change in a draft resolution or our willingness to join a drafting committee to overcome some problem in the draft under consideration.

Housekeeping at the OAS

The quota issue cast a shadow over the organization and was deemed a major political issue by the other member states linked to U.S. interest in sustaining a multilateral dialogue in the region. Some in the U.S. government thought this was simply a bookkeeping matter. In 1977, the U.S. still accounted for about 85 percent of GDP of the hemisphere and our population, well over 50 percent. As Brazilian Representative Silveira asked the ambassador and me at a session of the Permanent Council General Committee, "How can the U.S. be serious about wanting to work with Latin America and the Caribbean if the primary issue you are pushing is a reduction of your quota?"

Early on, Ambassador McGee became convinced that settling the quota question was critical to promoting a meaningful dialogue on the future direction of inter-American cooperation and in undertaking reforms to the structure and functions of the OAS.

With Pete Vaky's concurrence, we approached Ambassador Nander Pitty, then chair of the OAS Finance Committee, with a formula to reduce the U.S. quota symbolically from 66 percent to 60–61 percent. Ambassador Pitty had received instructions from Panama to treat me as "a friend" and agreed to work with us on the formula. He then discussed it informally with the Argentines, Brazilians, Colombians, Mexicans, and Venezuelans. None of them was enthusiastic about proposing to their governments even a small increase in their own quotas, but agreed to support such an initiative if the United States "showed flexibility." Ambassador McGee and I talked informally with several other delegations and prepared a policy paper for review at the State Department and NSC. We got clearance to make an offer of flexibility at the June General Assembly in Washington, D.C., and we wrote language in Secretary of State Cyrus Vance's address that would open the way for the General Assembly to authorize the Finance Committee to consider a new schedule of quotas based on a "flexible formula."

At the last minute, the secretary consulted an advisor, not Assistant Secretary Vaky or Ambassador McGee, on the propriety of his discussing budgetary matters in his address. He found that the quota was a matter of "housekeeping" that detracted from his central message on support for democratic institutions and human rights. Without advising Assistant Secretary Vaky or Ambassador McGee, he cut the paragraph from his statement. Hence, he left the impression with Ambassador Pitty that U.S. policy did not support the "flexible formula." As a result, Ambassador Pitty and the other countries took the matter off the table, and the proposal was not raised at the General Assembly. An opportunity to eliminate a major cause of friction had been lost because the impact of "housekeeping" on broader issues of policy was not appreciated.

The failure to resolve the "housekeeping" issue left the impression that the U.S. had lost interest in the OAS. Coupled with strong support for the Inter-American Development Bank (IDB) and declining participation in the OAS development councils, the question that Ambassador McGee, all of our staff, and I received at almost every OAS session was, "What does the U.S. plan to deal with in the OAS?"

Shortly after the General Assembly, the Permanent Council met to organize its work for the next fiscal year. Ambassador Pitty approached the U.S. delegation and proposed that I be nominated to be chair of the OAS Finance Committee. He reasoned that the quota issue remained unresolved and that, with the U.S. as the committee chair, the committee could work out a formula that could be considered at the next General Assembly in La Paz, Bolivia. After consulting Assistant Secretary Vaky, State Policy Planning, and Bob Pastor at the NSC, Ambassador McGee told Ambassador Pitty that the U.S. would be a candidate for the post. Pitti consulted the Mexican and Brazilian delegations, and they agreed to support the proposal and to name senior members of their delegations to serve as the other two officers of the Finance Committee. Vaky urged me to work out a formula to put the quota issue behind us.

Shortly after I was elected, I received a call from the State Department budget office that succinctly advised me that, despite inflationary pressures, the department was not prepared to accept even a one-dollar increase in the request for funds for the OAS in the next fiscal year. They expected me, as chair of the OAS Finance Committee, to deliver a budget at the same or a lower level than in the current fiscal year.

The OAS budget presentation was a sound, solidly justified request that called for an almost 10 percent increase in expenditures, and proposed integrating the OAS personnel and retirement systems into those of the United Nations—a proposal presented by the U.S. government some years earlier but resisted by most Latin American delegations because of the costs involved. I took the draft budget to the budget specialists at the State Department for instructions. They conducted a summary review in a quarter of an hour, said that it looked to be sound and told me that no matter how good the budget presentation, their instructions from the White House Office of Management and Budget (OMB) were "not one additional cent for any international organization in the next fiscal year."

When I convened the Finance Committee, the Peruvian delegate said that his government was facing a severe budgetary crisis
and would not be able to agree to any increase in the OAS budget
over the current fiscal year. That led two or three other delegations
to make similar statements and a decision to hold the OAS budget
for the next fiscal year to the same level as the current year and table
consideration of the OAS joining the UN personnel and retirement
program. OAS Assistant Secretary for Management Ron Scheman
said that, given inflation and increases in some fixed costs, it was
not possible to avoid an increase. That led to a decision by the committee to conduct a line-by-line review of the proposed budget.

That evening Ele and I had dinner with Mexican vice chair of
the committee, Marcelo Vargas, and his wife. We agreed that the
measures taken that afternoon had been draconian. Then Marcelo
quietly told me said that his mission had been authorized to accept
the Scheman proposal as presented, as had the Brazilians and Colombians, provided the U.S. would take the lead. He intimated that
if the U.S. delegation had been more flexible, the three delegations
would have moved to approve the Scheman's draft with some minor changes. I did not tell him that my instructions coincided with
those of the Peruvian delegation but I sensed that he suspected.

The Budget Committee met all through the brutally hot summer
of 1978, even when the air conditioning broke down. We reviewed
each and every position and expenditure, made cuts in every unit
of the secretariat, denied a cost-of-living increase, and postponed
essential repairs whose costs escalated over the years. I was very
concerned and sought to have my instructions changed—but without success. After eight weeks, the committee agreed to a budget
that was a few thousand dollars above the current fiscal year. The
State Department budget specialists were not pleased with the result because of the slight increase. I was not happy when I learned
that, under pressure from the secretary of state's office, the guidelines for the UN and the UN agencies had been changed to permit
U.S. support of a budgetary increase equivalent to the rate of inflation along with the cost of living adjustments for the staff. I am
certain that my colleagues in the other delegations to the OAS were
similarly informed—and what a policy message this "bookkeeping" matter sent to the other OAS member states!

After the budget was approved, the committee focused on pressuring countries to pay up their arrearages. The OAS reported that ten countries were in arrears, including the United States. The U.S. withheld 15 percent of each annual quota as leverage on member states to resolve the quota issue. So, I worked with representatives from five countries—Argentina, Brazil, Colombia, Mexico, and Venezuela—on a proposal to reduce the U.S. quota to 61 percent. We worked up a draft, but none of the countries would allow me to surface it without some high-level indication from the U.S. that it was prepared to be flexible. Try as we might, neither Pete Vaky nor Ambassador McGee could get any high-level support. The quota issue was tied up with other budgetary issues between OMB and Congress. Secretary of State Vance once again called it a "housekeeping" matter and refused to become involved. In 1979 at the General Assembly in La Paz, when my mandate as Finance Committee chair ended, the quota issue remained with us. The OAS budget had been substantially weakened. It was clear that the "housekeeping" issue had delivered a policy message on the importance the U.S. attributed to the multilateral forum it had created in the Western Hemisphere.

Our Life in Washington

The winter of 1978 was very difficult for Ele. After Guatemala and Panama, the winter seemed almost unbearable. She seemed to catch cold whenever she went out. Since her mother and grandmother had both died after breaking a hip, she was afraid of slipping on icy streets. With her health problems, she decided not to drive for fear that she might lose control of the car. I am such a terrible driver that we decided to live without a vehicle. We decided to rely on public transportation and cab services. It was not until Dr. Latimer finally eased her pains that her spirit revived.

Those early months of 1978 were also filled with concern and uneasiness about our finances. Inflation was eating away at our meager savings, and entertaining expenses in Guatemala and Panama had demanded money out of our reserve. My salary had been frozen for the past several years. I was one of the "asterisk" officers who couldn't be paid more than a member of Congress, that is, my salary would be shown as X amount with an asterisk—and the asterisk would show that, based on the cost of living index, the salary that should have been paid was Y amount. All Ele could see was money flowing out and, being frugal by nature, she reacted negatively to our incurring new expenses.

As the winter was ending and the exercises prescribed by Dr. Latimer were taking effect, Ele began to liven up. We had been able to live within her budget, the houses in Tulare were finally rented, and the two farms were showing a small profit. She began to venture out. She made the rounds of the brokerage offices and began looking for a new broker since her mentor, Jim Staggs, had dropped from sight. One morning, just by chance, she went into the office of Bache & Company on Connecticut Avenue and was introduced to a young broker, Rob Wright; they gelled and Rob has been our principal broker for nearly fifty years. She lunched with her old colleagues at the Department of Labor; if they had invited her to rejoin them, I would have encouraged her to accept.

Then, in early April, almost on a whim, she went to a meeting of the American Association of Foreign Service Wives (AAFSW) and was inspired by the work plan laid out by its dynamic president, Lesley Dorman. Ele's years overseas had reaffirmed her belief that the prevailing State Department rules on spouses and families needed to be overhauled. She was a victim of the State Department's refusal to allow spouses and families to attend briefings on the next post of assignment, and had seen the effects of the personnel system's lack of attention to the special needs of spouses and children. And, she believed that effective overseas assignments demanded the enthusiastic support of spouses and families. Ele used to say, "The department got two bodies and two brains for the price of one."

At that AAFSW meeting, Lesley Dorman laid out a plan to provide spouses with a manual to help them understand foreign service rules and regulations and provide them information on how to deal with personal, financial, and medical problems as foreign service spouses. She also called on the State Department to set up an office to service family needs. The following day, Ele called Lesley and volunteered to join the group working on the manual. She told me that this AAFSW project was where her skills and experience could best be used and we could tighten our belts if necessary to live within the budget.

She came to life. Every evening for the following months, she told me about her work with and admiration for the extraordinary group of foreign service wives who had lived the issues they were seeking to set right. The project was called "What Do I Do Now?" It explained the rules and regulations of the State Department that governed their lives in the service and provided advice about how to deal with problems they might face at post, or if they were widowed or divorced, or had financial and legal concerns. Ele took on the financial issues, including those emanating from U.S. and foreign service regulations as well as managing family investments. She researched the regulations, analyzed the economic challenges facing foreign service wives, and then made a detailed study of various investment opportunities. She talked to stockbrokers, Treasury officials, bank executives, insurance agents, and estate planners. She sat in on a course by Julia Montgomery Walsh and other noted Washington financial managers. She prepared notebooks full of information and drafted succinct summaries for review by her colleagues. I can remember no time in our married life when Ele felt more fulfilled and happy.

Those ladies did an extraordinary job. The publication they produced not only provided foreign service spouses with essential information to cope with their assignments but enhanced their status. It also led to the establishment of the Family Liaison Office to service families and to integrate them into the mainstream of the Foreign Service.

AAFSW became one of the passions of Ele's life. After the publication was completed, she continued to work with the association. She applied for a job in the Liaison Office, but was not selected. I urged her to run for one of the offices of the AAFSW, but she felt that she could better serve by working on special projects, like the preparation of a series of legislative reforms to protect the rights and interests of widows and divorced wives.

Lesley Dorman's next challenge was to enhance the legal rights of foreign service spouses. The State Department traditionally saw the role of the spouse to be support of their FSO husbands, be a gracious hostess, and "help" the ambassador's wife on her social and charitable projects. It discouraged wives from working while assigned abroad, and many foreign countries prohibited the employment of FSO wives in their public and private sectors. So, it was almost impossible to develop a work record while overseas that would qualify them for future job opportunities when on stateside assignments. In addition, many families often found it difficult to save or invest much money while abroad.

The impact of those realities was especially difficult for divorced wives. Ele had seen several tragic cases where wives had helped their husband's career, some rising to the level of ambassador, only to be divorced when the husband's fancy turned. Some of those former wives became destitute. Ele had deep concerns about the equity of the foreign service rules that terminated pension and health benefits to ex-spouses on divorce since they left too many in dire circumstances. A divorced wife, cut off from pension and health benefits, only received the alimony specified in the court settlement, and that alimony ceased on the death of the former spouse. Ele joined the working group that was preparing a legislative package for protection for widows and divorced wives. Their proposal included a provision that after ten years of marriage, a divorced wife would be entitled to a percentage of her former husband's pension and to continued health benefits in addition to the alimony she was awarded by the court on divorce.

Once the proposal was in draft, Ele and I introduced it informally to Congressmen Dante Fascell (then chair of the House Foreign Affairs Committee) and Claude Pepper (chair of the House Committee on the Aging). Shortly thereafter the AAFSW leadership met with the congressmen, who agreed to sponsor the enabling legislation in spite of the opposition of State. The legislation was passed as part of the State Department's appropriations bill. Many of my colleagues did not like it then, and some still have harsh words for it and the Tragens' association with it.

Once the legislation was passed, Ele and her colleagues at AAFSW worked with a group of Air Force officers who spearheaded the inclusion of similar provisions in the Defense Department appropriations bill, and then a group of civil service workers who had the provisions made part of the civil service body of regulations.

For nearly twenty years, until her health deteriorated in the early 1990s, Ele wrote a column for the monthly AAFSW Bulletin on "What Do I Do Now?"—advising foreign service spouses on investment strategies, dealings with stockbrokers and lawyers, preparing family budgets, and other subjects relevant to household financial and economic issues. For many years when I would visit an embassy, one of the wives would ask me, "Are you related to Ele Tragen?"

In 1991, First Lady Barbara Bush and the wife of Secretary of State Susan Baker hosted a tea in honor of those AAFSW ladies who in the late 1970s prepared "What Do I Do Now?" and the legislative package. I am so pleased that the work was recognized at the highest level of our government and that Ele was able to attend.

The OAS Agenda

The work at the OAS maintained its traditional slow pace as the member states sought some direction from the U.S. on its intentions and objectives. I worked with Luigi Einaudi on policy papers to allow us to define new U.S. positions, starting with the quota issue. We could not get authorization to change positions on critical issues and continued to vote no on economic and development proposals that required additional commitments by the United States. The mission could not provide that sense of direction because it could not get authorization to take positions on critical issues. I recall one issue on which I (not the ambassador) was authorized to abstain, rather than voting no, with the comment that U.S. was committed to shared leadership in the OAS, and that the day of hegemony by any member state was over.

When we expressed concern about the OAS financial situation, the question of arrearages would inevitably arise, and we were the largest debtor. Countries like Peru would respond that they supported the OAS and would pay their arrearages as soon as the U.S. paid up. And, the OAS finances could not be separated from the increasingly severe economic contraction occurring throughout the region at the end of the Vietnam War due in large measure to declining U.S. purchases of Latin American raw materials.

On one issue, human rights, we were authorized to aggressively call for OAS action. The membership was almost evenly divided between those counties with military dictatorships and those with elected civilian administrations. The U.S. supported the Charter provisions that committed the member states to the defense of human rights, and to support action against military dictatorships on all cases of abuse brought up in the Permanent Council. When we discussed measures to promote human rights through the OAS Human Rights Commission, we ran into the dilemma that, while we were making speeches of support, we had not ratified the treaty establishing the OAS Court of Human Rights.

As strongly as I supported our position on human rights, I was concerned that we did not have a new "overarching" strategy, in Pete Vaky's words, to replace the AFP. How could the U.S. call on the other member states to take the measures on human rights and other issues when their perception was that the U.S. had little interest in Latin America and even less in the workings of the OAS?

Ambassador McGee tried to open a dialogue with officials at the White House on U.S. positions at the OAS by accepting assignments to speak around the country in support of the Carter-Torrijos Panama Canal Treaty and the importance to the U.S. of inter-American cooperation in the Cold War. He also lobbied on the Hill to convince former colleagues to vote for ratification of the Canal Treaty. He encouraged the press to cover his statements in the Permanent Council in which he spoke of its historic role in pressing the U.S. to negotiate and sign the treaty.

As part of his effort to rally White House interest in the region, Ambassador McGee in 1977 won Vaky's approval to invite senior White House officials to meet with the Latin American and Caribbean ambassadors. In May, on the eve of the 1977 General Assembly, he invited President Carter to lunch at the OAS with the representatives of the member states. The president's calendar was already booked, and his aides suggested that National Security Adviser Zbigniew Brzezinski would be an appropriate substitute. Vaky and McGee then worked on the national security adviser, including a call from Secretary of State Cyrus Vance, to convince him to agree. They were warned that he had little interest in Western Hemisphere affairs, but he agreed. Secretary General Alejandro

Orfila arranged an elegant table and a menu with specialties that Brzezinski was known to enjoy at lunch. Vaky, McGee, and I met with the several key delegations on the topics to be raised in friendly discussion after lunch.

About noon, on schedule, Brzezinski arrived in an official car from the White House and was met at the marble entrance by the chair of the Permanent Council, the secretary general of the OAS, Assistant Secretary Vaky, and Ambassador McGee. They escorted him to the Hall of the Americas where the assembled representatives were introduced to him. Lunch went well, with polite conversation. Then at one o'clock, when the chair of the council planned to open the dialogue, Brzezinski announced that he had an emergency that required him to leave. He said goodbye from his seat at the table. The entire assemblage accompanied him to the main entrance and watched him leisurely walk up, in the bright sunshine, the five blocks from Constitution Avenue to Pennsylvania Avenue and his office. I could feel the blood draining from the inter-American arena.

A Brazilian colleague commented a few days later that the image of Brzezinski walking up the street, away from the OAS, made it clear to his government that the U.S. had lost interest not only in the OAS but also in multilateral inter-American relations in general.

McGee made one more effort to awaken high-level support at the White House. Working with Carmen Votaw, the U.S. representative to the Inter-American Commission of Women, First Lady Rosalyn Carter was invited to attend the Commission's 1978 inaugural session. Mrs. Carter made room on her tight schedule with arrival at 11:00 a.m. and departure at the end of program by 11:30 so she could attend a previously scheduled luncheon. Mrs. Carter arrived on time, and gave a short address on inter-American cooperation and support for the commission. The Bolivian president of the commission, Gabriela Touchard, then delivered a thirty-minute tirade, accusing the United States of indifference toward the region. The First Lady was late for her luncheon and turned down any further invitations to meet with groups at the OAS. After these two incidents, Ambassador McGee was unable to interest anyone in the White House in attending OAS meetings.

The incident was a tragedy because Mrs. Carter was interested in Latin American development and made several trips to the region, often accompanied by Peter Bell of the Inter-American Foundation. On occasions when Ele and I had been invited to the White House, Mrs. Carter talked to us about developments in the region, especially about schools and grassroots problems. When the Costa Rican youth symphony gave a concert on the Ellipse, Ele and I were talking to one of the young artists when the First Lady came by and I served as her interpreter. Her questions about life in Costa Rica reflected considerable knowledge of and interest in the region.

The 1978 OAS General Assembly was held in Washington. Secretary of State Vance appeared only once to welcome the delegates and deliver the U.S. position paper from which he deleted the quota proposal. Vaky and McGee occupied the U.S. chair except for one session, which Deputy Secretary Warren Christopher attended. The principal issue was a resolution in support of democratic political institutions and protection of human rights, which was drafted jointly by Colombia, Costa Rica, and the United States. The resolution was directed at the Dirty War in Argentina, torture while interrogating political prisoners in Brazil, and the repression in Chile. To pass the resolution we needed seventeen votes.

When introduced at the General Assembly, draft resolutions were sent to a working group. Mark Dion and I were the principal U.S. negotiators. The representatives of the English-speaking Caribbean states announced their support for the draft as presented. The key countries we needed to win over were Mexico and Venezuela. Obviously, the military dictatorships and authoritarian governments tried to bottle it up. Venezuela, then the most vocal opponent of military governments, wanted stronger language and political/economic sanctions. Mexico said that the draft as presented represented "intervention in the internal affairs of member states," and called for weaker, less specific language. With great care, we found language that Mexico and Venezuela could support. When the draft resolution was voted out of committee, we were not sure that it would pass when brought to the floor. Our head count was a tie. Then, Vaky put pressure on a couple of countries, especially Haiti—the Baby Doc dictatorship. The resolution passed by one or two votes, Haiti's vote being critical. To this day, I don't know what was promised to Baby Doc for his vote.

In the year between the eighth and ninth General Assemblies,

Costa Rica nominated the distinguished U.S. human rights expert, Judge Thomas Buergenthal, to be a judge of the Inter-American Court of Human Rights even though the U.S. had not ratified the protocol that created the court. For the U.S., two clauses stood in the way of our ratification: one that outlawed the death penalty, and the other, the use of the words "right to life." Since the United States was not a party to the protocol, getting votes for Buergenthal was difficult in spite of his qualifications. Some countries, especially from the English-speaking Caribbean, argued that no U.S. citizen should be considered for appointment to the court until the United States ratified. Working with Costa Rican Ambassador Echeverría, we finally rounded up the votes, more in support of Costa Rica than the United States.

At the closing session of the eighth General Assembly, Bolivia had offered to be the site of the ninth Assembly. Bolivia was a military dictatorship that had cooperated with Chile's Pinochet, Argentina's Varela, and Brazil's Geisel in Operation Condor, which had been responsible for assassinating opposition figures from various South American countries on the streets of, *inter alia*, Paris, Buenos Aires, and Washington. OAS protocol required that the "gracious invitation" be accepted by acclamation, sometimes with the expectation that circumstances would force a country to withdraw before the assembly was held. Most of the democratic countries, especially the English-speaking Caribbean countries and the U.S., were lukewarm to Bolivia's offer, but it was accepted. Few delegations believed the assembly would be held there.

In the year between those two General Assemblies, Ambassador McGee made a major effort to broaden U.S. relations with the delegations and improve the mood in the council. When his counterparts from military governments approached him about measures their governments might take to improve relations with the U.S., especially on human rights, he welcomed them to his office. He and I were visited by generals from Uruguay, El Salvador, and Peru to see whether, through the multilateral channel, they could begin to improve their relations with the United States. The generals outlined measures their governments were willing to take under the OAS Charter. The State Department was cool to those approaches and we were never able to set up even informal meetings between visiting generals and senior human rights officials. When the Uruguayan representative to the OAS and senior generals of the Uruguayan junta laid out for us in an hour-long presentation their fellow officers' desire to reestablish civilian rule, Ambassador McGee called senior State Department officials to join us and they declined. I shall never forget the sadness and dismay on McGee's face. In the Senate, he had been well known for bringing senators together and brokering deals. He couldn't understand why no one wanted, at least, to talk.

Social Dimensions of the Job

As in each of our earlier assignments, the work at the mission became an almost seven-day-a-week job. There were many official functions, including official visits of Latin American presidents and Caribbean prime ministers to Washington, commemorative occasions at the OAS, member states' national days, and receptions hosted by the fifteen or so observer states to the OAS. In addition, we were frequently invited to cocktail parties and dinners at the residence of representatives of other delegations. Sometimes I went alone because Ele was just not up to going out—and sometimes we didn't get to the event because taxis didn't show up.

Those two and half years saw us involved in some memorable events. The charismatic smile and warm greeting of John Paul II are etched in my memory. The solemn grandeur of the ceremony of the Unknown Soldier at the Arlington National Cemetery almost moved us to tears. The OAS Columbus Day memorial celebration at which the Caribbean speakers lambasted Columbus for bringing smallpox and slavery to the New World gave new meaning to the Age of Discovery. The Central American National Day, after the agreement to end the El Salvador-Honduras Soccer War, awakened new hopes. The formal opening of the OAS General Assembly in the presence of the chief executive of the host country always gave me a special thrill—and it was at the General Assembly in 1978 that I had my first opportunity to meet President Carter.

Ele and I received two invitations to the White House. The first was in the fall of 1978 for the concert of the Costa Rican Youth Symphony and the second in 1979 for an inter-American celebration.

These two events were both quite informal without receiving lines and the president and First Lady just mingled among us. The president walked by once or twice, but Mrs. Carter stopped to chat. I believe that, with her strong role in the executive mansion, the OAS could have gained a powerful ally if her invitation to the Inter-American Commission for Women had not turned out so unfortunately.

In the summer of 1978, the U.S. became chair of the Permanent Council. Ambassador McGee and his family left in July for six weeks at his vacation home in the Grand Tetons and I subbed for him. The chair of the Council was assigned a Lincoln limousine and, while I subbed for him, the limo took us to all the events that summer that required the presence of the chair of the Council. Those six weeks almost spoiled us as we were whisked from event to event, not worrying about taxis or parking spaces. But when Ambassador McGee returned we quickly became re-accustomed to the realities of life.

One of the duties of the deputy U.S. representative to the OAS was to serve as the U.S. representative on the board of the Gorgas Memorial Hospital in the Panama Canal Zone. The board meetings were held at the Pan American Health Organization, for which I had worked as personnel officer in the early 1950s when it was still called the Pan American Sanitary Bureau. The hospital had been founded during the building of the Panama Canal to treat cases of yellow fever. It had become a hemispheric medical research center on tropical diseases providing training for doctors, nurses, and techniciansworldwide. The hospital played an important role in Ele's and my life and to serve on its board was very special. I attended several meetings of the board and participated in the initial discussions about its future status once the Canal Zone reverted to Panama. The Republic of Panama held the hospital in high repute and was as eager as its board members to see it continue.

In early 1978, I was surprised to find myself named as one of the first recipients of the AID lifetime honor award for my work in development. At a ceremony at the State Department, AID Administrator Gilligan honored three of us. Ele joined me at the ceremony and we were deeply appreciative of the recognition. As I said then in accepting the award, I could not have done my job without the advice and support of my wife. Receiving the award seemed to be additional vindication after our encounter with columnist Jack Anderson.

Time Away from the Job

After Ele's health began to improve and with her involvement in AAFSW activities, we had one of our long family talks. Ele had become aware of my growing disillusionment with U.S. government policies on Latin America and the Caribbean, and urged me not to become bitter. She suggested that I take more time enjoying the rich cultural environment of Washington. She also proposed that we start thinking about what we wanted to do with the rest of our lives. We blocked out time for ourselves and made Sunday our special day together as we had in Bolivia, doing things we wanted to do—completely separate from the State Department and the OAS. Sundays we frequently went to the National Cathedral for 11:00 a.m. services and then spent a quiet day with friends or went down to the Smithsonian.

We spent many a weekend with Dorothy and Chet Guthrie until they retired to Sebastopol, California. They became like family and we talked out many of our concerns with them; we spent Thanksgivings, Christmases, and trips to Cap'n John's on the Eastern Shore of Maryland for oysters and crabs together. We also relaxed many an evening over dinner and bridge with Faye and Frank Sherry and joined them at the Corcoran and other prime galleries at which Faye's paintings were on exhibit. Elizabeth and Harold Walker, then retired, called often to check on us and periodically drove us to their home in Northern Virginia for dinner and a lively discussion of politics and developments in the labor movement. Frances Humphrey Howard had sold her home in Virginia and moved to a nearby apartment, and we had several family dinners with her and daughter Anne. Fran even tried to lift my spirits when I was particularly low about the absence of high-level interest in the hemisphere. She set up a dinner at the Democratic National Club for Ele and me to meet Deputy Secretary Warren Christopher and his wife. That Saturday night, I ordered a taxi half an hour before the time set for dinner. The cab never arrived. After calling unsuccessfully for help from friends who lived nearby, I had to cancel. I often wondered what might have happened if the cab had arrived.

Twice in 1977, Fran took us to Bethesda Navy Hospital to visit her brother, Hubert Humphrey, where he was being treated for cancer. His wit and wisdom were a treat and he never seemed to tire of talking about world affairs. He asked penetrating questions about the OAS and Latin America, and often gave me details about the genesis of some policy or another. He took us on walks to see other patients whose spirits he tried to uplift. Fran and her brother had the same infectious positive spirit.

Ele attended annual stockholder meetings of companies headquartered in Washington and once or twice to ones in Baltimore and Boston. At the JW Marriott annual meeting in 1978, she made a suggestion from the floor that caught the attention of the corporation leaders. Ele pointed to the support by the shareholders of the corporation's transition from its Hot Shoppe origins to a hotel company and proposed that the company invite shareholders to submit suggestions that they thought would add to its future growth, greater efficiency, and profitability. Bill Marriott, who was conducting the meeting, asked her to send him a copy of her suggestion in writing. In the coffee session following the meeting, Alice Marriott, the matriarch of the clan, sought Ele out and told her how much she supported her idea. Ele sent the suggestion to Bill Marriott and the following year she was named "Shareholder of the Year" and was given five shares of stock. The picture of that presentation sits in my living room to this day.

Ele balanced her life between official requirements and taking care of the Tragen family finances. She made her annual farm trips in 1978 and 1979, spending six weeks each year in South Dakota and California. She worked closely with the farm tenants on projects to increase production and profitability. In 1978, after substantially increasing her income from both farms, she advised her tenants that she was curtailing many of her managerial responsibilities because of continuing medical problems.

When in Washington, she went once or twice a week to brokerage houses to get the latest information about stock trends. She used to tell me at night that she was constantly looking for material to use in her AAFSW columns while at the same time, trying to make us some money. Ele became known in our OAS official circle as the financial whiz. At dinner parties with colleagues in other missions evening conversation often revolved around investment opportunities. Economic conditions throughout the hemisphere were difficult and most of our colleagues peppered her with questions about their family's finances. Few of the wives were concerned with such matters, which often meant that Ele was talking with my counterparts while I made soft talk with the wives. It worked out very well because Ele helped me build the personal relationships that are so crucial to effective on-the-job relationships. Within the U.S. Mission, Ele was also well known for her financial acumen. She helped several of our colleagues in making decisions about personal investments.

When we came back to Washington in late 1977, Ele called Mildred Pepper, the wife of Representative Claude Pepper. The Peppers lived in the East Tower of our complex while we lived in the West. Mildred checked on Ele during that difficult winter when Ele was not well and took her to lunch at the House dining room and the Democratic Women's Club. When Mildred became seriously ill in 1978, Ele visited her several times until she passed away in 1979. The congressman invited us to her memorial service at the National Cathedral, at which we were presented to Speaker of the House Tip O'Neill, and Barbara Bush, two who eulogized Mildred that day.

In the 1980s we continued to see Congressman Pepper and he told me about the transformation of his congressional district with the advent of Cuban and other Latin American voters. I tried on several occasions to help him memorize some Spanish phrases for his talks to constituents. Oh, how he tried to work the Spanish words into his thick Alabama drawl, but he never quite got the hang of it! No matter how he said it, his constituents recognized the dedication and great heart of Claude Pepper and re-elected him until he died. Ele and I attended his funeral and told each other how fortunate we were to have spent time with him.

We felt the same way about Gale McGee. We had the privilege of being invited to holiday celebrations with Loraine, Gale, and their children. The McGees treated the office staff as friends and hosted office parties in which Loraine would participate, and those official parties were always warm, personal occasions. Ambassador

McGee missed his senate seat and frequently had lunch with old friends on the Hill. Those were usually one on one, and sometimes in response to the request of someone at the White House or the Seventh Floor for help in answering a senator's question or getting him to change a position. I came to appreciate his perks of being a member—or a former member—of that august body. Going up to Capitol Hill with former Senator McGee was a unique experience. All of the guards knew him and he got royal treatment—no lines, no waiting. When we had lunch once or twice in the senate dining room, most of the lunch was absorbed by greetings from old friends. He was "Gale" to everyone who came over to the table and discussions were always personal, with an occasional question about some legislation with which Gale had been involved.

The U.S. Mission had a very limited entertainment allowance. Almost all of it was for the use of the ambassador and he would periodically host a reception, usually on the eighth floor of the State Department in the ceremonial rooms. Once, he called an old friend and obtained use of the Octagon House for the U.S. official reception during a high-level OAS meeting. Ele and I had not been in the lovely old building but admired its unique shape and decoration. We were thrilled to have the McGees walk us through the Octagon and allow us to be co-hosts at its graceful entrance as the foreign ministers and Council representatives entered into this National Heritage site.

Those were among the best times of this assignment. McGee brought together a dedicated senior staff that enjoyed working together. The ambassador created an open and friendly environment. He set high standards for building good working relations with our counterparts. All of us were committed to a dialogue in the OAS on effective inter-American cooperation.

Unsettled Central America

In 1977, when I began my assignment, Ambassador McGee and Assistant Secretary Vaky asked me to pay special attention to Central America in view of the ten years I had served there and my working relationships with many of its leaders. I was appointed the U.S. representative on the Ad Hoc Committee on the El Salvador-

Honduras War. It had been set up in 1969 in the aftermath of the Soccer War to try to help the countries work out a peace treaty and revitalize the Central American Common Market. In fact, little or nothing had been done—as a Salvadoran leader said to me, we were just forgotten and left to fend for ourselves. The old axiom in the OAS was, if the U.S. loses interest, nothing will happen.

In the first few months of 1978, when I asked Central American delegates about the status of negotiations to end the war, I found that not much progress had been made toward a settlement. Both sides, with military officers as presidents, needed a formula to save face. Most responses would usually include a rebuke to the United States for not stepping in to "induce" the parties to settle the dispute even though we were extricating ourselves from Vietnam.

In mid-1978, I was called to a meeting of the Ad Hoc Committee to witness the signing of an agreement to end hostilities. Envoys from the two countries gathered in an OAS conference room to agree to terms similar to those that had been proposed by mediators for several years. What caused the change of heart in the barracks was unclear, but both countries were suffering economic turndowns and needed urgent help. El Salvador was on the verge of civil unrest, precipitated in part by the military stealing the 1972 election and in part by the economic and social unrest caused by tens of thousands of Salvadorans expelled by Honduras at the onset of the Soccer War. Unfortunately, ending the Soccer War had little effect on the situation in Central America. The deterioration had gone too far.

By then, Nicaragua moved onto the OAS center stage. Nicaragua was on the OAS docket because neighboring countries, especially Costa Rica, felt threatened by Somoza and feared aggression on their borders. Inside Nicaragua, the Sandinistas, with support from Cuba, were at war with Somoza. Somoza had little support in the Council. Even though he had been elected president, the democratic bloc of OAS members deemed the election fraudulent and called him a dictator. The military-led governments barely tolerated him. Most of the Latin and Caribbean representatives considered him to be a "U.S. puppet" and frequently intimated that it was up to the United States to end the fighting. However, in the U.S. government, Central America remained a low priority and merited little high-level time and attention.

At the OAS, Somoza was seen to be losing support at home with few friends among his neighbors. Many believed that he had undermined the settlement of the Soccer War to enhance his image as the strongman of the region. He flaunted his influence and his ties to U.S. military and political leaders, and his neighbors resented it. His opponents, the Sandinistas, took to the hills and withstood the attacks of the Somoza's elite National Guard (the Nicaragua Armed Forces). Coupled with the effects of the 1972 earthquake and the corruption of the regime, support for Somoza crumbled. The *coup de grâce* was the assassination of Dr. Pedro Joaquín Chamorro, the widely respected Conservative newspaper editor. Costa Rica, Mexico, Panama, Venezuela, and the Caribbean States were outspokenly anti-Somoza and said in the OAS Permanent Council that any change would be better than the existing regime. Some, like Colombia and Venezuela, were concerned about Castro's influence over the Sandinistas, and sought U.S. support for opposition leaders that had a more democratic political orientation.

However, attempts to mobilize collective action to remove Somoza under the OAS charter were opposed by Mexico, citing the non-intervention clause. Ambassadors from military-led governments told us that their governments were opposed to the Sandinistas because of their links to Castro and often noted that Castro had shot many career military officers after he took power. While they privately favored the early departure of Somoza, they staunchly supported Mexico to avoid setting a precedent for multilateral action that might later be used against them. They would urge Ambassador McGee and me, "Just you take care of it."

Then, in 1976, there were a series of incidents along the Nicaragua-Costa Rica border. Costa Rica called for a Meeting of Consultation of Foreign Ministers to consider Nicaraguan aggression against its northern border. At the meeting, the member states agreed to send a fact-finding mission to verify the charge. My predecessor Robert White was part of that three-country team. The Meeting of Consultation charged Nicaragua with hostile acts against Costa Rica and ordered it to cease and desist.

The OAS Human Rights Commission independently sent a team to investigate human rights abuses in Nicaragua and the assassination of Dr. Chamorro.

Then, in mid-1978, President Carazo of Costa Rica called for reconvening the Meeting of Consultation to investigate additional acts of aggression by the *Guardia Nacional*, including the shelling of the Costa Rican side of the San Juan River, which demarcates the border between the two countries. U.S. intelligence reports on the alleged incidents were not conclusive, and there were some indications from sources in Costa Rica that President Carazo had staged them to press his case against Somoza.

Under the circumstances, Ambassador McGee and I recommended that the U.S. not take part in the fact-finding mission. We were afraid that, if indeed the evidence could not support the allegation, the U.S. would be accused of trying to protect Somoza and keep his discredited regime in power.

In mid-1978, Secretary Vaky asked me to join the inter-agency task force working on Nicaragua. I found that some participants from several government agencies were reluctant to turn their backs on Somoza, a long-time ally, however discredited. Even the State Department representatives were more concerned about the impact on Castro and the Cold War than finding a solution that, while protecting U.S. Cold War interests, would replace Somoza with a moderate, pro-West regime. The discussions became circular and inconclusive. After attending a couple of sessions, in which I was able to hear very little and found it difficult to follow the reasoning, I asked the secretary to be relieved of the assignment and concentrate on working with member states at the OAS on seeking a multilateral solution.

In the fall of 1978, the OAS fact-finding mission reported that it had investigated the allegations and believed that Somoza was responsible for the actions that had occurred on the Costa Rican side of the border, but that the evidence was not conclusive. At the Meeting of Consultation, the democratic bloc of countries (with U.S. concurrence and Mexican abstention) passed a resolution calling upon Somoza to resign in order to stabilize peace in Central America, and for the creation of a new interim government to pave the way for free democratic elections. I was a member of the working group that drafted the text.

The Nicaraguan ambassador, Sevilla Sacasa, uncle of Tachito, rejected the resolution publicly, but quietly advised Vaky, McGee, and me at the end of the session that he was prepared to help put together a three-person junta to replace his nephew as head of state. Sevilla Sacasa later told me that he could not convince his nephew to accept "a gracious way out." Tachito hunkered down. Tachito believed that the U.S. would come to his rescue.

While the report of the fact finders was equivocal, the report of the Human Rights Commission clearly spelled out the abuse of human rights by Somoza adherents.

Throughout the next several months, the Sandinistas continued to advance against the *Guardia Nacional,* and in the OAS, were gaining support from the Caribbean governments, Venezuela, and Panama. Mexico remained non-interventionist but privately looked favorably on the Sandinista advances. I reported regularly to Vaky and Luigi Einaudi on the shifting positions of the Latin American and Caribbean delegations. We spent considerable time reviewing the possible options open to the U.S. government.

One afternoon, after a particularly difficult Permanent Council session, Vaky asked me if it wasn't time for me to consider a change in assignment and offered me the post of deputy assistant secretary for South American Affairs. I said that I wanted to see the Nicaraguan crisis through and suggested that he consider another senior colleague, Sam Eaton, for the job. In retrospect, as events played out, it was another questionable career decision that I probably should have made differently.

Throughout the second quarter of 1979, the Sandinistas made steady progress. Somoza was increasingly isolated. The Meeting of Consultation was reconvened. Working with Vaky and Einaudi, the mission was tasked to put together a draft resolution for presentation at the meeting. The U.S. position was for the OAS to call upon all member states to isolate Somoza, to deny his regime economic and military assistance, to force him to resign, and to set up an interim pro-democratic government to replace him.

In our consultations with the other member states, we found that seventeen were ready to take strong action: Colombia, Costa Rica, and eleven English-speaking Caribbean states, Panama, Suriname, the U.S., and Venezuela. The other sixteen were non-committal or opposed to any action by the OAS that might set a precedent for multilateral "intervention in the internal affairs of a member state." None of the countries expressed support for Tachito, but they were deeply concerned about authorizing such action under the OAS Charter.

My discussions with those states favoring action showed they were prepared to send a clear message to Tachito that he must go and invest his powers in a multi-party junta that would prepare the groundwork for open elections at a time certain. It was also evident that none of the countries was prepared to support the creation of a multinational OAS force to maintain order in the country until a new government was elected. When we broached the idea of an OAS multinational force with the Colombians, Costa Ricans, Panamanians, and Venezuelans, they asked us outright if the U.S. purpose was to keep Somoza in power. As the ambassador of Panama told me, "An effort by the U.S. to create an inter-American force will be interpreted by my government as a U.S. effort to keep Tachito in power in spite of his violations of the Charter." Ambassador McGee and I reported to Vaky that any resolution calling for the creation of an inter-American force to intervene in Nicaragua was doomed to failure.

It was also clear that an enforceable resolution must be endorsed by the larger states of Latin America, especially Brazil and Mexico. We believed that with some pressure we could induce several smaller non-committed governments to fall into line, but that would not be enough. Vaky and McGee authorized me to work with the key delegations in preparing a draft resolution that would meet our objectives and bring delegations like Brazil and Mexico on board. We wanted a resolution that would pass quickly with the support of every corner of the hemisphere. I spent a week consulting daily with the Brazilians, the Colombians, the Mexicans, and the Venezuelans and working with them on every word and phrase.

The advocates of action proposed that the Meeting of Consultation send a delegation to Managua to tell Tachito that he had violated the Charter by the attacks on Costa Rica and he must resign and set up a multi-party junta. Mexico and Brazil were not prepared to go that far. However, they would agree to a high-level OAS Mission, including the U.S., to "ask" Somoza to leave and pass power to a junta. They proposed relatively weak wording; they finally agreed to consider stronger language that Colombia proposed and said that they would consult their governments whether they could vote in favor or abstain, rather than vote no.

In the meantime, we were told by various delegations that Nicaraguan Ambassador Sevilla Sacasa would of course vote against any resolution, but had prepared a list of names for a possible post-Tachito junta. The list included outspoken opponents of Tachito, including a senior National Guard general , and a leading opposition conservative political leader.

After we reached agreement on the potential text, Colombia, Panama, and Venezuela advised us that they wanted the U.S. to introduce it. Then they would move the appointment of a high-level working group to review it immediately so that a commission of foreign ministers could fly to Managua the following day to "ask" Somoza to depart.

The Panamanian ambassador also alerted us in private that, if the U.S. took any action to support Tachito, it would accredit the Sandinista spokesman on foreign affairs, Father Miguel d'Escoto, as a member of the Panamanian delegation. He reminded us that his government considered any effort to create an inter-American military force would be seen as action to keep Tachito in place. We duly reported this to Secretary Vaky.

By the evening before the meeting, we told the Brazilian, Colombia, Mexican, and Venezuelan delegations that the draft resolution was now being reviewed by senior U.S. government authorities. Before I left for home in the late evening, Vaky had reviewed the draft and submitted it to the Seventh Floor and the NSC for final clearances.

The following morning, Secretary Vaky asked me to review the proposed text with the representatives of Jamaica, Barbados, and Trinidad and Tobago to ask for Caribbean support. I was briefing Ambassador Jackman at the Barbadian Mission at about noon when I received a call from Vaky to return to the State Department at once.

When I arrived, Secretary Vaky told me that the NSC had determined that the proposed draft was not acceptable and that Secretary Vance would present a new U.S. draft resolution calling for the immediate creation of an inter-American military force to go to

Nicaragua and stabilize the military situation. I was speechless. No matter what happened now, I had lost faith in the decision-making processes of my own government.

It was 4:00 p.m. when the Meeting of Consultation of Foreign Ministers was called to order. Secretary Vance asked for the floor and made the U.S. presentation, to the consternation of Mexico, Brazil, and the democratic delegations. He had barely finished when Father d'Escoto took the seat of Panama, which by order of precedence at this Meeting of Consultation was seated next to the U.S. delegation. There had been no time to advise other delegations of the change in the U.S. position, and the impact, especially on those with whom I had been working for almost two weeks, was violent. Colombia and Venezuela accused the U.S. of duplicity and moved to convene a committee of inquiry into U.S. motivations.

The Meeting of Consultation went into disarray. Vance departed and was replaced by Deputy Secretary Christopher and other Seventh Floor and White House officials. They and Vaky went into consultations with the Andean foreign ministers in side rooms on the second floor of OAS headquarters. Ambassador McGee and I were left dangling. Several hours later, they came to an accommodation, and the proposed U.S. resolution was never mentioned again. McGee had a severe diabetic reaction and had to leave. Ambassador Jackman came over to say that he understood what had cut short our noon discussion. Christopher and Vaky never consulted McGee or me while they were being harangued by the Andean foreign ministers in the meeting room. After McGee left, I waited in the hall outside, feeling totally discredited. The session ended at about midnight. Christopher and Vaky left the room and went back to the State Department. I looked for a taxi to go home.

The Meeting of Consultation ended the next day without a clear resolution, just a repetition of the call for Somoza to step down. Later Vaky told me that the session with the foreign ministers had been bitter and that Christopher could not understand their reaction. How could they believe that the U.S. intention was to keep Somoza in power? Weren't they more concerned about the potential threat to the all of us in the hemisphere if the USSR and Castro weren't thwarted? If he had consulted with the U.S. Mission before the meeting, we could have explained the reasons why we should have pursued the original course and achieved our objective without calling for inter-American military intervention.

The days following the meeting, I was inundated by phone calls from newsmen who wanted to know what had happened. Several, like the veteran Latin American specialist Jerry O'Leary, had been aware of the efforts that had been made prior to the meeting. I remember his comment, "The decision to call for military intervention had nothing to do with Latin America, but was related to events in the Middle East and Iran. The U.S. had to appear strong and aggressive in the inter-American arena to send a message to protagonists in other regions where we had strategic interests more important than in the Americas."

This experience soured me on further assignments. McGee and I had not even been invited to brief Secretary Vance, nor had the reasons for the abrupt change of course been shared with us. I told McGee and Vaky that I thought my utility to my government had been undermined. Vaky told me to be patient. He had proposed my appointment as ambassador to Costa Rica and would do everything possible to make it happen.

That evening when I told Ele, she urged me on principle to consider retiring from the Foreign Service. She had watched the impact on my wellbeing and mental state over the past several weeks and was deeply concerned. After a lengthy family discussion, we agreed that I would not take any precipitous action and would see how the next weeks played out. Frankly, after the debacle at the Meeting of Consultation, I was not very optimistic about the prospects.

We also agreed that I should consider an alternate course if I decided to resign. We decided that the alternative should be to return to California and that I should approach our family lawyer about buying into his firm in Tulare. He and his partner had developed a thriving practice, based primarily on water rights and farm management law. Because of our own farms, I had developed considerable knowledge of the subject matter and, with a couple of special courses, I could quickly be ready to practice. The following week I sent him a letter to explore the prospects.

After the Meeting of Consultation, Somoza did not resign. The U.S. military support he expected from his friends in the Pentagon did not materialize. The *Guardia Nacional* ran low on equipment and ammo. Shortly thereafter in July 1979, he finally resigned, turned over power to one of his cronies, and flew to his second home in Miami. The Sandinistas moved quickly into the vacuum and took charge. Could a different outcome been shaped? We shall never know.

I do know that Central America did not appear on the agenda of the OAS for the rest of my assignment. And, yes, Somoza was given exile in Paraguay where he was assassinated. Rumor had it that Paraguayan dictator Stroessner ordered the hit after Somoza made passes at Stroessner's mistress. In exile, Somoza had only his long-time mistress Lenora with him. His wife Hope had abandoned him years earlier and moved to London. He had discredited his brother Luis and forced him into exile. Only his friends in some high places in the U.S. had stayed with him, but they could not save him from himself.

A Changing Life

While the Central American tragedy unwove at the OAS, Ele and I were facing our own dilemma at home. The developer and owner of our apartment complex, Mr. Gelman, died and his widow decided to convert the property into condominiums. The Towers of Cathedral Avenue had been built in the late 1950s as "middle-income residences." In fact they were upscale: two fourteen-story towers with over 300 apartments in each tower, connected by elegant glassed passageways to a central lobby. The Towers had finely appointed meeting rooms, an Olympic-sized outdoor swimming pool and an area that had formerly been a top-flight restaurant.

The decision to go condo was made in late 1978 when frustration with my job was mounting, and we began talking seriously about returning to California. Ele was deeply concerned about our razor thin financial resources. Mortgage rates were high and my salary, even as an asterisk FSO-1 (the top of the scale), was barely covering our regular monthly expenses.

We were renting a lovely two-bedroom, 1,800 square foot apartment. It went on the market for $130,000—almost twice as much as our savings account. Ele calculated that if we purchased our unit, we would have to take out a mortgage at 7 or 8 percent, and that, based on my salary and the anticipated condo fees, would leave us with less than $100 a month in disposable income. Her Scottish blood just wouldn't allow for that.

In light of the uncertainty about our future, she set about to find a financial formula that would give us some breathing room. The Carter "malaise" gripped the real estate market, and property values in Washington were down. She reviewed rents around town and the price schedules for smaller apartments on sale in the building. A one-bedroom 1,000 square foot apartment was available for $70,000, and the Bank of America in Tulare offered us a secured loan at 1 percent for that amount. Ele told me that we could afford to buy a one-bedroom condo. We negotiated to purchase a unit down the hall and obtained the secured loan. She calculated we could pay it back in full if we stayed in the Foreign Service or in Washington. If we decided to return to Tulare, we could sell it and pay off the loan immediately after the sale.

We completed the transaction just before Ele went on her 1979 farm trip and I left to attend the 1979 OAS General Assembly in La Paz, Bolivia. We were to move just before Thanksgiving, but the developers gave us an extra couple of months because our two-bedroom unit didn't sell. Ele went to South Dakota and California. She inspected the farms and negotiated farm agreements for 1980. She inspected her mother's and grandmother's homes and made detailed plans for their rehabilitation when and if we returned to California. She talked at length with our lawyer and obtained information from the State Bar on the courses I would have to take to qualify as a specialist in water and farm agricultural law.

The OAS General Assembly in La Paz

The preparations for the 1979 OAS General Assembly were routine. The contentious issue of Somoza had been removed from the agenda by the Sandinista victory. The emotional issue of Bolivia's outlet to the sea would come up and the member states would call on Chile to restore to Bolivia a corridor of land to the Pacific to compensate for the lands Bolivia had lost to Chile during the 1870 War of the Pacific. There would be a resolution on human rights and democratic institutions that would require negotiation at the meeting. No one anticipated any surprise diplomatic initiatives in La Paz. Most delegations just talked about surviving the altitude.

Prior to the General Assembly, the annual conferences of the IA/ECOSOC and CIECC were convened on successive weeks in Barbados to approve their annual reports to the General Assembly. President Carter named me ambassador for the month of August 1979 to lead the U.S. delegations to both meetings.

The two meetings were quite tumultuous. The IA/ECOSOC wrestled with the depressed economic conditions throughout the region. In both meetings, the Caribbean hosts pressed the U.S. for substantial commitments of funds for projects they considered of high priority for their development efforts. Latin American countries particularly wanted funding for OAS technical assistance in helping them prepare project proposals for submission to the international lending agencies (the IDB and the World Bank) for financing. Again, my instructions were to vote against all such proposals. At CIECC, when I tried to explain the U.S. budgetary process that inhibited U.S. support for those proposals, the Brazilian delegate said that was an internal U.S. matter and not relevant in an inter-American meeting. My fellow delegation members and I spent hours in negotiating sessions working out appropriate diplomatic language for saying "no."

During that month in Barbados, the tension of the meetings was broken by the support I received from U.S. Ambassador Sally Shelton. We had worked together in Washington when she had been deputy assistant secretary for Caribbean Affairs. She understood my concerns and frustration. We had long conversations about U.S. policy and her current assignment as ambassador to several Caribbean islands. She took me on a tour of Barbado, which had been one of the most important jewels of imperial Britain—the original sugar island on which the sugar-for-rum-for-slave trade had emerged. Barbados had its own parliament in 1690, abolished slavery in the first half of the nineteenth century, and installed universal education by the latter half of the nineteenth century. History had made Barbados unlike any other island in the Caribbean, and Sally acquainted me with the high points of this unique country.

For each of the meetings, the government of Barbados also held receptions in honor of the delegations, one hosted by the governor general and one by the prime minister. They were in the gracious, tropical buildings, with elegant gardens and stately rooms with portraits of Her Majesty Elizabeth II; Barbados had a uniquely English touch. I had met Prime Minister Tom Adams, formerly a union leader, through AFL-CIO Secretary for Latin American Affairs Serafino Romualdi. We had a short chat about the economic and social problems and his plans to develop tourism as a source for desperately needed foreign exchange earnings. Then, he told me that the reports from his delegates at the meetings were that the U.S. was not being helpful and asked me why. I told him that the U.S. was still feeling its way to a post-Alliance for Progress policy and that he should be patient.

September was dedicated to completing the documentation for the General Assembly, which was scheduled for mid-October. We spent several long nights negotiating in the General Committee of the Permanent Council. Assistant Secretary Vaky presented the agenda and working papers to Secretary Vance two weeks before the meeting. Secretary Vance had to cancel one briefing session after another because of the press of other business—much of it related to Iran and the deposed Shah. So, it was agreed that Vaky, McGee, and I would brief the secretary aboard the plane en route to La Paz.

Our delegation assembled at Andrews Air Force base for a daylong flight to the Altiplano, my first visit there in nearly a decade. The secretary advised us that he would be in La Paz for the inaugural session, a bilateral meeting with the president of Bolivia, the opening reception, the delivery of his statement on the U.S. position, and one or two bilateral talks with foreign ministers. He expected to leave by the end of the second day. He said that Vaky would take the U.S. chair for most of the meeting, and that all he really needed to know was about critical issues that might arise. He met with us for about thirty minutes and then turned to other papers. Ambassador McGee and I spent the rest of the trip going over the documents with Pete Vaky. It was then that Vaky told us that he was to retire in November on our return from La Paz.

On our arrival at El Alto, Secretary Vance's plane was met by officials of the Bolivian Foreign Ministry. It is always a unique experience to land at 13,600 feet: you feel light-headed and it takes time to adjust to the air pressure and lower oxygen levels. I didn't have that opportunity. I was the fourth or fifth to descend from the plane—and everything had been quite formal until then. When the Bolivian chief of protocol saw me, he called out "Erving" and gave me a not-very-protocol hug and called to his companions that I was back in Bolivia. It set the tone for my attendance at the General Assembly. Vaky and McGee just smiled and Vance looked a bit confused by the breach of protocol.

For the week we were in Bolivia, I ran into old friends and former colleagues everywhere I went. At a reception at the new National Museum across the street from the National Palace on the Plaza Murillo, I ran into several friends who had been past presidents of Bolivia and members of the military juntas that had replaced them. In the decade since my tour as AID director, there had been three presidents and two military juntas, and I had personally known and worked with most of the people involved.

The General Assembly moved forward without a hitch. Walter Guevara, a good friend, was the acting president of Bolivia, and he made a strong speech advocating democratic institutions and values. The Bolivian government submitted a resolution for hemisphere-wide observance of human rights and support for representative democracy. I joined the senior-level working party to convert the Bolivian proposal into the declaration of the General Assembly. I was also allowed to occupy the U.S. chair when the United States supported Bolivia's aspirations for a sovereign access to the sea. The newspapers printed a picture of me voting, with the caption in one newspaper reading, "Old friend votes for Bolivia."

One significant change occurred in the life of the OAS during the meeting. Since the early 1960s when the U.S. had decided not to present a candidate for secretary general (SG) or assistant secretary general (ASG), the practice had been for the SG to be from a South American country and the ASG from a Central American country. In Bolivia, the U.S. opted to support a Caribbean candidate for ASG. The election was between the sitting ASG, Dr. Jorge Luis Zelaya Coronado of Guatemala, and Ambassador Val McComie of Barbados. The vote was very close, but McComie won. The U.S. hoped that a new Caribbean presence would shake up the organization and broaden its appeal throughout the hemisphere.

The last evening of the General Assembly, we celebrated at a dinner hosted by President Guevara, and the delegations toasted Bolivia's commitment to a new era of democracy and progress. The dinner broke up about midnight and we went to bed firmly convinced that the assembly had been a positive step in stabilizing elected government in our host country as well as around the hemisphere. When we awoke the following morning, the hotel was surrounded by Bolivian troops. Colonel Albert Natusch Busch had staged a coup, arrested President Guevara and his escort on his way home from the dinner, and taken over the presidential palace. Natusch Busch closed the airport at El Alto and all the delegates were confined to the Sheraton Hotel in which the meetings had been held. Not even a Hollywood screenwriter could have scripted a more bizarre end to the meeting.

That morning, before the military surrounded the hotel, Secretary General Orfila left in a private plane for Mendoza, Argentina, to visit family and friends there. That left lame duck ASG Zelaya Coronado to negotiate the departure of the thirty-three delegations now left stranded. Zelaya's first problem was with whom he could deal. All the contacts with whom the OAS had been working had been replaced. No one, including most of the senior military, knew much about Colonel Natusch Busch, who by then had ordered tanks into the streets of La Paz and soldiers with orders to shoot to kill.

Breakfast in the hotel was a scene of great preoccupation. All of the delegations had had their flights cancelled and communications were in the hands of the rebels. Rumors were rife about violence in the streets, and the assassination of now ex-President Guevara and his cabinet. Some said that this was a pro-Castro coup aimed at the U.S. delegation. Even one Venezuelan quipped that it had been my picture in the press that prompted the coup.

Secretary Vaky had already returned to Washington, leaving McGee and me to look after our delegation. McGee sent me to Zelaya, who was besieged by all the other delegations. Everyone wanted to get out of La Paz before "fighting started in the streets." Zelaya was very calm and advised me that he had reached officials in the Foreign Office and the presidential palace and was negotiating a procedure to take the delegations to the airport and arrange for planes to take us to Lima, Santiago, or Buenos Aires. He told me to have our delegation packed up and ready to leave, keep calm, and await further instructions. So, McGee and I assembled our colleagues to await news.

About noon we were called to the lobby of the hotel and told that army trucks would arrive at about 1:00 p.m. to take us to El Alto where we would board Lloyd Aero-Boliviano planes for immediate departure. Colonel Natusch had assigned an officer to ride with each delegation, and each delegation had to ensure that only members of its delegation were on the truck assigned to it. Any variation from that norm would be severely dealt with.

So, in the early afternoon, a fleet of army trucks arrived and we were loaded, delegation by delegation, in alphabetical order, onto the trucks. Little respect for foreign ministers or ambassadors! In our case, Ambassador McGee sat with the driver, I climbed up the back of the truck with the rest of our delegation and we had to shoo away members of the other delegations for whom trucks had not yet arrived. We were driven up through the heart of town, past an array of World War I and World War II tanks and heavily armed young soldiers menacingly pointing their weapons at the road all the way up to El Alto.

When we arrived at El Alto, Zelaya directed departure plans. Some of our delegation was routed to Santiago because the plane to Lima was already full. Our passports were checked and we were escorted to our plane. We arrived in Lima about dinnertime and were met by the U.S. Ambassador to Peru, Harry Shlaughterman. He had made arrangements for most of our delegation to stay at the Sheraton Hotel and invited Ambassador McGee and me to spend the night at the embassy. He had booked our flights to Washington the following day. We recounted to the ambassador and his wife Carol our adventures in La Paz, especially the irony of the dinner on Saturday night as the coup was taking place.

When we arrived in Washington, we learned that former President Guevara and his cabinet had not been abused and that many had left Bolivia. Colonel Natusch lasted two weeks until his military colleagues displaced him. It was another tragic chapter in the history of a country that had had more presidents than years of independence.

Assistant Secretary Vaky retired shortly after our return from

La Paz. He was succeeded by William Bowdler, with whom I had worked for many years. In the interim, John Bushnell was acting assistant secretary and alerted me that the prospects for my appointment as ambassador to Costa Rica were not good. He said that the Foreign Service was going to recommend another career officer, Frank McNeil, whom I knew and respected. That recommendation relieved me of my commitment to Vaky. I told John that I would be retiring at the end of my assignment to the U.S. Mission.

When I told Ambassador McGee of my plans to retire, he asked me to help him find a replacement and not to leave until the replacement could be brought on board. We had a long talk about the events of last two years, and I made it very clear that I had been distraught by the decisions of the past several months, especially on Nicaragua, and believed that a country as great and important as ours needed not only global policies and strategies but also long and short-term regional strategies and tactics to further U.S. interests. I felt that the administration had lost sight of our long-term interests in the Western Hemisphere and the advantages to us of inter-American cooperation and development in achieving our global objectives.

That evening I phoned Ele in California to advise her of the action I had taken.

A few days later, Secretary General Orfila on his return from Argentina called me over to his office. He said that he heard that I was planning to retire and asked me to consider taking an assignment as executive officer of the Secretariat for the Inter-American Economic and Social Council. It was second highest post in that secretariat—a "political post" reserved for a U.S. national. He advised me that he had discussed the appointment with Ambassador McGee and reminded me of problems in the secretariat that led a succession of incumbents to resign, including differences with the Brazilian executive secretary, Dr. Diego Figueiredo, a cousin to the then president of Brazil. I agreed to consider the proposal.

Ele returned from her farm trip shortly thereafter. We had another one of our long family conferences. Ele was equivocal. On the one hand she wanted to stay in Washington to continue her work with the AAFSW and to begin writing about her life and experiences in Latin America. On the other hand, she was interested in returning to Tulare and helping me get started in a second career in law practice. Buying into the law practice required more cash than we had in our accounts and she was loath to borrow. The OAS job and my pension from the U.S. Foreign Service would allow us to accumulate funds needed for both the buy-in and the long-term move back to Tulare. After several days of weighing the alternatives, we decided that I should take Orfila's offer.

I submitted my retirement application to the Foreign Service, effective February 29, 1980. I located my old friend and colleague, Herbert Thompson, one of the most competent fellow officers I knew, and asked him to consider the OAS mission post. He and Ambassador McGee hit it off at once. Herb could be available on May 1, 1980, so the ambassador arranged for me to receive a temporary sixty-day appointment to keep me on board until Herb was available. As it worked out, we had almost a two-week overlap, much to Ambassador McGee's delight.

We had a quiet Christmas season. We moved into our new, smaller apartment. Secretary General Orfila told me that, because of budgetary restraints, I could not take up my new post until the next OAS fiscal year that began July 1, 1980. We agreed that the OAS would hire me from Tulare, California and bring Ele and me back to Washington, D.C. It fit Ele and my needs just about perfectly.

When word of my retirement made the rounds, AID asked if I would consider going to Peru as AID Director. Ele and I talked it over and decided that I should decline the offer. Then I was offered a spot in the AID central office, which we decided not to consider because a year at the OAS would generate enough money to cover the funds needed to buy into the law practice. So, we stayed with our original plan.

Retiring from State on February 29, 1980 involved filling out papers and turning in our diplomatic passports. I stayed on the job until April 30. Ambassador and Mrs. McGee gave us a wonderful farewell party at the mission and a dinner at their home. I was also awarded a Superior Honor Award from the State Department for my service at the U.S. Mission.

A few days later, we closed up our new apartment and flew back to Tulare for two months.

29

The Inter-American Economic
and Social Council

The seven weeks we spent in Tulare were idyllic. The weather was delightful: 70–80 degrees during the day and cool for sleeping at night. Both houses were unrented and we had the grounds to ourselves. We picked the Santa Rosa plums, the apricots, and the grapefruit from the trees, occasionally having to fight off the crows to obtain our prizes.

We maintained a leisurely schedule, with late breakfasts and early dinners. Most of our dinners were spent with Elizabeth La Cell, now retired as Tulare City librarian. Almost every afternoon about 4:30 p.m., Elizabeth drove over in her Pinto, and we would explore all the eateries in Tulare and nearby Visalia. We spent weekends with Mimi and Bus Hoffman at their home at Bass Lake in the mountains. Jean and Jim Leonard came by for lunch and invited us for a weekend with them in Hanford.

Many a morning we walked the seven or eight blocks to downtown where we took care of our personal affairs or reviewed the house rental and farm accounts. We made two trips to Pixley Farm with the county farm agent to check the ranch. We had a couple of meetings with our lawyer to clarify the terms of my buying into his law practice and even set a probable date of September 1981 for my joining the firm. Two or three Saturday afternoons, we went to matinees at the Tulare Theater to see old-fashioned double features while the kids ran up and down the aisles.

We had a wonderfully restful time. There were no urgent phone calls from Washington. In fact, the only long distance call we received was from the personnel office of the Organization of American States to say that my appointment papers had been signed and that United Airlines would fly us back to Washington by July 1, 1980.

We returned to D.C. in the midst of the first heat wave of the season. It was 90 degrees with humidity about the same. When we arrived at the Towers, we learned that the air conditioning system in the 632-apartment complex had collapsed and was to be replaced as soon as possible — probably over the next four to six weeks.

When I opened the door of our one-bedroom apartment, the heat and humidity raced out to greet us. The apartment had been locked up for seven weeks. I opened the windows and the screen door to the balcony; there was no cross ventilation and the humid air seemed to hang there and grip us. There was not even a rustle of air in the dogwoods in Rock Creek Park outside our balcony. Once the bags were in, I looked at Ele and said, "What are we doing here? Why didn't we stay in Tulare?"

Just then the phone rang. It was Faye Sherry. The desk clerk on duty downstairs had alerted her to our arrival and she had prepared dinner to welcome us back. We freshened up and went up to their apartment. The beautiful two-bedroom unit had cross ventilation, and Frank had rented two room air conditioners that made the environment quite livable. Faye had prepared a wonderful gourmet dinner and we had a pleasant evening. Frank gave us the phone numbers of the company that rented room air conditioners and told me to call first thing in the morning.

We went back to our hothouse at about 11:00 p.m. We put sheets on the beds, took quick showers and spent the night rolling on the sheets while perspiration poured off us. It must have been 4:00 a.m. before either of us really fell into a deep sleep. Awake at 8:00 a.m., I called the air conditioner company and learned that it did not have a single room conditioner available. He put us on his waiting list, and asked me to call back on Thursday. When I asked if he knew of any other companies that might be renting air conditioners, he gave me a couple of numbers. When I called them, I was told that they had room air conditioners for sale, but could not make delivery before the following week. Quite despondently, we unpacked and I walked up the hill to buy some groceries.

When I returned, I found Ele talking in the hall with our long-time neighbors, the Yates. Sidney was a congressman from Chicago. They had taken us to receptions at the Smithsonian Institution where he served as the House of Representatives' member of the board of directors. They learned of our return that morning and came to our rescue. The House of Representatives was recessing for the month of July, and they were going home to Chicago on July 2. They offered us the use of their master bedroom until the first week of August when the congressman had to return for a hearing of the Appropriations Sub-committee of which he was chair. Their Good Samaritan act made our day and month.

Tuesday and Wednesday went by—somehow. The heat and humidity persisted. Ele went to brokerage offices during the day and stayed as long as she could. I went to the office and stayed until 6:00 p.m. Breakfasts and dinners were designed to involve as little cooking as possible. Each night we resisted going to bed for as long as we could and then slept on a sheet with another one covering us. And when we got up in the morning, we were sweaty and almost as tired as when we went to bed. We took a lot of showers.

Thursday morning, after I had left for work, the Yates rang the bell. Ele took the keys and bid them a happy trip home. She took some sheets down to the Yates master bedroom for her first long nap since our return to D.C. I was at the office and had to wait until the evening for the bliss of my first good night's sleep since we left Tulare.

Now an OAS Staff Member

On July 1, I reported for duty at the OAS personnel office. There were the usual papers to sign, and I had a short talk with Ron Scheman, the director of Management, whose budget I had decimated when I was chair of the Committee on Budgetary and Administrative Affairs. He pointed out that, if the OAS were in the UN system, I would be receiving a higher salary and would be participating in the UN's more generous retirement system. Under the OAS rules for an appointment such as I was receiving, I would not be entitled to join the retirement system but only the Provident Fund which took 5 percent from my monthly paycheck and matched it with 5 percent from the OAS. I didn't really mind since I expected my tenure would be for only about a year, and then we would be returning to Tulare.

Then, the executive secretary of the Economic and Social Secretariat was advised that I was ready for work, and I went down to his office where Diogo de Figueiredo and his right hand man, Gilvandro Raposo, were awaiting me. They invited me to join them for a *tour d'horizon* of the Secretariat and their views about my role. Speaking in Portuguese, Diogo told me that his compatriots in the Brazilian Mission to the OAS had briefed him on my career and that he had reluctantly acceded to the decision of the council that a U.S. specialist had to be named executive officer since he really wanted Raposo to be his deputy and planned to use him in that role.

Raposo looked sternly ahead through this declaration. He said that he would work with me and that he would not let his personal relationship with Diogo interfere with my carrying out the duties of executive officer. He said that my predecessor and he had had a very rocky relationship, and hoped that he and I might get along better. I replied in my *portuñol* (a mixture of Portuguese and Spanish) that I wanted us to work together. I suggested that without disrupting the present flow of work, they allow me a few weeks to acquaint myself with the Secretariat's program and get to know the staff members while Raposo and I worked on our relationship.

For the next three weeks I quietly acquainted myself with the secretariat members and their work. The Secretariat was at a crossroads. In the Alliance years, it had been the most important operating arm of the OAS, with several hundred economists, technicians, and support staff and large budgets, based on annual voluntary contributions from the U.S. and a few other member states. When the Nixon administration ended the Alliance, several Latin American states, led by Panama, tried to revive it and resume large flows of financial and technical aid from the United States. However, the U.S. was prepared to consider a much less ambitious program only if the Latin American countries reformed their economic systems as they had promised to do under the AFP. Most of the countries had kept in place strictly regulated economies attuned to the nineteenth century mercantilism, with tinges of Marxist state planning controls. Most had not adopted fiscal and institutional reforms or adopted policies that promoted growth and open market economies.

In 1976, Panama proposed a special session of the OAS General Assembly to define a new inter-American cooperative effort for development in lieu of the Alliance for Progress. The Economic and Social Council (CIES) was tasked with preparing a working paper for that special session. Four years later, the countries had not reached a consensus on the working paper.

The current draft was prepared primarily by the chief economist of the OAS Secretariat, José Luis Restrepo, and reflected the prevailing views of the Latin American and Caribbean countries that the U.S. should be the primary source of funding. I had participated as ambassador and chief of the U.S. delegation in its analysis at the 1978 and 1979 CIES meetings; I had raised serious concerns about the absence of commitments by Latin American and Caribbean countries in the draft paper of policy and fiscal reforms and measures to strengthen domestic institutions as well as its focus on U.S. financial aid rather than an inter-American financial partnership. In the winter of 1979–80, as I was retiring from the State Department, David Lazar (then director of Program Planning for the Latin American Bureau of AID) was coordinating the U.S. review of the latest revision of the working paper.

Unfortunately, that revision was essentially a restatement of the earlier drafts. It barely touched on the inadequacies of Latin American and Caribbean governments in the management of their finances, their shortages of technical and administrative resources, or the absence of domestic policies and incentives to promote sound investment of resources. It also said little about what the countries needed to do cooperatively under the direction of IA/ECOSOC. There was little about "we" acting together and few commitments to resolve critical domestic issues in the developing countries that needed to be addressed for a sustained flow of aid to be effective and meaningful. The paper attacked U.S. conditions for supplying aid, especially congressional restrictions on the use of U.S. funds to purchase equipment, supplies, and technical expertise from sources in member states, widely known as the Hickenlooper Amendment of 1961.

Part of the paper dealt with eight areas in which the IA/ECOSOC should concentrate its development programming over the next decade: the food problem; natural resource development, including ecological considerations; energy, including alternatives sources; illiteracy and education; human settlements and environment;

transfer of technology; international trade; and finance. But, its tone had the feel of a shopping list of "wants" rather than a definition of priority actions to deal with the population explosion, accentuated rural-to-urban migration, and fiscal crisis.

At the end of July, Diogo and Raposo invited me to join them in a discussion of the new draft, which was to be the centerpiece for the next CIES meeting. He reminded me that the Brazilian government had been active in the drafting process and had not supported many U.S. comments or suggestions, especially those related to reforms and resource mobilization by Latin American and Caribbean governments themselves. I told them that I was skeptical that the paper in its present form could go very far. I then reminded him that when I sat in the U.S. chair, our serious disagreements with the Brazilian delegation was over the prospects of Latin American countries effectively using external resources without making critical policy and institutional decisions. I also urged them, from our vantage point as ECOSOC officials, to press for the inclusion of a framework for cooperation among governments, in the ECOSOC forum, that defined objectives and spelled out the policy, institutional, and program initiatives each government should undertake to make them better able to utilize external assistance effectively. With such a framework, the Secretariat would have a solid base for working with both recipient and donor governments.

Diogo and Raposo said they understood my position, but doubted that the Latin American and Caribbean delegations were prepared to amend the paper substantively to accommodate the concerns of the United States. They told me that they, not I, would represent the CIES Secretariat in the deliberations in the IA/ECOSOC working party reviewing the draft. They also told me that Diogo was working on a new paper for the working group since he was not satisfied with the draft under consideration. Knowing the U.S. position and hearing Diogo's approach, I saw little hope that the Special General Assembly would be convoked in the present political environment.

The discussion then turned to my role in the CIES Secretariat. I suggested that I concentrate on managing the technical cooperation portfolio and helping them reshape the structure of the Secretariat. The organization had been designed for the "glory" years of the Alliance for Progress, but today, the portfolio was substantially smaller and the Secretariat needed to be realigned to reflect the reduced budget. I proposed that they authorize me to present them a proposal in the next few months for reorganizing the Secretariat in the post-Alliance setting. They agreed. They would concentrate on the Special General Assembly and I, on the technical assistance role of the Secretariat. My initial appointment was for six months to one year, and that assignment suited me just right. As I moved into this assignment, Diogo, Raposo, and I developed a close working relationship.

In the end, the working paper was not agreed upon. The Special General Assembly was never convened. The OAS member states moved the inter-American development agenda to the IBD and World Bank.

The Executive Officer

On the first day on the job, Raposo showed me into a lovely, sunlit office around the corner from the offices of Diogo and Raposo. It overlooked a tree-lined patio and DACOR Bacon House. He also introduced me to my secretary, Marta Bellis, an Argentine who was fluent in all four official languages of the OAS. She not only took my dictation in three languages and corrected my Spanish and Portuguese, but also prepared first drafts of many routine interoffice memoranda. Marta also briefed me on the politics and intrigues of the Secretariat. She knew all the personalities and all the tribulations that had "induced" my predecessors, including David Lazar, to resign after short incumbencies.

That afternoon, Marta gave me the organization chart of the Secretariat that Diogo had approved in 1979 and the program plan that Raposo had laid out for 1980–1981. The organization chart was essentially unchanged from the Alliance years, except that the staff was substantially reduced. I set my first task as meeting and assessing each person on the organization chart and reviewing with her/ him the projects they were supervising. To avoid any misunderstandings, the following morning I suggested to Diogo and Raposo that they introduce me as the new executive officer as a show of solidarity. Diogo agreed and called a special meeting of all the Secretariat staff.

On my third day on the job, I made a courtesy call on Secretary General Orfila. He welcomed me and said that any time I wanted to meet with him, I should contact his political adviser, John Ford. John, a retired U.S. foreign service officer with extensive Latin American experience, founded the Latin American Group (FLAG), the only monthly luncheon discussion group in Washington that concentrated on inter-American relations.

Next I called on Assistant Secretary General Val McComie, with whom I had worked when he was Barbadian ambassador to the U.S. and the OAS. That afternoon, just before the Fourth of July, I also called Ambassador McGee and my successor, Herbert Thompson, to notify them that I was in my new job.

On my fourth day, I scheduled meetings with each member of the Secretariat during the slow months of July and August. The General Assembly was over. The Permanent Council was not in session. Preparations for the Economic and Social Council were just beginning. There was no more propitious time to begin my in-depth learning about the Secretariat. And I made sure that Raposo understood what I was doing.

My first meeting was with the program staff—Fernando Rodriguez and Victoria Espinoso, two Chilean economists, whose experience included the busy Alliance years. They were as competent and well organized as any program officers with whom I had worked in AID. They walked me through CIES's internal project approval procedures and the annual request to IA/ECOSOC for funding. Then they reviewed country by country for the period 1965 to 1976 the multi-million dollar authorizations and the specific projects; Fernando's assessment highlighted the reasons for delays in project execution, frequently because of limited in-country institutional capability or lack of trained technicians. It was a story of declining income and programming. Since all contributions for the CIES development programs were voluntary, it was up to each state to determine how much it would contribute. The principal contributor by far was the U.S. government, and its contributions had declined sharply in recent years.

He then reviewed the situation of the eight regional training centers that IA/ECOSOC had created to provide graduate training in specialized fields not covered at that time by Latin American universities: integrated development of water and land resources; regional development planning and implementation; tax and fiscal policy; public administration; tourism; social development; statistics; and international trade and export development. Fernando pointed out that several of the centers had run out of funding, and he made projections of the costs to activate each one, including instructors and fellowships. He also showed me charts depicting the sharp decline in recent years of government requests for fellowships and training, which he attributed to governments' need to use the substantially lower foreign aid funds for more pressing immediate problems.

Fernando next introduced me to changes being made in requests for technical assistance. During the Alliance years, each country program had been defined in a joint planning exercise. In the post-Alliance years, countries simply sent in a list of projects they wanted funded. Fernando was consolidating requests scattered among different divisions into one meaningful project. For example, he had brought together requests on agroindustry, rural development, and urbanization in a given country into one regional project. His redefined projects included policy, administrative, financial, and staff commitments that governments needed to make as the *quid pro quo* for CIES funds. Those consolidated projects had grown to about 30 percent of the annual CIES budget.

Next, I met with Diogo's three senior advisers: Dorel Callender, the Caribbean specialist; Elba Kybal, Integration Advisor; and José Luis Restrepo, the OAS's senior economic adviser.

Dorel Calendar, a Jamaican diplomat, had first-hand knowledge of the political, economic, and social situation in the English-speaking Caribbean countries and had worked with many key government officials and leaders of the Caribbean integration movement, the Caribbean Community (CARICOM). She briefed me on the leadership in the Caribbean countries and described how many had worked together in the struggle to end colonialism and then formed rival political parties to promote their own ambitions in the competition for national leadership. She laid out a very troubling economic and social panorama facing those newly independent parliamentary democracies, with budgetary strains and revenue shortages that prevented them from building critical infrastructure and funding essential health and social programs. She identified limited sources of energy as a major development bottleneck, and pointed out that most countries in this post-colonial era focused on public sector programs to provide jobs, not private investments and international tourism, the two most likely sources of foreign exchange. She thought that the number one priority in the Caribbean had to be job creation in the face of a rapidly increasing population whose impact had been kept in check by large-scale emigration to Canada, Great Britain, and the United States.

Elba Kybal, an Argentine-born economist, was a walking encyclopedia of the status of the economic integration movements in the hemisphere. She worked with the Central American Common Market (CACM), the Andean Community (CAN), CARICOM, and the South American common market group that later became MERCOSUR. She laid out development data that demonstrated the importance of economic integration to the development of the smaller countries and why CIES should give high priority to support for sub regional integration movements. She also described the problems these groups were facing and the national rivalries that impeded the solution to key issues, including U.S. political and economic measures that she believed exacerbated differences between the countries in favor of what she described as "short-term U.S. bilateral interests."

I had to wait for over a week to meet with José Luis Restrepo as he was working on the paper for the Special General Assembly. Over the past decade, he had risen from a staff economist to the principal adviser to the secretary general. He had in-depth knowledge of national and sectoral development programs as well as the capabilities of most of the Latin American governments to mount and sustain development programs. I had worked with him for years, sometimes as a critic when sitting in the U.S. chair, but I always respected him as an objective and talented economist. He lamented the departure of many senior Latin American and U.S. economists who were once the backbone of the OAS advisory group. He felt that if some of them had been induced to stay, they could have played a major role in bridging the gap between the United States and the other member states. Jose Luis briefed me on the disarray of both CIES and the preparations for the Special

General Assembly. He described the impact on the region of the decline in economic activity at the end of the Vietnam War, which led to a severe financial crisis caused by declining budgets and declining export earnings. This was exacerbated by the upsurge in military governments and the exodus of key economists and technicians who had been trained during the Alliance years— they had left their jobs, attracted by the higher salaries and job security at international agencies. Their replacements were often neophytes, some economic nationalists supported by the military, who were adopting policies and programs contrary to the progressive measures taken during the Alliance years. Almost all the countries were beset by budget deficits and unfavorable balances of trade. Export earnings were declining and foreign exchange reserves precariously low.

José Luis reviewed with me the situation in each of the member states, and said he was particularly concerned about the depth of the economic downturn in the less-developed countries. He emphasized the need for a broad new policy framework for inter-American cooperation—what Pete Vaky had called an "overarching" strategy. He felt that without a strong development component in that framework, the gains made during the Alliance years were bound to be erased. He avoided any comment on U.S. policies. Jose Luis believed that the future of CIES in development assistance depended on an agreement between the OAS and the IDB in which the IDB would finance certain CIES activities that would assist countries in preparing projects of interest to the IDB. Although CIES had created the IDB, the two entities had not maintained a close working relationship. With the powers of the OAS secretary general carefully circumscribed, his ability to open a dialogue with the president of the IDB was limited. José Luis recognized that promoting a coordinated inter-institutional approach was a long shot, but it was the best alternative open to the OAS.

As I completed each of the three interviews, I reported my findings to Diogo and Raposo. As the weeks wore on, Raposo and I came to talk more and more about the situation in the hemisphere and what the role of the CIES Secretariat might be. Diogo expressed interest and went back to preparing his own paper to replace that being prepared by José Luis Restrepo.

Then I turned to interviews with the chiefs of the eight operating divisions. I asked Victoria Espinosa of the Program Office to schedule them and join me whenever she was available. The meetings were with: José Luis Restrepo, chief of Development Programming; Ricardo Murúa of Rural Development; Stahis Panagides of Rural Sector Programming; Kirk Rodgers of Regional Development Programming; Henry Laurant of Public Sector; Alberto Insúa of Social Development; Renato Tovar of International Trade; and Medina Torres of Tourism.

The two divisions with the most active technical assistance portfolios were Regional Development and Rural Sector Programming, and they were advising governments on planning and implementing significant regional sector projects, ranging from river systems to increasing agricultural and mining production. The two areas overlapped but communication between the two divisions was haphazard.

The Public Sector had evolved in the later years of the Alliance into an important advisory service for governments on measures to improve their public administration, especially fiscal management and civil service development. In the past two years, as funding dried up, this critical sector had fallen on hard times.

The Tourism Program in the late 1960s had been one of the most successful Secretariat operations. It had stimulated significant private sector investment and foreign exchange earnings in a region where both were in short supply, but now this activity had faded away.

The Division of International Trade was as much a research arm of the Secretariat as it was an advisory service for the member states. It had built a comprehensive database on trade between and among the member countries as well between the region and the rest of the world. It worked with member governments in improving their trade statistics, including marketing patterns, and commodity prices. There was no record of its providing assistance to governments on measures to expand, diversify, or improve their trade capability or attract new investment capital.

The Division of Social Development was the vestige of the Labor-Trade Union program but had no operating field projects.

When I finished this initial program review, I sat down with

Diogo and Raposo and suggested that we consider a different structure for the Secretariat. I was very careful not to be a gringo in someone else's candy store. I tied my proposal to the 1979 priorities set by CIES and the discussions in the working group for the Special General Assembly for Development. When I finished my presentation, Diogo authorized me to prepare a new organization chart and a revised plan of operations. He set up a review group that included Raposo, the program officer, an office director, and himself; and he asked me to prepare a paper for consideration by January 1981 to give the group ample time for reaching a decision prior to the preparation of the 1982 fiscal year budget.

Reorganization

The core of my organization plan was based on the 1979 IA/ECOSOC Declaration of Barbados, which instructed the Secretariat to strengthen the regional training institutions and to concentrate its advisory services on "helping member countries to expand their financial base and mobilize domestic resources to sustain development efforts through (a) expanded tax, budget, and fiscals systems; (b) better project preparation capability to attract external financing; and (c) increased income from international trade and export promotion."

It defined CIES's mission to be advising governments in the preparation of projects that made them eligible for financing by worldwide, hemispheric, and sub-regional financial bodies. It instructed CIES to concentrate its assistance in four priority areas: social development, energy, tourism, and food. In social development, it identified the need for employment generation, manpower planning, skills training and vocational education, industrial health and hygiene, social security systems, labor schools, and workers' banks. In energy, the goal was development of alternative sources of energy and conservation of existing resources. In tourism, the focus was on the lesser-developed Caribbean countries and helping them create jobs, earn foreign exchange, and build the base for more diversified development. In food, the objective was to boost food production and improve nutritional levels. Education and health were not included as priorities because those sectors were the province of the Council on Education, Science, and Culture (CIECC), and the Pan American Health Organization (PAHO). CIES was instructed to consult CIECC and PAHO if any ECOSOC projects contained health or education components.

In preparing my proposal, I studied the records of CIES starting in 1962 when it was essentially a forum with little or no technical staff or experience in development programming. It was in 1963 that CIES began forming a staff of economists and technicians to implement the Alliance for Progress. While they were still in the initial stages of training professional staff, CIES was called on to advise countries on the preparation of national development plans, building public and private sector institutions, and identifying projects for funding. The records also showed that few of the Latin American countries had in place the institutions and trained personnel needed to prepare and implement complex development plans. The reports also revealed significant differences from country to country, but also some striking similarities, such as, accelerating rural to urban migration that had spawned large-scale urban unemployment, substantial population increase as a result of improved health programs, and a poor level of public education.

The review of the workflow and activities of each CIES staff divisions for the past decade showed a sharp decline in the work of most divisions, only Regional Development and Rural Sector Development Planning had maintained high levels of project activity. That activity was due to the funding received from the IDB for the preparation of projects IDB considered promising for further IDB loan funding. In public administration, the requests for assistance in raising tax revenues and improving tax collection process also had remained high, but funds to respond to those requests dwindled.

In all the other divisions, as their technical assistance portfolios declined, middle level technicians had rapidly found comparable jobs at the World Bank, the IDB, or the UN Development Program. Many of the senior officers found it difficult to find equivalent posts and several divisions were left with chiefs and few, if any, technicians. Reducing the number of divisions would require finding assignments for several surplus division chiefs, and that raised administrative problems under OAS personnel regulations and some practical ones since a few division directors had been at logger-heads for years and others had strong political supports.

Before I put my ideas on paper, I talked informally with colleagues at AID and the IDB—not about the reorganization *per se,* but the potential interest of their using the reorganized Secretariat for working with them in project development and their disposition to funding that work. While the responses were equivocal, there were not negative.

In early January 1981, I presented a draft report to the executive secretary. He reviewed it, asked some questions, and convened the review group. The group met a couple of times and introduced some revisions. The revised draft was then discussed with the secretary general before putting it in final form. The review process was similar to that followed in the U.S. government, except it was in a multilateral environment. In February, it was formally approved.

The new Secretariat had two permanent coordinating committees to support the executive secretary and the executive officer in planning, programming, and operating the Secretariat: Policy, Planning, and Program chaired by the executive secretary and Program Operations chaired by the executive officer.

There were only three operating departments, instead of eight divisions. Five division directors were eliminated; most of those whose positions were eliminated chose to retire or resign. The first of the three divisions was the Department of Regional Development, Energy, and Natural Resources, which combined functions that had been previously scattered. It covered the Barbados Declaration priorities of energy, food, and tourism. Its task was to advise member states on policies, strategies, and planning of integrated projects for designated geographic areas within countries and multinational frontier areas, including infrastructure, agricultural, food, environmental protection, population projections, and energy prospects. The department's goal was to assist member states in preparing bankable projects for funding by international lending agencies, including preparing cost/benefit analyses.

The second was the Department of Integral Social Development and Manpower, which again brought together activities dispersed through several former divisions, and it responded to the top priority of the Barbados Declaration. Its role was to help member states define strategies and policies; strengthen institutions; prepare projects to providing skill training for their rural and urban populations; raise productivity and living standards; and increase the participation of people in the benefits of development. Its mission was to help governments design programs and projects for funding by international lending agencies.

The third was the Department of Institutional and Financial Resources, which would advise member governments on policies and programs to broaden and increase their financial resources, improve public administration, and create incentives for private investment needed for effective long-term development. It again brought together a range of activities that had been dispersed among several former divisions. It covered the remaining priorities set forth in the Barbados Declaration.

The reorganization also reduced seven advisory offices to two: the first was the Development Studies Unit to prepare economic and financial studies mandated by the CIES, including those on commodities and regional integration movements; and the second was the Planning and Program Office to assist the executive director, the executive officer, and the three departments prepare annual programs, appraise results, and prepare progress reports to CIES.

The proposal was presented to the 1981 meeting of IA/ECOSOC as a streamlined Secretariat focused on implementing the Declaration of Barbados. The objective also responded to the comment of the then Executive Vice President of the IDB Ray Sternfeld, "Our money is out there looking for projects to fund—instead of good projects coming to the Bank for funding." IA/ECOSOC unanimously ratified the proposal at its 1981 meeting.

As we were reorganizing CIES, the Reagan administration was taking office. At the OAS, John Ford was our primary source of information about the key officials with whom we would be working. All of us expected major policy changes and we hoped that Reagan would revisit the importance of support for development initiatives in the hemisphere in the face of the Sandinistas in Nicaragua, the economic crises causing political unrest in a score of countries, and the possible effects those events might have on the balance in the Cold War.

It was fascinating for me to observe the change in the U.S. administration from the vantage point of an international organization. My coworkers at the OAS were mostly Latin American and Caribbean, and had quite a different perception of what was going on in the U.S. than my former colleagues in the U.S. government. Even the most liberal who praised Carter for his support for human rights gave him little support for his policies on development. None of them had much affinity for Castro or the USSR, but all of them believed that the U.S. did not understand the complexity of the economic, social, and political changes taking place south of the Rio Grande. They understood that the odds of another Alliance for Progress were minimal, but they hoped the new administration might sponsor a new initiative for inter-American cooperation to deal with the current array of problems.

After the restructuring was approved, I spent considerable time talking with associates in the U.S. government, like David Lazar, who was confirmed as AID's director of Program Planning for Latin America, and urged them to reconsider their assessment of cooperation and coordination with CIES in development programming and implementation. When I briefed the new ambassador to the OAS, J. William Middendorf, he asked penetrating questions and offered me his support in advising higher echelons at the State Department and the White House of the new orientation of CIES. Many of those favorably disposed were skeptical about the capability of CIES, given its previous track record. Moreover, at that time, they were more concerned with what policy changes the new administration might take in the scope and direction of bilateral aid, than support for multilateral donor organizations.

So, as I told Ele, my job now was to provide the leadership inside the Secretariat to make the technical staff as effective as possible in providing practical technical support needed by Latin America and the Caribbean. That meant bringing together the technicians of the different disciplines in the new departments and inducing them to work as unified teams, and not as separate, sometimes competing, project groups.

Our New Place of Life

The schedule at the OAS was different from that in the State Department. Yes, I arrived at work every morning at 7:30 a.m. Yes, I had a steady flow into my in-box. Yes, I had daily meetings with my colleagues and senior officials of the member states. Yes, there were headaches that seemed interminable and problems that just didn't seem to have solutions. Yes, I was frequently out of the office on business at the State Department, the Inter-American Development Bank, the World Bank, and the International Monetary Fund and even to Capitol Hill. But I seemed to be able to get my work done in nine to ten hours a day. I could plan regularly to take a rush hour bus and be home by 6:30 p.m. And my weekends were virtually free except when I was the duty officer or there was a meeting of CIES.

That meant that Ele and I had more time together to do things that we wanted to do. We could plan our own social life without the threat of an emergency that would call me back to Foggy Bottom. At the Secretariat, I was on duty as the "Officer of the Day" once every six weeks and that required me to go to the office on Saturday mornings and stay close to a phone the rest of the week. But that was manageable. Even on those duty Saturdays, I would arrange to meet Ele downtown, and we would go to the National Gallery, the Smithsonian, or occasionally a matinee at the National Theater.

We did have some official social obligations. We went to celebrations of member states' national days, sometimes at the residences of the representatives, sometimes in the Hall of the Americas at the OAS building. Once or twice a year, we were included in Secretary General Orfila's guest list for a dinner or reception. Ele often came to the office to help host a birthday or farewell party. But we were really in control of our own lives in a way that we had not enjoyed since the early 1950s.

We did very little entertaining in our small one-bedroom apartment. When we invited people for dinner or to play bridge, I had to almost stack furniture to fit everyone and everything in. But Ele and I were thinking of the job as a short-time experience and really expected to go "home" to Tulare when the brief assignment was over.

We kept in touch with my former colleagues in the U.S. Mission and were included in office parties. Herb Thompson, my successor at the mission, and I lunched regularly as much for personal as for business purposes. And we joined the mission in mourning when Gale McGee died from complications due to his diabetes, shortly after he completed his appointment as U.S. representative.

Ele continued to write her monthly column for the AAFSW, *"What if?"* which advised wives on how to deal with various kinds of economic and personal crises. To prepare her column, she continued to attend lectures on investment strategies, tax policy, business practices, and international trade. She was invited to the White House conferences on entrepreneurship and small business development. Her visits once or twice a week to her brokers were as much for information for her columns as they were to invest for us—and she had more funds to invest than at any other time in our married life, thanks to my State Department pension, my OAS salary, and the increased income from the farms and two rented houses. In our investments, she practiced not putting all our eggs in one basket, with a diversified asset base to protect us from financial crises. I can still hear her telling me that we need to spread the risk. In the early 1980s, for the first time in our lives, we felt quite financially secure. Her foresight and financial acumen allowed us to look forward to a comfortable retirement.

Ele kept very detailed accounts of all the investments. She balanced the monthly checkbook. She queried the brokers whenever some matter troubled the Tragen portfolio. She would brief me almost nightly on developments and point out concerns about a stock or the impact of a U.S. Treasury or IRS decision on one of our holdings. She would call congressional offices or even the White House to seek answers to the problems she identified, or to give them a piece of her mind about some proposed legislation or course of action. I well remember the evenings when I came home to find her on the phone with then South Dakota Representative Daschle (he represented the district in which the South Dakota farm was located) about a proposed change in agriculture policy that she believed would negatively affect the farms. I heard her tell a staffer in our Tulare Congressman Bob Mathis's office that the information he was giving her was inaccurate, and insisted she talk directly with Bob, whose father had been her family's physician and whose brother was her personal physician. Bob called her later to apologize.

Ele no longer felt constrained as the wife of a foreign service officer. She told me one night in 1981 that in the years we were in the Foreign Service, she did not assert herself for fear that it might affect "the job." Since El Salvador, she felt that she was "on stage" as my wife and never felt comfortable expressing her own views because, like me, she was a representative of the U.S. government. Since my retirement, she now felt free to do it her way. She added, "Don't ask me to be a foreign service wife any longer, just let me be Ele who now has only her own life and interests to live."

Implementing the Reorganization

Diogo asked me to take charge of implementing the reorganization and help establish effective working relations among the three department directors. Any reorganization is hard. Sometimes we reorganize just to reorganize. Not this time. It was a substantive change. Some former division directors left us and others agreed to work within the new structure. Several technicians were assigned new scopes of work. Refocusing the staff to our new objective of helping countries plan and carry out multi-purpose projects whose future funding would come from another agency was a major challenge.

For the Department of Regional Development, Energy, and Natural Resources, not much help was needed. It made the transition quickly and effectively. The department was already organized to do the job. Its director, Kirk Rodgers, and the deputy, Newton Cordeiro, had built an interdisciplinary staff and oversaw projects in eight countries that involved integrated rural development, food production, strengthened government institutions, more efficient use of water and energy supplies, infrastructure building, community participation, and expansion of employment opportunities outside of agriculture. Kirk and Newton had negotiated sizable financial and personnel counterpart contributions from the countries to match those provided by IA/ECOSOC. They knew how to prepare loan requests for the World Bank, the IDB, and the International Fund for Agricultural Development (IFAD) and had received funding from them to provide technical assistance in loan implementation.

On the other hand, getting the other two departments up to operating speed presented very serious challenges, made even more complex by fiscal austerity and shortages of seasoned technicians.

The focus of the new Department of Institutional and Financial Resources was very different from their former mission of advising governments on the preparation of national development plans. The new emphasis was on public sector organization and operations, fiscal and tax policy, and investment strategies. Most of the available staff had little expertise in those subjects. The department was headed by José Luis Restrepo and Henry Laurant, the former director of Public Administration. It brought together projects in a dozen countries that included advice on systems for collecting income taxes and customs revenues, maintaining national accounts, and setting up fiscal controls and government information systems. Its database contained detailed profiles on the fiscal and monetary structure of each country, the institutional set-up, the steps forward that had been taken and the capacity of the staff. It also illustrated that, in countries without civil service, a change in government meant that far too many technically-trained staffers were let go and improvements in public administration were often wiped out. While the situation varied sharply from country to country, the records indicated that very few member states had tackled the central fiscal and monetary issues that were constraining their growth potential. Most faced immediate fiscal crises and cash flow shortages.

The department staff had good analytical capabilities to diagnose institutional, fiscal, and monetary problems in the countries. Unfortunately, most of the specialists and economists who had experience in providing technical assistance had moved on to other jobs, and it was necessary to reorient and provide training for the remaining technicians. We faced a major on-the-job training challenge. To help in this undertaking, several technicians and I became active participants in the American Society of Public Administration (ASPA). With the support of Mel Spector from the State Department and OAS Director of Management Ron Scheman, we organized round-table discussions about strategies, tactics, policies, and procedures for introducing reform packages and invited senior U.S. administrators to participate. Even the comptroller general of the United States, Elmer Staats, found the subject matter interesting enough to join a couple of the sessions.

The Department of Integral Social Development was essentially new and required in-depth guidance in designing its program and presenting a package of services that responded to country priorities. It was no secret that the Department of Social Development was my special interest. I had always been focused on people and their role in development. I believe that that the ultimate goal of development is to benefit people and raise living standards and that job creation is critical to providing income and hope to people while the process of change takes place. Social instability means political instability, which in turn inhibits the development process.

The only socially-oriented division in the former organization was the OAS labor program that focused on trade union training. It had no experience with manpower, employment service, worker skills training, or community development programs. We had in effect to start from scratch.

I had hoped that Stahis Panagides, who had been the chief of Rural Sector Planning, would take over the post, but he received an offer from the IDB and moved on. The deputy representative of Venezuela to the OAS, Josefina Rodriguez, had experience with manpower programs in her home country, and her government was a major supporter of social development. I proposed to Diogo that for both professional and political reasons, we consider naming her director for two years. Venezuela and Brazil could provide a necessary voice for the department in the meetings of IA/ECOSOC and perhaps help us obtain the funding needed to staff properly this critical area of the CIES's work. The government of Venezuela agreed to a detail, and she became the director.

During the Alliance years, there had been few projects that dealt with social development, especially in urban areas. Little consideration had been given to projects dealing with the massive rural-to-urban migration underway or to improve living conditions in urban areas. There were some loans for water and sanitation projects, but almost none aimed at helping the people to cope with the massive changes taking place. The challenge facing the new division was how to help governments design strategies and tactics — right now! Josefina and I decided that our effort should be directed at two levels: (1) advising governments on the design of long term programs to provide people and communities with the tools to help themselves, especially through skill training to take advantage of employment opportunities, and (2) helping government create conditions favorable to grassroots self-help action programs, such as cooperatives and community improvement projects. We wanted to draw on the experiences of the Inter-American Foundation and Penny Foundation, credit unions and cooperatives, as well as proposals by Peruvian Hernando de Soto to legalize the informal business sector and develop micro lines of credit for small manufacturers, businessmen, and handicraft producers.

Josefina proposed that the department begin project activities on a small scale — by responding to pending country requests (1) for technical support for worker and grassroots micro lending projects that OAS, AID, and other organizations had successfully supported during the Alliance years and (2) for manpower short-term skills training projects to alleviate the critical shortage of semi-skilled and skilled workers in the less developed countries. For those activities, we requested funds to hire two or three specialists.

However, the OAS budget crisis prevented our hiring, even on short-term contracts, experts we identified in Argentina, Chile, Bolivia, and Mexico. We were able to contract a former colleague from the Inter-American Foundation, Anthony Gomes with extensive Latin American grassroots field experience, including credit unions and micro-finance, and to interest the U.S. Department of Labor to detail, at no cost, skill training specialists to prepare short-term skill training courses for Caribbean countries.

The interest of the Caribbean member states in social development projects led us to contract a demographic specialist, Loy Bilderback, from Fresno State University to provide us an overview of population trends and the composition of the work force in that region. In less than a year, he provided us with not only the overview but also a historical framework that provided basic data for long-term manpower programs. His studies confirmed that the Caribbean countries had an overpopulation problem, and were exporting their populations, on some islands at the rate of 50 percent.

Emigration was the safety value that kept a cap on civil unrest and provided remittances that saved many families from extreme poverty. They also correlated the improvement of public health facilities, especially in the former British colonies, with the large increases in population and provided evidence that the public education system paid little attention to providing the growing population with essential skills training.

After analyzing Loy's studies, in cooperation with the OAS Council for Education, Science, and Culture (CESC), we inventoried the training facilities in several countries and sent a mission to identify the immediate needs for skilled workers. These studies showed an immediate need for several thousand semi-skilled workers for the emerging tourist industry alone, including hundreds of technicians needed for maintaining air conditioners, elevators, electrical systems, modern plumbing, and television. They recommended setting up short-term training programs at the same time as steps were taken to modernize vocational school curriculum

Creating hundreds of new jobs in a country of a few hundred thousand people could be an important stimulus to economic development and help stabilize social and living conditions. With the assistance of the U.S. Department of Labor, a project was designed for a series of discreet, short-term courses to be conducted in different Caribbean countries. Those courses would provide the trainee with basic skills and knowledge that allowed him/her to do key elements of a job, and set the stage for the second, third, and fourth levels of skill training to raise him/her over time to be a journeyman. The target trainee was to be a young adult, who required income to meet family obligations. This approach was similar to that I had hoped to introduce in El Salvador in the mid-1950s.

Then I looked for funding. I knew that the Caribbean governments could not provide cash resources in view of their budgetary crises. I contacted David Lazar at AID, Ray Sternfeld at the IDB, and my classmate from UC Berkeley, Jim Grant at UNICEF.

It was not until late 1983 that, with a grant from AID and help from the U.S. Department of Labor, we could eke out enough to run the trials. Trainers tailor-made the courses. The governments provided facilities and helped select the trainees. We had no funds to cover living expenses for people in training for the short three-four month courses, and none of the countries had employment services to line up jobs for those in training. When you are learning by doing, you don't always have all the building blocks in the right places to get the job done the way you would have wished. But we tried. We provided the first segment of critically needed skills. The end result was that some unskilled people became semi-skilled, and every one found better paying jobs than they had before training.

As we were bringing together the new CIES program, Secretary General Orfila periodically invited Diogo and me to brief him. Orfila was sufficiently encouraged by our progress that he suggested that, when we were ready, he would join us in a visit to IDB President Antonio Ortiz Mena and Vice President Sternfeld to explore an institutional arrangement for IDB funding of CIES projects. That support from the secretary general was a major stimulus for moving our efforts forward.

By 1983, all three departments were beginning to put together some inviting projects when a political crisis in the OAS led to the resignation of Secretary General Orfila. All our plans were suspended until a new secretary general was selected. In 1984 Deputy Foreign Minister of Brazil João Clemente Baena Soares was elected to succeed Orfila. Diogo told me that Baena was not interested in supporting the OAS economic development program, and saw IA/ECOSOC and CIES as expendable. Rumors ran quickly around our small Secretariat and several key technicians found other employment. Then, Josefina's two-year detail to the OAS from her government ended, and there were no funds available to replace her. By mid-1984, the future of CIES was under a shadow.

Time for Friends

Friendships have been important components of our lives, and this was a period in which we were able to enjoy them. In 1981, we took a summer vacation in Hawaii and California. Ed and Lois Faison were settled in Honolulu. Chet and Dorothy Guthrie had sold their Bethesda, Maryland home and returned to California where they bought an apple orchard in Sebastopol. So we decided to see both couples on the same trip.

We flew to Oahu where the Faisons welcomed us to their home at Kailua and we spent several days with them lolling in the sun and being tourists. Then we visited the islands of Kauai, Maui, and Hawaii before returning to San Francisco where the Guthries met us and whisked us up to their aerie on a hill in Sebastopol overlooking the Sonoma Valley. I don't know which part of the trip was the more enjoyable. We had a total break from our routine and really recharged our batteries. We loved the Sonoma and Napa Valleys, and began rethinking retirement in Tulare. Chet and Dorothy even showed us some properties that were for sale and we discussed possible financing.

Their daughter Gail and her husband Bob Thomas moved from Alexandria, Virginia to Sebastopol, and Gail founded an innovative personnel management advisory company, with specialized software she had designed based on her years of experience in the federal government. She invited me to join her board of directors, and Secretary General Orfila approved my accepting the offer. That required me for the next couple of years to fly out to San Francisco every few months for board meetings; Ele accompanied me once or twice. Sometimes, my nephew Gary Meyer, who was living in Mill Valley, would meet me at the airport and take me up to Sebastopol. After Chet and Dorothy died, our interest in Sebastopol also passed.

Another long-time friend and, my mentor in El Salvador, Bill Schenk was chair of the Economics Faculty at the University of South Alabama in Mobile. Bill and his wife, Hildreth, came to Washington early in 1981 for a meeting of the International Executive Service Corps, and we were assigned to the same panel on the role of the private sector in development planning. Following two days of discussions, Bill and Hildreth took Ele and me on a spectacular weekend soaking up the splendors of southern Virginia, including visits to Williamsburg, Yorktown, and Jamestown. On our drive back to Washington, Bill invited me to South Alabama University to participate in a seminar on the Alliance for Progress. Secretary General Orfila authorized me to participate and Ele and I spent a week with the Schenks in Mobile. My seminar presentation was so lively and well received that Bill scheduled a repeat performance on the following day. After the second seminar, Bill took us down to the Gulf of Mexico where I enjoyed the best prawns I can ever remember as we picnicked on the warm sand. Before returning to Washington, we drove over to New Orleans through Confederate country and Jefferson Davis's last residence. In New Orleans, we met a former colleague from Bolivia, then a professor of Economics at the Louisiana State University, spent two days and nights exploring the sites, music, and cuisine of that unique city.

Our close friends, David and Nancy Lazar, lived just a few miles away across the District Line in Bethesda, Maryland; every few weeks, we had dinner together and occasionally shared a night at the theater. David and I had a special meeting place: the library he had built in the basement of his Bethesda home—the library I had always wanted but never had. He called it the "Orfila Memorial Library," because he funded its construction with the termination package he received from the OAS when he resigned from the same post that I now occupied. We spent many hours in that library talking about the world and our lives.

In 1983, David was named AID representative to the Organization for Economic Cooperation and Development (OECD) in Paris. Nancy opted not to go with him since she was earning her masters as a law librarian. David's residence in Paris was a government-leased, furnished, full floor apartment in an elegant building in the 16th arrondissement, just a few blocks from OECD headquarters. A few months after David's assignment, the OECD invited the OAS to participate in a roundtable on Latin American development, and suggested that I be one of the participants. I stayed with David for a week. It was the first of four visits we made to Paris during his incumbency there. I say we, because Ele joined me each time I went to Paris.

In 1984, the OECD invited me to return for a panel on development. This time we took our annual vacation at the end of the meeting. David took us on a weekend drive through the mustard fields to Normandy, Giverny, Rouen, Honfleur, and Deauville. During the week, Ele and I took the fast train to Grenoble and Lyons. We also mastered the Paris Metro and began our exploration of as many corners of the city as we could. We found a small Norman-run restaurant on the Île de la Cité with the most delicious menus at prices we could afford. We made friends with the two sisters who prepared the food and ran the establishment; our poor French was enough to earn us a warm welcome on each visit and a special treat at the end of each meal. We took David to the restaurant on the last day of our first visit and he became a member of their family.

We often had dinner with Nancy while David was in Paris. At one of the dinners, Ele picked up the sounds of discord between Nancy and David. She warned me not to pick sides in the dispute and let them work out the arrangement that was best for them. They divorced after David returned from Paris. While we remained friends with both, David remained a very special part of my life, an alter ego with whom I could discuss almost any issue and get help in finding a constructive way out.

In these early 1980 years, we also had some wonderful times with Francis Howard and her equally talented daughter, Anne. Fran now lived in the Colonnade, an apartment complex around the corner from us. Fran was working with National Institutes of Health and was a sponsor of the Washington Opera. Her invitations allowed us to meet a broad cross-section of exciting people in the mainstream of Washington political, cultural, and scientific life. She was generous in her invitations to dinners, receptions, and events at home and at the Kennedy Center. Her enthusiasm, always finding the bright side to a problem in the tradition of her late brother Hubert Humphrey, enriched our lives and gave us special pleasure. Ele and I had learned over the years how to walk into a room and introduce ourselves to each and every person, but Fran had a special grace of sweeping into the room, lighting it up, and making friends. Fran was a committed internationalist and was always probing to find new ways we could improve relations among countries.

By 1980, Fran's son Bill had settled in Minnesota and Anne, now graduated from university, was developing her own public relations firm on Connecticut Avenue, not far from my office. We had lunches together quite regularly, often at the OAS or at one of the "in" spots on Connecticut Avenue. When Anne had a client with Latin American interests, I did my best to help her prepare proposals or presentations.

Anne introduced me to Nancy Deale Greene, a foreign policy

specialist and adviser to the Pentagon who firmly believed that better foreign policy would result from "dyads," teams of men and women working together, rather than cadres made up of just one or the other sex. Nancy, the wife of famed TV actor Lorne Greene, sponsored several workshops in collaboration with the Pentagon and chose me to be her "dyad" partner. I believe that we had three weekend workshops in 1982 and 1983 at which several groups were asked to resolve specific foreign policy issues related to the Cold War; some groups were all male, others female, and two or three of them "dyads." In the final sessions, we would compare approaches and try to ascertain whether the "dyad" produced superior results. I'm not sure whether "dyads" were superior, but the experience was memorable.

Nancy and Lorne Greene became friends. We had dinners together when they came to Washington and found a wonderful Chinese restaurant not far from our apartment where we could talk and eat at leisure. They would invite us to their hotel, the Jefferson, for informal get-togethers, often with senior Pentagon officials with whom Nancy worked. At two or three of them, Ele reunited with her Tulare high school friend, Admiral Elmo Zumwalt, who, although a year or two ahead of her, had come to know each other fairly well through Ele's cousin, David Leonard. On those evenings, Ele and the admiral would go off into a corner and spent considerable time talking together.

Anne Howard arranged for me to be a member of the U.S. delegation invited by the Congress of Venezuela to the two-hundredth-anniversary celebration of the birth of Simón Bolívar. The Congress invited congressional leaders from all over the hemisphere and Spain to the event, including opposition leaders from Latin American countries governed by military dictatorships. All the delegates were housed in the Hotel Tamanaco and met together for breakfast and cocktails. I met many old friends and some new acquaintances like Chedi Jagan, then the opposition leader in Guyana. There was a cascade of receptions at the Congress, Miraflores Palace (the Venezuelan White House), and the residence of the president of Venezuela. There were seminars on and formal tributes to Bolívar that ranged from his legacy to assessments of U.S. policy in the hemisphere, the Cold War, and the outlook for democratic development in Latin America and the Caribbean.

Before we went to Caracas, Anne introduced Ele and me to her new beau, Dennis Tristani. Dennis was the scion of a Puerto Rican family and his grandfather had been the late Democratic Senator Dennis Chavez of New Mexico. Ele and I were thrilled to be included in dinners with Dennis, whom we liked from day one. When Anne asked us if we thought that she should marry Dennis, our answer was a resounding affirmative.

Anne and Dennis were married in the Bethlehem Chapel of the National Cathedral. Ele and I were seated between former democratic presidential candidate George McGovern and then U.S. ambassador to the United Nations, Jeanne Kirkpatrick. The two were old friends who had worked together in the 1960s as foreign policy advisers to Senator Humphrey. However, their views of the world and the role the U.S. should play in it took radically different courses in the 1970s. As we were seated in the wedding chapel, the two greeted each other warmly before they commented on some current international happening on which they had quite different positions. Ele and I sat discreetly as the friendly exchange played out, ending with a couple of sharp-edged bullets—and I can still hear McGovern saying, "Irving, don't you agree with me?" while the ambassador joshed back that I couldn't have such bad judgment.

We also enjoyed a second memorable wedding at the National Cathedral in the early 1980s—that of Paul Vaky, the youngest son of our colleague Viron "Pete" Vaky. It was held in the same Bethlehem Chapel and was a special family occasion. My recollection of the wedding and reception is of the smiling parents and the beautiful bride and handsome groom.

In the early 80s, a warm, special friendship with Margaret and David Frederickson blossomed. They were from Tulare, and Margaret's parents, good friends of Ele's family, had attended our wedding reception in Tulare that hot August night in 1947. David was a newsman and event organizer who worked in the Ford White House, spent the late 1970s with the Ronald Reagan campaign, and was now an official in the Reagan White House They lived in the Cathedral East apartment complex up the hill from us. Over those four years we became close friends, sharing Christmas and New Year holidays, much as we had in earlier years with the Guthries. Whenever Margaret's mother Eleanor came to town, she and Ele would take the day together to visit the Smithsonian or the National Gallery of Art.

It was disappointing that we could not share much time with many of our foreign service colleagues since most lived in Maryland or Virginia, and the Tragens did not have a car. Arranging for dinners often entailed logistical problems, such as bus schedules and meeting points. Sometimes one of our friends would pick us up and deliver us back home even though it required an hour's driving time each way. One couple we did see periodically was Arthur and Lucille Brown, my cousins from San Francisco who lived in Northern Virginia. Lucille's parents were Uncle Mo and Aunt Tillie who had visited us in Mexico City. Arthur's brother Warren had been my high school and college buddy.

We had no such logistical problems with Faye and Frank Sherry, who lived just one floor above us. We dined and played bridge with them regularly. My recollections of the many hours we spent with the Sherrys in their elegant, pastel-shaded apartment, adorned by the intriguing canvases that Faye had painted, are of wonderful conversation, delightful dinners, and sound advice—all the indicia of true friendship.

Another friend in the Towers was Edward Gingold, a veteran government lawyer, who had done graduate work in Spain, and had great interest in the Foreign Service. I met Edward at the bus stop one morning as we were going to work and a strong friendship developed and exists to this day. We had dinners together with Edward and his then roommate, Chris Railey (a grandson of Louisiana's Huey Long), sometimes at the Towers and sometimes, thanks to Chris's convertible, at one of the "in" restaurants around the Washington area.

The ever-present friend was Elizabeth La Cell in Tulare. Every Sunday afternoon, Ele would receive a call from her. If we went to the National Cathedral in the morning or visited the Smithsonian, Ele would hustle us home by the appointed hour for the call from Elizabeth. She stretched out on her bed to hear the latest news from Tulare and reports on her houses before detailing the events of her week. Elizabeth was her connection to her roots.

For Ele and me, July 1980 to the fall of 1984 was our closest time together. We enjoyed our friends, we enjoyed life, and we enjoyed each other.

Relations with the Missions to the OAS

In my job, I had working relations with almost all of the missions of the member states to the OAS. My assignment as deputy U.S. representative to OAS and ambassador to IA/ECOSOC had helped me established contacts with most of the Latin American and Caribbean delegations. Almost every day, a representative of one or another country was in my office to discuss the status of an existing project or the prospects for a new one in which his government had special interest.

The United States remained the most important OAS member of the IA/ECOSOC and CIES. The U.S. was the principal source of funds and a critical voice in defining the focus of its activities. I spent considerable time with that delegation.

After the election of President Reagan, William Middendorf was appointed to succeed Gale McGee as U.S. representative to OAS. Middendorf had a deep interest in the OAS and, shortly after his appointment, he invited John Ford, Ron Scheman, and me to a lunch at the State Department. He told us that he would use his considerable influence at the White House and on the Hill to strengthen the U.S. relationship with the inter-American system and pay up U.S. quota arrearages. That was a real shot in the arm. Middendorf was able to enlarge the staff of the U.S. Mission and assemble a strong team. He kept Herb Thompson as the deputy until Herb's retirement in 1982, and then had his replacement appointed with ambassadorial rank to facilitate relations with counterparts from the other member states. He arranged the appointment of Robert Schuler as his economic officer; Bob was a seasoned economic reporting officer who knew Latin America well. He also appointed a very bright young Roger Noriega as his aide.

For me, the appointment of Bob Schuler was a positive development. I had worked with him in ROCAP when he had been economic reporting officer in Honduras. His analytical ability and integrity made him an objective reporter with a bent for identifying key problems. Bob's observations were especially helpful when CIES was preparing documents for IA/ECOSOC meetings and they helped us shape proposals that avoided negative U.S. reactions. While my primary assignment was to oversee the technical cooperation component of the CIES program, Diogo usually asked me to draft documents for the IA/ECOSOC meetings. He would tell me the thrust he wanted, and I tried to find language that met his instructions without conflicting with what I knew about the U.S. position.

In 1981, IA/ECOSOC convoked a special meeting on the financial crisis that was engulfing almost all of the member states in the steepest downturn since the great depression of the 1930s The economic forecasts predicted no growth throughout the region in face of substantial population increases, widespread unrest caused by urban unemployment, and middle class demands for better public services. Many governments faced unprecedented financial shortfalls, and countries like Argentina and Mexico were facing imminent default on their national debt.

Spearheaded by Brazil, Peru, and Venezuela, the Special Meeting was convoked for Caracas in early 1982. Its agenda basically called on the United States, developed countries, and international lending agencies to channel large dollar assistance to Latin America and Caribbean countries to help alleviate budget deficits and foreign exchange shortfalls. They felt that they had leverage to pressure the U.S. in the Cold War to come to their assistance.

The agenda did not call on Latin American governments to commit to making fiscal and monetary reforms that were critical for putting their economies back on an even keel. My contacts in the U.S. government, including Middendorf and David Lazar, stated that the United States would not respond without commitments by the Latin American and Caribbean governments to reform fiscal and monetary policies and practices that contributed to and were exacerbating the crisis. I stressed it in discussions with Diogo and José Luis Restrepo. As an international civil servant, I understood my position, but I wanted to facilitate an agreement. Bob Schuler gave the same message to his counterparts in the drafting group that prepared the documents for the meeting. Middendorf tried to assemble a high-level U.S. delegation. He asked colleagues at the White House, the Federal Reserve, and Treasury as well as executives of major banks. Very few accepted. He did put together a strong enough mid-level U.S. delegation to attract every economic and finance minister from Latin America and the Caribbean.

Unfortunately, the only Latin American countries that were committed to adopt those difficult and painful reforms were Chile and Colombia. The other government delegations stuck to their instructions to call on the U.S. and the international community to provide substantial new resources. Argentina and Venezuela led the charge, but I sensed that several governments were eager for a confrontation with U.S.

I also noted significant changes in the negotiating environment. At the IA/ECOSOC meetings in the mid-1960s, I almost always could find colleagues in the Brazilian delegation with whom I could talk about finding a compromise or a way out of an impasse. At this meeting, the Brazilians listened politely and looked straight ahead. At first I attributed to it my being an OAS Secretariat member, not a member of the U.S. delegation. But then I came to realize that the Brazilians no longer looked at the U.S. as their partner but as a potential competitor.

In addition, the Mexican delegation had a different feel to its participation. In the 1960s, it had strongly defended the multilateral inter-American forum as a potential shield against unilateral U.S. actions. At Caracas, the language and interventions of Mexico seemed far more protective of its bilateral relationship with the U.S. and skeptical about the potential usefulness of the OAS and IA/ECOSOC. Indeed, a Mexican, Antonio Ortiz Mena, had been elected president of the IDB, in which Mexico and the U.S. were working closely together. So, why confront the U.S. at a meeting of CIES?

Colombia was the country trying to build bridges, but there were few who were ready to follow. The only country with a position close to the U.S. was Chile, but it was isolated, especially by the Caribbean countries and Venezuela because of the Pinochet government human rights record. As the meeting evolved, instead of coming together, the gap between the U.S. and the Latin American and Caribbean delegations grew wider. I sat through the sessions, listening to the discussion in which the countries talked through and past each other. The final document, prepared mainly by José Luis Restrepo, contained a solid analysis of the economic crisis in the region and then called on the U.S. and the international financial community to provide additional resources, without calling for reforms by Latin American and Caribbean governments. It was a diplomatic standoff that underlined the divisions in the hemisphere, not an expression of mutual interest in working together.

Another opportunity had been lost. The Caracas meeting was the last significant IA/ECOSOC meeting during my assignment with CIES. In many ways, it struck the death knell of CIES as a forum for serious negotiations on hemisphere-wide economic issues. In addition, the OAS member countries looked not to CIES, but the IDB (now with investors from Canada, Europe, and Asia as well as the U.S.) and the World Bank as the primary sources for project and program assistance and the International Monetary Fund for financial guidance and monetary support.

The annual IA/ECOSOC meetings in 1982, 1983, and 1984 were essentially housekeeping exercises in which the Secretariat reported on a declining number of projects and an increasing default on financial pledges by the member states. The Secretariat continued to manage about sixty projects in twenty-two countries. Some were in the public sector management, especially public finance and taxation. A few were in social development, especially on manpower in two Caribbean countries. The most significant and comprehensive were in regional development and energy, and many of them were financed not by the IA/ECOSOC but by the IDB and World Bank.

Between 1982 and 1984, I made a number of field inspection trips. After the 1982 IA/ECOSOC meeting in Asunción, Paraguay, I inspected projects in Paraguay, Uruguay, Argentina, Chile, and Peru. Regional development and energy projects had substantial support and counterpart funding from the countries; the projects were multi-sectoral, including waterway management, energy development, agricultural production, and transportation networks. There were only a few small social development projects in urban areas, and some of the regional development projects had significant manpower and farmer participation segments.

In my CIES years, the OAS had national offices, headed by a representative of the secretary general. Established in the early years of the AFP, the country offices were similar to those of the UN. The host governments treated the OAS representative as an ambassador. He oversaw all OAS business in country, including the servicing of projects and project personnel in country. My country visits were coordinated with the representative, and he or she accompanied me on most of my discussions with senior officials and visits to project operations. The representatives usually had excellent political connections in country. Many were personal friends of the presidents and key political figures. In Argentina, the representative was a retired army major with connections at the highest level of government. So, he was able to arrange high-level meetings with ministers and senior officials in addition to reviewing specific projects. In Chile, Paraguay, Peru, and Uruguay, I suspect that my access to the projects was similarly facilitated by the connections of the OAS representatives. I got insights and inside information that I would not have been given if I had still been a U.S. government official.

An example of the importance of the relationship between the OAS country representative and the national leadership occurred after the Caracas meeting on the Latin American financial crisis. The OAS representative asked me to stay on for a couple of days to meet with President Herrera Campins at his residence. The president told me of his concern about the Guajiro border region with Colombia, where he reported extensive smuggling and the threat of confrontation with Colombia. He asked for the technical services of the OAS Regional Development Department to prepare a plan for the socioeconomic development of the area, on both sides of the border. He said that the OAS was a neutral organization that both countries could support and that successful projects by the department in both countries made it the most acceptable entity to work with. I went with Venezuelan officials to visit Maracaibo and then the frontier area in Táchira for a look-see.

When I returned to Washington, Secretary General Orfila gave me the green light to consider a proposal. The formal request for a project was received just as the secretary general resigned and Herrera Campins was completing his term. The project was never really implemented, and I wonder what might have happened if a major development project for that area had been drawn up and funded by the IDB or World Bank: would a prosperous frontier area have helped suppress the smuggling and cross-border drug trafficking?

Some of the most interesting projects that I inspected were OAS assistance to governments on tax policy, planning, and institution building. I visited the planning and tax administration offices in many countries. The contrasts between countries were startling: some were still running pencil and paper operations, with incomplete lists of taxpayers and tax collections. The most complete data shown to me related to property taxes, customs revenues, and export taxes, with very little on corporate or individual income taxes. In countries like Argentina, Colombia, and Mexico, some state-of-the-art electronic equipment had brought some progress. Chile, on the other hand, had a fully operating tax system. The Chilean technicians, some of them trained at the University of Chicago, gave high praise to their OAS advisers. I saw an electronic data collection operation, with records on every taxpayer in the country, detailed maps showing property ownership, coupled with projections of anticipated income based on expected production per acre and world prices. Chile had a system for identifying tax fraud, and I received a briefing on the first two prosecutions for tax evasion in Chilean history. This was a demonstration that the tax reforms sought by the U.S. at Caracas would work effectively in Latin America if there were political will, and if the OAS was capable of providing tax specialists to advise on getting the job done.

A special field trip I made was to Grenada right after the U.S. ouster of Castro-leaning Prime Minister Bishop. Acting Prime Minister Nicholas Brathwaite asked for an OAS team to help him evaluate the needs of his government for technical assistance. Secretary General Orfila appointed me to lead a team made up of Dorel Callender and a representative from the Education, Science, and Culture Council (CIECC). The acting prime minister told us at our initial working session that he and his cabinet colleagues would prefer to have the OAS, not the U.S., direct and coordinate the assistance his country needed to recover from the economic and social problems that the overthrown Bishop administration had bequeathed them. He gave us *carte blanche* to meet with every government official and discuss their needs.

Fortunately, Grenada had the British system, and all the permanent civil service chiefs had remained in place under Bishop and provided continuity for government operations. My team visited every ministry and observed their staff and operations. We drew up a detailed package and presented it to the acting prime minister on our last day in country. He was enthusiastic and called in his cabinet to review it with us. He called Orfila to thank him for the work our team had done and the package we presented. Nothing substantive happened after our departure. When Orfila presented the OAS package to the U.S. government, he was advised that there was no interest.

In addition to my work at the Secretariat, Secretary General Orfila authorized me to accept an invitation from Clarence Moore to join the editorial staff of *The Times of the Americas*. The *Times* had been started by the Moore family in Cuba and transferred to Florida when Castro came to power. It was one of the few weekly U.S. newspapers that dealt exclusively with developments in Latin America and the Caribbean. The job paid me no salary or stipend, but it gave me an opportunity every few weeks to publish articles on development issues in the Americas.

The secretary general also authorized me to work with Pete Vaky on two papers for the Aspen Institute study on governance in the Western Hemisphere—a topic I had always considered of critical importance to democratic development in the hemisphere.

When Orfila was succeeded by the Deputy Foreign Minister of Brazil, Baena Soares, he requested status papers on CIES policies and operations. He brought several key aides from the Brazilian foreign ministry, Itamaraty, to help him analyze the workings of the OAS. Everyone was apprehensive. I expected to receive notice that my post was to be eliminated, and Ele began to plan for our return to California.

Baena Soares' aides and I got along very well. Raposo noted that they preferred working with me rather than with Diogo. I found myself spending a great deal of time in the secretary general's side office, helping two Brazilian Foreign Service officers put together the new secretary general's plan of operations. The OAS staff remained in place during this initial assessment, except for the retirement of John Ford and the replacement of Ron Scheman by veteran U.S. diplomat, Ambassador Robert Sayre as director of Management. Sayre was a career U.S. Ambassador and someone with whom I had worked over the years.

The new secretary general never talked directly to me about my status, but his aides told me that they expected that I would not be asked to resign in the near future. One of them told me that they had received favorable reports on my performance, and that Baena Soares looked to me to help "break in" the new CIIES executive secretary. Then, he announced the departure of both Diogo and Raposo. I heard rumors about the political negotiations going on with key countries about the appointment of a new executive secretary with experience in international finance and that the leading candidates were Mexican or Argentine.

A few weeks after Diogo and Raposo left, Baena appointed Mexican economist, Julio Gil-García, to be executive secretary. I prepared the briefing book for him and set up meetings with all the key staff. He proved easy to work with, and asked sound, probing questions about the program and the work of the Secretariat and its relationship with IA/ECOSOC. We spent the next few weeks working closely together, especially on preparations for the annual meeting of the IA/ECOSOC scheduled for September. Gil-García took special care in reviewing the agenda and the working papers. He was meticulous in his analysis and impressed me with his knowledge of the issues.

In May, the secretary general called to tell Julio about an invitation from the OECD in Paris for the OAS to participate in a high-level review of economic and social development in Latin America and to present a paper on progress and problems in the region and a summary of its programs. Baena Soares suggested Julio or I go. Julio proposed that I go since he was still breaking into the job and needed the time to get ready for IA/ECOSOC. When I asked if he would allow me to take a two-week vacation after the OECD meeting, he was agreeable. He said that I would be more useful to him in a month when I could help answer his questions after he completed his review of the organization, staff, and pending issues.

With that news, Ele and I contacted David Lazar in Paris to see whether he could accommodate us for the meeting and in June. He welcomed us in early June.

The OECD meeting was an in-depth discussion of conditions in the region. The outlook was very pessimistic. The representative of the UN Economic Commission for Latin America (ECLA), a senior official from the IDB, and I provided much of the up-to-date information. The OECD made estimates of resource inflows that the region would need. Spanish and French government representatives discussed with me the potential role that they might play in working with the OAS in funding some specific country projects. In my report to Baena Soares, I suggested that the Secretariat take the lead in opening discussions with those two countries for their technical and financial support for specific Secretariat's programs in social development and public administration.

After the meeting, Ele and I went by rail for ten days in Copenhagen, Stockholm, Uppsala, Oslo, and Bergen. Ele had been there before and she was initiating me to this area of Europe. How I enjoyed the Tivoli, the lakes of Sweden, the gardens of Oslo, and the Hanseatic vestiges of Bergen! We walked all over the city centers, rode buses and trams, watched the changing of the guard at royal palaces and parliaments, and enjoyed excellent meals. We stayed at hotels that Ele had frequented on her earlier visit. The rooms were just as she remembered them, but the prices had skyrocketed. In 1965, she had stayed at the Royal Viking in Oslo for $5 a night in a room barely large enough to crawl out of bed without hitting the wall and the toilet practically under the shower; the same room was now $150 a night. Except for sticker shock, we had a wonderful time with Ele as our guide.

On our return to Washington, with Julio taking charge of the Secretariat program, we enjoyed a quiet summer in which we again made plans to return to California. We were now in our mid-sixties and the retirement age at the OAS was sixty-five. We braved the heat of summer to enjoy the Smithsonian and all the other cultural events at Wolf Trap and mall concerts.

Then, in early September, Adolfo Nuñez, a former Peruvian diplomat who was special assistant to the secretary general, called me to tell me that the secretary general wanted me to come to his office immediately. My voice apparently reflected my concern, and Adolfo reassured me by saying he had a new assignment for me.

30

Entering the Inter-American Drug Arena

When the call came from the Secretary General that September afternoon, I thought that it was to tell me that my job
was being eliminated. In Europe and all that summer we had prepared ourselves for the return to California. We had considered
the new situation in CIES, the OAS budget crisis and my age *vis a
vis* the OAS retirement age. We had concluded that, when the time
came to retire, I should explore the prospects for joining a Washington think tank working on Latin America and, if nothing were
available, we would return to our base in Tulare. Now, everything
changed when the purpose of his call apparently had nothing to do
with my departure from the OAS.

The Mission in Bolivia

As I entered his office, the secretary general introduced me to Bolivian Representative to the OAS Ambassador Fernando Salazar Paredes. He explained that the Permanent Council's working group on
drug trafficking had been reactivated in March 1984 when the Permanent Council agreed that the seriousness of the drug problem
required the moribund committee to be reactivated. The working
group consisted of Argentina (Raúl Quijano), Bolivia (Fernando
Salazar Paredes), Panama (Roberto Leyton), Peru (Luis Marchand
Stens), the United States (J. William Middendorf), and Venezuela
(Edilberto Moreno), and it selected Ambassador Salazar to be its
chair.

He then advised me that the working group received a note
from the government of Bolivia requesting the OAS to send an

independent commission to review Bolivia's efforts to combat coca-cocaine trafficking. The note cited the criticism of its efforts from various sources. The interest of Bolivia was to demonstrate its commitment to combat illicit trafficking. The Permanent Council had responded favorably to the request and formed a three-country commission, headed by the attorney general of the Dominican Republic (Antonia Rosales) with Panama (former Representative to the OAS Juan Manuel Castulovich) and the United States (retired U.S. Foreign Service Officer Samuel Eaton).

The secretary general advised me that the government of Bolivia and the three commissioners had agreed to my being secretary of the commission and that an OAS lawyer, Alberto Tolosa, would serve as an adviser to the commission. He then informed me that the commission planned to leave for La Paz in ten days and, effective immediately, I was to work with the Bolivian ambassador in preparing the documentation and work plan for the commission. The Bolivian ambassador added that he hoped the commission could begin its work in October and present a report by January 1985. The commissioners would meet a few days before departure for Bolivia, and his government's arrangements for the in-country investigation could be ready by mid-October. There was no inquiry about my interest.

As I listened to the secretary general, I was recalling that every effort by the U.S. to raise the drug trafficking issue in the Permanent Council had been rebuffed by the Latin Americans. The United States blamed its escalating national drug problem, both trafficking and abuse, on the flow of marijuana and cocaine from Latin America. The Latin Americans blamed the problem on the demand in the U.S. and the enormous profits being made in that market that fueled the supply. For almost a decade, the OAS had finessed discussing the issue. Now, Bolivia, which was a major supplier of coca leaf, was finally putting it on the agenda in a form that could not be ignored or avoided. I was pleased that the working group was functioning and that a dialogue had opened at the OAS.

Before the meeting broke up, the Bolivian ambassador handed me several documents prepared by his government on the situation in country, its current legislation, a report by his government's law enforcement authorities, and a list of the key government officials engaged in combatting coca leaf production and trafficking, headed by the minister of the Interior.

After leaving the secretary general's office, I phoned Ele to tell her the news. I told my secretary, Martha Bellis, to cancel my appointments and that I would not be back that afternoon. That evening when we discussed the new assignment, neither of us was concerned about any threats to my personal safety. We both agreed that the government of Bolivia would make sure that nothing happened to the commission. We also decided that Ele should make her annual farm trip in early October and try to get back to Washington before I went to Bolivia. As it turned out, she was in Tulare while I was in Bolivia. We returned to Washington almost simultaneously.

Ele was genuinely excited about the assignment. She had become increasingly concerned about the drug-related violence in Washington, with holdups even in our Wesley Heights neighborhood, reputedly to obtain money for drugs. She had read reports by the Yale Institute on drug and alcohol addiction and actually knew a lot more about the problems than I. We didn't realize that night that for the next decade, my work life would revolve around the issue of drug trafficking and that this new assignment would impact the rest of our lives.

The following morning, I met with the Julio Gil-García and effectively terminated my work as executive officer of the Secretariat. I then met with Alberto Tolosa and received copies of papers in his files on the deliberations of the working group and began studying the Bolivian drug problem. This was before the Internet; I had to rely on the documents provided me by the Bolivian ambassador, materials in the Columbus Library of the OAS, reports of the United Nations Commission on Narcotic Drugs, and unclassified documents from the U.S. government. I asked Ambassador Middendorf for his assistance in getting reports from U.S. government agencies, and he set up appointments for me with State Department and DEA officials with specialized knowledge of Bolivia and with a specialist at the Library of Congress, Raphael Perl. It was Perl who provided me with the most comprehensive background information, including special reports that his office had prepared for members of Congress. Almost all of the information available came from U.S. sources. This was a problem, because I wanted to make sure that I had a balanced view and maintained my objectivity since I was part of an international organization, not the representative of the United States.

The picture was not unexpected. The instability that had characterized Bolivia's political life since its independence in the 1820s plagued its actions to deal with drug trafficking. The national police had been militarized in 1965 and was not a strong professional organization. There had been little progress in improving rural economic and living conditions in the two decades since I left Bolivia and public sector institutions servicing small farmers were rudimentary. In this setting, Roberto Suárez Gómez, known affectionately throughout Bolivia as the Godfather, had organized coca leaf production in the north central area of the country known as the Chapare, a promising farming area north of Cochabamba in which the MNR governments of the 1950–60s had established colonization projects. Miners and their families had been forcibly resettled under those projects. The miners knew little about farming, much less in a subtropical area far different from their arid homeland on the Altiplano. The colonization projects lacked the technical services and credit facilities needed for the new farm families to build productive income-earning farms. From the inception of the colonization effort, the Chapare was an area of discontent and anti-government sentiment. To the people of the Chapare, the Godfather provided credit, seed, fertilizer, and fixed prices for their crops.

The second largest area appeared to be the Yungas, another area of anti-government sentiment. As I related in Chapter 19, one of my first field trips in Bolivia as USAID director was to the Yungas and confronted the animosity that failed project of the late 1950s had sown. Coca leaf remained the main cash crop in the region and the Godfather once again provided not only the market but also credit for the crop, the seed, and fertilizer and expert advice on increasing productivity per acre.

Suárez, their multimillionaire neighbor, also built hospitals and schools, provided money for local governments to build roads and bridges and subsidized local charities to help those in need. He also provided free technical services for farmers to grow subsistence food crops for themselves. Even though he also provided strong-arm protection for the farmers who worked with him and punished

those that didn't, he had built a. Robin Hood persona with the dis-
contented subsistence farmers of the Chapare and the Yungas.

Bluntly put, the question that the commission was to answer
was whether the government of President Siles Suazo was combatting to the best of is ability drug production and trafficking. Or, was
it turning a blind eye, or even abetting, Roberto Suárez Gómez in
the production of and trafficking in coca leaf before he delivered it
to a Colombian cartel. What a challenge!

The commission met for the first time in late October 1984. At
the initial session, the Dominican Chair Antonio Rosario said that
he expected it to conduct a serious investigation, no whitewash; he
prepared a plan of action that included visits to Chapare and direct
talks with farmers and police, not merely attending briefings by
government officials. He also scheduled field visits to observe the
methods and procedures used to locate and destroy illegal crops.
He asked me to brief the commissioners about the situation in Bolivia, especially the operations of Roberto Suárez Gómez and the
evidence of his relationship with the Colombian cartels. Once the
commissioners agreed on a plan of action, they asked me to arrange a private meeting with Bolivian Ambassador Fernando Salazar Paredes. At that meeting, the chair outlined the work plan and
the importance the commission attributed to the full cooperation of
the Bolivian authorities. The Bolivian ambassador assured the commission that his government had air and land vehicles available to
facilitate its work.

The following day we left for Bolivia. Our plane took us to Santa Cruz, not the capital, La Paz. We were met by the minister of the
Interior and various other officials responsible for combatting drug
trafficking. We were taken to a luxurious hotel where the minister,
surrounded by a bevy of lovely young ladies and dapper young
men, feted us with a cocktail party and an elegant dinner.

After the toasts at dinner, the chair told the minister that the
commission intended to begin work immediately and laid out his
schedule for the next few days, including a visit to the Chapare and
discussions with coca farmers and local officials there. The minister seemed astounded by the request and reported that the Chapare was far too dangerous for the commission to visit, but that the
government would provide in-depth briefings by the key officials

at the table on the conditions there and the government efforts to control them. The chair insisted that the government provide transportation tomorrow to go to Cochabamba and drive to the Chapare. There was real tension at the table until the minister promised to look into the possibility of meeting the commission's request—indeed, he acted as if he had never been advised by Ambassador Salazar Paredes of the plan of action that the chair had spelled out less than two days earlier at OAS headquarters.

The tension was exacerbated after dinner when the minister indicated discreetly that the lovely young ladies and men were at the commissioners' disposal for the rest of the evening. That provoked the Dominican to call the commissioners and staff to his suite where he advised us that he questioned the minister's seriousness and that in the morning, he would decide whether to terminate the visit or not. Either the government acceded to our plan of work or we would return to Washington.

The following morning, the minister advised us that he had to return to La Paz and left us in the hands of his deputy who would accompany us to Cochabamba and make every effort to take us to the Chapare. The chair was assured that the government would comply with his plan of action and provide the transportation and other logistics support that we needed. The minister told us that the conditions in the Chapare were very unstable and he could not guarantee our safety if we persisted with our intention of making a visit.

After the minister departed, the commission received a series of technical briefings on the production and trafficking situation in Bolivia and the region. Throughout the briefings, much of which was a rehashing of information the commission had already acquired, the chair persistently asked about transportation to the Chapare. About lunchtime we were advised that a plane was available to take us to Cochabamba as soon as the weather permitted. Well, the weather didn't permit it until the next morning. We had more briefings in Cochabamba, were taken to a government operation where confiscated coca leaves were being destroyed, and then shown a seized cocaine lab in the process of being dismantled. That night we were back in Santa Cruz for "our own safety."

The commission spent a day or two longer in Bolivia being

shown operations of the Ministry of the Interior to curtail production and to combat the inter-country movement of processed coca leaf. To every inquiry about more field visits, we were advised that the region was too unsafe for us to enter. I should add that the bevy of lovely young ladies and dapper men remained in our hotel and were very attentive. When queried by the chair, Bolivian officials told us that arrangements could be made for returning to Cochabamba, but that there were no plans for the commission to discuss preliminary findings with President Siles Suazo or the minister in La Paz.

When we returned to Washington, the chair said that we had no basis for answering the questions either about the effectiveness of the efforts by the Bolivian government or its possible involvement in the trafficking of coca leaf and/or cocaine. We had not gathered significant information about the government's relations with Roberto Suárez Gómez, and he was certainly not comfortable with the performance of the minister of the Interior and his associates. We had no evidence to prove or even imply complicity, nor had we uncovered any information that demonstrated that the government was not involved in or cooperating with the drug merchants. He instructed me to write a diplomatic report that thanked the government of Bolivia for its cooperation and noted the efforts of the commission and the government, but to make it equally clear that we did not have enough evidence to make a judgment on the effectiveness of the government's efforts.

I wrote the report over the next couple of weeks in consultation with the chair, who had returned to Santo Domingo. He and the other two commissioners met one last time to review an almost final draft. They made the necessary adjustments and additions over the course of a weekend. The chair submitted the final report to the secretary general for presentation to the Permanent Council. Baena told me that he was pleased with the objectivity and clarity of the report, but was concerned about its implications on the situation in Bolivia and the potential impact on inter-American relations.

I know that neither the Bolivian ambassador nor the government of Bolivia was pleased with the report. The minister of the Interior resigned, as did several of his associates. It had a sufficiently equivocal effect in the Permanent Council that Bolivian Ambassador Fernando Salazar Paredes found it necessary to sponsor another initiative to demonstrate to the U.S. and other member states that Bolivia and the government of Hernán Siles Suazo were committed to combat the growing drug trafficking menace.

When the commission submitted the report to the secretary general, it was the holiday season. I had returned to my office in the Secretariat of the IA/ECOSOC when the secretary general sent word that he would see me on his return in mid-January and suggested that I take a vacation until January 15. I wasn't sure what the cryptic message meant, so I told Gil-García that I would support him and the Secretariat in any way that he thought advisable, especially in the preparation for the next IA/ECOSOC meeting that was scheduled to meet in Washington in April 1985.

Our New World

Ele and I had a special season. Ele helped my secretary Martha Bellis put on a lovely Christmas party for my CIES colleagues. We attended several receptions at Latin American embassies, and Ambassador Middendorf invited us to attend his party for the staff at the U.S. Mission to the OAS. We celebrated Christmas Eve with Margaret and David Frederickson and many of their colleagues from the Reagan White House. We enjoyed a family evening with Fran Howard and her family; her son Bill, his wife, and children had come down from Minneapolis while Anne and her husband, Dennis Tristani, had come up from Puerto Rico. We went to the National Cathedral on Christmas Day and treated ourselves to dinner at the Occidental in downtown Washington. New Year's Eve we spent with a lovely champagne dinner and party with Faye and Frank Sherry.

We spent most of that Christmas season discussing how the cycle of our lives was changing again. No longer in the U.S. Foreign Service, we were not awaiting reassignment after two or three years at post.

We stripped away all the outside issues and concentrated on us. Our conversation was very personal and almost introspective. Both of us realized that we were passing from middle age and that we had not realized the dreams that we had dreamed for ourselves.

I no longer had hopes of being appointed to head an embassy in Latin America. Ele felt that she had not lived the career she had seen for herself as a writer. Ele reiterated that she was done playing second fiddle to my job as she had for the last thirty-eight years and that she was going to concentrate her energies and skills on developing her own interests. In turn, I pointed out that I had tried to support every initiative she undertook, from rescuing her family farms and insuring the financial underpinnings of her family and ours. She called that insensitive to her ambitions. I was offended and blurted out that each had needed to make choices, not all of which turned out to be right or even in our long-term interest. We ended up considering every alternative for the future, from living separately to immediately returning to California, but we never went to bed angry at each other. I think that we not only became more conscious of what we needed to do for each other, but also we deepened our love and respect for one another. It was the reality of two aging people in the winter cold of Washington, D.C., where we would live out the rest of our working lives.

We also discussed our health problems. Since returning from Panama, Ele had never felt well. Doctors couldn't identify the cause of her malaise, but she had a broad array of aches, pains, and bouts of listlessness. She also told me for the first time that she was terrified of falling and breaking her hip—since both her mother and grandmother had succumbed after falling and breaking hips. She also had basal cells on her face that had to be removed and fear of their recurrence kept her from enjoying summers in the sun on the seashore or at our Towers pool. I had liver and prostate problems that kept flaring up, causing mood changes and complicating our lives. Then, too, we had not found a doctor in Washington who inspired the confidence we had felt for Dr. John Latimer, who had retired. Ele especially missed being able to consult regularly with Dr. Euguene Matthias, her Tulare physician who diagnosed her amoebas when the Chilean doctor had called them "cancer."

As we talked, we came to grips with our new reality and its implications for our lives. We agreed that as long as the OAS continued my job, we would remain at the Towers in our current apartment. We also agreed that Ele's time would be her own. I urged her to spend her time writing the novels about Latin America that she had roaming around in her head. She also told me that she would continue preparing her monthly "What If?" column for the Bulletin of the AAFSW—it required her to keep current on the financial world in order to ensure she provided up-to-date information for foreign service spouses to deal with their financial and legal problems. Ele also discussed the need for her annual trip to South Dakota and Tulare since the management arrangements she set in place for the farms and houses no longer demanded so much of her attention. Ele and I were together almost every minute and I believe that we came closer together than we had ever been before. Ele told me a few weeks before her death how important those days had been for her and her peace of mind.

Adviser to the Secretary General

I returned to work on January 15, 1985 expecting to resume my duties as executive officer of the Inter-American Economic and Social Council (CIES). I scheduled a meeting with the department directors to catch up on project developments over the past few months. I also asked for a briefing by the staff working on the preparations for the 1985 meeting of IA/ECOSOC programmed for April in Washington, D.C. I had no sooner laid out a work plan with my secretary when the secretary general called me to his office. My secretary turned to me with a quizzical look on her face and asked, "*Qué pasa?*" (What's going on?), to which I replied, "*Quién sabe?*" (Who knows?).

Baena Soares advised me that the last OAS General Assembly adopted resolution 699, which called for the convocation of a Specialized Conference to prepare an inter-American convention on drug trafficking. The General Secretariat was to work with the Inter-American Juridical Committee, headquartered in Rio, in implementing the resolution. The government of Venezuela had agreed to prepare an initial draft from which the Specialized Conference would work. The resolution had placed the inter-American drug problem high on the Permanent Council's agenda. He expected the Permanent Council to refer resolution 699 to the General Committee, which in turn would set up a working group to provide policy guidance and oversight to the General Secretariat on implementing it.

A convention is a document drawn up by legal experts that establishes the legal norms and procedures for inter-governmental cooperation to deal with a specific problem. When adopted and ratified by the member states, it becomes legally binding on the ratifying states and must be incorporated into their national body of laws.

The secretary general said that he had decided to appoint me his permanent adviser on drug issues and to be his representative in the General Committee on resolution 699. We talked for nearly an hour about the situation in the hemisphere and my very limited knowledge about and experience in the subject matter. He said that I no longer was assigned to CIES and that I would have a new office.

My agenda changed immediately. I had to read up on the international drug problem, with special emphasis on the situation in the various member countries. Thinking about a convention had to wait until I understood the problem better. My immediate priority was to identify what books to read, what people to interview, and what reports to analyze. I had to learn very fast.

When I went home that night, Ele and I had a long talk about the implications of the new assignment. First of all, we were relieved that I had a job for at least the next year or two. Then, drawing on her work in the early 1950s with Allied Youth, she suggested that I contact the Yale Institute of Alcohol and Drug Addiction for its studies on drug addiction. She also offered to help me develop my reading list. We also identified the United Nations Information Center, the Library of Congress, and the State Department as prime sources for information on the scope and dimensions of the illicit trafficking of drugs and drug addiction in the Western Hemisphere.

The secretary general invited me to join him at the first meeting of the Permanent Council in 1985. The council acted just as he anticipated. The following week, the General Committee renewed the mandate of the working group and named the same countries to membership that had participated in 1984: Argentina, Bolivia, Panama, Peru, the United States, and Venezuela, with Bolivian Ambassador Salazar Paredes as chair. Baena Soares then informed the working group that he had selected me to be his advisor on inter-American drug trafficking, and that I would work directly with it in its consideration of General Assembly resolution 699.

In its first meeting, the working group instructed the secretariat to prepare a working paper by no later than September 1. I was to coordinate my work with the Inter-American Juridical Committee. The working group determined that it would present a plan of work and timetable for convening legal experts to the next General Assembly, which was scheduled for Cartagena, Colombia in December. I had my marching orders. Within days, Marta and I were moved to new office space, with barely enough room to turn round and no view!

One of my first jobs was, as required by resolution 699, to contact the Inter-American Juridical Committee for its suggestions and the name of its specialist with whom I could work. Some three months later, I was told that the committee had no interest in the subject matter and therefore would name no specialist to work with me. I also sent send notes to each of the thirty-three representatives to the OAS requesting their assistance in identifying the key offices and officials in their countries engaged in combatting drug trafficking and drug abuse. Most had no information available in Washington and forwarded the request to their countries. Marta and I followed up every couple of weeks since the information was slow in coming—in some cases, apparently, it was difficult for the countries to identify those responsible.

That spring, I remember reading and analyzing materials in Spanish, French, Portuguese, and English about the complex network of criminal organizations engaged in the drug trade from the Triads and Yakusa in Southeast Asia to the Italian and French Mafia in Europe and the Medellín and Cali cartels in South America. I read books on the CIA involvement in poppy production in Afghanistan in order to finance the opposition to Soviet occupation. I read of the Golden Triangle and the history of the U.S. cocaine epidemic in the first decade of the twentieth century. I read books and documents on international efforts to confront and control both trafficking and drug use.

The international dimensions of the opium/heroin problem went back to the nineteenth century Opium Wars and British mercantilist policy in Asia. I found myself revisiting a seminar when I was a teaching assistant at Berkeley on economic history that dealt with mercantile policies of Britain and its war on China to force it to import Indian-produced opium poppy and hemp to improve its balance of trade. I reviewed the efforts of British Prime Minister Gladstone to stamp out the opium trade that burgeoned in the late nineteenth century. It was Britain who promoted the first inter-governmental meetings in Shanghai (1909) and The Hague (1912) to generate inter-country cooperation to confront the problem. It was Britain who in the League of Nations sponsored the creation of the first international commission to deal with drugs. Britain led the League of Nations to adopt three conventions between 1925 and 1936.

When the United Nations was created, the drug issue was on its agenda. In 1946, the Economic and Social Council created the Commission on Narcotic Drugs (CND) and adopted the Protocol of Lake Success that recognized the three conventions adopted by the League of Nations and empowered the CND to enforce them. The CND spearheaded international cooperation to combat trafficking and use of opium, cocaine, and marijuana, leading to the drafting and adoption of the Single Convention on Narcotic Drugs of 1961 and its Protocol of 1972 that brought together the prior conventions since 1909 in one document. Then in 1971, the commission approved a sister convention on psychotropic substances.

In 1961, the CND created the International Narcotics Control Board (INCB) to oversee the implementation of the Single Convention and to establish a reporting system on the implementation efforts by the 135 countries that had ratified the Single Convention. In 1971, the United Nations also established the Fund for Drug Abuse Control (UNFDAC) to provide funds to help countries design and implement programs to comply with the two conventions and specific objectives adopted by the CND.

Reading UN reports, I found that the UN had given CND an assignment to draft a new comprehensive convention to deal with all aspects of illicit trafficking in narcotic drugs and psychotropic substances and to strengthen the two existing conventions. Once I read of the process underway at the CND, I had serious concerns about the desirability of the OAS starting a competing process. Writing an inter-American convention is a cumbersome process that requires several years of negotiation. It is drafted by a committee of legal and subject matter specialists—usually one or two from each member state and working in four languages (English, French, Portuguese, and Spanish). Its cost is high because of the number of meetings required and services required of interpreters, translators, and support staff. Reaching agreement on legal principles and precise words is usually difficult because of differences between civil law practiced in Latin America and common law in the U.S. and the Caribbean. Once the instrument is agreed upon, it must be ratified by the member states, a process that usually requires another several years. On a topic as controversial as drug trafficking and drug abuse, there was a real possibility that national legislators would finesse the issue and put off taking action.

By the second month on the job, I began asking members of the working group why we needed to repeat in the inter-American arena an exercise already underway in the UN. Indeed, I questioned whether there wasn't something else the OAS could consider that might help countries deal with the immediate problems they faced with the growing drug trade and rising rates of addiction. I suggested that, since drug trafficking and drug abuse was a worldwide problem, would it not be preferable that the UN prepare a worldwide convention to strengthen those already in force, and concentrate OAS efforts on working with member states to apply its provisions, rather than seeking to draft another that would be exclusive to the Western Hemisphere.

When I expressed those concerns to Ele, she helped me hone my arguments and urged me to talk to the secretary general. When I met with him in early April, Baena Soares proposed that, before making such a recommendation, I should go to Vienna in May to attend the 1985 meeting of the CND and observe the status of negotiations on the new UN convention. He wanted to know how serious and determined the CND effort was before raising my concerns with key OAS delegations.

Baena Soares authorized me to brief the working group on my work to date. So, I reported to them on the sketchy and incomplete reports that I was receiving from the member states on national efforts to deal with the problem, the lack of interest by the Inter-American Juridical Committee, and the work of the CND and its preparations for a new worldwide convention. The working party unanimously recommended that I go to Vienna and report back to it.

The 1985 CND Meeting in Vienna

The secretary general's office arranged for an invitation for me to attend the 1985 meeting of the CND in Vienna as an observer. The meeting was scheduled for the last two weeks in May. The secretary general also authorized me to take a three-week vacation in Europe before returning to work. So, I contacted Dave Lazar in Paris, and he invited Ele to join him in Paris while I was in Vienna.

This was my first visit to Vienna, and I was like a kid in a candy store. I had read about the great Central European capital, and now I would have a chance to experience it. I spent the overnight trip on Pan Am to Vienna reading brochures on the city and refining the questions that I wanted to raise with the staff of the CND, INCB, and UNFDAC. After spending my first day catching up on lost sleep, I received directions for taking the subway to the UN center.

The guard at the entrance found my name on his list. I was photographed and given an ID card to wear at all times while on the UN premises. Then I was directed to the building that housed the CND, and l took an elevator up to the floor on which Tamar Oppenheimer, CND Director, had her office.

I was the new boy on the block and had a great deal to learn about CND operations, including its focus and bureaucratic politics. I knew no one at either the CND or INCB or UNFDAC. The only people in the UN in Vienna whom I knew were Director General of the United Nations in Vienna Margaret Ainstee (later Dame Margaret), whom I had met in Bolivia in the mid-1960s, and Director of the Division of Technical Cooperation of the United Nations Industrial Development Organization (UNIDO) Santiago Quijano Caballero (later Colombian candidate for UN secretary general), who had been UN resident representative in Bolivia.

My first appointment at the CND was with Director Tamar Oppenheimer, a Canadian career UN officer who had been transferred recently from New York to take charge of this politically sensitive operation. Tamar spent an hour with me; she told me later that she had set aside ten minutes for a formal welcome. She said that I seemed like an old friend and she took the time to give me an overview of the UN operation, the relations among the three entities, and an introduction to the key personalities.

As we finished, she called in two U.S. citizens on the CND staff, Bill Beachner and Paulson Bailey. Bill directed one of the CND divisions and Paulson was a senior member of the conference staff. They briefed me on the prospects for drafting the new international convention, introduced me to several CND officers and set up appointments at the INCB and UNFDAC. Bill took me to lunch at the UN cafeteria—some of the best food I had ever eaten and at prices I could afford. By the end of the second day, I was becoming acclimated to the Vienna routine.

After lunch, Bill informed me that CND operated on a very tight budget and its core activity was preparation and holding of the annual meeting at which governments appraised the effectiveness of the conventions and the need for further international efforts to combat drug trafficking and drug abuse. He added that CND provided only limited services to governments on planning national programs, usually conducting one or two regional training courses per year and occasionally advising individual governments, on anti-drug information campaigns. He also described the CND evaluation process for assessing the effectiveness of country programs and CND projects.

The next day, Paulson introduced me to the structure of the annual meeting and its operating rules. Then, he briefed me on progress in drafting the new convention. He pointed out that the earlier conventions had banned the use and trafficking in narcotic drugs and psychotropic substances without establishing international measures to deal with the powerful criminal syndicates that controlled their production and movement across national frontiers into world markets. He told me that the Western European bloc and the United States were playing the central role in the drafting and negotiations. He showed me the schedule of technical and political meetings set up to move the process forward. Based on his experience with negotiating patterns at the CND, he estimated that it would be three years before a final draft would be prepared.

After leaving Paulson, Akiro Fugino of the INCB explained that the INCB was a worldwide body of experts who advised the CND annually on the status of the drug problem. It presented an annual report to the CND, country by country, on progress and problems in controlling production, distribution, and use. It also identified critical measures that the CND needed to take and those required of the member states. He introduced me to the reports of the INCB and went over in detail the information and statistical data that the board asked annually of the countries, ranging from in-country production to seizures and addiction rates.

He then showed me the annual reports from Latin American and Caribbean countries, which were sketchy at best, primarily providing data on arrests and seizures. Only Colombia and Mexico seemed to have collected any data on drug use. Production estimates seemed more like guesses than technical assessments, and Akiro reported that the INCB sometimes had to use data from INTERPOL and U.S. Drug Enforcement Administration (DEA) rather than incomplete national reports. He then told me that the INCB had a small budget to advise national reporting agencies in various regions of the world on INCB data requirements and train national statisticians and other technicians. When I asked him about the INCB's assessment of the most dangerous focal points in the world, he said Southeast Asia, Colombia, and Afghanistan. He expressed special concern about new large-scale poppy production in Afghanistan and called my attention to some recent books on CIA encouragement of that production to finance the movement to oust the Soviets from that country. I spent two days reading INCB reports, paying special attention to the data from Western Hemisphere countries. Few countries reported and the reports were not consistent from one year to the next and most were summaries of police records.

At the end of the first week, I met with the famous Italian prosecutor of the Mafia, Dr. Giuseppe di Gennaro, the director of UNFDAC, which had been created to provide financial and technical assistance to member countries on suppressing illegal drug production, drug trafficking, and drug abuse. Contributions to the fund were voluntary and most of them were from Italy, Western European and Scandinavian countries, and the United States. The annual U.S. contribution was about two million dollars. Dr. di Gennaro was not enthusiastic about the OAS becoming involved in an area where he believed the UN had established a functioning program. He suggested that the OAS actively support UNFDAC and work with it in identifying projects that it could fund and in encouraging OAS member states to contribute to the fund. He then asked his deputy, Hans Emblad, to brief me on UNFDAC projects and their potential usefulness for the OAS members.

The projects Hans described were primarily in Southeast Asia and aimed at reducing the production of opium poppy. Hans had worked on one in the Chiang Mai region of Thailand, in which UNFDAC provided technical assistance and some funding to oust the warlord of poppy production and induce the farmers to replace poppy crops with other cash crops. Hans commented that, once the Thai government had established strong military control in the area and deposed the poppy king, he and his minions had moved their operations to supply the Chinese triads across the border to Myanmar, where UNFDAC expected to initiate a new project replicating the effort in Chiang Mai.

When I asked about projects in the in the Western Hemisphere, Hans said that there been only a few small projects, the most important in Colombia to reduce cocaine production. He reported that the results to date had not been promising because of inadequate government support, the power of the Medellín and Cali cartels, and the effects of the ongoing civil war. When I asked why there were so few projects in the Western Hemisphere, Hans replied that UNFDAC projects were dependent on voluntary funding, and most of its funding came from European governments whose interest was the source of most of the heroin on the streets of Western Europe, the Golden Triangle in Southeast Asia.

By the end of the first week, I understood that the CND and UNFDAC essentially reflected the interests of the European governments and their priorities. In the corridors, I heard a lot of gossip about the tension between the CND and UNFDAC and the rivalry between Tamar Oppenheimer and Giuseppe de Gennaro. I also had serious doubts about the interest of the UN bureaucracy in supporting a comprehensive effort to combat drug trafficking and drug abuse in Latin America and the Caribbean.

Since it was my first visit, I wanted to explore the fabulous city, its palaces, museums, and parks. During the weekend, I took streetcars and buses to various corners of city, walked the boulevards and absorbed the charm. At dinners at Paulson's downtown apartment and the Beachners' suburban home I met delegates from various countries and heard their views of the drug problem and their expectations for a new UN convention.

On Monday the annual meeting of the CND opened with statements from key delegations on drafting a new convention. I marveled at the adroitness with which Tamar moved the agenda forward. As an observer delegate, I sat with the representative of the Palestine Liberation Office and some non-profits. I made friends with Franceska Haller from the Zurich-based *Mut zur Ethik*, who introduced me to representatives of a score of the European non-profits, known in the UN as non-governmental organizations, or NGOs. They were urging the CND to place greater emphasis on demand reduction. I also met a young member of the German delegation, Baron von Harsdorf, a police official who was about to spend a year on detail in the CND. I was invited to the British, German, U.S., and Italian receptions for the delegates as well as those given by Margaret Ainstee and Tamar Oppenheimer. I talked about the drug problem with delegates from Pakistan, Malaysia, India, China, and Japan as well as those from Latin America and Canada. By the end of that second week, I was convinced that Tamar would move the new convention forward on the schedule she had set.

I also concluded that CND and UNFDAC interest in and information on the drug problem in Latin America and Caribbean was minimal. That conclusion served as the basis for the report I would present to the secretary general and the working committee. I began to identify a role for the OAS that would not compete with the UN, but complement its program. I was convinced that the Western Hemisphere did not need a special legal framework, but rather needed to adopt and enforce the worldwide norms of existing conventions and the ones about to be drafted. The OAS should help the member states build up their capability to enforce the UN conventions and deal with the complex drug trafficking issues they were facing.

After the meeting, I flew to Paris where I shared with Ele and David my impressions and conclusions. Dave arranged for me to meet on Monday with the OECD specialist on drug trafficking. I found that his impressions of the CND meeting coincided with mine. He showed me the OECD database that contained almost no information about the cocaine trade. Even without that data,

OECD estimated the illicit drug trafficking in recent years to be in the range of US$300–400 billion, probably second only in volume to international trade in military arms and equipment.

For the rest of our time in Paris, the three of us enjoyed the great city. We spent a day with Bobette Orr, the niece of Faye and Frank Sherry, who was then assigned to the commercial section of the U.S. Embassy. Ele and I took the TGV to Grenoble to savor the Isère Valley, followed by an overnight train to Barcelona for three sun-splashed, quite warm June days walking Rambla, the twisting lanes in the central city, the museums, and the old Olympic village. We marveled at the Sagrada Corazón and the Gaudi architecture. We dined on wonderful Catalan seafood, heard a group of Andean singers in the plaza, and watched a bullfight on TV with commentary in Catalan.

When we returned to Paris, Dave told us that his tour in Paris was coming to an end and that he wanted a special celebration for all of us to remember. He took us to the fabulous Cascade restaurant near the Bois du Boulogne. We drank champagne as we toasted our friendship. It was a very special evening.

Designing an Inter-American Program

On returning to Washington, I prepared a succinct report for the secretary general that called competition between the OAS and UN in drafting a convention on drug trafficking counter-productive and recommended that the OAS support the UN in its efforts to define world-wide legal standards and procedures for combatting drug trafficking. I pointed out that the timetable for a new worldwide convention had been set, and I believed that a final draft would be ready to submit to countries for ratification by the summer of 1988.

I also reported that the information provided by the member states to both the OAS and the INCB was sketchy at best, and told us little about the problems faced by member states in dealing with drug abuse and drug trafficking. I also pointed out that CND, INCB, and UNFDAC did not have the staff, funding, or interest to provide the support that OAS member states needed. So, I recommended that the OAS effort be focused on filling that void by creating a hemispheric program to help member states better understand and confront the threats posed by drug trafficking and drug abuse and promote inter-country cooperation in the undertaking.

The secretary general's response was to review the General Assembly's mandate, which read, "To instruct the General Secretariat to prepare, in consultation with the Inter-American Juridical Committee, by collecting and taking into account all of the background materials available on the matter, and on the basis of the draft convention presented by the government of Venezuela, an inter-American draft convention against drug trafficking for consideration by a specialized Conference." The secretary general was concerned that my proposal was not consistent with the mandate and advised me to talk with the working group. He was skeptical that the working group would agree with my approach.

When I sent my report to the chair of the working group, he suggested that I discuss it with the working group. Before the meeting, I consulted Ambassador Moreno of Venezuela because it was his government that had promised to prepare a draft convention that would serve as the working document for the Specialized Meeting, and his government would have to agree with my appraisal of a worldwide convention. I also consulted the new U.S. representative to the OAS, Ambassador Richard McCormack, who embraced my proposal. He said that the U.S. was not interested in having the OAS duplicate the work underway in Vienna, and that he had been instructed to find a way to build regional cooperation against trafficking through the OAS. I also received a call from Brazilian representative to the OAS, Ambassador Castro Alves, who, while not a member of the working group, was a key member of Permanent Council and close friend of the secretary general. He told me that Baena Soares had informed him of my approach and he asked me to explain my proposal to him. We had a lengthy discussion during which he asked a number of salient questions.

Within two weeks Ambassador Salazar called a meeting of the working group. The Venezuelan representative advised the working group that his government was committed to the drafting of a single worldwide convention and recommended that any action by the OAS be supportive of the process then underway in Vienna. Argentina, Panama, and Peru welcomed the Venezuelan statement and endorsed the approach proposed in my memo. The working group interpreted my proposed to be consistent with resolution 699, and gave me eight weeks to submit the documents needed in order to convene the Specialized Conference on the Drug Crisis in the first half of 1986.

I was called upon to present four papers mandated by resolution 699. My deadline was to present them to the secretary general by late August and their submission to the working group by mid-September. The OAS General Assembly was to convene in December in Cartagena, Colombia. Any matter to be considered at the assembly had to be approved by the working group and the Permanent Council. If not, consideration of the drug issue and the convocation of the Specialized Meeting would be delayed for another year. Fortunately the OAS had just installed the latest computer equipment and Marta had become a specialist. She put my drafts in the proper format for presentation to the General Assembly and Ele helped edit the drafts. OAS Director of Management Robert Sayre also assigned me a summer intern to help with clerical tasks.

The first of the four papers was an analysis of inter-American and international conventions and resolutions on drug trafficking and drug abuse. I drafted an outline covering the provisions for international drug control, the possible contents of an inter-American convention, and the implications of establishing an Inter-American Narcotic Drug Convention. Since the resolution required me to consult the Inter-American Juridical Committee, I asked it for comments on the scope of work and suggestions on its contents within sixty days. In late July the committee advised that it had no expertise in the subject matter and no comments on my proposal.

The other three studies dealt with the drug situation in the Americas. The first was to examine the economic and social impact of coca leaf production on the economies of the producer countries and the probable problems that would be created by the elimination of any surplus above legal or traditional uses in the producer countries. The second was on the demand for drugs, especially cocaine, and possible measures for reducing that demand. The third was on mechanisms for inter-American cooperation to control drug trafficking and drug abuse.

I cleared a detailed outline for the three with CIES executive secretary and the chair of the working group, Ambassador Salazar Paredes, who was also the chair of the Permanent Executive Committee of IA/ECOSOC. Ambassador Paredes gave me an even tighter deadline: namely, presentation to the working group for approval at the 1985 Meeting of IA/ECOSOC, two months before the General Assembly. He then added another study to my workload: a proposal to create a special inter-American fund to assist countries affected by the cocaine problem.

In the socioeconomic paper, I presented a systemic analysis of the supply of cocaine in its six inter-related components: coca leaf cultivation; coca farmers; the processing of coca leaf into cocaine; illicit trafficking as a big business; the impact of the coca-cocaine trade on member states and their development; and money laundering.

The paper on demand reduction examined the demand for coca-cocaine throughout the world. It also reviewed potential actions to reduce demand by controlling the distribution of the drug, confiscating the profits made on illicit trafficking, and promoting inter-American cooperative efforts to curtail demand.

Both papers described the sophisticated business model used by international criminal syndicates to integrate production, processing, and transport to the marketplace. They laid out the huge profits emanating from that business, primarily at the marketplace in developed countries. They illustrated the increase in market value of a pound of coca leaf, which in Bolivia at the farm site was worth about one dollar, raising it three dollars after being processed into cocaine in Colombia, then up to ten dollars on the streets of a U.S. or European city. They showed that the enormous profits of the criminal syndicates dwarfed the resources available to law enforcement in most Latin American countries.

The paper on inter-American mechanisms called for the establishment of an Inter-American Commission to assist member countries in dealing with the supply and demand problems defined in the papers. I tried to model it on the Inter-American Commission on Human Rights, with somewhat similar scope of operations and powers.

The drafts of those three papers were completed by the end of July. Ele worked with me in the drafting and editing, frequently calling my attention to points that needed further explanation or clarification. After the secretary general reviewed the drafts, he gave me a green light to submit them to the CIES executive secretary and Ambassador Salazar Paredes for their consideration.

The papers were approved by the Secretary General and submitted to the working group on schedule. Ambassador Salazar Paredes called a meeting of the working group, which accepted the reports and designated them as the working documents for the Specialized Meeting. The group agreed to meet again after the delegates had received the comments of their governments and their instructions on place and date for the Specialized Meeting.

At the subsequent meeting, each delegate reported that his government had been pleased with the documents. One representative said that it was the first time his government had received such a clear analysis of the drug problem and international efforts to deal with it. I especially remember Ambassador Castro Alves of Brazil, who was not a member of the working group, turning to me and saying in effect, "Now I understand the drug problem as an inter-country criminal operation that concerns us all, not merely Bolivia, Peru, Colombia, Mexico, and the United States."

As I left the meeting, the Spanish and Canadian observers to the OAS approached me with their commendations for the work presented. They said that their governments were pleased with the quality and scope of the documents and wanted to express their support.

The studies were also approved by the September 1985 IA/ECOSOC meeting. The CIES executive secretary was instructed to cooperate with the secretary general in his presentation to the General Assembly and to support the convocation of the Specialized Conference. It recommended inclusion of funds in the 1986–87 OAS budget to hold the Specialized Meeting in 1986.

The working group met one last time before the OAS General Assembly. At that meeting, the Brazilian ambassador offered Rio as the site of the Specialized Meeting. Having completed its review of my reports and with the IA/ECOSOC resolution adopted, the working group recommended to the Permanent Council the convoking of the Specialized Meeting in Rio de Janeiro in April 1986. At its next meeting, the Permanent Council unanimously adopted the recommendation and convoked the meeting.

Since the only business at the General Assembly related to drug trafficking was the Permanent Council's recommendation on the site and date of the Specialized Meeting, there was no reason for me to go to Cartagena.

Ele's 1985 Farm Trip

A few days later, Ele flew to Aberdeen, South Dakota, on what proved to be her last visit with Mr. Barnes and her last inspection of the farm. She was pleased with the improvements made by Mr. Barnes to reinforce the tree barrier to combat wind-induced soil erosion and to build up the soil and its moisture content. The county agent advised her that the farm was in excellent condition. She and Mr. Barnes agreed on an extension of the lease and an increase in the annual rental.

Then she flew to Las Vegas to change planes for Fresno. At the airport, she met her friend Billie Heller, who took her in Liberace's limo to attend a lunch on the Strip in honor of the renowned entertainer. Billie enlisted Ele's commitment to work with her on the U.S. Commission on Women's Rights and its planned conference in Washington, prior to a worldwide meeting in Europe. Liberace's welcome that afternoon was the last time either of us saw him. At the airport, while she waited for her United plane to be called, she placed a loose quarter in a slot machine and hit a jackpot. Quarters flowed all over the floor, and several people came over to help her pick them up, She had won thirty-five dollars in quarters—and she still had a roll of ten dollars of those quarters in the top drawer of her bureau when she died nearly twenty years later.

In her visit to Tulare, she quickly handled the farm business and concentrated her time on her continuing health problems. Since the hysterectomy, she never regained the same vigor and resilience of former years. She talked out her concerns with Dr. Matthias, because she trusted him more than any other doctor. When I asked her about the visit, she never quite told me what was discussed or what his advice had been, but she seemed disturbed. Ele spent almost a month in Tulare, and I don't think that it was a very positive experience. We talked every few days by phone, but she seemed to been marking time. She and her friend Elizabeth La Cell had their nightly dinners, but she made no effort to see other friends or relatives.

Ele arrived home in time for Thanksgiving, and she was eager to rest. The trip had been very hard on her. She was listless, and was having thyroid problems again. The disease had plagued her since she was a teenager, and now her long-time medication seemed not to be effective. She just asked me to let her be and make no plans for the holidays. I found myself doing most of the chores, from marketing to laundry, to give Ele more time to rest. With my own schedule clear through early January, I was delighted to go along with Ele's wishes. The office was essentially closed. The secretary general and the members of the working group were in Cartagena. My secretary had been conscripted to work for the secretary general at the assembly. The offices of all the delegations of the member states in Washington closed for the assembly and the holidays. I went to the office only for a few days to catch up on the backlog, get my files in order, and make plans for the work required for the meeting in Rio in April.

That Christmas season rolled by very quickly. There were some parties with the Fredericksons, the Sherrys, our good neighbor, Edward Gingold, and a few other friends. We learned that Nancy and David Lazar had decided to separate; we had a lunch with each one. Every nice day we tried to go to one of the exhibits at the Smithsonian or the National Gallery.

The Rio Meeting

It was mid-January before the pace of work began to pick up. My first significant call was from Brazilian Ambassador Castro Alves. He invited me to go over the reports I had prepared for the Specialized Meeting. He questioned me in detail about the segments of the paper dealing with the coca-cocaine drug trade, from production, processing of coca leaf into cocaine, inter-country illicit transportation, and marketing to consumption, the marketplace, and laundering of profits. He then raised issues about specific areas and mechanisms for inter-American cooperation to combat trafficking. We discussed the implications of the proposals for creating an inter-American drug commission and an inter-American fund.

He suggested that, to facilitate the discussions to be held in Rio, I prepare a draft resolution that incorporated the recommendations contained in the five papers.

The representatives of Bolivia, Mexico, Peru, and Venezuela called me for similar discussions. They all raised questions about the scope of inter-American cooperation. The Bolivian, Colombian, Peruvian, and Venezuelan showed special interest in creating an inter-American fund to help the producer countries deal with the drug problem in their countries. The Mexican was very skeptical about setting up a fund and even more skeptical about the interest of the more opulent countries, especially the U.S., in contributing to it.

I also had several meetings with U.S. Ambassador to the OAS, Richard McCormack. From the outset, he was an enthusiastic supporter of an OAS role in the combatting the drug trade. He named Richard Hines as his personal liaison with me; Richard was an experienced foreign service officer with whom I had worked during the ROCAP years.

Ambassador McCormack and Richard kept me abreast of their own problems in getting U.S. government support for an OAS program and the creation of a new fund. The U.S. government had been pressing the OAS for nearly a decade to develop policies and programs to combat illicit trafficking. Now that a potential program had been designed, the worldwide office in the State Department responsible for drug policy and programs was having second thoughts. They favored concentrating all programs in the CND; and they had allies throughout the State Department who were skeptical of the OAS's ability to mount a useful program. U.S. support for an OAS program was iffy.

With the pressure to prepare a draft resolution for the meeting, I did just that. The draft included a statement of principles and objectives, proposed measures for each government to implement, and priorities for action by the OAS, including creating an inter-American drug commission and a fund. I revised my draft several times in January and reviewed it with the secretary general in February before making copies available to each member of the working group, the ambassador of Brazil, and several other interested ambassadors.

As we prepared for the meeting in Rio, it was clear that most Caribbean and Central American member states were not going to participate. Some cited budgetary constraints. Others said they had no specialists. Several representatives said that their governments had no drug problems and saw no need to attend. I was frankly concerned we might not have a quorum of half the thirty-three member states to convene the Specialized Conference. In addition, I had no indication of the caliber of the delegates, in other words, would they be specialists who dealt with the drug trafficking and drug abuse problems in their countries, or generalists like the members of the Permanent Council? Above all, I was not sure what the U.S. response would be. The Brazilian ambassador to the OAS was the optimist who told me not to be concerned.

I went to Rio pretty much as the only OAS subject matter specialist. The OAS conference staff planned for a very controversial five days, with long night sessions. The setting was the Copacabana Hotel, where the delegates and staff were also housed.

When the meeting opened that Monday, there were twenty-two country delegations. The key countries sent senior government officials and specialists. Only a few were represented by their ambassador to the OAS or to Brazil. The UN sent UNFDAC director, Giuseppe di Gennaro. The Foreign minister of Brazil was elected chair.

The chair invited the OAS chief conference officer and me to meet privately with him at the first coffee break. He proposed a change in the agenda. He suggested that we hold off on setting up any working groups until after the member states had made their presentations. He wanted to get a feel for the mood of the delegations and then decide what committees might be needed. We agreed.

Then the countries made their statements. The first sixteen strongly supported the analysis and document presented by the working group. All of them, including Venezuela, supported the work of the CND to draft a new UN Convention and deemed any similar effort by the OAS unwise. Almost all included in their statements support for an inter-American program based on the proposals in the working documents. I believe that the U.S. was the seventeenth speaker, and its position was similar to that taken by preceding countries. The eighteenth speaker was the new Sandinista foreign minister of Nicaragua, and his statement coincided point by point with the presentation of preceding speakers.

Once the national statements were read, the Brazilian foreign minister stated that there was a consensus among the member governments, and proposed that further discussion be suspended while a drafting group composed of chiefs of several key delegations prepared a final document. There was unanimous consent and the agenda for the meeting was suspended.

The foreign minister then announced that the conference would meet to hear presentations by the UN and other observers, but that he would be engaged with the drafting group. He suggested that I concern myself with the presentations by the UN and other observers. That afternoon some delegates attended the session, but most were engaged in the drafting process or trying to learn what was being negotiated. Di Gennaro, the director of UNFDAC, made an impassioned appeal for the OAS to delay any regional action and promised to allocate ten million dollars a year from UNFDAC for projects in Latin America and the Caribbean. Several observers talked about the need for greater attention to and action on demand reduction. But the dynamic center of the conference was the office of the Brazilian foreign minister and at his side was the Brazilian representative to the OAS, Ambassador Castro Alves.

My OAS Secretariat colleagues and I were not used to being excluded from deliberations at OAS meetings, and we were somewhat uneasy. I learned from a friend in the Brazilian delegation that the previous week, my draft resolution had been analyzed and revised by Brazilian specialists and that their revised text was the basis for the work of the drafting group. They explained that they wanted the final document to appear to be an initiative of the member states and an example of inter-American solidarity.

That evening, the chair invited me to meet with him and his advisors. He told me that agreement on the text had been made easier because the members of the drafting group were already familiar with my proposal. He outlined the changes that he and his advisors had made, namely, the proposal for creating an inter-American fund was eliminated, as were several proposed lines of inter-American action. The Brazilian delegation had added a role for the Inter-American Juridical Committee, which was headquartered in Rio. Finally, the name of the proposed mechanism would be the Inter-American Drug Abuse Control Commission (CICAD).

In little more than twenty-four hours, the foreign minister reconvened the conference to present a final draft agreed upon in advance by all twenty-two delegations. The document presented by the chair was *The Inter-American Program of Action of Rio de Janeiro against the Illicit Use and Production of Narcotic Drugs and Psychotropic Substances and Traffic Therein*. The conference adopted it unanimously, and requested the Permanent Council to present it to next OAS General Assembly in Guatemala in November for approval and implementation. The conference adjourned two days earlier than scheduled—an event without parallel in OAS history.

After Rio

On my return to Washington, the secretary general sat down with me to consider the next steps for implementing the Program of Action of Rio de Janeiro. The program had to be presented to the General Assembly for approval, and a statute had to be written to spell out the scope of work and authority of CICAD. He instructed me to meet with the working group to prepare the necessary documentation and set up a timetable to ensure that it was ready in time for the General Assembly in November.

He also asked me to work with the director of Management, Ambassador Bob Sayre, to prepare a budget and staffing pattern for CICAD. I stressed that CICAD would need at least five professionals with knowledge of and experience in the subject matter. I said that no current member of the OAS staff was qualified and that we would require new hires. He was skeptical that the governments would authorize an addition to the budget to cover the hiring of new OAS staff.

I met with the chair of the working group, and set up a schedule of meetings in order to have the necessary draft resolutions ready in time for the GA. The group met in early May and instructed me to have a draft resolution ready for its consideration in July before the summer break.

My meetings with Bob Sayre and the budget officers were not

promising. The organization's financial situation was not good. The economies of the Latin American and Caribbean countries were still in recession and the U.S. was not disposed to increase its contribution, even a voluntary one earmarked for CICAD. Sayre asked that I put together my proposed staffing plan by mid-July and said he would help in any way possible.

I spent the two weeks in May, with the advice of the OAS Legal Office, drafting the statute, using the Statute of the Inter-American Human Rights Commission as my model. I sought to create a flexible body of no more than seven member states that could design and develop an action program aimed at building cooperation among member countries to combat drug abuse and drug trafficking. I presented my proposal to the working group just days before the secretary general sent me on a new assignment to Vienna.

He had received an invitation for the OAS to attend the May 1986 meeting of the CND. He asked me to officially present the final report of Rio Meeting to the CND and to reiterate the intention of the OAS to cooperate with the United Nations in combatting illicit narcotic drug use and trafficking. I was also to report back to him and the working group on the progress being made in drafting the new worldwide convention on drug trafficking.

Since there were two major drafting groups at work in Vienna, I obtained the secretary general's permission to include Ele on the OAS delegation. He authorized her participation if I paid her transportation and expenses. I did and I duly registered her as the alternate OAS observer representative.

I was home from Rio for barely a month when Ele and I were off for Vienna. We took the metro at Schwedenplatz every weekday morning for two weeks to attend the sessions. Ele sat in on the discussion of the proposed text on demand reduction. I attended the drafting session on dealing with the disruption of supply from producer countries. Ele became a favorite of the prime minister of Malaysia when she called drug addiction "Twentieth Century Slavery" and he proposed Ele's language be incorporated into the convention. We were later invited to the Malaysian Embassy for a reception. Her intervention was reported in a Swedish newspaper.

When I officially presented the report of the Specialized Conference of Rio de Janeiro to Tamar Oppenheimer, I emphasized the interest and intent of the OAS secretary general to cooperate and coordinate with the CND, INCB, and UNFDAC to improve the scope and completeness of reporting from Latin American and Caribbean countries and to develop regional and national policies and programs in support of the UN conventions. Tamar accompanied me to a meeting with Margaret Ainstee, the UN director-general in Vienna, at which I reiterated the OAS secretary general's interest.

Ele and I had a wonderful time. We toured Vienna and environs. We were invited to dinners and cocktails by various delegations as well as friends working at the UN. We lunched daily at the superb UN cafeteria, often with delegates from participating countries or with observers, especially those from NGOs.

The secretary general authorized me to take two weeks' vacation following the CND meetings. This time we used Eurail to explore Bavaria and Southern Germany—Passau, Regensburg, the Rhine-Danube Canal, and more of the Rhineland. We then went north to Hanover, Hamburg, the Ruhr, and Lubeck before returning to Vienna for the trip home.

On my return to Washington in mid-June, I went right to work with the working group. The statute covered the principles and objectives of CICAD—its membership and their election; its headquarters, powers and jurisdiction; its operating rules; and the composition of its secretariat. The only major issue was over the composition of the CICAD Commission. My draft called for a commission of seven member states, with the commissioners elected by the General Assembly for three-year terms. The terms were to be staggered so that there would an election at each General Assembly. It was clear from the discussions that seven was not acceptable; some wanted all member states to participate; others saw the need for a smaller executive group to get CICAD going. Several argued that the drug problem did not affect all the countries (as was evident from the attendance at Rio of only twenty-two member states). Ultimately, a compromise was reached at eleven.

Before the working group recessed for the summer, it approved the draft resolution for the General Assembly on the Program of Rio. It also requested the cooperation of the Inter-American Juridical Committee with CICAD in accordance with mandate of the Program of Rio. It then adjourned for 1986.

Ele and I developed a routine for the summer that year. I spent my time preparing papers for the General Assembly. Ele joined Billie Heller at the national conference on women and economic opportunities for them. She also participated in a White House economic conference that predicted storm clouds for the next few years. That made her uncertain about how to handle our personal investments as well as the advice she was giving in her monthly AAFSW column.

In the fall, Ele made one last trip to Tulare. Elizabeth La Cell had become a cancer victim, and this was the first year that she was really alone. Many of her friends had passed away. With others she had grown apart. There was no need for her to make farm and other business decisions. She cut short her stay and rejoined me the week before I left for Central America.

In Guatemala, the most important item on the agenda of the General Assembly was the Program of Rio. It was adopted unanimously, as was the statute. The Inter-American Juridical Committee sent a resolution pledging its cooperation. Argentina, Bahamas, Bolivia, Brazil, Colombia, Guatemala, Mexico, Panama, Peru, the United States, and Venezuela were elected to be the first members of the commission and given instructions to get CICAD moving.

But when it came to a budget, the GA authorized about US$400,000 for the first year, substantially less than what I had originally requested. All of the money was to be transferred from other OAS activities and all the staff reassigned from other OAS offices. There was no flexibility to hire specialists with experience in the subject matter.

Once the GA acted, the secretary general announced my appointment as the executive secretary of CICAD. A new chapter in our lives was about to open.

31

The Inter-American Drug Abuse Control Commission (CICAD)

On January 1, 1987, CICAD began operations. Its mission was to promote inter-country cooperation throughout the Western Hemisphere in the War on Drugs by directing the implementation of the Program of Rio de Janeiro approved by the OAS General Assembly in 1986. The enemy was the technically adroit, well-armed, and well-financed criminal organizations that controlled the supply of narcotic drugs and psychotropic substances and targeted that supply to money-making markets.

The effort in the Western Hemisphere complemented the worldwide campaign by the United Nations to fight the criminal organizations and to interrupt the production, manufacture, and commerce of cannabis (marijuana); heroin derived from opium poppy; cocaine; and designated psychotropic substances. At the UN Commission on Narcotic Drugs, negotiations were underway for a new worldwide convention to provide the legal framework for governments to bring the threat under control.

Cocaine, and marijuana were native to the Western Hemisphere. Heroin was primarily produced in Southeast Asia—the Golden Triangle of Thailand, Myanmar, and Laos—and Afghanistan, and was controlled by powerful local warlords in concert with the Triads based in China and the Mafias of Western Europe. Cocaine was derived from coca leaf, native to the Andean countries of Bolivia, Colombia, and Peru and trafficking in it was controlled by powerful cartels primarily based in Colombia and northwestern Mexico. Cannabis was produced in many countries, but the primary sources in Latin America were controlled by organizations in Colombia and Mexico.

The criminal organizations posed a threat to the sovereignty of several countries around the world. They were accumulating ever-greater income from their growing markets in North America and Europe, and were using it to build sophisticated marketing systems to deliver more drugs to more customers. In the process, they were corrupting public officials and were pressuring financial institutions to launder their profits. The trail of corruption in Latin America, the Caribbean, and the United States was being uncovered at an alarming rate.

Few Western Hemisphere countries were truly engaged in combatting the threat, except for those directly affected by drug production and manufacture. Until the mid-1980s, most of Latin America and the Caribbean considered the problem to be that of the United States and other consumer countries, and presumed that addiction would not affect them or their people. In face of their relatively weak financial and economic development, with relatively small GNPs, they did not believe that their countries would likely become targets of the profit-driven drug traffickers. Hence, when CICAD came into existence, many OAS member states had only a passing interest in the subject.

The United States had been wrestling with mounting drug use since the early 1960s. The Drug Enforcement Administration (DEA) had been created in 1963. The House of Representatives created a bipartisan select committee to consider measures to deal with problem, and the U.S. Senate established its own subcommittee. The primary focus was on law enforcement—intercepting the flow of narcotic drugs from abroad and meting out stiff sentences for drug offenders—even though those prison sentences seemed to have little deterrent effect on users. News reports increasingly covered widespread use of narcotic drugs and psychotropic substances in federal, state, and local prisons. Measures to reduce demand were minimal even though President and Mrs. Reagan addressed the nation about their concern at the increase in drug use among youth and spearheaded a campaign among young people to heed Mrs. Reagan's advice, "Just Say No."

In Colombia, the cartels waged war on the government, and one of the major rebel groups, the FARC, was reputed to have entered the drug trade to finance the purchase of arms. In Bolivia,

Colombia, and Peru, government programs supported by international agencies and the U.S. government, seemed unable to reduce production of coca leaf or contain the power of the cartels to convert that leaf into cocaine and move the cocaine to world markets.

Into this world, the OAS General Assembly created the Inter-American Drug Abuse Control Commission (CICAD) in November 1986 and proclaimed an Inter-American Alliance to combat Drug Trafficking. At the same time, it rejected an initiative to create a special fund for the CICAD program, and approved a budget of less than half a million dollars, from monies originally earmarked for other OAS activities.

My mandate as executive secretary was to activate CICAD and develop a meaningful program. With the limited budget and a staff of ten with no prior experience with the subject matter, what kind of a program could be designed to implement the Program of Rio?

Getting Started

In early January 1987, CICAD opened its doors in gerrymandered space on the eighth floor of the General Secretariat Building. When we assembled that day, we were six people, most of whom were beginning to work together for the first time: The deputy executive secretary, Samuel Echalar—a career OAS conference officer; my secretary, Marta Bellis; Anna Chisman, a career OAS translator and former president of the staff association; Marta Ramos, Sam's secretary; Jorge Rodriguez, a finance specialist; and me.

Samuel Echalar, a Bolivian, had been selected by the secretary general in consultation with the Permanent Council's working group. He was a veteran OAS officer whose specialty was planning, organizing, and managing conferences—skills we would need in building CICAD.

Anna, British-born and Oxford-educated was my choice after we had a long discussion that reflected her deep concern about drug issues, an understanding of their political and social implications, and a special interest in demand reduction—one of the critical elements of the problem. Her experience in preparing and translating documents were skills we would need in moving forward the CICAD program.

Marta Bellis had been my most competent secretary/administrative aide for five years, and was a proven asset. The other secretary, Martha Ramos, a well-qualified secretary, had been seconded by the personnel office to serve as Sam's secretary. Jorge Rodriguez was well-qualified and provided us the administrative and managerial skills we needed for managing CICAD.

It took us nearly a year to put together the core staff that built CICAD. We arranged the transfer from personnel of Ruth Connolly, a veteran OAS officer from the U.S., whose experience fit our need for setting up an Inter-American information center, and Ricardo Zavaleta, a Salvadoran statistician from the CIES, fit the bill for setting up the statistical program. In 1988, two more conference officers were assigned to our staff: Rudy García, a Cuban émigré, and Gabriel Gualteros, a Colombian. In 1989, the secretary general reassigned Caroline Casselman, a U.S. national in his office, to help us respond to the increasing demand for information about CICAD from governments and private entities.

Once assembled, that core staff remained in place for the eight years I served as executive secretary. The only two changes were the result of promotions for the first two secretaries: Martha Bellis became secretary of the secretary general and was replaced by Ligia Guillén, a Bolivian, who became indispensable to me in doing my job. Marta Ramos was promoted to be the secretary to the executive secretary of CIES. Rosemary Vasquez, an Uruguayan, replaced her and became a solid member of our staff.

None of us had professional background or experience in the subject matter of drug trafficking and drug abuse. We had to educate ourselves. We had to improvise and learn together—both the new subject matter and how to work with each other. I did most of the initial training, beginning with the background documents and policy papers prepared for the Rio meeting. I briefed my colleagues on the impact of cocaine on Bolivia, Colombia, Mexico, and Peru and that of marijuana in Colombia and Mexico. Opium poppy production at that time was not significant in any of the OAS countries. I showed them that almost every member country was affected in one way or another by the shipment of illicit drugs across national boundaries en route to the burgeoning markets in North America and Europe and called their attention to empirical evidence that narcotic drug use was growing rapidly in the larger cities of Latin America. I described how money was being laundered at each step of the drug chain, but most heavily in the United States.

While we were learning, we had an immediate deadline to prepare the first meeting of CICAD in April 1987. Barely operational, we had to design a format for the CICAD meetings; revise the draft statute to reflect the provisions of the Program of Rio and the General Assembly resolution; prepare draft bylaws for the fledgling commission; and prepare background and policy papers for CICAD to consider. We recognized that a poor beginning could be the end of the Program of Rio. It was a unique challenge.

Sam took charge of convoking the meeting, advising the eleven member states, working with the OAS Conference Office to make the logistical arrangements, preparing the draft rules of procedure, and lining up the personnel needed for servicing the meeting. Sam negotiated the use of the Chamber of the Permanent Council to inaugurate the opening session.

Anna worked with me on drafting the CICAD statute and bylaws, as well as background and policy papers. We reviewed the statutes and bylaws of other OAS bodies and consulted the OAS legal advisor, and then vetted our drafts with the working group to make sure there would be no problems with the Permanent Council.

Our most difficult task was to prepare proposals to orient the work of CICAD and its substantive program, and that was my job. I drew on the Program of Rio. Chapter III called on member states to (1) create national drug control commissions to formulate national policies, plans, and actions to combat drug trafficking, (2) promote cooperation between the public and private sectors to prevent drug abuse and treat the addicted and to (3) set up national funds to combat drug abuse and drug trafficking.

Chapter IV called on CICAD, with the support of the Inter-American Juridical Committee, to (1) prepare bilateral and multilateral legal instruments to combat drug abuse and drug trafficking, covering extradition and cooperation among judicial, police, and custom officials; (2) promote the harmonization of laws among the member states; and (3) promote cooperation and coordination among judicial, police, and customs officials that dealt with illicit drug trafficking. Chapter IV also empowered the OAS to create a data bank, a documentation center, and regional training centers to prepare national officials to better deal with education on prevention.

In assessing the various possible lines of action that CICAD might consider, I reviewed projects being carried out by both the CND and UNFDAC. While CND sponsored periodically seminars for government officials on policy and law enforcement, most UNFDAC projects dealt with curtailing production. The UNFDAC projects were expensive and the results not promising. I felt that CICAD should not try to duplicate those existing efforts.

A month before the first meeting, the secretary general gave me a green light to set up the regional data bank and documentation center as called for in Chapter IV. Prior to the meeting, Ruth Connolly was assigned to work on the documentation center and Ricardo Zavaleta on the data bank. Their initial efforts were to explore what other documentation centers and data banks existed in the region, how they were organized and operated. The UN and U.S. information centers and data banks were consulted. The CND and INCB were requested to provide us information about its information center and data bank and its manuals so that the CICAD structure and operations would be as close as possible to theirs. Notes were sent to each of the member states asking for detailed information on such organizations in their respective countries. Similar requests were sent to OAS observer states (Canada, Spain, Japan, France, Morocco, and Saudi Arabia) for information about their programs. What we reported to the first session of CICAD was that we were getting started.

In addition, for the first meeting of CICAD, we put together a package of working papers to enable the eleven delegates to initiate their consideration of the policies and programs that they wanted CICAD to undertake. The most significant focused on its possible role in assisting countries to prepare critical laws to combat drug trafficking and drug abuse and in harmonizing the legal provisions in force in the member states. I prepared that paper because the Inter-American Juridical Committee advised CICAD that it lacked resources to participate and proposed that CICAD itself develop policy proposals, just keeping it informed. I shared the response with the secretary general and the Brazilian delegation since Brazil had a special interest in the organization that was headquartered in Rio de Janeiro.

The First Meeting of CICAD

As that first meeting approached, to say that I was apprehensive is an understatement. We were a newly assembled group of generalists who had never worked together before and were learning the subject matter. We were being called on to build a new mechanism within an international organization in financial crisis, with barely enough resources to cover our salaries and a few supplies. We were entrusted with the mission of supporting members from eleven countries to establish a new organization and program. All we knew about the eleven delegates was they worked in one or another facet of the drug abuse and illicit trafficking problem, but we knew little about them or how they approached or evaluated the inter-American drug problem.

Ele knew how uneasy I had been since CICAD opened its doors. I shared with her my doubts about my own limitations in the subject matter. There was really no one to guide me—unlike the other posts I had occupied. There were no established guidelines about how to mold our staff together. I had doubts about my ability to provide the leadership to work with the members in implementing the Program of Rio.

On that morning when CICAD assembled for the first time in the Permanent Council chamber, we met each of the CICAD members for the first time. Two were legislators, one was a jurist, several were senior officials dealing with the interdiction of illicit drug traffic, and two were senior advisers to heads of state. Few of them had even met each other before that morning. None had prior experience with the OAS or other international forums. None had worked with officials of other Latin American or Caribbean governments. One or two had worked with the U.S. government on drug interdiction projects.

The secretary general opened the meeting, welcoming the members and stressing the challenge given them to implement the Program of Rio, and assured them of his support. The assistant secretary general also greeted them. Then the two senior OAS officers returned to their offices at the coffee break and I was left to initiate the work of setting up the new commission.

During the coffee break, I talked to the members about the election of their officers and asked how they wished to proceed. I found that most delegates favored that their first chair be from Colombia, given the dimensions of the problem afflicting that country. With several delegates, we approached the Colombian delegation and met its chief, Deputy Minister of Justice Dr. Alfonso Soler Mantilla, a judge widely respected for his courage in convicting traffickers. He was reluctant to assume the chairmanship of CICAD, but after some convincing by other delegates, agreed. With his election, the work of CICAD began. Peru's Deputy Minister of Justice Lucio Galarza was elected Vice Chair.

Sam and I invited the two of them to lunch so that we could review the agenda and help them analyze the topics that needed to be covered. Sam explained the proposed rules of procedure that were designed to be informal and promote discussion among the members. Our objective was to encourage the members to interact with each other and share their views and concerns. Sam and I answered their questions and made clear that our role was to support them.

After lunch when we reassembled, Dr. Soler created a less formal atmosphere. After approving the Statute and Rules of Procedure, CICAD agreed to meet twice a year although most OAS bodies meet once a year. I urged that it meet twice a year in order to get the dialogue going and establish a presence. I also feared that, if it met only once a year, CICAD would be run by the secretariat, not the representatives of the member states. Two meetings a year placed a heavy load on our small staff, but we could adapt. CICAD decided to hold one meeting at headquarters in Washington, D.C., and the second in one of the member states.

Then, the chair invited the members to make brief presentations on drug trafficking and drug abuse in his or her country and the measures being taken to confront them. In their presentations, most Latin American and Caribbean members implicitly or openly blamed the United States for the problems their countries faced, while the U.S. delegate blamed the problems on the avalanche of drugs coming in from abroad and the failure of Latin American and

Caribbean countries to interdict and curtail the flow. They listened to each other in a session that ran much longer than planned.

On the second day, the discussion focused on the activities CICAD should carry out to implement the Program of Rio. This discussion was far more substantive than the presentations the first day. The Latin Americans called on CICAD to focus on demand reduction and urged the United States to take strong action to curtail its burgeoning drug market. The United States, in turn, proposed that CICAD emphasize measures to impede the movement of drugs into the U.S. market. Profound differences, yes. However, when discussions focused on the threat posed by organized crime, almost all the members began talking a common language and identified similar targets. They began talking to each other and shifting the tone to what could we do together. While skeptical about what CICAD, with its limited resources, might be able to do, they decided that CICAD had to try. So, they called on the secretariat to prepare an options paper on the program alternatives for the next meeting.

Drafting a strategy paper with options for the members to consider was by itself a complex undertaking. But preparing a paper with the limited resources available made it even more perplexing. I drew on the studies I had prepared for the Rio meeting that indicated that only a handful of countries had established high-level bodies to deal with the narcotics problem. Few had national drug policies and many dealt with the problem through uncoordinated police and health activities. Few countries had legislation adequate to control the sophisticated drug syndicates, especially on money laundering. My studies had turned up evidence of corruption by drug money from Alaska to Cape Horn.

So, in drafting the paper for the second meeting of CICAD, I proposed five initial lines of action that could lay the groundwork for inter-governmental cooperation and through which CICAD could assist the member states: first, to establish in each OAS member country a high-level government entity to deal with the drug problem; second, to enact legislation needed for combatting the drug cartels and for harmonizing legislation among the member states; third, to initiate in-country demand reduction programs; fourth, to build the Inter-American Data Bank to provide governments with essential information for policy making; and fifth, to create the Inter-American Documentation Center to provide information on worldwide activities that dealt with the drug problem.

At the second meeting, the members agreed to develop the five lines of action as the initial phase of its operations and to make its presence known throughout the hemisphere.

During my eight years as executive secretary, it was through those five lines of action that CICAD helped national governments build and strengthen their institutional and planning capability and put in place relevant laws and procedures. They established CICAD's presence as a forum in which differences in perceptions and policies could be talked out in the search for common ground in achieving a shared goal. Over those eight years, our annual budget, including voluntary contributions we could raise from member countries (the U.S., Canada, Mexico, Argentina, Chile, and Brazil), observer states (Spain, France, Germany, and Japan), and other sources, never reached $1 million. The powerful drug cartels spent much more money on one Go Fast drug boat than CICAD received in its entire budget over those eight years. The cartels hired MBAs to run their operations; we had no money to hire experts or support staff. The drug traffickers bought their "influence" and public relations; we had to write pamphlets and publish them as an adjunct to our other activities,

That CICAD became recognized as one of the more effective agencies of the OAS gives me great personal satisfaction. Equally gratifying were the words of the Canadian ambassador to the OAS when he reported that the effectiveness of the Inter-American Human Rights Commission and CICAD were important considerations in his government's decision to join the OAS in 1989. Although I had retired, I took pride in 1996 when at the summit of Heads of State of the Americas in Miami, less than ten years after its inception, CICAD was recognized for its efforts and entrusted with implementing decisions reached at that meeting, including making annual assessments of country performance in combatting narcotic drugs.

CICAD Meetings

Its semi-annual meetings usually lasted two days. Physical arrangements for each meeting were the responsibility of Sam Echalar. The executive secretary prepared the agenda for each meeting in consultation with the chair of CICAD. The agenda was shaped to stimulate open discussion among the members. In the formative years, the agenda usually revolved around the implementation of the five lines of action.

Each meeting began with a report by each member on recent developments in his/her country and tended to be non-controversial sliding over critical issues, but they provided information essential for understanding conditions and policy trends in the countries. They highlighted the increasing seriousness of the drug situation, country by country and throughout the Western Hemisphere. The few questions or comments made during presentations often touched on similar issues or problems that other governments were facing. Initially, few presentations touched on the need for help from another country to deal with some aspect of the drug problem even when that help might be critical to its resolution. The agenda for the remaining day and a half focused on progress in implementing the lines of action and facing specific problems that had arisen since the last meeting. Most comments in the initial sessions remained general and tended to be uncritical, seldom casting aspersions. However, the longer the members worked with each other, the more open their communications became. Then the discussions could become very specific and sometimes heated. As executive secretary, it was often my job to find common ground that the various countries could accept. Getting eleven governments to agree was often delicate and time-consuming.

It was at the third meeting held in the Hotel Antigua in Antigua, Guatemala that Anna, Sam, and I first sensed that the members felt comfortable working with each other. In a very informal environment, they ate together, met over drinks in the evening, and got to know each other. They reached a series of informal understandings for initiating activities under the five lines of action that they summarized in the CICAD document *Declaration of the Americas against Drug Trafficking*.

In those early meetings, the U.S. member played a central role. To the Latin American and Caribbean members, the constructive participation of the United States was critical. The eleven delegates sat around the table facing each other. They could see each other's reactions, and that led to some tense minutes in those early meetings.

They watched for the reaction of the U.S. delegate. Fortunately President Reagan appointed former Florida Senator Paula Hawkins, and she was used to working in deliberative bodies and knew the subject matter, having chaired the U.S. Senate subcommittee on drug trafficking and drug abuse. She had a reputation for being forthright and critical of Latin American efforts. So, when she reacted and talked out issues frankly, she helped set the stage for open discussions. She served on the commission for nearly seven years, through George H.W. Bush's presidency.

Senator Hawkins was aided by Richard Hines, a career U.S. foreign service officer, whose experience in Latin America helped the senator immeasurably in building relations with her fellow members and in advising her on how best to address controversial measures on the agenda. Richard was also my primary day-to-day channel for appraising the U.S. government's reaction to possible measures that CICAD planned to take. Richard's support of CICAD in those early years was inestimable.

Senator Hawkins' political credentials gave her ready access to key offices in the U.S. executive branch and on Capitol Hill. She arranged briefings for the Senate Subcommittee on Drug Trafficking and the Select House Committee chaired by Congressman Charles Rangel. She set up a meeting for CICAD to brief the majority and minority leaders of the Senate, as well as a special session with the Republican leadership of the Senate, led by Robert Dole. In part because of the contacts that Senator Hawkins helped establish, Secretary General Baena Soares in mid-1988 assigned one of his senior liaison officers, Caroline Casselman, to develop a public information program, including briefings for interested senators and congressmen.

Relations with the UN Programs

At its first session, CICAD instructed the secretariat to maintain close working relations with the CND, INCB, and UNFDAC. CND was invited to participate in each CICAD session. At the close of the first session, CICAD asked me to go to Vienna to present a written and oral report to the CND on the results of its meeting. At meetings at OAS headquarters in Washington, an official from Vienna or New York occasionally attended, but they rarely participated in one outside of Washington. The CND was also invited to provide experts for all CICAD technical meetings.

During my eight years as executive secretary, CICAD was represented at each annual meeting of the UN body and presented a detailed report of CICAD plans and operations. We tried to convene CICAD meetings at times that did not conflict with those of the CND, and Sam Echalar was sent to Vienna to coordinate meeting schedules and compare the structure and format of meetings. Anna also went to Vienna to meet with the CND's experts on demand reduction to encourage joint programming in the Americas. CICAD recognized that pooling and coordinating the use of our limited human and material resources could broaden our impact and help stretch our limited budgets. CICAD was able to draw on the expertise of the CND and INCB and use their models to shape the inter-American documentation center and the data bank, and its experience with evaluating country performance.

In addition, my colleagues and I contacted UN specialists working in Latin American and Caribbean countries. We followed developments in all CND and UNFDAC projects and noted that reports by CND field specialists were often less optimistic than those by representatives of the U.S. State Department, the U.S. Department of Justice, or the DEA.

The Emerging Role

The Program of Rio did not authorize CICAD to assume an action role in intercepting the trafficking of drugs or eradicating production, nor did it authorize resources to build an intelligence capability to penetrate the powerful drug cartels. Coupled with the decision not to create a special operations fund, CICAD had to see itself primarily as a forum in which the member countries could discuss strategies and tactics to combat drug trafficking and drug abuse, with its subsidiary activities designed to strengthen its role as a forum.

Thus, from day one, CICAD was the inter-American forum on the drug problem, and every activity it undertook, including the five lines of action, was to enhance its effectiveness as that forum. The agenda for each CICAD meeting was aimed at stimulating discussion on inter-governmental cooperation to deal with the drug problem. The five lines of action were designed to project CICAD beyond its semi-annual meetings and make it known throughout the Western Hemisphere, and provide it with data and experience to better assess its options.

The environment for the forum was challenging. Latin America and the Caribbean had very different perceptions of the problem from that of the United States and had quite different approaches for dealing with it. Only one or two had established national policies or programs. All were wary of U.S. intentions in supporting CICAD and, with a U.S. national as executive secretary, they expected that CICAD would reflect U.S. policy. On the other hand, U.S. authorities questioned the seriousness of the Latin American and Caribbean anti-drug efforts, and were concerned that CICAD would become a spokesman for Latin American and Caribbean complaints about U.S. actions. Neither side had confidence in the other or in the secretariat.

For those reasons, my colleagues and I tried to make the meetings and the agenda as technical as possible. Certainly each topic had significant political ramifications, but it was by working on technical measures that members could find common ground. The lines of action provided concrete activities that facilitated discussion around the table of policy issues and possible areas of inter-country cooperation. The constant challenge from the first CICAD meeting in that spring of 1987 to the sixteenth meeting in Santiago, Chile in October 1994, which was my last, was to shape technical actions to enhance the capability of the forum to reach a political goal of inter-country cooperation to combat drug trafficking and drug abuse.

By the fourth meeting, during the chairmanship of Venezuela's Sonia Sgambatti, the discussion warmed up. That was the first meeting where I remember members talking about political, not technical, issues, such as corruption, inefficient police work, lack of communication within countries and with neighboring countries, and other critical deficiencies in national efforts. And that was the first meeting where a Latin American said to the U.S. delegate that his country didn't trust U.S. intentions and felt that the United States didn't trust his country enough to share information. The U.S. response was strong and pointed to the human tragedies caused by the narcotic drugs coming from Latin America. That exchange turned out to be pivotal: afterwards, discussions became more open and constructive.

The fifth meeting was held in La Paz, Bolivia and focused on strategic and practical measures to facilitate inter-country cooperation. It took five meetings to build enough confidence in the forum for the topic to emerge as a felt need. In La Paz, I sensed that the Latin American delegates had become committed to the existence of CICAD and saw it as a useful inter-American mechanism.

The initial meetings in 1987 and 1988 met with skeptical reactions by most members of the Permanent Council, the OAS permanent staff, and the press. Few thought CICAD would last more than a year or two. Little by little, attitudes changed as word spread of the discussions in the forum and progress under the lines of action. Observer countries like Canada, France, and Spain not only attended the sessions but also regularly consulted my colleagues and me about the flow of work and CICAD's position and activities. On several issues, Sam, Anna, and I received feedback that the discussions in CICAD were being echoed in other OAS bodies and in bilateral discussions among member states. In addition, observer countries like Canada (before becoming an OAS member in 1990), France, Japan, and Spain became active supporters of CICAD, providing funds for specific lines of action.

After only two years of existence, the respect for its efforts led the OAS General Assembly to convene a meeting of ministers at Ixtapa, Mexico, April 17–20, 1990, to reaffirm support for CICAD and to recommend to OAS member governments that they cooperate with CICAD in implementing the lines of action. It was the Western Hemisphere's complement to the Seventeenth Special Session of the UN General Assembly on Drug Trafficking held in 1989, and provided the opportunity for the governments at the ministerial level to reassert that drug trafficking, including money laundering, was a criminal activity that the OAS member countries had a collective responsibility to combat. It also reaffirmed that CICAD was the chosen OAS mechanism to exercise that collective responsibility. The Ixtapa meeting approved the five lines of action that CICAD had adopted in its exercise of that collective responsibility.

First Line of Action: Legal Development

The line of action was designed to harmonize the legal provisions and operating procedures in OAS member states to fight illicit drug trafficking. To promote harmonization, CICAD called on all member countries to adopt and apply the conventions of the United Nations to provide a common legal framework. CICAD set its role as advising member states on the compatible and consistent application of the provisions of the conventions in member countries. It was my responsibility to develop this line of action.

First, I worked with member countries to prepare documentation to request that national congresses adopt the UN conventions. By 1991, nearly every government in the Western Hemisphere had adopted all the UN conventions.

Second, we worked with OAS member states to create high-level national drug agencies to plan and coordinate national action against illicit drug trafficking and drug abuse. By 1994, most had established such agencies, often in the office of the president.

With the conventions in place and high level commissions in formation, the emphasis in the line of action shifted to assisting member countries to harmonize norms and operations for combatting pivotal criminal actions of drug traffickers. The first dealt with the production and marketing of precursors and chemical substances used in the manufacture of narcotic drugs and psychotropic substances. The second was money laundering. In both areas, CICAD followed the guideline policies and operations recommended by expert groups set up by G-7 heads of state. The third was on judicial procedures when requested by a member state.

Harmonizing norms and standards on precursor chemicals was

funded by a special grant from the U.S. government and the UN Drug Control Program (UNDCP), which was established when the UN merged CND, INCB, and UNFDAC into one body. Those funds allowed CICAD to convene a committee of high-level inter-American experts to appraise the worldwide norms contained in the G-7 Model Regulations to Control Chemical Precursors and Chemical Substances, Machines, and Materials and adapt them to the reality of the Latin American and Caribbean environment. I had been a member of the G-7 task force and was coordinator of the CICAD committee. The result was the Inter-American Model Regulations that, at the 1990 Ixtapa meeting, were adopted for uniform application in the Western Hemisphere, and the secretariat was instructed to assist member countries in adopting and implementing them.

CICAD then worked with the INCB, INTERPOL, the U.S. Drug Enforcement Agency (DEA), and the UNDCP to conduct four sub regional workshops and training programs to help member states understand and apply the model regulations. DEA and the Royal Canadian Mounted Police (RCMP) provided lecturers and other assistance.

My workload as both executive secretary and manager of this line of action led me in 1990 to ask the secretary general to hire a legal specialist to work with CICAD. The secretary general approved my request and CICAD recruited a Canadian lawyer, Michael Sullivan, who was conversant with both the Civil Law of Latin America and English common law practiced in the Caribbean countries, the U.S., and Canada. Michael became the first Canadian citizen member of the OAS staff after Canada joined the OAS a year earlier.

The second substantive area that CICAD tackled was money laundering. After the G-7 adopted worldwide standards and procedures to apply uniformly the provisions of Article 5 of the 1988 United Nations convention on controlling money laundering, CICAD called for the formation of an expert group to adapt the global standards to the conditions in the OAS member states. Several of the inter-American experts had participated in the G-7 deliberations and they facilitated the drafting of a CICAD document consistent with that of the G-7. It was titled "Model Regulations Concerning Laundering Offenses Connected to Illicit Drug Trafficking and Related Offenses."

In 1992, the OAS General Assembly approved those model regulations and recommended that the member states enact them as national law. Following the General Assembly, CICAD, with funds contributed by the U.S. and other countries, undertook a series of sub regional workshops and training programs to help member states understand, adopt, and apply them. Michael and I organized and participated in workshops and training programs in the Southern Cone, the Andean countries, Brazil, Central America, and Mexico. We also advised ministers and legislators on adapting them to meet specific constitutional and other legal requirements.

In the early 1990s, based on its concerns about the escalating violence related to drug trafficking, largely supported by gun purchases in the United States, CICAD sought to convene an expert group to prepare model regulations on gun sales to drug cartels. When CICAD presented its proposal to the Permanent Council, the Council declared that the issue transcended the drug arena and determined that it, not CICAD, was the appropriate organ to consider this critical subject.

On judicial procedures, using our own limited resources, Michael and I conducted sub regional and regional workshops and provided advice to governments on improving the collection, safeguarding and presentation of evidence against traffickers, expediting court proceedings, and setting appropriate sanctions and penalties commensurate with the crimes.

CICAD's work on precursor chemicals and money laundering led to invitations to participate in workshops and seminars in Belgium, France, Italy, and Spain in which I made presentations on the CICAD program and participated with UN, EU, INTERPOL, and host country specialists. After a workshop in Paris, the French police offered its cooperation with CICAD in the Caribbean Basin. During a seminar in Brussels on precursor chemicals in Latin America, the European Community offered to work with CICAD in upgrading Latin American capacities to identify and control illicit substances being smuggled into the countries. Discussions in Brussels and Paris were inevitably followed by some of the most palatable meals of my life, often in small, out-of-the-way restaurants. The flavors linger in my memory.

DEA's Director of Operations against Precursor Chemicals,

Gene Haslip, invited me to participate in DEA workshops in Italy and Spain. They were usually four-day events with senior officers of the host country police forces and offered opportunities to identify potential future collaborations with CICAD in assisting OAS member states.

In the fall of 1992, I was invited to participate in the Vatican Conference on Illicit Trafficking and Drug Abuse. The conference, held in a Vatican meeting room just steps from St. Peter's, was the first major effort by the Vatican to combat drug abuse. The meetings included some of the most eminent authorities from the four corners of the earth; Queen Sofía of Spain attended every session. Just being in the setting of the Vatican was moving, and being able to have escorted private visits to the Sistine Chapel, the Treasury, and the Museum made it a once-in-a-lifetime experience. The final evening, the delegates sat with the Pope at a concert in the incredibly beautiful new concert hall. After the concert, the Pope expressed his appreciation for our contributions to the Vatican's efforts.

I had to thank an old friend for being included in the program: Edilberto Moreno, who was then the Venezuelan ambassador to the Vatican. He had been a friend from the time we first met in 1960 when he was private secretary to President Betancourt of Venezuela. In the mid-1980s, as the Venezuelan ambassador to OAS, he had been a leading proponent of the creation of CICAD.

CICAD's work in legal development led to my participation in two other memorable conferences that dealt specifically with the role of the mafia and organized crime in drug trafficking: the 1993 UN Crime Prevention and Criminal Justice Program (UNPAC) on mafia issues, held in Sicily, and its 1994 follow-up meeting at Courmayeur, Italy, at the base of Mont Blanc.

The meetings were the consequence of the brutal assassination of Judge Giovanni Falcone and Judge Paolo Borsellino by the Cosa Nostra as reprisals for their role in prosecuting drug traffickers and disrupting their illicit activities. The focus at the Sicilian conference was the Italian government's measures to combat the Cosa Nostra and other mafias in Southern Italy and Sicily. The discussions transcended the Italian problem and probed into the drug trafficking activities of organized crime throughout the world, including the Triad, Yakuza, Russian mafia, and the Medellín and Sinaloa cartels.

I presented information compiled by CICAD about the Latin American scene.

Second Line of Action: Demand Reduction

At its first session, CICAD placed high priority on action to reduce the demand for illicit drugs. One delegate called it "the human side of the problem" and proposed that CICAD focus on educating young people about the consequences of drug abuse and drug trafficking.

The data CICAD was collecting showed that almost every country in the Western Hemisphere was experiencing a rapid increase in the use of cocaine, marijuana, and other drugs and that arrests for drug use were rising. Some delegates expressed concern about the apparent availability of drugs on the streets of their major cities and brought newspaper reports of increasing numbers of young people using drugs. All the Caribbean and Latin American delegates reiterated their belief that drug trafficking would not be substantially reduced until the U.S. took decisive action to reduce drug use in its national territory.

The question of whether supply encouraged demand or demand encouraged supply was irrelevant. The crux of the issue was that both supply and demand had to be attacked. CICAD, with its limited resources and limited law enforcement and intelligence capability, was not equipped to deal extensively with curtailing supply, but it could try to develop programs dealing with demand reduction.

The responsibility for putting together a plan of action fell on the shoulders of Anna Chisman. She compiled information on efforts in schools, churches, and communities throughout the Western Hemisphere. She identified organizations that worked on the problem in the member states, interviewed specialists and observed programs in operation. Anna compiled a directory of facilities in the Western Hemisphere, most of them in Canada and the U.S., with only a handful in Latin American and the Caribbean. Her office computer became a treasure trove of information about relevant policies and programs. She found private organizations that worked extensively on treatment and rehabilitation, but on prevention, she found that almost no effort had been made by either governments or the private sector in spite of the call by U.S. First Lady Nancy Reagan. She established working relationships with counterparts in other international organizations and the U.S. and other governments, as well as with key officials in the Inter-American Council for Education, Science, and Culture (CIECC). She spent 1987 and 1988 becoming an expert on the prevention and treatment of drug abuse.

Building on her investigations, Anna prepared a series of background and policy papers on the situation in the member states. The evidence demonstrated that families and communities in every corner of the hemisphere were wrestling with the human disasters caused by this twentieth century plague. The problem affected rich and poor, people in urban and rural areas of developed and underdeveloped countries. She spelled out a role for CICAD to play in formulating and implementing measures to reduce demand that could stimulate inter-country cooperation on not only demand reduction but other aspects of the drug problem.

At the third meeting in Antigua, CICAD approved a plan to implement this second line of action based on a strategic paper prepared by Anna. The paper's underlying premise was that only by reducing demand, especially in the more opulent economies, could there be a substantial reduction in the drug trade. The enormous profits made in the more developed countries outweighed the risks and were the lure for drug traffickers to deliver the supplies. To undermine this alluring business, a major effort had to be made to shrink the market by reducing consumption.

In addition, Anna's evidence showed that the drug traffickers were building markets in producer and transit countries to supplement their established markets in the more developed countries. Hence, demand reduction efforts were needed throughout the region. The evidence also showed that one-shot campaigns had not worked. A sustained comprehensive effort of education for prevention, especially for young people, and treatment and rehabilitation for those already addicted, was the remedy. Mobilizing community support was an essential ingredient for such an effort.

Working with CIECC, Anna planned and organized four workshops on demand reduction and education against drug abuse. The first workshop was held in Uruguay in May 1988 and was inaugurated by Uruguayan President Julio Sanguinetti, who made an impassioned plea for an inter-American crusade to protect the youth from drug abuse. The second was held in Grenada in November 1988 under the co-sponsorship of CARICOM and was opened by the prime minister. The third held in Mexico for the Central American countries and Mexico was opened by Mexican President Salinas de Gortari and attended by Mexican Minister of Education Ernesto Zedillo. The fourth was held in July 1989 in Argentina and was opened by President Carlos Menem.

Those four workshops, attended by experts and specialists from almost every country in the hemisphere, provided the substance and direction for a comprehensive education program against narcotic drug use that could be incorporated into the regular school curriculum. Anna integrated the results of the four workshops into a comprehensive action plan that national drug commissions and ministries of education and health could install in public and private schools in each country. Her proposal also included machinery for sharing information on results among countries. It defined a clear anti-drug message for the young and spelled out policies and procedures for dealing with drug abusers in school systems. It set guidelines for curriculum, teacher training, instructional materials, and parent and community involvement. It also included on-going research to improve program effectiveness as experience dictated.

The Ecuadorian government invited all OAS member states to meet in Quito in June 1990 to consider the results of the four workshops. The plan of action was the principal document. The Ecuadorian government gave special status to the meeting, and President Rodrigo Borja Cevallos not only inaugurated the meeting but also asked for special briefings on progress and results. The Ecuadorian member of CICAD, the minister of Justice, and the minister of Education worked together to mobilize logistical and public support for the meeting. The delegations from the member states included key education and anti-drug officials. The CND sent its chief demand reduction specialist, and the Spanish government and several NGOs sent accredited observers. The meeting was front-page news in Ecuador and newspapers from several Latin American countries had special correspondents covering the event.

I remember the meeting as one of the most stimulating since the

Alliance for Progress days. The focus was on programs that could be carried out anywhere in the hemisphere, whether in developed countries like Canada and the United States, or the least developed like Haiti, Honduras, and Bolivia, to educate young people to resist using drugs and offer them other incentives and activities to involve their energies and imaginations. It included mechanisms for mobilizing resources for positive efforts by governments and NGOs to fight drug abuse. The discussions were down-to-earth and dealt with the real situation in the countries of the Americas, not academic theory or wishful thinking. The participants talked frankly about the obstacles they faced, from the political framework in which they worked, to the deficiencies in their education systems, weaknesses in teacher education, and lack of job opportunities for young people.

The product of the meeting was the Inter-American Program of Quito: Comprehensive Education to Prevent Drug Abuse. It included proposals recommended by the four workshops and provided the framework for formal and non-formal education to prevent drug abuse and included parental and community participation. It called on CICAD to reinforce and complement country efforts by informing and advising country officials on specific innovative practices and activities that might enrich national and local programs.

The program was enthusiastically endorsed by the OAS General Assembly, and significant efforts were initiated in a few countries. However, in spite of efforts by CICAD and a few Latin American presidents during my term as executive secretary, we were never able to raise the funds needed to give life to the Program of Quito. I accompanied Latin American presidents and chiefs of National Drug Commissions while they requested funding from international and bilateral lending agencies. Loan officers of those agencies said the proposals were too "soft" or "inchoate" to define or evaluate and turned down funds needed to begin trial operations.

One of my greatest frustrations from my years as executive secretary was that I was unable to obtain adequate funding for this line of action. I continue to marvel at Anna's resourcefulness in finding ways and means for moving the Program of Quito forward. I remain convinced that only when demand is minimized will the drug problem become manageable. Protecting youth from the human and societal tragedy of drug abuse must be a priority whether drugs remain illegal or are afforded some degree of legitimacy. Inadequately developing and funding prevention programs is unforgiveable and bad public policy.

The second area of demand reduction that Anna tackled was treatment and rehabilitation. She compiled a hemisphere-wide database on universities that prepared doctors, nurses, and technicians to deal with addicts and on facilities that were engaged in treatment and rehabilitation. Her goal was not only to identify their resources but also to ascertain their interest in cooperating with CICAD in training needed Latin American and Caribbean technical personnel.

The Program of Rio called on CICAD to establish inter-American centers to assist member governments in training specialists needed to deal with the drug problem. She began exploring prospects with Johns Hopkins University in Baltimore, the Yale Institute of Alcohol and Drug Addiction, and the Addiction Research Foundation at the University of Toronto. When she contacted Johns Hopkins, its renowned specialist on drug treatment and rehabilitation, Dr. Wallace Mandell, not only advised us in planning the CICAD program but also invited us to meet with the Latin American and Caribbean Humphrey fellows in the Johns Hopkins Graduate Program and inform them about our plans.

By the mid-1990s Anna and I weighed the possibility of creating an inter-American center at Johns Hopkins but did not discuss the idea with Dr. Mandell because of uncertainty of funding. We felt that we would need resources to both fund training of Latin American and Caribbean candidates and support their programs when they returned to their home countries.

On every trip that Anna and I made to the Caribbean or Latin America, we visited schools and treatment centers to review their programs to see whether they were potential sites for training centers or capable of providing inputs to the demand reduction line of action. We saw two programs as potential inter-American training centers—the first was the *Centros de Integración Juvenil* (Youth Integration Centers) in Mexico, which rehabilitated addicts and advised public health and education authorities on measures to prevent addiction among youth; and second was the program to prevent drug abuse in Brazil directed by Professor Cândida Rosilda de Melo Oliveira. Budget limitations prevented us from establishing those centers.

Third Line of Action: Community Participation

CICAD set community mobilization as its third priority line of action. Several members reported to CICAD that drug traffickers were trying to buy public support, portraying themselves as Robin Hoods by funding community projects or giving to the Church. They called on the staff to identify measures that could be taken to unmask the criminals and align the community with the suppression of illicit trafficking and drug abuse.

Anna and Carolyn Casselman took the lead in exploring what could be proposed to CICAD. They contacted mass media technicians and public relations specialists on how CICAD could spearhead the dissemination of information to the various sectors of each country's population. They explored the vehicles available for a long-term campaign to inform and educate people about the multiple threats that drug trafficking posed to the health, wealth, and stability of their societies.

They enlisted the support of the U.S. Information Agency (USIA) and organized satellite conversations of groups from various countries on measures that might be taken to increase awareness of rising drug use and the effects of drug trafficking. In 1987, in the Dominican Republic, a group of corporate and private sector leaders from twelve countries met to advise CICAD on what actions it might promote and support. Seminars were held for journalists in the Caribbean, Mexico-Central America, and South America on measures needed to awaken public awareness. A consultation was held in Miami with corporate executives from a dozen countries.

Out of these meetings came a proposal for using a variety of traditional and non-traditional media to attract the attention of key elements of the media, corporations, advertising companies, and private voluntary groups to address the drug problem, especially as it affects youth. The underlying message was to reduce tolerance for drug traffickers and support for prevention, treatment, and rehabilitation efforts by both the public and private sector.

Through contacts in the Inter-American Press Association, Anna and Carolyn were able to obtain traditional press, radio, and TV coverage of CICAD events and visits by CICAD officials to cities throughout the region. They sponsored teleconferences, computer simulations, and other techniques to reach private anti-drug groups and universities and drew on the work of private and public information organizations to gather research on targeting key groups and to evaluate our media efforts. As part of this effort, CICAD encouraged national drug agencies to schedule interviews on TV and radio and meetings with newspaper publishers and business groups for CICAD members and me. In addition, in all of the workshops and public events in which CICAD took part, messages were included to generate public support for prosecuting drug traffickers and identifying the havoc they were wreaking.

With funds from the Inter-American Development Bank, CICAD conducted a survey of the drug problem among the street children of Bogotá, Caracas, Cochabamba, La Paz, Lima, and São Paolo. This was the initial phase of designing and implementing a multi-country Andean program to mobilize public and private action to deal with the festering problem. With the Inter-American Children's Institute, a program called "Youth Encounters" was undertaken to train youth leaders to recognize the symptoms of drug abuse among their peers and offer them information on constructive measures to counter the attraction of drugs.

Once again, CICAD operated on a shoestring. We had no budgetary resources to design and sustain a full-scale action plan, and relied on voluntary contributions from member states, observers, and international agencies to fund those activities we were able to carry out.

Fourth and Fifth Lines of Action: The Inter-American Data Bank and the Inter-American Drug Documentation and Information Center and System

The fourth and fifth lines of action consisted of building the Inter-American Data Bank and Uniform Statistical System, and the Inter-American Drug Documentation and Information Center and System. Their objective was to build a comprehensive body of information that would facilitate more effective decision-making at the hemispheric, regional, national, and local levels.

When CICAD was created, there was no hemispheric database, only a smattering of information about arrests, addiction, and other aspects of the problem. Only a few countries collected data on drug trafficking and drug abuse as part of their national statistical programs. There were very few public or private documentation and information centers.

As the first step to setting up the Inter-American Data Bank and Regional, Statistical System, Ricardo Zavaleta, as CICAD's statistician, took the UN statistical system as the starting point. He spent well over a year becoming acquainted with the data being published in the countries, and the gaps between that data and UN requirements. Ricardo, in his years at CIES, had established good working relationships with the directors of statistical services in most of the Latin American and Caribbean countries, and those contacts responded positively when CICAD in 1989 convened a meeting to discuss the creation of an inter-American drug data system. Thanks to financial support from Japan and Spain, we were able to finance the event.

At that meeting, the Inter-American Uniform Statistical System was created. An agreement was reached to set up a hemisphere-wide effort to collect vital data, harmonize criteria, establish common definitions, and install a uniform system for collecting, storing, and publishing data—all compatible with those of the UN.

The Mexican national statistical agency, INEGI, agreed to be our partner in the implementation of this line of action and provided technical training and advice, through CICAD, to other member states. Mexico financed an annual training program at INEGI headquarters, and CICAD provided scholarships through grants financed by Spain. By the early 1990s, CICAD was able to produce meaningful annual statistical reports on the drug problem in the Western Hemisphere. In 1995, CICAD began publishing a comprehensive annual report on drugs and drug trafficking in the Western Hemisphere, with comparable data from thirty-four governments.

Ruth Connolly took on an equally challenging assignment in creating the Inter-American Drug Documentation and Information Center and System. She used her computer, one of the first in the

CICAD offices, to track down and establish contact with the existing public and private drug information centers in the thirty-four OAS member states. She built working relationships with them and encouraged them to work together. Ruth Connolly worked alone for several years until we are able to obtain funding for an aide in the early 1990s, Sofía Kosmas of Panama.

In early 1991, CICAD sponsored the creation of the Inter-American Drug Information System. Agreements were negotiated with public and private national organizations on the design of a hemisphere-wide network of drug information centers, procedures for sharing information, and a common methodology for bibliographic data, electronic format, and information gathering and processing. The agreement also provided training for technicians from cooperating agencies throughout the region and for assistance in developing materials for national and local programs. Over twenty organizations were in the network by the mid-1990s, and they provided CICAD and the member states a specialized collection of materials, publications, and audio-visuals on the drug problem attuned to the needs and conditions in the member states.

Other CICAD Activities

While the five lines of action were the core of the CICAD program, they were not its only activities.

One of CICAD's first special programs was a police-training program sponsored by the Royal Canadian Mounted Police (RCMP). In 1988, as evidence of its support for CICAD, the government of Canada offered to conduct a training program for Latin American police officials engaged in combating drug trafficking. It had become an annual event by the time I retired. RCMP also conducted separate training programs for its English-speaking Commonwealth partners in the Caribbean.

The course consisted of a three-week program at the RCMP Academy in Ottawa, Canada. It was conducted in Spanish and Portuguese, and covered almost every component of police work required for combatting the drug problem—investigation techniques, intelligence, on-site surveillance, evidence control, forensics, and reporting. For the officers from Latin America, the forensics laboratory was a highlight—and CICAD received requests from several countries for assistance in setting up or improving their own national laboratories. The first RCMP instructor, Wayne Jeffreys, became one of the first contractors CICAD hired. He helped us design courses and provided technical support for national laboratories in several countries and also led discussions at workshops on precursor chemicals.

The U.S. DEA not only cosponsored four training programs in the early 1990s on precursor chemicals, but it included CICAD in its many country police training programs. Through this contact, the French government cosponsored with CICAD in 1992 and 1993 training programs for Latin American and Caribbean customs officers at its Martinique Training Center. This comprehensive course was designed to acquaint Latin American and Caribbean enforcement officers with smuggling techniques of drug traffickers, the identification of chemicals used as precursors, and techniques for investigating their potential diversion of licit chemicals for illicit purposes. The course drew on French and European experience that complemented those provided by Canadian and DEA programs.

In 1992, CICAD convened in Lima the Inter-American Conference on controlling coca leaf production. In 1991 Bolivia, Colombia, and Peru proposed that CICAD examine the problems of coca leaf cultivation and possible measures to help farmers substitute coca leaf production with other crops and/or sources of income. Technical support for the conference was provided by UNDCP and US-AID drawing on their experience in advising on such programs in various Southeast Asian and South American countries. Most of the working papers were prepared by CICAD staff. The only in-house assistance we could afford was a young intern, Jorge Rios, then a Bolivian student in Washington, D.C.; Jorge now is the head of the worldwide UNDCP program in this field.

President Fujimori of Peru inaugurated the meeting and high-level government officials from most OAS countries attended. The conference report called on CICAD to assist member states in planning and implementing alternative development programs, but once again the necessary funding never arrived.

Throughout my years as executive secretary, I tried to respond to each request for assistance that we received from a member state. I attended national conferences, assisted national offices in drafting legislation, and participated in consultations with legislative bodies considering such legislation. In all I provided technical services or participated in conferences or workshops in every OAS member country except Dominica, Guyana, and Suriname.

A Long-Term Strategy

The Program of Rio called on CICAD to establish a strategy and program for inter-American cooperation to combat drug trafficking and drug abuse. The organization of the forum and the initiation of the five lines of action were to provide the setting and means for the member states to explore what that strategy should be and how it should be implemented.

CICAD began the process of determining that strategy at its the second session in the fall of 1987 when I was instructed to prepare a working paper on the strategic options. That paper provoked some sharp differences among the delegates and led to the creation of a working group that included several countries, including the United States. Several more drafts were produced, but no consensus. Some members wanted a multi-country effort to combat drug trafficking and the drug cartels with the active leadership of CICAD; others, including the U.S., favored bilateral action, with CICAD providing a forum for mobilizing regional support for the bilateral actions. In the absence of consensus on the role of CICAD, the second and third chairs of CICAD, Dr. Sonia Sgambatti of Venezuela and Dr. Anibal Aguilar of Bolivia, focused the meetings more on the progress under the five lines of action than on strategy. At each meeting the staff was called on to prepare additional strategy papers for CICAD to consider.

When the special meeting was convened at Ixtapa, Mexico, the agenda included the preparation of a long-term strategy. In his opening address, the president of Mexico, Carlos Salinas de Gortari, called on CICAD to build on the five lines of action and recommend a long-term strategic role for CICAD.

After Ixtapa, the debate on strategy continued in the CICAD meetings. At the eighth session, after Ixtapa, the fourth chair of CI-

CAD, Dr. Alberto Lestelle of Argentina, said that the five lines of action had created a solid operational base and called on his colleagues to deal with the threat to national sovereignty posed by the growth of organized criminal syndicates financed by the drug trade. From that meeting forward, while covering progress on the lines of action, CICAD's clear priority was strategic. The agenda and discussions at the table and in the corridors focused on the strategic framework that CICAD needed to create to promote effective cooperation to deal with organized crime at the center of the drug trade. That was the central theme of Lestelle's successors: General Jorge Carrillo Olea of Mexico, Dr. Augusto Durán of Uruguay, Mónica Nagel Berger of Costa Rica, and Dr. Guillermo Villalobos of Chile.

Devising a strategy was an enigma. CICAD did not have resources or intelligence capability to take on the drug cartels. The staff of CICAD had barely enough resources to carry out the five lines of action, much less mobilize those needed to undermine the power of traffickers. Moreover, few governments matched the concentrated resources of the drug cartels; and the traffickers took advantage of weak economies and political instability to circumvent law enforcement, especially in Central America. The traffickers chose where and how to operate by selecting countries and regions favorable to their interests and where poorly paid public officials and police were easily tempted by a small cut of the huge profits.

From 1990 to 1993, CICAD delegates met informally and wrestled with strategic issues. Sessions included meetings at *Los Pinos* (the Mexican White House) in Mexico and at the *Casa Rosada* (the Argentine White House) and at the Congress in Buenos Aires. The frankness with which the delegates discussed the real conditions and capabilities of their countries often surprised me, a gringo who happened to be the executive secretary of CICAD. The issues remained how to strengthen the capability of governments to confront the menace, and the appropriate channels, multilateral or bilateral, for providing critical assistance from intelligence to operations.

Those years of discussion led to a strategic statement, the Declaration of Santiago, at its sixteenth session in Santiago, Chile, in October 1984. CICAD defined its role as the vehicle for promoting inter-country cooperation to combat drug trafficking and drug abuse through advising and assisting countries to upgrade their legal and institutional capability to the level needed to combat effectively the drug traffickers. The strategy called for coordinated efforts throughout the hemisphere to reduce demand and to bring the people of the Americas together to face a common threat to their health and wellbeing. It did not address the source of financing for multilateral action, and implicitly left it to bilateral efforts to implement. The Declaration of Santiago reflected the maturity CICAD achieved in its first eight years of existence.

CICAD ultimately did not have enforcement powers to promote and coordinate the in-country actions and inter-country cooperation needed to achieve the goals set in the Program of Rio. Those powers reside in the member states.

What CICAD achieved in those first eight years earned the respect of governments of not only member countries but also many in Europe and Asia. That explains why CICAD was invited to participate in conferences, seminars, and training programs in France, Malaysia, Sweden, Italy, Spain, the Vatican, INTERPOL, the European Community, and the OECD.

That is why, after only six years of existence, all the thirty-four member states of the OAS insisted on their right to be members of CICAD, originally set up to be run by only eleven member states. That is why in Miami in 1996, at the summit of the chief executives of the Americas, the presidents of the American republics bestowed on CICAD the strategic role of evaluator of the efforts of the thirty-four member states in dealing with drug trafficking and drug abuse. While CICAD was not delegated the power to enforce its findings, it was empowered to recommend measures needed by each member state to enhance the effectiveness of its efforts.

32

CICAD and Our Lives

Those eight years took a heavy toll on Ele. I was often on assignment outside of Washington, sometimes up to eight months per year. I was totally absorbed by the job and often on assignments that she found dangerous. CICAD almost immediately transformed the lives of two childless people in their mid-sixties, and the comfortable routine of our life prior to CICAD evaporated. I didn't realize the effects that the job had on her. I do now because she told me about them in the last years of her life.

Changes

1987 started out well. We celebrated Christmas Eve with the Fredericksons at a fabulous buffet in honor of the head chef at the White House. We went to the National Cathedral on Christmas Day and then to an open house at Fran Howard's for a reunion with Anne and Dennis who had come up for the holidays from Puerto Rico. We spent New Year's Eve with dinner and bridge at the Sherry's and toasted in 1987 with great anticipation. Elizabeth La Cell called on New Year's Day, and Ele talked with her for over an hour about plans for the New Year; but little did we know that within months Elizabeth would be carried away by cancer.

That long winter, I worked from dawn to dusk at getting CICAD up and running. Ele and I had breakfast and dinner together every day. On an occasional sun-filled but cold weekend day, we would brave the elements and go to an exhibit at the Smithsonian or the Corcoran or a matinee at the Kennedy Center. Our life remained relatively unchanged. Ele worked on investments and her

AAFSW columns while I was at work. After the first meeting of CI-CAD in the spring of 1987, I was sent to Vienna to advise the CND in Vienna of the results of that meeting. I took Ele with me again as the alternate OAS observer. She attended the committee meetings that I couldn't attend. All went well on our two-week Eurail vacation to Regensburg, Hannover, Hamburg, and Lubeck. Then everything seemed to change.

When we returned home in mid-June, Ele got her Sunday call from Tulare, not from Elizabeth, but from her close friend Barbara Milnes, who told her that Elizabeth was in Los Angeles for cancer treatment and that the diagnosis was terminal. I had never seen Ele more shaken. She said very little, and assured me that she was all right. I was so absorbed by the work required to get ready for the second meeting of CICAD that I gave little further thought to the impact of the news on Ele.

The summer seemed to rush by. Ele's basal cell problems made it difficult to spend time with friends at the Towers pool. That summer, I spent a couple of hours every Sunday at the pool while Ele stayed upstairs, pining for the calls from Elizabeth that never came.

Then in preparation for the second session of CICAD, I was working seven days a week. Ele was left alone much of the time and decided that she would make her annual farm trip, even though she had little actual business to transact. When she arrived in Tulare, she learned that Elizabeth had just died. When she called me that night, she could hardly talk. I urged her to come back to Washington. She said she wanted to see her favorite doctor, Gene Matthias, check the houses, talk to the banks, and inspect the farm. I didn't press her to change her plans because, once Ele made a decision, she was seldom prone to change it. What she didn't say then—why should I come back when you have no time for me.

Ele and I talked several times in the next few days, often with her voice shaking. Then one evening she broke down and I could almost hear the tears rolling down her cheeks. She felt shattered and all alone. She asked if she could cut short her trip and come "home." This was the first time I ever remember her calling Washington "home." Up to that evening, home was always Tulare. I told her that she did not have to make the farm trip anymore unless she wanted to do it for pleasure. She got a reservation for the following morning.

I met her at the airport. Ele was not the same person who had left for Tulare a few weeks earlier. Tulare had been an important dimension to her life. Now the roots of her life had dried up. In the 1960s, she considered joining the city planning office when the city was redeveloping its downtown district. She toyed with running for political office when some friends approached her. When Ele's long-time family friend Budgie Sturgeon visited us in Bolivia, he told us of his plans to create a city museum to record the history of the Tulare community. He asked Ele to join him in developing the project. In the 1970s, a friend on the county commission urged her to consider applying for a senior post that was open. Throughout our married life, she made plans for rehabbing her mother's and grandmother's houses, including space for a home law office for me. She talked about displaying her Latin American handicraft collection and using it as a cultural center that would draw the Anglo and Latin American communities closer together. In the late 1970s, she planned to return to Tulare on my retirement from the Foreign Service and we laid plans for my buying into a Tulare law firm. Those dreams evaporated with Elizabeth's death. The last cord had been severed.

That first week back in Washington, she hardly said anything and ate very little. She mainly stayed in bed. I went on with my busy schedule, not really realizing how deeply Ele was grieving. I was happy having my Ele home. I didn't understand until years later how blind I was to her needs.

The only bright spot in this difficult period was the advent of two people into our lives: my nephew Gary Meyer and his partner Ray Zacharias. Ele and I had had passing contact with Gary since he was a small boy. We had confused perceptions about him because we really didn't know him. We were overseas and he was in San Francisco.

Then on one of our home leaves, we had lunch with the family at Fisherman's Wharf in San Francisco. Gary's mother, my sister Jackie, had already died, as had my father. Our lunch included my mother, my niece Lynne, her then husband Marvin, Gary, and the two of us. It was Gary's wit and sense of humor that kept the lunch lively and enjoyable—Ele and Gary had a sophisticated, nuanced exchange going all through lunch. After lunch, Gary took Ele and me to his apartment to know each other better.

Then, some years later, Gary visited us in Guatemala for a few days where for the first time we talked seriously with him and were able to make firm judgments. In fact, we not only liked him but also found that we had many common interests. In the early 1980s, he visited us in Washington and told us that he was gay. Ele, Gary, and I had dinner one evening at which the good feelings we first felt in San Francisco and then again in Guatemala seemed to intensify. It seemed strange that after so many years, we suddenly felt a coming together. Even then, we seldom communicated between visits. After that, we would see each other periodically when I was in the Bay Area. Gary lived in Marin County, and once or twice met me at the San Francisco Airport when I was traveling to a meeting in Sebastopol.

Then, in 1987, before Ele went on her traumatic trip to Tulare, Gary called to tell us that he wanted us to meet his partner, Ray Zacharias. Gary and Ray picked us up on a rainy Saturday morning. Ele liked Ray from the first greeting. Ray's specialty was horticulture and he had many interests similar to those that Ele enjoyed. Ray wanted to see the National Arboretum but bad weather ruled that out. So, we explored the National Botanical Gardens and the nearby Congress, with Ele and Ray walking and chatting together. When the weather began to clear, we went off to Baltimore's Inner Harbor for a very late lunch, with Ele and Ray in the back seat talking and laughing all the way.

That day, Ele and I felt that we indeed had forged a special kinship. My mother had told me when I was a lad, "You are stuck with your relatives, but you can choose your friends." That day, we chose family as friends. At home that night, Ele told me that she had had a wonderful day and that "our nephews" were very dear. Over the rest of her lifetime—and now mine—they became our family.

Two Trips Together

It was late November 1987 before Ele seemed to get back into a routine. My long days were spent on finalizing the documents for the second meeting of CICAD, which was held in Washington in late November. I noticed that Ele went down to the brokerage houses a couple of times a week and prepared an article for the AASFW. But as Christmas approached, she just seemed unable to get into the festive spirit until the Fredericksons invited us to a Christmas Eve buffet where we met some of David's colleagues from the White House and the Republican Party, who regaled us with stories about events in the White House and plans for the upcoming 1988 elections. Ele's eyes lit up for the first time in weeks when she talked politics with some of the guests. She seemed to be sparkling for the first time in months.

The New Year entered with the usual cold and ice of Washington, D.C. I was off to the office every morning, but the weather kept Ele pretty much confined to the apartment in January and February. I invited her to join me at the third meeting of CICAD to be held in Antigua, Guatemala. I knew how much she enjoyed Antigua and how pleased she would be to see old friends like Barbara and Hank DuFlan, whose home was just around the corner from the Hotel Antigua where CICAD was to meet. Ele responded enthusiastically and the DuFlans invited her to stay with them during the meeting.

March in Antigua, the land of eternal spring, was delightful. The meeting lasted two days and was much more relaxed than the first two sessions had been. Ele joined me at the official lunches in the gardens of the Hotel Antigua, with the marimbas accompanying the folk dancers. The government of Guatemala hosted a reception, which was a bit tense, because the delegate of Venezuela, Dr. Sonia Sgambatti, got herself elected chair of CICAD, instead of supporting the delegate of the host government, as is OAS tradition. Ele helped me that night to smooth over the situation and console the Guatemalan delegation. For several years thereafter, the first question by a Guatemalan delegate was about Ele and her health.

After Guatemala, the preparation of documents for and reports on CICAD was demanding. First, I had to prepare for the UN meeting in May, at which it was anticipated the UN Convention on Illicit Traffic in Narcotic Drugs and Psychotropic Substances would be finalized. OAS Secretary General Baena authorized me to take Ele with me to the meeting as part of the OAS delegation, so long the OAS did not bear any of the expenses.

Ele was delighted when I asked her to accompany me again to Vienna where she thrived on interacting with the delegates. She spent much of April and early May making plans for the trip to Vienna and a one-week vacation after the meeting ended since CI-CAD activities in June required my presence.

In May 1988 in Vienna, we stayed once again at the Pension Swiza at Schwedenplatz and rode the subway out every day to the meeting. Ele once again covered the meetings on demand reduction and by the NGOs while I tried to keep track of the negotiations on key issues in the subcommittee on production and trafficking that were holding up agreement on the text. Since we were not members of a government delegation or representatives of a UN agency, we were not permitted to participate in the negotiating sessions. We mingled with delegates in the halls and at social events, sharing bits and pieces of information and perceptions of problems and progress. She often called my attention to corridor activity at which different texts were being passed around. We were a good team and as well informed as most of the government delegations.

Late one afternoon, one of Ele's NGO contacts told us that one of the key delegations had acceded to the U.S. position on the wording of the remaining critical provision and that the U.S. had agreed to another, and that now at last, the draft could be brought to the floor for approval by acclamation. A member of the Canadian delegation confirmed the news and reported that the UN staff was putting the text in final form.

The following morning Ele and I received the text in the six official languages. We just had time to read the English version before going into the final plenary. We identified the compromises and noted that the consumer countries had prevailed in focusing action under the convention primarily on production, processing, and transport, with minimal demands on them to reduce demand. Even so, we found it a strong document.

Ele and I were invited to the formal signing ceremony in the Hofburg Palace in central Vienna following unanimous endorsement of the proposed convention, after which it was then submitted to the UN Economic and Social Council and the General Assembly for approval before submission to the UN member states for ratification as international and national law. It was a historic moment. We left the Hofburg with high hopes for prompt ratification, followed by determined action across the world to diminish perceptibly, if not wipe out, illicit drug trafficking.

With only a week's vacation after the meeting, we stayed in Vienna and made short trips in Austria and to neighboring countries. At dinner with a member of the West German delegation, Baron Christoph von Harsdorf, we were encouraged to visit Salzburg when his wife, Elizabeth, offered to have her mother to show us around. We accepted her offer and were overwhelmed to learn Elizabeth was the granddaughter of the Baron of Nurnberg and a Russian Grand Duchess. So, the first trip we planned was to Salzberg.

We told our plans for the week to the manager of the Pension Swiza and were told of an affiliated pension in Salzburg and a one-day excursion to Budapest. She also suggested that we consider taking an all-day round trip train ride to Graz and Ljubljana, Yugoslavia. We firmed up our plans for the week including our first venture across the Iron Curtain. Those trips about depleted our available traveler checks.

Our first day trip to Budapest was in a station wagon with one other another U.S. couple. We were apprehensive on the trip to the border until we were joined by a Hungarian In-tourist guide whose English was impeccable. After outlining the arrangements for our visit and the places to be visited, she coyly added, "Please note that everywhere you visit, you will not see anyone smiling." Our travelling companions groaned about being herded around by a "Communist." Ele and I heard a quite different message.

We made the grand tour of an elegant city in disrepair, with shabby unpainted buildings on what appeared to have been once vibrant boulevards. We visited the Opera House, the Parliament, the palaces of Buda, and grand churches. When we got to the great square and the monument to Hungary's heroes, the guide advised us perfunctorily that they were Hungary's tribute to the Red Army that liberated the country from Nazi Germany. When Ele and I accompanied her to get some bottled water, she said that the monuments had little or nothing to do with the Russians, but were to honor her Magyar ancestors. Our fellow travelers from the U.S. did not get her point. When we visited the mighty Hapsburg palace in Buda, the guide pointed out the old ladies selling their embroidery for pennies at the main entrance, and commented, "That is communist prosperity!" When we had very mediocre lunch in one of the poshest restaurants in the city, the guide apologized, "This is the best we have to offer today." On the way back to Vienna, once we left Hungary, our travelling companions announced their relief at the departure of our communist guide. Ele and I believed that she had told us how unhappy she and her countrymen were with communist rule in her country.

Tuesday morning we went to Salzburg and returned Wednesday through the lake region of the Attersee and Traun. Elizabeth's mother met us at the train—an elegant lady dressed in tweeds and low-heeled walking shoes. After a light lunch at her apartment, she led us on a fabulous encounter with Mozart, the guilds of Salzburg, concert in the church with near perfect acoustics, and tea at the Elefant Hotel where Ele had stayed in 1966. She left us in the late afternoon, while we took a car out to the von Trappe villa. We had enjoyed a truly unforgettable day.

Thursday, we made train reservations to Graz and Ljubljana. The ticket agent warned us that there was some unrest in Yugoslavia and that we would be told at Graz whether the train would go any further than the border. Slovenia was talking succession from Yugoslavia and Belgrade was very unhappy. We made it only as far as Graz.

That Sunday we flew back to Washington and Ele spent a week sending thank you letters and nurturing friendships that lasted for many years.

Ele's Concerns

Our return to Washington marked the beginning of one of the busiest periods of my work life. CICAD was afire with work. I was committed to making CICAD an effective inter-American vehicle, and I felt challenged twenty-four hours a day, seven days a week. I tried never to falter, even when my hearing was at low ebb and my lip reading not too reliable. I was often too tired at night to share time with Ele.

That summer and the years that followed, Ele spent much of the time by herself and increasingly stayed inside our small apartment. She read the newspapers and used the telephone to express her opinion to offices of senators and representatives as well as the White House and federal government agencies about what she thought needed to be changed. I thought she was very much alive and active, but didn't notice that she needed personal attention. I was frequently away for weeks at a time. On birthdays and anniversaries, I was often on a field trip or attending CICAD workshops, symposia, and training seminars throughout Latin America and the Caribbean; or accompanying drug enforcement officers on raids of coca labs in Peru and Bolivia; or visiting border control posts in Ecuador and Venezuela. What I had promised not to do just a few short years ago, I was doing all over again.

Ele knew the trips were publicized by the OAS, local governments, and the U.S. Information Agency to demonstrate that CICAD was alive and active. Ele reasoned that the drug traffickers were also aware that I was around. That worried her deeply. She never said anything while I was on the job, but once retired she poured out her relief that I was no longer so exposed. She told me that every time I left on a trip, she braced herself for the news of my demise. She related my trips to the work accident that killed her father when she was nine and the fall that caused her Uncle Tom's death in 1935 when she was a teenager.

She was also concerned for her own safety alone in Washington, D.C. The daily newspapers were full of stories of crime throughout the city. She read of cars being stolen just outside our balcony. Those reports were compounded by newspaper accounts of the violence of the Colombian drug mafias. She followed the exploits of the Pablo Escobar of the Medellin cartel and read of the Miami drug wars. In Ele's mind, the reports now touched us directly, especially me on each trip to Latin America or the Caribbean. While I told her that I was always met by government officials and escorted by police or military during my visits, she remained uneasy. Being alone as much as she was, she became reluctant to take risks, even to ride the Metro bus. We had discussions about those concerns, but I really didn't realize during those years how deeply those events and my absences had affected Ele.

In the fall and winter of 1988–89, Ele made every effort to make it as festive as possible. We accepted invitations for a few Christmas receptions at various embassies and at the OAS. She helped us put on a Christmas party at CICAD. But she remained concerned about personal safety, especially when we were out at night. That was reinforced when scheduled taxis failed to appear twice that Christ-mas season. The first was at an embassy reception across town where a member of the host's family ended up driving us home. The second time, Ele in high-heeled evening shoes and her heavy Persian lamb coat had to walk several blocks to a bus stop and wait twenty minutes in the bitter cold after waiting almost an hour for the taxis that never arrived. Thereafter, when a reception or party was in the late afternoon or evening, she would frequently ask me to go alone. Our budget still did not allow us the luxury of hiring a car and driver for fifty or a hundred dollars for an evening—and Ele controlled the budget.

That Christmas season was intensely cold; on New Year's Eve, Ele caught a chill when we left a dinner outside of the city, and its effects stayed with her almost to March. One antibiotic worked on one problem, and then she needed another for the second. So, in March 1989, she did not feel well enough to accompany me to the fifth session of CICAD in La Paz. Before I left for La Paz, I filled the refrigerator with juices, meats, fruits, and vegetables that I knew she enjoyed. When I arrived home ten days later, I found that she had eaten very little and had not left the apartment building even to get her hair done or to see the doctor. This was the first time that I mentioned my concerns to a few of our close friends, who told me that Ele had been turning down their invitations to lunch or din-ner even when they had volunteered to pick her up. I also discov-ered that she had not prepared an article for the AAFSW for several months and had not talked to our brokers for weeks. I was deeply concerned, but Ele kept telling me that she was getting better and asked me to let her recover in her own way.

A Trip Gone Sour

When the sun returned in April, Ele seemed to perk up. When I asked her if she wanted to go with me to Vienna again in mid-May, she seemed elated. When Margaret Frederickson's mother, Eleanor, came from Tulare for a visit, Ele was up and running to the Smith-sonian, the National Geographic, and other museums for day-long visits, and Ele regaled me each night about their adventures. Fol-lowing Eleanor's visit, Ele's interest seemed revived and she pre-pared an article for the AAFSW and made a couple of investments.

So, I was very upbeat about our pending trip to Vienna. I had good progress by CICAD to report and planned to propose areas in which we could work closely together. I had a wife eager to participate in the meeting and to enjoy life once again. Ele and I also made plans for a two-week vacation after the UN meeting. She decided we would go to Northern Italy, including Trieste, the Dalmatian coast, and the northern Italian cities of Verona, Milan, Turin, and Genoa. Ele pored over maps, guidebooks, and cultural reports, and prepared a two-week Eurail itinerary.

When we arrived in Vienna in mid-June, the manager of the Pension Swiza surprised us with the large suite in the attic. When we told her of our plans to visit northern Italy before returning to the U.S. from Vienna, she suggested that we leave all but one suitcase at the pension during our train trip, and she would reserve a room for us on our return to Vienna.

The CND meeting lacked the excitement of earlier years. The convention was approved by the UN and a bureaucratic battle was underway between Tamar Oppenheimer of CND and Giuseppe di Gennaro of UNFDAC over the control and direction of the UN Drug Program. Tamar advocated a single unit that integrated the CND, UNFDAC, and INCB, while Giuseppe proposed maintaining three distinct bodies, each with its own autonomy. The two were overtly wooing the delegates and lining up votes. It became clear that by the end of the first week that Tamar would prevail when the Italian delegation began to lean toward a single unit, with Tamar as the chief. Ele and I did not engage in the discussion—for, as Ele reminded me, CICAD would have to deal with whichever of the two prevailed.

When I reported to Tamar and Guiseppe on the progress being made by CICAD, I was rewarded with polite comments and then a description of their different positions on the future organization of the UN drug effort. I was frankly disappointed at the lack of interest—disappointed enough to tell Ele at lunch that day that I would not return to the CND meeting in the future. Ele calmed me down and reminded me of bureaucratic politics and the importance of never making hasty decisions one later regrets.

Ele and I attended various committee meetings and lunched with different delegates and UN staff members. There were few cocktail parties and receptions and few opportunities to meet with delegates off the floor. The government and NGO delegations were much smaller. The German delegation did not include the Harsdorfs that year; they had gone to Chile with the German Christian Democratic Foundation, *Misericordia*. We had dinner invitations from the Paulson Baileys and Franseska Haller of the Swiss NGO *Mut zur Ethik*, but most evenings we had dinner at small restaurants near our pension.

Summer had arrived early that year. Vienna in June was hot and humid, and our attic suite at the pension was very warm, with no air conditioning and poor cross-ventilation. Sleeping was difficult, and several days Ele stayed in the room to catch up on sleep in the mornings. We hoped that the weather in northern Italy would be more springlike.

On the Saturday following the CND meeting, we took the overnight train to Trieste and were quite comfortable in our first class, air-conditioned compartment. When we arrived in Trieste that Sunday morning, we were met with a blast of hot air — Trieste, as all of northern Italy, was experiencing one of the hottest Junes of the twentieth century. At the tourist office at the railway station, we were able to book a lovely, high-ceilinged room with overhead fans at a hotel on the central piazza, and were much more comfortable than in Vienna.

We had a leisurely Sunday exploring the city — riding buses and following up on tips in our guidebook. We visited the lovely Miramare Castle on the Adriatic that had been the home of Maximilian and Carlota before their ill-fated venture as Emperor and Empress of Mexico. Seeing Miramare and its remembrances of the tragic pair were quite moving. I must also confess that I was also impressed by the bevy of Scandinavian bare-breasted women who sunbathed on the ledges and rocky beaches surrounding Castle.

Early Monday morning, we went to the travel agency to book an overnight tour through the Istrian Peninsula to Split with its Roman ruins. The tourist agent advised us not to book any trip to Yugoslavia at that time because of political unrest. Since the last thing that we wanted was trouble, we just decided to leave Trieste the following day and head to Verona. Why Verona? The answer was its location as a rail hub, the terminus of the rail line to Vienna through Innsbruck with easy access to almost every part of Northern Italy.

We arrived in the city of Romeo and Juliet on a very hot morning. We learned that the opera season was opening on Saturday and that hotel rooms were as scarce as hen's teeth. At the Italian tourist office, we were able to book a room at a pension not far from the railroad station but not in the city of Verona itself. The room was available for only three nights, which meant that we would have to move on Friday. We had two glorious days—walking through the Roman ruins in which the operas would be performed, visiting museums and churches, joining the romantics at Juliet's balcony, and sipping Campari on the piazza. In spite of Verona's charm, the heat and humidity tired us quickly.

On Friday, on the advice of tourists we met in Verona, we moved on to Brescia, a one-hour train ride. Our check of the railway grid showed that we could reach Lake Garda, Lake Como, Milan, Bologna, Ravenna, Cremona, Parma, Turin, and Genoa in a couple of hours from Brescia. We found a lovely, quaint and comfortable small hotel across from the train station, with a superb dining room, only a few guests (most of whom were Italian), and at a price well within our budget. Our large, well-appointed room and bath overlooked the garden and its roses and fruit trees. We lucked out.

In spite of the continuing heat and humidity, those eight days were a kaleidoscope of wondrous experiences. We rode mail boats around enchanting Lake Garda and Lake Como, with exquisite lunches at small restaurants at the water's edge. We toured Genoa in the rain, and visited Columbus' home. We saw the city center and theater at Parma, and enjoyed special dishes featuring Parmesan cheese. We walked the streets of Cremona and visited violin shops. We had lunch in Bologna en route to Ravenna to be awed by the most spectacular mosaics that we had ever seen—whose green and gold tiles still sparkle in my mind. We spent a day just roaming around Brescia and visiting art studios. Another day we toured Milan and enjoyed the Galleria, La Scala, the Duomo, and the elegant shops. Our one unfortunate episode came in Turin, where we had planned to visit the Royal Palace and the birthplace of modern Italy, when we were besieged by a group of gypsies and had to call on the *carabinieri* to rescue us and escort us back to the train station with our sightseeing left undone. Ele and I often spoke Spanish when we needed directions and were treated as if we were speaking a dialect, and sometimes were asked where in Italy we lived!

When we boarded the train Saturday afternoon on our way back to Vienna, we were two very satisfied tourists. On our Eurail pass, we had a first class compartment. I had tried to buy a berth but was told none was available; later I learned that obtaining a berth often required a special sweetener for the ticket vendor. We had to share the compartment to Venice and then had it exclusively to Vienna. Our companions from Brescia to Venice were delightful Italian students, who not only spoke English but also shared their wine and sandwiches with us as we discussed everything from fashion to world politics. When they detrained in Venice about midnight, the compartment seemed very quiet.

Ele stretched out on one of the seats. I arranged her pillow and a lap robe and she dozed off. I had a stomach cramp and went to the bathroom. Ele thought that I had returned to the compartment when she felt someone pat her side. She thought nothing more of it until the conductor came to check our passports and Eurail passes as we approached the Austrian border. Ele had put them in her bag and placed the bag under her legs as she stretched out. Now, she reached for them and they were gone. We frantically checked our bags and awakened to the fact that we had been robbed, probably while I was in the restroom. We were both in shock.

The conductor brought the security officer to our compartment and we were told that we would be put off the train at the next stop, the last station in Italy before entering Austria. No ifs or buts.

When we arrived at the station about 4:00 a.m., we were taken to the police office where we made a declaration of our loss: both our passports, both our Eurail passes, and all $1,500 of Ele's travelers' checks.

The police took our statement and provided us a copy. They advised us to take our copy of the statement and obtain new passports at the nearest U.S. Consulate, which was in Milan. We were also advised to return to our last hotel in Italy because no other hotel was likely to have the passport information that Italian police regulations required for hotel guests. They allowed me to call the U.S. Consulate to report the theft and of our forced return to Brescia. The consular officer instructed us to be at the consulate at 8:00 a.m. Monday morning.

The police chief escorted us to the stationmaster and explained what had happened. The stationmaster said that there would a train going back to Brescia at about 6:00 a.m., and we could board it. When I tried to buy a first-class ticket using an American Express card, he said that his station did not accept credit cards. Fortunately, I had some travelers' checks in my name, just enough to buy second-class tickets back to Brescia and on to Milan. I knew the hotel took American Express.

The sad story of our return to Brescia is forever etched in my memory. As we stoically rode in an over-crowded, non-air conditioned, second-class train back to Brescia, we had barely slept over the past twenty-four hours. I found Ele a seat while I stood most of the way to Venice. A second-class compartment in an un-air-conditioned train on a hot day is not pleasant and, when crammed from stem to stern with families and their meals, it was downright uncomfortable.

When we arrived in Brescia in the late afternoon, we had not even had breakfast. We were tired, unsettled, and apprehensive. And Ele was barely talking to me. Our plane was due to leave Vienna for Washington on Tuesday morning, and we appeared to be stranded in Italy. The hotel found a room for us, and the owners helped me call Pension Swiza in Vienna to tell them why we would not be arriving on schedule. I also called the consulate to advise that we were now in Brescia and told them the name of our hotel. The owner even phoned the American Express office to report the robbery and arrange for me to get a cash advance.

Monday morning, we took the 6:30 a.m. express to Milan and arrived in time to be at the consulate at eight. The chief consular officer was Janet Jackson, a colleague with whom I had worked during my State Department years. She invited us into her office. When we told her what had happened, she said that in her consular district every weekend, about seventy-five U.S. passports were stolen and that each passport could bring five to ten thousand dollars on the black market.

The consul general could not have been more helpful. She arranged for us, together with some ten other theft victims, to go to a nearby photographer who took passport photos in accordance with U.S. standards. She issued new passports by 11:00 a.m., had her administrative officer book a flight back to Vienna at 4:00 p.m., allowed me to call the manager of the Pension Swiza about our flight plans, invited us to lunch in the consulate dining room, and allowed us to ride in the consulate station wagon to the airport when it was making its official run to pick up the mail. She saved our day.

The manager of Pension Swiza could not have been more helpful when we reached Vienna. She had prepared a light dinner, delivered our stored suitcases, and made arrangements for a taxi to take us to the airport in the morning. While we didn't sleep much that night, I felt that divine providence had stepped in and saved us from the abyss.

The flight home from Vienna went well. When we arrived in our apartment, Ele just looked at me. She said absolutely nothing. I prepared cold drinks and, as she sipped hers, she quietly sighed— no crying, no talking, just looking weary and relieved.

For the next few days, while I went to work and took care of the follow-up with American Express on her travelers' checks and did paper work related to the loss of passports and Eurail passes, Ele remained almost in shock. I noticed that she might occasionally fix herself something to drink, but she ate almost nothing except what I prepared for her. It must have been a week before we began talking normally together and the impact of the robbery ebbed away. Now I believe that I should have sought medical help for her, but at the time, I thought that time would cure all.

No Time for Anything but CICAD

For me, being back on the job quickly erased the trauma of the "great train robbery." CICAD was holding a series of workshops on prevention of drug abuse. Anna Chisman had prepared a unique workshop involving teachers and anti-drug specialists in examining various approaches and techniques to discourage pre-teens and teenagers from experimenting with drugs. Leading up to the workshop, the U.S. Information Agency (USIA) invited Anna and CICAD to participate in a satellite conversation with teachers and teenagers from Bolivia, Peru, and the U.S. on drug abuse. Following that event, we went to workshops and meetings in Miami and the Caribbean.

Simultaneously, Sam and I were preparing for the sixth meeting of CICAD in Washington scheduled for November, for which I had a special assignment to prepare an options paper on CICAD's long-term strategy. I was also named the OAS and CICAD representative at a series of meetings at the UN in New York to prepare for seventeenth special session of the UN General Assembly on illicit drug trafficking scheduled for February 1990.

I soon moved past my trauma over the train robbery, not Ele! She kept reliving the experience. When I noticed that she seemed disturbed and asked if I could do anything, she would just nod or smile, often reminding me of that day on the train in Northern Italy. She seemed content to stay in our apartment.

It was not until I took three weeks off for the Christmas season that she appeared to be emerging from the shock of our Northern Italy misadventure. So, I asked her if she was up to accompanying me to New York for the Special General Assembly on Drugs in February, to Buenos Aires for the seventh session of CICAD in March, and to the hemisphere-wide workshop on education for prevention of drug abuse, to be held in Quito, Ecuador in May. She declined New York because of the winter weather, but responded favorably to Buenos Aires and Quito. Since I would be in Quito during the CND meeting, I asked Sam to make CICAD's annual report to the CND. I hoped that the "great train robbery" was behind us. Winter passed quickly.

I went to New York for the preparatory sessions at which the plans for the Special General Assembly were agreed upon. CND Director Tamar Oppenheimer introduced me to many of the government and NGO participants. The U.S. ambassador to the OAS arranged for me to meet U.S. Ambassador to the United Nations General Vernon Walters, and I had the privilege at the Special General Assembly to accompany him as he greeted several CICAD delegates. His fluency in Portuguese, Spanish, and Papiamento was astounding. He explained to me that he had been born in Trinidad and that he had learned those languages very early in life. The meeting was full of strong talk against drug trafficking and drug abuse and a ringing resolution, but very little additional financial or other resources for finding practical solutions to the causes and effects.

Following the Special General Assembly, the Peruvian member

of CICAD arranged for me to meet UN Secretary General Pérez de Cuéllar from Peru, who had won election over our friend, Santiago Quijano Cabellero of Colombia. I briefed him on CICAD. That was a memorable experience for me.

Latin American Trips

In the winter of 1989-1990 my staff of nine and I had to prepare for two major meetings at the same time. In early March 1990, a special Inter-American meeting on the drug problem in the Americas was convened for Ixtapa, Mexico, and the seventh session of CICAD was to be held in Buenos Aires in late March. We had to prepare the documentation for both meetings as well as organize the logistics for them. Anna and I drafted most of the papers for Ixtapa, dealing with both the UN and CICAD programs and the strategy options for CICAD. Fortunately, Sam was able to obtain assistance from the OAS conference office for the logistical requirements of Ixtapa so that he could concentrate on Buenos Aires.

Ixtapa was a high-level policy meeting of foreign ministers and senior government officials in which almost all the OAS member states participated. It followed the format of the UN Special Assembly and produced a twenty-point program for CICAD and the countries of the Western Hemisphere. It laid out a schedule of work for the next several years.

Two weeks after Ixtapa, Ele and I left for Buenos Aires, leaving the cool weather of mid-March in Washington for late summer heat and humidity. In Buenos Aires, the Argentine member of CICAD, Dr. Alberto Lestelle, took special care of Ele. He was aware of the Italian experience and made sure she was well-protected. He took us on special excursions that included a day on the Río Tigre, one of Argentina's most scenic rivers, a barbeque at an *estancia* for lunch, and a visit to Our Lady of Luján in her sanctuary. On the days when CICAD was in session, while he set up lunches for the CICAD members with leaders of Argentine administration and congress, he arranged lunches, museum visits, and shopping trips for the wives. Each evening there was a special dinner—one in the Boca, another at the Opera House, and a third at Tango Dinner Theater. Ele seemed relaxed and contented throughout our two weeks in Buenos Aires.

Argentine President Menem opened the meeting at the Casa Rosada. He made a strong statement in support of CICAD and joined the delegates in an informal discussion over *mate* and coffee. Lestelle was elected chair of CICAD and Mexico became the vice chair. The meeting centered on country views on the long-term strategy for inter-country cooperation and gave the secretariat another heavy workload.

When we arrived back in Washington, Anna, Sam, and I spent a week analyzing our new assignments and set deadlines for draft papers and other materials that CICAD had requested for its next meeting. The six weeks between Buenos Aires and Quito flew by. I hardly had a day off and saw Ele only in the evenings and perhaps for part of a weekend. Anna and I were also preparing for Quito. Anna and I briefed Ele for the work at Quito and invited her to work with us there, rather than just observe. I sent Sam to the CND meeting in Vienna to brief them on CICAD developments.

In Quito, Ele participated in working sessions and seemed as excited as I. Midway through the meeting, I noticed that she was uneasy and was constantly looking around the room. She asked me a couple of times about the police protection being provided by the Ecuadorian government, and she fretted about the personal safety of the participants. She later told me that, at a dinner with friends from I House-Berkeley, they expressed concern about our safety with all the publicity being given to the meeting, especially with the Colombian FARC guerillas across the border. Other Ecuadorian friends warned her to be especially careful and not to leave the hotel or meeting area alone. That awakened old fears and spoiled the meeting for her. I must admit that those concerns never entered my mind during the meeting, and I apparently did little to soothe her worries.

For Ele, that concern colored the rest of our stay in Quito. It was so telling that when the minister of Justice, his wife, and daughter took us out to the Indian market in Otavalo, Ele did not even leave the vehicle. It was so unlike our previous visits to Otavalo when she and I had walked for hours among the carpets and wall hangings suspended from the trees in the open-air market place. This time, she merely looked out the windows of the station wagon, and remarked how beautiful the textiles were and how striking the colors.

When the minister's wife offered to walk with her to get a closer look, she said a polite thank you, but no. Later she told me that she thought that walking around the market place would make us sitting ducks for anyone who might want to pick us off.

This growing sense of insecurity pervaded Ele's life. On our return to Washington, she became increasingly reluctant to accept invitations outside our apartment building. When I asked her to join me at an embassy reception, she would often cite a recent article about crime in the Washington Post and remind me of the occasions when we ordered Yellow or Diamond cabs that didn't show up.

Shortly after we returned from Quito, I left her alone again as I escorted the chair of CICAD, Alberto Lestelle of Argentina, to the OAS General Assembly where the recommendations of Ixtapa and Quito were on the agenda. While we called on foreign ministers to explain the importance of their strong endorsement of both Ixtapa and Quito and the need for additional funding for CICAD, Ele sat alone in the apartment. The items dealing with CICAD came up late on the GA agenda, so we were tied down for the full two weeks of preliminary and plenary sessions.

The General Assembly gave unanimous support for the Ixtapa and Quito recommendations, called on member states to implement them, and instructed CICAD to work with member states in the implementation process. But, no additional funding! It meant more workload and less time for me to be with Ele.

That also meant that, to carry out the mandate, I had to raise additional extra-budgetary funds—another assignment that took time that I should have spent with Ele. Most of the next eight months I spent on trips to Latin America, Caribbean, and Europe lining up contributions for specific activities. With the assistance of U.S. Ambassador to the OAS Dick McCormack and Richard Hines, we obtained the funds for the four workshops on precursor chemicals and counterpart funding from member governments for the in-country costs. With the assistance of DEA's Gene Haslip, we lined up European and INTERPOL specialists for the workshops. The Canadian government financed the participation of its forensics laboratory specialist Wayne Jeffreys. The four workshops themselves required at least two weeks of preparatory work and a week in each host country. The demands of the job consumed my attention, and I did not notice the impact of my absence on Ele.

Next came the planning for the CICAD expert panel on money laundering. Although Michael Sullivan had joined us and helped ease the load in preparing the documentation and work plan, I still had to find the financing and oversee the logistical arrangements. For the meeting of the expert panel to draft the CICAD model regulations, I turned to the U.S. government again since we were using the G-7 prototype as our guide, and the U.S. played a major role in its formulation. When officials at the State Department were reluctant to fund an OAS expert panel, I had to call on colleagues in the DEA and the U.S. Department of Justice to help me make the case. Ambassador McCormack and Richard Hines once again came to CICAD's support. After several weeks of difficult negotiations, the U.S. approved the monies. Then Michael and I also lined up OECD, Canada, U.S., and Mexico to provide experts at their expense to work with CICAD in the drafting process that produced the Model Regulations Concerning Laundering Offences Connected to Illicit Drug Trafficking compatible with those produced by the G-7. That required another eight months of time in which I could give only causal attention to Ele.

At the same time, I was working with Anna to obtain funding from the IDB to implement the Program of Quito through trial projects in education for prevention in selected urban and rural settings in Latin America and the Caribbean. President Enrique Iglesias of the Inter-American Development Bank (IDB) named my good friend John Elac of his staff to work with Anna and me on the preparation of the request. We understood the odds we faced in putting together a "soft" proposal to experiment with different approaches. We could not provide the bankers with cost/benefit analyses and had to find alternative measures to meet the IDB criteria. Anna, John, and I worked on draft after draft of a project for consideration by IDB officials. After John retired in mid-1991, Anna and I struck a stone wall. We failed to raise the funds, but once again my attention had been diverted from Ele.

When I returned from an assignment, I would ask Ele if everything went well while I was away. She told me about items in the *Washington Post* or the *New York Times* that had caught her eye and of phone calls she made to the White House and members of Congress to tell them how she felt about a particular issue. When I asked her about the stock portfolio, she would comment that she didn't like the feel of the market and was apprehensive about making any investments. When I asked her about developments with the AAFSW, I would get evasive answers until she finally told me that the new editor and she didn't seem to be on the same wave length. However, she talked little about herself or her feelings.

Over those many months I tried to get her to work on her ideas for books, write op-ed articles for the Tulare Advance Register, her hometown paper, or talk to David Frederickson about some way she might use her journalistic skills. I knew how skillful a writer she was and tried to make her see that she could make her points more effectively working as a journalist. She seemed cool to any suggestion that might interrupt the routine into which she had settled.

However, there were some events that I could induce Ele to attend. She always came to the Christmas and birthday parties at CICAD that Anna and my secretary Ligia organized. She enjoyed their companionship and knew that I would always be with her on the trip back to the apartment. She also agreed to small dinner parties at embassies, especially when someone offered to pick us up. I remember one such dinner party in the late fall of 1990 at the Spanish Embassy when the ambassador invited me to make a presentation on CICAD at a forthcoming Ibero-American Conference in Madrid. He turned to Ele and added that his government extended an invitation to her as its guest. I knew how much Ele enjoyed Spain and thought that she would jump at the opportunity, but she responded that she appreciated the invitation but thought that I should go alone. And I did travel alone in December to Madrid.

A change seemed to occur after the winter of 1990–1991, when CICAD and the Tragens received an invitation to attend the annual INTERPOL meeting in Washington, Ele agreed to accompany me to the inaugural and closing sessions as well as various social events planned over the three-day meeting.

At the inaugural meeting, she met the chief of INTERPOL and they had a long conversation about the international crime scene. He was impressed and invited us to attend a working session the following morning dealing with inter-country cooperation to intercept narcotic drugs. Ele and I were then invited to participate in almost all of the working sessions, in many of which CICAD had initially not been included. At the working sessions, she took extensive notes, and frequently raised questions that received serious attention. At the social gatherings, delegates from various countries approached her to thank her for her insightful questions. And the head of INTERPOL invited us to visit him at his headquarters outside of Lyons.

After the INTERPOL meeting, Ele was more animated than I had seen her in almost a year. Before the meeting, she had told me that she would not go with me to Vienna for the annual UN meeting. After the meeting, she changed her mind and said she would go. So I reserved a room in the Pension Swiza and had Ele certified as a member of the OAS/CICAD delegation. Because of the schedule of CICAD meetings, I could only arrange for a short vacation after the UN meeting and a trip to Prague the weekend between meetings.

Ele attended most of the sessions with me, participated in the subcommittee on drug abuse, and met with some of the NGO representatives. The UN meeting dealt more with bureaucratic matters related to the merger of CND, INCB, and UNFDAC into the United Nations International Drug Control Program (UNDCP) and updates by countries on progress in ratifying the 1988 convention, not new substantive issues. Midway through the conference, I felt Ele's attention waning. The high point of trip was our excursion to Prague, with the golden domes of the medieval city and the explosion of freedom on the Charles River Bridge.

After Vienna, I had almost no time with Ele at home. I flew back and forth to Mexico City for meetings on CICAD strategy with the chair of CICAD, the Mexican drug czar, General Jorge Castillo Olea, and a trip to Rio de Janeiro to represent CICAD on a panel of the fourth International Symposium on Victimology, of which the Brazilian member of CICAD, Dr. Esther Kosovski, was an officer.

One big event that awakened Ele's enthusiasm in the fall was the tea at the State Department where First Lady Barbara Bush and Susan Baker, wife of the secretary of state, honored the AAFSW ladies who had championed the rights of female foreign service officers, foreign service wives, and families. She commented that night at dinner that she felt that she had accomplished something in our lifetime.

Ele's Last Trip to Mexico City

I had many sleepless nights that summer drafting the paper on the strategic role CICAD should play in combating drug trafficking. Its focus included both law enforcement and the Program of Quito. I had to bridge the different positions of the U.S., Canada, and Latin American and Caribbean countries on the role that CICAD should play; differences among the countries in the working sessions had been substantial. The CICAD Chair, General Carrillo Olea of Mexico, provided me with very qualified reinforcements from his staff, especially Jorge Tello Peón.

The discussion of the paper was held in a hotel at the edge of Chapultepec Park. The participants included Alberto Lestelle of Argentina, the past chair of CICAD; Augusto Durán Martinez of Uruguay, the vice chair of CICAD; Richard Hines, the alternate U.S. delegate; Mónica Nagel Berger, the minister of Justice of Costa Rica; Guillermo Villalobos, the executive secretary of the National Drug Commission of the post-Pinochet government in Chile; Gabriel De Vega Pinzón, the chief of the Colombian National Drug Commission; and Esther Kosovski, the chief of the Brazilian National Drug Commission. The discussions lasted for several hours at a time and reflected sharp differences. Jorge Carrillo Olea and Augusto Durán Martinez kept bringing the discussion back to the core question: how could CICAD contribute to inter-American cooperation to combat the drug cartels? The reality was that the U.S. did not favor a multilateral approach and wanted to continue bilateral operations. What the CICAD members were searching for was a viable formula for using multilateral machinery to deal with the United States, to complement or supersede bilateral arrangements. All of them recognized the limited resources and facilities at CICAD's disposal, but they explored how far the U.S. was prepared to use multilateral machinery. In those long hours, I came to appreciate how concerned all the CICAD members were about the ever-greater presence of the drug trafficking in their countries.

What they did not talk about at the table was the capability and resources that the Latin American and Caribbean governments had available to take down the well-organized and financially powerful syndicates, or the specter of corruption. They did raise concerns about the reliability of national agencies to work with each other and the possibility of information leaking to traffickers about inter-country cooperation. I noted how the members talked to each other indirectly and how they understood the underlying conversation.

When the session ended, General Carrillo Olea pressed me to have a revised strategy proposal to present to the next meeting of CICAD scheduled for late November at OAS headquarters in Washington. The meeting had worked in Spanish and my revised draft was in that language; now Anna took over for translation into English and Portuguese.

When we had drafts of the strategy paper available in all three languages, General Carillo Olea invited me to return to Mexico City for one final review before the meeting of CICAD. He invited me to bring Ele as a guest of the Mexican government. She accepted.

During this final working session, Ele and I were housed at a hotel across the street from offices of General Carillo Olea. Most of our working sessions were held in the offices of the Mexican attorney general, but we also met at *Los Pinos*, the Mexican White House in Los Pinos. One morning, we briefed the president of Mexico, Carlos Gortari de Salinas. Another morning I accompanied Carrillo Olea to a meeting with the National Security Council of Mexico, which Carrillo Olea had previously headed. There was no doubt of the high-level interest of the government of Mexico.

While I was working, the wife of Carrillo Olea and his aide, Cibeles Marín, took very good care of Ele. They accompanied her on visits to museums and handicraft exhibits. Ele had been offered a car and driver, but turned them down. There were late lunches or dinners every day after the afternoon session. Ele appeared to be enjoying herself.

On the third night, we had dinner at an elegant restaurant in the Lomas and got home about midnight. Ele seemed fine. At about 4:00 a.m., she woke me screaming, weeping, and shaking. She seemed disoriented and kept crying out, "Where am I? What is happening to me?" I tried to hold her and calm her down. She did not recognize me for a while and fought me off. It seemed like an eternity before she became composed and I could ask her if she was all right. I took her to the bathroom and helped her wash her face. She was ashen color and her walk unsteady. I asked her if she wanted me to call the hotel doctor. She said, "Please, no." I got her back to bed and sat beside her as she fell back to sleep. A couple of hours later as morning approached, she awoke and asked me to let her spend the day in bed. She said that she felt very weak and was not up to seeing anyone. I asked her if she wanted breakfast and she said, "No." She said that she would call for room service when she felt hungry.

I left her about 9:30 a.m. As I left the room, she asked me not to tell anyone of the events of the early morning. When I arrived back at the hotel at noon, she was still in bed and emotionally distressed. She asked me to take her home as soon as possible and to excuse her from any further engagements. At first I thought that something had happened the previous day that had frightened or upset her. She never told me if something specific triggered the upset or whether her concerns about our safety just welled up and shook her to the core. What I do know is that Ele's health took a turn that morning and she never regained that special sparkle that had been her leitmotif.

On our return from Mexico City, Ele spent more and more time in bed. I finally talked her into seeing doctors to find out what had happened to her that night in Mexico City. Ele had never been a good patient; she didn't trust doctors if she didn't really believe in them. I asked her if she wanted to go to Tulare to consult Gene Matthias and she said no.

I arranged appointments with two specialists; neither one seemed to take her seriously. She compounded their lack of interest by balking at taking certain tests or raising questions about their diagnoses. I accompanied her to several appointments and watched her reactions. She told me that she was not convinced that they were interested in helping her. We finally ended up booking an appointment with a GP whose offices were in our apartment building. He was only an elevator ride away.

After he examined Ele and analyzed the lab tests, he told us that he believed that Ele had suffered a TIA, or minor stroke, that morning in Mexico City, and that it had affected her motor skills, her sense of balance, and the urinary system. He placed her on several medicines and reduced certain others she had been taking since her surgery in 1970. He warned her that she would have a greater propensity for falling and urged her to stop using high heels. And he advised me to restrict my travel schedule because my wife needed care.

Over the next three years, Ele had some good days, but she also had a great many bad days. None of the medications prescribed seemed to work, and some of them left her depressed. Her constant concern for a bathroom led her to stop going shopping downtown—and how she used to love to go shopping to find a bargain almost more than making a purchase. She gave up her beautiful high heels for flat shoes, but she still had several falls, two serious enough to require hospitalization. Then, her magnificent auburn hair started to fall out.

Her periods of dejection seemed to come more often. Ele had always been my shining light, the sparkle that made life exciting. Now, she felt that her life had been wasted. I remember coming home one evening in 1992 and finding her sobbing in bed. That was the first time in forty-five years of married life that I ever saw her sobbing. Angry, annoyed, mad at me—many times, but sobbing, never! She told me that she felt that her life had been a failure and that she never achieved what she had wanted for herself. Reminding her of her success in turning around her family farms, in investing our resources, in writing her column with the AAFSW, and just being the anchor of our family seemed to alleviate her. Eventually she dropped off to sleep, and awoke the following morning in much better spirits. But the periods of dejection returned, especially when she felt she was left alone.

That year, she met a widow living on our floor with whom she developed a strong friendship. The lady had been a senior government official until cancer forced her to retire. She and Ele spent hours together discussing the economy and politics. Neither lady left the building often and spent their mornings reading the newspapers and listening to the news on TV and radio. Two or three times a week, one or the other would ring the other's doorbell and

they would have tea and talk. That turned out to be effective therapy for both of them until the other lady died. During that interlude,
Ele's physical health did not improve, but she seemed less dejected.

I cut back on my travels, but I could not eliminate them. CICAD
leaders called on me as their executive secretary to represent the
commission at international symposia and technical meetings, and
the executive secretary had to appear at most workshops and meetings convened by CICAD. In those years, my work demanded that
I take trips from Kuala Lumpur to Rome as well as from Ottawa to
Montevideo, and many places in between.

It was in those difficult times that we renewed our discussion
of retirement. Ele analyzed the returns on our investments—stocks,
muni bonds, farms, and other investments—and said that by the
spring of 1995, if we lived in Tulare, we should have enough income to cover our needs for the rest of our lives. We presumed that
Ele would outlive me. We agreed that we should return to California in spring of 1995 and then rehab the two houses in Tulare to our
needs. The die was cast.

The Work Keeps Coming

In spite of my best intentions, the demands of the job kept me on
the road. In February, I represented CICAD at a British Commonwealth workshop on drug trafficking in Kuala Lumpur, Malaysia,
where I made a detailed presentation on the Program of Rio and
the Model Regulations on Precursor Chemicals. The British and
South Asian organizers were looking at CICAD as a possible model of multi-country cooperation for replication in South East Asia.
We had long discussions in the sessions at the fabulous Shangri La
Hotel, but I was skeptical that the countries were prepared to move
beyond the UN-assisted program of substituting the production of
opium poppies with other cash crops.

A week after my jet-lagged return from Kuala Lumpur, I was
in Punta del Este, Uruguay for the tenth session of CICAD. Even
though it was only two weeks before the meeting in Punta del Este,
my concern for Ele's health led me to take several days off. The
weather was downright nasty, and Ele did not want to go out. So,
I stayed with her, only leaving to buy groceries for the two weeks I

was to be away. I left with considerable trepidation. I still remember walking round in a daze, trying to finish up the preparations for Uruguay and taking care of household requirements while getting over the Malaysian trip's impact on my biological clock.

After returning from Punta del Este, I shared with David Lazar my concerns over Ele's reclusive behavior. He suggested that we include Ele in our lunches, and she joined us several times over the next couple of years. David also suggested that I take a few hours off each week to take Ele on excursions downtown, to see exhibits, or visit brokers. I was working sixty-hour weeks, so I rearranged working hours to make additional time to be with my Ele.

In May, I went to the UNDCP meeting in Vienna at the specific request of Tamar Oppenheimer, now the confirmed director of UNDCP. I did not realize that that would be her last year as director. The UN retirement age was sixty, and she was about to receive her golden handshake. Those discussions were especially interesting because Tamar had concluded that international drug programs had to pay more attention to demand reduction and less to crop substitution. She proposed a closer relationship with CICAD, including assigning one or two UNDCP technicians to work on implementing the Program of Quito and with national drug commissions to design and carry out experimental demand reduction programs that could serve as a model for other regions of the world.

When I returned from Vienna, Anna and I spent months revising the request to IDB for funding to include the participation of UNDCP and national drug commissions. Ultimately, IDB turned down any regional funding for the prevention program and proposed that CICAD and UNDCP work with countries in presenting proposals as part of their education sector plans. This required rethinking the premises and proposals of Quito and most unfortunately coincided with the time that Tamar retired as director of UNDCP. Anna then began to explore with national officials the prospects of including projects on prevention of drug abuse as part of national education sector loans. I spent as much time with Ele as I could.

I was on the road again in June to accompany Augusto Durán Martinez, then chair of CICAD, to the OAS General Assembly in

Nassau, Bahamas. CICAD presented a detailed report on actions taken to implement Ixtapa, the proposed Model Regulations on Money Laundering, and the schedule of workshops to help countries implement them. The interest of the delegates was very high, and they praised CICAD, adopted the model regulations, and authorized CICAD to convene an expert meeting on alternative development as soon as possible. Governments' interest in the work of CICAD led to a decision to increase the number of commission members from eleven to fifteen. But again no increase in our budget was authorized.

After Nassau, I spent most of the summer of 1992 in Washington, and Ele seemed to be getting back to her old self. I took as much time off as I could to be with her. With me present, she seemed more inclined to accept invitations. And, she began to make plans on rehabbing her houses on our retirement.

In the fall, I was invited to chair a panel at the Vatican Conference on Youth Drug Abuse. Ele was invited by the Vatican to accompany me, but she declined. She never got over the trauma of the robbery on the train. On my return from Italy, I took vacation for the rest of the year and spent the time with Ele, talking about our lives and the impending changes in the federal government and at the OAS.

The U.S. Administration Changes

Bill Clinton was elected U.S. president and many of my contacts in the U.S. government changed. OAS Secretary General Baena Soares would complete his second term in 1994 and could not be reelected. We knew that changes would be coming to CICAD as well and that after nearly six years, my days as executive secretary were coming to an end.

My most immediate concern was CICAD's relationship with the U.S. government. The primary supporter of CICAD in the U.S. government had been the U.S. representative to the OAS, Ambassador William McCormack, a political appointee. He had told us at the U.S. Mission's Christmas party that he would be returning to private life. The U.S. member of CICAD, former Senator Paula Hawkins, a republican, expected to be replaced. Her deputy, Richard Hines, a career officer and pillar of support for CICAD, was up for re-assignment. My working contact at the Department of Justice, Paul Vaky, the son of my long-time colleague and friend, Ambassador Viron "Pete" Vaky, expected to stay on, as did Gene Haslip and other colleagues at DEA. However, their bosses were likely to change. I wondered that December how the Clinton administration would react to CICAD.

I also wondered about my status at the OAS. I was five years over the retirement age and a political appointee. The OAS budget was very tight and eliminating my post would allow for significant savings. Then, too, even though this was the last year of his administration, Secretary General Baena Soares might be pressured by the new U.S. administration to appoint someone of its confidence to my CICAD post.

In spite of the impending changes, CICAD's work plan for 1993 demanded attention, including four workshops on the Model Regulations on Money Laundering, a meeting of experts on alternate development, and a seminar in Mexico on demand reduction. In addition, CICAD was to meet in San José, Costa Rica, for its thirteenth session in March and in Washington in November for its fourteenth. So, my calendar for the year was very full. As best I could estimate, I would be on the road for about five months — which was not conducive to my helping Ele at home.

In late January, I decided to talk to the secretary general. I told him that I was wearing out and that I needed to spend more time at home and that I planned to retire no later than April 1995. He reminded me that his term was over in mid-1994 and said he would not replace me for so long as he remained in office. He also agreed to let me set my own pace. He was very affable, and joshingly called me in Portuguese "his drug trafficker."

Then, with Michael Sullivan, we laid out a schedule for the four money laundering control workshops, starting with one in Mexico for Mexico and Central America, a second in Barbados for the English-speaking Caribbean, a third in Buenos Aires for the Southern Cone, and the fourth in Quito for the Andean countries. To allow me more time at home, Michael replaced me as the principal CICAD legal expert for the workshops and the principal contact for U.S, OECD, Canadian, and UN experts who were to conduct the workshops.

I concentrated on the preparations for the CICAD session in Costa Rica. The primary item on the agenda was the long-term strategy of CICAD. With the change of administration in the U.S., and with no principal U.S. delegate named, the U.S. held up its response to the working paper that was completed in Mexico. Thus, the meeting in San José became essentially a reporting session. Nonetheless, the logistical work getting ready for San José imposed a heavy load on the staff since membership had been increased from eleven countries to fifteen, and the amount of papers to be produced and distributed mounted. That was also to be the last CICAD for my deputy, Sam Echelar, who had reached the OAS retirement age.

When CICAD convened, Costa Rican Minister of Justice Mónica Nagel Berger was elected chair of CICAD for the year. It set the fall of 1994 as the deadline for a decision on the strategy statement and instructed me to speed up the workshops on money laundering control, develop national projects on education for prevention that met the criteria of the IBD, publish the first inter-American statistical compendium on the drug problem by early 1995, and to begin the operations of the inter-American drug information system as soon as possible.

My staff and I worked through the closing dinner that the government of Costa Rica hosted and the CICAD members toasted Sam on his retirement before he ran back to oversee the shipment of the documents back to Washington on the early morning American Airlines flight. At the closing dinner, the U.S. delegation advised us to hold off our departure because a ferocious nor'easter was pounding the East Coast of the United States. All of the airports from North Carolina north had been closed, and there was speculation that the problem would persist for several days. We talked it over about midnight and agreed that we all had family reasons to get back to Washington as soon as possible. I was especially concerned about having left Ele alone for the week.

When we queried American Airlines, they advised that the American flight to Miami would leave on time since all airports would be open by mid-morning, and flight connections would be on time. When we arrived in Miami, the message was totally different. We were instructed to pick up our luggage and proceed to a holding area where thousands of passengers from scores of other flights were already crammed together. We were told that all flights north along the Atlantic Coast were suspended indefinitely and that, because it was an Act of God, the airlines assumed no responsibility for the assembled masses in the holding area and each of us was responsible to find accommodations in the Miami area. No, American had no information on when connecting flights would be rescheduled. No, American could not help us advise our loved ones of the delays.

In that swirling mass of humanity, we were very upset. Our colleague Rudy García, a Cuban American, went off to seek help from a friend who worked in the airport. We calmed down when Rudy rejoined us and advised that his friend told him about a motel not far from the airport where we could get six rooms for a couple of days. It was run by a friend and a "rental by the hour" establishment—a popular stop-in for a quick assignation. Rudy's friend had cajoled the owner to do a Cuban favor for a Cuban friend—and we booked six rooms at very favorable daily rates.

Then we rented a car and loaded all our bags and boxes into it. We left the angry mob behind, and arrived in about ten minutes to a not-too-new motel, with bright flashing lights announcing rooms available. The contrast between my elegant tropical room at the Hotel Cariari in San Jose and this one was striking—and I could not be sure when my motel room had last been cleaned. Yes, the bed had fresh linens and there were clean towels but bits and pieces left by recent occupants were on chairs, tables, and in corners.

Anna Chisman had a cell phone and she called her husband in Washington, who in turn advised each of our families. Rudy took charge of contacting American Airlines every few hours for the latest news, and through another Cuban friend, found out how to get us on the priority list for departure when the airports up north were reopened. With those details worked out, our hardy band of six settled down to enjoy Miami, Little Havana, the waterfront, and Biscayne Bay. Mid-afternoon, Rudy reported that American would be operating a connecting flight to Washington early Monday morning and that through his friend, we and our boxes were booked on it. Anna called home and the word was spread to our awaiting families. That Sunday night I did not sleep very much, as there was a continuous parade of cars looking for a room for a few hours of rest and recreation.

When I arrived home Monday and told Ele of our adventure, she barely reacted at all. She said that she was relieved since she had spent the two days very concerned that one of the Colombian cartels would find out about our being stranded and take the opportunity to put CICAD out of business. Frankly my colleagues and I hadn't been concerned about our safety. Indeed, the motel in which we were stashed was hardly one where even the most menial cartel operative would have lowered himself to stay.

On my return to Washington, Richard Hines advised me that Harriett Babbitt, wife of the new secretary of the Interior, was the new ambassador to the OAS, and that Robert Gelbart was the new assistant secretary for International Narcotics Matters. Richard set up appointments for me to meet with each of them.

I met with Ambassador Babbitt first. We had a lengthy discussion of not only CICAD but also U.S. relations with Latin America and the Caribbean and the pivotal role of the U.S. in the OAS. Her knowledge of Latin America was impressive and her commitment to the OAS strong. She assured me that the support that CICAD had received from Ambassador McCormack would continue.

My subsequent meeting with Bob Gelbart was a surprise. He reminded me that we had met in Bolivia when I was AID director and he was a Peace Corps volunteer, one of the twelve "disciples" of the community development adviser whom I had sent home. He also reminded me that he had been one of those volunteers who had sought to have me removed until New York Senator Robert Kennedy had told him that my actions were justified. He said that as his career in the Foreign Service had placed him in positions of responsibility, he now understood why I had acted. After I briefed him on CICAD and its program, he informed me that he had been appointed the new U.S. member of CICAD and asked for the background on the strategy paper and the positions of the other members. This was in stark contrast to his predecessor who had opposed the creation of CICAD and had never attended a CICAD meeting. Gelbart took an active role from day one and, while he kept Richard as his alternate, it was Gelbart, not the U.S. Mission to the OAS, who made the key decisions from that day forward.

On the Road Again

After San Jose, I spent a few weeks in Washington before I was on the road again. There was the workshop on money laundering in Central America, a technical meeting on demand reduction in Mexico, a training program on controlling precursor chemicals jointly sponsored by the French government and CICAD in Martinique, and a visit to Lima on arrangements for the Expert Meeting on Alternative Development to be held in September. The schedule was so packed that I arranged to have Anna represent CICAD at the UNDCP meeting in Vienna and to assist Mónica Nagel Berger, the chair of CICAD, at the OAS General Assembly in Managua, Nicaragua. I had to leave Ele on her own again for weeks at a time, but asked David Lazar to check on her every few days. I also missed several opportunities to consolidate my relationship with Gelbart. But, I was the only one on our small staff who could do the required tasks.

The meeting in Martinique was a practical, realistic, and comprehensive seminar of lectures and on-the-job demonstrations that exposed the participants from Latin America and the Caribbean to the experience of French customs and the measures they take to control drug smuggling and precursor chemicals. Most of the Latin American countries lacked the structure and organization of the French customs with its trained professional staff that made the system work. Several of the Latin American participants told me that they had been exposed to most of the technical processes before, but that their supervisors resisted applying them.

The technical meeting on demand reduction had been arranged by Jorge Carillo Olea, past chair of CICAD. Anna and I met with representatives of the *Centros de Integración Juvenil*, a Mexican NGO that had been working on treatment and rehabilitation of drug users in Mexico for twenty-five years, as well as specialists of the Mexican Ministry of Education. We discussed their programs and the youth to whom they were targeted. Mexican Minister of Education Ernesto Zedillo (later president of Mexico) informed us of programs his ministry was using in high schools to dissuade young people from experimenting with drugs. I was so impressed with the program that I suggested we explore its applicability to Spanish-speaking school children in California, especially in farm areas where exposure to marijuana was high. The minister expressed interest in the idea and authorized his aides to work with Anna to see whether we could put a proposal together.

Coincidentally, an official of the Mexican Embassy in Washington, who had been aide to Carrillo Olea during his term as CICAD Chair, was being transferred to Sacramento, California as consul. Carrillo Olea arranged for him to meet with me while Anna worked with Mexican ministry specialists on a proposal that the Mexican government agreed to include as an activity in its education sector plan for which it would be seeking external funding.

During that visit to Mexico, I spent several hours with Carrillo Olea discussing illicit drug trafficking throughout the Americas. I told him about my special concern over the situation in Central America, the weakness of law enforcement, the lack of public sector programs to deal with precursor chemicals or money laundering, and evidence of pay-offs by the drug traffickers. He said that his intelligence people were equally worried. We talked about the need to create a professional police and customs system, not only in Central America but also in Mexico. I proposed that CICAD try to design a special program for Central America, and he in turn said that, if I could set up a project, he would do his best to get CICAD some funding from his government.

On returning to Washington, I joined Sam in getting ready for the special meeting on alternative development that the governments of Bolivia, Colombia, Mexico, and Peru had pressed CICAD to convene. All four were producers of narcotic drugs and had experimented with alternative development projects, with assistance from USAID or UNDCP, to wean farmers from producing them.

I had resisted CICAD involvement in this dimension of the drug problem partly because of the UNDCP commitment to it, and partly because experience with AID that taught me the high financial and technical investments required for a successful program. A successful alternative development operation had to provide *campesinos* with a crop that has a reasonably comparable market price to coca leaf, poppy, or marijuana—backed up by financing for seed and other inputs, technical assistance for cultivation, access to the market, and a police presence sufficient to neutralize the power of the drug cartels. For most of the affected countries and their governments, putting all the pieces together had to be a multi-year, multi-million dollar commitment to build the institutional in-frastructure, develop the technical know-how, and train the staff needed. Conducting such a program was beyond the technical and financial resources of CICAD.

On the other hand, drug traffickers had the resources in hand to provide the seed and technical expertise for the cultivation of the crop and to purchase the crop at a price well above that of any other traditional cash crop. They also had the power to sabotage an alternative development program, buy politicians and enforcement officials who got in their way, and back up their interests with co-ercion that usually was more terrifying to the *campesinos* than local law enforcement.

After Sam and I completed the paperwork required for the Lima conference, I had to make a three-week trip. First I was to spend several days in Bogotá for meetings with the national drug commission and Colombian officials on strategy discussions and briefings on the agenda for the Lima conference. Then I was to go to Lima where Sam and I would complete arrangements for the con-ference. Finally, I would go to Mexico City for the first workshop on money laundering.

Ele was particularly concerned about my going to Colombia. I felt very uneasy about leaving her alone in Washington and asked my nephews Gary and Ray if they would mind having Ele be their houseguest in Houston while I was on the trip. They said, "Delight-ed!" They had bought a beautiful big house in the Woodlands, and had a guest suite available for her visit. I found an airline routing Washington-Houston-Bogotá-Lima-Mexico-Houston-Washing-ton on Continental that could not have been more convenient and cost about the same as going through Miami. Boy was I happy that Ele would not be sitting for three weeks in our small apartment in Washington worrying about me and my safety!

This visit was my first to Colombia as CICAD executive sec-retary. Earlier requests by the Colombian government for a visit, or for any CICAD activity in Colombia, had been vetoed by the director of the OAS national office for security reasons. This time, the secretary general authorized me to accept the invitation by the Colombian national drug commission. Our meetings included high-level government consultations with aides to President Gaviria and members of both houses of the Colombian congress.

In Lima, I met with officials of the Foreign Ministry. President Fujimori's brother was present at all of the sessions, along with key officials from the Ministry of Agriculture and Rural Affairs. I was briefed on the government's plans and expectations. After assuring us that all the resources CICAD needed would be provided, the Peruvians confirmed that President Fujimori would personally open the meeting and advised us that he, who had been rector of the National School of Agriculture, had keen interest in replacing coca production with other cost-competitive crops and expected the meeting to provide him with a list of cash crops that competed with coca leaf on the world market. I was frankly quite concerned because I doubted that the meeting could produce such a list.

After Lima, I flew to Mexico City for the first workshop on money laundering at which CICAD introduced the model regulations. Michael Sullivan managed the workshop and carefully tested the way in which model regulations could best be explained to the Mexican and Central American participants. They were from countries at very different stages of financial development and technical enforcement capability. From their reactions, it was clear that their perceptions of the complex subject varied substantially.

The discussions raised constitutional, operational, and procedural problems for the officials of the various countries. They spelled out the institutional weakness of their country's banking and law enforcement establishments, but made little mention of the endemic corruption in the region. Their discussions helped us realize the problems CICAD faced in making a dent in the money laundering flows from the illicit narcotics trade. After one of the sessions, I expressed my concerns to Jorge Carrillo Olea and he reminded me of our earlier discussions about the imperative need to assist almost every country participating in the workshop address the critical institutional weaknesses of their law enforcement establishments. At that meeting, I started to design a CICAD program for Central America. At the end of that meeting, Michael and I began to revise the structure and organization of the future workshops, but not the message.

After Mexico City, I spent the weekend in Houston. I found a very relaxed and totally contented Ele. She had loved the house and the attention that Ray and Gary had showered on her. Both of them worked all day during which time she could just enjoy herself. Her companions were the three household pets — two large dogs, Matilda and Duncan, and a nineteen-year old cat, Teddy. Ele told me that she got a boost from the antics of the three pets and their control of the household. Gary and Ray took Ele out to dinner; on outings to shopping centers, museums, and art galleries; and sightseeing in the Woodlands and Houston. She visited a nearby retirement community run by Marriott, the Forum, which she felt was a distinct possibility as our retirement home.

In spite of my determination to spend more time at home with Ele, the workload for the remainder of 1993 had me packing and unpacking my suitcase on a regular basis. The big event was the meeting of technical experts on alternative development. Some of the most eminent specialists of the UN, AID, and other international organizations led workshops that analyzed the experience in Southeast Asia and Latin America. President Fujimori opened the meeting and his brother attended all the sessions and reportedly briefed him on the presentations and discussions. The meeting and social events were held in the Sheraton Hotel to maximize the safety of the participants, for Peru was still combatting the subversive movement, *Sendero Luminoso*. The meetings ran well into the evenings and I remember leaving the sessions just in time for either a cocktail party or dinner. Our staff worked almost around the clock to make sure that at each morning session, the participants had the documents in English and Spanish from the evening before.

The meeting in no way changed my perception of the problem and the complex institutional, financial, and organizational inputs needed to carry out successful alternative development projects. The success in Chiang Mai, Thailand was almost overshadowed by the transfer of production to sites in Burma, where strong military repression of illicit production did not exist. The experiences in Bolivia and Colombia led to the conclusion that the savvy *campesinos* joined alternative development programs and then went over the hill to produce illicit coca bushes that kept the drug traffickers placated and their wallets open.

Following Lima, I observed seminars in São Paulo, Rio, and other Brazilian cities on a new education program aimed at preventing drug abuse by high school students that was sponsored by the Brazilian National Drug Council and its specialist, Dr. Cândida Rosilda de Melo Oliveira. Three days of working in Portuguese taxed my not so fluent knowledge of the language but left me quite energized by the reaction of the students. I suggested that Cândida lobby her government to include a request for including her program in the new education sector loan package about to be submitted to the IDB for funding, since CICAD had no funds of its own to offer.

Back in Washington, we had to get ready for the November meeting of CICAD. The strategy and longer-term CICAD activities were the central theme and we prepared for the meeting without Sam, who had retired. So, the post of assistant executive secretary was open, and the OAS secretary general, whose term was ending in mid-1994, decided not to fill it in order to allow his successor to make the selection. Sam's retirement just placed heavier workloads on Anna and me. So, for the next three months I stayed very close to home and the office.

In addition to preparing the papers for the meeting, I spent a considerable time with Assistant Secretary Gelbart explaining the positions of the various Latin American and Caribbean members on the proposed strategy for CICAD. As assistant secretary, he oversaw the work of the narcotics attachés and specialists in embassies throughout the region, and he was prepared to use those in-country contacts to help him win support for policies and positions that the U.S. would take in CICAD. Gelbart's direct involvement set the stage for bridging differences that had held up CICAD's decision on strategy.

At the November session, all the members finally reached a consensus on strategy. Many Latin American delegates told me that Gelbart's presence had made that possible. CICAD decided to hold its fifteenth session in Mar de Plata, Argentina, and its sixteenth in Santiago, Chile, and that at the sixteenth session, it would complete the work on its strategy statement. I was assigned the task of preparing the statement for Santiago and clearing it with all the members.

At the same time, Ele and I were solidifying our plans for retirement, and reaffirmed the date for my leaving CICAD as April 1995. I was concerned about the selection of my replacement. I knew that the choice would be a political decision, but hoped I could identify a candidate who already knew CICAD and shared my perception of its role as the forum for inter-country cooperation and dialogue, and not try to impose U.S. policies and priorities on reluctant partners.

I had found three very talented prospects. Richard Hines of the U.S. Mission to the OAS had worked tirelessly with me from the inception of CICAD and was extremely effective in bridging differences on critical issues. He was a foreign service officer and, like me, had had little field experience working on drug issues, but knew the subject matter and the Latin American participants.

A second prospect was Paul Vaky, the young lawyer from the Justice Department who had been working with Latin American governments to improve enforcement capability to deal with drug issues. Paul had lived much of his life in Latin America and was astute in dealing with Latin Americans. He had participated in several workshops and assisted me in handling some delicate confrontations between U.S. and Latin American delegations.

The third was Raphael Perl of the Library of Congress. Raphael was the subject matter specialist on international narcotics matters at the Congressional Research Service. He prepared most of the reports for committees of congress on the drug situation in the region and was well respected by congressmen on both sides of the aisle.

However, I found out very quickly that as retiring executive secretary, I had little or no input to make on personnel decisions that were politically sensitive. The choice of both the executive secretary and the assistant executive secretary would be political judgments made by the incoming OAS secretary general. My input would be nil. *Sic transit Gloria!*

The Final Year

After the November CICAD meeting, I met with Mónica Nagel Berger, the chair of CICAD; Guillermo Villalobos of Chile, the vice chair; and Alberto Lestelle of Argentina, a past chair. They were very upbeat about CICAD and very generous with their comments about my work. On the other hand, I don't believe that I had ever felt as wrung out as I did that day. The impact of the pressure and pace of the last several years made me feel very old and exhausted. I told them that I would be retiring the next year and that Ele and I planned to return to California. They urged me to stay with them until CICAD formally adopted the strategy statement on which we had worked so hard. When I went home that night, I knew that it was only a matter of time before this chapter of our life would be closing.

The Dominican member of CICAD, Vice President of the Dominican Republic and Chair of the National Drug Commission Jacinto Peynado Garrigosa, asked CICAD for assistance in building the commission's program and in helping him explain to members of his congress the need for legislation on precursor chemicals. He said that his government knew that its territory was being used for the transshipment of drugs and that drug use in the country was rising.

In response, I went to Santo Domingo after Thanksgiving to advise the National Drug Commission on organization and staffing. I used my visit to focus Dr. Peynado and the commission on demand reduction as much as on law enforcement. I was also requested to meet with key committees of the Dominican congress to advise them on pending legislation. Many of the measures in the proposed laws raised serious problems for the legislators, and my role was to help them understand the real world situation that required the measures proposed. I had been doing this sort of job in country after country over my eight years as executive secretary. I recognized that here, as in many other countries, I was multi-lateral window dressing that the Dominicans were using to support legislation that the DEA was pressing them to pass. CICAD, the inter-American presence, was a political convenience. On returning from Santo Domingo, I took leave for the rest of the year.

Ele talked to me about her interest in Houston as our retirement home. She had enjoyed the people, loved having the nephews nearby, and was impressed by the facilities and environment at the Forum. So we called Gary and Ray to see if they had room at the inn for two tired travelers over the holidays. When they said yes, we packed our bags and made our way southwest to Texas.

It was a wonderful interlude. Gary and Ray took time off to show us Houston, the museums, and sights. We saw the Christmas lights as we accompanied them to parties. We visited the Forum and I was very impressed; and Ele, after looking at my pension, our social security, and our outside income, opined that we could afford to live there. After she told Ray and Gary of her interest, they advised that they did not intend to stay in Houston much longer. They loved their house, their neighbors, and neighborhood and had reasonably good jobs, but the heat and humidity was wearing on them. They planned in the reasonably near future to return to Denver, where they had met and where they preferred to live.

With that information, Ele and I reconsidered all the factors and decided that our only viable option was to return to California when I retired and to rehabilitate the houses in Tulare. We had good working relations with banks and financial institutions in the area, and we had nineteen lift vans of our belongings stored in a nearby warehouse in Visalia, including many of the Latin American handcrafts that she had been accumulating. So, when we left Houston at the end of 1993, we settled on returning to Tulare, California.

The first two months of 1994 were spent getting ready for the fifteenth CICAD meeting in Mar del Plata at the end of Argentina's summer. With the economy booming, finding hotel rooms and hiring temporary staff was a major challenge, even with pressure placed on major hotels by the Argentine government. It was almost at the last minute that we were able to pull all the pieces together and get instructions out to the members about hotels and meeting rooms.

Ele did not travel with me to Mar del Plata. Anna and Rudy handled the logistics and oversaw the staff provided for the meeting by the Argentine government. The meeting went well, with no hitches or surprises. Guillermo Villalobos of Chile was elected chair of CICAD. The final draft text on strategy that had been my charge was adopted and submitted to the governments for final comments. The sixteenth meeting of CICAD was convoked for mid-October at Santiago, Chile, with the adoption of the strategy paper as its core issue.

During the session, I learned that the U.S. government had been pressuring the president of Colombia, César Gaviria Trujillo, to run for OAS secretary general against the Costa Rican foreign minister. Friends in the Argentine Foreign Ministry told me that their government had already pledged its support to the Costa Rican, but the U.S. was urging them to switch. They said that the election of an ex-president seemed more prestigious for the inter-American system, but they had made a formal commitment to Costa Rica. I just listened, as the political play moved onto center stage.

Back in Washington, the rumors abounded. The OAS Secretariat reacted to the speculation by almost grinding to a bureaucratic standstill. Besieged with financial problems, the world around CICAD was not conducive to getting much done. That spring, we did carry out a workshop on money laundering in Quito and a statistics-training course in Querétaro, Mexico.

After the Quito workshop, the Colombian government asked me to stop over to meet with congressional leaders on legislation being drafted on money laundering. The head of the Colombian National Drug Commission took me to meet with advisors to President Gaviria. As the meeting was breaking up, one of the advisors commented that Gaviria liked to form his own teams whenever he took charge of a new organization. He in essence alerted me that my days with CICAD were numbered. Frankly, that did not bother me because my own plans called for retirement in the first quarter of 1995.

In May, Secretary General Baena Soares asked me to attend the UNDCP annual meeting in order to report on the emerging CICAD strategy consensus and to hurry back to attend the forthcoming OAS General Assembly in Belem do Pará, his hometown. I had not attended the General Assembly the preceding year, and Baena Soares sent word that he expected me to attend this, his last as secretary general.

The OAS General Assembly was a tribute to Baena Soares. The only major item on the agenda was the election of his successor, and the U.S. twisted enough arms to get Gaviria elected over the Costa Rican foreign minister. Gaviria's term as president of Colombia was to terminate almost simultaneously with the date of his inauguration as the new secretary general of the OAS.

On our return to Washington, retiring Secretary General Baena Soares instructed me to move ahead on all CICAD's pending activities, but to initiate no new ones. He asked me and all other senior OAS officials to prepare detailed briefing papers for the Gaviria team. While the date of his arrival was uncertain, a few of his immediate advisors from the Executive Office of the Presidency of Colombia would be arriving shortly to ensure an orderly transition. An aura of uncertainly engulfed the Secretariat as it does in any government whenever there is a change of administration.

The chair of CICAD pressed me on the arrangements for the upcoming CICAD meeting in Santiago, and, without Sam, Anna and I had to do all the advance planning. Meanwhile, the Mexican member of CICAD was urging me to put together a project for Central America and made a small grant earmarked for that activity. I barely finished the briefing paper for the Gaviria team when I had to go to the workshop on money laundering control for the English-speaking Caribbean. After the Caribbean workshop, I had one last commitment to fulfill for the retiring secretary general—a presentation on CICAD at the *Mut zur Ethik* Conference in Zurich before I had my first formal meeting with Gaviria's advance men.

One of the first statements from Gaviria's team was a reiteration of the message in Bogotà—the new secretary general always put its own team in place and wanted to shape his own policies. One of Gaviria's men, whom I had met in Bogotá earlier that year, told me, "Your term ends when Gaviria takes over," but assured me that it was nothing personal. I told him that I certainly respected and understood the need for a new team, but reminded him of the long debate in CICAD over long-term strategy, which was to be sealed in Santiago in October. They said that they would consult Gaviria and let me know.

When Gaviria took office, he named Anna acting executive secretary. However, in light of the Santiago meeting and my role in the process of reaching a consensus, I would be given a contract as a consultant to CICAD through the sixteenth session in mid-October. I regret that the new secretary general never invited me to review the briefing paper with him. One of his aides did review my paper and told me that it was one of the most useful that had been prepared for the new secretary general. He also told me that the secretary general had no one in mind to appoint as executive secretary or assistant executive secretary, but that later in the year he would consult the member states about possible candidates. He said that the secretary general had received the invitation to attend the Santiago session, but his schedule prevented him from attending.

My last official assignment for CICAD was the Santiago meeting. The strategy statement was adopted. The member states were very generous in their comments on my tenure as I closed this chapter of my life.

PART V

THE TWILIGHT YEARS (1995–)

33

Home to California

November 1994 ended my tenure with the OAS and CICAD. For the first time in our forty-seven years of married life, neither one of us was employed. We were on social security, pensions, and the income from our investments. We rolled over my OAS Provident Fund into an IRA. Thanks to Ele we had a financial cushion for our old age.

Those days in November 1994 remain bittersweet. On returning from Santiago, Anna and I prepared the final report of the sixteenth meeting and laid out the plan of work to follow up on the decisions made. Anna was now in charge and she was doing three jobs: Sam's, hers, and mine. I wanted to help.

The member governments with which I had worked were very generous in their messages of appreciation, but several also sent farewell presents, including a special edition of the poems of Gabriel Mistral and a pair of silver spurs from Chile, a silver gaucho's belt and knife from Argentina, a traditional indigenous medal of good fortune from Canada, a silver letter opener from Mexico, and a lithograph from the RCMP. They are all part of my most precious possessions. My colleagues in CICAD gave me a farewell party. The State Department scheduled a farewell lunch in the formal dining room on the eighth floor. The National Drug Commission of the Dominican Republic invited me to a meeting in Santo Domingo at which its draft law on money laundering was finalized and the country joined the inter-American statistical system; then I was awarded the Order of Columbus, one of its highest honors.

Actually, it took me several months to realize that I didn't have to go to the office every day and that someone else was now respon-

sible for CICAD. For over two months, I went to the office to prepare a detailed report for my successor on the background and evolution of CICAD. Then, in mid-January 1995, when my password
and ID for entering the OAS building were canceled, I realized that
my ties to the OAS had been irretrievably cut.

After New Year 1995, Ele and I began planning our return to
California. Under the OAS staff rules, we had until June 1995 to receive OAS funding for the move back to our designated residence.
Ele seemed truly excited. She contacted friends in Tulare and Visalia for the names of architects and building contractors with whom
she could discuss her plans for renovating the two houses. She
worked on sketches for redesigning the layout of the houses and
for converting her grandmother's home into an office and guesthouse. Every night when I came home, she had new plans for me
to consider. Ele had a new mission and she was delighted to be the
new center of our family attention.

We made plans to go to Tulare in March as soon as I returned
from a one-month contract that UNDCP offered me. I was contracted, with a Bolivian newsman, to evaluate the impact of a project financed by the Italian government to provide firsthand experience to
newspaper editors and reporters on the human devastation caused
by the drug trade and to encourage them to publicize the effects in
their newspapers and magazines. The evaluation required field investigations in Uruguay and Argentina and then a trip to UNDCP
headquarters to present the report. The results as we found them
were inconclusive, with no evidence that the exposure of the editors and reporters had substantially influenced editorial policy of
important newspapers or other media. Our recommendation was
that the project not be extended.

On my return from Vienna, I found a vibrant Ele. She had made
reservations to fly to Visalia and arrangements to get to Tulare. She
also told me about a contractor who was "booked for the next several months but would be available by the summer." She showed
me her most recent plans for the houses and her expectation that
the remodeled houses would be ready by the end of 1995.

The Break-In

As we prepared to leave for Washington National Airport, Ele had a briefcase full of plans—not only for the houses but also for writing about her life. She talked about having the time to reread her letters to her mother and to Elizabeth LaCell that were locked in footlockers in her small Tulare apartment. She seemed excited and happy.

When we arrived, it was a sparkling spring day. A good friend, Barbara Milnes met us and drove us leisurely to Ele's small apartment in back of the houses that were to become our retirement home.

On the trip from the airport, Barbara and Ele talked about contractors and the economic situation in Tulare. Barbara warned her that most of the contractors had work and that Ele would have to be very persuasive to get one of them to commit to her before the fall. She also named a few scoundrels that Ele should avoid. As we approached the house, she and Barbara were joking about the challenges and the work ahead.

Ele gave me the key to the apartment. I tried the key and it wouldn't open the door. Ele took the keys from the incompetent and was equally unsuccessful. After three or four tries, Ele looked around and saw that the door had been jimmied and one of the windows broken and replaced, and that an electrical wire was running to the main house. She and Barbara decided to go to the real estate office that managed the property while I stayed with the luggage.

They returned a half hour later with an apologetic agent. Ele had not been told that six weeks earlier burglars had broken in and cleaned out the apartment. The agent changed the locks but chose not to advise Ele since she knew that she was coming in the near future. Yes, the break-in had been reported to the police. No, the agent had not notified the insurance company. Ele was furious.

The door opened onto a scene of total devastation. Almost every piece of furniture had been stolen, and the floor was a heap of papers and broken items through which cockroaches and other little beasties were cavorting. All the burglars had left were an overstuffed living room couch and matching chair, the refrigerator, the box spring and mattress to the double bed whose frame they carted away, and one or two other items apparently too heavy to move. They had emptied and absconded with eight footlockers in which Ele had so carefully organized and filed her letters. They carried away the family desk in which Ele had stored family records. They stole boxes full of family treasures and linens Ele had acquired for her "old age." I remember as vividly today as I did that late March day the chaos and rot in the room, and the blank, empty look in Ele's eyes that replaced the life and vigor that had been there only an hour earlier. For the next three days, she said practically nothing and just stared blankly straight ahead.

Barbara gave Ele a hug. I gave the real estate agent a piece of my mind. I made a place for Ele to sit, and went to work. With Barbara's help, I called the insurance agent and asked him to file a claim. Then I called the Tulare police for a copy of the police report. Barbara bought us some sandwiches that I put in the refrigerator, and then went to Sears to buy us towels and linens to replace those that had been stolen. Then, I called the president of the real estate company managing the property and learned that she had been ill for several weeks and had left the agent in charge. There was no one else to blow up at.

So, I set out to clean up the mess and assess the damage. That afternoon, a policeman came by with the report that he had made. He said that unfortunately there had been a wave of break-ins by young drug addicts seeking money to feed their habit. He said that drugs had become a major source of crime in Tulare. The insurance agent came by and Ele signed the claim without ever saying a word. I called Mimi Hoffman, Ele's closest friend and found that she was at her home in Maui. And Ele just sat and stared straight ahead.

All I remember of the next two days was working to clean up and killing cockroaches, ants, and other bugs. I cleaned the bathroom on hands and knees. I contacted the tenants in the two houses in front of the apartment when I began to wonder how the desk, the dining room table, and chairs were removed without someone hearing. After all, the main houses a few feet away were occupied and someone should have heard something going on!

When I talked to the tenants, they said that they had heard nothing and seemed genuinely upset. They brought us food for dinner. The police came by to see if they could be helpful.

Then, the insurance agent called to say that, because the claim had not been made within thirty days of the break-in, the company denied liability and canceled the policy. When I called the company, the Tragens were accused of "constructive abandonment" of the property in spite of our written contract with the real estate company to take care of the property. The insurance company told us that our recourse was with the real estate agent. Well, no one from the real estate office came near us in those horrendous days.

Ele did not speak for three days. Her eyes were glazed over. Her doctor, Dr. Matthias, had retired and I knew of no one to call. She basically stayed in bed while I worked to clean up the two rooms and make a definitive list of the losses including items of more sentimental than cash value, including the 1860 model of the reaper that Ele's grandfather had patented and old family pictures and albums. All in all, the material loss was not great, probably only a few hundred dollars, but for Ele, the emotional loss was immeasurable. Its effect scarred her irreparably. During those three days, I only left her for a few minutes at a time to buy food or run errands.

On the third day, Ele looked sadly at me and said, "I never want to live here again. I never want to live here again." Not a tear. Not a gesture. An important part of my dear Ele had died three days before and she lost her verve for life.

It took several more days before we could talk rationally about the future. We had nineteen lift vans full of personal and household effects in storage in Visalia a few miles away. Some were full of the Latin American handicrafts she had been collecting for the past forty years. We could not abandon them.

We decided to look for a retirement community in the area. We called Barbara and she directed us to a real estate agent. He took us around for several days but we saw nothing remotely close to what we might consider. The most interesting was a senior community in mobile home park in Visalia, but the deal just didn't seem for us. We went to the Bank of America, whose staff seemed to know more about what was going on in the area than anyone else in town. We talked to several officers about senior facilities they knew of in Tulare and nearby communities. The nearest they could recommend was a church-run facility about a hundred miles away that was more assisted living than for the independent seniors that we considered ourselves to be.

We were almost despondent when on Palm Sunday, we went to lunch in Hanford, a nearby community where Ele's favorite cousin, Jim Leonard, lived. The Leonards took us to church and brunch. Ele seemed much calmer, even renewed, that day, and I hoped that she was now getting over the trauma. After brunch, Jim drove us around Hanford and showed us a new townhouse development, Greenfield Village, of thirty-five houses that one of his friends, Dan Humason, managed. It had a pool and a community center and was by far the best prospect we had seen.

Ele said that she was interested in learning more about Greenfield Village, and Jim called Dan, who picked us up in Tulare the following Tuesday and showed us a house all on one floor; it met Ele's criteria of no stairs. It was about 1,800 square feet with two bedrooms, two baths, a study off the kitchen, and a small backyard. It was attached to the neighboring houses on both sides, and backed up on Dan Humason's house located outside the Village itself. Dan told us that the condo dues covered the landscaping and front garden maintenance, the maintenance of the exterior of the houses, the pool, and the community center. When we asked the purchase price, it was very close to what we expected to get for our apartment in Washington. Ele said that she wanted us to buy it. So, on the way home from Hanford, we reached a deal to buy our next home in Greenfield Village in Hanford.

Getting Settled in Hanford

The last two months in Washington were not easy. Ele fell into a deep malaise and seemed indifferent to what was going on. I had to organize the packing up of the apartment, including sifting through Ele's accumulated press clippings on topics from Watergate to Bill Gates. I found myself doing almost all the household chores, and having little time to do much else.

I received a couple of job offers, one in Coral Gables and one in D.C. I didn't really consider them because of the burden of the nineteen lift vans in Visalia. It was a time when possessions seemed to preempt other considerations.

Most of April and May was dedicated to getting our household and personal effects in order. Nothing seemed to be going well.

When the movers came in, Ele was not well and stayed in bed during the packing. The apartment was up for sale, but the market was very weak and not one offer had been made in three months.

The trip to Hanford was long and weary and the adjustment not easy. I had to put Ele to bed almost immediately as she seemed distraught. She had turned bitter, responding negatively to almost every suggestion or comment directed to her; for, this was not how she had planned to live out her life and she wasn't happy.

The shipment from Washington arrived in late May during one of the hottest late Mays recorded in the area. It was 110 degrees the day the moving van appeared. Everyone said that it was dry heat and not as bad as humid heat. I won't argue the point, but it was hot. The furniture and barrels were offloaded, and we discovered that the space in the dining room was too small to hold our beautiful blonde mahogany glass-topped table, and I had to assign it to the one-car garage. A hundred boxes with our dishes, linens, Latin American handicrafts, paintings and books joined the table in that small, un-air conditioned space. The movers unloaded the truck and bid me a fond adieu. It was my job to unpack the boxes at my leisure.

The shipment did not arrive in the condition we had hoped. Not all the boxes arrived, and several pieces of furniture were damaged. I could not find some items listed on the inventory. I contacted the insurance agent who recommended someone to do the repair work and then clashed with him when the repair work was shoddy. I tried to shield Ele from the trials and travails.

May stretched into June and the hot weather persisted. I spent several hours every day in the garage unpacking, and I did the shopping, cooking, and care giving. When I was almost at my wits' end, Jim Leonard introduced us to Milt Woods, the competent and helpful jack-of-all-trades who came to my relief. St. Milt, as Ele and I came to call him, came to my rescue in the unpacking process, in repairing damaged furniture in his workshop, hanging paintings, and identifying inadequate repairs by cabinetmakers recommended by the insurance company. During the eight years we lived in Hanford, it was St. Milt who found answers to the glitches that kept arising in our household.

Ele's listlessness led me to ask Jim and Jean Leonard about a

doctor. Their doctor said that he would take no more Medicare patients, and of course our primary insurer was Medicare. So, with St.
Milt's help, we were able to book an appointment with his family
doctor whose office was a block away from our home at the Hanford Medical Center. I made an appointment for both of us. Ele did
not respond much to the doctor or his examination. I recall that he
prescribed an increase in her thyroid medications and some vita-
mins, but her apathy continued.

Jean Leonard tried to help out by inviting Ele to the Hanford
chapter of the American University Women's Association. Almost all of the members were teachers whose interests revolved
around school and family. When Ele returned from the meeting,
she thanked Jean but declined to join the group, saying that their
interests were quite different from hers. Jean and Jim also introduced us to several other friends who invited us to dinners and
local events over the years. Jean and Jim became close friends and
always were there to lend a hand when we were in need. Jim also
invited us to join his Great Books Group, which met once a month.
Ele and I looked forward to the monthly discussions, but her stamina for evening sessions was so low that she opted out after a couple
of sessions.

What did light up Ele's eyes and spirit was a weekly call from
her boys—Ray and Gary in Houston. She was eager to talk to them
about their week, and she made no secret of her affection for both
of them and her preference for living at the Forum in the Woodlands. When the phone would ring on Sunday afternoon, as soon as
I answered, she would call over to me, "Is it Gary and Ray?" When
I said yes, she would say, "Pass me the phone." And they would
talk for easily half an hour about events in Houston, the dogs, and
their plans. In the telephone conversations, she would tell the boys
all about her week in Hanford, and would discuss national politics
and just about anything that concerned her.

One of her most pressing and immediate concerns was what
to do about those nineteen lift vans in storage in Visalia. As usual,
the expense of continuing to pay storage weighed heavily on her;
as she would tell the boys and me regularly, "We need to eliminate
all unnecessary bills since Irving isn't working anymore." Since I
am such a poor driver and she didn't want to drive anymore, we

had chosen not to buy a car, but rather depended on the very limited public transportation and taxi services in Hanford. There was limited direct inter-urban transit connection between Hanford and the neighboring communities of Tulare and Visalia, less than thirty miles apart.

When Ele told the boys of her concern, Gary and Ray agreed to help us out. Gary volunteered to fly out in September for a week so that we could check the contents of the lift vans, and decide what we should keep and what needed to be sold now that our plans for living in the Tulare houses had been scrapped. I remember how relieved she was when the boys agreed and we set the date.

Before Gary's planned arrival, I worked to make space in the garage for the stored items we planned to keep. Lord, it was hot in that garage! My schedule was tight because one of the commitments I made before leaving Washington, with Ele's agreement, was with ILANUD (the Latin American Institute of the United Nations for the Prevention of Crime and Treatment of Offenders) to participate for a week in mid-August in planning the initial activities of its newly established Central American drug control program, CEDEJU, in San Jose, Costa Rica.

It was mid-September when Gary arrived in Hanford to help us sort through the nineteen lift vans. The heat had abated somewhat. In the cool warehouse, it was almost comfortable. Gary rented a car and ferried us every morning for a week to the Visalia warehouse. Ele supervised the segregation of the contents into three piles: the items to be used in Hanford; the Latin American handicraft collection, and items to be disposed of. At the end of the first day, a fourth pile was formed of those items that Ray and Gary might want. Each lift van seemed to present special problems. Some contained household effects from Ele's mother's and grandmother's houses. Some were charming nineteenth century antiques that had come with the family from Dennison, Iowa. Some were kitchen appliances and dishes that dated from the 1920s and 1930s. Many of the antiques seemed to catch Gary's eye and were set aside for his possible use. Some Ele decided she could use in her small Tulare apartment to replace items that had been stolen a few months earlier. Many just did not seem worth keeping. At the end of the first day, the office manager of the storage company suggested that the items we did not want be consigned to a Visalia auction company, and we agreed to call in the auction company. It was Thursday before we completed filtering through the collection of three lifetimes—and determining what items went where. Most, including all the handicrafts, came home to Hanford. Some antiques went to Houston. The rest the auction company sold. Our garage runneth over! October and November had me once again in the garage and once again trying to fit all pieces together.

When the boys invited us to spend Christmas with them in the Woodlands, Ele jumped at the opportunity. Ray and Gary fixed up a suite for her with many of her grandmother's cherished items and she was elated. We had a full schedule of museums, galleries, dinner parties, and delights that brought back smiles that had been very rare since the break-in. Since it was Christmas, I told Ele that we would go on a shopping spree at Nieman Marcus and her Christmas present would be all the special things that she set her heart on; Ele led me on a merry chase looking at all the clothes and lingerie, until she settled at the Estee Lauder counter where she sampled different kinds of make-up and finally decided on the mix of cosmetics she wanted for herself. She dressed up that night for a Christmas party next door and she looked just exquisite. She gave all of us a wonderful Christmas gift just looking at her. I was hopeful that my dear Ele was coming out of her dark days.

Unfortunately, once we were back in Hanford, Ele seemed to re-enter her shell. The onset of the Tule fog didn't help. The Tule fog is dense grey, almost blinding, and it settles over the southern San Joaquin Valley for days or weeks at a time. This was my first winter in the Tule fog, and it was depressing to go for days without sunlight. Everyone seemed testy or depressed and there was very little social activity, especially for people like us without immediate family nearby. Civic events like art shows and band concerts were put off until March when the fogs tended to diminish. St. Milt came over regularly to check on us. That winter was particularly dreary and Ele seldom got out of bed unless she had to.

Central American Center for Legal Development on Narcotic Drugs and Drug Trafficking (CEDEJU)

In 1994, ILANUD, the Latin American Institute of the United Nations for the Prevention of Crime and Treatment of Offenders, and CICAD agreed to set up CEDEJU to improve cooperation and coordination among Central American governments to combat the drug problem. ILANUD was chartered by the UN Economic and Social Council in 1975 and funded by the government of Costa Rica. It cohosted with CICAD several regional workshops and technical meetings, and had adequate facilities and staff. The Mexican government donated funds to CICAD to initiate CEDEJU activities. While Ele and I were still in Washington, the then director of ILANUD had asked me to be the technical adviser to CEDEJU. Ele and I talked it over and decided that we could not move to San Jose, but that I should take the job if it could be done through periodic trips to Central America. Knowing how tight the budget was, I agreed to work *pro bono* for a couple of years, spending no more than a week a month in Costa Rica, with ILANUD paying my travel and per diem expenses. The program was scheduled to begin operations in January 1996.

In the summer of 1995, the long-time director of ILANUD retired and his principal assistant, Cristina Rojas, was expected to be named his successor. They selected Dr. Benjamín Odio, a well-respected Costa Rican lawyer, to head up CEDEJU. They invited me to join them in August 1995 to plan the initial operations of a three-pronged program aimed at improving cooperation among the legislative, administrative, and judicial branches of the seven regional governments in dealing with drug trafficking and drug abuse. The three-pronged program included: (1) meetings of legislators from the seven countries (Belize, Costa Rica, El Salvador, Guatemala, Honduras, Nicaragua, and Panama) on legislation needed to deal with the problem; (2) workshops for executive branch officials responsible for enforcing the laws, and (3) roundtables for judges to explore common standards for dealing with drug cases. The goal was for ILANUD to spearhead a long-term regional program for better inter-government cooperation and coordination to combat trafficking and drug abuse. It was hoped that the results of the first phase of operations would be sufficiently promising to attract further financing from UNDCP, the U.S., Mexico, and others.

In March 1996, I made my first week-long trip to Costa Rica and found that another Costa Rican—a recently retired UNDCP official from Vienna, not Cristina—had been selected as director of ILANUD. Benjamín was concerned because of reports that the appointee had quite different interests. I urged him to withhold judgment and proceed with the development of the project as originally planned.

In the next few days we visited the seven countries of the Isthmus and met with the heads of national drug commissions, justices of the Supreme Court, key legislators working on drug trafficking and related criminal issues, and heads of the police and customs. My work at CICAD facilitated our getting many appointments and ILANUD contacts opened the doors to the others. We laid out the nature and scope of the problem in the region and explained the project and its objectives. Our reception in each country was quite different. In some, there was polite agreement, colored by skepticism that the region was ready for such an approach. In one, we felt differences in not only the perception of the problem but also the capability of national entities to participate effectively. In two or three countries, there was genuine interest and offers to cooperate. In Panama, which had more sophisticated and effective anti-drug programs than in the other countries, judges, legislators and National Guard leaders offered to work closely with CEDEJU in planning and conducting workshops. The chief justice of the Supreme Court offered to co-host with CEDEJU a meeting of Supreme Court justices. Those were the responses we expected.

On returning to San José, we decided to take advantage of the Panamanian interest and to start the program with a workshop in Panama for police and customs chiefs on measures to tighten law enforcement efforts and to build closer formal and informal inter-country cooperation. In the process, Benjamín worked with the Panamanians and other law enforcement officials to put the workshop together. He approached the DEA and the RCMP for their participation. He located first-class hotels for workshops that provided low rates in the off-season and was able to schedule meetings at costs that permitted our limited budget to be stretched a long way.

The Panama workshop was followed by other training sessions, seminars, and consultations. During 1996, I made five week-long trips to Central America to attend workshops and planning meetings. The discussions illustrated how different the policies and procedures were in the seven countries. The officials in the neighboring countries did not know each other and had only superficial knowledge of what was going on across their own borders. The first CEDEJU meeting of judges was the first time that the judges from different countries had met each other and had an opportunity to compare how they prepared their cases, how their judicial police forces operated, and how trials were conducted. Six of the countries based their legal systems on the civil law and Belize on English common law. Each of the six civil law countries had very different rules of procedure, and I was fascinated to listen to them contradicting each other or questioning a local variation on similar code provisions.

Those meetings provided empirical evidence of accelerating drug trafficking and money laundering in the region and that no country, except Panama, had legislation in place to deal with them. So, Benjamin decided that CEDEJU had to commit its remaining limited resources to make legislators from the seven countries aware of the imminent threat to all seven countries of the region and encourage them not only to draft relevant legislation but also to make that legislation compatible throughout the region for more effective law enforcement.

Money laundering was the topic chosen for workshop. Benjamin and I visited the national congresses to identify the key legislators in each country working on criminal matters and invited two participants from each country—most of whom had never met before the workshop. It held three sessions. The CICAD Model Regulations and the Panamanian legislation were the basic working papers. The Panamanian delegates laid out the threat of drug trafficking and money laundering, and Benjamin led the discussion on legislation and proposed that they draft a model law that all seven could adopt. By the third meeting, they hammered out a comprehensive proposal to deal with money laundering, and agreed to work with CEDEJU in presenting it to their respective congresses. Unfortunately, ILANUD abolished the CEDEJU program before any further action could be taken.

As CEDEJU became operational, the new director and Benjamín Odio were at loggerheads. Benjamín found himself working alone as he began implementing project plans. The director refused invitations to participate in any CEDEJU activities. He refused to allow Benjamín to draw on ILANUD finances or to contact the ILANUD funders, especially UNDCP, even though contacts in Vienna advised me that it was looking for projects to fund. My trips to Central America were colored by the tension between the ILANUD director and Benjamín, and my hopes for an effective regional program gradually dissolved.

After the last session of the legislators working on money laundering, with CEDEJU almost out of funds, I suggested to Benjamín that we travel to Mexico City to report to the Mexican authorities on the results of the grant that their government had made to CICAD and hopefully promote a second tranche. In Mexico City, the government of Ernesto Zedillo had changed all of the senior policy and enforcement officials engaged in combatting drug trafficking and the current team was not informed about the origins of the Central American project. The principal advocate of the project, General Carrillo Olea, was then governor of the State of Morelos, and we arranged to brief him. He promised to intercede on behalf of CEDEJU with the attorney general and the foreign minister. Unfortunately, the events at ILANUD prevented any follow up.

In February 1998, Benjamín called to alert me that he was resigning. He had attended a meeting called by DEA and presented a request for funding. It was rejected when the director of ILANUD disavowed it. I was asked to prepare a final report within thirty days. I was saddened by this turn of events because I believed that Central America needed such a regional effort to deal with drug trafficking and drug abuse. The initial reactions by participants, from Sandinistas to conservatives, had been positive. I also regretted that I was no longer able to work with my Central American colleagues, especially Benjamín and his family who had made me feel part of the Odio family.

I'm Still on the Road

During those first three years, I had the commitments with not only CEDEJU but also *Mut zur Ethic* in Zurich. The trips to Zurich were usually for two weeks once a year. I would be invited to participate on a panel at the international forum on drugs sponsored by *Mut zur Ethik*. I also agreed to be an advisor on its campaign for a Drug Free Youth in Switzerland. I tried to get Ele to travel with me, but she frequently declined.

In 1966, when invited to present a paper on the drug problem in the Western Hemisphere, I replied that I would be able to attend only if Ele were to accompany me; so she was named to a panel that dealt with treatment of drug addiction. This was the first year that I attended a Zurich meeting without having to rush back to Washington to get ready for a CICAD meeting. So, our hosts arranged an in-depth review of the drug scene in Switzerland, a briefing in Bern on canton-by-canton policies on narcotic drugs, and a daylong conference in Zurich on the Canton's program to decriminalize drug use. In Zurich we met with officials, policemen, and social workers who had differing views on the effectiveness of its program to provide free heroin to addicts, housing in District 5, and a subsidy of 2,500 Swiss Francs (500 more if they had a dog) as deterrents to their resorting to crime to feed their habit. Then we went on a walking tour of District 5, Needle Park, and free drug dispensaries. Ele was very attentive and asked some penetrating questions, but she tired very quickly and had to return to our hotel. We had a light dinner in our room and the next morning she seemed quite disoriented again. I had to cut our plans for staying another week in Zurich and flew Ele back to Hanford.

Once back in Hanford, I made appointments with doctors to evaluate Ele's health. The results were very disappointing. Our GP attributed the condition to thyroid imbalance. A change in thyroid medication dosage had no visible effect except to induce Ele to want to sleep longer.

I became frustrated. This was not my Ele. She had other problems that seemed to me unrelated to thyroid, especially the sadness in her eyes that had not gone away since the break-in. When I pressed her to do something, she would often lash back at me and say, "Let me live my life my way." It was one of the most difficult periods in our married life.

A few weeks after our return from Zurich, I was invited to participate on a panel at a prestigious national seminar on money laundering in Miami at the Fontainebleau Hotel. I convinced Ele to go with me. The prime mover of the seminar was Charles Intriago, formerly an adviser to Dante Fascell, when he was chairman of the House Foreign Affairs Committee.

Dante Fascell, then retired from Congress, was the chair of the plenaries. He encouraged Ele and me to join him for much of the seminar. Unfortunately Ele tired and did not attend many of the sessions. As we were leaving for the airport, Dante, whose wife Marie had recently passed away, came over to tell how concerned he was about Ele's health and urged me to keep a close eye on her.

That concern permeated most of our life during 1996. When I tried to make appointments with doctors, Ele objected. So, I focused on finding activities to whet her interest, hoping she would snap back. Knowing her interest in politics, through Jim Leonard, who was Treasurer of the Kings County Democratic Party, we arranged for her to attend meetings of the County Democratic Party and, through our neighbors the Evans, the Republican. Knowing her interest in history, we joined the Kings County Historical Society and went on trips to points of interest. Knowing her long-time association with Elizabeth LaCell and the Tulare Library, we joined the Hanford Friends of the Library. Unfortunately, she tended to tire easily and seemed to lose interest, even in subjects that once had delighted her.

This was also the first time that we had become aware of our own mortality. Ele asked me if our wills were adequate instruments for disposing of our possessions on our demise. We began to study trusts. While we procrastinated in making a final decision, we worked out how we wanted our assets to be used on our passing and prepared an inventory of them. Some of the more significant were the paintings, textiles, ceramics, straw, and other handicrafts that had been acquired over our many years in Latin America. There were over three thousand pieces in the collection. We knew that we could not display them or even store them appropriately in our little town house, and decided that one of our priorities would be to find a permanent home for them. Ele contacted a curator at the Smithsonian who had seen pieces of it and she wrote back that the Smithsonian would welcome receiving them, but warned us that the Institution had no immediate plans for a museum of Latin American handicrafts, and that Ele's collection would probably be warehoused for the foreseeable future.

When we went to Houston for Christmas, we talked to the boys about our concerns and plans. They promised to help us find a permanent home for the collection. Gary made a computer review to identify institutions that we might contact. One of them was the Houston Natural History Museum and the boys took us to meet with one of the curators who expressed great interest in the collection. He told us one of Houston's long-term projects was to build a five-story museum of Latin American art and culture, but he warned us that the proposal might not get off the drawing board for some years. I wanted a site that Ele could see in her lifetime— and I was not too sure how long that would be.

When we returned from Houston, I told Ele that I was terminating my consultancies after one final trip to Zurich in June and would spend all of my time with her in Hanford. The next several weeks we spent on family projects, including the status of our investment portfolio, organizing the handicraft collection, and the steps required for setting up a trust.

We had an interruption in that planning when in March Dave Frederickson called to tell us that the dean of the University of the Pacific (UOP) School of International Relations, Marge Inman, would like to talk with me about joining the advisory council she was forming on school policy and programs. Dave said that he and his wife Margaret were available to accompany us. UOP is located in Stockton—only a two-hour train ride from Hanford. Ele agreed that we would both go. Our meeting with Marge went well, and I agreed to join the advisory group.

We also met two of David's colleagues at UOP, Beata and John Evey. John was the vice president for development of the university. Ele asked David and John whether the university might be interested in receiving her Latin American handicraft collection since it had the School of International Relations and had once been the home of Covell College, a prestigious center of language and cultural education on Latin America. With that possibility and my relationship with the school, Ele suggested that we might consider moving to Stockton. Unfortunately neither worked out.

I sensed that my being home revived Ele's spirits. She became interested in Hanford civic affairs and accepted invitations to dinners sponsored by the Hanford Historical Society and had us join its tour to the Pacific Northwest that fall. We visited the devastation caused by the eruption of Mount St. Helens, and enjoyed the museums and rose gardens of Portland, and marveled at the Cascades, Mount Hood, and the sequoias. Ele took it rather well, except her recurring need to be close to a restroom. I was optimistic that Ele was on the road to recovery.

Late that summer, we also had a surprise visit from my cousin, Susannah Harris, and her husband, Jay Wilson, who lived in Oxford, England. Susannah had left California for college at the University of Pennsylvania and worked for years at a secondary school for young women in Lahore, Pakistan. Jay was an Anglican priest whose mother was in a retirement home in nearby Turlock. We had two fantastic days getting to know each other, talking politics and social issues, and visiting nearby sites of interest in the Hanford area, including the world-famous Center of Oriental Art and Culture on the outskirts of Hanford.

We spent the rest of the year in Hanford and looked forward to a fruitful 1998. We had Christmas Eve with the Leonards at the home of Edie and Joe Bercher, friends who had lived in Spain and were active in the international student exchange program. St. Milt had us over for dinner. We spent a quiet New Year at home. We agreed that we would concentrate on three priorities: finding a permanent home for the Latin American handicraft collection, setting up the trust, and keeping Ele well and happy.

Ele Breaks Her Hip

In early May, *Mut zum Ethik* requested my participation in a meeting on the plebiscite on drug free youth, and, with Ele's agreement, I agreed to this one last assignment.

On a Monday, just two weeks before I was to leave for Zurich, our neighbor Jane Morrow invited us to go grocery shopping with her in her car. I accepted, but Ele was resting in bed. Before I left, Ele asked me to leave my keys at home since there had been a wave of pickpocketing. When I returned, I rang the bell and there was no answer. I began to panic and then climbed over the fence that separated my neighbor's yard from ours. When I reached the glass door–picture window of the bedroom, I saw Ele lying on the floor, crying from pain. My neighbor called 911 and the team arrived in minutes. They broke the lock on the glass door to the bedroom and rushed to Ele's aid. She told them that she had stumbled coming back from the bathroom. Their diagnosis was that she had broken her right hip. I rode with her in the ambulance to the emergency room at the Hanford Community Hospital. Jim Leonard joined me while Ele was taken for X-rays and other lab tests. The ER doctor advised us that the surgeon who did hip replacements would not be available for at least forty-eight hours, and that meant that the hospital would try to make Ele as comfortable as possible until Thursday morning. When I asked him how bad the fracture was, he said that it was bad but reparable. He asked me to please go home while they sedated Ele and moved her into a room. When we were allowed to say goodnight, she seemed very fragile and sobbed that her grandmother and her mother had died after they broke their hips. Early Thursday morning, the surgery was performed successfully.

The next several days, I walked many times between our home and the hospital. It was Saturday morning when they assigned her a room and I was allowed to spend time with her. I spent almost every hospital visiting hour with Ele and was shunted to the waiting room when it was time for therapy or tests. On Sunday I was with her as the nurses tried to get her to sit up and even move from her bed to a chair. She was so weak that I almost ached from her straining.

On Monday, she began physical therapy. I remember a very handsome, young South Carolina man who came in the mornings. He had a warm, inviting manner and Ele responded to his instructions; by Thursday she was walking a bit down the hall with him. In the afternoon, a Brunhilde-type physiotherapist came in. Ele did not respond well to her manner; she accused Ele of not trying hard enough. That lady turned out to be the supervisor of the physical therapists and one powerful presence at the hospital and in its outpatient services.

I decided to cancel the trip to Zurich, but Ele urged me to go. She pointed out that she would be in a convalescent home for a month for physical therapy and that it might be better if I were not there during that first week. So, we agreed that I would make the trip as planned.

Then I looked for a rehab center. A neighbor worked at what was reputed to be one of the best-rated in town. She said that she would keep an eye on Ele for me if Ele went there. Jim Leonard and I reviewed other facilities in the vicinity. The best was in Visalia, thirty miles away; but without a car that would mean that I could not spend much time with Ele during her convalescence. So, after considerable discussion, Ele and I agreed to move her to the facility at which our neighbor worked. On the Friday before my departure for Zurich, I moved her by ambulance. I spent Friday and Saturday with her and worked out the physical therapy schedule that was to speed her recovery. Jim and Jean Leonard agreed to look in each day, and our neighbor promised to ensure that Ele got special care.

I arrived in Zurich on the Sunday and our meetings began Monday. But that day, Jim called me to say that Ele was not doing well, and, in a second call that evening, urged me to return to Hanford as soon as possible. I explained my concerns to my hosts and to my eternal gratitude, they arranged through Swiss Air to fly me back on Tuesday. On my arrival in Hanford, Jim explained to me that the physical therapy sessions had not taken place because Ele apparently had some other problems that made her too weak to get out of bed. Our GP had left town on a hunting trip and his replacement was not responding to Jim's calls for him to visit Ele as soon as possible. When I saw Ele on Wednesday, she was peaked and fragile. The head nurse at the convalescent home thought she had an intestinal infection, but could give no medication without a doctor's approval. I then spent hours trying to reach the substitute doctor as his nurse kept advising me that he was tied up tending to other patients. Then, I blew up and let loose a flow of invectives that made the head nurse blush. But it worked. The doctor called and promised to see Ele as soon as he could.

I spent all evening Wednesday at the facility waiting for the doctor and left only when visiting hours were over. The doctor did not arrive until Thursday afternoon. He agreed that she had a bad infection and said that she urgently needed medication. However, he left town the following morning without leaving a prescription for the medication.

Friday morning when I arrived at the convalescent facility, the head nurse told me how concerned she was. So, I got on the phone to the doctor, whom I was told, had left town and another doctor was taking his patients. So, I spent most of the day tracking down the substitute who, when I reached him, very cavalierly responded, "She is not my patient, I am already overbooked for today." At which I fired forth another volley of four letter words and told him that I was taking Ele back to the ER at the hospital.

As the afternoon passed that Friday, Ele seemed to fall into a deeper and deeper semi-coma. About 4:30 p.m., she closed her eyes and quietly said "goodbye." The head nurse broke into tears. So I called the doctor's emergency line to let him know what was happening while the head nurse ordered an ambulance. I had us back in the ER by 5:30 p.m. This time I stayed with Ele in spite of the protestations of the ER staff. No doctor came to see her for nearly two hours while she drifted in and out of consciousness. Finally, the ER doctor arrived and asked why he hadn't been alerted to Ele's condition. He then asked me to please go home. He needed to give his full attention to the patient for the next several hours because her kidneys were not functioning properly. He promised to call me if he needed me, but he said that I would be better off at home than in the ER waiting room. After waiting for about an hour without word from the ER staff, I drearily walked the block back home for a sleepless night. Saturday morning about 6:00 a.m., I was back in the ER and learned that Ele was resting comfortably. I was allowed to see her for a minute and was told that she would be heavily sedated for the next day or two. The doctor urged me to let her rest. All I remember of the rest of Saturday was giving a report to Jim and Jean Leonard, St. Milt, and our neighbor Jane. I guess between jet lag and worry, I just passed out until early Sunday morning.

When I awoke Sunday, I went down to the hospital to check. I was told that Ele was doing much better, but that she was still not fully awake. Jean and Jim came by to take me to church and lunch and back to the hospital. Ele looked so much better, especially the color of her skin and the ease of her breathing. We talked to the doctor who had taken care of her in the ER and intensive care. He thought that she would need at least another week in the hospital before she could be released. He was scheduling physical therapy for her hip starting on Wednesday but warned us that the infection had delayed her recovery by several weeks.

It was Monday or Tuesday before Ele recovered full consciousness. Her first words to me were that she wanted to go home. She would not agree to go again to a convalescent facility. So, I began working with the hospital on its outpatient program and my role in it. I was to become the primary caregiver. The outpatient program would provide nursing care three times a week for up to ninety days, as well as physical therapy to strengthen her right hip and help her to walk. I obtained a wheel chair and a walker as well as instructions about her diet, including the exclusion of certain foods high in potassium and sodium. I was drilled on how to help Ele get in and out of bed, use and clean bed pans, apply salves to avoid bed sores and do a host of other things that she would need while recovering at home.

I brought Ele home a week later and began a routine that would last almost until her death. This seminal event brought us closer together and deepened our affection for each other. It was not an easy time for either of us. I frequently had to cajole her to try harder. She would sometimes get angry with me for not being sympathetic enough to her problems. No human relationship is easy and the most difficult of my life had been to watch this wonderfully intelligent, independent lady become wholly dependent on me. Before my eyes, she shrank from a size 12 to an 8 petite, from almost 5'4" to 5'1."

From July to mid-November, I never was certain if Ele would survive the night. I took her vital signs regularly and called the outpatient nurse at the first sign of fever. She was using a catheter, which caused her one infection after another. I shall always be grateful to the outpatient service, since the nurse always responded as quickly as she could. During those four months, I don't remember ever falling sound asleep. I could almost sense whenever Ele changed position. I did not need to hear when she needed help — somehow I just knew it.

Complicating my concern was that I was never quite sure what her underlying illness was. I knew that she had suffered kidney damage from the infection she had in the convalescent facility, but her doctors gave me various different diagnoses. The doctor on duty in the emergency room who essentially saved her life that Saturday night told me that she needed dialysis, while our GP suggested other treatments. Friends who were acquainted with dialysis said that she was too frail for the treatment. In hindsight, maybe I should have taken her to Stanford Hospital or UC San Francisco for analysis, but I truly believed that she was receiving appropriate attention and treatment from doctors who knew her medical history.

Around Thanksgiving, Paul Leonard, Jim and Jean's son, returned to Hanford after graduating from medical school in Guadalajara. Paul was also a pharmacist. I asked Jim to have him stop over and check Ele's condition. As I made the suggestion by phone to Jim, Ele perked up. Paul came over and checked her records and medications. He suggested that two medications were counteracting each other, and he sounded more like our GP than the ER doctor. I cut out the medicines and Ele responded almost immediately. When Paul returned the next morning, Ele was more alert than she had been in weeks and almost free of pain. He got her out of bed and she walked a bit with him. I felt that it was a turning point.

That night she slept well and responded enthusiastically to suggestions by the physical therapist when he arrived later that day. Ele had not responded to Brunhilde, her outpatient therapist, and Brunhilde had cut us out of Medicare services. So, I hired a male physical therapist recommended by one of the outpatient nurses. He and Ele hit it off—his bedside manner was positive, not threatening as Brunhilde's had been. I was delighted when Ele said to him that morning that she wanted to exercise and try walking. For the first time since she had returned home, she seemed to be doing better. A week later, the outpatient nurse told me that she felt Ele was finally on the road to recovery, and that her services could no longer be justified under Medicare regulations.

In spite of our optimism in November 1998, Ele never fully recovered. Our last four and half years in Hanford revolved almost entirely around Ele's health. She was in and out of the hospital several times, once for almost two weeks. I remember the sleepless nights when I had to call for emergency help or a nurse to help me administer medications. I remember the hours spent in doctors' offices and the lack of precision in the diagnoses we were given. I was hesitant to leave her alone even when I went shopping, so I hired caregivers to sit with her whenever I was away. Ele was never alone in the house after she came back from the hospital. She once told me that she had hated my snoring until she broke her hip— and then my snoring was her reassurance that I was nearby if she needed me.

The one day I never had a problem getting her up was the day when she had her appointment at the beauty parlor. That day, I would get her breakfast in bed while she watched television. Then, I would help her take her shower, get her dressed in a pants suit and wait for the senior citizen Hanford City bus that took us to the beauty parlor in the mall. I would do the shopping for our family needs at the mall while she was being attended to. Then we might have a snack before heading home. Though those were difficult and trying years, I would not trade one minute of them.

Our friends in Hanford were very attentive. Many of our neighbors in Greenfield Village would stop by to say hello, or offer to take me to town or shopping when I needed a ride. Our neighbor across the driveway, Melissa Hill, often dropped in to chat and take us to dinner. The Humasons around the corner frequently left fruit or other goodies for Ele. The Evans in the adjoining group of town houses often included us in trips to Fresno or to the coast. Other neighbors dropped off casseroles or desserts. In fact, through Ele's illness, we had become part of Greenfield Village. So, at the annual homeowners association meeting, I was elected secretary of the HOA and became one of the active board members. Ele asked me not to become involved in the HOA and reminded me of that whenever problems with fellow homeowners arose.

The Trust

Once Ele was past the crisis, we set out to put our house in order. Priority number one was to set up the trust to govern the disposal of our assets on our demise. Jim Leonard introduced us to Neil Helding, a well-respected local lawyer. Neil came to our home and discussed the usefulness of a trust for us. He was our man for the job.

Our first in-depth conversation was about how Ele wanted to distribute our assets. I felt that since Ele had played so critical a role in building them up, she should play the key role in deciding how they should be distributed. We reviewed our family relationships and agreed that, since we had no children, we wanted the bulk of our assets to go to charitable purposes—to be used to help people and to contribute to greater understanding among people. So, over the next six weeks, we reviewed our options and settled on three. The first would be an endowment to a U.S. institution to maintain and enhance Ele's Latin American handicraft collection and to use the collection to promote better appreciation of Latin American arts and culture in the United States. The second would endow a chair at the UC Berkeley Law School on Comparative Law to facilitate greater inter-country understanding of the different legal systems; this gift would not only be a substantive contribution to better international relations but also express our appreciation to my law school for the role it played in building my career. The third would be an endowment to a university for geriatrics medical research. We provided Neil with all the information he needed to write the trust.

By April 1999, Neil completed the Tragen Revocable Living Trust, and Ele and I executed it. We named my nephew Gary as our successor trustee on the death of either one of us and as administrator on our deaths.

With the trust in place, we began working with Gary and Ray on finding a home for Ele's collection. We touched base again with our contact at the Smithsonian who reiterated interest and her expectation that the collection would be put in storage indefinitely. We checked with the Houston Museum of Natural History on its interest, and sent letters of inquiry to several museums, including the Mexican Museum in San Francisco. Representatives from Houston and San Francisco visited us in Hanford and went over the collection and the terms of endowment. Both offered a permanent home. However, Houston reiterated that it would have to store the pieces pending a fund-raiser to construct a new building for its Latin American collection. San Francisco said that it was well ahead in its planning for a new home for the museum in the Mission Street cultural center next to the Holocaust Museum and across the street from the Museum of Modern Art. We were excited about the San Francisco possibility. So, in July, Ele and I made the trip by Amtrak to San Francisco.

The Mexican Museum had an extensive program for us, including visits to its temporary home at Fort Mason and meetings with key members of the board and staff. Gary joined us for a meeting and luncheon with the board at which we learned of deep divisions over objectives and interests between past and present board members. When Ele, Gary, and I met after the luncheon, we had serious concerns about its potential for serving as the permanent home for Ele's collection.

The following day, we were invited to City Hall to meet San Francisco Mayor Brown. He made a pitch for us to work with the Mexican Museum and promised full support from the city for the prompt construction of its new home. It was a very formal conversation until Ele asked the mayor if he remembered our dear friend Carlos Bee. The mayor warmed up to Ele and said, "Of course I remember Carlos." He told us several anecdotes about their relationship when the mayor was speaker of the California Assembly and Carlos was deputy speaker. Then, with genuine personal interest, he asked Ele about her collection and how she acquired it. The two of them talked for another quarter of an hour until his aides reminded him that he had other appointments waiting.

When we returned to Hanford and Gary to Houston, we talked at length by telephone about our respective reactions to Houston and San Francisco. We agreed that we needed other options. Gary told us that he and Ray had decided to move back to Denver in the near future and they would look for a possible institution there.

On his next trip to Denver, Gary found the Museo de las Américas, a small Hispanic community-based organization about ten years old. Its objective was to use art and culture as a bridge between the Anglo and Latin American communities in Denver and the Mountain States. José Aguayo, its executive director, called us and was definitely interested. We talked several more times on the phone about the collection and the terms and conditions of our making a gift, as well as the Museo's facilities for displaying the collection. On August 30, 2000, we signed an agreement with the Museo to give it the collection and a share of the Tragen estate and to make the Tragen Trust an emeritus member of the Board. Since Ray and Gary had then moved from Houston to Denver, Ele chose Gary to represent the trust on the board. Over the years, Gary has helped the board overcome several financial crises and in setting up necessary financial controls.

Later that year, José and several of his aides came to Hanford to pack up and move more than three thousand objects to Denver. Ray flew in from Denver to help Ele and me sort and catalogue the items gifted.

We were delighted that every item arrived and was integrated into the Museo's permanent collection. The Museo staff seemed genuinely intrigued by the objects and gave us periodic reports on their plans for an exhibit in 2001. That was especially pleasing for me because it meant that Ele would able to see her "babies" on exhibit in her lifetime.

We had an opportunity to visit the Museo in November 2000 before the exhibit was set up. We were invited to the Museo's annual gala. Gary and Ray helped me take care of Ele during the visit. The flight to Denver was hard on her, but she perked up when the boys helped her to the hotel and later at the gala itself. Colorado Governor Owens and U.S. Senator Campbell came to our table to thank Ele for choosing the Museo as the home for her collection. Without the boys, I don't think that I could have handled the evening as Ele had a relapse and almost passed away from us.

The first exhibit of Ele's collection was in the fall of 2001. Ele and I went to Denver for the inauguration. The exhibit was titled "Folk Art of Latin America," and hundreds of the pieces were on display. Ele cut the ribbon and was wheeled into the exhibit set up to look like a colorful Latin American market place. Her eyes lit up as she entered the exhibit, and I shall always remember the sheer joy she reflected on that happy occasion. On the bureau facing my bed is the picture of all of us at the entrance to the exhibit. Ele's smile says it all.

The second beneficiary of the trust was the UC Berkeley School of Law. In June 1999, Ele and I sent a letter to the dean of the Law School, Herma Hill Kay, advising her of our intentions. Shortly thereafter we received a call form Louise Epstein, the assistant dean for development, who said that in principle, the dean was interested and that later that summer the dean and she would fly down to Hanford to explore the prospects.

The two flew down to Hanford a few weeks later for a leisurely lunch with Ele and me. Ele explained our objective in setting up the trust and our choice of beneficiaries. I explained that my objective in setting up a chair on comparative law was to build another channel for inter-country understanding and to promote the rule of law among nation states. The chair would enable the Law School to establish a dialogue with governments and law schools around the world about each other's legal precepts and procedures and hopefully help chart paths for dealing with differences. We discussed the Law School's experience in comparative law with Korea, Japan, and China.

The dean told us that there was great interest in the UC Law Faculty in the subject matter and was prepared to create the Distinguished Professorship in Comparative Law. She explained that a "Distinguished Professor" was the terminology being used in the California University system for a chair, and that at least one million dollars would be required to create a professorship. I explained that, through Ele's management of our assets, we could assure her that one-third of the trust assets exceeded one million dollars. Having reached an agreement, we offered to prepare an initial draft of the proposed gift, and the dean promised to begin the formal approval process within the university to establish the Professorship.

Formalizing that agreement took almost a year. In late 2001, we agreed on a text to create the Distinguished Professorship on Comparative Constitutional and Administrative Law and a program fund to support the Professorship. A formal signing ceremony was held in Berkeley on February 22, 2002.

Since 2002, the university has replaced Distinguished Professorships with Chairs. I worked with former Deans Christopher Edley and Sujit Choudry to amend the February 22, 2002 agreement in order to create the Tragen Chair on Comparative Law, with a support program to conduct seminars and meetings at Berkeley or overseas, and to fund fellowships, research, and inter-country meetings.

The third beneficiary was geriatrics medical research. Ele and I were not certain how best to use our funds for this purpose. We initially considered an endowment for the UC San Francisco Medical School. In early 2000, Ele and I went up to San Francisco for initial discussions with the UC San Francisco Foundation and key members of the faculty of the medical school. We explored various alternative uses for our funds but never reached a firm agreement. After Ele's passing, I found the geriatrics research program at UC San Diego that Ele would have embraced. An understanding was reached with UC San Diego to endow a fund for geriatrics medical research, and that Fund was activated in 2018.

Preparing for Another Change

Ele and I remained in Hanford until January 2003. They were difficult years. Ele's health never recovered. We had some good spells, but most of those four years she was a convalescent and I, the primary caregiver. Ele was not an easy patient. She had a stubborn streak that came out of her strong will and deep pride. She had to be convinced that treatments were necessary or she just wouldn't cooperate. Often it would take hours of cajoling, persuasion, and sometimes intimidation to get her to do physical therapy or agree to a medical exam. I hired a caregiver to lend me a hand several days a week and be on call if I needed her. The Hanford Emergency Response Teams were occasional visitors when I could not handle a problem and I needed to move her to the hospital. As I remember those four years, my thoughts are filled with the day-to-day struggle to keep Ele going.

Ele had a few long-time friends like Mimi Hoffman, whom she especially wanted to see. Even though Mimi had suffered a stroke, whenever Ele needed her, bless Mimi's heart, she had her caregiver bring her over to Hanford. Once when I thought Ele was passing, Mimi came right over and helped me revive Ele's spirit and will to live. Ele always seemed to revive when lifelong friends like Mimi paid her a visit.

Part of keeping her spirit up was to organize special things. Jean and Jim Leonard made sure to invite us along when there was a good movie to see. They knew Ele loved pancakes and that mine left much to be desired. So, when they found a nearby senior center that had fabulous pancake breakfasts on Saturdays, they would arrange for us to join them. On some very difficult nights, Ele would tell me not to worry because she wanted her pancakes on Saturday. Almost more important to me was the assurance that the Leonards were there to help in times of emergency—and there were many such times in those fateful years.

The Leonards also took us many evenings to dinner at Edie and Joe Bercher's home. Edie worked with the international program for exchange of high school students and frequently had foreign students living at her home, and Joe was a colleague in the YMCA support group, Ysmen. Conversing with the foreign students always awakened Ele's interest, and evenings with the Berchers raised her spirits.

We had a special affection for St. Milt. Whenever we encountered a problem at our house, she would tell me to call St. Milt—she knew that he never failed her. He always dropped by whenever he was in the neighborhood to check on Ele and sometimes stayed to buoy her up or tell her an amusing story. St. Milt took us into his family and made sure that Ele was always welcome. When she felt she needed to go to Tulare, the County Court House in Visalia, or the Pixley farm on business, she would ask him if he was available, and I never remember him saying no.

Another close friend who became a constant source of support for Ele was our neighbor, Melissa Hill. As a lawyer and adviser to Kings County judges, Melissa brought a level of professional discussion to our home that Ele truly enjoyed. Melissa often dropped in after work to say hello, and frequently suggested outings that might be of interest to Ele. Sometimes she persuaded Ele to go out for lunches or early dinners or to the dinner theater in Fresno that once was home to Audra McDonald. Melissa invited us for a very special evening in Hanford when she put on a one-woman show at the old jail in downtown Hanford.

Melissa was a member of Rotary and arranged for me to speak at a Rotary luncheon on inter-American relations. At that meeting, I met Dean Osterling, the program chair, and found that his wife's, Barbara, and his interests in international relations and travel coincided with ours, and led to many events we spent together. He introduced me to his daughter, Lisa, and she chose me to be an adviser on her high school paper on Latin America. Dean and Barbara also arranged invitations for me to speak periodically at Rotary luncheons, churches and civic groups. His invitation for me to join Rotary had to be declined because of my concerns for Ele's health.

Whenever the Fredericksons came to Tulare to visit their mothers, they dropped by to see us, and we would go out to dinner. Ele loved to talk politics with David and Margaret and hear the latest gossip from the nation's capital. David worked out of his office in the National Press Club Building and was involved in the Bush advance planning team in 1999 and 2000. Living in Hanford, we felt quite isolated from the "big picture" since our neighbors seemed primarily interested in the local events. David and Margaret were one of our few remaining links to the environment we had become accustomed to when living in Washington, D.C.

David called me one morning in the spring of 1998, about the time my relationship with CEDEJU was terminating, and asked whether I would join a small group of specialists that he was bringing together to prepare a proposal for the government of Panama to celebrate the reversion of the Canal Zone to Panamanian sovereignty and the centenary of its independence. His group had been approached by a prominent Panamanian official, close to then President of Panama Ernesto Pérez Balladares, and asked its assistance for planning a year of national celebration Although I was skeptical of the request, the idea excited me and gave me something positive to work on that related to Latin America. Over the next eighteen months, I contributed to David's team by long distance with suggestions about Panamanians to contact, activities to include, and timing of events. I involved Ele and she helped me remember sites and personalities that enriched my suggestions. Unfortunately, the group's proposal was not completed until after the 1999 election in Panama and the president-elect, Mireya Moscoso had a different perception of how to celebrate the reversion and the centenary of Panama's independence. Although it was stillborn, Ele and I had had a lot of fun with the project.

The Fredricksons also arranged for us to receive an invitation to the University of the Pacific to attend the festivities in Stockton to honor Lech Walesa, the past president of Poland and hero of the

Polish Solidarity Movement. I hired a car for the drive to Stockton, and helped Ele pick out a new evening suit for the formal dinner. Half way to Stockton, Ele became disoriented and fell ill. When we got to our Marriott hotel, I had to put Ele to bed and call for a doctor. He gave her medicine, but she did not improve. When David in tux and Margaret in dinner dress knocked on the door to take us to dinner, it took Margaret one minute to appraise the situation. Margaret told David and me to go the dinner and she would monitor Ele. I was presented to President Walesa and we talked a few minutes about his years as a union leader and the popular movement that ended communist rule. I excused myself before dinner and rushed back to replace Margaret. Ele then fell into a deep sleep and seemed better in the morning. I withdrew from attending the meeting of President Walesa with the faculty and Advisory Council of the School of International Studies, and took Ele back to our doctor in Hanford who ran some tests and seemed baffled at what was going on in Ele's system.

Another friend who called us regularly from Washington was David Lazar. He was one of the few people whose judgment Ele trusted and felt she could rely on. When he would call, she would always tell me not to hang up until she had a chance to talk to him. One day in 1999, David called to say that he and Valerie Estes, later his second wife, were coming to Hanford for a visit. When they arrived, Ele's face dropped as she looked at him. Then she picked herself up and we went to dinner at Hanford's Imperial Dynasty Restaurant that for many years had been one of the few five star Chinese restaurants in the country. The Imperial Dynasty was in decline—its distinguished owner had died and the chef had moved to San Francisco—but we had a warm and intimate dinner. We talked about politics and foreign affairs, with David leaving the table occasionally for a cigarette. Ele lectured him as she had for nearly twenty-five years about smoking too much. David listened as he had so many times before—and at one point said that it was too late. When we said good night and we closed the door, Ele said to me tearfully, "David came to say goodbye. He is dying of lung cancer. We are about to lose one of our closest friends." David endured the cancer for several years, but he worried about Ele as much as she worried about him.

Every time there was a trip organized by the Hanford Historical Society, I talked Ele into participating. I encouraged her to join excursions to neighboring Valley cities and towns and would arrange for seats in the front of the bus that minimized the strain on her energies. I often took a wheel chair so that I could ensure that she would see the points of interest at each stop. I induced her to agree to go on a several-day visit to Los Angeles, Long Beach, and Catalina Island, by reminding her of her grandmother's love of Long Beach and of her experience there during the great earthquake of 1933. She made the trip well—with frequent bathroom stops. We stayed on the Queen Mary for several days while we took day trips to Catalina Island, the Getty Villa Museum, and to the beach nearby where she and her grandmother had spent so many happy hours when she was a youngster. On the way back to Hanford, we stopped at the Gene Autry Western Museum and the Norton Simon Gallery in Pasadena—how she savored the Raphael at the Norton Simon! When we got back to Hanford, she just conked out for several days.

In spite of the troubles whenever she traveled, Ele still longed to take trips. In early 2001, after looking at her art books, she asked me if I would take her to the Hermitage in St. Petersburg, whose Impressionists hanging there had caught her eye. I found a Baltic cruise on Holland America in mid-August that started in Copenhagen, went to St. Petersburg, and ended in Harwich, England. I reserved a cabin for a handicapped passenger, and Holland America arranged to provide meals that met her medical requirements. I purchased business class airfare and reserved a wheelchair for her at the airports. When I told my cousin Susannah and her husband Jay about our plans, they invited us to spend a week with them in Oxford; so I hired a car to take us from Harwich to Oxford. We spent four months buying Elle clothes for the trip and accumulating medical supplies she needed. She was delighted.

The trip did not go as planned. The flight over was long but comfortable. However, when we arrived in Copenhagen, our bags were not to be found. All I had in the hand luggage was a couple of changes of underclothes and her medications. The bags had not been found when we boarded the ship. Holland America located them in San Francisco and delivered them at our first port of call—

Tallinn, Estonia. We had needed a change of clothing since ours were wrinkled and dirty, and the ship gave us a clothing allowance to get a few essentials aboard ship. I made the purchases and gave Ele a bath before dinner.

The biggest disappointment came when I tried to buy Ele's tour of the Hermitage. We learned that the Hermitage had no facilities for handicapped people, not even an elevator to the second or third floors. They would not sell us a tour for Ele since they felt she could not manage the steep stairs, especially the flight up to the Impressionist collection on the third floor. Ele was very upset—doubly so that Holland America had not alerted us to problem before we bought the tickets.

We took shore excursions at each port of call. The first was Tallinn's medieval city and its great park where we witnessed a youth festival celebrating the independence of Estonia from the Soviet Union. We noted that many of the businesses had signs in both Estonian and Russian, and that there were vestiges of the Russian presence throughout the city—for after all, St. Petersburg was just a hop, skip, and jump away.

St. Petersburg, the imperial city, its cathedrals, small museums, and fortress caught our fancy, but all Ele could see of the Hermitage was its main entrance and the steep staircase she could not ascend. Ele rested in our cabin while I spent two hours navigating the Hermitage in the tow of a guide who "kept us moving." Frankly, after seeing the exhibits of Impressionists in Paris, London, and Washington, I was not impressed with the way the Hermitage displayed its treasures. Some wonderful paintings just did not have adequate settings. I gave Ele my impressions at dinner that night, but she did not disguise her disappointment.

Our third port of call was Helsinki and we toured the parks, the unique seaport area, the government center, and some comfortable suburbs; it seemed to be a city designed for people to live well. It rained at Visby and Stockholm, so Ele stayed aboard ship while I took city tours. Then the weather cleared and we had bright sunshine again at Warnemunde, Germany, as we made a half-day excursion along the Baltic coast. Back in Denmark, we took the tour to Odense to visit the birthplace of Hans Christian Andersen—and what a mistake that turned out to be! Odense is not a particularly picturesque spot, and the area around Hans Christian Andersen's home is paved with stones; for Ele in her wheel chair, it was sheer torture to be pushed over them. We tried walking, but their unevenness made it almost impossible for her to move. She wept all the way back to the ship. She needed a chiropractor, but all the ship's doctor could give her were some painkillers that did no good. When we reached Oslo the next day, she just stayed in the cabin.

When the cruise ended, we rode two hours to Susannah and Jay's Oxford bungalow. Susannah had rented a wheel chair for Ele and had the spare bedroom all set up for her. Unfortunately, with her bad back, she was in pain; but we had a fine evening of just talking and resting. Over the next several days we visited Blenheim Palace and many of the colleges and memorable spots in and around Oxford. With Ele's back still bothering her, we declined Susannah's suggestion that we stay on a bit longer and flew back as scheduled from London to Boston two weeks before 9/11.

Boston was a near disaster. I gave the wheel chair attendant twenty dollars to get us through customs and to the Delta gate for the connecting flight to Salt Lake City. He took us to the curb and said that the connecting flight was in a building up the hill to our left and that he had ordered a car to pick us up to take us there. We waited a half an hour but no car came and the time was fast approaching for our connecting flight to leave. A Boston policeman had been watching us and came over to ask me, "What's your problem?" On learning our situation, he stopped an airport vehicle and helped put Ele and me aboard. I suspect that the policeman or the driver called Delta because we were met at the entrance to the building and taken directly to the departure gate without going through the usual security checks. We arrived at the gate just ten minutes before departure. Ele was shaking as I settled her into her seat. We reached Hanford at 2:00 a.m. the following morning, and Ele was too tired to talk or eat.

The next morning I made an appointment with a chiropractor to treat her back. He immediately relieved her physical pain, but it took three more treatments before she could walk comfortably again. Needless to say, the cruise did not turn out as we had planned. Ele and I watched the horrors of September 11, 2001 on television. She quietly said to me, "We could have been at Logan

Airport if we had stayed on in Oxford as Susannah and Jay had suggested."

She remained weak and tired. I took her back to the doctor for more tests and examinations. He kept telling me that he could find no reason for her continuing inertia and lack of appetite. He made an appointment with a kidney specialist who, after examining Ele, warned me to adhere to a low-salt, no-potassium diet, but gave me no particulars about her problems. I was told to get her interested in new activities and to convince her that she needed to walk and exercise more. I was depressed and frustrated.

In the fall, we received an invitation from the Museo in Denver to return for the opening of a new exhibit of items from Ele's collection. We flew to Denver for a few days with the boys. Ele cut the ribbon to the now named Tragen Gallery of Latin American Folk Art, and saw an enchanting presentation of some of her favorite ceramic, textile, and silver handicrafts that lit up her eyes once again. She smiled as she moved from one area of the gallery to another.

The remaining days in Denver turned cold, and we stayed close to home except for a visit that Ray arranged to a nursery that specialized in growing poinsettias for Christmas. We took several shots of Ele sitting among the exquisite array of red, pink, white, and green flowers, reminding us of Christmas in Central America where poinsettias grow wild along the highway.

We returned to Hanford before Thanksgiving. On hearing of our return, Barbara and Dean Osterling invited us to join their family for the celebration. Ele was not doing well, but I decided to accept the invitation. Unfortunately, Ele had a bad day and could hardly sit up; the Osterlings helped her to settle down in a bedroom during dinner. What genuine affection the Osterlings showed Ele that day in spite of the burden the Tragens had added to their family occasion.

Ele perked up over the next couple of weeks and told everyone of her pleasure of seeing the exhibit in Denver and the thoughtfulness of the Osterlings. She seemed almost back to normal when we joined the Leonards for church one Sunday morning as the Christmas season started. She responded happily to family dinners with the Berchers and St. Milt during the season. She was smiling all through Christmas with the Leonards and the Berchers. While Ele tired quickly, she seemed to have enjoyed every minute. I had high hopes that her health was beginning to improve at last and that she would be ready for a wonderful, healthful 2002.

34

One Final Move

2002 opened on a happy note in spite of the thick Tule fogs and the sad aftermath of 9/11. Ele had truly enjoyed Christmas and seemed more eager to see people and go out than she had been for a long time. Her doctor reported that her medicals showed no further deterioration in her condition and, when he suggested additional exercises, she responded favorably. We had long discussions about our plans for the future, the status of our investments, and the U.S. political scene as the Bush administration reacted to 9/11. She was up almost every day and looked forward to her weekly trip to the mall and her hairdresser. We went to the movies a couple of times with the Leonards. Melissa took us to Fresno for a dinner theater and Ele held up well. Ele joined me in going to the Presbyterian Church when I was invited to give a talk about Latin America. When Melissa invited us to accompany her on a trip to her family home in Ventura, Ele said yes and remarked that she had not been there for many years; Ele even offered to help Melissa in working out some family problems.

Everything seemed to be upbeat that spring until the real estate agent called to say that the tenant in one of the Tulare houses was several months delinquent in paying the rent, and recommended that Ele start legal action to evict. Ele asked St. Milt to take us over to Tulare so that she could talk face-to-face with the agent. It was a beautiful spring day on which we went over for the discussion. Ele agreed to start eviction action and to use the attorney suggested by the agent.

As we were leaving, she decided that she wanted to check her apartment at the back of the house. We had refurbished it with leftover furniture. On entering the driveway, Ele said that something was wrong. Milt and I went over to the apartment and found that it had been stripped bare. There was no mess this time, just an empty space except for the heavy sofa and chair and the small refrigerator. It looked as if a moving van had systematically taken out the beds, chairs, tables, and personal belongings that we had arranged there. We tried to keep Ele in the car, but she insisted that she see for herself and she was visibly upset.

We returned to the real estate agent's office and Ele asked who had been checking on the houses and when. The record showed that the agent had found everything in place the preceding Friday when she entered the apartment. Then we checked Tulare police records that showed no unusual activity at the address since last Friday. So, there was no negligence on part of the agent. But how could a moving van or U-Haul take so many items out of the apartment without anyone noticing? After all, both houses were rented and the tenants were in town. We filed a claim with the insurance company.

We were both very upset, but Ele did not seem as traumatized as she had been during the terrible break-in in March 1995. This time, when we got back to Hanford, she quietly said, "I never want to go near the Tulare houses again. This is the time to sell them."

Ele put the houses up for sale shortly thereafter. She never visited them again. When they were finally sold after several months on the market for prices well below what we thought they were worth, she showed no emotion. She later told me in San Diego that she had never wanted to return to live in Tulare, but the houses were her safety net. If anything happened to me, she knew that she could afford to live in them on social security and our retirement income.

A few days after the second Tulare burglary, Melissa told us that she ready to make the trip to her family home in Ventura. With the overhang of the Tulare robbery, I thought it would be a good idea and talked Ele into going.

The trip started out well. I was up front with Melissa, but half way Ele was clearly unwell. Melisa suggested that we turn back, but Ele urged her to continue the trip. When we reached Ventura, I put her to bed in the bedroom on the main floor of Melissa's century old redwood mansion. I gave her medications and she fell sound asleep. I thought that she was just worn out. But, Ele did not respond and we canceled the sightseeing that we had talked about in Hanford. Ele loved being back at the ocean; and, when Melissa told us that she planned to move back to Ventura in the fall, Ele asked whether there were any senior living facilities that we might look at. So, we looked at several. All were for assisted living, and they did not appeal to us. On the trip back to Hanford, Ele seemed to rest quietly. After a shower and dinner, she fell into an uneasy sleep.

The next morning when I brought her breakfast, I asked if she had enjoyed the visit to Ventura. She looked quizzingly at me and asked, "What visit? I haven't been to Ventura in years." I reminded her of the problems she had had on the trip. She remembered our getting into the car but nothing else. This was the first time that I had become conscious that Ele was suffering from mental black-outs.

When I called our GP to tell him of Ele's black-out, he asked me to bring her in that afternoon for a check-up. He could find no medical cause for the condition I had reported. Then and there, I knew that I needed to get better medical care and chided myself for having waited so long to reach this conclusion. The next few weeks Ele's constitution seemed to be deteriorating. Almost every few days, I took her to doctors who kept reassuring me that they noted no significant change in her condition. I was increasingly skeptical of that diagnosis when she no longer seemed able to get to the bathroom by herself. I remember changing many a bed in the middle of the night.

Then, one evening in early September, Ele had a bad night. She could not get up and she wasn't responding to my efforts to help her. So I called 911 and the emergency crew helped me get her settled. She refused to go to the hospital emergency room, and I called a caregiver to help me through the night. The caregiver told me of a lady doctor who she thought was one of the best in Hanford. She warned me that the doctor was not taking any new patients and kept only limited office hours because of family commitments.

When I called the doctor's office, she agreed to see Ele if I could bring her there by 11:00 a.m. I called St. Milt and he agreed to take us to the appointment. After an initial examination, the lady doctor said that Ele was in critical condition and called for an ambulance. She told me that her kidneys were barely functioning. The next two weeks Ele was hospitalized. Twice in the first week, I received early morning calls from the hospital asking that I come immediately because of Ele's critical condition. Ele was not a cooperative patient and balked at being awakened at 1:00 a.m. for a procedure or lab test. I got calls from angry nurses once or twice asking me to ask Ele to cooperate. Thanks to that wonderful lady doctor , she improved enough to come home at the end of the second week.

When Ele came home, I hired a caregiver to come every day to help me. Ele had lost a great deal of weight and she seemed to have shrunk in size. I think that she knew how close a call it had been when she asked me to call Mimi Hoffman for what she called a last visit.

That same day, I talked to the boys in Denver about Ele's deteriorating health. I asked them if they could come to California and help me move from Hanford to some place with access to better medical care. They agreed to come as soon as they could arrange their schedules. Gary agreed to make an Internet search of medical facilities and senior living communities from La Jolla to Santa Barbara.

Thus began the last move of our life together.

The Choice Is San Diego

In early November, the boys drove us to La Jolla. Gary's Internet search had revealed several possible senior communities located near medical centers. We ruled out Los Angeles since I did not drive. The most promising appeared to be in the San Diego area, close to the highly recommended Scripps Medical complex and the medical school at the University of California San Diego.

As we drove to San Diego, we eliminated visits to the large-scale, widely-dispersed senior housing developments and narrowed the search to those that were more compact, with medical faciliteis not too far away. Ray took care of Ele on the trip, practically cradling her. It took much longer than we anticipated because of frequent stops for Ele's bathroom needs. I had contacted Sally Phipps Korkowski, the daughter of our dear Mexican friend Helene Phipps

Tubbs, who lived in San Diego, to help us locate facilities and possible medical care since she worked for Scripps Hospital in its program for counseling cancer patients.

When we arrived at our hotel, we had to wheelchair Ele to bed. Sally agreed to help us find appropriate medical care at Scripps if we chose to move there, but she was not knowledgeable about senior communities

The next day we looked at two facilities that appeared to meet our needs. The first was a an elegant high-rise building with two-bedroom units, dining room, exercise room, health care center, transportation, and all the requisites that met our needs. It offered continuing medical care for life, with accommodations for independent living, assisted living, and full-time care. We had lunch there and I was told that, even if we selected an apartment, it was likely that we would be assigned to an assisted-living unit in light of Ele's condition and that the management, not the Tragens, would make that decision.

The second was the Pacific Regent La Jolla, also an elegant high-rise. It was an independent-living senior condominium in which one purchased a condo and took care of one's own health requirements. It was located just five minutes from both Scripps and UCSD medical centers, had a dining room, exercise room, and other amenties. I could buy a unit and take care of Ele as I felt appropriate. We had to cancel other visits because Ele was too tired to continue.

For the next three days, we visited facilities in Carlsbad, Dana Point, Ventura, Montecito, and Santa Barbara, but none was more convenient for our purposes than the Pacific Regent La Jolla. We sought advice from friends along the way—I House friend, Tilak Lall, in Dana Point and Melissa in Ventura—but Ele didn't seem to recognize them.

When we returned to Hanford Friday morning, we put Ele to bed and sat down with her in the bedroom to discuss our reaction to the trip. All of us, including Ele, thought that our best bet was the Pacific Regent La Jolla and, with Sally's help, signing on with a first-rate specialist at Scripps. So, I called the marketing office at the Pacific Regent and asked if I could purchase the unit they had shown us but was advised that it had sold. However, another unit, suite 1303, would become available on December 1. I looked at Gary and he nodded to take it. So sight unseen, I agreed to the purchase and arranged to take possession after January 1, 2003.

My big chore was to bring together the money needed to pay for our new home. We had to sell the Hanford house in a down property market. We arranged for a secured loan with Bank of America. We sold some stocks and most of the gold coins that Ele had collected at bargain prices. By the end of December, we had accumulated enough to pay for our new home.

The last two months in Hanford were an almost daily crisis. I had a caregiver in every day to tend Ele. The lady doctor who had saved Ele's life recommended a kidney specialist in Visalia, and St. Milt drove us over a couple of times to see him. He practiced holistic medicine and believed that diet was key to Ele's recovery, even from her badly damaged kidneys. He gave me hope.

Packing up was exclusively my job. I had to segregate our belongings into several different categories. First, we were moving from a fairly large town house to an apartment of less than 1,100 square feet. I had to select what would go with us and what we would consign to an auction company to dispose of. Second, I had to select the clothing; not only was closet space limited, but Ele had gone from a size 12 to an 8 petite—she had a closet full of elegant clothes and scores of shoes with heels that she could never wear again. Third, I had to select those items that should be sent to Denver for the Museo to be added to the Latin American handicraft collection. Fourth, Ele's mother had collected American Indian memorabilia, and I had to find a collector who would treasure them as Ele's mother had.

When we emptied the house, we sent a moving van full of items to the auction house in Visalia, shipped several crates to Denver, gave several hundred books to the Friends of the Hanford Library, forty-eight boxes of clothing and linens to the Salvation Army, sold Ele's baby grand piano, found a judge who collected American Indian art and artifacts, and loaded a moving van for La Jolla. When we got to our new home, we barely fit it all in.

Our friends, especially the Leonards, St. Milt, the Osterlings, the Hummasons, and the Berchers, did everything they could to make those last two months as pleasant as possible. They had us to Thanksgiving and Christmas dinners, took us to church on occasion, and helped me through my daily chores. The caregiver stayed with us until the minute we left for La Jolla. The cavalcade of work and care of those two months was made bearable by the kindness of friends.

The Pacific Regent La Jolla

Gary flew out from Denver to help me bring Ele back to San Diego. He hired a car for Ele's convenience and made her comfortable in the back seat for the five-hour drive from Hanford to La Jolla, with plenty of time for necessary rest stops. We rented rooms at a small hotel for a couple of nights while Gary and I set up the furniture and made the space habitable for Ele.

When we finally moved her into the Pacific Regent, Ele looked around as if she had never been there before. She seemed totally disoriented and dismayed. She wanted to go back to her bed in Hanford. That first night in La Jolla, she literally shook. I held her for several minutes until she calmed down. She asked why I had brought her to "this place." I tried to remind her that we had visited the building some weeks earlier and that she had agreed that this was a good choice for us to live and to give her access to the medical care she needed. She looked at me and cried, "I have never been here before. I haven't been to San Diego since I was a teenager. I have never been on a trip from La Jolla to Santa Barbara."

The next morning she woke me to say that she wanted to go back to Hanford, to her own home. I tried to remind her that we had sold the home. She demanded that I buy it back. I knew that the purchase agreement with Pacific Regent gave us sixty days to cancel and to have the money fully refunded.

So, I called Dan Humason in Hanford and asked for his help. The next day he called back to say that the new owner would not sell, even at a profit since they for health reasons needed a house on one level. Dan then offered to help me find another house in Hanford. When I explained the situation to Ele, she said that she wanted to go back and trusted Dan to find an appropriate house. Dan called on Friday to say that he had located an elegant house that met our needs: all on one floor, two large bedrooms, modern kitchen and lovely living room. Ele and I had been to dinner at the house, and she had thought it beautiful. Dan said that the owner needed cash and would sell at a steep discount. Ele seemed pleased and said that she would like to live in that house. Dan promised to approach the owner on Monday.

That night, we were invited to dinner by two lovely ladies, Clara Wertz and Roselle Silberstein. Ele and the ladies engaged in lively conversation about politics, foreign affairs, and other topics. I had not seen Ele so animated for some time. She slept quietly that night and seemed quite content when I got her up that morning. Saturday evening we had dinner with another couple who had moved to La Jolla from the San Joaquin Valley, and Ele had another lively conversation about the differences in life in San Diego compared to the Valley. She seemed quite happy when I put her to bed. Sunday night, we had dinner with a group of long-time residents of the Pacific Regent and they talked about activities sponsored by the homeowners association, including visits to local museums and occasional excursions to nearby points of interest. When I took Ele upstairs that night, she was very contemplative and completely at ease.

The following morning, she woke me about 6:00 a.m., and asked me, "Can we afford to live here?" I replied that we certainly could. She asked, "Can we continue to save money for our old age?" I replied that we were in our old age and had enough monthly cash flow to be solvent for the rest of our lives. Then she said, "I think I'll stay. No need to go back to Hanford." Dan understood when I called him early that Monday morning.

Thus began our life in San Diego. Making friends was a wonderful experience at the Pacific Regent La Jolla. They enriched our lives, making certain that we were included in birthday dinners, family parties, and other events. They made Ele very happy and made both of us feel that we belonged. I took her to the concerts, play-readings, and other on-site events at the Pacific Regent. I encouraged her to go every night to the dining room for dinner, and invited neighbors and friends who lived nearby to join us. It gave Ele great pleasure in that last phase of her life and earned my eternal gratitude.

Ele and I settled into a routine. Thanks to Sally Korkowski, we quickly found a lady doctor specialist in internal medicine, noted for her diagnostic ability. She ran tests and asked the kidney specialist at Scripps to examine Ele. She again was not an easy patient. I had to accompany her to all the examinations and tests, and frequently had to cajole her into cooperating with the technicians.

Her medical problems seemed to escalate and diversify. Her gums became infected and her lovely teeth decayed. She lost weight in spite of the special diets that the doctors prescribed. She was perennially listless and slept up to fourteen hours a day. It was my job, as her caregiver, to get her up and around and to try to stimulate her interest and her will to overcome. Her new doctors were quite up front with me. They told me that she was a very ill lady and that she needed great care. The kidney specialist emphasized diet control and told me that more radical treatment was unwise in view of her overall health.

During 2003, we spent a good deal of time with Sally. She joined us for dinner at least once a week during the first half of the year. She also took us for rides and showed Ele different areas of San Diego County. She often joined us when Ele had a medical appointment at Scripps. Ele loved having her around as it reminded her of Sally's mother and the good times that she and Ele had had enjoyed for so many years.

Then, one morning, Sally's daughter called to say that her mother had suffered a stroke and was in intensive care at Scripps. When I told Ele, I watched her face drop and her eyes tear up. Sally was another link to a much happier past, and I sensed that Ele saw this news as another sad omen. I went to the hospital to join four of Sally's five children who assembled from various parts of California. I spent much of the next few days with them as Sally's condition worsened and they made the decision to remove life support. Rachel Noble, a friend on the staff of the Pacific Regent, sat with Ele while I was away. Each time I returned to Ele with the depressing news, she looked stoically ahead and said very little.

Ele was too fragile to attend the memorial service, but one of Sally's daughters and our long-time friend Billie Heller came by to see Ele after the service. All of us noted how deeply the passing had affected Ele.

Throughout 2003 and 2004, Ele was not getting any better.

Everything was a major effort for her, but we maintained the routine of going to dinner every evening. For dinner, I would bring down a pillow because she had lost so much size that she had difficulty reaching the table from her chair. She also got tired and seldom could last through dessert. So, I would bring her upstairs, settle her in bed, turn on the TV and return downstairs for my dessert.

Those were the years in which the outside of our twenty-four story building was in remediation to replace its skin because of a mold problem. For most of 2004, the building had a plastic cover over it that obstructed our view and access to sunlight. I tried to have an array of activities and TV shows to brighten Ele's day and divert her attention from the gloomy plastic enveloping our windows. Neighbors dropped by and stayed with her whenever I had to leave the apartment for more than a few minutes. Even the workman doing the remediation showed Ele great respect, and even lent a hand to help her whenever they had to work in our unit—and it never hurt that she always spoke to them in Spanish.

Given Ele's health, travel was out of the question. But I wanted her to believe that we might soon go on a trip. She lit up whenever I suggested that we revisit the Museo in Denver. When I proposed joining a group of fellow residents of the Pacific Regent on voyages to Alaska or Rio, she asked me to bring her maps and to point out the ports on the itinerary. When I raised the possibility of a trip to China, she got really excited. While we did some planning for longer trips, our experience with short outings showed how fragile she had become. She in her wheelchair went on day-long excursions to the Getty Museum in Los Angeles and the art museum in Santa Ana, but neither one went well as she tired quickly. I took her with me in 2003 to a luncheon with our fellow retired foreign service officers, but she had trouble sitting up through the program that followed lunch. After those experiences, she would opt out of invitations outside of the building. She would say, "You go." I usually didn't, but if I felt I needed to attend, I would arrange for someone to sit with her during my absence.

I also tried to shield her from problems and began to handle most of our investment challenges. I consulted her, but she seemed increasingly oblivious to developments. One problem I did have to involve her in was our 2003 federal income tax return. I had always prepared our annual declaration and never had a serious problem arise in fifty-five years, and Ele was adamant that no outsider should be privy to our tax information,

In 2003, I had my first encounter with the AMT, the Alternative Minimum Tax, and I misinterpreted the instructions. I think it was August when I got a letter from the IRS advising me that I had not complied with the AMT requirements and owed a lot of money, with penalties and interest. "If you wish to speak with an IRS agent about this letter, call this number." I did and made contact with a knowledgeable agent who immediately understood my problem and spent almost a full day working with me in preparing an appropriate amendment. He called mine a common misunderstanding, and gave me an address to send the correction with a check for amount due, plus interest, but no penalties. The IRS accepted my amendment, for which I was and am grateful.

That experience convinced me that I could no longer handle our income tax filing by myself. Through a friend, I was introduced to John Massey, his tax adviser. Over Ele's objections, I invited John to come by. When he did a few days later and after we discussed our situation, I left him with Ele. John and Ele talked for nearly a half an hour while I did some other paperwork. When I rejoined them, John and Ele had bonded. She trusted him and then and there authorized me to use John as our financial and tax adviser. Since then, John has guided me through the tax jungle.

One consistent source of pleasure in Ele's life was the weekly phone call from the boys in Denver every Sunday afternoon. Ele looked forward to talking to them and hearing about their adventures until in mid-2004, when she began to have trouble holding the phone because her fingers had shrunk so much. So, I would sit on the bed and relay the conversation to her.

One Monday morning, Gary made a quite unexpected call. He told me that the Museo de las Américas, the recipient of Ele's Latin American handicraft collection, was on the verge of bankruptcy and was considering closing its doors. Gary, as our representative on the board of the Museo, was very concerned about the fate of Ele's collection. Lack of fiscal discipline and over-optimistic income expectations had led to the crisis. Like so many small non-profits, the Museo had anticipated faster income growth and purchased properties for expansion; those mortgages were eating up the Museo's limited resources. Gary asked for instructions about segregating Ele's collection and moving it to another museum.

When I explained the situation to Ele, she just stared for a moment and then lamented that she was too "weary" to undertake a search for a new home for the collection and asked me what we might do to help save the Museo. I reviewed all our available assets with her, and we agreed that we could offer our accumulated E and EE U.S. Treasury Bonds. She then said, "Call Gary and ask him to work out a plan for putting the Museo on a sound financial basis and offer our bonds as the incentive to keep the Museo going."

While I checked on the tax consequences of giving E and EE bonds to the Museo, Gary worked with the board on a financial plan to save it, including the sale of properties not in current use and the adoption of stringent control over expenditures.

I discovered that gifting the bonds had serious income tax consequences because, on redeeming them, all of interest accumulated over the life of the bonds was subject to income tax as ordinary income. So, we set up a multi-year plan for cashing in the bonds and transferring the funds to the Museo. Ele and I agreed to redeem a fixed amount per year until the bonds were all cashed in, on condition that the Museo adhere to a stringent financial management plan. We also stipulated that the income from the redeemed bonds be deposited in an endowment administered by a third party, with only the annual income from the endowment available for use by the Museo. Gary was elected treasurer to oversee the initial implementation of the agreement. The Museo was kept alive and it has recovered.

We had barely finished the arrangements with the Museo when the tenant on the Pixley farm called to tell us that he was running low on water. The pump was set down at 520 feet and the well was running dry. Under the farm rental agreement, the Tragens were responsible for supplying the well water. We authorized him to bring in experts from the Edison Company and a well company to check the situation.

He reported a few days later that the stream from which we were drawing our water was running dry, and that the next possible source of water was a stream at below 600 feet. The cost for digging the well would be $16.00 a linear foot, but there was no assurance that an adequate water supply would be obtained at 600 feet. If we mortgaged the farm, we could probably raise $200,000 at 7 or 9 percent interest to begin the work as soon as the well digging company could fit us into its already overloaded schedule. Frankly, the cost overwhelmed us.

Then, I recalled a similar situation that a friend in Tulare had faced a couple of years earlier. He contacted the University of California/Davis and arranged to give the farm to the university— problems and all. The university found a purchaser who paid for the farm and took responsibility for repairs. In turn, the university set up a charitable remainder trust, with income for the donor for life and, on his death, the corpus would be used for a specified university program. I talked to Ele about the possibility, and she said that she preferred such a solution to our spending $200,000 on digging a new well.

So, I called the UC Berkeley Law School and offered to gift the ranch to help fund the agreement we had signed in 2002. I was put in touch with university's farm specialist who asked me to send him relevant information about the farm, the name of a USDA farm agent knowledgeable about the farm, and details about the soil and production history. Within a week, I was advised that we had a deal with a dairy farmer in the San Fernando Valley, who had sold his land to a developer and was looking for a new location for his dairy. Ele's reaction to the deal was subdued as she realized in less than one month, she had divested herself of another part of her roots.

The Last Few Months

2005 burst upon us with much promise. Ele and I went to the Pacific Regent's gala New Year's Eve party. Ele wore an elegant new dinner pants suit and I, my tux. Ele joined us in a glass of champagne before she retired for the evening. She seemed in be in good fettle when we attended two or three special musical programs in January and February. She went to every dinner for the first several weeks of the year and actively joined in conversations about recent developments in the Middle East and their impact on the U.S. financial markets.

I especially wanted Ele to have a memorable birthday. So I planned a special dinner for her eighty-third birthday on April 1, 2005. I invited several good friends—Ben and Polly Holmes, Roselle Silberstein, and Clara Wertz—to join us at dinner that night. On the afternoon of April 1, I took Ele to the beauty salon for a new hairdo and manicure, while Ben and I bought flowers for the table and a special dessert. As I was leaving the beauty shop, the attendant called for me to come back. Ele had passed out in the chair. We called 911 and Ele was revived. This was the second time in two weeks that she had passed out and I convinced Ele that she go to the ER.

Ben Holmes, a retired physician approaching his hundredth birthday, joined me in the emergency room. After nearly two hours, the ER doctor told us Ele's condition was critical and that her personal physician and the Scripps kidney specialist had been summoned. They also recommended that Ele be given a pacemaker as quickly as possible and undergo some other minor surgery to correct a small problem they had identified. Ben consulted with the ER specialist and then advised me to agree. To my questions about the causes of the two recent blackouts, the ER doctor thought that a pacemaker could help her avoid future blackouts and that, with a pacemaker, she should be going home in a few days. So, I agreed that Scripps go ahead.

I spent most of the weekend with her at Scripps Memorial Hospital. Neighbors at the Pacific Regent drove me to Scripps whenever I needed to go. She only poked at her food and was awake only for brief periods. The parade of nurses and technicians kept waking her and making her very cranky. Giving blood was especially painful because the technicians could not find her veins. While I was with her, I could calm her down and let the technician do his job.

On Monday they inserted the pacemaker. One of the doctors told me that she had not handled the anesthesia well. The kidney specialist came in for a special examination and some blood tests. I sat with Ele as she came out of the anesthesia.

On Tuesday she was given a battery of tests and examinations under the direction of the kidney specialist. I waited in the room while she was taken from one lab to another. I left her late that afternoon being prepped for minor surgery early Wednesday morning. Thursday I spent the day with her. She was semi-conscious and I left very uncertain about her prospects. Early Friday morning, I received a call from her lead physician asking me to please come at once to the hospital where I was told that Ele's body was shutting down and that there was no hope for recovery. She then asked me what I wanted the hospital and the doctors to do. I told the doctor to re-read Ele's medical power of attorney that instructed us to remove life support in such an eventuality as we were now facing. Ele looked up and smiled. I also told the doctor that I wanted Ele removed from the hospital as soon as possible and placed under hospice care to ease her last days. Then I just sat down to spend as much time as I could with my Ele. No one interrupted me, except a lab technician who came in to take blood samples, and whom I ordered out.

That evening, I called Dr. Doris Howell, the founder of the San Diego Hospice and a fellow resident at the Pacific Regent, and arranged for hospice care and a room at the health care center next door to the Pacific Regent. All that I needed was the release from the hospital and Doris would have a hospice nurse waiting for Ele. I phoned the boys and a few close friends and sent out emails to others. One longtime friend, Ana Rosa Cervantes, arranged to come down from Redondo Beach Sunday to say goodbye to Ele in person.

Saturday, I was in a daze. I went to the hospital expecting to oversee Ele's move to hospice care and was told that the paperwork for her departure was not ready. I left Ele semi-conscious about 5:00 p.m. About midnight, I was awakened by an angry nurse who complained that Ele was not cooperating again and would not allow the technician to extract blood. I blew up and screamed that Ele was dying and to leave her alone. The nurse was insistent and in a matter-of-fact tone insisted that I talk to Mrs. Tragen and ask her to cooperate. She gave Ele the phone. Ele angrily demanded, "Come take me home. I want a bath, and I want my hair done. Take me home or I will divorce you." Before I could reply, the phone was hung up. I dressed and called a cab. When I reached Ele's room, she had lapsed into a semi-coma from which she would never recover. I have never forgiven Scripps Memorial Hospital for the uncaring treatment given Ele in those critical hours.

I returned home before dawn Sunday morning and waited for Ana Rosa, her family, and my former Secretary Peggy Hook O'Rourke to arrive from Redondo Beach. Ele seemed unaware that we were in the room while they said their goodbyes.

The following morning, I called the hospital and was told that no instructions had been received to move the patient and that nothing could be done until her office received instructions from the doctor. I blew up. I then called our doctor's office and was told the doctor was not available. I blew up and recounted my Friday instructions that Ele be transferred to hospice care after I was told that her condition was hopeless. I think I yelled out the substance of the Saturday night conversation and demanded that the doctor take immediate action to remove Ele from the uncaring hospital.

I got to the hospital after 11:00 a.m. and went to the administration office where I was told quite matter-of-factly that no instructions had been received from our doctor. "Please check later."

I spent the day with Ele. I don't remember anyone coming into the room for a couple of hours until an administrative assistant came in to tell me that arrangements were being made for Ele's transfer, and asked for instructions about how and where to transfer her. I told her that I had given instructions to the doctor and the hospital administrator the preceding Friday. After the details were then written up, I kissed Ele good night and explained that I would see her later. I hoped she understood.

I rushed back to the Pacific Regent, confirmed the arrangements with hospice. Then I sat by the phone awaiting a call from the hospital. Finally, a call came at 4:30 p.m. advising me that the paperwork for Ele's discharge would not be ready until the following morning. I blew up again and called hospice.

Tuesday morning, about two hours later than scheduled, the ambulance finally brought Ele to hospice care. She was almost blue from the waist down. I went with her to a sunlit corner room where Ben and Doris joined me and helped me through the evening. Ele got her bath and a new hairdo. I sat by her side until midnight.

The next two days, Ele drifted from us. She ate or drank nothing and the hospice nurse told me it was a miracle that she was still alive. Ben and Doris were frequent visitors and were as dear to Ele and me as one could imagine. Before I left Ele Thursday night, I whispered to her that I might be late arriving Friday morning because I was to have a tooth extracted at 8:00 a.m. The hospice nurse promised to call me if there were any change.

Friday morning at dawn, I stopped by Ele's room en route to the dentist and I kissed her and said that I would be back right after the extraction. The hospice nurse said that she had barely moved during the night and that her vital signs were almost gone, but she had survived. I went to the dentist's and returned as quickly as I could. I told Ele that all had gone well and that I was fine. I kissed her and held her hand. Then I turned on her favorite daytime TV show, *The Price is Right* with Bob Barker. Halfway through the program, I looked over and she had stopped breathing. It was 10:30 a.m. on Friday, April 15, 2005. My soul mate, my better half, had passed.

The next few days were a whirl of sadness. I really wasn't sure what I should do. But I got great help. Hospice took care of the immediate arrangements for advising authorities, arranging for organ donations, and cremation. I informed family and friends, as well as the State Department and the insurance companies. Then I called our financial adviser, John Massey, who began to work with me on all the financial and tax details. So much of the planning that Ele and I had done presumed that I would die first, but now I had to make some difficult financial adjustments.

I wanted to have a private service in Ele's honor and memory. Ele had asked that she be buried in her mother's plot in Tulare. She also asked that there be no large service. So, I asked a friend at the Pacific Regent, Rev. Will Gotwald, a Lutheran Minister, to conduct a small memorial service, which about fifty neighbors and friends attended. Ben Holmes hosted a lunch at the Pacific Regent right after the service. It ended the saddest month of my life.

Over this period, the boys in Denver called almost every day to see how they could be helpful. I asked them to delay coming to San Diego until I was ready to take Ele's urn up to Tulare to be interred. I knew that I needed them at that most trying time in my life. Laying her to rest was the event I least wanted to do—much less alone.

The legal requirements a family faces at such a difficult time of one's life are extensive and not until I was fully engaged in my own did I realize how challenging they are. Fortunately, I had John

Massey to guide me and help me prepare all the documentation for the U.S. and California tax purposes. Since all of our assets were in the Tragen Trust, I needed to notify banks, brokers, county clerks, and corporations in which we held stock that Ele was being replaced as a trustee of the Tragen Family Trust by our nephew Gary Meyer, as Ele had ordained.

Gary and Ray flew in from Denver in late June and accompanied me to Tulare. Only a few friends were available for a brief graveside farewell. We had no ceremony or services, just a loving remembrance of the great lady who has been the central person in my life.

35

The Road Alone

In this last chapter of my life, I continue to live at the Pacific Regent La Jolla. Never a day goes by without my thinking about Ele or remembering some advice she gave me, or an incident with her that helped shape who I am, what I do, and why I act as I do. I remain committed to move forward the projects that Ele and I started together and to respect the principles that she and I established for us. This is my way of keeping her alive and with me. Time passes quickly, but memories are timeless.

I am grateful for my nephews Gary and Ray, my neighbors at Pacific Regent, and my colleagues from the Foreign Service and I House, as well as friends from Hanford, Tulare, and Visalia—friends have helped me fill the vacuum. They have enriched my life and strengthened my resolve to recount these experiences of Ele's and my life during our fifty-seven years of marriage.

Her spirit and interests led me to create and endow the Eleanor Dodson Tragen Award for the Foreign Service Spouse of the Year as my testimonial to the fact that I could not have done my job without Ele. It is a tribute to the contribution that she and other foreign service ladies have made to the Foreign Service and an incentive for today's foreign service spouses to continue the work of prior generations and use their talents to enhance the quality of life for the families of the Foreign Service today and tomorrow. The Award is open to all family partners—the spouses of today's Foreign Service with so many female, gay, and transgender officers.

Words cannot express my appreciation to DACOR (Department of State and Consular Officers Retired) for its endorsement of this proposal in 2006. My long-time friend and colleague, Richard

McKee, then DACOR's executive director, encouraged me to present it to the board, which adopted it and has administered it now for over a decade. The award is given annually at a ceremony at the State Department to a foreign service spouse who has made an outstanding contribution to the development, sustenance, and/or enhancement of the Foreign Service and the foreign service family. Nominations are requested from State Department offices around the world. The selection is made by a committee made up of Associates of the American Foreign Service Worldwide (formerly the American Association of Foreign Service Wives), the American Foreign Service Association (AFSA), the Family Liaison Office of the State Department, and DACOR.

I have participated in most of the award ceremonies, and have been delighted by the candidates selected. Some of the spouses were women with whom Ele worked; one was the husband of a foreign service officer, and another a pioneer in establishing the rights of gays, lesbians, and transgender to serve in the U.S. diplomatic corps. I know that Ele would be pleased to be associated with each of those recognized, and I am pleased that it will continue past my lifetime.

Moving Forward Our Lifetime Goals

In the last years of Ele's life, we set up the Tragen Family Trust and selected the three primary beneficiaries to receive its assets on my passing. I described in the last chapter how Ele and I made our choices. Not a day passes without my dealing with this stewardship or making decisions to ensure the integrity of the investment base that Ele had so diligently built up during her lifetime. I have been supported in this effort by my co-trustee Gary Meyer, my financial adviser John Massey, and my two brokers, Rob Wright and Penney Sick.

The first beneficiary is the Museo de las Américas in Denver, Colorado. Since recovering from its 2004 financial crisis, the Museo has played an ever more vibrant role in the cultural life of Denver. Three extraordinary board presidents—Olga Garcia, George Martinez, and Elizabeth Munoz—with the support of my nephew, Gary Meyer, have built a solid financial base for the Museo. Three gifted executive directors, Patty Ortiz, Maruca Salazar, and Claudia Moran, have built bridges to all segments of Denver society and sponsored a kaleidoscope of cultural events, especially its education programs on Latin American art for school children and its summer art training program for gifted youngsters. The association of the Tragen Trust with the Museo is a living memorial to Ele. Every time I see another exhibit drawn from the collection that she built is like reliving with Ele the adventure of discovering each and every piece on display.

The second beneficiary of the Trust is the Chair of Comparative Law at the University of California/Berkeley School of Law and its supporting program of seminars, fellowships, and research. Since Ele's passing, I have worked with Deans Christopher Edley, Sujit Choudry, Melissa Murray, and Erwin Chemerinsky, on measures for activating the Chair and program. In 2010, the UC Berkeley Law School awarded me a citation for my sponsorship of the chair and recognized its importance to the school's long-term international commitment and interests. In 2020, the program initiated operations. Complementing the chair, I also endowed a fellowship for a UC Berkeley Law School student to live at I House, where Ele and I met. It is my hope that the recipient will find his or her soul mate there as I found Ele. For their help in setting up the fellowship, special thanks to the law school development officers, Luisa Siravo and Stephanie Deaner, the director of I House, Hans Giesecke, and his predecessor Martin Brennan.

The third beneficiary is the University of California San Diego (UCSD) to support its medical research programs through the Eleanor D. and Irving G. Tragen Fund for Medical Research in Geriatrics. The current director of the program, Dr. Alison Moore, and I are engaged in discussions now on ways to make the fund as meaningful as possible to the long-term development of the UCSD medical research program.

In addition to the fund at UCSD, a percentage of the contributions from the Tragen Family Trust will be used to endow research at the Shiley Eye Institute, the program of the Mexico-U.S. Center, and a fellowship for a Latin American scholar at the Scripps School of Oceanography. Those were all activities Ele supported in her lifetime and, as she wished, I have continued to support them since her passing.

Life at Pacific Regent

In the years since Ele's passing, Pacific Regent has become my home and my neighbors like my family. When Ele passed, they closed in to support me and make sure that my grieving was not my undoing. I was never left alone. Almost every day, someone called to make sure that I had dinner plans. Others encouraged me to participate in a community activity or go on an excursion to see the wider world. I was constantly reminded that there were people who cared about me and wanted to help compensate for my loss.

I became a regular at the Monday bridge game and had Mickie Shugert as my partner for nearly a decade. Dr. Doris Howell—Ahli to those who love her—and Peggy Oechsle, her devoted cousin, got my neighbor Ham Loeb and I interested in the Doris Howell Foundation on women's health problems, and in the work of the San Diego Hospice and Palliative Care Center. For a decade, Sherm Smith, George Winters, and I shared our birthdays in May. Ben Holmes set up dinners with our fellow resident, Herbert Klein, the director of communications in the Nixon White House and former editor of the San Diego Union Tribune, and we pulled together a special lecture in which he talked about his role in Nixon White House and I talked about life in the Foreign Service; for over two years, we were invited to make presentations in San Diego, Stockton, and other sites. Maggie Petrick recruited me to be a member of our "crab leg" epicurean table where once every few weeks or so, we have a crab fest in our dining room. Alice Thomas, Madeline Winters, and Paul Sterner include me in Sunday brunches at the Yacht Club and Rancho Valencia. Leona Adler made sure I got good parts in the play-reading group—imagine me, an eighty-six year old Romeo, playing to Royal Academy-trained June Klein, the ninety-three year old Juliet! The distinguished acting teacher Mary Corrigan not only allowed me to play Big Daddy to her Big Mamma in our play-reading group but also invited me to be her co-reader of *Love Letters* and a *Christmas in Wales* in downtown La Jolla. Jack Bowsher offers me a ride on Thursday mornings to the San Diego North County World Affairs Council lectures.

Another aspect of my life at Pacific Regent has been my work on the board of directors of the homeowners association. Six months after Ele's passing, Lady Smith and Ben Holmes induced me to run for the board. They said that I could be useful and challenged me to make a contribution. I was elected for the first of several terms. Since Ele died, I have been engaged in HOA business, seven years as a board member and four as president. Those were turbulent times, in which the HOA rewrote most of its basic documents, carried out major repairs, and changed management companies. Our board sometimes worked eight-hour days. Many times, I felt as if I had been drafted into the practice of property law. It was a rewarding experience to work with my fellow homeowners toward a common purpose.

Sadly life is not eternal and many good friends have followed Ele out of my life after deeply enriching it. The average age in our community is about ninety, with a few in their hundreds. Each of us knows that we are in the twilight of our lives and many of us are widows and widowers. We have a table in the front hall on which a picture and a white rose are displayed to honor of each of our members on passing. Every time I go by the table and see a picture and white rose, I brace myself as I look to see which of my friends has left us.

Since Ele's passing, I have been occasionally invited to give lectures or participate in seminars on Latin America and U.S.-Latin American relations. My analyses of worldly affairs have earned me a free lunch or two at a service club or the World Affairs Council. Alas, at age ninety-seven, when talking with vibrant young people, I often feel like a Neanderthal who wandered in from some distant age when I'm only relating what happened to Ele and me just a few years ago.

Since Ele departed, I have visited many of the places that she and I had planned to enjoy together. I had the great good luck of finding Madeline Winter, travel agent par excellence, living at Pacific Regent. Starting in 2006, Madeline Winters took my interests and built them into memorable trips. She showed me the comfort of ocean and river travel, where your hotel takes you to see the sights and provides a dinner and bed, all without packing and unpacking every day. She arranged for trips to Alaska, Hawaii, around the Pacific Rim, through the Mediterranean, down the Danube to the Black Sea, around the Aegean and Black Seas, across the Atlantic to

Egypt and the Holy Land, and from Bangkok to the Taj Mahal. She also arranged land trips through China and Central Europe, those times on buses, not ships, but very enjoyable indeed. She and her late husband George even allowed me to join them on a few memorable Holland America trips to Honolulu and Rome. I will never forget walking the hills of Rome with George in his motorized wheelchair shaped like a small car that stopped traffic as Italian motorists gawked at his vehicle and even some got out of cars to help lift George's "car" over curbs. On all the trips, I felt Ele sitting on my shoulder, taking in the sights and the people.

It was on the sixty-day cruise from Fort Lauderdale to the Holy Land that I began seriously to write down my remembrances of Ele and my life. My tablemates kept asking me about my experiences living abroad, and enjoyed the stories enough to urge me to record them. I had already drafted what is now Part I of the book in response to questions from friends at the Pacific Regent about how Ele and I met. I really wasn't thrilled at the idea of putting my memories on paper, until I imagined how much Ele would have enjoyed the experience of revisiting Caribbean Islands and crossing over to Africa, savoring Marrakesh, steaming past fogged-in Gibraltar, finally seeing the Sphinx and Bethlehem, revisiting Venice, and finally feasting on the beauty of Madeira. So, on the trip home from Madeira, I sat down with my ACER notebook and began drawing shards from various corners of my brain. Much of the last seven years have been dedicated to writing, re-writing, and editing these remembrances.

In addition to my travels and this writing, I have strived to keep in touch with friends around the world. My computer and Internet are my great facilitators, although often I feel that the computer is an animate object using me! Once a year, I put together a holiday letter in December to say hello and remind them of Ele and me, and share with them the highlights of my annual adventures, joys, and pains. It is my way of saying that they all still matter to me and how grateful I am that they played roles in Ele and my lives.

Here I am several years later coming to the end of this wonderful cathartic adventure of reliving Ele's and my life together. This has made realize how fortunate I have been. I've had such loving and caring parents, mentors and friends, associates and stimulators, over so many years. I have searched every cranny of my brain to remember names and faces, but I am certain that many prized contributors to my life are left unnamed in the pages that I am now closing. That is one of tribulations of being ninety-seven years old.

My conclusion is very simple: for over fifty-seven years Ele and I had a partnership. Both of us had stimulating and challenging assignments. Neither of us accomplished what we had hoped for, but we tried. I may not be able to speak for Ele, but I know how much I have missed her and that I could not have done my job in life without her. Above all, I appreciate how wonderful and enriching it has been to have had Ele as my life partner!

CPSIA information can be obtained
at www.ICGtesting.com
Printed in the USA
JSHW011300200523
41983JS00005B/99